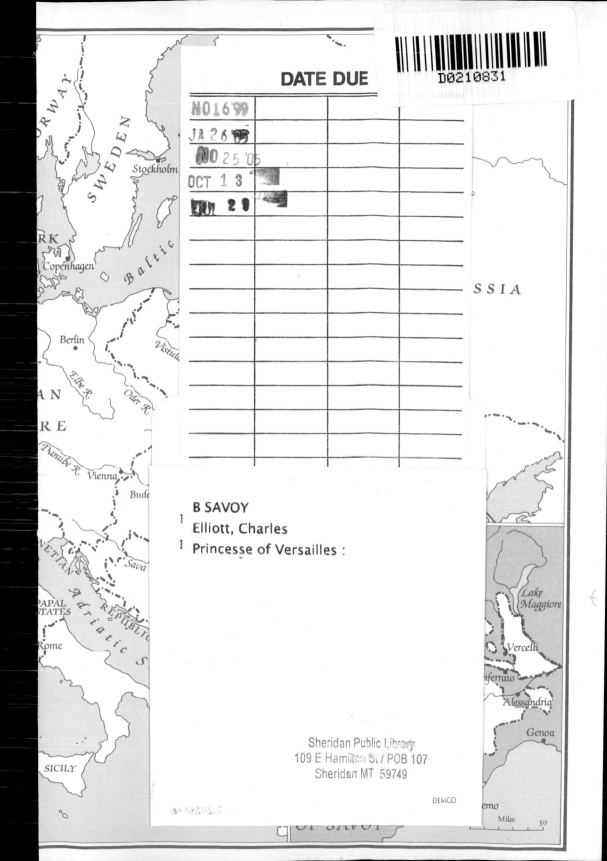

Princesse of Versailles

✦

Princesse of Versailles

The Life of
Marie Adelaide
of Savoy

CHARLES ELLIOTT

TICKNOR & FIELDS

New York 1992

For information about permission to reproduce selections
from this book, write to Permissions, Ticknor & Fields,
215 Park Avenue South, New York, New York 10003.

Library of Congress Cataloging-in-Publication Data

Elliott, Charles W.
Princesse of Versailles : the life of Marie Adelaide of Savoy /
by Charles W. Elliott.
p.   cm.
Includes bibliographical references and index.
I S B N 0-395-60516-4
1. Marie Adelaide, of Savoy, Duchess of Burgundy, 1685–1712.
2. France — Princes and princesses — Biography.   3. France — Court and
courtiers.   4. France — History — Louis XIV, 1643–1715.   I. Title.
DC130.M35E45   1992
944'.033'092 — dc20
[B]   91-41655
CIP

Book design by Anne Chalmers
Endpaper and text maps by Jacques Chazaud

Printed in the United States of America

AGM   10   9   8   7   6   5   4   3   2   1

TO DALE
with love and gratitude

ACKNOWLEDGMENTS

One of an author's more pleasant tasks in the final stages of preparing a book is acknowledging the assistance of others. In the research and writing of *Princesse of Versailles,* I am indebted to a number of people whose generous extension of time and knowledge has been invaluable.

I owe a special debt of gratitude to Dale Muller. From the very first outline and through countless revisions, her questions, her comments, and above all her unflagging enthusiasm provided true inspiration. With no exaggeration, she made this book possible.

I wish to thank Susan Gee Rumsey, whose fine craftsmanship was instrumental in shaping this book. Also Ann McAtee, who not only had the answers to more than a hundred questions, but also pointed me in the right direction — straight to Philip G. Spitzer, the most supportive agent anyone could wish for.

And last, to Caroline Sutton of Ticknor & Fields and to Natalie Bowen, I offer both my appreciation and my admiration. One hears too often the stale old chestnut "I couldn't have done it without you" — believe me, this time it is no cliché.

To all of you I doff my hat and say, with all my heart, thank you.

Contents

List of Illustrations

Princesse of
Versailles

❧

The House of Bourbon

HENRI IV (1553–1610)
m.
MARIE DE MEDICI (1574–1642)

CHRISTINE (1606–1663)
m.
VICTOR AMADEUS I of Savoy (1601–1637)

CHARLES EMMANUEL II (1634–1675)
m.
JEANNE DE SAVOIE-NEMOURS (1644–1724) (Madame Royale)

VICTOR AMADEUS II

ELISABETH (1602–1644)
m.
PHILIP IV of Spain (1605–1665)

MARIE THÉRÈSE (wife of Louis XIV)

PHILIPPE, duc d'Orléans (1640–1701) (Monsieur)
m.
1) HENRIETTA of England (1644–1670) (Minette)

2) ELIZABETH CHARLOTTE of Bavaria (1652–1722) (Madame)

PHILIPPE, duc de Chartres (1674–1723)
m.
FRANÇOISE MARIE, Mlle. de Blois (1677–1749)

MARIE LOUISE ELISABETH (wife of BERRI)

MARIE LOUISE (1662–1680)
m.
CHARLES II of Spain (1661–1700)

LOUIS XIII (1601–1643)
m.
ANNE OF AUSTRIA (1601–1666)

LOUIS XIV (1638–1715)
m.
1) MARIE THÉRÈSE (1638–1683)

2) Françoise d'Aubigné MADAME DE MAINTENON (1635–1719)

ANNE MARIE (1669–1728)
m.
VICTOR AMADEUS II of Savoy (1666–1732)

MARIE LOUISE

MARIE ADELAIDE

LOUIS, the Grand Dauphin (1661–1711) (Monseigneur)
m.
MARIE ANNE of Bavaria (1660–1690)

CHARLES, duc de Berri (1685–1714)
m.
MARIE LOUISE ELISABETH, Mlle. de Valois (1695–1719)

PHILIPPE, duc d'Anjou (1683–1746) (PHILIP V of Spain)
m.
MARIE LOUISE of Savoy (1687–1714)

LOUIS XV (1710–1774)

LOUIS, duc de Bourgogne (1682–1712)
m.
MARIE ADELAIDE of Savoy (1685–1712)

LOUIS, duc de Bretagne (1707–1712)

LOUIS, duc de Bretagne (1704–1705)

1

The State of France

LOUIS XIV NEVER really said, "L'état, c'est moi." But unquestionably, he believed it; and in the final decade of the seventeenth century, no one in Europe, from the mighty Hapsburg emperor Leopold to the little Princesse Marie Adelaide of Savoy, had reason to doubt that indeed the Sun King *was* France. For half a century, this dynamic personality, with all his intriguing contradictions, had dominated his people, inspiring them to new heights, forcing them into greatness, molding both royal absolutism and the modern nation. His success, in the eyes of his contemporaries, was phenomenal: in the early days of Christianity, Rome was the world's crowning achievement; in the twentieth century, New York; but in the *grand siècle*, it was the French king's seat of power at Versailles.

The apotheosis of Louis XIV as Apollo, the Sun God, was no hollow boast, but a logical development of the seventeenth century, a critical age in the history of European monarchy. The institution of royalty had met with serious challenge in almost every country on the continent. Portugal, Naples, and Catalonia all were scenes of bloody revolt. In England, one king (Charles I) had lost his head in a civil war, while another (James II) had lost his throne without a single battle. In France, the boy-king Louis XIV had endured several unsuccessful rebellions — known collectively as the Fronde — which emotionally scarred the impressionable youth and instilled in him a lifelong hatred for Paris and mistrust of the nobility. Before the tumultuous events of the seventeenth century, French kings had been more inclined to act as the most privileged of the privileged few rather than the country's chief executives, using their power to support one faction against another and sharing the spoils with their favorites. It was Cardinal Richelieu who first developed a higher, apolitical role for his monarch (Louis XIII), separating the king's private life from his function as the personification of the state. From 1661 onward, Louis XIV brought this conception of monarchy to its climax, refining it into a work of art and making himself the greatest "actor of majesty" the world had ever seen.

Such apotheosis could not have been achieved solely on the strength of Louis's will or ego, though both *were* colossal. In addition, it required a firm national foundation upon which to build, the very foundation that Richelieu had painstakingly laid: only France, the greatest power and influence of the seventeenth century, could have successfully produced the Sun King.

France exercised a complete and awesome dominance over Western European politics from 1643 (with the destruction of the Spanish army at the battle of Rocroi) to 1763 (with France's own defeat in the Seven Years' War); in the worlds of language, literature, and art, French predominance went unchallenged until the fall of Napoleon in 1815. Foreigners flocked to Paris, "the finishing school of Europe," and many remained there, preferring Parisian *joie de vivre* to the more dour aspects of their own countries. (The impact of French culture was so far-reaching and enduring that at the court of Catherine the Great of Russia in the late eighteenth century, an English bride, struggling to master her new husband's native tongue, was told such effort was a total waste of time: "except to speak to the servants," nothing but French was ever used.)

Manpower was a major factor in France's ascendancy. Its population in 1660 was a staggering twenty million, compared with five million each in England and Spain. Little effective resistance could be expected from six million Italians, or the two million citizens of the Dutch United Provinces. Only the Holy Roman Empire stood to offer potential challenge, with twenty-three million "subjects" — but it was an empire in name only, a loose conglomerate of rival German princelings, and the Austrian emperor himself was more concerned with the menacing Turk that battered relentlessly at his southern gates than with his Gallic cousin's dreams of aggrandizement. The seemingly inexhaustible supply of French human resources enabled Louis XIV and his military genius, the marquis de Louvois, to create the most

impressive war machine yet known to man: 150,000 strong in peacetime, 400,000 during war, the Grand Army patroled the map of Europe, ensuring that the Sun King's rays were felt in every corner of the
continent. The battle of Rocroi in 1643, which effectively reduced
Spain to a second-rate power, raised the Grand Army to preeminence,
and for over half a century (until the disastrous defeat at Blenheim in
1704) the Sun King's forces marched onto battlefield after battlefield
in absolute confidence of victory. As W. H. Lewis wrote: "The reform,
or rather the re-creation, of the French army remains one of the most
remarkable achievements of seventeenth-century France."

The extraordinary length of Louis's rule — seventy-two years, the
longest in European history — was also important for French supremacy. It added a unity of government and policy to the "unity of race
and soil," the growing spirit of French nationalism, although Louis
XIV initiated little in French foreign policy. Instead, he quickened the
pace and enlarged the scope of its age-old goal: to crush the power of
the House of Hapsburg. His early successes in this area were remarkable. The disablement of Spain and Austria's obvious fear, as it faced
the Turkish menace to the south and the Grand Army to the west,
lulled the Sun King into dreams of a universal monarchy — a France,
under permanent mobilization, extending eastward to the Rhine and
surrounded by a ring of vassal states, a Europe where French influence
was paramount — a dream eagerly embraced by twenty million Frenchmen.

Louis XIV's outstanding development of the French diplomatic system, and the general practice of diplomacy, had marked effects as well.
Not only did he bring this branch of government to a new level, he
forced the statesmen of Europe into a new consciousness of the fledgling principle of balance of power. The international alliance of
1688 — an unparalleled binding together of seven nations in the face
of a single enemy — is ample indication of the fear and dread that
France evoked in its neighbors.

Louis XIV's efforts at internal aggrandizement were generally no
less successful. The reasons offered for the building of Versailles are
many and varied — from the creation of his own life's monument to
the emasculation of his nobles to the psychological intimidation of
Europe — but possibly its greatest consequence was to raise the prestige of French craftsmanship to unscaled heights. Hundreds of artists
were kept at work for years on the king's several châteaus, and such
architects as Le Vau and Mansard and the landscape genius Le Nôtre

subsequently found themselves in high demand across the continent. The king's generous subsidization of the Gobelin factory helped to make French tapestries the most highly prized in Europe, and the silk weavers at Lyons blossomed under his patronage. If it became impossible for contemporary rulers to envision anything but the monumental monotony of the Versailles façade when they constructed their own royal dwellings, it was because the French model afforded the very finest and latest in artistic achievement.

Music and literature flourished. The king was passionately devoted to music, and an orchestra was seldom out of earshot. He woke each morning to the sounds of a band in the Marble Courtyard below his windows, and his daily routine, from official audiences to informal walks through the gardens, was accompanied by the strains of Lully and Couperin. Molière exposed the hypocrisies of his age, with the king's continued support and encouragement; even Racine thrived, despite his suspected Protestant leanings. From the stirring tragedies of Corneille to La Fontaine's enchanting fables, from the disarming wit of Mme de Sévigné to the caustic reportage of Saint-Simon: never before or since has France produced finer drama, prose, or letters, but never before — and seldom since — has it had so inspirational a leader.

The head of this emergent state, the font and raison d'être of this rich and complex culture, was himself no less rich in complexity. The Sun King's consideration and generosity were hallmarks: an old courtier, confessing himself bankrupt and forced to leave court, was quietly awarded a pension and told, "You and I have known each other too long to separate at a time of life when neither of us can afford to make new friends; don't desert me." But it was the same considerate Sun King who forced his wife to live on intimate terms with each of his mistresses. On the subject of women, Louis XIV was no less paradoxical: his lifelong weakness for beautiful women was legendary, and his reliance on them for solace and pleasure never left him, but for all their considerable influence elsewhere, the king's women were firmly excluded from politics. The twenty-year-old king once assured his friends: "You are all those of my kingdom of whom I am fondest, and in whom I have most confidence. I am young, and women usually have great power over men of my age. I order all of you, if you notice that any woman shows the least sign of managing me, to warn me. I shall then need only twenty-four hours to get rid of her." Never did he give cause for warning. Forty years later, even his second wife was forced to admit, "The King does not wish to hear matters of business spoken of except by the Ministers; I must keep my opinions to myself."

Louis XIV's extraordinary chameleon nature created a variety of postures. The one presented in the autumn of 1696 — the fifty-eight-year-old grandfather waiting impatiently in his château at Fontainebleau for the arrival of his grandson's fiancée, Princesse Marie Adelaide of Savoy — while new and unexpected, was just another facet of the Sun King's intricate character.

Louis XIV was born on September 5, 1638, and ascended the throne at the age of five.[1] The regency was entrusted to his mother, Anne of Austria, but power quickly devolved on her certain lover and possible husband, Cardinal Mazarin. This Italian-born naturalized Frenchman (despite his ecclesiastic title, he was not an ordained priest) had been Richelieu's protégé; with the latter's death in 1642, and with the willing compliance of the love-starved queen-regent, Mazarin became the virtual ruler and unofficial king of France for the next twenty years. Though unscrupulous and blatantly avaricious, Mazarin continued the work of centralizing the French government inaugurated by Richelieu, and the France he bequeathed to young Louis on his deathbed was well established as a united nation.

Louis was twenty-two at the time of Mazarin's death. Though the regency had officially ended with his attainment of majority in 1651, the young king showed no inclination to assume the burdensome duties of government. His days were absorbed in the pleasures of the chase, whether on horseback or in the boudoir, and the exuberant young hedonist was content to leave the administration of his state in the prime minister's capable hands. But at half past two on the morning of March 8, 1661, Cardinal Mazarin died, and the reign of Louis XIV effectively began. The king was told the news by his nurse when he woke that morning. In view of his later life, his first act was astonishing: dressing quickly, he locked himself in his study, and the king who would henceforth never spend one moment of solitude remained sequestered with his thoughts for over two hours. The king that emerged from the study was no longer a puppet — neither was he the grand monarch as yet, though it might be romantic to cast him as such. He was a zealous young idealist, and one determined never again to relinquish his power or his birthright. To the assembled heads of departments he announced his intention to personally discharge all the duties previously undertaken by the cardinal. In the future, no departmental decisions could be final without the king's express consent; no requests, benefices, or offices would be conferred without his sanction; never again would he appoint a prime minister or allow a churchman to sit on his council. "You will assist me with your advice," he declared, *when I ask for it.*"

The startled ministers bowed politely and withdrew, to criticize this latest royal whim in private and wait for the novelty to wear away. But they were destined to wait in vain — for the next fifty-four years, Louis XIV alone was the government of France.

By our standards, it was a government oppressive in its centralization. Three councils, each presided over by the king, prepared and presented the information upon which Louis XIV based his decisions. The five-member Council of State met three times a week to deliberate the major questions of state policy. The Council of Dispatches oversaw the management of provincial affairs, and the Council of Finance controlled taxation and regulated expenditure. The function of these councils, however, was merely to advise, never to inaugurate: as one frustrated minister later commented, for every twenty proposals submitted in council to the king, Louis XIV would agree to nineteen and object, in principle, to the twentieth — as an exercise of his royal prerogative.

On the local level, government was taken away from the negligent and largely irresponsible nobility and conferred on royal intendants; these officials, who often doled out harsh punishments to the local petty tyrants, were enormously popular with the common people. Under Louis XIV, feudal law, which had fragmented the French for centuries, was at last replaced by monarchical law, the final stage of Richelieu's plan and a laudable achievement: the Code Louis survived the vicissitudes of 1789 and the Reign of Terror until its replacement, in the nineteenth century, by the revisionary Code Napoléon.

Physical appearance, then as now, was no small factor in the seventeenth century's concept of monarchy. Louis XIV *looked* like a king; his dignity, grace, and extraordinary looks were so pronounced that one admiring ambassador declared that even had he been a lowly peasant, Louis de Bourbon would have stood out from the crowd. In his prime, Louis XIV was the physical embodiment of France — or certainly all that France wished itself to be. His contemporaries invariably described him as tall — and the fact that he was actually only five feet five inches high is further evidence of the powerful impression he conveyed. On his twentieth birthday, one of his mother's ladies-in-waiting, Mme de Brégis, wrote gushingly: "He is the most gallant and honest man in the world. He is better made than other men; tall and of such an excellent build that he need not grow any more to achieve perfection . . . Since beauty is that which pleases, one can say that [he is] the most handsome man alive. His legs and feet are so perfectly made that no one should worry that they are there to walk over us." Nor was the national infatuation restricted to the female sex; one male court official, who began his description with the objective pronouncement that the king possessed "a proud but sweet-natured face," was inspired to write: "His pallor [the result of measles in 1647] has remained to contrast with the beautiful coral of his mouth by comparison with which roses pale and from which oracles and graces pour." He added that all agreed that "to know the grace and majesty of this entirely royal and august body, one must see him mounted, or in a ballet, where the advantages of nature and habit are so obvious." Young Louis XIV was an excellent dancer, a superb and passionate horseman. His love for the hunt (which would endear him to Adelaide) was so great that even after breaking his arm at Fontainebleau, he followed the hounds in a carriage rather than forgo the pleasures of the chase.

In the pleasures of another chase, the young king was equally avid. There is rich irony in Louis's sexual initiation: at the age of eighteen, returning from his bathroom, he was waylaid by one of his mother's waiting women, Mme de Beauvais, and for the first and last time in his life, Louis was the seduced and not the seducer. A romantic streak quickly surfaced and within a year he had fallen desperately in love with Mazarin's niece, the darkly beautiful Marie Mancini. The handsome young couple were not cynical sophisticates, and the practical, worldly arrangement of such liaisons never occurred to them: far from establishing Marie as *maîtresse en titre* (the king's acknowledged mistress), Louis proposed to Marie in the summer of 1658, promising to make her his queen. Whatever the cardinal's true feelings on this undreamed-of elevation within the ranks of his family, the queen mother's horrified reaction quickly destroyed all hope for the match. The regent firmly informed her son that it was his duty to France to wed the daughter of the king of Spain. After many a tearful protestation, Louis reluctantly consented. Marie, her mother, and her sisters were exiled to Italy, thus ending Louis XIV's first, finest, and purest love.[2] It was his initiation into personal sacrifice for the good of the state — a lesson the young king never forgot.

The chosen bride, Marie Thérèse, the infanta of Spain, was the queen mother's niece and Louis XIV's first cousin. She was short and frumpy, her vapidly pretty face ruined by a mouthful of blackened teeth, rotting from an overindulgence in chocolate. As a result of centuries of Hapsburg inbreeding, she had the mentality of a child (the imbecilic Carlos II of Spain was her half brother), and despite twenty years at her husband's court, was never able to fully master the French language. Her pleasures were equally infantile: she had a passion for little dogs, and these pets were given servants to walk them, carriages for their transport from one royal palace to another, and food from the queen's own table — at a cost of four hundred écus a year. She also took great amusement in dwarfs and kept half a dozen of them in her suite, addressing them as "my heart," "my son," and "poor baby." Louis XIV could hardly be expected to find marital contentment with such a wife, though he did grow quite fond of Marie Thérèse, privately indulging her like a simple and spoiled daughter and never failing publicly to treat her with all the honor due her rank. He took his ceremonious main meal with her daily, although he found her clove-scented gravies and garlic-nutmeg stews revolting. Once every fortnight, he performed his conjugal duties: the next morning, before a smirking court, a glowing Marie Thérèse would take communion and pray fervently for an heir. Like the rest of France, she adored her handsome, charming husband, and though she suffered agonies of jealousy, never criticized or rebuked him. (On her death in 1683, Louis XIV sighed to Mme de Maintenon, "Poor woman, this is the only time she has ever given me any trouble.")

With the birth of his son, Monseigneur the dauphin, in 1661, the succession was secured, and the king was able to "resume the chase" in good conscience. First he fell in love with his sister-in-law Minette, the first Madame (Adelaide's maternal grandmother).[3] Minette's husband, Monsieur, was a notorious homosexual and had already abandoned his wife's bed for that of the handsome, self-serving chevalier de Lorraine. But indifferent or not, Monsieur had no wish to play the cuckold. Outraged by his brother's public affront to his dignity, Monsieur voiced his shrill complaints to their already disapproving mother. To avoid the queen mother's censure, Minette devised a somewhat odd deception: she would continue to see the king without raising suspicion, for Louis would pretend to be infatuated with one of her ladies-in-waiting.

Her choice of decoy, Louise de La Vallière, was even more surprising, for while Louise was not noticeably beautiful, she was extremely feminine, with large blue eyes, luxuriant fair hair, and a pouting, sensual mouth. The result was predictable: within months, Louis was indeed in love with La Vallière. (There is a sense of ironic justice in the fates of Louis XIV's women: Minette introduced him to La Vallière; La Vallière, in her turn, invited Mme de Montespan into their private circle; and lastly, it was Montespan who brought Mme de Maintenon to the king's attention, insisting on her appointment as governess to their children.)

It has often been noted that the beginnings of Louis XIV's love for La Vallière and for Versailles were coincidental, but the latter passion far outlasted the former. By 1668, as the massive enlargement of the royal palace began, Louise de La Vallière's position as *maîtresse en titre* was clearly in jeopardy. One contemporary described Louise as having "no bosom and few brains," and the shame of bearing three illegitimate children had increased her innate shyness. The king was obviously tiring of her, and to keep her restless lover amused, Louise invited a friend to join in their trysts, a friend who could be counted on to make the witty, clever remarks she herself could never think of.

The friend was Athénaïs, marquise de Montespan, "the most ravishing, the most wise, and the most charming of all the ladies at the court."[4] Athénaïs was extremely ambitious as well; deftly she supplanted La Vallière in the king's bed, then his heart.

Brilliant and voluptuous, Montespan held the king's affection through ten stormy years and nine royal babies. Her decade marked the apogee of the court of Louis XIV; Versailles continued to expand and awe all Europe, with the wit and valor of its men, the beauty of its women, and its own sheer magnificence unrivaled throughout the world. But these royal lovers were not romantics, like Louis and Marie Mancini, or young idealists, like Louis and Louise de La Vallière. Montespan was too self-assured and self-seeking to inspire real love, and Louis XIV had begun to coarsen and harden with age. As one shrewd courtier observed, the king felt it merely due his position to have the most beautiful woman in France for his mistress. As middle age encroached, the king began to find Athénaïs's wit taking on a sharper edge in private, where it was often directed at Louis de Bourbon the man and lover. He spent less and less time in Montespan's silky boudoir, more and more in religious or philosophical discussions with the unprepossessing, newly created marquise de Maintenon, who was destined to be his second wife. Athénaïs had given birth to a daughter in 1668, the first of her four surviving children by the king. Children bored and irritated La Montespan (a trait she rather stupidly flaunted before her lover, an inveterate father and later doting grandfather), and she had no intention of rearing the girl herself. She suggested that her friend, Françoise d'Aubigné, the widow Scarron, be appointed royal governess. Interestingly enough, Louis at first objected to Mme Scarron: he disliked that kind of carping, intellectual woman, he told his sister-in-law, the second Madame.[5] Nor was the widow herself much taken by the proposal, expressing great reluctance to get entangled in the shifty, covert accommodation of royal bastards. Montespan, to her later regret, persisted on both fronts: of the two, Louis XIV was certainly the easier to manage personally, but after her confessor assured the pious widow there was no sin in raising a bastard child under the express command of the king, Mme Scarron relented. Montespan's downfall had begun.

Françoise d'Aubigné was born in a prison in Poitou in 1635. Hers was, however, a family of the old, provincial nobility. Her grandfather, the admirable Théodore Agrippa d'Aubigné, had been a Huguenot leader and a great friend of Henri IV, a poet and historian, and author of the noted satire Les Tragiques, an eloquent, indignant protest against the vices and corruptions of the early seventeenth century. But her father, Constant (titled baron de Surimeau after a property inherited from his mother), was wild and dissolute, adept in the art of forgery. His life after 1627 was spent in one jail after another: first at La Rochelle, where he was cursed and disinherited by his father, then at Angers, Poitiers, and Bordeaux — where he seduced and later married Jeanne de Cardilhac. Joining her jailed husband at Niort, Jeanne gave birth on November 27, 1635, to their only daughter.

Released at last, Constant d'Aubigné sought his fortune in the French Caribbean, and in 1645 he boarded a ship with his wife, their ten-year-old daughter and infant son, and sailed for the island of Marie Galante, off Guadeloupe. Little Françoise fell ill and nearly died en route, but an even greater crisis awaited the family. The ship arrived in port to find that the hostile natives had chased all the French settlers off the island. The d'Aubignés were forced to seek refuge on Martinique where, two years later, Constant died. His destitute widow was able to scrape together passage to take her children back to France. She settled in Paris and died soon afterward.

The orphaned Françoise now found herself farmed out to various provincial relatives. Officially the ward of her aunt, Mme de Neuillant, young Françoise was educated at an Ursuline convent; born a Huguenot, she converted to Roman Catholicism at the age of sixteen, although she was never able to rid herself of certain Protestant prejudices, like distaste for the rosary and dislike for the saints. But the humiliations of her early life did not embitter the girl, and her "bright and cheerful disposition" soon brought her to the attention of the poet Paul Scarron, who entered Françoise's life in 1651. She was sixteen, beautiful, and penniless; he was forty-two, successfully established as a man of letters, and horribly arthritic. In the prologue to one of his books he described himself for his readers: "My figure was well made, though small. My malady has shortened it by a good foot. My head is rather large for my body. My face is full, while my body is that of a skeleton. My sight is fairly good, but my eyes protrude, and one of them is lower than the other . . . My legs and thighs form at first an obtuse, next a right, and finally an acute angle; my thighs and body form another; and with my head bent down on my stomach, I resemble not badly the letter Z . . . To sum up, I am a condensation of human misery."

Faced with the choice of Scarron or a convent, Françoise did not hesitate. They were married in April 1652. Though hardly in love with her husband, Françoise proved a dutiful, caring wife, nursing her dying invalid and presiding capably over the literary circle that frequented their Paris home. The chevalier de Mère, a distinguished writer and their steady guest, described the seventeen-year-old Mme Scarron in a letter to the duchesse de Lesdiguières: "She is not only beautiful and of that kind of beauty which is always pleasing; but she is also sweet-tempered, discreet and of a graceful disposition, trustworthy, modest and very intelligent, and she makes use of these gifts to amuse others and to win their sympathy." Women admired her no less: when Queen Christina of Sweden visited Paris, she invited the Scarrons to call upon her, and afterwards complimented the poet on his choice of wife.

Given Scarron's infirmities, it is highly unlikely that their marriage was ever truly consummated; the poet himself wrote that he was so lame that he could neither turn around in his bed, nor flick away a fly if it chose to settle on his nose. Whether or not attempts at consummation were ever made, it is evident that when Scarron died eight years later, his widow considered herself still a virgin. Writing her younger brother, she remarked as late as 1678: "You will find it strange that a woman who was never married should give you so much information about marriage."

Scarron died on October 7, 1660. The will in which he left all his worldly possessions to Françoise was little more than a piece of scribbled paper, for there was not even money enough to cover his funeral. Faced with assets of ten thousand francs and debts of twenty-two thousand, Françoise fled to security behind convent walls, while creditors seized her furniture and art works, and stripped bare the maison Scarron. She appealed to her godmother, Mme de Motteville, wife to the duc de Navailles: could she intercede on Françoise's behalf with the queen mother to ensure the continuation of Scarron's royal pension? These efforts were successful, though hardly prompt: shortly after his mother's death in 1666, Louis XIV stipulated that, in her memory, the widow Scarron (the first time he had ever heard her name) would receive a yearly stipend of two thousand livres.

Her story might well have ended there, but Françoise's wit and keen intelligence had earned her the friendship of the powerful marquise de Montespan, and when Athénaïs's thoughts turned to the rearing of her royal offspring, this needy and gifted friend seemed to her a most logical candidate. Here Montespan's judgment did not err: greatly afflicted by her own childlessness, Françoise Scarron was able to vent this frustration in the care of the growing royal troupe, proving herself a born educator. A second royal bastard, the duc du Maine, entered her nursery in 1669, and despite his many subsequent failures and disappointments, she loved him as her own for the rest of her life. Louis XIV began to notice just how well Mme Scarron was bringing up his young son, how selfless and devoted her service was. Her conscientious attentions were all the more impressive when Montespan's eldest daughter died, and the governess displayed a grief far greater than the mother's. "She knows how to love," the king remarked. "There would be great pleasure in being loved by her." For her part, Françoise now began what she would later describe as her "long struggle for the King's soul."

Slowly Montespan grew concerned: she knew there was not the slightest chance the king would ever lure her virtuous friend into his bed, but their deep conversations on religion and morality, increasing with each passing day, were no longer to be tolerated. She set about finding a way to rid herself of this highly improbable, but insistent, rival. A duke was discovered, willing to marry the royal governess (for an appropriate dowry), but Mme Scarron declared herself perfectly content to remain a widow. Next, Montespan offered her friend a prestigious position as abbess of a convent, but Françoise declined to quit the world, and the king himself intervened, concurring that the governess indeed deserved a reward for such faithful and excellent service while expressing an aversion to her departure from court. In 1675, he presented her with Maintenon, a moated château between Chartres and Rambouillet — and Françoise Scarron became the marquise de Maintenon. The entire court laughed at Montespan's fit of pique; they punned upon the word *maintenant* ("now"), but they also sat up and took notice of this budding royal favorite. Mme de Sévigné wrote her daughter: "This dame de Maintenon or de Maintenant passes every evening between eight and ten o'clock with His Majesty. M. de Chamarande escorts her there and brings her back quite openly."

Maintenon's rise and Montespan's fall reflected the tremendous change Louis underwent as he passed what we would today term a midlife crisis. On September 5, 1678, he celebrated his fortieth birthday. The vibrant young Sun King was now middle-aged, and while the years had left his grace and regal bearing unimpaired, his lithe figure had definitely thickened, and his once luxuriantly natural chestnut hair was now replaced with elaborate wigs. Louis's innate sense of dignity began to prick his conscience: what had been attractive, even inspiring, in the amorous exploits of a vital young monarch now seemed to rest rather foolishly on an aging roué. He might recall fondly his nocturnal escapades, scrambling in and out of garret windows on the roof of the Louvre, midnight trysts in the scented arbors of Saint-Germain, but he recognized and accepted that such adventures belonged to an age now passed.

Religion, too, began to play a more important role at Louis's court. The king's Catholicism is one of the more intriguing aspects of his character. From infancy, his mother had instilled in him a lasting fear of the devil, and in his reign of seventy-two years, Louis XIV missed daily mass only once — having instead to undergo a fistula operation. Yet his knowledge of Church dogma was virtually nonexistent; his sister-in-law, the second Madame, noted that he "has never read the Bible, and believes whatever he is told . . . He doesn't wish to have the fatigue of finding out for himself what religion really is." Archbishop Bossuet, caught off guard once, admitted that the king's degree of religious enlightenment was on a par with that of a charcoal burner. Mme de Maintenon, who undoubtedly had a greater insight into Louis XIV's religious creed than anyone else, wrote: "He wants to accommodate religion to himself, not himself to religion; he wishes to observe all its externals but not its spirit."

This obsession with externals, which pervaded every aspect of the king's life, had its roots in the mysterious pageantry of the Catholic ritual, and his attitude of "accommodation" is more understandable when we realize that his rigid and narrow-minded religious creed served to emphasize and heighten his deep conviction that as king of France he held a particular personal relationship with God. Versailles etiquette decreed that during church services, the court should kneel with their backs to the altar, facing the king above in his private pew, and that only Louis XIV should face front, the effect being, according to one observer, "a sort of subordination, for the people appear to adore the King, and only the King to adore God." Louis did not need the pious Mme de Maintenon to urge the revocation of the Edict of Nantes; with his growing religious zeal and his uneducated bigotry, religious tolerance in France was already doomed.

The threat of eternal damnation, so easily defiable in one's twenties, grows imminently more terrifying as the decades pass. Louis XIV began to find his conversations with the virtuous Maintenon — lofty discussions on general morality as well as the dangers facing his own immortal soul — far more satisfying than the witty banter and vicious gossip of La Montespan. Not surprisingly, a strong and often heated rivalry developed between the two ladies, as the spiritual and the physical warred for possession of the king. "It is a real aversion," wrote Mme de Sévigné. "It is bitterness, it is antipathy, it is black, it is white."

Then Montespan made the fatal error of crossing Mme de Maintenon on the subject of the royal bastards, an area in which her exemplary conduct was irreproachable. When the king was forced to intervene, he came down firmly on the side of the governess, to the great surprise and undoubted chagrin of the mistress. The transfer of influence was complete. Montespan could no longer delude herself that the royal heart was hers, and though she continued to reside at Versailles, her relationship with Louis XIV had ended.

By 1681, when Louis discarded the marquise de Montespan forever, Mme de Maintenon's ascendancy was unchallenged. Her subsequent actions are perhaps the most admirable of her career, for despite persistent pressure from the king — whose religious fervor never entirely stifled his physical passions — she refused to replace Montespan as *maîtresse en titre*. She urged the king instead to return to his long-suffering queen, and surprisingly, she was successful. The dim-witted Marie Thérèse, having endured her husband's blatant infidelities for over twenty years, now received the prodigal with undisguised delight, and her gratitude to the royal governess was boundless. Louis XIV at last discovered domestic contentment, but his poor queen was allowed only two years of connubial bliss. In July 1683, Marie Thérèse developed an abscess under her arm. The doctors administered powerful emetics and bled the woman remorselessly; her condition deteriorated rapidly.

On the morning of July 30, the court was witness to an amazing sight — suddenly Louis XIV, tears streaming down his face, appeared at the doorway of the queen's bedchamber, "much distracted," and *ran* through the Hall of Mirrors toward the chapel, to fetch the viaticum for his dying wife. One hour later, Queen Marie Thérèse, forty-five years old, expired — in the arms of Mme de Maintenon.

Less than three months later, the royal governess underwent her final metamorphosis: Françoise d'Aubigné, the widow Scarron, then the marquise de Maintenon, became the second wife of Louis XIV.

The actual date of their secret marriage has never been determined, but evidence points to the early autumn of 1683 at the château of Fontainebleau, where the court had retired following the death of the queen. Early in September, Maintenon's brother had proposed himself for a visit, and she wrote begging him not to come to Fontainebleau at present: "The reason which prevents me from seeing you is so valuable and so marvelous that it ought to bring you nothing but joy." A young niece, Mlle d'Aubigné, who lived with Mme de Maintenon at court, later remembered that she had never seen her aunt so nervous or edgy as during the autumn sojourn; this emotional turmoil was apparently resolved, however, by September 20, when Mme de Maintenon wrote her confessor, Abbé Gobelin, that her agitation was at last ended and that she looked forward to telling him of her newly found peace of mind and happiness — in the meanwhile, she prayed that "she might put them to good account."

After her death, a prayer was allegedly discovered among Mme de Maintenon's private papers; its authenticity has never been certified, but its expression is so characteristic that one cannot help but hope for its validity. Purportedly it was composed by Maintenon herself at Fontainebleau following the secret wedding:

Lord God, Thou hast placed me where I am, and I submit myself to Thy providence without reserve. Grant me grace that as a Christian, I may support its sorrows, sanctify its pleasures, seek in everything Thy glory, and help the salvation of the King. Prevent me from giving way to the agitations of a restless mind . . . Thy will, O God, not mine, be done; for the sole happiness in this world and the next is to submit to it without reservation. Fill me with this wisdom and all other spiritual gifts necessary to the high place to which Thou has called me; make fruitful the talents Thou hast been pleased to give me. Thou holdest in Thy hands the hearts of kings, open that of the King that I may set therein the good that Thou desirest; enable me to please, console, encourage, and even, if it be necessary to Thy glory, to sadden him. Let me hide none of the things he might learn from me which others have not the courage to tell him. Let me save myself together with him; . . . [let me] love him in Thee and for Thee; and let him love me in the same way. Grant that we may walk together in Thy paths without reproach till the day of Thy coming.

In all her years as the king's wife, she never forgot this prayer.

While the court had no way of guessing that a secret marriage had indeed taken place, a significant change was noticed that autumn, both in Mme de Maintenon's status and the king's attitude toward her. In the past, he had addressed her politely — and correctly — as "Marquise." At Fontainebleau he began to call her "Madame" just as he had always addressed the queen. Further, the former governess now sat in the queen's box in the royal chapel, using the late queen's prayerbook, and while she always dined alone at Versailles, she now presided at the head of the table at family dinners in the king's country houses. In the court hierarchy she remained behind the duchesses in precedence, yet more than one contemporary remarked that, on being received in Maintenon's rooms, one felt unmistakably in the presence of a queen. Throughout the last thirty years of the reign, speculation of Mme de Maintenon's true position continued, and whether secret wife or final mistress, few dared to cross the formidable lady.

Mme de Maintenon's marriage was a morganatic one — as a mate of inferior status she acquired no new rank, and any offspring (she was forty-eight when she married Louis XIV) owned no hereditary rights. The king's attitude toward public recognition was straightforward and favorable; the few trusted advisers to whom he confided his marriage and his plans had great difficulty in dissuading him from granting his second wife full rights and crowning her queen. They argued a loss of prestige for the monarchy, and pointed out how extremely disconcerting the royal family and the court would find it suddenly to be curtsying to a former governess. In the end, Louis acceded.

Mme de Maintenon's attitude on acknowledgment is less clear. She herself often admitted that, above all things, she loved "to be honored, to be respected and enjoy consideration." What more honorable position was there than queen? She expressed constantly her contempt for fawning, ingratiating courtiers, yet she fully expected the obeisance of all who approached her apartments in supplication. Perhaps the perceptive Madame, who heartily despised Maintenon, hit upon the answer in a letter to her aunt, June 8, 1692: "The King's old monster has enjoyed this great power for a long time. She is not such a fool as to get herself acknowledged Queen; she knows her good man's temper too well. If she did such a thing, she would soon fall into disgrace and be utterly lost."

No less intriguing than the question of acknowledgment is the consideration of the emotions involved. After the Sun King's death, Maintenon said, "He loved me, it is true, but only as much as he was capable of loving, for unless a man is touched by passion, he is not tender." But her remark seems unfairly harsh. As a king, Louis XIV was one of those few human beings destined never to know disappointment in *les affaires de coeur* — women dreamed of surrendering to his advances, and men threw their own wives in his path as a way to royal favor. Yet for thirty years he remained faithful to his prim, almost spinsterish wife; pledging to love and honor her alone, he never broke that promise. (At seventy years of age, Maintenon complained bitterly to her confessor that the king insisted on his conjugal rights daily, sometimes twice a day. She cried, "These distressing occasions are too much for me," and asked if she might refuse. The abbé replied that while he too would prefer to see her in the chaste condition of the brides of Christ, it was her holy work to preserve the king from sin and possible adultery: "Your bedroom is the domestic church to which God leads him in order to uphold and sanctify him without his knowledge." In a letter after the king's death, she exclaimed: "What a martyrdom I have endured!")

Once again Maintenon's true feelings are not so easy to discern. Her renegade father, shiftless brother, and paralytic poet husband had left her with little respect for men. To the girls at her school at Saint-Cyr, she warned, "Flee from men as from your mortal enemies . . . The majority of men who [flatter] girls do it in the hope of finding some means of ruining them." Her opinions on marriage were similarly low: "It is the state in which one experiences the most tribulations, even under the most favorable circumstances . . . One finds so few good [husbands]; in truth I have known only two, and were I to say only one, I should not be exaggerating." Toward her royal spouse, Maintenon felt gratitude, devotion, even perhaps veneration — but not real love. Imbert de Saint-Armand once discoursed on women of Mme de Maintenon's type, declaring them "seldom enamored of the men to whom they owe their fortune. In general, they prefer to protect than to be protected. They find it sweeter to inspire gratitude than to experience it. What they like best is to show their superiority . . . They are happy when the roles are inverted, when it is they who dominate, protect, oblige." In Saint-Armand's view Maintenon "was too much indebted to Louis XIV to be in love with him."

Several little notes the king addressed to his secret wife are still in existence, though significantly, all of her correspondence to him has been destroyed. Always written in the most courteous of terms, Louis's notes are charming requests for the privilege of her company, for a walk with her, or a meeting, the hour and place of which are left for her to choose. His many fine qualities attracted her to him, his merits won her admiration, but her heart was as immune to love as his was receptive. She once said, "I love the King as a brother, and I want to see him perfect, so that God may bless him" — probably the most honest explanation of her complicated feelings.

For above all, husband and wife were united by a driving concern for the king's immortal soul, and her position as keeper of His Majesty's conscience was emotionally necessary to them both. Louis XIV could not live without a woman, and there was Mme de Maintenon. Maintenon ached to glorify her God with earthly works of conversion and guidance, and there was Louis XIV, the most needy and deserving of sinners. French historian Henri Martin wrote: "There was a harmony of mind and manners between them, which was destined to increase with age; and her regular, gentle, and serious beauty, heightened by rare natural dignity, was essentially fitted to please Louis. She loved consideration as he loved glory . . . Like him she had the individuality of vigorous and self-seeking organization, yet she was capable of lasting, and solid, if not ardent, affection. She was at once less passionate and more constant than the King, who was to be, in friendship as in love, truly constant to her alone."

At Versailles, Louis XIV created for himself an exclusive and artificial world. The glorification of Apollo, the Sun God, became one with the glorification of Louis, the Sun King. Center stage was wherever the Sun King happened to be, and Louis's days were carefully orchestrated to ensure that the pomp and ceremony expected from a king of France would be visible to the greatest number of sycophants. From the moment he woke until he was put to bed, Louis XIV was never alone, never without a raptured audience. He accepted without question that his life was to be played in public — that as the living personification of the State, he relinquished the mortal right of privacy. His stroke of genius was to codify the mundane doings of his daily life, creating rigid ceremonies from such simple actions as rising and dressing in the morning, then attaching such importance to these shallow rites that veteran courtiers and illustrious noblemen fought for the "honor" of holding the king's candlestick while he prepared for bed. The seventeenth century was a world of externals; it was show, not substance, that counted — and Louis XIV provided a show that has never been equaled.

The king was awakened each morning at eight by his First Valet of the Bedchamber, whose duties included sleeping in a trundle bed outside the gilded railing that protected his master's Bed of State. Until her death, Louis's former wet-nurse was allowed to kiss him on the cheek each morning; she was followed by the First Physician and the First Surgeon, who monitored the king's health meticulously. Louis sweated profusely during the night, and being naturally fastidious, had his body rubbed down with spirits each morning.[6] From a side door, the Royal Wigmaker entered with two wigs, a short one for the king to wear during his dressing ceremony, and the first full-bottomed wig of the day. At quarter past eight, the Grand Chamberlain entered the Royal Bedchamber, and with a great flourish reopened the damask curtains that the masseurs had closed. This signaled that the *lever*, the "rising," had officially begun.

The coveted *grande entrée* was the privilege of accompanying the Grand Chamberlain into the king's bedroom. It was the right of the king's brother and his son, the male Children of France, and a jealously guarded honor for a handful of trusted courtiers. As the Grand Chamberlain presented His Majesty with a miniature font of holy water, these chosen few were permitted to speak with the king and seek his favor. After the king had recited his prayers from the Office of the Holy Ghost, the *grande entrée* came to an end. Louis XIV rose from his bed, put on his slippers and dressing gown, and signaled that the *seconde entrée* should commence. This was the privilege of entry for the lesser nobility, and within moments, the room was packed with courtiers anxious to watch their lord dress.[7] The king donned his undergarments, stockings, garters, breeches, and shoes, all with "consummate grace." When the moment came to put on his shirt, it was handed to the senior ranking nobleman present by the First Valet, and only then offered to the king. Louis was shaved every other day (the barber being one of five hundred attendants to the king who were given free board and lodging at the palace); he kept his wig on throughout and afterward splashed his face in water mixed with wine, then dried it — apparently without any assistance from the admiring throng.

The king then ate a light breakfast of bread and wine to fortify himself — for there still remained the *grand lever,* during which each remaining article of clothing was handed to him by members of his family or honored favorites. These procedures were rigidly prescribed by etiquette — for example, *only* the First Valet of the Bedchamber was to help the king with his right coat sleeve and *only* the First Valet of the Wardrobe with his left. The Master of the Wardrobe put on the king's neckcloth, but only the Royal Cravatier could arrange it. Once Louis had been handed — in proper sequence — his hat, his gloves, his lace handkerchief, and his cane, the *grand lever* was completed.

Mornings were devoted to business: Louis XIV administered the orders of the day, then granted interviews with his ministers in the royal study. Daily mass was said at half past twelve, and Louis expected the full attendance of the court. He attended council meetings every day, except Thursdays and Fridays: Thursdays were reserved for private audiences and Fridays he was closeted with his confessor.

The fashionable dining hour of the period was noon — doubtless this came about because the king himself ate at one o'clock, forcing his courtiers to bolt down a quick repast before attending their master's luncheon. Since the king's main meal of the day was not served until evening, this dinner was a small affair. Small in terms of dishes, not in terms of ceremony, for watching the king eat was a favorite form of entertainment, not just at Versailles but in the capital as well, and crowds of Parisians rode out daily to slowly and reverently file past the royal table where the king nibbled at meats and salads, washing them down with watered Burgundy wine. (Louis XIV never drank undiluted wine, nor any kind of liqueur, coffee, tea, or chocolate: if he felt thirsty during the day, he sipped on ice water flavored with orange blossoms.) Given the distance between the dining room and the kitchens — servants bearing the royal repast had to cross the entire distance of the Great Courtyard, ascend one flight, and traverse several rooms before reaching their destination — it is highly unlikely that Louis XIV ever tasted hot food.

With dinner over, and if there were no council meetings scheduled for the afternoon, the king went off to his private rooms to play with his beloved dogs and feed them biscuits. He then changed his clothes and prepared for his favorite time of the day. Louis XIV was a passionate "open-air man," and was never happier than when he was outdoors, regardless of the weather. (Prolonged absence of fresh air gave him headaches, which he attributed to a childhood surrounded by heavily scented courtiers; all his life he felt an aversion to strong perfumes.)

Louis spent the afternoon hunting in the park or walking in the gardens. Hunting with the king was by invitation only, although such expeditions were hardly intimate since the king maintained a pack of five hundred staghounds. A stroll through the gardens was open to anyone, and drew a large crowd, albeit a reluctant one — if we are to believe Madame when she says that the king, Mme de Chevreuse, and herself were the only people at court who could walk twenty paces without puffing and sweating.

Returning from his afternoon excursion, Louis would disappear into Mme de Maintenon's apartments, either to visit privately or work with his ministers. The king's secret wife apparently had mixed feelings about these daily visits, as she confessed in a letter to Mme de Glapion: "So I am alone with him, and have to listen to his troubles, if he happens to have any, and bear with his melancholy and his vapors. Sometimes he bursts into tears, which he cannot control, or else he complains of illness. Then some Minister arrives, who is often the bearer of bad news, and the King works with him. If they wish me to be a third in their consultation, they call me. If not, I withdraw a little distance, and it is then that I say my afternoon prayers." Wisely, however, she kept such feelings from her royal spouse.

Three evenings a week, from seven to ten o'clock, Louis XIV held an *appartement* — the king was "at home" to his court. The evening's entertainment began with a concert, followed by billiards (at which Louis was a master) and card games. "Formal informality" was the keynote: sitting in the presence of one's superiors was permitted, as was cutting in at any card table, and guests were free to wander through the state rooms as they liked. The king mingled easily, chatting with courtiers and making jokes, inviting one man to the gaming tables and another to the sumptuous buffets of iced liqueurs in the Room of Abundance. *Appartement* evenings were high spots in the lives of Versailles courtiers. These glittering entertainments were rapturously described in the contemporary newspaper, *the Mercure de France*: "There is a great stir and animation. Diamonds and jewels sparkle in the dazzling luster of chandeliers. People are ecstatic over the resplendent toilettes of the most beautiful women in France . . . A perfume of elegance and aristocracy." But this thrill was far from universal. One courtier wrote: "The entertainments seem to lack spontaneity and appear stiff and formal, with a sense of constraint reigning over the pleasures." Madame found little pleasure in her brother-in-law's gala soirées:

> The *Appartement* is an absolutely intolerable experience. We all troop into the billiard room and squat, no one uttering a word, until the King has finished his game. Then we all get up and go to the music room where someone is singing an aria from some old opera which we have heard a hundred times already. After that we go to the ball. Those who, like me, do not dance have to sit there for hours without budging for an instant, and can neither see nor hear anything other than an interminable minuet. At a quarter to ten we all follow one another in a quadrille, like children reciting a catechism.

But despite such scattered grumblings, an *appartement* was an eagerly awaited event, a chance to mingle with the great and powerful, perhaps even to speak to the king himself. (In the later years of the reign, Louis ceased to put in an appearance at these evenings, deputizing his grandchildren to take his place while he worked with his ministers in Maintenon's salon until supper, but even with the absence of the Sun King, attendance did not slacken.)

Supper was served nominally at ten, though more often than not state business detained the king; Madame, required by etiquette to attend and partake of this meal, complained that usually they did not eat much before eleven-thirty.

For a man so strictly abstemious all day long, Louis XIV's food consumption at supper was astonishing. (Mme de Maintenon once said that if she ate half as much as her husband did at supper she would be dead within a week.) The king would begin with large servings of four different soups — one of them always *soupe Colbert* made with poached eggs, his particular favorite. In the next course, Louis "elegantly" consumed a whole bird (chicken, partridge, or sometimes duck), accompanied by a plate of truffles and a large dish of salad. After a generous serving of garlic-flavored mutton, he downed two large slices of ham. A pastry course followed, complete with preserves and crystallized fruit, then the meal was rounded off with a large platter of cheese and hard-boiled eggs.[8] This gargantuan repast was shared with the entire royal family and always taken *au grand couvert* — in the presence of the full court.

When supper was finished, the king returned at last to his rooms to prepare for bed — but do not think this was accomplished without the sort of ceremonies that had governed the rest of the day. The *coucher,* or "retiring," was no less complex than the *lever.* It began with the king receiving the curtsies of the ladies of the court. When they all had bade him good night, the king would make a sweeping bow, then retire to his closet for an hour's private conversation with his family. By the time he returned to the royal bedchamber (after bidding good night to his dogs), he found the gentlemen assembled for the *grand coucher.* Quickly he said his prayers, then glanced about the room to select the recipient of the day's most distinguished favor: holding the candlestick while the king disrobed. The lucky courtier received his taper from the First Valet of the Bedchamber and held it proudly while the king removed each garment and handed it to the appropriate attendant. In his nightshirt at last, Louis bowed to the assembly and watched them depart. But the day's rites were still not over, for the *grand coucher* was followed by the *petit coucher,* one of the more tiresome rituals: while the king's hair was brushed, those with the right of entry were allowed to approach and speak confidentially with their master — most often to ask for money or office. It is to Louis's credit that every petitioner was listened to with kindness and patience, even if his hopes were not always crowned with success.

The *petit coucher* closed with a ceremony that only the very elect were permitted to view, one too characteristic not to mention: ready for bed, the king now sat upon his *chaise percée,* while the gratified Gentlemen of the Bedchamber (who paid up to fifteen thousand louis d'or for the honor) watched His Majesty relieve himself. The call of nature answered, Louis XIV retired for the night, secure and happy in the knowledge that tomorrow would be just like today.

While the king's secret marriage to Maintenon was a matter of conjecture at court from the mid-1680s on, the changes at Versailles resulting from the marriage were very real. Almost overnight, a radical difference in tone was apparent, as Louis settled into middle age and the almost bourgeois domesticity that his pious bride demanded. Maintenon's growing influence produced a cleaner, better court, but one that grew progressively more dull. The endless rounds of ceremonies and aimless pageantries were not abandoned, but greater and greater emphasis was placed on religious services. Plays and operas were soon banned during Lent, and there was talk of doing away with court theatricals altogether. Talking and laughing during mass (tolerated for decades) was severely frowned upon, as was neglect of one's Easter duties. Piety was definitely in fashion, although one wag observed that "the saints of Versailles became the sinners of Paris." Madame complained: "The Court is growing so dull that people are getting to loathe it, and the King imagines that he is pious if he makes life a bore to other people." Inevitably, religious hypocrisy flourished, and the king who twenty years earlier had protected the topical Molière and laughed heartily at the exposure of the charlatan Tartuffe was now the king who ended all religious tolerance and insisted on the extermination of inoffensive Alpine Protestants. It has been suggested that the fashion for virtue was set by the piety of the late queen and the goodness of the late dauphine, but the real motivation was the king's new conscience, safely, permanently ensconced in her apartments overlooking the Marble Courtyard.

A decade earlier, the king was living in mortal sin with Montespan; now he exhorted women to live devoutly and spoke "so well against patches that even the greatest coquettes dare not wear them." Ten years before, ostentation in costume was de rigueur; now, "a sober suit ensures a man a welcome at Court, whereas to be gaily dressed will earn you a slightly but perceptibly chilly reception." Amusement was still available: evening card parties, gondola rides down the canal, symphonies in the state rooms. But as the century drew to its close, one vital ingredient had disappeared from these entertainments — fun. La Bruyère complained of the all-pervasive melancholy, and Mlle de La Fayette agreed: "Always the same pleasures, always the same hours, and always the same people."

Madame held the king responsible for the court's decline. "He is letting himself go," she wrote her aunt in 1694. "He is visibly sinking, and appears fat and old. His face has changed so that he is hardly recognizable; it becomes more lined from day to day." But with Mme de Maintenon in firm control, Madame had scant hope for any improvement. "All reasonable and honest persons are dissatisfied," she wrote in the autumn of 1696, "but nothing can change the existing state of things."

Unbeknownst to Madame, something could. Change was on the way, jostling over the country roads and heading for the border town of Pont-des-Beauvoisin. A little girl of ten was about to revitalize the dying court of the Sun King.

2

"This Fortunate Marriage"

HER NAME WAS MARIE ADELAIDE and she hailed from the small Alpine duchy of Savoy. Her life would be brief — a scant twenty-seven years — yet it would profoundly affect the Sun King and, thus, the State of France.

Her father was Victor Amadeus, fifteenth duke of Savoy. For over six hundred years, his family had ruled in the province straddling both sides of the southwestern Alpine range between France and Italy. The Romans had called this territory Sabaudia, from which Savoy is quite possibly corrupted, but romantic etymologists insist the name is derived from the Latin *salva via,* or "safe pass" — a reference to the relative ease and security afforded along its road through the heart of the Maritime Alps.

This strategic location earned Savoy's rulers the nickname of "Gatekeeper," since it was within their power to grant or deny access to the safe pass from both sides. The lords of Savoy guarded the door to Italy, checking French aggrandizement on the peninsula; they also staved off Gallic conquest by the land-hungry Holy Roman emperors. For centuries, these crafty gatekeepers had exploited the value of their friendship, reminding the major European powers that the door to the safe pass, if sufficiently greased, was capable of swinging in either direction. None of these gatekeepers was craftier, or more enterprising, than Victor Amadeus.

He was born in Turin, May 14, 1666, the son of Duke Charles Emmanuel and his second wife, Marie Jeanne of Nemours. The infant prince inherited the fine looks of his mother's House: a fair complexion, blue eyes, and pale blond hair. His birth occasioned great rejoicing in the capital, with all of Savoy relieved to see the succession thus secured. Yet no sooner were the bonfires extinguished than rumors spread of the child's extreme frailty. The country, the court, and above all his anxious parents trembled for this delicate baby. Charles Emmanuel summoned every eminent doctor on the continent; professional opinion was often contradictory, and a cure, at best, elusive. The distraught mother watched helplessly as physicians pricked veins and administered purgatives that merely aggravated her son's condition. Disgusted in the end by what seemed to her "little more than quackery," the duchess sent the doctors packing. She had learned of a village doctor, Petechia, who condemned the practice of bloodletting as a panacea to illness and who had achieved local prominence with simple, logical "home remedies."

Petechia was duly called to the palace in Turin. He examined the wasted child and straightaway abolished all remedies previously foisted on him. He put the boy on a strict diet of light biscuits called "grissini," a Piedmontese specialty, and devised a daily program that included plenty of fresh air and exercise. It was a miracle to seventeenth-century eyes: the prince improved at once. Though his health throughout childhood, and even in early manhood, would scarcely be robust, still Victor Amadeus thrived under Petechia's regimen and the doting eyes of Duchess Marie Jeanne.

The maternal feeling the duchess so patently displayed sprang more from dynastic concern than pure affection. Her son was the heir, and would one day rule; regardless of the size of his domains, she would be the mother of a sovereign. She had recently suffered a miscarriage, which the doctors declared had rendered her "incapable"; now her efforts to preserve and nurture her only child doubled. Nothing would be permitted to keep him from his destiny — a destiny in which she expected a lioness's share.

If young Victor Amadeus was smothered with attention from his mother, he was all but neglected by his father. The duke had rejoiced at his son's birth, though like his wife he found it difficult to separate the child from his birthright. He was able, in their rare private moments, to see the boy inside the prince, a boy hungering for parental approval. But the private life of a man had to give place to the public role of a ruler, as the duke well understood; the duchess might lavish undistracted attention on the boy, but Charles Emmanuel had no time to spare from the pressing urgencies of state. So Victor Amadeus grew, fussed over by his mother and pampered by her ladies, respectfully ignored by his father and his court.

The court of Charles Emmanuel, wrote one British expatriate in 1670, was "the jolliest of any in Italy." It was certainly the most democratic. In an age of court factions and favorites — when a Mazarin or a Sarah Churchill could overwhelm their slavish, too mortal monarchs and assume absolute authority — Charles Emmanuel proved himself remarkably in command. He showed an almost revolutionary lack of concern for rank and privilege, boasting that he preferred a man's qualities to the circumstances of his birth. Nor was his boast hollow. Intelligence and ability ensured entry to his circle: the French ambassador sneered at the humble origins of Truchi, the minister of finance, "his father a plowman, very many of his relations exceedingly poor, not worth a cow or pig," but was forced to admit him "a man of elevated parts . . . incomparably the greatest in office, in esteem, in veneration, of anyone here." When genius did appear in the ranks of his nobility, Charles Emmanuel exploited it to the fullest. The exemplary marquis de Pianesse, who served as chief minister for several years, "quitted the world and retired in a religious house to lead a private life," but Charles Emmanuel refused to do without the man's talents; he called daily at the monastery for advice and insisted the marquis keep his seat on the Council of State.

The duke had every need for trusty, competent advisers. His ostensible ally and protector, Louis XIV, had been inculcated by Mazarin with the notion of total Savoyard dependency on France. He envisioned himself a benign father figure, who could wink at the foibles of his prodigal stepson (actually cousin), but who expected obedience in everything. That the tiny duchy might long for self-sufficiency or resent French intervention was unthinkable to the Sun King. Time and again, he demanded troops for his continuing struggle with the Austrian emperor. He expected Savoy to place its frontier forts and citadels at the disposal of the Grand Army, when necessary to place them entirely under French control.[1] A frustrated Charles Emmanuel had no choice but submissive compliance, for what chance had his tiny realm against the forces of the French army? What moments of anguish he endured, watching the greedy French control his fortresses at Pinerolo, La Perouse, Angrone, and Lucerne, dreaming of that day of independence he seemed destined never to enjoy. He had but one hope — the fair-haired little prince — for he knew there would never be another child; ill health or no, young Victor Amadeus was Savoy's only future. Carefully the duke bred his heir with a passion for freedom, a lesson the boy never forgot.

The duke, thirty-eight years old in 1675, was in superb physical condition: "vigorous, lively, and active," also "generous and liberal," observed the French ambassador. He thrived on an abundance of exercise — a trait he transmitted to his granddaughter Adelaide — and he loved hunting "above all things." Often his zeal overcame his common sense, with harrowing results. Once, while he was attacking a stag, his horse was suddenly gored by the struggling animal. The convulsions sent Charles Emmanuel flying through the air and onto the stag's horns. The hunting party watched with horror as their liege lord grappled with the buck. Then dread turned to amazement: of the three combatants — horse, stag, and duke — Charles Emmanuel alone emerged from the fray with his life.

Such strenuous exertion could not fail to leave its mark. In early June 1675, the duke was suddenly taken ill, owing, it was said, to the shock of witnessing a riding accident involving his young son. In spite of (more probably, because of) all medical efforts, his condition rapidly deteriorated. By June 10 he realized he was about to die. He anguished at the thought of leaving so young a successor. He had long accepted that his wife felt more love for her son's position than for the boy himself, yet he was determined she should be regent. He bitterly recalled the disastrous regency of his own mother, whose unlimited power and pro-French policy nearly provoked a civil war, and he resolved not to repeat the mistakes of his father. Despite great pain and a struggle for consciousness, Charles Emmanuel spent his dying day selecting the most able men of his land to assist the duchess in her guardianship. On June 12 he signed his last will, naming the members of his newly created Council of Trustees: the venerable Truchi was appointed, as was the duke's illegitimate uncle, Don Gabriel (considered by many the most qualified person to head the regency). Also named were the archbishop of Turin, the lord chancellor, and the marquis du Bourg — gifted men all, and all firmly committed to the duke's policy of future autonomy.

It was the last, finest gift of Charles Emmanuel to his son and his people. Within hours he was dead, and Victor Amadeus, aged nine, was duke of Savoy.

For almost a decade, Duchess Marie Jeanne — or Madame Royale, as she now styled herself — governed as regent for Victor Amadeus.

Technically, the young duke's minority ended on May 14, 1679, his thirteenth birthday, but on that day, he shocked the court of Turin by announcing his intention to leave the reins of government in the "capable hands of his Regent-Mother."

Shock is indeed a most appropriate adjective, for in the four years since Charles Emmanuel's death, relations between mother and son had degenerated into contempt and thinly veiled hostility. The reason for this was simple enough: power had corrupted Madame Royale.

Her husband's death effected the realization of all Marie Jeanne's ambitions. She had secretly resented her exclusion from politics during his lifetime. Suddenly, everything was transformed — the days of envy on the sidelines were over, and every noble in the land rushed to court her favor. The business of reigning was an intoxication, and she met the role of regent with zest and extraordinary competence (barring her highly unpopular pro-French leaning). She appeared to cooperate with and rely upon her husband's Council of Trustees, though she soon made it plain that she viewed the group as an advisory board, and that in a difference of opinion they, and not she, were expected to concede. She was determined that her court should sparkle and that she should be its brightest star; and so it happened. With a circle of sycophantic courtiers fawning and praising her endlessly, Madame Royale found it all too easy to wish that her present life might continue forever. After all, her son was very young and still very frail; the possibility he might never reach manhood was all too real. She who depended upon him for her very position now concluded that he must be made to depend upon her: one day she might begrudgingly share authority, but she had no intention of surrendering it.

There was, however, one flaw in the enchanted vista that rose before Madame Royale, and that was the insecure foundation upon which all her calculations were based. She failed to take into account the exceptional tenacity and intelligence of her son.

Victor Amadeus endured with resignation the years of his mother's rule — years in which her neglect and indifference instilled in him an almost pathological hatred. He possessed a discretion extraordinary for his age. Not long after his accession, the French ambassador wrote: "This prince is reserved and secretive; it is difficult to divine his real sentiments, in spite of the trouble that one takes to ascertain them; and I have observed that he admits people to his friendship whom I am aware he has regarded with aversion." His shrewd, analytical mind had quickly perceived that court adulation devolved on his rank more than his person (a lesson his mother taught, but unfortunately never grasped herself). So, logic told him, if no one could view him apart from what they stood to gain, then no one could be trusted. Logic also told him that, at thirteen — however legal his claim — he was no match for his formidable opponent. And so he waited, watching and learning.

Had Madame Royale controlled her love of power and been content to live peacefully with her son, she might have enjoyed her position much longer than she did. But carried away by pride and a penchant for intrigue, she cast aside all prudence; ultimately, her downfall was her own doing.

She pushed to marry off the young duke, preferably to some foreign heiress whose position would require the couple to live away from Turin, but Victor Amadeus steadfastly resisted her pressuring. When Louis XIV offered the hand of his niece (and sweetened the prize by pledging to recall the three thousand soldiers he had illegally stationed inside Savoy-Piedmont) Madame Royale reversed her tactics: if marriage would not remove her son from the duchy, then she would do everything in her power to delay it. But time had now run out for the regent.

On September 14, 1684, the eighteen-year-old duke rode out of the capital to Rivoli, his country seat near Turin. Ostensibly it was a shooting party, but he brought with him a large company of soldiers and those members of his suite he felt he could trust. Meanwhile, the official documents announcing his assumption of control had been drawn up and signed, and now waited at the palace for publication. Somehow Madame Royale learned of the plan; the day she had always dreaded had arrived. Before the duke's letter notifying her of dismissal could be delivered, she sent a letter of her own to Rivoli. She wrote that, as the duke had attained an age when he no longer needed her assistance in the administration of government, she remitted to him all authority, and that "should he still wish to leave it in her hands, her decision was inviolable." It was a stunning about-face, but her unexpected tact and meek surrender rescued a potentially volatile situation. The documents were peacefully endorsed by mother and son, and a smooth transference of power was effected.

Victor Amadeus had triumphed, and the thrill of victory — coupled with his mother's surprising acquiescence — overpowered his desire for vengeance. It was whispered at Versailles (where their hostility had been widely discussed) that the duke now treated Madame Royale with marked coolness and had even accused her of misappropriation of public funds — but these rumors were unfair and inaccurate. Nowhere in the duke's correspondence with his mother through this period is there anything to suggest a breach, nor any indication that his grudging respect for her real capabilities had dissipated. Quite the contrary: only days after his takeover, Victor Amadeus wrote the former regent: "Letters from Your Royal Highness will be always of great value to me, and I am much obliged for the one Your Royal Highness has done me the honor to write by means of the Marquis de Bresse. I have been informed of the interest taken by Your Royal Highness in the successful issue of affairs . . . These tokens of goodwill are most precious to me, and the gratitude I feel is only what is due from a son who is deeply attached to Your Royal Highness." Certainly it was not an effusive letter, but then it was not in Victor Amadeus's character to be openly emotional. Most definitely it was not the letter of a vindictive winner. Power and authority now rested with him alone — still the young man was keen enough to recognize his mother's talents and to envision the use of those gifts for his own ends.

The duke was already politically shrewd, yet he was human: it was noted that "without disguise, he rejoiced at the termination of her rule." And after rejoicing, his thoughts returned to marriage. Despite his innate francophobia, he recognized the international prestige an alliance with the House of Bourbon would bring. Negotiations began.

The bride Louis XIV had designated was his niece, Anne Marie d'Orléans. She was the younger daughter of "Monsieur," the king's only brother, Philippe, duc d'Orléans. Her mother, Monsieur's first wife, was the beautiful and tragic Minette, Henrietta Marie of England. This first duchesse d'Orléans, daughter of the executed Charles I, possessed considerable charm and grace, and had captured the affection not only of her brother-in-law Louis, but of the entire French court. The only person at court who seemed immune to Minette's delightful personality was her husband, a notorious homosexual who openly preferred the company of handsome young noblemen to that of his lovely wife. Nevertheless, conjugal duty prevailed: Marie Louise (destined to be the first wife of Carlos II of Spain) arrived in 1662, and on May 11, 1669, arrived a second child, Anne Marie.

Barely one year later — June 30, 1670 — the exquisite Minette was dead. The court, and all of Paris, suspected she had been poisoned by her husband's jealous lover, the chevalier de Lorraine. The postmortem examination stated peritonitis as the cause of death, but few accepted this theory and all mourned her loss. Louis XIV ordered the sort of funeral usually reserved for crowned heads. Bossuet preached a funeral oration considered by many the most eloquent in history, and the diarist La Fare noted sadly that "in losing the Princesse, the Court lost the only person of her rank who was capable of liking and distinguishing real merit."

The two little princesses Minette left behind were not destined to be motherless for long. Much against his will (and to the chevalier de Lorraine's disgust), Monsieur was married to the indominable Charlotte Elisabeth, princess of the Palatinate, in 1671. If her bridegroom inspired scant affection with his mincing airs and his heavily rouged cheeks, the second duchesse d'Orléans — also called Madame — was drawn to his poor, neglected daughters. They in turn came to love her deeply. Within two years of her arrival at Versailles, Madame wrote to her aunt, the electress of Hanover, about little Anne Marie: "She was but two years old when I came to France. I can therefore say I am the only mother she has had: she loves me as such, and I look upon her as my child." Monsieur, whatever other emotions he maintained, experienced gratitude and a grudging admiration for this stolid German woman who turned his palace at Saint-Cloud into a home.

Anne Marie's cozy childhood was shattered abruptly in 1679, when her older sister, Marie Louise, was selected to marry the king of Spain. The sisters were devoted to each other, and their grief at being parted only increased their extensive popularity at Versailles. The little princesse was brought up suddenly to the adult realization that a similar destiny — "banishment" from the world she knew and loved — one day awaited her. She grew quiet and reserved, intensifying her devotion to her doting stepmother and sometimes indulgent father.

Of the two girls, Marie Louise was said to have inherited their mother's striking good looks, and Anne Marie, her charming manner and sweet disposition. One might be tempted to dismiss as partial Madame's claim that Anne Marie was "one of the most amiable and virtuous of women," but there is the more objective Mme de Faverges to second the opinion, praising the princesse's "air of dignity tempered by an expression of goodness." In 1684, the year of her engagement, she was just fifteen, not particularly beautiful or intelligent, but "of the type of beauty found in the House of Bourbon." Her face was soft and oval, with a high forehead, an aquiline nose and smiling lips. Her thick black hair fell in long curls across "white and shapely shoulders."

Of course, all this information had been transmitted to a curious court in Turin, where the prospective bridegroom still vacillated. Victor Amadeus was young, but not naïve: he recognized that the Sun King's proposal was more an order than an offer, his intention being to reestablish the now waning French influence in Turin. This was Victor Amadeus's dilemma. He understood that Savoy could not yet oppose mighty France, that he must continue to equivocate and wait; when at last he was forced into acceptance, he swore to avoid the pitfalls in which French brides had trapped his father and grandfather.

In January 1684 he wrote his ambassador, Ferrero, in Paris: "I wish to inform you that it is my intention that Mademoiselle should leave Paris at the beginning of April. I tell you this in confidence so that you may undertake those steps you think best in this affair." In confidence, for secrecy was vital: the terms of the princesse's dowry were still unfinished, and Victor Amadeus was determined to hold out for the greatest settlement possible. While assuring Ferrero he was "quite satisfied at the way in which you are managing the formalities," he urged the ambassador to keep working on the dowry terms, simultaneously advising him not to make Savoy appear too greedy and not to offend the French negotiators, since "if France is not moved by friendly dispositions, no claims or requests would alter her decision, for I have had reason to know by experience that His Majesty and his Ministers are inflexible in matters on which they are determined."

Ferrero duly requested an audience and was received by Louis XIV at Versailles on January 27, 1684. Formally he sought the hand of the princesse, and the king gave assurance that the match was agreeable to him. Louis expressed his "immense satisfaction" on the projected marriage; referring to the esteem and affection he had always felt for the House of Savoy, he remarked, "It is Mademoiselle's good genius as well as her education that has brought her this fortunate marriage, in which I hope that all parties will be satisfied." Ferrero turned next to the delicate matter of the French troops still stationed in Piedmont. The Sun King flashed a dazzling smile and replied that "as his wish was always to oblige others when it was possible, he had given orders to his troops to cross the mountains back to France."

Ferrero withdrew, and Louis XIV remained for some time alone in his study with Monsieur. Finally, Anne Marie was summoned and informed of the duke's proposal. The king told her he would not reply without her consent, adding that Monsieur, "who was a good father, was also of the opinion that no engagement must be contracted with

the Duke of Savoy till he was assured of Mademoiselle's approval."
Louis XIV explained that "though this marriage would not make her
a queen, she need not be less happy for this reason, as at the Court of
Savoy nothing she required would be wanting. She would find the
same habits and customs as in France, by which she would feel less
regret at leaving her own country." The Sun King may have persuaded
himself the final decision rested with his niece, but his court was not
so deluded: "The King added that if he himself had a daughter to
marry, she would have had to accept the Duke of Savoy, who was not
only a great Prince, but a gentleman as well" — hardly a subtle attempt to sway her choice. To no one's surprise, the princesse consented: with an obedient curtsy and tears in her eyes, Anne Marie
answered that she had no will save the king's and her father's.

Reaction to the engagement at Versailles was unanimously favorable. Madame rushed off to write her aunt the happy news, remarking
she only hoped "a similar good fortune awaits my own daughter."[2]
Monsieur sought out the Savoyard ambassador, and told Ferrero he
hoped "his daughter would prove to be a comfort to His Royal Highness, as besides her sweet disposition she had the advantage of a good
education" — one of his rare compliments to Madame.

In Turin, the duke's subjects were no less enthusiastic: "The news
was announced last week to the town by a salvo of artillery and
bombs," the French ambassador reported. "The Princesse's portrait
was placed on a chair in the Throne Room, and all the Court claimed
the honor of kissing the Duke's hand."

Learning that his suit had been accepted, Victor Amadeus was
moved to write his future bride proper phrases of affection and interest; he encountered instead the seventeenth-century royal bugaboo:
etiquette. Nowhere were its strictures more strictly enforced than at
Versailles. How one rose in the morning and retired at night; how one
ate or drank, made love or war; when one sat and when one stood;
when to speak, and more importantly, with whom; even how to knock
on a door ("One must gently scratch the doors of the chamber, not
rudely strike them. Moreover, if one wishes to pass out when the doors
are closed, it is not permissible to open them oneself, but they must be
opened by the usher." — from *Etat de France*, 1694): everything was
ruled by etiquette. And these rules were scrupulously observed: every
gentleman in Europe attached great importance to the tenets of etiquette, for they defined his rank and station, and thus provided a
petrified stability to society. To our modern, egalitarian minds, they
provide an inexhaustible study of the ludicrous.

Victor Amadeus's epistle of love reached Ferrero in Paris in early February, falling immediately under the strictures of French etiquette. It was, of course, unthinkable for the ambassador to simply hand the letter to its intended recipient: Ferrero was obliged to inform Monsieur of his possession and its contents; Monsieur in turn informed his daughter of the letter's existence. Now arose the first procedural problem — for no man was allowed to enter the princesse's apartments. Monsieur graciously consented to bend the rules for this special occasion. But a second and more serious obstacle surfaced, for etiquette stated unequivocally that no fiancée could receive communication from her betrothed unless that gentleman had previously been presented to the king. Obviously Victor Amadeus could not satisfy this requirement — and it devolved on his emissary and now proxy, Ferrero, to request the necessary audience of presentation. Louis XIV was a very busy man, and several days elapsed before the king could receive the Savoyard ambassador (to the intense annoyance of the curious young bride). At last, the mandatory presentation was made, and Ferrero hurried off to the apartments of the impatient fiancée. Still, etiquette was unrelenting: the letter was handed to the princesse, who then requested formal permission from her father to open the envelope. Having finally satisfied all the requirements of this implacable man-made god of order and decorum, Anne Marie was reported to have blushed as she read her future husband's declarations.

But this wasted time was trivial in comparison to the lengthy delays and complications that ensued over the marriage contract itself — though here blame rests not so much with etiquette as with the characters involved, the cunning Sun King and the crafty duke of Savoy. Much correspondence and several weeks of wrangling passed as the combatants each tried to best the other. At last a satisfactory compromise was reached: Louis agreed to settle ninety thousand francs on Anne Marie, plus sixty thousand francs' worth of jewelry. In addition, 240,000 francs were appropriated from the interest on the marriage settlement of Anne Marie's late mother; on receipt of this money, Victor Amadeus was to renounce all future claims to his father-in-law's property. For his part, the duke of Savoy guaranteed his bride a settlement of forty thousand francs, a yearly allowance of one hundred thousand francs, and more than eighty thousand francs' worth of jewelry as her private property.

The wedding date was set for April 19, 1684. On the eighteenth, the marriage contract was signed in the king's study at Versailles. Surrounded by the Children and Grandchildren of France, Louis XIV listened intently as the terms of the contract were read aloud. He signed the document, then handed the pen to his son. The dauphin's signature was followed by those of Monsieur and Madame, then by the duc de Chartres (the bride's stepbrother). Lastly the pen was given to the bride herself, and the alliance was concluded. There followed a brief betrothal ceremony performed by Cardinal de Bouillon; given the physical distance that separated the young couple and the fact that the wedding ceremony would be held on the morrow, this served little purpose save to satisfy the formalities of etiquette. The solemnities ended with a magnificent banquet for the entire court in the state apartments.

The next morning, Anne Marie wrote for the first time to her new mother-in-law. Her letter to Madame Royale was graceful and touching in its simplicity. It clearly revealed that the princesse had remained fresh and unspoiled amid the luxuries of Versailles: "19 April 1684: I so earnestly wish, Madame, to gain your affection that it has given me intense pleasure to receive your kind expressions of sympathy for me. I trust that my conduct will persuade you better than my words of my desire to please you and to live with you in such a way that will contribute as much to your satisfaction as to my happiness. I sincerely hope that my obedience, attentions, and affection, when they are known to you, will not lessen the sentiments that I would wish to believe you will feel for me."

The wedding ceremony began shortly before noon. The ambassador of Savoy went first to fetch the young duc du Maine (Louis XIV's acknowledged illegitimate son), who had been chosen proxy for Victor Amadeus. Together they arrived at the princesse's apartment, where the excited bride awaited. She was dressed in a stunning gown of silver brocade, trimmed with lace and covered in jewels. Her train — nine yards long — was cloth of silver, powdered with diamonds and pearls, and so heavy that three adults were required to carry it. Around her neck was a splendid rope of pearls that Victor Amadeus had sent following their engagement (valued by the *Gazette de France* at thirty thousand pistoles). The proxy bridegroom was no less suitably attired: the duc du Maine's suit of black Venetian velvet was covered almost entirely in diamonds and trimmed with narrow rose-colored ribbons of silk. His plumed hat (also rose-colored) was studded with one million francs' worth of diamonds and pearls.

With Maine on her left and the Savoyard diplomat on her right, Anne Marie entered the apartments of Mme la dauphine,[3] where the princesses of the blood had assembled. The august body then marched ("according to their rank," the *Gazette* was careful to point out) toward the chapel; the king and his suite joined them in the Hall of Mirrors, and one hundred Swiss Guards lined the steps of the Great Staircase, down to the chapel doors, each saluting the bride as she passed by.

The remainder of the court awaited the bridal party inside the chapel. Cardinal de Bouillon, holding a magnificent crozier, sat in a gilt chair with his back to the altar as Anne Marie and Maine advanced down the aisle and the rest of the royal family took their positions. The bride and (proxy) groom knelt together on velvet cushions; it was noted that the king stood beside his niece throughout the ceremony, rather than taking his customary place at the royal prie-dieu, a signal token of his affection. When asked by the cardinal if she accepted the duke of Savoy as her husband, the bride stood and curtsied — first to the king, then to her parents — before nodding consent.

At the close of the nuptial mass, the marriage register was set before the king. He duly affixed his signature, then gave his hand to the new duchess of Savoy; leading her out of the chapel, he escorted her to one of his own carriages. The *Gazette* reported the new duchess was "bathed in tears" and "made some remark in so low a voice that it could not be overheard . . . The King seemed to reassure her with that persuasive manner which is such a charm of his." Kissing her three times — an unusually demonstrative gesture on his part — he put her in the royal coach, and she was driven across the Versailles courtyard. Instead of entering the palace by the usual door, she was taken to the Courtyard of the Princes, to signify that now she entered Versailles not as a member of the French royal family but as a foreign princess.

The conflicting emotions of the day overcame the ingenuous Anne Marie: reaching her father's apartments, she fainted and her maids hurriedly cut open the laces of her gown. The bride was allowed a few hours of rest and an intimate visit with her parents and the king before presiding over a magnificent wedding supper. As evening drew on, the time approached for Anne Marie to begin her journey to the border. When her father arrived on the doorstep to escort her down to the waiting convoy, "the young Sovereign threw herself at his feet to implore his blessing; both father and daughter were in tears, but Monsieur at last raised her from her knees, kissed her, and after a touching farewell with Madame, Monsieur started with her on the journey as far as Juvisy."

The last rays of sunlight transfused the marble palace, and the carriage wheels clattered loudly through the cobblestone courtyard; the duchess of Savoy wept quietly on her father's shoulder, and departed from Versailles forever.

The young bridegroom had left Turin and arrived at Chambéry on May 1, there to await his wife's arrival. Early on the sixth, it was learned that Anne Marie had reached the Savoy border at Pont-des-Beauvoisin, some thirty miles west of Chambéry. Immediately, the duke assembled his escort, and to the sounds of fife and trumpets, and the beating of drums, he marched forth with a company of guards and archers, pages and servants.

Anne Marie had only just finished her meal in Pont-des-Beauvoisin when sounds of the approaching procession reached her party. She was informed that the duke himself was riding to meet her. Emotion overcame her: heedless of protocol and the great god Etiquette, she impetuously gathered up her skirts and ran — ran! — out to the street and straight into her husband's arms. Victor Amadeus was shocked and disarmed by this public show of feeling. Her spontaneity moved him deeply, and he responded in kind to her embrace; the Savoyards, prepared to receive a haughty princesse of the highest refinement, were stunned by the spectacle before them.

After a brief rest, they began their journey back to Chambéry. They approached the town just before sundown, and were greeted with a display of fireworks that illuminated the dusky sky. The entire city turned out to welcome its new mistress. Passing through the Chambéry gates, the bridal couple rode immediately to the royal chapel, where they received a nuptial benediction from the archbishop of Grenoble. As they walked from the chapel to the nearby castle, they stopped often to acknowledge the wild acclamations of the crowd. Anne Marie was allowed only five minutes to rest before attending a *grand souper* for the duke's suite and the town officials. Well past midnight, husband and wife were ushered to the royal bedchamber, and the archbishop arrived for the traditional blessing of the marriage bed. Though obviously exhausted, the new duchess remained on her knees throughout the interminable ceremony. While the first light of dawn crept over the hillside, the bride and groom were finally permitted to go to bed.

From that moment forward, every interest and ambition of Anne Marie, duchess of Savoy, was centered in Victor Amadeus alone. To him she gave her absolute trust. The tragedy was that she loved a man with whom she had no real chance for happiness: she offered him wholehearted devotion, and he returned heartless contempt, moodiness, and callous indifference. Though she would suffer deeply, Anne Marie would also learn to suffer silently — and if she failed to win her husband's undivided affection, she never lost his esteem or respect.

The morning of May 10, the duke and duchess reached the country seat at Rivoli, where Madame Royale and the court of Turin waited to receive them. Madame Royale met the newlyweds in the courtyard of the villa and greeted her new daughter-in-law with a well-rehearsed show of affection. When they walked upstairs to meet the court, she deferred to the new duchess in the position of honor — the right side of the staircase — but Anne Marie refused to take precedence, an artless gesture that more than favorably impressed her imperious mother-in-law and her husband's watchful nobles. En masse the royal party set off for the capital, arriving that same evening.

The *Gazette de France* reported later (May 24, 1684) that as the ducal couple entered Turin, "the town was ablaze with the light of illuminations and fireworks. The cannons were fired three hundred times as a salute and the same number of rockets were discharged." The golden glow of novelty lingered pleasantly through those first summer months: the duchess, receiving the formal compliments of the Senate, the Chamber of Commerce, and the other official bodies of the town during her first week, charmed each and every representative, capturing hearts that remained hers forever. The ambassadors of Milan and England each vied to outdo the other in extolling her praises, complimenting her wonderful self-possession and the surprising extent of her knowledge, her appreciation of the fine arts in Turin, and above all, her elegance and refinement.

She, in turn, was delighted with her new home, for Louis XIV had spoken accurately when he had promised she would not feel an alien in Turin. Essentially French in character — in 1684 French was more widely spoken than Italian — Turin had been labeled "the antechamber to France," and invariably foreign travelers, impressed by the "agreeable and sociable manners of the place," were reminded of Paris. Anne Marie visited the shops and homes of her new subjects and soon the enduring love and loyalty of the common people was hers. Notwithstanding the relationship of their lovely young mistress to the dreaded Sun King, the Savoyards wholeheartedly shared Louis XIV's enthusiasm for "this fortunate marriage."

But inside the private apartments of the palace, the honeymoon had ended. Victor Amadeus found the affairs of state competing for attention with his new bride. During their first months of married life, Anne Marie made little attempt to mask her impatience when her husband was constantly called away to attend to the pressing business of government. She looked forward with eagerness to the rare short hours when Victor Amadeus might throw off his burdens; she assumed that he shared in her wish to pass their leisure time together.

But the new husband did *not* share this wish. Little by little, with mounting remorse, Victor Amadeus realized that the total independence he had envisioned still eluded him, that he had merely exchanged Madame Royale's chafing shackles for the silken cords of domesticity with which his wife now meant to bind him. What pleased the duke best was freedom from emotional obligation. Anne Marie's ingenuous charm and selfless devotion made him uncomfortable, and he discovered that her company was not the distraction he thought he required. To her dismay and confusion, the duchess saw increasingly less of the duke.

Much of this estrangement was rooted in an unacknowledged issue that preoccupied them both. Victor Amadeus cared little whether he would come to love his wife, but he cared greatly that his wife should give him an heir. Summer ended, Christmas came and went, and still the duchess showed no signs of pregnancy. The tension between the couple mounted, relieving itself in trivial outbursts of pique that avoided the fundamental problem.

For her part, Anne Marie prayed desperately for a child. She felt instinctively that an heir would promote her heart's desire — winning the love of her adored husband — but she was cursed with the type of constitution that made conception difficult. It was a trait that she would sadly pass on to her daughter Adelaide: both women would suffer a history of debilitating miscarriages, difficult pregnancies, long and painful labors.

At last, Anne Marie's prayers were answered; late in March 1685, she announced to her husband that she was expecting a child. Victor Amadeus was overjoyed, and for a few short months returned his wife's deep love with kindness and something akin to affection. He demonstrated great concern for the duchess's prenatal health and safety; while basking in her husband's newfound solicitousness, Anne Marie virtually retired from public life at his request.

Spring passed in Savoy, then another golden summer. By autumn, the duchess had taken to her bed. On the evening of December 5, 1685, the first labor pains began. Despite all the precautions, labor proved extremely difficult; by the afternoon of the sixth, there were fears both mother and child might die. Throughout, Victor Amadeus never left his wife's bedside. At last, the moment arrived. The attendant court pressed closer, craning their necks, silently begging God to send an heir.

And the duchess gave birth — to a girl.

The Gnat and the Lion

THE ARRIVAL OF LITTLE MARIE ADELAIDE brought about a (temporary) reconciliation of her parents. Having ascertained that his daughter was healthy and well formed, the duke's attentions were focused on his dangerously exhausted wife. He ordered a camp bed placed in her room; to the court's great surprise, he remained there for several days until she had passed out of danger.

Neither parent expressed disappointment at the birth of a daughter, although Victor Amadeus's feelings appeared somewhat ambivalent. We are told that he "showed great interest in the little Princesse, and often went to see how she was." Still, he canceled the scheduled fireworks and bonfires, and all official ceremonies of congratulation.[1] Motherhood had a profound effect on Anne Marie: not only did she have a new infant on whom to lavish her thwarted affections, she seemed also to have a new husband. His care and concern throughout her ordeal revived her hopes for intimacy.

Each Sunday of carnival season in the early months of 1686, the duke held a gala ball at the palace, and twice a week he organized small dances for Anne Marie in their private apartments. Every diplomatic dispatch of the period emphasized his model behavior as husband and father. His happiness at his daughter's safe delivery and his confidence that sons would soon follow affected his own role as son: even Madame Royale was somewhat forgiven, and began taking a larger part in the incubating family unit.

Marie Adelaide (or more simply Adelaide, as her mother preferred to call her) was christened in the royal chapel on December 27. Her grandmother and great-uncle, the prince de Carignan, were sponsors; near the gilded font stood the marquise de Saint-Germain, newly appointed nursemaid to the infant princesse. To the radiant Anne Marie, standing proudly beside her handsome young husband, the baptism seemed to usher in both a new year and a new era: henceforth, they would live in contentment, peace, and harmony.

Perhaps they might have — were it not that Anne Marie's uncle was the king of France.

From the very day of his wedding, Victor Amadeus found the French attitude toward his tiny realm growing increasingly more unbearable, for Louis XIV expected the duke to grovel and fawn at the "honor" of marriage into the Bourbon dynasty. Recent developments further strengthened his insistence on Savoy's deference. The year 1684 had been a watershed for the Sun King. With impunity, he had robbed the Holy Roman Empire of the eastern bank of the Rhine, and had removed Spain as a first-class power. Holland was still too weak from its English wars to give any protest, and the victorious English king, Charles II, was his secret pensioner. The French army was the finest in the world; French influence predominated Europe. To be crossed by an insignificant little prince (and a family member as well!) was ludicrous. The mighty Sun King simply would not tolerate such independence.

Sadly, the "lessons" he deemed necessary to bring the duke to heel served only to further alienate Victor Amadeus. In the decade following 1685 — the first ten years of Adelaide's short life — the duke's relations with France would run full spectrum, from ally to enemy and back again. Sainte-Beuve likened Victor Amadeus's dealings with Louis XIV to the gnat that infuriated the lion, though he felt him completely justified: "The cunning and constant duplicity employed by the Duke would merit only detestation and blame, had not Louis XIV drawn it entirely on himself by his abuse of power, and justified his weaker rival in paying back the proud and powerful monarch with all the ruse of which he was capable." The image is particularly apt in its vividness — for ten years the industrious little Savoyard gnat buzzed tormentingly about the head of the overproud French lion; aroused at last, the old lion swung a mighty paw at the obnoxious annoyance and settled back into his lethargy. Sure enough, within moments, the gnat returned with dogged persistence.

One glaring example of the Sun King's overbearing interference occurred in the autumn of 1685, as the duchess entered her seventh month of pregnancy. Victor Amadeus announced his intention to visit Venice, and Louis XIV was instantly alarmed. Though the duke maintained this was nothing more than a pleasure trip, the French king feared a ruse. He knew the emperor had never ceased his attempts to woo Savoy from the French sphere into a German alliance, and he suspected the "pleasure trip" to be a mask for secret negotiations. Savoy's strategic importance was too great to risk. Blustering with omnipotence, the king of France absolutely forbade the duke of Savoy to enter the Venetian republic — threatening to send eight thousand troops into Savoy should his order be ignored. The French ambassador, d'Estrades, stretched his diplomatic talents to their fullest in order to soften the blow of this ultimatum; Victor Amadeus listened politely and acquiesced with good grace. Inside, he seethed with resentment.

The duke's anger barely had time to cool when a second and more humiliating incident occurred. His uncle, Prince Emmanuel Philibert de Carignan, expressed a wish to marry Caterina d'Este, a princess of Modena. The duke approved the match, but warned his uncle to expect objection from Versailles (Savoy would not be allowed to ally itself with any but of the Sun King's choosing), and he requested that the negotiations be kept top secret. The contract was virtually complete when the scheme was discovered by France. Predictably, Louis XIV was enraged and curtly ordered the duke to stop the proceedings and prevent the marriage from taking place. Victor Amadeus was put in an awkward position: secretly he sided with his uncle, but he knew well enough the Sun King could only be appeased by a public attempt to dissuade him from the marriage. However, the prince de Carignan himself was under no obligation to bow to French dictates and firmly refused to abandon his intended. The couple were married, and Louis XIV exploded — not so much at the wedding itself, but at the blatant contempt for his orders. It was time for another "lesson."

The first victims of the Sun King's ire were the bridegroom's sisters, the old princesse de Carignan and the princesse of Baden. The former, who had lived peacefully in Paris for many years, was forbidden to appear at court; the latter was ordered to retire to Rennes in virtual exile. To further express his displeasure, Louis XIV expelled the Modenese ambassador from Versailles, then sent scathing instructions to Victor Amadeus: first, he was to banish the prince and his bride from Turin, then he was to arrange an immediate annulment.

While forced to comply with the king's demand for banishment, Victor Amadeus refused to open annulment proceedings without first

consulting the Church on the marriage's legality. An assembly of ec-
clesiastics headed by the archbishop of Turin met and declared the
union lawfully binding. The prince and his bride enjoyed the ultimate
victory — their marriage sanctioned by the Church — but at the time
it seemed a small one, forced as they were into exile. The resentment
of the common people was obvious as the ill-starred couple left Turin;
it was insignificant compared to that of the again defeated Victor
Amadeus. (The hurt and surprise that Louis XIV expressed at the
duke's eventual defection from the French camp only points up the
myopic self-absorption with which he governed France.)

Louis XIV had appointed himself master of the duke of Savoy's
family. Now he intended to prove that his jurisdiction extended into
the duke's state as well. His interference would have disastrous effects:
four thousand innocent Protestants would be killed, and Victor Amadeus's already tenuous loyalty to France would be destroyed. Very
nearly destroyed as well would be the "fortunate marriage" the Sun
King himself had engineered.

Nestled in the Maritime Alps of Piedmont was a small religious colony
called the Waldenses (after their founder, Petrus de Waldo). This band
of simple farmers subscribed to Calvinism, their freedom of worship
guaranteed by the dukes of Savoy since the early days of the seventeenth century.

Then, one month before Adelaide's birth — on November 18,
1685 — Louis XIV revoked the Edict of Nantes, promulgated by his
grandfather, Henri IV, in 1589, which promised freedom of conscience
to French Protestants. These Huguenots were now given a choice of
conversion, persecution — or permanent exile. An estimated one hundred thousand fled to England or Holland, Protestant Scandinavia, or
the New World — or across the southeastern border of France into the
Waldensian valleys.

This was more than the Sun King could tolerate, and Victor Amadeus was summarily ordered to destroy the thriving colony of heretics.
The duke's Catholicism was remarkably free of the Sun King's bigotry
and he had no wish to turn on his own subjects. For three months, he
stalled, cleverly placating the French ambassador with empty promises
of compliance. At last, an outraged Louis XIV exhorted d'Estrades:

> I see that your negotiations are quite ineffectual. All the same, you are
> to tell the Duke that as long as he allows the Huguenots to live on the

confines of his estates, his authority is not sufficient to prevent the desertion of my Calvinist subjects. He can judge for himself that I shall not permit matters to remain as they are, and as I shall probably suffer some annoyance from the insolence of these heretics, it is just as likely as not that he will find an alteration in my sentiments towards him, which hitherto have been most friendly. I am confident that the Duke will seriously reflect over what I have said.

The duke's reflections were grim indeed, but there was no avoiding an ultimatum from the Sun King. On April 22, 1686, he reluctantly marched out of Turin at the head of an army of French troops, thoughtfully provided by his wife's uncle — eight thousand holy crusaders against thirty-seven hundred farmers.

It was over in a fortnight, the entire countryside depopulated. Men and women were tracked down and bayoneted on the spot. More than one thousand children were torn from their parents and placed in Catholic homes to be raised in the One True Faith. The imprisoned "rebels" suffered horribly through deprivation, torture, and starvation: more than seven hundred died in one month at the castello di Verrua. Louis XIV callously remarked to his ambassador: "It is very fortunate for the Duke of Savoy that illness is saving him a great deal of trouble with the rebels of the valleys, and I have no doubt he will easily console himself with the loss of subjects who can be replaced with others far more loyal and dependable." After two years of incarceration, free passage from the country was granted the remaining Waldenses: forty-two half-living men and women — the remnants of a proud mountain culture — straggled into Switzerland.

In June, the French force withdrew from Savoy. From Casal, Maréchal Catinat dutifully reported the duke's compliments to Versailles, declaring himself "highly satisfied at the terms in which the Duke showed his attachment to Your Majesty."

The terms were all for show. Victor Amadeus had been forced to bend and grovel before the mighty Sun King. His country had been devastated. He was bitter and disillusioned; hatred for France seared his very soul. Someday, he vowed, he would be avenged.

Religious massacre in a distant Alpine province ostensibly could have little effect on an infant princess, but the changes produced within the ducal household because of that religious massacre were of enormous consequence to Adelaide. Victor Amadeus was no longer able to disassociate his wife from her monstrous uncle; all pretense of affection was abandoned. Still, an heir was required and, early in 1687, the duchess was again pregnant. When, on August 15, a second daughter, Marie Louise, was born, the duke made no attempt to conceal his disappointment from his wife. All celebrations were again canceled, and reports of his callous disregard for the blameless Anne Marie inevitably reached Versailles, where Madame wrote of her stepdaughter: "Her husband is so savage that I fear he will end by going out of his mind."

Monsieur was outraged by the duke's emotional abuse of his daughter. He demanded that his brother take action, and Louis XIV, motivated by sincere affection for his niece, responded with a harsh missive on the proper respect due a princesse of France.

In retaliation, Victor Amadeus took himself a mistress.

Jeanne Baptiste, contessa di Verrua, was ravishingly beautiful and unscrupulously self-serving. French by birth and well trained in the arts of love, Verrua quickly perceived the advantages of a liaison with the duke of Savoy, and she played her hand with all the dexterity of a Montespan: for almost one year she resisted the duke's advances, fanning his ardor to a fevered pitch. At last assured of his emotional enslavement, she succumbed. "Last Wednesday," the French ambassador, d'Arcy, wrote to Versailles on January 20, 1689, "Mme di Verrua was for the first time at the Opera in a dimly lit box above that of the Duchess of Savoy; the Duke was always with her . . . Her husband, the Conte, and her uncle, the Abbé, who were in one of my boxes, appeared interested in watching the Duke's movements . . . though I cannot gather that the undeniable love of the Prince for Mme di Verrua has caused either disapproval or trouble in the Conte's house."

Victor Amadeus was shameless in his infatuation. To have his love at his side during his annual expedition to Nice, he insisted his wife accompany him — and bring along Verrua as her lady-in-waiting. Shortly before their planned departure, word reached Turin of the death of Anne Marie's sister, the queen of Spain. The duchess was prostrate with grief and begged permission to retire for a time to the country alone. Without his wife in Nice, there was no justification for his mistress's presence: with supreme insensitivity, Victor Amadeus insisted Anne Marie still make the journey.

The motley party — the self-obsessed lovers, the grieving wife, and their embarrassed entourage — started south in early May. They stopped in several towns and villages along their route where, according to ancient custom, the duke claimed one thousand livres in fealty from the inhabitants. This proved a wise measure, for their expenses in Nice quickly rose to over six hundred pistoles a day (an exorbitant sum for a prince already noted for his parsimony).

In Nice, the lovers cavorted with reckless, shameless abandon while sad Anne Marie locked herself away, mourning the loss of her sister and pining for her two little daughters. The conte di Verrua, along as the duke's equerry, left after the first week (d'Arcy informed Versailles), "being apparently disgusted at his wife's conduct, which, if not absolutely criminal, is, to say the least of it, very bad and imprudent."

When the court returned to Turin in August, Anne Marie was happily reunited with Adelaide and Marie Louise, and the contessa de Verrua found herself pregnant. With her lover's connivance, her next step was bold and dramatic: under the cover of night, she escaped from her husband's home, took sanctuary in the convent of the Sisters of Mercy, and severed all communication with the Verrua family. The court was scandalized, none more than d'Arcy, who informed Versailles: "The morning after Mme di Verrua had entered the convent, the Prince, as if quite astonished himself, turned to the Duchess and said, 'Well, Madame, what do you think of this extraordinary resolve of Mme di Verrua, who, as report says, has entered the Convent of the Sisters of Mercy? Surely you will agree with me that she merits some interest should be shown her?' . . . The only reply the Duchess made was to bend her head and drop her eyelids."

The humiliations inherent in the role of deserted wife were just beginning; neither Anne Marie's silent tolerance nor Louis XIV's outraged lectures on morality could stem the course of the affair. The birth of a son to Verrua in January 1690 strengthened her hold over Victor Amadeus, and greatly increased her unpopularity in Turin. Ruthlessly she used the boy without the slightest show of maternal feeling: she coerced Victor Amadeus into settling on her a life annuity of twelve thousand livres, then into appointing her First Lady of the Bedchamber to the duchess. This afforded her a luxurious apartment inside the palace; it also forced poor Anne Marie into daily contact with her more successful rival.

Characteristically, the duchess accepted this painful state of affairs without protest. She could not, did not, lower her dignity with ugly scenes or jealous fits. In fact, her demeanor with the contessa was so sweet and generous that the startled (and shamed?) Verrua responded with the greatest respect and courtesy in the duchess's presence.

During this difficult time, one ambassador described the duchess: "She is a Princesse of great virtue, who has studied the Duke's character, and has found the surest way of adapting herself to it . . . In spite of himself, the Duke has been forced to render to her wisdom and her merits all the justice that is due her . . . She leads a very retired life, and takes no part at all in any sort of affairs."

A very retired life indeed, for however tolerant, Anne Marie was only human, and life away from the ducal palace — where Verrua so obviously held sway — was infinitely more preferable. She had adopted the Savoyard taste for open air and country living, a trait already highly apparent in the vivacious young Adelaide. Fortunately, the royal family maintained several residences outside Turin, scattered about the lush countryside. Most striking of them all was Valentino, a fine Renaissance building in the center of a large park; other favorite haunts included the Villa at Rivoli, Charles Emmanuel's shooting box near Veneri, and a magnificent country seat at Moncalieri.

But the favorite residence of them all, the place Adelaide considered home, was the charming Vigna di Madama.[2] Built in 1649 by Cardinal Maurice of Savoy, it passed on his death to his nephew's wife, Duchess Ludovica Maria. Thereafter, it served as dower house for the duchesses of Savoy.

French in style, the large, four-storied central building included a magnificent double staircase — an imitation of the famed Horseshoe Staircase at Fontainebleau. French influence was also reflected in the extensive grounds, with the gardens laid out in terraces up the sloping hill behind the house; here and there the shaded groves were spotted with fanciful temples and picturesque belvederes. Less than thirty minutes from Turin, the Vigna, with its magical gardens, its acres of fragrant vineyards and blooming orchards, remained for centuries a favorite haunt of Italian royal children — and none enjoyed the hours of peace and recreation there more than Anne Marie's two daughters. In later years, after both had left their childhood home, they often referred in their letters to the enchanting gardens still lingering in their memories.

Amid this natural beauty, the deserted wife lived in partial retirement, indulging in the unaffected pleasures of the countryside, taking long walks through the orchards and pastures with tiny Adelaide. Here she escaped the humiliations of a failed marriage, creating a happy home life for herself and her two little girls. And here she inculcated Adelaide with a love of informality that would never leave her.

Life at the Vigna for Marie Adelaide, a graceful child with a lively curiosity and abundantly high spirits, was delightful indeed. Away from the stifling formality of the court of Turin, she explored the natural wonders of the countryside, making friends with the simple peasants that tilled the vineyards and worked the farms. For long hours she chirped gaily with dairymaids as they sat side by side churning butter. Bred with such indifference to rank, Adelaide would never be completely at ease within the ossified etiquette of Versailles, much like her eighteenth-century cousin Marie Antoinette, though Adelaide would move through its machinations with far greater success. She inspired the protective affection of everyone at the Vigna with her kindhearted manner and her genuine, unaffected cooperation.

The little princesse showed a keen love for animals: she was taught to groom her own horse and to milk the cows in the Vigna's dairies. (All her life, she took delight in making her own cheeses.) She sewed and knitted with great skill and genuine flair; Mme de Maintenon would later assert there must have been "some waiting woman, to pay her court, [who] taught her these things," but in truth it was the lonely Duchess Anne Marie.

There was a serious side to life at the Vigna. The education of the princesses was the official responsibility of their governess, the princessa della Cisterna. But she preferred to "supervise" her charges from the court of Turin and left their daily instruction to their undergoverness, the diligent Mme Dunnoyer. From the beginning, Adelaide displayed a greater aptitude for play than learning, and Dunoyer frequently expressed exasperation at her pupil's erratic spelling, her clumsy, almost infantile scrawl, and her rudimentary knowledge of history; much later, Adelaide noted wryly that her poor undergoverness "took an immense amount of trouble with very little result." The duchess was clearly untroubled by her daughter's lack of scholastic achievement. Though extremely well educated herself, she placed little value on book learning for women; her daughters were taught instead to use a spinning wheel, producing threads of fine wool and silk with which they learned the art of embroidery. For this vibrant older daughter with inexhaustible wells of energy, exercise of the mind took second place to that of the body, and her doting mother seldom sided with the frustrated Dunoyer.

But moral education was an altogether different matter. The duchess personally undertook the religious instruction and training of her daughters, and in this Anne Marie was an exemplary teacher. Little Adelaide learned to love and fear God in his heaven and Louis XIV, his regent on earth, to obey her confessor in everything, and above all, always to display in public the dignity and composure expected of a princess. Anne Marie's complete acceptance of faith was also passed on to her daughter; fortunately, she had at her disposal one of Christendom's most treasured relics, housed in the Chapel of the Sindone in the capital.

The chapel, designed by the Italian genius Guarino Guarini, was a baroque temple of dark brown marble, relieved only by the cream-white statues of the dukes of Savoy. Within its thick, cooling walls, in the soft glow of a thousand candles and the pungent smoke of incense, Adelaide had her first exposure to the religious mysticism still prevalent in the seventeenth century. The chapel enshrined the fabled Holy Shroud of Turin, believed to be the winding cloth used by Joseph of Arimathea to wrap the corpse of Jesus Christ. It had first appeared in France sometime during the fourteenth century, a spoil of battle taken during the looting of Constantinople. Originally the property of one Geoffrey de Charney, seigneur de Lirey, the shroud was given by Charney's granddaughter Marguerite to Duke Louis of Savoy in 1453, for reasons never satisfactorily explained. (One charming, but apocryphal, contemporary explanation was that Marguerite "gave the cloth to Duke Louis because when she was returning to Burgundy the relic-bearing mule stopped at the gates of Chambéry [then capital of Savoy] and refused to budge.")

As the focal point of the chapel, the shroud was carefully wrapped in red silk and kept on the altar in an ornate chest bearing the royal coat of arms. On rare occasions, the sacred relic was exhibited in the Ceremony of the Holy Shroud. At that time, the winding sheet — measuring fourteen feet three inches by three feet seven inches — was stretched wide and attached to a specially constructed frame that displayed its entire length. Amid pomp and reverence, it was placed before the high altar of the adjoining cathedral and the public was permitted to view it.

No Savoyard doubted for an instant the shroud's authenticity, and today, even with the aid of twentieth-century techniques, science is at a loss to explain the phenomenon in a logical way. The material is linen, commonly used in ancient Palestine for graveclothes, and investigation has uncovered traces of a Middle Eastern variety of cotton; while very pliable, it is loosely woven in a herringbone twill, and resembles the coarse cloth used for the making of sails. The image of a body is stamped indelibly upon it and it is evident that this body indeed suffered crucifixion, and more. Scourge marks cover the back and chest, reminiscent of the pattern inflicted by a flagrum, a multi-thonged Roman whip. A large flow of blood from the left side indicates piercing of the body with a spear or lance, and rivulets of blood that encircle the head suggest a crown of thorns.

It is the placement of the bloodstains on the victim's arms that argues most persuasively for the shroud's veracity — for these wounds are placed, not on the hands, but on the wrists. Research with cadavers in the mid-1930s established that the bones in the hand could not sustain the weight of a hanging body; a medieval forger would have been ignorant of this and would have followed artistic tradition, placing the wounds in the center of the palms. Miracle or master sham — the controversy that still rages is of our century's devising; the seventeenth held no such agnostic doubts.

After public display, a holy vigil was kept each night for a week by the highest nobles of the land. In the final rite of the ceremony, the shroud was carefully examined by the archbishop for signs of disintegration. Any required repairs could be performed only by the reigning duchess of Savoy, using golden needles and the finest of silk threads. For Anne Marie, this was an occasion of intense religious fervor. Deeply imbued with piety, she was easily and profoundly moved by the mysteries of her faith, and she performed her task with reverence.

Adelaide, a wide-eyed spectator at this impressive ceremony, was filled with a simple piety, a childlike reverence and love for God that never deserted her; after she arrived in France and her education was entrusted to Mme de Maintenon, the latter described her great relief to discover that she had merely to say "That would be sinful" for Adelaide to reply "Then I will not do it." The hedonism at Versailles would often sidetrack the naïve young princesse, but the early training of her saintly mother would never entirely desert her.

The pleasant ennui of country living was punctuated with expeditions into Turin and visits to Madame Royale at her townhouse, the Palazza Madama. For the two little princesses, excitement itself seemed to emanate from the very person of their grandmother. Still beautiful, witty and gay, still surrounded by the cream of Turin society, Madame Royale found in her granddaughters the delight that had eluded her in their father and she indulged them outrageously. In her glittering salon, the entrance of these young innocents signaled the exit of etiquette and decorum: hilarious rounds of blind man's buff (Adelaide's favorite game) delighted the princesse, and she would squeal with glee as handsome army officers grabbed her by the legs and "sledged" her across the polished parquet floor. Her mother, the duchess, felt out of place with Madame Royale's sophisticated, carefree circle, and made infrequent visits; but for her daughter, grandmama's court was an enchanted oasis.

Adelaide's world was almost exclusively female. The young princesse saw but little of her father, whom she nicknamed (with a mixture of awe and intimidation) *Le Grand,* "The Great One." Deprived of a father's love and presence during her formative years, she unconsciously craved the missing attention: the eagerness to please, which characterized her life, perhaps sprang from this need, as did her deep affection for father figures such as the French diplomat Tessé and, more significantly, Louis XIV.

For by the age of five, experience had taught the little princesse that home life meant an adoring mother whom one adored in return, and a father whom one worshiped and feared — and seldom saw.

With her mother and grandmother both devoted to the Sun King, there is no reason to doubt that from a tender age Adelaide was aware of her splendid possibilities at the court of Versailles. Nor had these possibilities gone unnoticed in the appropriate circles: when the little princesse recuperated from a bout with scarlet fever, the dauphine — Louis XIV's daughter-in-law — wrote of her concern for the patient to Madame Royale, "not only because she is our cousin, but because we are given to understand that she says she will never be happy unless she marries our son."

But events in the great world outside the Vigna seemed inexorably set on confounding Adelaide's future happiness. The gnat and the lion had not yet made peace, and for the little princesse, for her parents and her country, the road ahead was obscured and treacherous, rife with detour and diversion.

Victor Amadeus suffered severe depression following the Waldenses massacre, and at its root was fury at his own impotence in the face of French bullying. The horrible scenes he had witnessed and his own inability to resist foreign intervention painfully exposed his position as puppet to the mighty Sun King. His desire to throw off the abominable yoke became obsessional. Louis's lessons had molded the duke's character and granted him clear-sighted objectivity: he recognized that his defection could be only subtly and covertly achieved, since the very existence of his tiny realm was at stake.

His first step on the road to independence was taken in late January,

1687. During an evening court, he took aside the French ambassador, d'Arcy, and confided his intention to spend the forthcoming carnival season in Venice with his cousin, the elector Max Emmanuel of Bavaria. D'Arcy was visibly taken aback and remonstrated. The duke picked up the challenge, asking point-blank if the ambassador was under orders from his master to oppose such a trip; when d'Arcy replied that he had no such orders, but ventured to anticipate the king's objections, Victor Amadeus smoothly reassured him of the "continued respect and esteem" he felt for his wife's uncle, then reminded him of his friendly submission when a similar holiday had been proposed in 1684. Refusing to alter his plans — which he maintained were inspired purely by amusement — he closed the interview.

Louis XIV *did* object to the proposed adventure, and he doubted at once the innocence of its nature. His reasons for alarm were not difficult to understand: his Dutch archenemy, William of Orange, had been working ceaselessly to forge what would become the first Grand Alliance to check the growing French domination of Europe. The emperor, the prince of Lorraine, and the elector of Bavaria had already joined with the Dutch United Provinces, and the republic of Venice was known to be favorably considering the alliance. It was William's dream to include Spain and Savoy in the general mobilization; in Madrid and Turin, diplomatic relations with the collective allied rulers had taken a marked turn. The Sun King felt confident that sufficient pressure could be exerted to maintain Spanish neutrality (his niece, Queen Marie Louise, had another two years left in her short life), but his Savoyard nephew-in-law, with his history of troublesome behavior, posed an entirely different problem. He understood from d'Arcy the futility of objecting to the Venetian holiday. To Victor Amadeus, he remained silent on the subject; to d'Arcy, he gave orders for strict surveillance of the duke's every move along the journey.

The duke left Turin on January 30, 1687, and at once his actions appeared to justify the Sun King's apprehensions. Arriving in Milan on the thirty-first, he immediately called on the conte de Fuensalida, governor of the Milanese States. Fuensalida was well known as an Austrian sympathizer, and Louis XIV frowned suspiciously on their private conference. He was no less displeased to learn that in Padua the duke met with his cousin, Prince Eugene of Savoy, a rising soldier in the imperial army and a personal favorite of Emperor Leopold.

On February 5, the duke arrived in Venice, joining the elector of Bavaria. One month later he was back in Turin; in that interval, the

Sun King received several alarming reports of "long and private conversations."

Anne Marie was overjoyed at her husband's return. All of Turin paid compliment to the duke on the fine reception his journey had met. Only Louis XIV was displeased with the duke's successful visit, sniffing the faint whiff of defection.

By 1689, clouds of war appeared once more on the horizon. With the Sun King's invasion of the German Palatinate, Victor Amadeus was ready for his rupture with France.

William of Orange, now King William III of England, had convinced Emperor Leopold of the importance of Savoy in the Grand Alliance, and Prince Eugene of Savoy was dispatched from Vienna to Turin, to sway his cousin over to the allied camp. The terms offered Victor Amadeus for his commitment were considerable: restitution of Pinerolo, which the French had held illegally for more than fifty years, as well as the liberation of the fortress of Casal, occupied by French troops under Maréchal Catinat since pre-Waldenses days. In addition, England pledged an annual subsidy for the duration of the war, while Austria promised troops to protect the safe pass from French reprisals following the duke's defection.

Victor Amadeus was most interested but, true to form, he delayed evasively. He commended the generosity of the proposal, but as war had not yet been declared, he "could not help but consider it premature" to draw up an official treaty of conditions, and he added pointedly that he would be pleased to establish a "friendly understanding with the Emperor to guard against future contingencies." The allies then decided to sweeten their enticements: on February 8, 1690, two imperial decrees were issued — the first bestowing on the Savoyard ambassador the full rights usually accorded only to the representatives of kings, the second consenting to the duke's purchase of certain imperial fiefs he had long coveted.

Louis XIV was hardly ignorant of the sharp turn events were taking at his southeastern border. His agents already had intercepted a letter from Victor Amadeus to the elector of Bavaria, in which the duke informed his cousin he could keep Maréchal Catinat "employed" long enough to give time for the arrival of the promised Austrian troops. With the publication of the imperial decrees, the Sun King accepted the possibility of Savoy's defection as future certainty. The miserable poverty in large areas of the duchy, still recovering from its debilitating religious massacre, and the great disparity between French and Savoyard forces convinced Louis XIV that diplomatic reasoning was unnecessary. Instead, he hurried to bring matters to a crisis: Catinat was ordered to formally request the duke's assistance on yet another religious expedition.

Victor Amadeus saw the approach of his long-overdue showdown with Versailles. True to the plan outlined in his intercepted Bavarian letter, he set about delaying tactics. While unwilling to part with the smallest portion of his limited army, he dutifully dispatched a force of five hundred men, with the secret injunction to postpone their arrival at Casal for as long as reasonably possible.

The French were not deceived. Under one false pretext after another, Catinat's army advanced steadily on Turin; by mid-May, his force of seven thousand was encamped outside Orbessano, a few miles from the capital. From there, he announced he had another communication from Louis XIV and demanded that a state minister be dispatched to hear the Sun King's orders. These orders were simple and overwhelming: the surrender of the fortresses of Verrua and Turin — in other words, the capitulation of Savoy.

Victor Amadeus rose to the occasion with calm imperturbability. He sent a secret communication to Governor Fuensalida in Milan, apprising him of the dilemma and calling for assistance. He notified the Austrian ambassador of his adherence to the anti-French league and requested an immediate dispatch of Austrian troops to stave off his country's annihilation. Then, with cold, unemotional calculation, he wrote to Louis XIV in his own hand, avowing his respect and allegiance; he pledged his willingness to hand over the two citadels, should the king *personally* request him to do so, as proof of his sincerity. In sending this conciliatory epistle directly to Catinat, for forwarding to Versailles, Victor Amadeus gained the time he so desperately needed.

In the interim, word arrived from Milan: Fuensalida was sending three thousand horse- and eight thousand foot-soldiers under the command of the comte de Louvigny. Acknowledgment from the emperor also arrived, and on June 4, 1690, the duke of Savoy signed the treaty that bound him to the League of Augsburg.[3] Austria pledged an immediate six thousand troops; Savoy agreed to cooperate with the empire against France and to make no terms hereafter without the emperor's express consent.

Louis XIV's response to the duke's stall now reached Catinat's camp (much earlier than he expected) and was delivered to the ducal palace by the French ambassador. In it the king expressed his pleasure at the duke's acquiescence and concurred that Catinat should take immediate control of the fortresses. Overstrained and overworked, Victor Amadeus lost his habitual self-control: he raged violently, protesting against the occupation of Verrua and Turin, and crying that his words had been deliberately misinterpreted, that his consent had been conditional.

Catinat was not deluded: he gave the duke twenty-four hours to come to a decision — surrender the forts or he would open hostilities. Further delay was now impossible. The minister of war announced that "owing to the extremity to which he has been pushed by the King of France, the Duke has been finally compelled to accept offers of assistance from foreign troops."

France and Savoy were at war.

In Turin, the War of the Palatinate was inaugurated with a display of patriotism, a dramatic scene of the type for which Victor Amadeus exhibited real flair.[4] The duke, in full state surrounded by his ministers and entourage, his duchess (six months pregnant) at his side, addressed an assembly of over four hundred nobles in the council chamber of the ducal palace. He spoke with moving sincerity, reiterating the many intolerable insults he had suffered from France and justifying his alliance with the league. He disclosed that the Milanese troops under Louvigny had already crossed the frontier and that daily he expected succor; he ended his speech with a stirring declaration: "Though the allied armies come to my aid, I place much greater reliance on the valor and devotion of my nobles and people, to which the Princes of Savoy have never appealed in vain." The council chamber resounded with joyous cries of "Viva il duca!" As the royal couple made their way out onto the Piazza Castello, they were met with even greater acclamations of loyalty and devotion.

Dissension evaporated with this promised deliverance from French domination; the pope, Alexander VIII, publicly commended Savoy's defiance of the Sun King, and the clergy of Turin offered their gold and silver church ornaments to help defray the war expense. (More important, from William III of England arrived the first monthly subsidy of twenty thousand crowns.)

Toward Anne Marie — resigned that her husband and her uncle were finally at war — the duke was swept up on a wave of affection and concern, confessing to one staff member: "It is the Duchess only who seriously fills my thoughts in this state of affairs." Given her advanced state of pregnancy, Victor Amadeus's pattern of attention and neglect was fast becoming predictable, but to the common people, whose love for the duke's good wife was exceeded only by their hatred for the duke's evil mistress, the improved relations in the royal apartments, coupled with the prospect of the long-awaited heir, added even greater incentive to the war effort. (Sad to tell, the general wish for an heir was not to be fulfilled: within weeks of the war declaration, Anne Marie prematurely gave birth on June 25 — the son she had finally produced was stillborn.)

But fervent patriotism alone is not enough to win a war, and the supremacy of the Grand Army was once again apparent. The battle of Staffarda on August 18, where the duke "took part in battle for the first time and did wonders of bravery," was a disastrous defeat for the allies. Four thousand dead, fifteen hundred wounded, and two thousand taken prisoner — nearly one third of the duke's forces wiped out in one battle.

Staffarda proved ominous: throughout the summer, Victor Amadeus was forced further into retreat, surrendering Saluzzo, Savigliano, and other fortified towns in quick succession. Catinat advanced relentlessly — by the end of September, Victor Amadeus was compelled to recross the Po and take refuge outside his capital. As in the Palatine, the French minister of war, Louvois, gave orders to burn and destroy *everything*. Catinat wreaked devastation: across more than half of Savoy-Piedmont, Catinat's scythe ravaged the land and extinguished life.

Gloom and depression enveloped Turin as 1690 ebbed and the duke's weary, defeated soldiers straggled back to their winter lodgings. Throughout the capital and countryside, the jubilant optimism that had launched the war now lay trampled beneath the heavy boot of the invincible French army. From every quarter — even the pope himself — came despairing entreaties to sue for peace, yet the duke's commitment remained irrevocable. However, the weakness and irritating cowardice of the court around him, the enforced inertia of the winter months, and his aching for action all worked together to produce another profound depression.

Anne Marie, once more pregnant, tried to rouse him from his solitude and his morbid reveries; for the first time, Victor Amadeus broke his pattern of prenatal solicitude, further evidence of the overwhelming melancholy that gripped him. He passed the holidays in the domestic circle at the Vigna: Adelaide celebrated her fifth birthday, baby

Louise scampered about the gardens, and the duchess glowed with the radiance of expectant motherhood. But the duke remained unmoved by the budding charms of his family; after the New Year, he left his wife and daughters to their arcadian life and returned to Turin and the arms of the contessa di Verrua.

At the meeting of the League of Augsburg in March 1691 in The Hague, Victor Amadeus demanded greater reinforcements to ensure that the devastation of 1690 would not be repeated, and anxious lest they should lose his commitment, the allies complied: Austria pledged to double the expeditionary force; the elector of Bavaria, a distinguished commander, offered to personally take charge of these troops; William III of England not only repledged his monthly subsidies but immediately dispatched five battalions of Protestant emigrants under the duke of Schomberg.

But the second campaign proceeded as woefully as the first. The desperate rush to fortify the defenses of Nice failed, and the city fell to Catinat only days before reinforcements arrived. The pattern of defeat and retreat was renewed. Systematically, towns and villages fell or surrendered to the indomitable invaders. From the surrounding hills outside Rivoli, Victor Amadeus watched as the French heartlessly razed his favorite palace. Still the allies could not check the French advance on Turin.

Panic reigned throughout the capital, and evacuations trebled once it was known that the duchess (who would never leave Turin unless the situation were truly grave) had departed for Vercelli in the east, under orders from the duke. Victor Amadeus was concerned that the duchess, fast approaching delivery, should be removed from the threat of siege. The arduous journey proved too much in her advanced condition, and before Vercelli could be reached, Anne Marie gave birth prematurely to her second son, who died that same day.[5]

Close as he was, Catinat did not attempt to capture Turin. Following the destruction of Rivoli, he turned his force southeast, taking the city of Carmagnola on June 9. His next action, an attack on the city of Cuneo, met at last with defeat, due as much to the determined resistance of the besieged city as to the timely arrival of fresh imperial troops under Prince Eugene of Savoy. Facing a loss of four thousand men (including fifty officers), Catinat was forced to abandon his cannon and ammunition and retreat across the river.

Less than a month after Cuneo, word arrived in Savoy of the death of the French war minister, the detested Louvois. While no one seriously believed the rumor that he had been poisoned at the instigation of Victor Amadeus, still it helped to stoke the bitter animosity between enemies.

But any further success in this second campaign was undermined by the Austrian Maréchal Caraffa, the emperor's plenipotentiary to Italy — a man determined, whatever the circumstances, to keep Austrian soldiers out of danger. His continual obstruction of tactics put the remainder of the campaign in jeopardy; more damaging in the long run, it ignited the duke's disenchantment with the allied cause.

Only one fortress, Montmélian, still remained under Savoyard control, having bravely resisted French siege for over a year. Victor Amadeus proposed an immediate march to the rescue. The elector concurred, Schomberg as well; but Caraffa, loath to expose his Austrians to the impressive number of French troops amassed along the Po, refused to quit Turin. Montmélian was doomed; unrelieved, the garrison surrendered. All of Savoy except Turin and environs was now in French hands.

Victor Amadeus was incensed at this loss, and furiously complained of Caraffa's "overbearing vanity and most insolent behavior" to Vienna. When Prince Eugene corroborated with angry letters of his own, Caraffa was recalled and replaced with General Caprara, a particular favorite of Eugene's. To further placate Victor Amadeus (technically now a duke without a duchy), the emperor officially appointed him supreme commander of the allied troops in Italy.

With a united high command, the allied force in Italy was able to recapture Rivoli and the cities of Avigliano and Carmagnola before retiring for the winter. The sight of his countryside devastated by the retiring Catinat served to steel the duke's resolve, and when, in February 1692, Louis XIV dispatched an envoy to Turin to propose a separate peace, he dismissed the emissary with the proud boast, "Monsieur, I have but to stamp my native soil with my foot, and more soldiers than I require would emerge."

Sadly, even Victor Amadeus knew this was not true, and the bitter defeats of the first two years were repeated in 1692. Then, in August, he fell ill with smallpox. For two weeks, his life hung in the balance — and his disheartened troops, bereft of his stirring presence, quit the field and retired to their winter lodgings. The duke's recovery was followed by two serious relapses, and it was not until March 1693 that he was able to return to the war council.

His feelings had undergone a change. Just as his bouts with smallpox had left scars across his body, his massive defeats (and their causes, both real and imagined) had scarred his soul and twisted his mind. The odious Austrian Caraffa he held responsible for the crippling loss of Montmélian, and from there it was an easy step to the conclusion that the loss of his lands had been due entirely to imperial apathy. Although the allied troops achieved a major victory over the French at Santa Brigida on August 1, 1693, the gnawing fear that his cause was being neglected by the league festered in the duke's mind.

His suspicions were rooted firmly by October 4, when the overwhelming defeat of the allies in the battle of Marsaglia produced as severe a shock to Victor Amadeus as Staffarda had three years before: ten thousand allied soldiers dead, including the marchese di Parella, one of Savoy's finest generals. The English commander, the duke of Schomberg, was severely wounded and died shortly afterward in Turin. The French had lost two thousand men; an exultant Louis XIV congratulated Catinat: "I always expected a great success . . . but in the splendid victory you have obtained over my enemies you have surpassed all my hopes, increased my esteem for you, and you have proved yourself worthy of my trust by the way you have served the state."

On the field outside Marsaglia Louis XIV, the French lion, had squashed the pernicious gnat with his heavy paw. If the gnat were ever to rise again, Victor Amadeus knew that it could only be through cunning and dissimulation.

The duke of Savoy retired to Moncalieri for the winter. There, in the first months of 1694, he reflected on the vicissitudes of war against the Sun King. His country lay in ruins: whole villages had been annihilated by the French invaders, and the carcasses of slaughtered livestock rotted in the scorched, barren fields. The threat of famine was everywhere, and a severe frost that winter seriously damaged the vineyards and sapling orchards. No longer could he ignore the anguished pleas for peace from his ministers. More important, no longer could he find solace or support from the League of Augsburg, which had seemingly abandoned the Savoyard cause. Slowly, doubtless painfully, he began preliminary negotiations: *if* France were willing to meet him on several points, he *might* consider a separate peace.

Louis XIV, despite his successes in northern Italy, also faced impending crisis. Five years of warfare against a united Europe forced the Sun King (and his subjects) to acknowledge the immense strain being placed on the French economy; as Mme de Sévigné wryly noted: "France is perishing to the sound of Te Deums." In 1693, French state revenues totaled 81 million livres against an expenditure of 219 million. To further intensify matters, both 1692 and 1693 had yielded exceptionally poor harvests, and at the front, French generals began to whisper among themselves of the poor quality of transport supplies.

And so, heartily tired of war and resolved to separate the duke of Savoy from the League of Augsburg, Louis XIV was prepared to make large concessions to guarantee the return of his erstwhile satellite.

Victor Amadeus was understandably concerned that news of his negotiations be kept from Emperor Leopold, in view of his 1690 pledge to make no terms with France without Vienna's consent. Announcing a pilgrimage to Loreto, in fulfillment of a vow made during his bouts with smallpox, the duke met covertly with an envoy from Catinat, the Venetian ambassador, and the papal nuncio. The major terms for peace were broached: the duke was adamant that the towns and fortresses now in French hands should be returned unconditionally, and he desired (and needed) the recognition of Italian neutrality for the remainder of the war. Catinat's envoy held no authority to confirm such requests, but had been instructed to emphasize French willingness to cooperate, and when Victor Amadeus left for Turin, the preliminary arrangements had been accomplished to his satisfaction.

Victor Amadeus returned to his capital confident that an agreeable settlement could be reached. He did not return alone. Disguised as a member of his entourage was the French governor of Pinerolo, the comte de Tessé, commissioned to conclude the second phase of the peace talks. Tessé was an ideal choice for the mission: quite apart from being tall, good-looking, well bred, amiable, and kind, he was a diplomat of great charm and ability. In the field of war, he had proven himself an able soldier; at the peace table, he was fair and honest — and when the question of a marriage alliance entered into the plan, he showed himself a true friend to Adelaide with his understanding, his sympathy, and his gentle encouragement.[6]

Determined as he was to keep secret his plans for redefection, the duke had insisted that Tessé's true business in Turin be camouflaged. He first suggested that the diplomat accompany him in the guise of hostage. Tessé was less than thrilled with this idea, hastening to remind both the duke and Louis XIV of a similar incident where, "by some unfortunate misunderstanding, not rectified in time, one such hostage had recently been hanged." Instead, Tessé disguised himself as a simple postilion on the duke's coach. Unnoticed, he made his way into Turin and was admitted to the palace through a back stairway. He remained there, in the highest secrecy, for several days, conferring for long hours with Victor Amadeus and his secretary. His departure for France signaled a truce between the French and Savoyard forces; when he returned with the counterproposals from Versailles, he was still incognito, although this time not in the demeaning role of coachman.

Louis XIV chose at this juncture to make an inspired offer of marital alliance. The king's oldest grandson and heir after the dauphin was a boy of thirteen, the duc de Bourgogne. Adelaide had recently celebrated her tenth birthday. Louis XIV proposed that the re-alliance of France and Savoy be cemented by the union of these children. To the French policy maker, this idea was doubly beneficial: the promise of a brilliant destiny for the little princesse would lull her ambitious father into submission, and Louis XIV would obtain a bride for his future heir — and ensure the propagation of his royal line through the eminently appropriate daughter of his beloved niece Anne Marie.

As the Sun King anticipated, Victor Amadeus was dazzled by the proposal. His daughter one day queen of France, the highest position on the European chessboard to which she might aspire! Himself — father of a queen of France! Ironically, the Sun King imagined the match would keep Savoy under control, while Victor Amadeus imagined that through his firstborn he might one day control France. Still, the bait was eagerly swallowed. On May 30, 1696, a separate peace between the king of France and the duke of Savoy was signed in Turin.

Louis XIV agreed to evacuate Pinerolo (a condition the duke had earlier imposed on the emperor), with the stipulation that the fort be razed at once. Nice and Villafranca were immediately returned to Savoy; Montmélian and Susa would be restored upon the publication of the treaty.[7] These stipulations, coupled with the subsequent marriage contract, formed a French conciliatory package of sizable proportions.

For his part, the duke of Savoy pledged his efforts to extract from his former allies recognition of Italian neutrality; should the league refuse this, he would join his forces with Catinat's, taking command himself, and receive a monthly subsidy of one hundred thousand crowns for the remainder of the war. In a secret clause, the duke bound himself to aid the Sun King in expelling the imperial army from the whole of Italy. His reward for this would be his long-desired acquisition of the duchy of Milan.

Victor Amadeus was now faced with the unenviable task of announcing his redefection to his former confederates. The members of the Italian high command were duly summoned to the ducal palace; Victor Amadeus found himself confronted by men who had grown to revere his military talents and derive inspiration from his valor and strength of purpose, men who had ardently prayed that smallpox might not remove their beloved leader.

> Messieurs, our paths now somewhat diverge, but I shall find occasion to show you marks of my esteem. I have done everything possible to secure for you good winter quarters; I hope, in future, you may find even better ones; but please, not in Italy . . . It is time for my country, and if possible, for the princes, my neighbors, to enjoy the rest I have endeavored to procure for them. I trust your masters will consent . . . Should they refuse, to my great regret, I shall proceed against you, at the head of a French army, and with all the vigor that has won your respect hitherto. Yet, messieurs, since I hope to retain your friendship, let us, pray, dine together.

That evening, Victor Amadeus dined alone. Later that night, with no apparent remorse, he remarked to a lady of the court: "You may be sure of one thing: from now onwards, we are all French."

Following the Savoyard peace proclamation, the League of Augsburg declared an immediate truce for the summer months of 1696. During this time, the emperor tried desperately to woo back the wayward duke, offering his younger son, Archduke Karl, as a bridegroom for Marie Adelaide. But wife to a second son offered scant compensation in Victor Amadeus's eyes, and he spent the months of truce trying to extricate himself from further obligation to the league. With impatience (and a good deal of bravado), he ordered the allied troops to evacuate his country. This demand was not crowned with success. Nor were his hopes for the acceptance of Italian neutrality: the temporary armistice expired on September 15 and fighting resumed in Milan. Without the slightest compunction, Victor Amadeus, former generalissimo of the allied armies, became supreme commander of the French army in Italy.

Undeniably, Savoy's defection from the League of Augsburg led to its disintegration, and made possible an ultimate French victory. The allies struggled to rise from the ruins of the league and found themselves defeated as much by their own xenophobia as by the Sun King's army. No sooner did fighting resume than they agreed to a suspension of arms pending the proclamation of a general peace.[8] Ironically, despite all the reversals it had suffered, the tiny state of Savoy had decisively asserted itself, emerging with France as the only true victors of the war. Singled out for the pacific overtures of the Sun King, the duke had succumbed; in doing so, he encompassed the defeat of the entire allied cause.

Throughout Europe, the duke of Savoy's name was invoked only with derision and contempt. Hatred was most intense in England — and all the more after it became known that the Savoyard ambassador in Paris had been commanded to acknowledge the overthrown Catholic James II as rightful king of England.

The prevailing attitude in The Hague was one of disgust, and the duke's ambassador, Conte della Torre, wrote anxiously on November 6: "The people are very excited, and are beginning to ask what business I have here; they are indignant that I should be allowed to remain, and wish me to be turned away. This sentiment runs so high that a plot has been discovered to pillage my house and tear me to pieces. [The Government] at first gave orders for my safety, and to spare me from insults, ordered a patrol of infantry and cavalry all the night through; but it is a remedy that instead of pacifying the conspirators only embitters them the more."

But revulsion by the world at large went unheeded in Turin, where a grateful populace celebrated the return of peace with an elaborate succession of fêtes and fireworks that lasted through the autumn. The cost of peace had been high, both in terms of independence and general reputation. But once again, the House of Savoy had saved its country by the only means available. The gnat had *not* been obliterated — as the lion would quickly come to find.

And best of all were the prospects that awaited young Adelaide.

4

Waiting in the Wings

ON A WARM AFTERNOON early in June 1696, the comte de
Tessé, for the first time, publicly entered the city of Turin. Perhaps to
recompense for the mean disguises forced on him in earlier visits, his
official entry occasioned the pomp and panoply the world had come
to expect from the emissaries of the mighty Sun King: in a magnifi-
cently gilded carriage, Tessé drove into the palace courtyard amid an
escort of ten mounted gentlemen and followed by a train of thirty
mule-drawn baggage carts. Having successfully concluded the strug-
gles of war between his master and the duke, Tessé's diplomatic gifts
were now shifting to implement the second phase of Louis XIV's grand
design — the betrothal of Princesse Marie Adelaide to the duc de Bourgogne.

Although these objectives — peace and a bride — hinged upon each
other, the relative ease with which the first had been accomplished by
no means guaranteed facility in the second. The adversaries had been
desperate to end the fighting — Victor Amadeus ready to stake his
international reputation and Louis XIV willing to make historic concessions. Peace restored, both found themselves with time and an opportunity for more leisurely competitive bargaining. Separately, each
resolved to employ his considerable talents to best the other; the smug
old lion and the undaunted gnat prepared for yet another encounter.

While as eager for this marriage as his French opponent, Victor
Amadeus intended to play every card fate dealt. Count Mansfield, the
special envoy of Emperor Leopold, entered Turin the same day as

Tessé. His mission was to woo back the duke to the anti-French camp by an offer of marriage with the emperor's younger son, Archduke Karl; failing this, he was to do everything in his power to deter the Bourgogne suit and prevent a marital alliance with the Sun King. Victor Amadeus had no serious intention of settling for an archduke without prospects when the future crown of France was his alternative, but he used the Austrian envoy's presence to manipulate his French counterpart, leaning favorably toward Mansfield whenever Tessé — or his master — appeared too obdurate. And though an Austrian alliance was doomed to failure even before Mansfield's arrival, the count's second objective, to destroy the French plan, nearly came to pass — though responsibility for this rested on none other than the prospective father of the bride. Throughout the summer months, Victor Amadeus argued every term and condition, and more than once very nearly aborted negotiations altogether.

The first obstacle encountered on Adelaide's road to France was actually one of relative simplicity, memorable more for its comic element than anything else. Tessé's arrival to press the official suit for Adelaide's hand necessitated his formal presentation to the royal family. In the eyes of the public, this was a first meeting; in reality, the elderly statesman had been coming and going covertly for several months, was very familiar with the duchess and her two little girls, and had already earned a conspicuous place of honor in Adelaide's affections. With Mansfield lurking about, the duke feared his daughter might betray the length of his secret dealing with France by acknowledging her old friend. Mansfield's embassy might not have a chance, but Victor Amadeus did not wish to drive him off the very first day. The little princesse was given strict instructions that before the court she was to indicate in no way that she had ever before set eyes on Tessé. The precocious ten-year-old did not disappoint her anxious father: in the glittering council chamber, before a large assembly of unsuspecting nobles and the Austrian ambassador, Marie Adelaide played to perfection her role in this official charade.

Problems far more difficult arose once negotiations began in earnest. Among the first was the question of Adelaide's succession rights in Savoy. At this date, the duke was still without an heir, and was nettled by the thought that his lands might one day be claimed by France on his daughter's behalf. (These fears were not altogether groundless, since Louis XIV's bloodiest and costliest conflicts — the War of the Palatinate and the War of the Spanish Succession — were both the result of such claims, on behalf of his sister-in-law and his wife, respectively.)

That Adelaide was to formally renounce her rights of succession was mutually agreed; it was in the method of this, and the implications of the method, that disagreement occurred. Victor Amadeus insisted that the renunciation be included not only in the marriage contract but also in the peace settlement now in its final stage. He reasoned that its inclusion in an international treaty would make it all the more binding — the thorny question of the Spanish succession already loomed on the horizon, and Louis XIV had made sufficiently clear to Europe the little value he placed on promises made in a simple marriage pact. On the other hand, he wanted the renunciation as part of the marriage contract *only* — rather obviously justifying all of the duke's apprehensions. The issue was batted back and forth between Versailles and Turin; in the end, the Sun King's will prevailed and no mention of Adelaide or the Savoyard succession was made in the published treaty of Ryswick. Having conceded in this, Victor Amadeus arranged for the relevant clause in the marriage contract to be surrounded by the most complicated and theoretical guarantees his ministers could devise, to ensure that his patrimony would never fall into French hands. It was a waste of time and effort: to this convoluted exclusion clause, the wily Tessé added the words "au préjudice des mâles de la maison de Savoie," and explained in a secret dispatch to Louis XIV: "This means, should all the princes of Savoy die, our princesse will not lose her rights, and by those few words, the succession remains open to her." Small wonder the duke continued through the summer to watch France with suspicious eyes.

Adelaide's extreme youth posed another problem for the diplomats. As she had not reached the "age of puberty," she could not legally take the oath required to finalize her betrothal. Several weeks were thus wasted, waiting for a special dispensation. Pope Innocent XII finally granted his permission, because "she is gifted with knowledge and discernment far beyond her years" — a lovely, but rather unlikely, compliment for a little girl of ten.

Happily, a dowry for the princesse proved an issue far easier to resolve: France did not require one, and Victor Amadeus felt no inclination to make an offer. However, as a face-saving device, an appropriate sum was mentioned in the marriage contract — exactly the same figure stipulated in the peace treaty as French reparation to Savoy. Brazenly, the duke wrote to His Holiness that he was marrying off his daughter without costing himself a penny; Tessé reported to Louis XIV that the frugal Victor Amadeus had been seen "wreathed in smiles" and smirking exultantly before the long mirror in his study.

The greatest storm rose over the subject of native attendants to accompany the princesse into France — an unexpected clash since the duke now diametrically opposed the very position he had maintained when his own bride came to Savoy twelve years earlier. At that time, Victor Amadeus had categorically refused to allow Anne Marie to bring *any* French attendants across the border. The bride had wept, her father had fumed, and her uncle had blustered — and in the end, the duke of Savoy had won.

Now Louis XIV demanded that Adelaide enter France unaccompanied by any of her Savoyard ladies. Her parents were aghast: the duchess for reasons purely maternal; the duke, for others more complicated. Anne Marie wrote her uncle plaintively that "the Princesse, a mere baby of eleven [actually she was ten and a half] should be accompanied by a Piedmontese doctor, a governess, and two maids, in order that she not be isolated from all those who know her." The king summarily dismissed her plea. Poor Tessé, caught in the middle as frantic letters flew back and forth over the next eight weeks, sympathized more with the concerned parents than with his implacable master. He tried to reason with Versailles: "M. de Savoie and Mme la Duchesse agree, in principle, with the King about the two or three women whom they wish to send to France with the Princesse. Yet she is only a child, and will cry at the least little thing, and they believe she will be sooner comforted by women whom she knows, if only to hand her her chamberpot. Everyone finds comfort in not having to keep up appearances before servants whom they know more or less intimately."

The Sun King's reply made it plain that he had no intention of compromising: "You must stick to your orders and insist on her being unaccompanied by anyone from Savoy." Louis XIV demolished the compassionate Tessé's arguments one after the other: surely the duke understood that "for the happiness and tranquillity of his daughter he should not request any of her serving women to remain with her. He knows himself the disadvantages that might follow." Tessé had proposed that the Savoyard suite might perhaps be allowed to remain with the princesse for just the first few months, but "the pain at parting will be just as great after the three or four months you suggest. She will much more quickly become accustomed to the ladies given her here, if there are no others better known to her. As for her doctor, when once he has informed those in my service regarding her constitution, his presence will be extremely unhelpful."

Tessé attempted to sway the duke with dilutions of this logic, but Victor Amadeus proved as inflexible as the Sun King. As a last resort, the king's letter was produced; afterward, Tessé reported to Louis XIV the anguished cry his missive had wrung from a previously well-hidden paternal heart: "This prince, who claims to be above personal considerations, was moved to tears, and I must confess that my own eyes filled also when, with a heavy sigh, he said, 'I shall never see my daughter again, and when she reaches France, there will be no one she knows well to give her a chamberpot and make her clean.' "

If the intensity of the duke's concern was startling and therefore suspect, Tessé himself, whose affection for the little princesse mounted daily, unflinchingly supported his position: "I do entreat Your Majesty once more to allow a few waiting-women (no more than two) to accompany her, and the doctor who understands her health. All here are agreed that they should return in six months time, or at the very latest, after her marriage. I can assure Your Majesty that this trifle has caused me more distress and anxiety than far more difficult matters." Tessé well understood his master and hastened to assure the king that the duke held no ulterior motives:

> It truly appears to me that in all this M de Savoie has no other purpose than a misplaced tenderness for his daughter. She is still a young child who will cry, and the prince seems unable to overcome his perhaps rather puerile fear that she will need some familiar servant to save her embarrassment in the early days, at moments of weakness, dirtiness, or indisposition. In every other respect, he thinks and speaks in exact accord with Your Majesty's desires, and accepts all you say as being reason itself. What he fears most is that his daughter, when she arrives at your Court, will be transported in such an ecstasy of delight that she may, so to speak, forget the mechanism of the human body unless some intimate woman is there to calm her in such moments of weakness.

If the fear that Adelaide might wet her pants before the king of France seems specious to our sensibilities, the duke's reluctance to send his daughter into France without the security of one familiar face, to abandon the ten-year-old girl in a strange and alien court, is human enough. Louis appeared to soften at Tessé's persuasions, though the envoy's less than tactful reference to Adelaide's frightened tears brought a stinging rebuff: "It would be far better for the Princesse that any tears occasioned by the parting should be dried before she meets me."

Still Victor Amadeus refused to negotiate any form of compromise; the little gnat, as irritating as before, once again provoked the French lion to raise a threatening paw. In a letter to Tessé written in his own hand, Louis XIV put an end to the annoyance:

> I had reason to suppose that, when he knew my mind, the Duke of Savoy would order all the women and other servants attached to the Princesse to return to Turin as soon as she came under the care of those ladies whom I have appointed to attend her. Since I now learn that he still speaks of letting them remain, you must state clearly that my desire for her happiness forbids me to consent. The Duke of Savoy himself says that he knows what disastrous consequences result from such misplaced compassion for princesses going to foreign countries. The pain his daughter may suffer at parting from the women who brought her up will certainly be forgotten when she arrives at Fontainebleau. She will learn, during the journey, to be happy with the ladies charged with her care, and the Duke of Savoy may rest assured that every attention will be paid to her upbringing once she arrives at my Court.
>
> A skilled hand [Mme de Maintenon] will complete the task of forming the intelligence of which the Princesse already gives proof. She will have the knowledge and enlightenment becoming to her future rank, and examples of the most perfect virtue will daily inspire her to love her duties. I have reason to believe that she will be guided by the principles thus instilled into her, and she will be taught those others that will ensure her a happy life. I persist in concluding that she would be greatly harmed by the counsels of women who accompanied her from Savoy, and since I am firmly resolved to send them all back, together with any officers, no matter what their rank, you must make every effort to persuade the Duke of Savoy to forbid their going further than [the French border].[1]

With this letter, the old lion assumed he had put an end to the matter. Victor Amadeus, with his usual subtlety, persevered slyly, pitting his will against the Sun King's: when Adelaide arrived at the court of Louis XIV that autumn, her "exclusively French" retinue included her Savoyard doctor and one Mme Marquet, her confidential maid.

The doctor was sent back to Turin immediately, but the unobtrusive Mme Marquet remained in her young mistress's service for another two years, slowly earning the king's respect as a "quiet, sensible woman." When at last she requested permission to return to Savoy and her family, he consented, saying, "She may do as she pleases, because there is no fear of *her* giving bad advice."[2]

Certainly the oddest aspect of the entire issue was the conduct of Victor Amadeus, his sudden concern for his daughter's emotional well-being and his continued resistance long after the other members of his family deferred on the subject. Madame Royale, as always, quickly sided with Louis XIV. Anne Marie, a far better mother than the duke had been a father, acquiesced early in the negotiations, just as she had in her own case a dozen years before. For her part, Marie Adelaide maintained that she did not care one way or the other — perhaps she was too excited, perhaps she was already intent on pleasing the Sun King in everything, perhaps she was just too young to realize what the argument entailed. Yet Victor Amadeus doggedly persisted with his attempts to alleviate the pain of uprooting; tardy as his fatherly attentions were, they afford us a glimmer of the paternal affection hidden deep in his heart, and help to explain in some way the lifelong love and reverence he enjoyed from both his daughters.

Despite her youth, Adelaide was far from ignorant of her intended future and shared fully the enthusiasm of her mother and grandmother. One incident in particular confirmed her inclinations. Spotting Tessé at the end of a candlelit corridor shortly before the official announcement of her engagement, the princesse mistook him for Count Mansfield, who had been lurking in the shadows so ominously all summer long. Running to her mother in tears, she cried, "What is *he* doing here? You will see that Papa will listen to him, just as he did before. He has no business with us now. Why won't he leave us in peace?" The poor girl's anxiety was, of course, ungrounded; while the duke had held the emperor's proposal as a trump card for several months, its effect was now academic, for the emperor himself had recently withdrawn his suit (on curious grounds: if his son had to wait another four years or so to consummate his marriage — in view of the princesse's age — he would certainly be driven to immoral conduct). The duchess dried Adelaide's tears and assured the little girl that her father had informed Count Mansfield he would accept no offer, however advantageous, that was contrary to "the inclinations of both mother and daughter."[3]

Negotiations closed at last, the marriage contract between Marie Adelaide, princesse of Savoy, and Louis, duc de Bourgogne, was signed on September 15, 1696. Just after ten in the morning, the entire court of Turin assembled in the ducal apartments. Tessé reported to Versailles that the ceremony was "most impressive." The duke was "powdered and habited in a handsome coat." The duchess, "whose countenance expressed ineffable joy," wore "a suitable quantity of diamonds," and Madame Royale was "adorned with all the jewels she possessed." The young fiancée wore a heavy gown of silver brocade; a diamond tiara crowned her rich chestnut hair. Tessé himself escorted Adelaide to mass in the royal chapel, writing proudly that she "acquitted herself of her duties with a facility that was astonishing." After mass, the court returned to the family's rooms, where the marquis de Saint-Thomas read aloud the marriage contract. A copy of the Gospel was produced, and after Adelaide and Tessé (acting as proxy for the duc de Bourgogne) touched the Scriptures "at every place where the contract of marriage is mentioned," the papers were signed — with the usual battle for precedence. Tessé reported to Louis XIV that Adelaide affixed her signature "boldly, modestly, and with dignity," even though he was forced to admit that her handwriting was "childish and clumsy." The doors to Anne Marie's Presence Chamber were thrown wide, and all who wished were allowed to enter and kiss the princesse's hand. The demonstrative nature of the Italians did not go unnoticed by the reserved Frenchman; Tessé commented, "I must say that I have never witnessed anything more resembling a turmoil than the sight of those hundred women and more than two hundred men, kissing one another indiscriminately, and showing all signs of heartfelt joy."

That evening, Tessé held an open house, offering a celebratory banquet for all who came to offer their congratulations. By sundown, every street in the vicinity of his embassy was blocked completely with carriages, and the crush was so overwhelming inside the house that the old diplomat was forced to take refuge at a neighbor's in order to finish his report to the king.

The reaction to the engagement in Paris was as joyous as in Turin. Countless Te Deums were celebrated in the hallowed cathedral of Notre Dame, and church bells pealed endlessly throughout the city. Fireworks displays commemorated the fortunes of peace, and the city poets outvied one another with their compositions in honor of the young couple.

Versailles was agog with excitement. The pleasure-hungry court of Louis XIV, stagnating in elegant and increasing ennui, anticipated the revival of brilliant state occasions, delightful fêtes, entrancing theatricals. Courtiers gobbled up every detail and description of their future mistress: Anne Marie, eager for Monsieur's opinion of his little granddaughter, had sent him her portrait and caused a huge sensation at Versailles. Tessé also sent a life-size portrait in oils; he studied his future queen minutely, and wrote to Louis XIV: "The more I notice the young Princesse, the more I am convinced that she is strong and has a good constitution. Whenever I see her, she blushes with becoming modesty, as if in seeing me she is reminded of the Duc de Bourgogne."

At the request of Mme de Maintenon, Tessé forwarded a tiny corset that belonged to Adelaide and a measurement of her waist on a satin ribbon; the industrious Maintenon set the royal modistes to work designing, stitching, and embroidering miniature gowns in the French style, with which to welcome and delight her young charge.

No one was happier than the Sun King himself. His pleasure was reflected in the betrothal gifts he lavished upon his prospective granddaughter-in-law: a capital sum of 200,000 gold crowns was set aside in her name, and she was assigned a jointure of 20,000 gold crowns per annum (to be augmented by a further gift of 50,000 crowns on her wedding day).

Only one sour note could be heard amid the general felicity — predictably, the disgruntled Madame. Writing her aunt, the electress of Hanover, she predicted: "I doubt whether the Princesse of Savoy will be happy here, for the Duc de Bourgogne is horribly reserved and ill-tempered, and she is certain to fall into the hands of bigoted old women, who will certainly disapprove of any pleasures or happiness that she may be given."

Such pessimism was nowhere to be found at the excited court of Turin. Anne Marie regained her former spirits, and seemed once again the lighthearted princess of years gone by. Gaily she occupied herself with Adelaide's arrangements. Tessé informed the king: "The Duchess cannot repress her great joy . . . and seizes every occasion to talk to me of Your Majesty [and] of her happiness." Memories long suppressed of an enchanted childhood at the Sun King's court came flooding back, to be endlessly recounted for her avid, impressionable daughter (though neither Marie Adelaide nor her mother could know that Anne Marie's Versailles of the 1680s bore little resemblance to Mme de Maintenon's Versailles of 1696). Even the duke's relations with his older child underwent a drastic change: carefully, with patent love and skill, he trained Adelaide for her future role. He explained thoroughly the meaning, purpose, and vast importance of the endless court ceremonies of Versailles, teaching her the intricacies of rank, stressing the necessity of that discriminating politeness her station would require. His lessons included a smattering of statecraft — and most important, how and when to hold her tongue (which astonished Louis XIV, who expected "idle, incessant chatter"). The duke's efforts were made easier by the fact that his wife had already indoctrinated Adelaide with the concept of royal divinity; Victor Amadeus reiterated that the king's word was God's law, and that her first and greatest duties were to serve, obey, and please the king.

And the little princesse, on whom all eyes were focused — what were her feelings? They are not difficult to divine: what ten-year-old child does not revel at being the center of attention, and for Marie Adelaide, such attention to her destiny brought with it so many unexpected blessings. A mother at last gay and carefree again, a father, so long absent, now so lavish with his time and instruction — in short, a set of parents. Relations between husband and wife improved markedly, for the impending loss of the first fruit of their union reawakened in the duke long-dormant affections. His liaison with the contessa di Verrua was temporarily abandoned as he spent more of his time in the domestic tranquillity of the Vigna.

The last golden days of summer passed in the flurry of trousseau preparations. With Anne Marie's Versailles breeding and her husband's notorious frugality, battles over expenditure were inevitable. The duchess could gush as much as she liked over the rich gold and silver brocades offered by the merchants Bistori and Giovannetti; the duke still held the pursestrings firm. His boast to the pope that he was marrying off his daughter for free was a hollow one, since Anne Marie had no intention of sending her daughter to the richest court of Europe without a suitably impressive trousseau. The finest in linens and lace were selected, at a cost of 24,000 francs, and 2,700 francs went for exquisitely embroidered petticoats. A gold and silver toilette service, valued at 9,000 francs, was ordered from the silversmiths Peretti and Sachetti. Shoes, ribbons, baskets — even a miniature sedan chair (1,600 francs) — nothing was neglected; while the duke surely blanched at bills totaling 54,000 francs, he might have found consolation in the depressed marketplace of 1696 had he known that in five years' time, when his daughter Marie Louise would prepare for her journey to Madrid, the cost for a similar outfitting would be more than double.[4]

The marriage contract stated that the wedding of Adelaide and Bourgogne could not take place before the princesse had reached the age of twelve. But it was also a condition that she be sent to France as soon as possible, for the Sun King (and Mme de Maintenon) intended to take charge of her supervision and train her as future queen of France.

Louis XIV pressed the duke to set a departure date, but Victor Amadeus was suddenly reluctant to part with his daughter. One wishes to ascribe his hesitation to the new parental solicitude he displayed, but more probably his plan was to keep Marie Adelaide as "hostage" to make sure that the Sun King first came through with all his contractual agreements. Tessé wrote to Louis XIV:

Regarding the departure of the Princesse, it is the way they have in this country of putting everything off until the last moment; and Monsieur the Duke acting on the principle, or from parental affection, desires me to remind Your Majesty that his daughter is very young, and the season very far advanced. He wonders whether it would not be best to wait until the spring before making her cross the Alps. I offered no hopes as to that, seeing that all she will need is six vests and a warm cloak to protect her from the elements. I pressed and shall continue to press him for her departure, and I beg Your Majesty to send me word that your eagerness to see the Princesse is such that you can accept no further delay.

His Majesty obliged, demanding that the date be fixed and announcing his intention to journey as far as Fontainebleau to greet the princesse in person. The duke was forced to commit himself, and Tessé reported: "After some painful sessions, which he and the Duchess spent weeping together, the Prince sent for me to say that the Princesse would leave whenever Your Majesty gives the word. Although affairs in this country are not easily brought to a head . . . I conclude that the Princesse could not depart before the first days of October."

Though "the first days of October" was still too vague for his liking, Louis XIV jumped on this pronouncement and ordered the immediate departure of the French cortège that was to greet Adelaide at the border. The Sun King reasoned to himself that the duke of Savoy would not be so rude as to keep such an impressive entourage, over six hundred people, cooling their heels along the frontier. (Alas, he credited Victor Amadeus with too much courtesy: the French retinue arrived at Lyons on September 19 and decided to wait there for word of the princesse's departure from Turin, word that did not come until October 12!)

Marie Adelaide's last week in her native land was one of splendid celebration. Every evening there were fireworks, generally accompanied by lengthy speeches and flowery odes — in one such oratorical display, the birth of the future Louis XV was predicted: a son who would grow to be "a Mars in battle, with the face of Cupid, the god of Love."

But apart from the excitement occasioned by such elaborate festivities, the last days in Turin were more arduous than enjoyable. From early morning until sundown the princesse received the endless deputations that arrived with formal addresses of congratulations; farewell compliments were tendered by representatives of the Senate, the guilds, and the city of Turin. On October 5, sitting with appropriate gravity beneath a golden canopy in her mother's apartments, Adelaide endured the felicitations of the entire ducal court. First, the Roman nuncio bestowed a (lengthy) papal benediction. Then, the marquis de Bellegarde, in a brilliant crimson robe of office, harangued her in French on behalf of the Council of State. Every courtier claimed the honor of kissing her royal hand — which grew positively painful by nightfall. As one wit noted: "Her grief at leaving her native city must have been sensibly mitigated by the respite from these wearisome functions which it afforded her."

The streets of Turin were mobbed with curious crowds the morning of October 7, 1696, as the little princesse set off for the Alps. The acclamations that started her journey were ample testimony to the enormous popularity of the House of Savoy. Adelaide drove through the capital accompanied by her mother and grandmother. Victor Amadeus had said his goodbye the evening before; whether he dreaded an emotional farewell or simply could not bear to watch her drive away, the duke spent the morning hidden away in his study. The parting of father and daughter had been surprisingly heartfelt: Marie Adelaide had cried bitterly when she kissed her father for the last time, and the duke had struggled for composure. In the end, duty prevailed — Adelaide had dried her tears and recovered her smile by the time the ladies of the household were ushered in to take their leave. These ladies were under strict injunction *not* to cry or further distress the little girl — though Adelaide herself was ignorant of this order. Apparently one, the contesse de Grésy, was unable to control her emotions; well over a year later, Adelaide wrote her: "I love you still the same. You were the only one of my mother's ladies who cried when I left home, and believe me, I shall never forget that."

Louis XIV had earlier suggested to Victor Amadeus that the duchess might travel with her daughter beyond the border, writing that it would afford him and Monsieur "the greatest pleasure" to see Anne Marie once again. The duke, irrationally afraid that his wife might complain of life in Savoy, refused to permit the duchess or Madame Royale to journey farther than Avigliano, where the Savoyard cortège stopped the evening of October 7.

Adelaide was again reduced to tears, forced to part from the two women most prominent in her young life. But her tears dried quickly. Tessé had often chided her that "a Duchesse de Bourgogne should not cry," and she wrote her faithful friend back in Turin that "though she wept much, she had remembered that he had enjoined her, in case she wept, to laugh immediately afterwards, and to bear in mind the position she was destined to occupy."[5]

Madame Royale and her daughter-in-law returned to Turin the morning of the eighth, and Adelaide was left in the care of the three court officials who would escort her to Pont-des-Beauvoisin on the border — the principessa della Cisterna, first lady-of-honor to the duchess and Marie Adelaide's official governess; the marchese di Dronero, grand marshal of the palace; and the conte di Vernone, the duke of Savoy's master of ceremonies (a position of no mean importance, given the convolutions of seventeenth-century etiquette).

The princesse was allowed one day to rest and compose her emotions. On the ninth, the entourage started across the Alps. The journey was a slow one, even by the standards of the period, owing to the excessive enthusiasm of the Savoyards. Every town and village along the way presented the departing princesse with welcoming speeches and congratulatory odes, and at each stop, Marie Adelaide conquered hearts with her grace, her obvious delight, and her guileless charm. At Montmélian (still under French occupation), she was received by the entire garrison under arms, and the governor personally escorted her convoy a considerable part of the way. Taking his leave, the governor requested her to name the password for the following day: without a moment's hesitation, Adelaide responded, "Saint Louis — for henceforth he will be my saint."

On the thirteenth, the French party struck out from Lyons; that same afternoon, the princesse reached Chambéry, the last major stop before the frontier. From there, the conte di Vernone reported back to

Turin: "This evening, the Most Serene Princesse has arrived . . . in excellent health, having met with no other mishap than the accidental entry of a gnat into her left eye, near Montmélian, which has occasioned her some annoyance, but caused little loss of time . . . I trust that by tomorrow she will be altogether rid of it." Adelaide's guardians had decided on a brief sojourn at Chambéry; Vernone explained to the duke:

> The stay which she will make here tomorrow is absolutely necessary, on account of the fatigue which one is bound to take into consideration in the case of one of such tender years, in order that she may remain in the same good health as when she left Turin, and that she may be conducted to Pont-des-Beauvoisin in the best possible [condition] . . . On Monday [October 15] the princesse will sleep at Echelles, where she will breakfast on Tuesday morning, and in the evening she will reach the Pont. These are two easy stages, to be undertaken with the intention that the princesse shall arrive there in good health, as we have recognized that to cover the remainder of the way by a long journey, as that to the Pont is, would not be to her advantage.

October 16, 1696, was the last day Marie Adelaide ever spent in Savoy. She awakened early in the village of Echelles; as Vernone had planned, the convoy took to the road shortly after the princesse had finished her breakfast. The few miles to the border were covered at an easy pace; at three in the afternoon, the entourage entered Pont-des-Beauvoisin. Across the river stood the Sun King's welcoming delegation.

The wait in the wings was now over. Within the hour, Adelaide would cross the bridge and enter France, the metaphoric "center stage" of the seventeenth century. Her mother's carefully imparted principles she had well absorbed; her father's training in statecraft and diplomacy no less. And just as well learned were the unconscious lessons of her parents: Anne Marie's pious resignation and unquestioning acceptance of pain and humiliation, Victor Amadeus's callous disregard for human feelings, his tenacity and his instinct for survival. From beneath the gilded luster of royal trappings, these two very human beings had provided Adelaide with the glimpse of a world far more real than that she was about to enter — a world of thwarted love and frustrated ambition, a world where, unlike fairy tales, princes and dragons were often indistinguishable. Though the princesse could not know it as her carriage rolled across the cobblestones to the medieval bridge at Pont-des-Beauvoisin, her education and her background would hold her in good stead, rescuing her from the ornate traps and plush pitfalls that would beckon in the years to come.

France — and the promise of a glorious future — awaited her.

5

A Perfect Princesse

OVERNIGHT, THE ENGAGEMENT of the duc de Bourgogne to the princesse of Savoy injected new life into Versailles. Courtiers who wallowed in the resplendent boredom of the last decade acclaimed the arrival of fresh blood and happily anticipated a new chapter for the Sun King's reign — if not a full return to the vibrance and gaiety of the sixties and seventies, at least something reminiscent of those glorious days. As always, they took their cue from their master: Louis XIV's childlike eagerness for Adelaide's arrival that autumn was observed with great pleasure and greater relief. Preparations abounded; shaken at last from gloomy melancholy, the Sun King — and Versailles — sparkled anew.

Of top priority — and just the type of meticulous planning at which the king excelled — was the creation of a household for the princesse. With Louis and his son officially widowers, marriage to the king's grandson would make her the first lady of the land and it was imperative that this household reflect, both in size and quality, her exalted position.[1] Adelaide's entourage was to consist of a *dame d'honneur* (lady-of-honor) with a corresponding *chevalier d'honneur*, a *dame d'atours* (mistress of the robes), five *dames du palais* (ladies-in-waiting), six *femmes de chambre* (waiting women), a first equerry, an almoner, and a confessor. The most important of these offices was the *dame d'honneur*, who would have complete authority over the little princesse as well as the rest of the staff, would take precedence over all ladies not of royal blood or married to princes of the blood, and would ride beside her young mistress in the king's own coach. Every court lady of suitable rank ached for the appointment, and dubious methods of canvassing were employed: Saint-Simon noted that "anonymous letters flew about like flies, libels and denouncements were everywhere."

Louis XIV was laid up in a sickbed, an extremely rare occurrence for him. A carbuncle on his neck had turned to anthrax, and his pains were excruciating. It was lanced by the surgeons several times — on one occasion, "eight snips of the scissors" — performed, of course, without anesthetic. His recuperation, under Mme de Maintenon's patient ministrations, was slow and (for once) private. "The King is seeing no one but his doctor and the old hag," Madame reported to her aunt in early September. "He shuts himself up in his study and never sees members of the Court . . . It is all vastly irregular." This irregularity afforded Louis XIV the chance to carefully arrange for Marie Adelaide's "proper" household, one that would meet fully with his wife's approbation since (as Saint-Simon observed) Maintenon "was resolved to keep the training of the little Princesse for herself, win her love, and teach her to amuse the King."

Together the royal couple reviewed the leading candidates for *dame d'honneur*. There was the capable duchesse de Créquy, lady-of-honor to Queen Marie Thérèse, or the duchesse d'Arpajon, who had performed that office for the late dauphine. Also under consideration were the maréchale de Rochfort, *dame d'atours* to the duchesse de Chartres (wife of the king's nephew) and the venerable duchesse de Ventadour, who had served as royal governess to both the dauphin and the duc de Bourgogne (and would later fill the same role for Bourgogne's son, the future Louis XV). But to the court's surprise, the office went to a "dark horse" candidate, the duchesse du Lude.

The duchesse du Lude did not come to the new household without qualification. Royal blood flowed in her veins, for she was a descendant of Henriette de Verneuil, one of Henri IV's several mistresses. She had married twice, first to the gallant comte de Guiche, and after his death, to the duc de Lude, grand master of the artillery; both marriages were childless. Although the reformed Louis XIV criticized her use of rouge and patches, Lude was still acknowledged as one of the great beauties of the court. She was good-natured and generous, sophisticated and tolerant. With her considerable fortune, she maintained a large establishment and a bounteous table, and cut a dignified figure at court, where she was generally liked and respected. Her appointment was startling, however, because Mme de Maintenon had never shown her any friendliness and Louis XIV had pointedly disliked her, never once inviting her to his retreats at Marly or Trianon. The backbiting Saint-Simon insinuated that she won her position through bribery: Nanon, waiting woman to Mme de Maintenon, received a secret visit from Lude's waiting woman, Mme Barbesi, and was given sixty thousand livres to influence Maintenon's decision — though it seems highly improbable that the powerful Maintenon could be swayed by a mere serving woman to make any choice contrary to her own wishes. With her shrewd instincts for hidden character, it is far more likely that Maintenon recognized the duchesse's potential capability, and her selection proved to be a wise one: though the duchesse du Lude later had good reason to regret the honor (as Adelaide grew older she found Lude's supervision irksome and teased her ruthlessly), she filled her office with great distinction, saving her unappreciative little mistress more than once from social blunder and lending beauty and dignity to the fledgling household.

The position of mistress of the robes was awarded to Mme de Maintenon's niece, the comtesse de Mailly, "an enchanting siren." The comtesse had served in this station for the temperamental duchesse de Chartres and had been very unhappy there; Saint-Simon, predictably sneering at her lowly birth, was forced to admit that she was "extremely kind and sensible."

In the appointment of the five ladies-in-waiting, Mme de Maintenon's design grew clearer: Mme de Montgon, a plain woman who "sparkled with wit, grace and kindness," was the daughter of Mme d'Heudicourt, one of Maintenon's oldest friends; the comtesse de Roucy, "extremely plain but very glorious," had served with Maintenon in the late dauphine's household; the marquise du Châtelet, "virtue and piety's self, good, gentle, and of a merry humor"; Mme de Nogaret, also plain and rather stout, but "with a witty expression which made amends for everything"; and the marquise de Dangeau (at thirty-two, the youngest of the group), "pretty as the day, and built like a nymph, with all the graces, and a virtue above suspicion," and also a close friend of Mme de Maintenon. Obviously it was important that the women surrounding the young princesse be sympathetic to the king's wife, since to her was entrusted the ultimate responsibility for the future queen. As an assembly, this group of mature ladies were not conspicuous for their beauty, but as companions they were intelligent, virtuous, and delightfully amenable to becoming indulgent chaperons for the little girl.

Tessé, still stationed in Turin, was made first equerry in absentia; the Jesuit Père Lecomte, a former missionary to China, was appointed Adelaide's confessor. The most inspired selection of all, for the post of *chevalier d'honneur,* the senior gentleman of the household, was the marquis de Dangeau, husband of Adelaide's lady-in-waiting. Gambler, poet, soldier, best dancer in France, and author of an excellent Court Journal, Dangeau was a great friend of the king's and of the same age.[2] Mme de Maintenon realized that Dangeau, with his high spirits and delightful wit, would be able to make Marie Adelaide laugh (this would not be a particularly difficult thing to do); more important, he possessed sufficient tact to correct the little girl without upsetting her. Once again, Mme de Maintenon's instincts were correct: from the very start, Dangeau became a special favorite, and as a past master of blindman's buff (Adelaide's great weakness), he soon became her dearest playmate.

Since Louis XIV had made it abundantly clear that no Savoyard waiting women would be permitted to serve the princesse once she entered France, the selection of her six French maids was debated as diligently as every other appointment. For Adelaide's personal maid, Maintenon picked Mme Quentin, which would prove a tremendously advantageous choice. Quentin was no stranger to royal service: her husband was the king's barber and her brother-in-law, La Vienne, one of His Majesty's masseurs. Mme Quentin knew everything worth knowing about the workings of the court and everyone who mattered within it; no better guide could have been found for the little newcomer.

It was fortunate (since, after such careful deliberation, any changes in staff were unthinkable) that Marie Adelaide grew genuinely fond of all her suite and fully enjoyed their company. Later, she playfully nicknamed her ladies *mes puits,* "my wells" — wells of information, she said, and wells of silence, for they never made her any mischief; she might have felt differently had she known that her "wells" reported her every move to Mme de Maintenon.

There also remained to be settled the question of Adelaide's rank and title. As a foreign princess, she held no official rank at the court of France, nor would she until her marriage. This opened the door to all matter of problems of precedence: for example, her own table would be presided over by the senior-ranking duchesse du Lude, while Adelaide would find herself seated on a taboret well below the salt. Plainly, some special arrangement was required.

After much contemplation, Louis XIV announced that until the wedding, which would make her the duchesse de Bourgogne, Adelaide would be known at court simply as La Princesse, and since her eventual position as first lady was assured, would be accorded the full rights and honors of that rank without the title. To confer this dignity on his future granddaughter, the king was obliged to seek the acquiescence of his sister-in-law, Madame, the official first lady since the death of the dauphine. Surprisingly, Madame, who placed an extraordinary importance on her rank and privilege, agreed immediately; to her aunt in Hanover, she explained: "Now that it has been resolved that [Adelaide] will have precedence over me, it matters little whether it is sooner or later," adding sourly that "except for precedence, no other benefits have accrued to me from being first lady in the land." She also found in Adelaide's elevation this measure of consolation: should the king's marriage to Maintenon ever be acknowledged, to the princesse and not Madame would fall the humiliation of having to walk directly behind "the old hag."

Arrangements settled to his satisfaction, Louis XIV ordered the departure of the welcoming cortège set for September 17. That morning, the king gave an interview to the ladies of Adelaide's new suite. He urged upon them the honor and the responsibility of their charge and the great trust he had conferred in their selection. Anxious to eliminate any potential discord, he told these women, "You are old friends; from now onwards, you must be united." As they withdrew, he handed the duchesse du Lude a large bag of coins, for Marie Adelaide to disperse as charity on her passage through France.

That afternoon, the palace gates were thrown open and the convoy clattered through the Great Courtyard and down the road toward the border. A most imposing cortège it was: five splendid postilioned royal coaches, each drawn by six or eight horses, carried Dangeau and the ladies of the household; the king's equerry, the comte de Brionne; and the master of ceremonies, the Marquis Desgranges — as well as the king's personal physician, surgeon, and apothecary. Following in a train of less sumptuous carriages were the lesser members of the new household: the chaplain, clerk, and master of the horse, six pages, ten footmen, three gentlemen-in-waiting, eight waiting maids, two ushers, two tapestry hangers and three furniture movers, a coachman, four postilions, and eight grooms. To equip the princesse's kitchen en route there were four servants for gathering firewood and kindling and thirty-seven officers for her fruit and vegetable larders, her bakery, and her butler's pantry. There was a baggage master and his assistant, two billeting officers, four couriers, and a small orchestra. A large detachment of the palace cavalry escorted the entourage, assisted by Louis XIV's own Swiss Guards — a total party of more than six hundred people. (We must remember that Adelaide was only a princesse; for a king like Louis XIV it would have been inconceivable to travel on such a reduced scale.)

This enormous retinue awaited the princesse's arrival at Lyons, preferring urban comfort to rustic charm along the border. Word arrived on October 12 that the Savoyards had left Turin and were expected at the frontier within four days. Again the giant caravan was set in motion and reached the border the evening of the fifteenth, just as Adelaide, in Echelles, prepared to sleep her final night in her native land.

The morning of the sixteenth, the French suite was up early, busy with last-minute preparations, anxious and excited. A ceremony of great implication was about to unfold: France readied itself to welcome its future mistress.

Adelaide arrived at the border town of Pont-des-Beauvoisin at three o'clock in the afternoon, October 16, 1696. She was able to look back with genuine pride at her triumphant farewell progress through Savoy. Every town, every village, had greeted her with celebrations, with dazzling fireworks and florid orations. She had heroically endured endless lines of well-wishers and had greeted them all with the utmost kindness and grace, whispering her thanks in a small, shy voice. As one concession to the human side of royalty, few were allowed to kiss the hand of the princesse; the tremendous audiences in Turin had made it very sore indeed and her master of ceremonies decreed that henceforth only the highest born of each group would be allowed to touch the throbbing little paw.

At Pont-des-Beauvoisin, Adelaide was first taken to a Carmelite convent for a rest, some light refreshment, and to change her dress for the ceremony that awaited. At four o'clock, a sedan chair arrived to carry the princesse the last remaining yards. With impressive dignity, the ten-year-old girl took her seat and began her official entry into France.

The ensuing ceremony was in no way spontaneous: weeks of meticulous preparation had been spent by both the French and Savoyard masters of ceremonies, and once again the behemoth etiquette ensured countless complications. In the "battle" of protocol between Desgranges and Vernone, the major problem appeared to have been whether or not the French escort should advance into Savoyard territory to receive the princesse. Desgranges maintained that it should, citing Anne Marie's similar journey in 1684 as precedent. Vernone, who knew well enough his master's antipathy despite the alliance, argued against the French advance and pointed out that, unlike Princesse Adelaide, the duchess of Savoy had already been married before she entered her new homeland. Neither gentleman would budge on so vital an issue, insistent that neither side should encroach upon the other's territory or gain the slightest advantage that might later be construed as evidence of superiority.

At last a peaceable solution was discovered: since the western half of the bridge at Pont-des-Beauvoisin was considered French, and the eastern half Savoyard, the welcoming coach would be backed up halfway across the span, its front wheels resting in "France" and its back just touching "Savoy." In this way, the two escorts could both advance and yet remain on their native soil; Adelaide alone would enter the carriage, and all threats of encroachment would be eliminated. How wonderful it would have been had this solution put an end to all discord — and how foolishly naïve to think it might!

Crowds assembled on both banks of the river. Beside the carriage in the middle of the bridge stood the duchesse du Lude, Dangeau, and the equerry, Brionne.[3] As Adelaide's chair advanced, a detachment of Victor Amadeus's household guards, in scarlet jerkins astride their caparisoned horses, took up their positions along the river edge and gave the signal to the waiting trumpeters. At the foot of the bridge, the princesse halted the runners and dismounted to walk the last few paces into her new land.

What the conte di Vernone next described is a wonderfully ridiculous example of etiquette, for the rule that no one should speak, or even be introduced, to anyone but his or her precise national counterpart was strictly observed: "I said to the Comte de Brionne, 'Monsieur, here is the Marchese di Dronero,' and to the Duchesse du Lude, 'Madame, here is the Principessa della Cisterna.' The Marquis Desgranges said to the Marchese di Dronero, 'Monsieur, here is the Comte de Brionne,' and to the Principessa della Cisterna, 'Madame, here is the Duchesse du Lude . . . [and so on for some time].' Finally, the Marchese di Dronero said to the Comte de Brionne, 'Here is the Princesse of Savoy.' " But if Louis the king inflicted this tedious formality on the princesse, Louis the grandfather made thorough amends by arranging a delightful piece of theatrics for the little girl: as Adelaide took her first step on French ground, there was a roll of drums, an elaborate fanfare from the orchestra, and the roar of cannon fire capped by wild cheering from the Swiss Guards.

Brionne made a gracious speech to Marie Adelaide, first expressing the joy and pride he felt in the great honor of receiving her and then conveying the king's personal message. His Majesty had taken great joy in hearing of her many fine qualities and eagerly awaited her arrival. He felt already that he loved her dearly and that he meant to prove his love in every way he could. He vowed that she would find in him a tender, devoted grandfather, as well as the mightiest king in Christendom.

Adelaide thanked Brionne for his welcome; when the count inquired if she wished him to relay any messages to the expectant French court, she tactfully requested that he send her love to the king and his son. (It is telling that she made no mention of the king's grandson, her fiancé — pleasing the king was all in all to her, and at this point Bourgogne was still little more than a name.)

Brionne presented to her the marquis de Dangeau and the duchesse du Lude, then introduced the other ladies of the suite. A French page took the train of her gown from his Savoyard counterpart (who reportedly shed "abundant tears"); Brionne took her right hand and Dangeau her left, and the princesse was put into the coach amid deafening cries of "Vive le Roi et la Princesse de Savoie!"

An enormous crowd had gathered before Adelaide's lodgings in town and cheered madly as she stepped from her carriage. She was settled in her apartments and dined alone that evening with the principessa della Cisterna; downstairs, Lude and Brionne presided over two tables of guests, the French and Savoyard escorts. After the banquet, Brionne distributed the gifts he had brought from the king: gold caskets studded with precious stones, magnificent diamonds, bracelets, and a rich assortment of jewels. With respect to her former position as governess, Cisterna received a magnificent diamond bracelet valued at 31,000 livres, although lesser members of the entourage found their presents less munificent.

An international incident very nearly arose when it was discovered that Victor Amadeus had sent along an equerry named Maffei, to pen an account of the reception. The French had not been informed beforehand of this additional guest and therefore had no present for him. When Brionne offered him a sizable sum of money, Maffei sniffed that it was beneath his dignity to accept a "payment"; but the equerry recognized the French predicament and said he would be satisfied to receive a sword. Dangeau came to the rescue by presenting his own magnificent sword, with its diamond-encrusted hilt, and thus a crisis was averted.

That night, the duchesse du Lude displayed her fine breeding and tact by waiving her rights and allowing the little princesse to sleep with her old friends, Cisterna and Mme Marquet. Adelaide slept her first night of the future in the familiar arms of companions from the past.

The newspaper *Mercure de France* reported that throughout this momentous day, the princesse had never once appeared nervous or shy. When she was presented with the officers of her escort, she smiled at each "with most genuine kindness . . . From what she said, and from her general appearance, she seems much older than her age. She has a beautiful figure and great amiability. Her face shows her noble birth, with a lively complexion, and a coloring that is all her own. Her eyes are very fine, her hair a beautiful chestnut brown . . . Among her many charms, the princesse shows a readiness to please and a liveliness of mind that are truly astonishing."

The French nation's love affair with Marie Adelaide of Savoy had begun.

The French entourage started early on October 17, understandably eager to return to court with their little charge. Adelaide was awakened, fed, and dressed; then the moment for farewells arrived. The duchesse du Lude felt that these goodbyes should be strictly curtailed to avoid distressing the girl, but Adelaide herself insisted on speaking individually with each member of her staff, nobles and servants alike. The little princesse was on the verge of tears, struggling to retain her composure; still she thanked one and all for their decade of faithful service and their good wishes for her future. When one tactless courtier remarked that she would miss her old life and all her friends, the princesse was caught off guard and tears welled up in her large, dark eyes. She hesitated, at first muttered something inaudible, then confessed that she hated to leave her dolls and toys behind.[4] As the old principessa della Cisterna approached her former charge for one last kiss, Adelaide's control broke and she cried long and hard in her nanny's arms.

The Savoyard retinue withdrew and sadly prepared for departure. The duchesse du Lude consoled the weeping little girl, her arms protectively around her tiny frame. But neither Adelaide's training nor

Tessé's excellent advice deserted her: smiling through her tears at her new governess, she declared, "No, I shall be sad no more, since I know that I am going to be henceforth the happiest person in the world."

The journey through France was conducted on a scale of royal progress. The purpose of such grandeur was twofold: to display to her future subjects this newest member of the royal family, and to acquaint that new member with local dignitaries and the general conditions of the land her husband would one day rule. Her passage through Savoy had been but a pale prelude: with a flair so typically French, this royal progress became the occasion for grand ceremonial entries and loyal addresses, feasting and fireworks, and flowers strewn en route.

It was easy enough for the ten-year-old to wipe away her tears and enjoy her journey. Her French ladies were indulgent, kind, and supportive, and Dangeau was a delightfully funny companion. And to pass through village after village, church bells tolling wildly, gallant young nobles riding out to greet her train, cheering crowds lining up outside the towns, sometimes for distances of two miles in both directions, was more than just exciting — every new day was an exhilarating adventure.

After stopping the first night in the town of Bourgoin, the royal cortège arrived at Lyons at four o'clock, the afternoon of the eighteenth. They entered the city between a double file of young Frenchmen, and the princesse was greeted by the provost of merchants, who made a long and rather fulsome address: "Heaven could not reserve for you a more brilliant destiny . . . All France tastes in anticipation the fruits of the union of the two noblest families in the world. You, Madame, will restore to Europe that peace so much desired, and so long banished by the fury of war."

Amid the salvoes of cannon and musket and the pealing of cathedral bells, she was led to the Place Bellecour, to lodge in the city's finest house, owned by one M. de Mascagny. That evening all of Lyons was illuminated, and an impressive fireworks display was presented, which Adelaide watched with delight from her balcony window.

It had been arranged for Adelaide to remain at Lyons for three days. The entire first day was spent receiving visitors: the princesse was called upon by the curious city treasurer, the deputies of the parlement, and all the town notables, and for each deputation she had a gracious smile and a kind word. The next morning was devoted to religious edification: Adelaide visited the Church of Saint-Jean, where she was hailed by the canons of Lyons. She witnessed the initiation of a novice into the Carmelite convent, and at the Jesuit college, semi-narians recited verses in her honor.

That afternoon, the duchesse du Lude attempted to satisfy the curiosity of the vast crowd outside the house by appearing in an open carriage on the Place Bellecour with the little bride-elect. The more insatiable were further gratified that evening when the princesse dined in public — Adelaide's introduction to the ceremony of *grand couvert*. At Versailles, where the king dined in public daily and the adoring throng could observe His Majesty's elegant manners and deft mastery of the knife and spoon, this rite was as intricate and rigidly defined as every other aspect of royal daily living.[5] Happily, in provincial Lyons, the pageantry was streamlined, reduced to the sole ministrations of the duchesse du Lude. While Adelaide's private table manners were less than exemplary (and quite normal for a child of ten), she behaved admirably in public, eating moderately and daintily, first receiving the dishes proffered with suitably grave politeness, then smiling infectiously at everyone present.

Her sophisticated staff was greatly impressed, discovering with each new day that the little princesse surpassed their highest expectations. Letters of praise flew back to the court at Fontainebleau. The duchesse du Lude had melted at Adelaide's ingenuous confession — "I wish that you could have been in some little corner, when mama spoke to me of you, to hear all the kind things that she said to me" — and she soon extolled the princesse's "modesty, sweet temper and charming manners." Brionne was amazed to find the princesse conversing with her household as easily as if she had known them all her life. Dangeau wrote: "The more we see of her, the more the good opinion which we have formed of her increases," although he attempted to maintain some vestige of objectivity: "She is quite a child; but, with much childishness, she shows good sense and intelligence, amiability, and animation." Master of ceremonies Desgranges, thoroughly smitten, was thoroughly subjective: "On my part, I persist in asserting that she is not a child of ten at all, but a sensible woman, capable even now of managing a household. The serious little replies she makes to the compliments paid her are spontaneous, and assuredly not suggested to her." To demonstrate his point, he related an example of the little girl's charming tact: the entourage prepared to leave Lyons, and the lieutenant governor delivered a florid address to the princesse as she sat in her coach. As he neared the end of his speech, he dried up, suddenly and completely. Without hesitation, Marie Adelaide shifted slightly from her seat, glanced down at the red-faced official's notes, and gently whispered his concluding sentence. Afterward, she thanked the lieutenant governor with "such a dazzling and sympathetic smile" that the man declared himself her slave for life.

Louis XIV was entranced by this story, relating it in council and to half the court. Mme de Maintenon responded to these floods of praise with a letter to Dangeau: "You are giving us a most charming impression of the princesse; we are all impatient to greet her. You are clearly a man of many parts, as the story of the diamond sword [which he had presented to the extra Savoyard, Maffei] amply proves. If the Princesse is not deceiving us, we are fortunate in having a child with a sweet nature to bring up, and I am glad to hear that she is still babyish, because I do not think precocious children ever go far in life."

Years later, Maintenon explained to the students at Saint-Cyr her initial reservations: "People thought to please the King by inventing all manner of witty remarks which they said she had made . . . They thought it excessively amusing, but when the King and I were alone together, we said, 'The child must be a fool or a scatterbrain if she makes such retorts at her age!' And we were enchanted to find that, on the contrary, she was extremely shy, and at first, scarcely uttered a word."

But if the Sun King shared his wife's doubts about the wit and wisdom of the ten-year-old girl, there was no question of his "wild excitement" as her arrival drew near. The Savoyard ambassador, Govon, wrote to Victor Amadeus that the king's "impatience and loving tenderness are inexplicable." She was the sole topic of his conversation and he often interrupted council proceedings to relate the latest reports of her progress.

Sadly his euphoric anticipation was marred by a family squabble, the roots of which once again lay entrenched in etiquette. Madame, who had so readily consented to Adelaide's precedence, now entertained second thoughts on relinquishing her prerogative (one courtier quipped that doubtless she felt the king insufficiently grateful for her enormous sacrifice). Abetted by her imperious daughter-in-law, the duchesse de Chartres, she nagged incessantly at Monsieur to persuade his brother to reverse the order. The king naturally refused to change his decree, and the indignant Monsieur grew very disagreeable. Sulking loudly, he complained to all who would listen that his brother meant to keep the little princesse all for himself — though the greater part of the court secretly endorsed the king's order that Adelaide was *not* to mix with her grandfather's immoral crowd, either at Versailles or at Monsieur's country estate at Saint-Cloud.

Monsieur then demanded that his granddaughter address him as *Bonpère* instead of the correct *Grandpère,* whining that "Grandfather" made him sound like an old man. Finally, he decided to set out on his own and meet the princesse en route to Fontainebleau, motivated by the egotistical longing to be the first in the family to greet the little girl and even more by the wish to take precedence over her, even if only for one night. Again he was thwarted: just outside Montargis, he received word that the king himself was riding out to meet the cortège, and wisely, if ungraciously, Monsieur turned back and joined his brother's party.

The court was astonished by Louis XIV's sudden decision to end his wait and journey south to meet the princesse. Such condescension from the Sun King was extraordinary in itself, and all the more since His Majesty still had not fully recovered from his recent illness. But the king was simply tired of waiting and saw no reason to curb his impatience further.

Louis XIV departed early in the morning of November 4, and at four o'clock that afternoon arrived at the town of Montargis. Adelaide's party was not expected for another two hours, so the Sun King retired to rest and refresh himself; as the time ticked by and their meeting drew closer, his impatience grew so keen that he was soon up and out on the balcony, scanning the horizon for a sight of her party.

All this while, the cortège had continued its triumphant progress north through the heartland of France. City after town after village wildly acclaimed their new princesse, hailing their "dove of peace" and — more fantastically — their "long-awaited olive branch." To protect their little charge from overexertion, Lude and Dangeau had arranged a rest of five days (October 31 to November 4) at the village of La Charité. At ten A.M. on the fourth, the party set off for Montargis, fifty miles to the north.

Shortly before six o'clock, Louis spied the royal caravan from the balcony of his lodging. He quickly assembled the "brilliant suite" he had brought to greet the princesse — his legitimate heir, Monseigneur the dauphin, and his illegitimate sons, the duc du Maine and the comte de Toulouse; his cousin, the prince de Conti; his nephew, the duc de Chartres; and, of course, Monsieur. This august delegation descended into the street as the carriage drew up before them. When Marie Adelaide stepped from her coach, the old Sun King could wait no longer: rushing up to assist her, he cried, "Madame, I have awaited you with much impatience!"

The little princesse rose admirably to the occasion. In her sweet, clear voice, she replied, "Sire, this is the greatest moment of my life!" She attempted to kneel before him, but the king swooped her up and embraced her heartily. She kissed his hand "most tenderly" — and Louis XIV surrendered unconditionally.

The king turned and presented Monseigneur, then Monsieur; well instructed in the subtle differences in their ranks, Adelaide gave two kisses to her future father-in-law and one to her maternal grandfather. She was then introduced to the duc de Chartres, her step-uncle, and the other members of the royal party. After this, the king personally escorted Adelaide upstairs to the apartments prepared for her. Assembled there, and agog with curiosity, was a large contingent of nobles, "whom she saluted according to their quality; the princes and the dukes and peers she kissed," for her father's lessons on the niceties of French etiquette had been well mastered.

The tone of Adelaide's future relationship with Louis XIV was set at that very first meeting: when the princesse answered a question from the king, she addressed him as "Sire," but he cut short her reply, granting her the honor of calling him "Monsieur." By the time the royal party reached Versailles, "Monsieur" had been replaced by "Grandpère."

The *Mercure de France* reported that the king asked her many questions, "to which she replied very intelligently and clearly; during this conversation, the Princesse twice took His Majesty's hand, which she kissed very affectionately. In short, she did not appear in the slightest degree embarrassed." This ease and amiability profoundly moved the aging Sun King: all his life, the mighty monarch had known only the fawning adulation of sophisticated, self-seeking courtiers, and the unaffected familiarity of this artless child awakened in him the long dormant desire to be loved simply for himself. For the first time in his threescore years, Louis XIV felt the urge to protect, to cherish.

Leaving the princesse in her salon to receive the compliments of the mayor, the king retired to his room to rest till supper. There he penned a letter to Mme de Maintenon at Fontainebleau, a letter which tells almost as much of its writer as it does its subject:

I arrived before five o'clock; the Princesse did not arrive until six. I went to the coach to receive her; she allowed me to speak first, and afterwards replied extremely well, but with a little embarrassment that would have pleased you. I conducted her to her room through the crowd, letting her be seen . . . She bore this progress with grace and modesty. At length we reached her room, where there was a crowd and heat enough to kill us . . . I studied her in every way, in order to write you my impressions of her. She has the best grace and the most beautiful figure that I have ever seen: dressed to paint, and coiffured the same; eyes bright and very beautiful, the lashes black and admirable; complexion very harmonious, white and red, all that one could desire; the most beautiful hair, and a great quantity of it. She is thin, as befits her age; her mouth is rosy, the lips full, the teeth white, long and ill-placed; the hands well-shaped, but the color of her age. She speaks little, as far as I have seen, and shows no embarrassment when she is looked at, like a person who has seen the world. She curtsies badly, and with rather an Italian air. She has also something of the Italian in her face; but she pleases; I saw that in the eyes of all present. For my part, I am very satisfied with her. She bears a strong resemblance to her first portrait, not to the second. To speak to you, as I always do, I find her all that could be wished; I should be sorry if she were more beautiful . . . I say it again: everything is pleasing except the curtsy . . . I will tell you more after supper, then I shall remark many things which I have not been able to see as yet. I forgot to tell you that she is short rather than tall for her age . . ."

As Sainte-Beuve accurately noted, there is, in this rather detailed study, no mention of anything beyond simply physical characteristics — for above all, Louis XIV was concerned with externals, appearance over substance. What she was like was not so important as what she *looked* like; this letter foreshadowed the attitude the king adopted toward his granddaughter for the rest of her life: let her please everyone, let her be charming and amusing, and for the rest, let her do as she pleased — he would require nothing further.

Louis's first letter to the duke and duchess of Savoy after meeting their daughter has been lost, but the dispatch sent to Tessé at the same time leaves no doubt to the king's great pleasure: "Although I have already expressed to [Victor Amadeus] my satisfaction at finding in her all the qualities I was promised, you may add that I am perfectly delighted with her manners, disposition, and looks, the grace that accompanies her every movement, and the education she has received. I have no doubt of discovering that gentleness of spirit, and all those other qualities needed to enable her to profit by our care, and that being so good a subject, she will soon reach perfection . . ." It was clear enough to everyone present at Montargis that, in the eyes of this tired old man, that perfection was very near indeed.

It might be claimed, with a certain amount of justification, that at this time in his life, Louis XIV was "ripe for the picking," that anyone could have successfully conquered his heart, provided they were new, fresh, and unintimidated by Louis le Grand — but these requirements form a rather tall order, and the claim does injustice to the extraordinary charm of Adelaide's personality. The approach of old age had exacerbated the king's feelings of loneliness. The same Louis who, in his youth, had set himself apart as the state incarnate now longed for the security and affection of family life. His own children, legitimate or otherwise, had been a disappointment: the dauphin, dim-witted and lethargic, terrified of his august father, was hardly the type of offspring to inspire paternal devotion. As for the king's bastards, their very origin and anomalous rank created a barrier between the generations — while Louis XIV treated them as his children, it was impossible for them to treat him as their father. The king's pure and simple love for Marie Mancini (in the dimly remembered past) had demonstrated his capacity, if not his need, for deep and sincere affection — and therein lies the secret of Adelaide's conquest. The princesse of Savoy did not see, let alone love, Louis XIV, the great Sun King; she saw instead, and came to love deeply, a sweet and somewhat sad old man who melted every time she called him Grandpère. She regarded him as a grown-up playfellow, created especially for her benefit. Both of them would find the results of this love highly gratifying, for henceforth one of Louis XIV's primary objectives in life would be to ensure the happiness of the little girl whose love gave him cause for living.

Dining with the Sun King was an experience awesome enough to strike terror into the hearts of many seasoned courtiers, but Adelaide's remarkable composure, her ease and familiarity with Louis XIV that first night, amazed the curious spectators. It was noted that she never served herself without first offering the dish to the king and Monseigneur, and that she thanked the steward for each plate "with excessively dignified politeness." For more than one elderly observer, the princesse brought to mind her grandmother, the first Madame: the extraordinary charm and gentility with which Minette had captivated the French court a quarter century before seemed to live again in her delightful granddaughter. During their meal, the king playfully inquired what she thought of his son's figure — Monseigneur, who lived only for the hunt, the table, and the boudoir (in that order), was greatly overweight — but Adelaide gravely, and cleverly, replied that while the dauphin was certainly stout, she did not find him *too* stout, for she had expected him to be much larger than he really was. This was just the sort of remark that had won Minette the love of a young Sun King, and twenty-five years later, her granddaughter found it no less effective.

Memories of Minette were invariably accompanied by recollections of her daughter, the gentle Anne Marie; when Louis XIV returned to Adelaide's room after completing his letter to his wife, his first remark was to Monsieur: "I wish that her poor mother could be here for a few moments to witness the joy we feel." He sat the little girl in his own armchair and placed himself on a low stool beside her. Together, they passed the evening playing jonchets, an early form of cribbage. As the little princesse was taken off to bed, the contented old man exclaimed, "I would not have her changed in any way whatever!"

The next morning, Adelaide was awakened at six o'clock, and to her great surprise, the king himself attended her toilette; he greatly admired her hair, declaring it "the most beautiful in the world." At nine, he escorted her to mass, through a crowd estimated (excessively) at twenty thousand. Dangeau observed that "the Princesse prayed to God with an edifying piety," but her thoughts can only be imagined as she watched the entire congregation, backs to the altar, bowing low before God's regent — the kindly old man who knelt beside her and held her hand tightly in his.

Dinner was served at eleven, and afterward the royal party departed for Fontainebleau. Adelaide sat in the king's own coach, between Louis and Monseigneur. Monsieur and the duchesse du Lude sat opposite, and one place was left vacant for the absent fiancé — for the duc de Bourgogne was scheduled to meet them on their journey.

Outside Nemours, Adelaide was at last confronted by her future husband: the fourteen-year-old Bourgogne was overcome with embarrassment and totally forgot the compliments he had so carefully rehearsed. He kissed her hand twice, and as he took his seat in the carriage, she blushed. Then, absorbed as she was with her great-uncle the king, the princesse promptly forgot all about the prince.

The cortège arrived at the gates of Fontainebleau shortly before five that afternoon. Half the court had gathered outside, craning for a first glimpse of their future mistress as they lined the steps of Louis XIII's

Horseshoe Staircase and crowded along the terraces. The king stepped from the carriage, took the hand of the diminutive princesse, and led her up the stone staircase: to one courtier, she seemed to be a tiny puppet peeking out of the king's great pocket. At the entrance to the palace, Adelaide was introduced to Monseigneur's two younger sons, the thirteen-year-old duc d'Anjou and the ten-year-old duc de Berri.

A short service was held in the royal chapel, to celebrate the safe conclusion of her journey, then Adelaide was conducted to her rooms, formerly the apartments of the king's mother, Anne of Austria, one of the finest suites in the palace. Beneath the intricate sculpted ceiling of the great drawing room, Mme de Maintenon, the princesses of the blood, and scores of courtiers waited. Madame, no less eager to meet her step-granddaughter than the others, found the throng stifling, though amusing: "There was such a crowd, all pressing one another so that poor Mme de Nemours and the Maréchale de La Mothe were so violently pushed that they came on top of us, walking backwards the whole length of the room, and finally fell against Mme de Maintenon. If I had not seized the latter by the arm, the whole three would have rolled the one on the top of the other, like a pack of cards. It was exceedingly funny."

At last the little princesse entered the room; her dress, "immensely rich, embroidered with gold thread and studded with jewels" (and doubtless provided by Mme de Maintenon), excited universal praise, as did the grace with which she took her seat beneath the dais. Louis XIV and Monsieur, each at her side, took turns presenting the members of the court, whispering the appropriate ways for her to receive them: whenever a duke, a prince, or a marshal (or their wives) approached, Monsieur would give a little push and mutter "Kiss" — and Adelaide would graciously perform. These presentations continued for more than two hours; much of the court was still unintroduced when the little girl began to display visible signs of exhaustion and the remainder of the ceremony was postponed till the following day.

The tired princesse was taken to her bedchamber, where the most important introduction of the day was made privately. As Adelaide prepared for bed, Louis XIV and Mme de Maintenon entered through a secret side door. The elderly couple approached, the king introduced his wife, and then retired to allow them privacy to become acquainted. If Mme de Maintenon had feared disappointment (and she certainly had), five minutes alone with the enchanting child dispelled all her worries. Adelaide had been instructed by her parents to trust implicitly in Mme de Maintenon, to love and respect her, and earn her favor; but the child's open nature and genuine eagerness to please captured the heart of the old governess without ruse or flattery. Left alone, Adelaide immediately embraced the startled, proper Maintenon and jumped into her lap: "When I wished to resist the caresses which she was bestowing on me, because I was too old, she replied, 'Ah! Not so old!' " Adelaide quickly made it evident that hers was not a nature to flatter falsely or mince with words: "With a caressing air . . . she said to me, 'Mama has charged me to give you a thousand friendly greetings from her, and to ask your friendship for myself. Teach me well, I beg you, all that I must do to please the King.' These were her very words . . . but the gay, sweet and graceful manner which accompanied them cannot be described."

There was much about Mme de Maintenon to comfort and reassure a displaced child: her wonderful smile, her soothing voice and good-humored way of admonishment, her soft, petting hands — and above all, her fastidious cleanliness and delicious scent.[6] Maintenon possessed the gifts of a mother rather than those of wife or lover. Instinctively she sensed Adelaide's carefully concealed apprehension — a child thrust, alone and friendless, into an alien adult world — and her heart went out to the brave princesse. Whatever injunctions had been set by the duke and duchess of Savoy, Marie Adelaide offered sincere, unrestricted affection to her new guardian, and Mme de Maintenon, surprised, relieved, and delighted, responded fully. Her love for the princesse, while more objective than the king's, would prove as true and enduring.

As she kissed the child good night and returned to her own apartment, Mme de Maintenon surely felt optimistic. The king's increasingly low spirits had alarmed her; nor was she blind to the fact that, since his "conversion," he had lost his zest for living. Never for a moment did she doubt his love or need for her (they were equally convinced that the salvation of his soul rested entirely in her capable hands), but she knew that in many ways she had ceased to amuse him — and the possibility of a return to his former sinful ways horrified her. To Maintenon's mind, the king's favorable reactions to Marie Adelaide had been crucial; now, at last, she could sigh in relief. In the coming years before the child's marriage, she was determined that Adelaide should provide diversion for the aging king and a mutual occupation for them both. What responsibility, what pleasure, they would encounter together as they trained this child for the greatest of futures.

Euphoria flowed from her pen; before retiring that night, she wrote

Anne Marie: "She is perfect in every respect, which is a very agreeable surprise in a person eleven years old. I do not venture to mingle my expressions of admiration with those which alone ought to be counted, but I cannot refrain from telling you that, according to all appearances, she will be the glory of the age."

Maintenon's excessive joy "at the treasure we have received" compelled her to continue extolling the little paragon: "The Princesse need not speak to show us her wit; her way of listening and all the emotions of her countenance show us that nothing escapes her notice." And later: "Your Royal Highness will scarcely believe how much the King is delighted with her; he told me he had to restrain his feeling lest his happiness appear too excessive."

Amid the universal chorus of praise, one predictable voice held the jarring note. Madame, who prided herself on objectivity, delivered her own verdict to the electress of Hanover — "neither pretty nor ugly." She was pleased to discover the princesse possessed "a nice little figure, like a doll, lovely hair and masses of it, black eyes and eyebrows with long beautiful lashes," but her smooth skin was "not very white," and her mouth was "large with thick lips; truly the Austrian mouth and chin." Unlike her royal brother-in-law, Madame explored the girl's character as well: "[She] is as artful as if she were thirty years old. There is an envoy here from Savoy, her mother's riding master, whom she must know very well indeed. But she pretends she doesn't, hardly looks at him, and never speaks to him for fear the King might take offense and think she is still attached to her old country . . . She is certainly intelligent, one can see that in her eyes." And the future of this "perfect Princesse?" Madame had no illusions; citing herself and the Bavarian dauphine as examples, she was confident the novelty of the new toy would fade: "When we first arrived, we also were thought wonderful, one after the other, but they soon got tired of us."

Seldom had Madame predicted so inaccurately.

The court's departure from Fontainebleau had been postponed one day to allow the little princesse to rest and recover her strength. But as the rejuvenated Sun King proudly displayed his latest acquisition, this day of "relaxation" was everything but relaxing. Louis XIV escorted Adelaide to mass, then resumed the previous night's ceremony, further confusing the little girl with introductions to the remaining members of the court. She was allowed to dine alone with her staff; already she had begun to rely on them as a buffer against this great new world and they responded with total, devoted service. Adelaide then paid her first formal visit — to the comfortable and no longer formal Mme de Maintenon.

Louis XIV had been apprised of Marie Adelaide's great love of the outdoors, and he shortly arrived at Maintenon's salon to treat his "two favorite ladies" to an afternoon drive. On their return, the princesse felt strong enough to face the visits of ceremony required by her station. With strict observance to the orders of rank, she called upon Madame, the princesse de Conti and Mme la duchesse (the king's illegitimate daughters), and the duchesse du Maine. Back in her own rooms, she then received visits from Monseigneur and his sons Anjou and Berri; Monsieur; and finally, the duc de Bourgogne — who was granted permission to visit his fiancée, chaperoned by Lude, once each week.

Louis XIV set the court's return to Versailles for the next day, November 7. He was anxious to be back at his favorite residence, now that the quarterly cleaning was finished and the "bad airs dissipated." He was even more anxious to show off his fabled palace to his entrancing new playmate. As the massive entourage prepared to quit Fontainebleau, the king summoned the little princesse to the private chamber of Mme de Maintenon — *ma tante* ("my aunt") as Adelaide had begun to call her already.

He informed her that he was setting aside three hundred livres a month as "pin money" for the princesse, and he presented her with a dazzling set of diamonds from the Crown collection. The princesse was overwhelmed: despite her tender age, she understood the implication of the jewels. The marriage contract had been framed with the understanding that final acceptance was dependent on the Sun King's approval of Adelaide's person, and that even at this late date, he was free to send her back to Savoy. With Louis XIV's well-known abhorrence of disagreeable scenes and disputes, and Victor Amadeus's well-known parsimony, property of the Crown of France would never have been offered unless the possibility of Adelaide's return to Turin no longer existed.

The princesse was sent ahead from Fontainebleau with her ladies by separate coach, but the king arranged to join her at Plessis. He wanted to see for himself her first reaction to Versailles and the splendid rooms he had redecorated for her. Shortly after five in the afternoon, the royal coach reached the Place d'Armes, and Adelaide first beheld Versailles.

6

The Glory of the Age

THE MODERN VISITOR to Versailles is struck first by the incomparable size of the palace complex. From the central Marble Court (which only the royal family was privileged to use) at the apex of the main building, the two arms of the eastern front sprawl, widening past the large Royal Court and into the larger Great Courtyard; perpendicular to these arms, the north and south wings stretch out seemingly without end. On the other side of the palace, the garden front alone measures almost two thousand feet. Time has faded the brilliant and carefully planned coloring of the château, bequeathing us a monochromatic (though grand) sepulcher, but for Adelaide and her contemporaries, the immensity of Versailles was further enhanced by the vivid blending of golden stone and deep red brick, its elaborate iron grillwork sparkling in fresh gold leaf. If this immensity seems ostentatious today, we must realize that during the reign of Louis XIV the palace was home to ten thousand people. Under one large roof, the Sun King assembled his nobility, his government, and the countless scores of servants both required. From 1682 until 1789, Versailles was the seat of administration as well as the principal residence of the court, the true capital of France.

Size alone would ensure Versailles a place in history, its cost as well (estimated at 400 million francs). Its wealth of artistic decoration — Le Brun's beautifully geometric walls of precious marbles in alternating colors, his magnificent carved ceilings, even the fabulous solid silver furniture (alas, sacrificed in the War of the Spanish Succession) — or Le Nôtre's inspired gardens also would have guaranteed distinction. Yet what makes Versailles unique is that it manifests one particular age — the *ancien régime* — and nothing else. The historian G. F. Bradley noted: "The curse of most historical buildings is that they contain too much history: the mind wanders restlessly from century to century and finds no central and solid halting place." This is certainly true of Fontainebleau, which housed four centuries of French kings and emperors, or of the Louvre, which owes so much of its charm to its eclectic progression through eras of architecture. But Versailles was fossilized, as it were, almost from its very inception. It is a celebration — the monument — of absolute monarchy, and wherever else it fails, its most astonishing effect is that it remains to this day the truest representation of its creator.

In contrast to its lofty personification, the origins of Versailles are humble. The Sun King's father, Louis XIII, discovered the site while hunting in the forest nearby, and in 1624, bought the property and erected a modest hunting lodge — the seed and central core of the future palace. It was his favorite residence until he succumbed to tuberculosis in 1643; during the minority of Louis XIV, it stood deserted and forgotten.

It has often been remarked that in 1661, the young Louis XIV fell in love twice: with Louise de La Vallière (his first *maîtresse en titre*) and with his father's beloved haunt at Versailles. The former passion waned predictably by the end of the decade; the latter not only stood firm, but increased through the years. Louis XIV never disclosed his reasons for building at Versailles — and with his well-known love of open air and exercise, and his growing preoccupation with gardening, the selection of this molding old lodge set in marshy ground, which Saint-Simon declared "the gloomiest and most thankless of places; without view, without woods, without water, without soil," was inexplicable to the ministers and courtiers alike. Build in Paris, they urged. But the king had no liking for his capital — it reminded him of the penurious years of his minority, of the Fronde uprisings and the humiliations he had endured at the hands of rebel nobles; he had vowed secretly never to live there again. Perhaps it was the challenge of wresting Versailles from nature that appealed to his megalomania: how fitting for the Sun King to transform the earth, "tyrannizing over nature and subduing it by the force of art and money." Perhaps the place revived some dim remembrance of the father he had scarcely known.

Whatever the reason, the spot held a special charm for Louis XIV, and that charm, coupled with the Sun King's indomitable will, over-rode all objections. The ministers argued there was no town, so Louis created one; the aesthetes declared there was no suitable view, so Louis dug the Grand Canal and created the most exquisite park the world had yet seen; the court complained the air was unhealthy, but since the Sun King felt perfectly well there, nothing further was said on that score.

Still the evolution from modest hunting box to seat of the government was a gradual one. It began with a compromise between the king and his finance minister, Jean-Baptiste Colbert. Colbert (who was also the superintendent of buildings) had argued eloquently for the renovation of the Louvre as a more suitable expression of Bourbon majesty (his logic — "Oh, what a pity that the greatest and most virtuous of kings should be measured by the scale of Versailles" — rings today with wonderful irony). Very well, the king countered, he would consent to the construction of a new east front at the Parisian palace if Colbert would agree to "modest renovation" of the lodge and redecoration of its gardens. The bargain was struck in 1662, but the "compromise" quickly proved one sided: while expenditure on the Louvre's colonnade was held under strict control, twenty kilometers away (and to the finance minister's horror), one and a half million francs were spent during the first year alone.

It was the king's original intention — or so he maintained for fifteen years — that Versailles was to be his private hermitage, an appropriately elegant hideaway where he might escape the formality of court life and indulge in arcadian pleasures with his wife, his mistress, and a select group of intimates.[1] Yet it also provided an ideal setting for the magnificent *grandes fêtes* that Louis XIV presented to celebrate the French military ascendancy in the high noon of his reign.

The first of these great entertainments, known as "The Pleasures of the Enchanted Isle," was held in the Versailles gardens in the summer of 1664. More than six hundred people were invited to enjoy the festivities, which opened with an elaborate fanfare and the appearance of the king (in gold-, silver-, and jewel-encrusted armor, a scarlet plume in his helmet) in the guise of Charlemagne's paladin, Roger, coming with his knights from their enchanted island to entertain the Sun King's court. Roger was followed by Apollo himself (allegorical incongruity never bothered Louis XIV); in tribute to his earthly counterpart, the Sun God was borne in an immense glittering chariot drawn by four caparisoned horses and escorted by twenty costumed attendants.

The afternoon saw a tournament, won by the marquis de La Vallière, Louise's brother. After a ballet performance, the guests found a sumptuous banquet awaiting them in one of the torchlit groves. The next afternoon, they were treated to a performance of *La Princesse d'Elide*, by the king's protégé Molière (the author scoring a triumph in the role of the idiotic valet Lycisas); that evening, in the vestibule of the palace, the guests enjoyed the premiere performance of Molière's new work, *Tartuffe*. As the second day had been devoted to drama, the third was taken up with music and dance: the ballet music provided by Jean-Baptiste Lully (another of the king's protégés) immediately established him as the court's favorite composer.

On July 18, 1668, Louis XIV celebrated peace with Spain in yet another Versailles extravaganza. "The Grand Royal Divertissement" was one day only, but Louis spent over one hundred thousand livres (not including the cost of the elaborate costumes he provided for the guests). After a performance of Molière's latest, *Georges Dandin,* and an opera-ballet composed especially for the occasion by Lully, guests were invited to promenade through the newly completed gardens. For their refreshment as they strolled, tables beckoned from the groves, spread with trays of fresh oranges and currants, and delicacies of marzipan, spun sugar, and crystallized fruits; trees along the pathways were wired to hold baskets of peaches and plums, to be "picked" and nibbled as one walked. A temporary building, the Salle de Verdure, was constructed for the royal banquet, and supper was served on small silver tables, amid garlands of flowers and leaves, hundreds of candles, and rows of sparkling fountains that lined the walls. In another building (also raised for the day, with walls of marble and porphyry), the evening ball was held: couples danced in the warm glow of candlelight, or sat in private boxes tiered around the floor, listening to the music. Just before daybreak, the company moved outside again, and over the gardens beheld a dazzling and dramatic display of fireworks: the last *feu d'artifice* to explode above them was the king's cipher, the inverted L, traced in gold and silver stars. The divertissement was the most memorable celebration ever to take place at Versailles; it also marked the end of the château's first stage of development.

Even as the last of the divertissement's burnt-out fireworks were carted away and the temporary buildings dismantled, orders were issued for major construction to begin on the main house. The earlier renovation was handsome indeed, but failed to solve the problem of space, a problem more acute with each visit as the king invited larger numbers of his court to play there with him. With France at peace, the Sun King could return to his cherished and secret project, establishing himself outside Paris.

He was adamant that, whatever improvements were made, his father's unpretentious dwelling must remain intact, and this posed no small architectural problem. Architectural genius Louis Le Vau at last devised a neat solution: the eastern, or town-facing courtyard front of the original château was left untouched, but the remaining three fronts of the inverted-U building were encased in a giant "stone envelope" that effectively doubled the size of each wing. For his new garden façade, Le Vau abandoned all use of the brick that lent the courtyard its delightful gradations of color, and designed instead a majestic baroque front of stone, glass, and coupled Ionic pillars capped with statues and carved urns.

The envelope was completed by 1671, when the decoration of the new state apartments began in earnest under the direction of Charles Le Brun. Seldom has an artist been given such encouragement to lavishness as the Sun King offered Le Brun, and the result — the fruit of ten year's labor — was a dazzling display of consummate French decorative art.

The state apartments comprised a suite of five large reception rooms extending along the northern front of the main building. Each was dedicated to a god of antiquity whose planet revolved around the sun: Venus smiled benignly from the ceiling of the large buffet room, while Mars hovered significantly in the Grand Chamber of the Guards. The throne room, last in the suite, was devoted appropriately to Apollo; across Le Brun's coffered ceiling, the Sun God arose from the waves in his golden chariot while his mortal counterpart below dispensed royal justice from a solid silver throne.

The walls of these sumptuous rooms were hung with priceless Gobelin tapestries, glorifying the Sun King's achievements in war and peace, or lined with geometric panels of alabaster, porphyry, and colored marble. Plush rugs from Persia and Savonnerie carpets were spread across the polished parquet floors.[2] Rock crystal candelabra and priceless porcelain vases gleamed side by side from gilded pedestal tables; paintings by Titian and Veronese vied for the eye with marble clocks and busts by Bernini. Europe gasped at this unrivaled display of French refinement — yet Louis XIV's vision was by no means fully realized.

In 1677, the king first revealed his intention to make Versailles his permanent residence. The vision developing since the days of the Fronde now lay within grasp. With his enchanted fairy palace as the lure, Louis XIV would ensnare the still potentially dangerous nobility; under his roof and his ever watchful eye, their effective resistance could be eliminated. The prize was to live amid unmatched splendors, to breathe the heady atmosphere of the Sun King himself; the stake was emasculation and total subjugation — the nobility eagerly paid its price.

The next year, a royal commission to undertake the third and greatest stage of construction was granted to Jules Hardouin-Mansard (Le Vau had died before the completion of his envelope). Over the next two decades, Mansard transformed the entire palace: Louis XIV, with his impeccable sense of style and short memory, criticized Le Vau's "nonwork" on the eastern courtyard front as incongruous with his more splendid garden façade, and so a face-lift — more accurately, a roof-lift — was performed to unify both sides of the building. To accommodate the bureaucracy the king intended to transfer, Mansard designed two buildings of office space flanking the Royal Courtyard. To house the growing population, two enormous wings were constructed, sprawling to the north and south of the central U-block, once again doubling the already extensive garden front. Two sweeping concave buildings were erected across the Place d'Armes, one for the royal coach horses, the other for the riding horses; the magnificence of these stables inspired the elector of Hanover to complain that the horses of the king of France were better housed at Versailles than he was in Germany.

Mansard's south wing, overlooking the Queen's Garden and the Orangerie, combined living and working space beneath one long roof. It came to be known as the Princes' Wing, for it was home to the princes of the blood. In addition to the king's brother, Monsieur, and his son, the dauphin, Louis XIV's illegitimate children (and their households) were accommodated here. Five royal bastards had survived the vicissitudes of seventeenth-century childhood; three others had died in infancy and one, Louise de La Vallière's son, the comte de Vermandois, had been exiled to Normandy in 1682 at the age of fifteen, following his implication in a homosexual scandal in the palace.

Eldest of the king's love children was La Vallière's only daughter, the ravishing Marie Anne, "the most beautiful woman at the court of France," thirty years old at the time of Adelaide's arrival. Marie Anne had been married at the age of fourteen to Louis, prince de Conti, but had little use for her adoring husband; an early widowhood left her free to devote her time to her half brother, the dauphin, and her energies to making mischief. In both pursuits, she was aided, if not directed, by her half sister, Louise Françoise, known to the court as Mme la duchesse. The eldest daughter of Montespan, Mme la duchesse (twenty-three in 1696) was pretty and witty, and the naughtiest member of the rising young "fast set" of Versailles. Married to Louis, duc de Bourbon (another Conti prince), she despised her husband, an ugly, dwarfish drunkard, and openly conducted a love affair with his younger brother. She was an inveterate prankster: she once procured a small petard and exploded it outside Monsieur's bedroom window, and more than once was caught smoking in the royal apartments. Although on more familiar terms with her father than his other children were, she was continuously called before the king and chided for conduct unbecoming a scion of the House of Bourbon. Like her half sister, the princesse de Conti, she reveled in her royal (if ambiguous) position and deeply resented the intrusion of a ten-year-old upstart.

The remaining three bastards happily felt no such animosity for the little princesse. Nineteen-year-old Françoise Marie had achieved a respectability denied her older sisters when (in 1692) she married her cousin, the duc de Chartres, Monsieur's only son and heir. (Madame, horrified that her son should be compelled to marry a bastard, reacted to their engagement by publicly boxing her son's ears in a gallery at Versailles.) The duchesse de Chartres grew quite fond of the little princesse of Savoy, as did Louis XIV's youngest son, the comte de Toulouse.

Less clear were the feelings of the king's other son by Montespan, the duc du Maine. Twenty-six-year-old Maine held a special place in the royal heart since he had been raised by Mme de Maintenon, who loved him dearly all her life and kept him on good terms with his father. Her task was not always easy, and at the time of Adelaide's arrival, those terms were very strained: in the final campaign of the late war, he had been accused of cowardice and inability, and (despite Maintenon's support) Louis XIV and the entire court accepted the charge.[3] "His name had fallen so low," Saint-Simon wrote later, "that such a man as the duc d'Elboeuf could insult him publicly, and with impunity. D'Elboeuf, choosing a moment when he had a good audience, asked M. du Maine where he would be serving next year, because, wherever it was, he solicited the honor of serving with him; and when thanked, and pressed for his reasons for the request, replied with a long bow that with M. du Maine, a man could be sure of not being killed." For Maine to have expressed any reservations about his father's new pet, while struggling to rehabilitate his reputation, would have been the grossest of follies. Wisely, he kept out of sight, sequestered in his country seat at Sceaux or locked in his apartments in the Princes' Wing.

These were the most illustrious occupants of the south wing. They were, by no means, the only residents: in addition to the fifteen "flats" that made up the principal floor, there were fourteen other apartments in the attic story. On the ground level, there were shops and offices, and of necessity, Mansard designed a less imposing building (today a military hospital) between this wing and the town to hold the kitchens, pantries, and accommodations for fifteen hundred servants.

The corresponding north wing, called the Nobles' Wing, housed the scores of courtiers drawn into orbit around the Sun King. While its main floor contained apartments of size and elegance, generally assigned to the more illustrious noble families, the bulk of this building was a labyrinth of dark, narrow corridors and tiny rooms (windowless, more often than not) where one froze in the winter and fried in the summer. Demand for accommodation far exceeded supply — nobles often took rooms in town and waited for years for a vacancy to occur — and proud families forsook their spacious country dwellings to exist in airless little suites above communal latrines, so great was the irresistible magnetism of Versailles and its creator.

The haughty duc de Saint-Simon, who prized his rank as peer of the realm above all else, maintained that he possessed one of the finest "nonroyal" apartments in the château: three small rooms deep within the maze, overlooking a stinking courtyard, with a low and dark entrance hall, and two tiny closets without windows. The hall and closet spaces had been cut in two horizontally, to provide servants' cubicles, so that a man of average height could just barely stand erect. Since the duke needed his three best rooms to fulfill his social obligations, he was compelled to sleep in the first of the windowless closets, and use the second as his private study, writing by candlelight day or night. Incommodious as this sounds, Saint-Simon's suite was so highly prized that once a neighbor duchess begged its loan for a wedding reception that promised to be too large for her own small apartment.

But if Mansard condemned the average courtier to squalid conditions, he more than compensated with the new apartments created for his lord and patron, in particular with his spectacular conversion of the garden façade along the central block. Under Le Vau, the two upper stories of this front had been deeply recessed, creating an enormous terrace that traversed the ground floor, separating the king's apartments on the north from the queen's to the south. Mansard enclosed this terrace, then raised and arched Le Vau's windows to complement the new, grander proportions. Inside this space, he created the fabled Hall of Mirrors, his finest achievement at Versailles.

Together with its salons of War and Peace at each end, the Hall of Mirrors extends along the entire west façade — 240 feet long and 33 feet wide, its incomparable ceiling arching to a height of 40 feet. Light pours through the seventeen high arched windows, splashing onto seventeen corresponding mirrors along the opposite wall. Luxuriant red marble pilasters, with gilded bronze bases and intricate gold capitals, divide the archways; each bay of three openings is broken by marble niches, housing classical statuary and adorned with trophies in thick bronze relief. In the reign of Louis XIV, the gallery was lined with solid silver console tables and flower tubs (the king had a mania for orange trees, and year round his rooms were filled with them); the highly polished parquet floor was covered with Savonnerie carpets. At night, three thousand candles flickered in the massive crystal chandeliers, while hundreds of smaller candelabra lined the walls. The ceiling by Le Brun was an enormous pictoral ode to the glory of the Sun King: the large central panel commemorated the year 1661, when Louis XIV took the government into his own hands, and the smaller flanking panels celebrated the various triumphs of his personal reign.

Mme de Sévigné, visiting the new Hall of Mirrors, proclaimed it "unique in the world." Today, it is still undisputedly splendid, but cold and lifeless; the twentieth-century visitor, awestruck by such petrified magnificence, forgets that this vast empty gallery once teemed with life. The archbishop Bossuet labeled Versailles "the city of the rich": the Hall of Mirrors was its main street. During the day it was crowded with the great and the small — noblemen clustered to whisper the latest court gossip while servants ran to and fro, bearing tokens and messages. Curious country folk crouched inconspicuously in its arched recesses (for Versailles was open to all, regardless of rank[4]), eager for a glimpse of the king on his way to the chapel or the council chamber; these guests were rewarded as often as not with the procession of the royal dairy cows, herding through the marble hall toward the nursery, to provide fresh milk for the Children of France.

The hall was always lined with rows of sedan chairs, plushly up-holstered and stamped with the royal emblem: with the enormity of his palace complex, the lord of Versailles thoughtfully provided his de-pendents with a baroque "taxi service," and for a few coins, the in-significant courtier could indulge himself in the luxury of being carried through the endless maze of corridors. Members of the royal family maintained their own private sedans, but this right was theirs exclu-sively, and more than one weary noble, longing for his bed down the hall and up the stairs — some half mile off — availed himself of the "municipal cab."

The suite of rooms to which Louis XIV conducted the wonder-struck princesse of Savoy — the queen's apartments — was located on the first floor on the north side of the central block. It was created by Le Vau for Queen Marie Thérèse, but she occupied the finished suite for only one year. Following her death in 1683, the rooms were assigned to the king's daughter-in-law; since the dauphine's death in 1690, the apartment had stood vacant. Its windows looked out on the *parterre du midi*, a terrace of fountains and flowerbeds, embroidered in bright and varied colors, that led to the Orangerie and the Swiss Lake.

The apartment consisted of four large rooms. The guard room, with white and red marble inlays accented by bold frames of ebony marble, was among Le Brun's finer accomplishments. Here the royal guard kept watch night and day, and the room was cluttered with gun racks and laced with screens, to hide the soldiers' camp beds and tables. The next room, the largest in the suite, was the dining room; despite her tender age, Adelaide was expected to fulfill the required duties of her station, which included dining in public (although Mme de Maintenon mercifully ruled that the little girl should perform the *grand couvert* only once every fortnight). In the adjacent drawing room, dubbed the Salon of Nobles, the princesse received important ambassadors and members of the court, while overhead the god Mercury, in the com-pany of Eloquence, Poetry, Vigilance, and Learning, smiled down from Michel Corneille's coffered ceiling. Last was the bedchamber, where the future wife of a future king could repose in appropriate grandeur, separated from the ever present throng by a carved and gilded balus-trade; a hidden jib-door to the right of the bed alcove led to a small retiring chamber, a bathroom, and a secret passageway to the king's apartments.[5]

That night, Marie Adelaide slept for the first time in the room where she would later welcome her husband, give birth to her children, and within fifteen years, die. The next morning, Louis XIV took the first opportunity of escorting the princesse through the gardens. Of all Versailles's countless treasures, the king was most proud of the royal park; he even wrote a book himself, *Presenting the Gardens of Versailles,* which opened with these instructions: "Leave the chateau . . . and go out onto the terrace. Stop for a moment at the top of the steps and gaze at the way the flowerbeds are laid out, at the ornamental lakes and at the fountains." Louis XIV, with his obsessive precision, adored this vista — and the perfect symmetry and balance with which André Le Nôtre had laid out the entire park. Nor has the magic of this landscape ever palled. In 1869, Mark Twain paid his first visit to Versailles and wrote: "You gaze, and stare, and try to understand that it is real, that it is on the earth, that it is not the Garden of Eden — but your brain grows giddy, stupefied by the world of beauty around you, and you half believe you are the dupe of an exquisite dream."

The son of the superintendent of the royal gardens in Paris, André Le Nôtre had studied architecture before turning to gardening, and his genius drew heavily on this earlier training. The formal garden style that he created at Versailles was revolutionary in its effortless coordination of buildings and grounds. The Parterre d'Eau (literally, "Flowerbed of Water") is one stunning example of Le Nôtre's art: by laying two large basins of water that span the entire western front, he brilliantly extended the façade with the pools' reflections, providing a subtle transition from palace to the extensive gardens beyond as well as balancing the panorama that concludes (at the other end of the axis) with an even greater expanse of water, the Grand Canal. Le Nôtre avoided monotony in his carefully balanced groves and flowerbeds by exploiting the uneven nature of the ground: the swampy hillside was shaped into terraces and ponds, steps and great open staircases. La Fontaine extolled Le Nôtre's genius: "He had the power to command Nature; she obeyed him because he asked of her what she was able to give."

The gardens, like the palace, were dedicated to Apollo, and the Sun God is presented in the two finest of the fifteen hundred fountains (today, only three hundred remain). The Pool of Latona, at the foot of the majestic staircase leading from the Parterre d'Eau, depicts the young god together with his sister Diana and Latona, their mother, as Latona pleads with Jupiter to punish the disrespectful peasants of

Lycia. Jupiter obliges, and the Lycians are transformed into frogs. The fountain, with more than sixty jets, rises to four tiers inlaid with red marble and adorned with ingenious, half-human, half-batrachian figures imploring divine clemency.[6]

Below the Pool of Latona, the royal avenue rolls gently down the sloping ground some two hundred yards, a wide carpet of lawn (hence, the nickname Tapis Vert, "Green Rug"), alternately bordered with classical statuary and monumental marble urns. At the foot of the royal avenue, in a large, half-moon basin, lies the Fountain of Apollo, counterpart to the Pool of Latona. In this magnificent composition (executed from a drawing by Le Brun), Apollo rises from the water on a chariot drawn by four horses, as around them tritons and dolphins announce the return of day; the grouping was originally gilded and could be seen glistening in the sun from the palace windows. The gushing waters of this fountain create three majestic fleurs-de-lis that jet dramatically fifty feet into the sky — and require a million gallons of recycled water an hour.

Le Nôtre understood the vital role water performed in his landscaping: a garden of perfect symmetry required the constant play of water to achieve harmony and eliminate dullness. But the existing supply of water at Versailles was inadequate to meet his heavy demands. It was impossible to keep all the fountains running for more than three hours at a time, and even with this economy, there were frequent breakdowns in the system. "You must arrange for the pumps at Versailles to work properly," the king snapped at his superintendent of buildings. "When I come back I want to find them in a condition that will not exasperate me by their breaking down all the time." After the consideration and rejection of several proposals, including diverting the Loire River to Versailles (this was abandoned when it was realized it would entail finding a way to make the river flow uphill), an extraordinary system known as the Marly Machine was devised. A system of fourteen enormous water wheels and 221 pumps carried water from the Seine valley over the hills of Louveciennes to the gardens of Marly and Versailles. Thirty thousand soldiers were employed on this project, which cost over eight million livres — the loss of lives during construction was "prodigious" (according to Mme de Sévigné), but Louis XIV wanted water, and cared not a whit what it took to get it.

Between the fountains of Apollo and Latona, wooded thickets, crisscrossed with pathways, ran parallel to the principal axes. Since Louis XIV spent almost every waking moment outdoors during the summer months, Le Nôtre created a series of concealed groves and open-air glades to function as "rooms" throughout the park. They served in various ways — as ballrooms or theaters, refreshment stops, pleasant diversions, or secluded trysting points — and were often furnished with tables, vases, large candlestands, even with chests of drawers inlaid with precious stones. The Rockwork Grove, once called the Ballroom, held a marble dance floor encircled by a ditch decorated with shells. Tiers of rockwork steps rose around the arena for courtiers to rest on various levels while water cascaded around them and sparkled in the light of a hundred crystal candelabra. Open-air concerts and light suppers were given in the Colonnade, a circular peristyle of thirty-two columns of Languedoc marble, alternating in slate-blue and pink, paired with an equal number of pilasters, and supporting an arcade of white marble. Inside each archway stood a white marble bowl with a jet of water spouting from the center, splashing softly as accompaniment to the royal flutes and oboes.

Other grottoes were devoted to more simple amusement, such as the Labyrinth in the southeast corner of the gardens. With its intricate maze of tall shrubbery and its charming seclusion, it had been a highly popular spot for rendezvous in the high noon of Louis XIV's Court of Love; Marie Adelaide grew particularly fond of it because it was dotted at every turn with (thirty-nine) fountains depicting the fables of La Fontaine. In the Queen's Grove, trellised alcoves held animals from Aesop's Fables, realistically painted lead sculptures — another spot guaranteed to delight the little girl.

Louis XIV was especially taken with tulips and each year (during peacetime) he imported four million bulbs from Holland to flame yellow and crimson in his private grotto, the King's Garden. To indulge the previously mentioned royal penchant for orange trees, Mansard erected and Le Nôtre filled the colossal Orangerie: its main hall, five hundred feet long and lit by thirteen arched windows, was flanked by two smaller galleries, each over three hundred feet long. In cold weather, the Orangerie housed two thousand orange trees — as well as more than a thousand oleanders, pomegranates, and palms.

But for the little princesse of Savoy, the most intriguing of all the gardens' delights was the royal menagerie. Located near the end of the Grand Canal's southern arm, this six-sided compound, walled and segmented into compartments around a central building, housed His Majesty's private zoo: from the safety of balconied windows, one could view the king's collection of bears and wolves, pelicans, gazelles, lions and tigers, camels — even a pair of elephants. The aviary was the finest in France — abounding with hummingbirds, cockatoos, parrots and toucans, ostriches, flamingoes and birds of paradise — and three thousand birds roosted in the pigeon house alone. There was, in addition, a poultry yard, and farms for horses and cattle. Beneath the central building was a large rock grotto, to be entered at the visitor's risk: pipes were hidden in the walls and floor, and a turn of the appropriate tap squirted ice-cold water in the face (or up the legs) of the unsuspecting guest. The young Sun King had delighted in this prank; now the old grandpapa performed the trick to Adelaide's squeals of delight. In fact, the princesse was so entranced with the menagerie that the king gave it to her on the spot — together with the miniature hunting pavilion facing it — so that she might give "tea-parties" there for her ladies, and more important, for him.

Louis XIV was overjoyed to discover that Adelaide shared in his love for the outdoors. At once, he altered sections of the park to suit her pleasure: two courses were laid out for *mail* (a game resembling golf), which Adelaide was fond of playing, and a switchback railway with a golden chariot was installed along the steep slope near the southern boundary, for her exclusive enjoyment. When the little girl requested a swing set, an elaborately gilded machine suddenly appeared on the grounds of Marly.

Louis's infatuation with little Adelaide mounted with every passing day; at the end of her first week at Versailles, Sourches noted in his journal: "The King is enchanted by her ways, and shows for her an astonishing affection." Royal exuberance transfused Versailles with new life, and happily Louis's rejuvenation was infectious. "Everyone is becoming a child again," Madame wrote her aunt, confessing that she herself had spent the day before yesterday playing blind man's buff with her step-granddaughter. "Yesterday, it was the turn of the Dauphin and the Princesse de Conti . . . what think you of such company?"

The entire court was clearly delighted with its new princesse: her freshness, her ingenuous blend of timidity and merriment, precocity and childishness, and her unaffected friendliness were refreshing beyond measure. Even Sourches, who remained her strongest critic throughout Adelaide's life, conceded that "her slightest actions are imbued with intelligence . . . her manner is serious and gentle, and she already knows how to mingle high spirits with royal dignity. Yet she is still only a child, and loves to play with dolls."

She was acknowledged as the king's darling — she was also a little girl approaching her eleventh birthday. One courtier discovered her, playing alone with those dolls, one afternoon in the glittering Salon of Peace. (Officially this was one of the state apartments, but it was quickly assigned as a playroom for the princesse.) It did not occur to him to make an observation on the presence of the hoped-for glory of the eighteenth century within the walls of the undisputed glory of the seventeenth; instead, it struck him that she appeared "like a tiny bee, lost in the center of a gigantic golden hive."

Tiny, yes — but already a queen bee.

7

A Royal Education

ADELAIDE'S HONEYMOON WITH FRANCE continued through her first year at Versailles. With each passing day, Louis XIV loved Adelaide more; bringing pleasure to his small enchantress became a major preoccupation. Govone, the Savoyard ambassador, reported to Victor Amadeus that Louis "visits her regularly twice a day, not ceremoniously, but from affection, since his attention is continuously occupied with providing her amusements suitable to her age" — amusements exceeding the child's wildest dreams. Govone was permitted to follow while the king explained to his darling the delights and intricacies of the palace gardens — "This spectacle was, for me, a simple spectator, a true gourmet's banquet"; more significantly, he reported yet another honor bestowed upon the little conqueror. Louis XIV, nearing sixty, toured his gardens in a special wheeled chair, drawn by two Swiss Guards. He was "pleased to permit the young Princesse to walk by his side on foot," but "when he perceived that she was tired, [made] her enter the sedan-chair with him." Though the royal chair was wide enough to accommodate two, no one had ever been allowed to share it with the king. "The Princesse opened her great dark eyes wide at the honor, and made no attempt to conceal her pleasure."

Every day the king unveiled fresh novelties. He took Marie Adelaide to visit the royal riding school, where the pages performed equestrian feats for her enjoyment. He walked with her in the perfumed air of the Orangerie, and through the Versailles orchards where the finest peaches in the world were grown. He arranged deliciously private picnics alfresco in the parks' more picturesque glades. Adelaide enthusiastically shared the king's passion for hunting and was soon a permanent figure at the chase: too young to ride alone, she stood beside Louis in his *soufflet,* a lightweight two-person chariot drawn by six ponies, which he drove "with much skill and at remarkable speeds."

When the king taught her to fish and she took to it seriously, it became the latest court craze. She snagged baskets of "monstrous fine carp" from the Grand Canal and sent them to the king's table with her compliments. Arriving for a visit to Fontainebleau, the impatient little angler sprang from the carriage and ran directly to the Carp Basin, while her footman, laden with bait and rods, struggled to keep up. No less plentiful or varied were the indoor amusements: jugglers and magicians, a puppet theater, jonchets — and endless rounds of blind man's buff.

On November 13, Adelaide paid her first visit to Marly, the king's private retreat. Like his father with Versailles, Louis XIV had chosen its site while out hunting. It was an open, somewhat marshy place, but surrounded by a fine forest and commanding a lovely view of the Seine valley. Le Nôtre was called again to metamorphose nature, and Mansard and Le Brun to re-create their magic on a smaller scale. They built their complex on rising ground looking south toward the river, the land falling away before it in terraces bounded by rows of trees and ornamented with a series of widening artificial lakes. Twelve evenly spaced pavilions were constructed, six on each side of the water. Each was divided into two apartments, one above the other, connected by an oval staircase, and paneled and furnished in crimson satin; these guest rooms were fully equipped, down to nightshirts and hairbrushes. All dozen pavilions were connected by arbors of sweetly scented shrubbery, opening into the gardens behind.

At the crown of these fragrant pathways stood the main house. The château was a masterpiece in the art of trompe-l'oeil: the façade was painted to appear adorned with busts, with gold and blue bas-reliefs, and with red marble pilasters, skillfully disguising its diminutive size and intimate nature. Louis XIV wished for a private home for himself and his family, so the château contained only twelve apartments, each decorated and furnished in a different color. Those select guests received in the main house were entertained in a huge octagonal salon that occupied the building's inner core. It was a splendid but confusing room; half the walls contained windowed doors to the radiating vestibules, and the other half were covered in identical false doors of mirror. After a few turns around the floor, more than one baffled nobleman forgot how to reach the gardens again.[1]

Because of its modest size, only a fraction of the court could visit Marly at a time; a weekend there became a highly prized mark of royal favor. Louis XIV took advantage of Marly's appeal to continue his subtle debasement of the once proud nobility: an invitation to Marly came only by *asking* for it. The formula was simple — as the king approached a group of hopeful courtiers, each in turn, with tense expectancy, asked the required question, "Marly, sire?" A graceful nod of the royal head signaled assent, the assurance of a place in one of the pavilions and an opportunity to sample the enchanting delights of the Marly gardens.

Most delightful of all, however, was the intimacy of the Sun King, for at Marly Louis XIV allowed himself a respite from majesty and grew something close to human. He gave animated supper parties, and often amused himself by throwing bread pellets at the ladies, who on this occasion were permitted to retaliate. One evening, surrendering to the jocularity of the moment, he began to toss oranges and apples until one, thrown with a good deal of force, hit Mlle de Viantais, a young maid-of-honor to the princesse de Conti. The indignant woman responded instinctively, grabbing a bowl of dressed salad and hurling it at the royal head — with astonishing accuracy. Louis, dripping with soggy lettuce, merely laughed.

Princesse Adelaide was captivated by Marly; to the king's gratification, she admired the splendid perspectives, the arbors and great pools, and countless fountains with their endless cascades of sparkling water. When later she expressed a wish to return to the enchanting retreat *alone* with "Grandpapa" (another unheard-of presumption), the doting king arranged for their private expedition the very next day.

"The Princesse understands how to attach the hearts of His Majesty and Mme de Maintenon more and more closely to her," Govone informed Victor Amadeus in mid-November. "His Majesty continues to relate to me with tenderness the questions and answers which are exchanged between himself and the Princesse, and to say how rejoiced he is at finding such childish ways joined to a fund of good sense." The weeks passed, and glowing reports still flowed to Turin: "[3 December 1696] The Princesse continues to give further and stronger proofs of good sense and good conduct, in demonstrating the lively affection which she feels for His Majesty. Moreover, the affection which the King entertains for her grows stronger every day. Mme de Maintenon does not cease to tell me of the satisfaction of His Majesty, of herself, and of the whole Court."

A glance at Dangeau's journal for the month following Adelaide's arrival shows how quickly her supremacy in the king's heart was established:

> 12 November: On leaving the Council, the King sent for the Princesse . . .
>
> 13 Nov: The King went to dine at Marly, and took there the Princesse, with Maintenon . . .
>
> 15 Nov: The Princesse went to Meudon to dine with the King . . . After dinner, the King took her into the gardens . . .
>
> 17 Nov: The King returned early from Meudon, and on his arrival went to see the Princesse . . .
>
> 18 Nov: The King went out shooting and returned early. When he had entered Mme de Maintenon's apartment, he sent for the Princesse and gave her [more] Crown Jewels . . .
>
> 21 Nov: After dinner . . . the King sent immediately for the Princesse to come to him in Maintenon's apartments . . .
>
> 24 Nov: The King went to the chase, but bad weather caused him to return at three; he went to the Princesse's apartments, where he remained a long time . . .

Her conquest was total — she became as necessary to the king of France as food or exercise. The marquis de Sourches watched the little girl with her grown-up playmate, and observed how willingly his royal master succumbed to her innocent attentions: "She claps him round the neck at all hours, jumps upon his knees and torments him with all kinds of playfulness."

Mme de Maintenon was no less enamored of the princesse. Soon an increasingly larger part of Adelaide's day was spent with "*ma tante*" in Maintenon's apartments across the hallway from her own. They chatted happily for hours on end: as the former governess brushed Adelaide's long chestnut tresses, she would tell her the fables of La Fontaine, carefully explaining each moral. Sometimes she read from Perrault's recently published collection of stories, *Tales from Mother Goose,* or thrilled the rapt young listener with recollections of her childhood days in the French Caribbean. There developed a comfortable intimacy between them, a closeness much deeper than many a mother and daughter have known. Mme de Maintenon, touched by Adelaide's wholehearted trust, lavished the princesse with love, and more important, with watchful and sensible care during her first years in France. It is to Maintenon's great credit that this early training enabled the princesse to survive the heavy royal spoiling that would later threaten to obliterate the finer side of her character.

The cynical faction at court remembered still — if the king did not — that this perfect princesse was the daughter of the chameleon duke of Savoy. Madame doubted the sincerity of Adelaide's devotion and perceived in the ten-year-old a streak of Machiavelli: "She pays no attention to her grandfather [Monsieur] and hardly looks at my son and myself; but as soon as she sees Maintenon, she smiles and runs to meet her . . . By this you can see how politic she is already." Saint-Simon also questioned the truth of her affection for the king and his secret wife: "Never had princesse, arriving so young, come so well-schooled and better capable of profiting by the instruction which she had received. The Duke of Savoy, who possessed a thorough knowledge of our Court, had depicted it to her, and had taught her the only way to make herself happy there . . . From the very moment of her arrival, she understood how to work to obtain this, nor did she cease so long as she lived." These suspicions, all too understandable in view of her father's turncoat tendencies, were held by only a small minority at Versailles, and to ascribe Adelaide's devotion to motives of self-interest and diplomacy is to do the young princesse a great disservice. From infancy, she exhibited a singularly sweet and lovable nature, a warm heart quickly responsive to kindness and affection. Unquestionably her parents had stressed to her the importance of gaining the favor of the royal couple. In a letter to Madame Royale in December 1696, Adelaide artlessly assured her grandmother: "I do what you ordered me about Mme de Maintenon." Such an admission might point to dissimulation were it not followed by the equally candid confession "I have much affection for her, and confidence in her advice." In the final analysis, it appears that the affection and loyalty the princesse displayed for her royal protectors was genuine. Mme de Maintenon's niece Mlle d'Aubigné, a shrewd observer and intimate companion to the princesse for years, later asserted, "It is impossible for me to doubt her affection for the King." She recalled that she once discovered Adelaide in tears; when she asked the reason for such grief, she was told that because of their advanced ages, Adelaide had suddenly realized that the king and Mme de Maintenon would probably die before her, "and the thought of their loss made her quite miserable." D'Aubigné admitted, "Hers was not a deep nature. She very speedily became attached to people, and the King, if it suited his mood, could be kind and gentle." For this charming little girl, the king's mood was always well suited.

December 6 was Marie Adelaide's eleventh birthday, and as a special treat, the king took her to Marly for the weekend. Govone was again witness to the tour of the grounds conducted by proud Grandpapa: "The King showed her everything, admiring her aloud, like a doting parent, encouraging her to hop, skip and jump and over and over again; telling her how charmed he was by her sweet nature, how she was exactly made for him." Later the king buttonholed the ambassador on the terrace, bragging of his little paragon: in a recent attack of toothache, she impressed one and all by calling all their fussing ridiculous and saying that she was far better qualified to manage her own health than the doctor was. The king reiterated that "the Princesse was absolutely his ideal," and as a sign of impatience to embrace her as a member of his family, he set the date of her marriage to Bourgogne for December 10 the following year, four days after her twelfth birthday.

Yet indulgent and catering as Louis XIV grew, he remained determined (with Mme de Maintenon's supervision) to keep his charge innocent and unsophisticated, at least until her marriage. Madame informed her German aunt that Adelaide "is kept greatly shut up; the King has forbidden us to ever mention the opera, the play, or gambling before her; I am quite sorry for the poor child." She need not have wasted her time on dubious sympathy; the "poor child" found her cozy evenings alone with the king and his wife, telling stories and singing old songs around the harpsichord, far more delightful than the wit of Molière or the lure of the lansquenet tables. Worldly pleasures would make themselves all too available once she had matured; till then, and for as long as possible, Grandpapa and his wife intended to keep the little pet all to themselves.

Family contentment blinded neither from the serious work before them. Even more than in maintaining Adelaide's naïveté, the king and Maintenon were jointly absorbed in the occupation of preparing a perfect queen.

The theory and implementation of royal education in France saw striking revision during the reign of Louis XIV, most of these changes being the inspired work of the king's secret wife.

Many of the Sun King's achievements appear even more remarkable when we learn that, for the boy Louis XIV, an education program was virtually nonexistent. The widowed queen-regent, busy first with her lover Mazarin and later with the suppression of aristocratic revolt, had neither the time nor inclination to develop her son's mental capacities. Anne of Austria taught her little boy his prayers and instilled in him a lifelong fear of the Devil and eternal damnation — then considered the business of education finished. The care and nurture of the boy king was left entirely to a gaggle of empty headed governesses, for whom education was little more than a word; years later, the king told Mme de Maintenon that these ladies' preoccupation with themselves and the latest gossip had resulted in such complete neglect that once he wandered away from their "watch," fell into a fountain at the Tuileries, and was only saved from drowning by a last-minute rescue from a passing court official.

The indifferent governesses were soon replaced with sycophantic governors. Their contribution to the royal intelligence rested chiefly with writing exercises — copying maxims like "Homage is due to kings; they act as they please" — and rote lessons from the *Educatio regia*, written especially for Louis XIV; it charged the boy to remind himself each morning he was about to enact God on earth, and to ask himself each night to what measure he had succeeded. The boy's keen mind quickly deduced that his exalted rank made any normal "master-pupil" relationship untenable: because of the subservient phrase forever on the lips of his governor-in-chief, Louis dubbed him "Maréchal Oui-sire," and he studied just as much as any other exuberant boy of ten would have, had he too been given tacit control of his own schooling. By the time the king reached his majority — at the age of thirteen — all pretense of educating him had been abandoned. His subsequent distaste for any reading (outside the realm of state affairs, which he studied voraciously) became so well known that it was a matter of intense court conjecture when once he read a fashionable romance.[2]

Despite this woeful void in his own training, as a young father Louis XIV conscientiously approached the education of his children. He vowed to make his son and heir "the most virtuous and accomplished prince in all Christendom," and personally devised a rigorous timetable for the dauphin, engaging the most learned and respected scholars in the land. Unfortunately, these pedants possessed neither the ability nor the inclination to communicate with the timid, slightly backward young prince; no less inspiring was the dauphin's brutal governor, the duc de Montausier, who once gave the terrified boy "five cuts with all his might on each of his hands" — for making the same mistake twice during the repetition of his lessons. Montausier liberally employed verbal abuse and physical violence in his attempts to instill learning, and the results were piteously predictable: one afternoon, the adolescent dauphin listened as a lady of the court related some misfortune that had befallen her. At last, he asked politely, "Do you have to write essays?" The startled woman replied that she did not; Monseigneur sighed deeply and said, "Ah! Then you don't know what real sorrow means." The heir to the throne escaped his schoolroom with a fear of books so great that it was matched only by his fear of the father who had permitted so torturous an education.

With Mme de Maintenon's engagement as the duc du Maine's governess in 1670, a truly innovative educator entered the royal household. Through her skill and handiwork, she transformed not only the royal schoolroom but ultimately the French educational system. Her way was not to cram facts and figures into an unreceptive mind, but to gently encourage inquisitiveness, to create first the desire for knowledge and then to satisfy it. She was fortunate that her pupil was bright and precocious — but in no way should this detract from her achievement, for her success with other, less gifted royal children was just as striking.

Perhaps the finest tribute to the royal educator came from the nonroyal pen of her niece, Mme de Caylus. Little Marguerite was rescued at an early age from the country, where she lived in impoverished obscurity with her parents, and raised at Versailles under her aunt's strict guidance. Years later, Caylus recalled:

> I was brought up with a care for which Mme de Maintenon cannot be too much praised. Nothing happened at Court without her causing me to make such reflections on it as I was capable of, approving me when I thought justly, and correcting me when I thought badly. My days were spent among masters, reading, and honest and well-regulated amusements. My memory was cultivated by obliging me to learn verses by heart, and as I was under the necessity of giving an account of my reading or anything I heard, I was forced to pay attention. In addition to this, I had to write a letter every day, either to a member of my family or some other person whom I might choose, and this I had to take to my aunt every evening, that she might either approve or correct it accordingly.

Marguerite de Caylus, quick-witted and highly intellectual, later shone as one of the brightest stars at the court of Versailles, and never failed to accord her aunt full credit for her success. Louis XIV was no less appreciative of his wife's tremendous accomplishments; he could offer no higher praise than to entrust to her capable hands the princesse of Savoy.

With Adelaide's arrival in November 1696, the royal educator felt once again transfused with a special purpose. The rearing of the king's bastards and the establishment of her school at Saint-Cyr paled now in comparison to this, her greatest challenge.

From the outset, she demonstrated the seriousness with which she undertook her obligation. While waiting at Fontainebleau for the king's return with the princesse, Mme de Maintenon took (for her) an unprecedented step: she summoned the Savoyard ambassador for a private audience in her chambers. The startled Govone appeared, and was questioned in great detail on every aspect of Adelaide's life in Savoy — her likes and dislikes, her health, her character, and, of course, her education. In common with her regal spouse, the royal educator placed great importance on detail and she assured Govone that nothing was too trivial for him to tell. After he described the quiet family life the princesse had enjoyed with her mother and sister at the Vigna, Maintenon was full of praise. Then she turned to her own concern for the little girl: she informed the ambassador that she intended to plant herself "between the Princesse and the world," until the child could learn for herself the ways of society. She announced her resolve to keep Adelaide from the fashionable (and immoral) court her grandfather, Monsieur, had assembled at Saint-Cloud; to gain her affection; to ensure that religion would play a major part in the role destiny had called her to — so that when the time approached, Adelaide would shine as a paragon before all Europe. Deeply impressed, Govone reported to Turin: "At which point, she launched forth into reflections of so high-flown a nature that neither my pen nor my memory is equal to their expression."

Before Maintenon ever set eyes upon her future charge, she laid ground rules for the little girl's training. To Dangeau, en route with the princesse, she wrote: "If her ladies continue to amuse her with a mixture of word games, activity games and a few serious lessons, they will not waste their time. Charades will accustom her to make conversation, and teach her to speak out; proverbs will sharpen her wits; blind man's buff will keep her healthy, and spillikins make her dexterous. Truly, it all sounds excellent to me, especially that she plays these games with intelligent people, who will instruct as they amuse her."

After meeting the princesse, Mme de Maintenon succumbed to her charm and goodness; she was also deeply shocked at Adelaide's ignorance. "She really knows nothing, not even how to write!" she complained — and Adelaide's first letter to her grandmother back in Savoy bears witness to her charge. Scrawled in something akin to hieroglyphics, full of punctuation and spelling errors, the brevity of the letter indicates how difficult and laborious correspondence was for the little princesse: "De Versaie, ce 13 Novembre 1696. Nous me pardonere Madame si je ne vous est pas écrit la peur de vous annuier me la fait fair je fini madame votre embrassan. Très humble très obeisantes petite fill, Marie Adelaide de Savoie." ("You will pardon me Madame if I have not written you, the fear of boring you [*ennuyer*] made me do it. I end madame embracing you. Very humble, very obedient granddaughter, Marie Adelaide of Savoy.") Grammar and spelling would improve slightly in later years, though the latter never kept pace with the improvement of Adelaide's vocabulary, and at the end of her life, she was still unable to spell "Versailles."

Worse yet, the princesse was totally indifferent to the idea of education. It was no display of obstinacy or rebellion — quite simply, she seemed incapable of absorbing even the most rudimentary of teachings. Such apathy toward mental improvement is hardly surprising, for nothing in the little girl's past had ever inspired her toward scholarship. In the arcadian years at the Vigna, the duchess of Savoy had attached far more importance to her daughter's spiritual and social education than she had to the mastery of languages or composition; now that Marie Adelaide was the darling of the French king and court, few would encourage her to waste precious hours of her day in a stuffy schoolroom — were she ever inclined to seek such encouragement. Clearly, this education was not going to be an easy one, but the royal educator was undaunted.

Maintenon's first action upon the court's return to Versailles was to engage for the princesse a writing master and a French instructor. Both were advised to keep their lessons short, for Maintenon had already observed that "our Princesse does not care for what is long." To teach Adelaide history (a subject of vital importance in any royal curriculum), Mme de Maintenon wisely enlisted Dangeau, the little girl's favorite household officer. Dangeau was supplied with *L'Histoire de l'Empire Romain,* by the Dominican monk Nicholas Coeffecteau, but the royal educator doubted that the princesse could ever make a serious dent in this dry and lengthy dissertation. "I think it will be enough to give her two lessons a day, one in the fables [of La Fontaine], another in Roman history. You, sir, know better than I that it is useless to think of making a learned woman out of her; we should not succeed." Understanding her pupil's inclinations and capacities, Mme de Maintenon accepted that her pill of learning must be sugar-coated: "We must limit ourselves [in the beginning] to instructing her in certain things that are necessary for her distraction." Consequently, a dancing master was provided, and a music professor to instruct the princesse on the spinet. Musical ability would never appear on a list of Adelaide's talents, but she quickly developed what would be a lifelong passion for dancing.

As she had told Govone, Mme de Maintenon was anxious to shelter Marie Adelaide from the loose morals of the court of Versailles. Beginning at the top, this meant a strict avoidance of the king's own daughters. Not that Mme de Maintenon was prudish with regard to the circumstances of their birth — far from it, for her deep affection for the duc du Maine proved she held no puritanical fear of illegitimacy. Quite plainly, she had good cause to worry: the princesse de Conti had recently been at the center of a public scandal involving poison, while her more flamboyant sister, Mme la duchesse, was brazenly cuckolding her husband with his own brother. In barring these ladies from Adelaide's presence, Maintenon unwittingly fanned their jealousies, paving the way for intense rivalry in years to come — but one can hardly fault the conscientious woman for her conviction that they were unsuitable company for her innocent young princesse.

Still, Maintenon quickly realized the potential disadvantage of surrounding Adelaide with nothing but mature, dignified companions, as she had originally intended. While she understood the necessity of these "chaperones," dull as they might seem to a high-spirited child, she saw, too, the great need for contemporary playmates. A second and younger group of ladies was appointed, "for the amusement of the Princesse." Saint-Simon's wife was one, though she was several years older than Adelaide; Mlles de Chevreuse and d'Ayen (daughters of the old nobility, whose parents happened to be close friends of Maintenon's) were the same age as the princesse, and Maintenon's niece, Mlle d'Aubigné (the future Mme de Caylus) was just one year older. These four young ladies had the welcome charge of responding to all invitations from the princesse — and they were called for almost daily, especially for excursions through the fairyland park of Versailles and outings to Marly. The fact that they were strictly forbidden, under any circumstances, to reproach or argue with Marie Adelaide made them delightful companions indeed for an exuberant and strong-willed little girl!

Adelaide made quick and lasting friendships with each of her new playmates; Marguerite d'Aubigné in particular became her favorite companion, which must surely have pleased the royal educator. The two girls were devoted to each other, though this did not prevent them from the occasional spat, sometimes violent. Once a boisterous disagreement had them rolling on the floor and hitting each other when they were interrupted by a message from Adelaide's confessor, Père Lecomte, who awaited her in the chapel to grant weekly absolution. With a gleefully malicious smile, Mlle d'Aubigné exclaimed: "Oh! I would not wish to be you for anything, having to confess with all that is on *your* conscience!"

Still Maintenon deemed haphazard morning lessons and a small company of contemporaries insufficient training for the future queen. After deliberation she announced her decision to the king: Adelaide was to be enrolled in Maintenon's school for girls at Saint-Cyr.

Just over a century before the cataclysmic events of 1789 and the Revolution, there occurred in France a double revolution in the world of female education: in 1686 (six months after the birth of Marie Adelaide), the abbé Fénelon published his *Traité de l'education des filles* and transformed educational theory; that same April, Mme de Maintenon opened the first girls' boarding school at Saint-Cyr, transforming educational practice.

Before the arrival of these two innovators, the prevailing ideas on female education (no less than education in general) had remained unchanged since the Renaissance. Children were considered an indispensable nuisance, a form of frozen capital requiring twelve to fourteen years of maturation before any dividends could be expected. The meager education provided was designed more to propel these miniature adults through adolescence as quickly as possible than to equip formative young minds with tools to combat the vicissitudes of life. Precocity was dearly prized for its promise of a shorter period of transition into the adult world; Louis XIV's decision that Bourgogne and Adelaide should be wed immediately after her twelfth birthday reflected as much his desire to declare the young girl a "woman" as to enfold her in his family.

Most well-born young brides of the seventeenth century came to their equally ill-equipped husbands with little more than a rudimentary knowledge of grammar and spelling (matched with suitable penmanship), an understanding of the rules of precedence, an ability to dance, to leave and enter rooms with dignity and grace, and to mindlessly repeat the parrot prattle of society. If a young bride was noble enough to merit presentation at court, she was expected to display some knowledge of history and philosophy (however superficial); still, it was far more important that she know how to carry herself appropriately. A sure grasp on the intricate rules of etiquette and ceremony was deemed ample compensation for deficiencies in science or literature. However beautiful or brilliant, Louis XIV's was not an intellectual court.

The most startling development in the Fénelon/Maintenon "revolution" was the transformed relation of teacher and pupil. Child welfare and training were to be undertaken *with*, not in spite of, the child. Under Fénelon's guidelines, the grim, inflexible governess who crammed and discouraged her small prisoners surrendered her rod to an instructress, "open, gay and familiar," whose primary task was to win the affection and trust of her pupils. Fénelon's rule for discipline was succinct: as few rules as possible should be set down, clearly explained to the child, and then adhered to scrupulously. Punishment should be only a last resort, and never used if either teacher or pupil had lost her temper; but, the abbé insisted, one should never merely threaten, but follow through with punishment. The child should be encouraged, freely and spontaneously, to seek instruction; casual conversation in itself could be highly instructive. Finally, Fénelon prescribed a balance of work and recreation throughout the formative years.

If much of Fénelon's thinking strikes us today as common sense, we must remember how startling and innovative he was for his time. Elsewhere, he succumbs to the misconceptions of his century: music was classified as a "corruptive influence" (apparently the abbé had in mind the sensuous melodies of Lully, the rage at Versailles), but if a girl was incurably musical, it was wiser to permit church music than to deny altogether any outlet. A girl *could* learn enough Latin to follow mass, but she ought to carefully conceal this knowledge. Italian and Spanish were strictly forbidden, for they provided access to dangerous literature — of which there was more than enough already available in

French! Naturally, Fénelon forbade the reading of romantic novels — not for reasons of morality, but with the surprisingly practical contention that as they bore no resemblance to real life, a girl nurtured on their fantasy was apt to be painfully disillusioned in adulthood.

As Fénelon's little girl became a young lady, added lessons polished off her character and prepared her for society. She learned to show no aversion to the company of dull people; since every person had at least one subject on which he or she was knowledgeable, it was a lady's duty to draw out that topic. She was never to gossip with her servants, but learned how to speak with them frequently and kindly about their own affairs; remembering that servility is "contrary to the natural equality of man," it was her moral obligation to make the yoke as easy and as pleasant as possible. In the final stage of her education, this incomparable young woman familiarized herself with the forms for leasing property, rent receipts, and the laws governing wills and inheritances.

Fénelon's paragon of womanhood might easily have remained a topic of intellectual speculation were it not for the fact that the secret wife of the king of France was herself a born educator and ardent reformist. Mme de Maintenon had first come to the attention of Louis XIV in the field of education. In the years that followed, she gained a husband but lost a job, and felt keenly the deprivation. She had long cherished the idea of helping young ladies, of saving them from the dangers she had faced in her own youth. When her fortunes rose and she found herself the most powerful woman in France, her private dream became a public debt to God for his bounteous blessings.

Luckily for Maintenon, seventeenth-century France had given birth to the idea of reciprocal obligation between people and state. To the king, the people owed their absolute loyalty; to his minister of finance, a portion of their purses; and to his minister of war, their arms and often their lives. Slowly it was realized that, in return for this allegiance, an obligation existed to the wounded, the dying, and most important, the survivors. The construction of the Hôtel des Invalides, the first military hospital and retirement home in Europe, was Louis XIV's first step in compensation; a program of government subsidization of military schools (for over four thousand noble orphans) was the second. Mme de Maintenon saw the opportunity of welding the king's growing sense of duty to his people with her own cherished dream: during a visit to the cadets, she remarked to her husband how sad it was that his care for the orphans of war was sexually discriminating. Years later, she described their subsequent discussion: she told the king that "the greater part of the noble families of the kingdom were reduced to a pitiable state, owing to the costs their heads had been forced to incur in his service; that their children required support to prevent them from falling into utter degradation; that it would be a work worthy of his piety and greatness to make a settled establishment as a refuge for poor young girls of rank throughout the kingdom, where they could be brought up piously to the duties of their condition." Louis XIV hesitated, pointedly remarking, "Never did a Queen of France do anything like this!" When the King's confessor, Père de La Chaise, enthusiastically endorsed Maintenon's idea, however, he gave his consent.

A property was purchased at Saint-Cyr, on the outskirts of Versailles, for three million francs in 1684: appropriately, Saint-Cyr has been called the king's wedding present to Mme de Maintenon. Mansard was commissioned to design the school complex, a two-year project estimated at a million francs. During the planning Mme de Maintenon wrote sourly: "I know the King's architects; they will give me a palace of exquisite external symmetry, lacking in every single convenience of a school." (As so often before, she was entirely correct.)

Quite the novelty from its inception, Saint-Cyr was eyed suspiciously by both Church and State. Was it a charity or a convent? And if a convent, what order?

Louis XIV disliked convents, and as he helped Mme de Maintenon prepare a school constitution, he made plain his intention that Saint-Cyr should not become one. France, he felt, needed more good mothers, not more good nuns. By his own suggestion, the mistresses of Saint-Cyr were not required to take the absolute vows of any established order — instead they took an oath to devote their lives to the education of their young women. Any religious vocation that surfaced among the students would be neither encouraged nor deterred.

Qualifications for admission were strictly prescribed in the constitution. The age for entry was between seven and twelve; leaving was set at twenty. Each applicant was required to prove four noble ancestors on her paternal side, and demonstrate evidence of impoverishment — also, she was to be free of epilepsy and the vapors.

The institute of Saint Louis at Saint-Cyr opened its doors on August 2, 1686. The headmistress, Mme de Brinon, with her staff of twelve, welcomed the 250 girls personally selected by Louis XIV. Under the constitution, Mme de Maintenon was designated spiritual foundress;

in truth, she was the unacknowledged headmistress, an arrangement unavoidable in the circumstances but sure to create friction with Mme de Brinon.

The day before opening, Maintenon had addressed a lengthy epistle to the Dames of Saint-Cyr. "God having willed to use me to assist in this establishment . . . I think I ought to communicate to the persons destined to bring [the girls] up what my experience has taught me about the means of giving a good education." Her experience and her knowledge were formidable. She saw too clearly the sexual prejudice of her age: "A young girl who knows a thousand things by heart will shine in company and gratify her relatives more than one whose judgment has been formed, who knows how to be silent, who is modest and reserved, and is in no haste to show her cleverness." But, however thankless the task, "we should think less of adorning their minds than of forming their reason . . . When the object is merely to adorn their memories, it suffices to instruct them for a few hours a day; but when we seek to form their reason, waken their hearts, elevate their minds, destroy their evil inclinations, in a word, make them know and love virtue, we must always be at work, for at all moments opportunities present themselves. We are just as important to pupils in their amusements as in their lessons." The girls were to be instructed in all the delicacies of honor, in discretion, generosity, humanity, and integrity; "virtue should be described to them as being both beautiful and agreeable, as it is."

Her methods echoed Fénelon: the use of fables and little stories to underscore a lesson was "very proper and useful," since instruction could and should be amusing while enlightening. "You must make yourselves esteemed by the children . . . Never scold them from illhumor . . . Treat fine natures with affection, be stern with bad ones, but harsh with none."

Mme de Maintenon viewed the establishment of Saint-Cyr as the culmination of her life's work and was obsessed with its success. After its opening, she wrote honestly: "Nothing is dearer to me than my children of Saint-Cyr; I love their very dust . . . I have no reluctance to be their servant if my service will teach them to do without that of others. It is to this I tend; this is my passion, this is my heart." She was as good as her word: despite the strenuous obligations of her position at court (unofficial as it was), she made time to visit Saint-Cyr every morning, and twice a week she devoted the entire day to her little girls. She would arrive at six in the morning, assisting in the dressing of the youngest students; the next twelve hours were crammed with class instruction to be assumed, interviews with the household staff, and visits to the sickroom.

Her patent devotion inspired the affection of students and teachers alike. One novice rhapsodized: "Often she gave two or three consecutive months to one class, observing the order of the day, talking to the class in general and to each member in private; reproving one, encouraging another, giving to all the means of correcting themselves. She had much grace in speaking, as in all else she did. Her talks were lively, simple, natural, intelligent . . . I should never finish if I tried to relate all the good she did to the classes in those happy days." Certainly, the universal adulation of Saint-Cyr more than atoned for its demands; as Imbert de Saint-Armand remarked tersely: "Mme de Maintenon is almost Queen of France. She is absolutely Queen of Saint-Cyr." Her words were taken as oracles, her letters were read like biblical epistles before the entire student body, and their recipients prized them higher than any royal commission. Scant wonder that Maintenon came to regard Saint-Cyr as "my great comforter," the place to relax and let fall her mask. At Versailles it was "painful to last too long, to live in a society of persons who do not know us," but at Saint-Cyr it was "very pleasant to retreat to a garden bench and find ourselves surrounded by fresh young souls, docile in letting themselves be trained, and eager for all that we will say to them."

Mme de Maintenon might not have responded so completely to Adelaide's emotional and educative needs had the golden glow of "those happy days" lingered beyond the school's first years. The royal educator prayed that it might: "Vive Saint-Cyr! May this establishment last as long as France itself, and France as long as the world!" But, as Mme de La Fayette noted cynically: "Sometimes the best-invented things degenerate considerably; and that establishment which . . . is the abode of virtue and piety, may someday, without any profound prophesying, be that of debauchery and impiety . . . To believe that three hundred girls can live there until they are twenty, with a Court full of eager young men at their very doors (especially when the authority of the King will no longer restrain them), to believe that young men and young women can be so near to each other without jumping the walls is scarcely reasonable."

But this external problem, the proximity of Versailles, was a source of far less grief to Maintenon than the continued rise of problems internally. By the early months of 1688, she had concluded that the cause of her troubles was Headmistress Brinon. Two years of the king's steady friendship, coupled with large doses of court flattery and her own innate arrogance, had turned Brinon's head completely; more than once, she had the audacity to question the judgment of Saint-Cyr's spiritual foundress. To take on a king's mistress was foolhardy; to challenge a king's wife — and one as patiently calculating as Maintenon — was sheer self-destruction. For almost a year, the royal educator waited for her adversary to miscalculate: when Mme de Brinon visited the spa at Bourbon in late October with an ostentatious display of pomp guaranteed to infuriate the Sun King, she had her weapon. On December 10, 1688, Mme de Brinon was dismissed from Saint-Cyr and ordered to retire to a nearby convent.

The removal of a proud headmistress was simple enough, but the removal of that pride she had spread throughout the school was another matter, one that came to a head only a month after Brinon's dismissal.

Under the former headmistress, the girls of Saint-Cyr had presented theatricals in the king's honor. Most of the songs and plays performed were of Brinon's composition and, since her talents fell short of her ambitions, were deadly dull. To spare her husband further boredom, Mme de Maintenon tactfully suggested that the girls might try their hands at real tragedy: "My object was to avoid the miserable compositions of the nuns." Corneille's *Cinna* and Racine's *Andromache* were thus performed before the king and a select audience on an improvised stage. If these adolescent muses were unable to convey the heroic pathos of Corneille, they were genuinely inspired by Racine's melodious verse. Louis XIV was enchanted and called at once for a new production. When Mme de Maintenon objected to so much "worldly amusement," the king charged Racine to compose a play *without* love scenes that might tempt the youthful cast. Racine answered his sovereign's command and, within a year, had composed *Esther,* based on the biblical story and (as requested) devoid of any love interest. He coached the cast himself, though many tears were shed before he declared his satisfaction. The king provided an orchestra, costumes, and stage decorations.

Esther opened in January 1689, before a truly royal audience: the king, his heir, and the entire royal family attended, plus the recently deposed James II of England and his wife, Queen Mary. For all but one, the evening was an unqualified success. *Esther* became the rage of the season, the troupe at Saint-Cyr the toast of the court, and six additional performances were scheduled.

But for Mme de Maintenon, the effects of *Esther* spelled disaster. Her sharp eyes caught the nonverbal communication across the footlights between her girls and the young officers crowding the pit. In the marbled halls of Versailles, she overheard all too clearly young guardsmen on winter leave discussing and comparing the charms of the performers, in terms she deemed highly unsuitable. Nor did the trouble stop there; the girls at Saint-Cyr, giddy with accomplishment, spoke of nothing but the court and its gallant young men. With each day, discipline grew lax and soon not only the structure but the very survival of the school tottered precariously. Criticism for Mme de Maintenon's experiment mounted; when the Dutch gutter press reported to Europe that she sought to retain her hold on Louis XIV by turning procuress and that Saint-Cyr was really nothing but a training school for courtesans, the royal educator resolved to act, and quickly.

Generously overlooking the failings of Mme de Brinon, she assumed all responsibility herself: "It is I who have spread the sin of pride through our house, and I shall be very fortunate if God does not punish me for it." Of course, she found responsibility more palatable when taken with a good dose of self-pity: "I wanted that the girls should have intelligence, that their hearts should be uplifted, and their reason formed, and I have succeeded in my purpose: they have intelligence, and they use it against us; their hearts are uplifted, and they are prouder and more haughty than is becoming in the greatest princesse . . . A simple Christian education would have made them good girls, out of whom we could make good wives; we have made *beaux esprits,* whom we ourselves cannot endure."

The royal educator applied a swift remedy: "As many little things have fomented pride, so many little things will subdue it. Our girls have been too much considered, too petted, too often deferred to. They must now be ignored in their classes; they must be made to keep the rules of the day; and little else must be talked of . . . Do not talk to them of pride, we must destroy all that without fighting it, by stopping the use of it; their confessors will talk to them of humility better than we." Consciously or not, she shed several of Fénelon's more progressive tenets; disheartened that her special children proved themselves too human, and disillusioned by the worldliness of the dames of Saint-Cyr, Mme de Maintenon conceded defeat and spent two years (1692–94) transforming Saint-Cyr from a secular house of education into a standard convent school.

Henceforth, the Dames of the Institute of Saint Louis would be regular nuns under solemn vows, charged with the solemn injunction to "keep [the girls] entirely confined to your own house, and never let them be seen by outside persons under any pretext whatever . . . Do not permit the presence of any man." All communication with Versailles was absolutely forbidden.

But if the royal educator's dream establishment, "the same prudence, purity and ignorance of evil as convents, but with none of their pettiness," had crumbled, it must not be assumed that she abandoned all interest in Saint-Cyr once it had been reshaped along more traditional lines. Her admonishment of one teacher in the new regime echoed the lecture preached in the early days of experimentation: "You must punish as seldom as you possibly can, and for this reason you must not see all faults," though recent experience compelled her to add: "It is now a question of bringing the young ladies to a footing of perfect obedience." She continued to devote a large part of her time to the school; indeed, with control now in the hands of the virgin brides of Christ, she felt her guidance and knowledge more vital than ever before. "Most nuns dare not utter the word 'marriage,' " she told one surprised group of students. "Saint Paul had no such false delicacy, for he speaks of it very openly . . . When young ladies have entered marriage, they find it is not a thing to laugh about; for it is the state in which we have most tribulations, even in the best marriage." Her low opinion of men was often expressed to her impressionable students: "Flee from men, as from your mortal enemies. Never be alone with them. Take no pleasure in hearing that you are pretty, amiable, or have a fine voice. The world is a malignant deceiver, which seldom means what it says; and the majority of men who say such things to girls do it in the hope of finding some means of ruining them." (Maintenon's opinion of the weaker sex was no more charitable: "Women only half know things, but the little they do know makes them usually conceited, disdainful, loquacious, and scornful of solid information.")

By 1697, the year of Adelaide's enrollment, the evolution of Saint-Cyr had been completed. With reforms established and illusions discarded, the royal experiment entered its golden period.

There were four class "dames" or teachers: each was assigned three assistants, and of these four, two were on duty at all times — for in the chapel, classroom, playground, or dormitory, no girl was ever again left unsupervised. Below the teachers came a great number of officers, some with purely religious posts for the convent, and others — the portress, the librarian, and the infirmière — attendant to the school.

The student body was divided into four classes, each of approximately sixty girls and each named for the color of ribbons worn on their uniforms. The youngest class was the Reds, girls seven to ten. This group studied elementary sacred history, catechism, reading, writing, arithmetic, and music — the last a concession to Louis XIV.

At the age of eleven, the student advanced into the Green class, where geography and mythology were added to their studies. Mythology might seem an odd subject in a convent school, but the innovative royal educator deemed a smattering of classical knowledge indispensable for a young lady of quality and breeding.

Mme de Maintenon always maintained that the Yellows, the next group, were the most difficult of all the classes. Its members were aged fourteen to seventeen, in the awkward transition of adolescence, and Maintenon noticed that in this class most of the girls found themselves in constant conflict with the mistress general. More often than not, the royal educator found herself called in to take appropriate measures — as always, she did not mince words: "I have heard of your disobedience . . . How can you suppose that we should allow such rebellion? What exception could there be to our rules? Do you think yourself necessary because you have a fine voice? No, certainly not; and you will leave the establishment if I hear anything more about you. Submit, if you wish to remain."

In the Yellow class, the girls' previous curriculum was augmented with a study of the French language and advanced religious instruction. On the lighter side, lessons in deportment and dancing were provided.

Maintenon considered that a girl's character was formed during the last phase of her development; consequently, the pupil reaching the Blue class (at the age of seventeen) found her study schedule greatly reduced. Moral instruction filled most of her days, sharing time with advanced needlework. To alleviate boredom, Mme de Maintenon allowed afternoons of poetry reading and amateur theatrics (but once burned, she stood firm: "Do not permit the presence of any man").

The Blacks, a subdivision composed of specially selected members of the blue class, acted as school prefects, under the direct supervision of the mistress general. In this capacity they washed and dressed the younger girls, made the beds, and worked in the offices, kitchens, and infirmary. The Blacks were the elite of the school, and to the best of their group went the greatest prize of Saint-Cyr: the post of secretary to Mme de Maintenon. The lucky winner of this office found herself transported for one term to the magical world of Versailles, in close proximity to the Sun King himself; whether it speaks louder for Saint-Cyr training or for Mme de Maintenon's hawklike vigilance, each of these secretaries emerged from this august experience unscathed.

When the time approached for a young woman to leave Saint-Cyr, she was faced with several possibilities, all of them promising: if she felt a religious vocation, she was admitted (at the king's expense) to one of the many royal abbeys. If she expressed an interest in teaching, she was awarded the first available vacancy at Saint-Cyr, remaining at the school as a Black until that time. If she chose marriage, her wedding expenses were paid for personally by Mme de Maintenon and (best of all) the king signed the marriage contract, raising the orphaned bride to the same rank as the daughters of France's most illustrious families. Whatever option the graduate chose, she was provided at once with a complete outfit of clothing and a purse of three thousand francs.

Despite a shaky beginning, Mme de Maintenon succeeded in her goal: at Saint-Cyr, she provided a system of education, revolutionary for its time, designed to inspire rather than discourage — and the exemplary women she produced fully justified her experimentation. The "cult of the child" that Fénelon envisioned on paper, she brought to fruition. Her work survived her, survived the destruction of Saint-Cyr (during the Revolution), and survives both in theory and practice today.

On November 25, 1696, Mme de Maintenon took Adelaide to pay her first visit to Saint-Cyr. The princesse was received with full honors: the assembly of three hundred girls, long ceremonial cloaks covering their uniforms, lined both sides of the entrance court as the royal carriage pulled up. The Superior, Mme de Payra, made a welcoming speech, then introduced the student body to their distinguished guest. Adelaide was given a complete tour of the school complex and the visit concluded in the refectory with the presentation of a charade (which she found especially delightful) and a choral concert.[3]

In his journal, Sourches noted Marie Adelaide's reaction to the school: "She returned in raptures, having been enchanted by seeing the little girls in the chapel and at their play. She immediately ran to find the King, who was working in Mme de Maintenon's room, and he was particularly pleased with her eager responses to his questions, and the respect with which she tempered her childish delight." She assured Grandpapa of her hope to visit Saint-Cyr again and, when pressed further, expressed a wish to study at the school. The king was relieved: he had told his wife the princesse would not be forced to attend the school against her inclinations, regardless of the royal educator's plans.

Although the princesse was entitled by age to study with the Greens (eleven to fourteen), Mme de Maintenon wisely placed her with the younger Red class, where the glaring defects in her education would be less noticeable. She began by attending the school once a week, usually arriving in the morning and spending the entire day sharing lessons, meals, and recreations; her attendance was soon increased to three times a week. Her course of study was outlined by the royal educator herself: religion first, then Roman history, classical mythology, harpsichord, dancing, and writing. She was issued a school uniform, treated without ceremony (though always with great respect), and addressed by the pseudonym "Mlle de Lastic."

It was an innovation (even if a reasonable one) for a princesse to attend Saint-Cyr, and Mme de Maintenon quite naturally feared that intimacy with their future queen might revive in her girls the fatal pride that had earlier threatened the establishment. Before Adelaide's enrollment, Maintenon warned the girls: "I should feel quite in despair if the daily appearance of the Princesse, with ladies whose station in life requires them to give, as it were, an air of worldliness, should revive any such tendency in you." But her fears proved groundless: Adelaide's simplicity and ingenuousness triggered the protective instincts of all, and never more than at school. The darling of Versailles became the darling of Saint-Cyr as well — often the girls supplied her with questions in advance so that she might memorize the answers before she was called upon. In her *Memoirs,* one Dame of Saint-Cyr wrote of Adelaide's sojourn there: "She was good, affable, gracious to everybody, interesting herself in the different duties of the Dames, and in all the occupations and studies of the demoiselles, subjecting herself readily to all the regulations of the establishment, even to silence."

Adelaide was blissfully happy at Saint-Cyr. She was thrilled to make so many friends of well-born girls her own age, and blossomed under the well-planned regimen devised by Mme de Maintenon. While hardly a brilliant pupil, she did enjoy catechism — because she already knew most of the answers and was able to show off a little. One afternoon, with the teacher's consent, she took over the class and delivered a lecture on the Last Judgment. One girl asked her where the Valley of Josaphat was located; Adelaide had no idea, so she pertly replied that the question was absurd since nobody cared to hear anything about the silly old valley.

She distinguished herself in the outdoor exercises with her gaiety, her agility, and her daring. Mme de Maintenon placed great emphasis on recreation for her girls, both to show them their defects and to win their confidence without appearing to ask for it. "Recreation," she wrote, "is what leads to union and removes partialities; that is what binds the mistress to her pupils . . . It is the time when edifying things can be said without repelling, because we can mingle them with gaiety." In the quiet gardens and groves of Saint-Cyr (with such appropriate names as Meditation Walk and Contemplation Cell), the princesse played games of hide-and-seek and ran races with the other students; often Maintenon herself was infected with the high-spirited fun, joining in for a game of Hunt the Pig.

Maintenon rigorously oversaw Adelaide's lessons as well as her recreations; even her school meals (taken with the Reds in the convent refectory) conformed strictly to the royal educator's philosophy. "Eat several kinds of soup; it is less harmful than eating a lot of meat without bread . . . Most women who have charge of children make the mistake of crying out against sweets. They are not unhealthy after a meal, provided one eats them in moderation." So she had written when the duc du Maine first came under her charge; twenty-five years later, her attitudes remained unchanged: every afternoon, Adelaide was served crayfish soup in a silver bowl, filet of sole or fried eggs, wholemeal bread with fresh butter, red currant jelly, cakes, a carafe of diluted wine, and a jug of sparkling water.

Once lessons were finished, Adelaide was free to do as she pleased, and the inquisitive little girl ran about the convent helping the novices with the housework or baking pies with the cook in the kitchen. She grew very close to the convent housekeeper and loved to work for her — picking over the fruits of the convent orchard, running messages, doing all sorts of odd jobs. It delighted her all the more when the housekeeper forgot her rank and began to order her about, scolding when she grew too mischievous and rewarding her assistance with a snack of dried apples and brown bread. Another favorite was Sister Marie, the old peasant woman who ran the school dispensary. Sister Marie had earned a permanent place in the princesse's heart when she miraculously cured an attack of indigestion by covering the little girl's stomach with the lid of a well-greased earthenware pot.

Life at Saint-Cyr for Adelaide had its serious side as well. She was required to take an active part in the religious life of the community and attend chapter meetings (though her age barred her from voting). When a newly professed nun was admitted into the order, it was Adelaide who handed her the veil; at funerals for the sisters, the princesse held one corner of the pall. Still she was an eleven-year-old with irrepressibly high spirits. Mme de Maintenon had given her but one rule — she could do as she pleased, provided she was punctual for all her lessons and did not disturb the timetable of the school — and this was broken almost as often as obeyed. One favorite caprice was to dress up in the nuns' habit and see how long she could escape detection. One day, with her best friend Marguerite d'Aubigné, she donned the long black robes and ornate gold crosses to spend the afternoon doing heavy manual labor in the novice cloister, the impersonation discovered only because the little girls were unable to stifle their giggles and observe the rule of silence.

In her *Memoirs,* as Mme de Caylus, Marguerite recorded her favorite story of the Saint-Cyr days: the princesse arrived with Mme de Maintenon for confession and dutifully took her place in line with the other students. Because of some ceremony she had attended earlier that day, she was still wearing court dress. From behind the grille, the priest heard the rustle of her silk gown, assumed the unseen penitent to be some jaded court sinner, and unleashed an appropriate admonition. Marie Adelaide listened in silence, then ran laughing to Mme de Maintenon, exclaiming, "*Ma tante,* I am enchanted with that confessor — he told me that I was worse than Magdalene!"

Six months after Adelaide began at Saint-Cyr, Mme de Maintenon sent a "progress report" to the duchess of Savoy: "I am astonished at the Princesse, and have never seen anything more extraordinary than her intelligence. It is not displayed in clever sayings, nor lively and surprising repartee, nor by such feats of memory as one sees in other children. She speaks little; but says nothing out of place. She listens without seeming to listen. She fears to displease, but does not seek to please too evidently." She was proud to report the princesse tractable: "When her women thought they perceived some signs of impatience at her toilette, it sufficed that she should be spoken to, and the fault was not repeated," and remarkably discreet: "She keeps a secret without betraying it by the slightest gesture." The princesse was maturing rapidly, and Maintenon felt she was "growing prettier every day. Her face is getting shorter . . . Her complexion is rosy and white. She has grown . . . and her figure is perfect. She is clean and neat, unlike most children. She dances very well, and for grace she has no equal . . . This is how she is at present," Maintenon concluded. "But who knows what the future may hold? She lives surrounded by a small group of respectable women, who speak to her with one voice. No one spoils her; on the contrary, everything is directed towards her training. It will not always be so, for traps are set for princesses as well as for ordinary mortals, and the more praise she receives today, the more envy will be stored up against her. I trust God will protect her." Fortunately, the royal educator did more than just rely on divine intervention: in sending Adelaide to Saint-Cyr, she provided the little girl with invaluable training (albeit more social than intellectual), a coterie of delightful companions, and best of all, scores of pleasant childhood memories to store up against the days to come.

Of course, Saint-Cyr occupied only a portion of Adelaide's days; this particular royal education entailed instruction in the role promised by destiny. While Mme de Maintenon concerned herself with providing the little princesse with grammar and the fundamentals of history, Louis XIV oversaw her training as future consort to a king of France. She was already the unofficial queen of Versailles, but not even the Sun King could ignore the fact that she was still a child. To demand that a little girl fill the exhaustive requirements of her exalted role was unthinkable, yet (at Versailles) equally unthinkable was a blatant disregard of the tyrannical etiquette that prescribed these very requirements.

After intensive discussion of the matter with his wife, Louis XIV adopted a middle course. Court ritual still would be observed but its scale would be greatly modified: Adelaide would perform her public toilette twice a week (on Tuesdays and Fridays, the days she did not attend Saint-Cyr), at which time the court was free to pay respect to its future mistress. She would also grant an occasional audience to the ambassadors and plenipotentiaries of the courts of Europe; for the time being, her official duties would end there.

And so Marie Adelaide entered the official life of Versailles, beginning with the ritual of the public toilette (the ceremony that Marie Antoinette would describe as "odious"). For Adelaide, these mornings began pleasantly enough: she was awakened at quarter to eight and would flit about her apartments in comfortable *déshabillé,* practicing on the harpsichord with her music master or dancing with Dangeau while her favorite fables from La Fontaine were read aloud.

Shortly after eleven the ceremony commenced, and the princesse was dressed for daily mass. Before a privileged audience of high-born ladies, she was handed the various articles of her court costume: first her shift of fine white linen, the color chosen to complement her delicate skin. Then her heavily boned corset, its four-inch opening securely laced together by the senior member of the household. Several petticoats followed, and lastly, the stiff body of the dress itself, sometimes rich Italian silk, sometimes intricately embroidered velvet. The ritual never varied, and often the dressing was slow and laborious, for the ladies who held the cherished right of handling the royal clothes were obliged on occasion to surrender their prerogative — even in midaction — to others of superior rank. For example, one morning the duchesse du Lude was detained elsewhere, and so a lesser attendant laced the royal corset closed. The woman had just finished the top knot when Lude arrived, completely upsetting the balance of rank. The laces were at once reopened, and poor Adelaide forced to endure the uncomfortable process again. Another child might have rebelled — the much older Marie Antoinette certainly did — but Adelaide viewed the public toilette as simply part of her job, the calling for which she had been specially chosen.

By noon, or once the duchesse du Lude was satisfied with Adelaide's appearance, a preordained signal was given. The doors to the royal bedchamber were flung wide, an usher cried "Service!" and the remaining members of the household and the attendant court filled the room. The princesse greeted her staff and kissed them individually while the fawning courtiers — still little more than strangers to the child — formed two lines on either side of the door. From there, they watched her don her jewels and have her hair brushed into the style the king and Mme de Maintenon believed the most becoming: pulled up from the back and dressed in elaborate curls atop her dainty head, adorned with ribbons and sparkling with diamonds. Throughout this performance, an orchestra provided music from the adjoining salon.

At the close of the public toilette, the crowd adjourned to the Hall of Mirrors, to watch the king escort the princesse to mass. While Louis XIV ate in public following mass, the ambiguity of Adelaide's position afforded her the privacy to dine alone in her rooms with the duchesse du Lude. Lunch was a hurried affair, for at two o'clock, the king was at her door for their daily outing. Returning at four, Adelaide was faced again with the duality of her status: often she was called upon to be "La Princesse," for it was at this time that she received the dignitaries of foreign courts. One such interview was given to the envoy of the sultan of Morocco, and the ambassador's harangue, if long-winded, was certainly typical:

> Madame, overwhelmed as I presently am by the generosity of the Greatest Monarch in the world, and drowned in the ocean of his munificence, my cup of joy should be overflowing. But the honor which His Majesty now does me of permitting me to pay homage to a Princesse whose merit so much greater than her age has been judged worthy of uniting her to the greatest prince on earth makes my happiness complete. May it please you, most high and excellent Princesse, that I join my voice to that of Europe, and that I go to acquaint the people of Africa with the striking merits of your illustrious person, of you who have come, the Star of the Morning — and the shining dawn of peace.

To her credit the Star of the Morning controlled her giggles till she was alone with her ladies.

When not required to play "La Princesse," Adelaide could be "the little girl" — a far easier role — left to enjoy a few hours with Grandpapa and his wife. The king would join her in Maintenon's rooms for a round of blind man's buff or a game of spillikins, sometimes to watch jugglers or a puppet show. Then he would work on state affairs while his ladies chatted quietly on the other side of the room. They talked of clothes — for Maintenon thought this a proper interest for a girl — or of Savoy or Maintenon's youth.

The royal educator always injected her recollections with a useful moral:

> We should never neglect to learn anything, no matter what . . . I never supposed that learning to comb hair would be useful to me. My mother, going to America, took several women with her, but they all married there, and she was left with no one but little slaves, all quite incapable of doing her hair. So she taught me to do it, and as she had a fine head of very long dark hair, I was obliged to stand on a chair; but I combed it very well. From there I came to Court, and this little talent won me the favor of the Dauphine; she was quite astonished at the way I handled a comb, and said she was never so well-combed as by me . . . You ought not think such things beneath you because you are a young lady.

Summer arrived and royal thoughts turned to the approaching wedding. Mme de Maintenon and the duchesse du Lude took the little princesse to Paris, to begin trousseau preparations. They entered the Porte Saint-Honoré and crossed the Pont Neuf to visit the convent of Port-Royale, where the nuns served a splendid collation for them. The jaunt combined a little shopping and a little sightseeing: Adelaide was taken to the Luxembourg Gardens, the quays along the Seine, and the recently completed Hôtel des Invalides. By her own admission, a second visit to town one week later was even more fun: it was devoted entirely to shopping, and the excited little bride-to-be picked out bolts of silk and velvet and presents of jewelry to distribute to her ladies.

Adelaide's first year in France drew to a close — a year of extraordinary success. She had captured the imagination of the common folk, who crowded round her carriage when she appeared in town, crying their undying love and devotion. She had impressed the court with her curious blend of sophistication and naïveté, and promised greatly for the future. The king and his secret wife were patently bewitched by their little treasure, thrilled by the progress she had made under their expert tutelage.

And though she saw him but once a fortnight, Adelaide had made yet another significant conquest, one that would hold her in good stead till the end of her life — her bridegroom, the duc de Bourgogne.

8

"The Holy Terror"

THE BIRTH OF LOUIS BOURBON, duc de Bourgogne, on August 6, 1682, was of more personal significance to Louis XIV than the insurance of dynastic continuation: the child was the first grandson born to a reigning king of France in 135 years. Determined not only to announce the birth, but to be the first to know the gender, the king had arranged a signal with the *accoucheur,* Jean Clément, to relay the baby's sex.[1] As the dauphine delivered, Louis would ask his prearranged question; for a girl, Clément would respond, "I do not know"; for a boy, "I do not know yet." When "yet" fell from the doctor's lips, Louis XIV turned to the hushed crowd of witnesses and cried, "We have ourselves a duc de Bourgogne!"

The new parents had special reason for relief at this successful delivery, for the dauphine had miscarried twice before. Marie Anne Christine Victoire of Bavaria had arrived at Versailles early in 1680 to wed the Sun King's heir. Her fiancé, a good-natured if somewhat indolent young man, had a perverse passion for ugly women, which proved fortuitous — for the bride turned out to be, in one courtier's words, "not just ugly, but grotesque." Sanguin, Louis XIV's chief maître d'hôtel, who was sent to Bavaria during the marriage negotiations, was compelled on his return to warn the king, "Sire, do not betray your emotions when you see her for the first time." Her skin was sallow, and her forehead spotted with brown blotches; her eyes were described as "neither large nor small, neither sparkling nor languorous." Her nose was fat and bulbous at the tip. Her hands, not her lips, were red, and her teeth — which gave the appearance of uniformity — were all rotten. Louis XIV, stunned despite his warning, gravely pondered just what sort of children so ill-favored a woman might produce, and prepared to abandon the entire project. But the dauphin declared himself perfectly pleased, and the wedding took place as planned.

The young woman's prior difficulties carrying a child to full term should have been seen as a warning during this third attempt, for her labor (in the middle of a grueling heat wave) was appallingly severe and lasted over thirty hours. More than once it was feared she would die, and the child with her. The king remained in her room throughout the night, feeding her chicken broth with his own hands, while the queen sent for the holy relics of Saint Margaret — by tradition reserved only for the queens of France. The expectant father crouched miserably in a corner chair, unable to watch his wife's suffering.

When the child was at last delivered at ten-thirty P.M., the crowds in and outside the palace went wild. Monseigneur recovered his spirits and kissed every lady within his reach. Even the king surrendered himself to the general exultation: not only did he grant the excited courtiers the unprecedented liberty of embracing his person, but as he withdrew for his own apartments the imperious Sun King allowed himself to be carried on their shoulders.

The abbé de Choisy described the tumultuous scene in the courtyard: "The common people seemed to have taken leave of their senses. Bonfires were lit everywhere in celebration of the event. Some chairmen were so bold as to break up their mistress's gilded sedan chair and burn it in the courtyard . . . adding to the blazing heap some pieces of paneling and flooring that were stacked there waiting to be installed in the gallery. Bontemps [the king's *valet de chambre*] came running to the King in a rage to tell him of this vandalism; but the King simply laughed and said, 'Let them be, we can soon order new floorboards.' "

Inside, however, the dauphine was still in agony. We are told that Clément "kept his head"; his subsequent actions provide an illuminating glimpse at the medical practice of his age. He called for a sheep and had it flayed alive in the room, wrapping the new mother in its skin — her ladies were understandably horrified, though Marie Christine was beyond caring at this point. Of course, the dauphine felt better at once. She was then given a cordial of orange juice and crushed almond, which had a soothing effect, and she expressed a desire to sleep. Clément was aghast: after so long and precarious a delivery, sleep must certainly be dangerous, so the exhausted creature was forcibly kept awake for several hours. Finally, her room was sealed off and she was ordered to remain in bed — throughout the heat wave — for the next nine days.

Such treatment was unlikely to inspire any young woman to a large family, yet the luckless dauphine did not shirk from her duty to the state. Philippe, duc d'Anjou, arrived on December 19, 1683, and Charles, duc de Berri, on August 31, 1685. But pregnancy — and medical practice — took their toll, and Marie Christine never fully recovered after her third child. "Ah, my little Berri!" she would sigh as she cradled her youngest. "I love you dearly, but you have killed me." Uncomfortable with the French court and melancholic, she shut herself up in her rooms and pleaded ill health. The doctors were convinced that her sickness was imaginary, a ruse to avoid her official duties, and so she received no sympathy from the king or the court. She complained that she would have to die to prove she was not shamming, and with her death in 1690 she was at last vindicated: the autopsy revealed that her lungs were ulcerated, her intestines greatly abscessed, and her stomach filled with gangrene.

The dauphin grieved, but not for long. Turning for solace to his half sister, the princesse de Conti, he soon fell in love with one of her waiting women. Mlle Emilie Joly de Choin had all the necessary requirements: the kindly Marguerite de Caylus called her "remarkably ugly" and left it at that, but Madame described her vividly: "She resembled a pug-dog; she was low-built, with short legs, a round face, a snub nose, and a large mouth filled with rotten teeth, the stink from which could be smelled at the other end of the room. Her breasts were horribly overdeveloped, but Monseigneur was enchanted by this phenomenon and used to play on them like drums." The happy couple were later married, but in such total secrecy that the absolute legality of their union has never been established. Not that there was any confusion in the mind of the heir: a letter from Monseigneur to Mme de Maintenon, dated July 19, 1694, clarified his feelings: "I was amazed that you spoke to me of my wife — amazed and taken aback. I am delighted that I am in favor; my only thought is how to please the King."

Not strictly true: for the rest of his life, Monseigneur appears to have been motivated by three concerns — food, hunting, and Emilie Joly, in that order. Certainly he gave little thought to his sons: after the dauphine's death, his complete indifference to them had led the king to take charge of the three boys. The dauphin, described by his aunt, Madame, as "far from being a fool, although he always behaved as if he were one," was content to live peacefully on his country estate at Meudon with his hounds, his horses, and his ugly second wife.

Little Bourgogne was seven when his mother died. He was required to attend her funeral and sprinkle holy water on the coffin, but mercifully spared the ordeal of the twelve-hour procession to Saint-Denis where the dauphine was interred. The prince's grief surprised the court; royal children had little communication with their illustrious parents, and the dauphine's sequestered last years had afforded even less contact than usual. Yet the boy's attachment was genuine: several months after Marie Christine's death, the prince's tutor read aloud to him one of the funeral orations that had been composed in her honor, when Bourgogne suddenly dropped from his chair and vanished under the table. The tutor assumed that he had fallen asleep, but when he reached under to retrieve his pupil, he found the proud boy trying to conceal his tears. This devotion for his mother would soon be transferred to his teacher, Fénelon, and in due time to his wife, Adelaide.

This capacity for affection was not the characteristic that first attracted the attention of the court of Versailles. Rather, it was the little prince's extraordinary temper. Saint-Simon painted this portrait of young Bourgogne: "This prince was born terrible, and in his early youth made people tremble. He would fall into ungovernable fits of rage, even against inanimate objects, would break the clock which summoned him to some unwelcome duty, or storm at the rain when it prevented him from going out. He was impetuous with frenzy; incapable of supporting the least resistance; obstinate to excess . . . He had an ardent inclination for everything which is forbidden the mind and body, and a biting, cruel wit, which spared no one and never missed its mark." Further, Saint-Simon felt the child already displayed alarming signs of insufferable arrogance and pride: "As from the height of the sky, he looked down upon men, whoever they were, as flies and atoms, and even his brothers scarcely seemed to him connecting links between himself and the human race, although all three had been brought up together in perfect equality." This acute sense of self-importance doubtless was the inheritance of his dynasty — one needs only a brief acquaintance with the megalomania of the Sun King to realize that his imperiousness, conspicuously missing in the timid Monseigneur, had reappeared with a vengeance in the next generation.

No measures were taken to curb Bourgogne's overweening arrogance. His governess, the maréchale de La Mothe, was a kindly old woman of sixty, given to petting and spoiling and perfectly unsuitable for a headstrong, willful little boy. The maréchale had been governess to Monseigneur twenty years earlier, and found the difference between father and son baffling; she dubbed Bourgogne "the holy terror," a nickname soon adopted by the entire nursery staff.

However irascible, the little prince was a delicate child, given to head colds and frequent fevers. Such maladies were common for children of the seventeenth century, living as they did in haphazardly cleaned houses with poor ventilation, but Dangeau recorded that the prince suffered over fifty such attacks in a single year and, to Saint-Simon, Bourgogne looked "puny, as though he would blow his very soul into his pocket handkerchief." Medical practitioners were no more kindly disposed to children than they were to parents; with bleedings, emetics, and purgatives, an ailing youngster died as often from the cure as the disease. In a letter from Saint-Cloud dated September 2, 1687, Madame informed her aunt: "Just now the Dauphin's two eldest, the Duc de Bourgogne and the Duc d'Anjou, are very ill with fever; this morning the poor little things were bled — I cannot think it is a good thing for such little children; the eldest is only five years old."

Another bout with illness is memorable as the only recorded instance of the dauphine's interference in the rearing of her sons. An argument raged over the use of the new medicine, quinine, found to be effective on fevers in adults but as yet untried with children. Both Louis XIV and Bourgogne's governess favored its application, but the dauphine categorically opposed experimentation on her child, and finally, the king conceded to his daughter-in-law. In his journal, Sourches commented: "In such cases, it is the event which decides. The Prince has regained his health without quinine, therefore the Dauphine was right. Had a mishap occurred, all the blame would have been hers."

Saint-Simon noted that little Bourgogne was "passionately fond of all kinds of pleasure." In particular, the boy loved to play soldiers with his brothers and carefully selected playmates from the ranks of the nobility. Because of his exalted rank, he was always the commander and, better still, always the victor. (His younger brothers, not being in direct succession, fared less successfully, and while the sweet-tempered Anjou supported their rough playing with amiability, the more competitive Berri was often downright vindictive to his oldest brother.) Bourgogne displayed such enthusiasm and zeal for these games that the king decided to let him "play soldier" in earnest; when he appointed his six-year-old grandson to the musketeers, the boy was delirious with joy.

The musketeers went everywhere with the king: they guarded his tent during military campaigns, and his private apartments at Versailles and Fontainebleau. They were divided into two companies, the Grays and the Blacks, named for the color of their horses — the Grays were the senior troop and, rank for rank, held superiority. The king had unwittingly assigned Bourgogne to the Blacks, and with the boy's burgeoning pride, some sort of scene was inevitable. Sure enough: one day, at Fontainebleau, Bourgogne was selected to march with his compatriot Gray to receive the order of the day from the king. On discovering that *he*, the first Grandson of France, was to stand on the left (inferior) side and remain silent, the prince flew into a rage so violent that it nearly came to blows. The king himself intervened, and asked his grandson if he wished to change regiments. The boy paused, thought long, and finally answered that, as heir presumptive, he rightfully belonged to both troops and should be given a piebald pony.

If Louis XIV assumed that the rigors of an actual regiment would dampen some of Bourgogne's youthful ardor, he was greatly mistaken. The little prince threw himself into the task of mastering the drills with such passion (not to mention success) that one rainy morning in June 1689, as the king entered the Royal Courtyard at Versailles to review his musketeers, he was greeted with the sight of his grandson and heir, present and correct — and one month shy of his seventh birthday. Sourches was suitably impressed. Though the rain refused to lighten, "the Duc de Bourgogne continued undismayed to exercise with his troop, showing a precision, steadiness and skill, far beyond the usual for boys of his age . . . It was really astounding to see a child, not yet seven, behaving as coolly and confidently as young men of twenty-five . . . The spectators rejoiced to see such strong evidence that when he grows up, the young prince will have developed the proper inclination for war." The next day, however, he noted that little Bourgogne had caught a cold.

Not only the spectators were impressed — Louis XIV was deeply moved. He had long since abandoned all hope of making anything out of his fat, lethargic son, and his hopes and ambitions were transferred to his grandson. The boy already displayed more aptitude than his father had when twice his age. It was clearly time to take him from the nursery and from the gaggle of indulgent old women who quaked before his fits of temper — time to place the boy under the supervision of men who would train him for the glorious role he would someday play. Louis XIV belatedly accepted his responsibility for the disastrous education that had been foisted on the dauphin. He was determined not to make the same mistake twice.

The afternoon of September 3, 1689, the duc de Bourgogne was summoned to the royal apartments and summarily informed by his grandfather that the time had come to bid goodbye to the maréchale de La Mothe. The young prince was understandably upset at being removed from the safe familiarity of his governess, the nursery, and his brothers; the knowledge that they would eventually join him in his new, all-male establishment was no more comforting than might be expected for a high-strung boy of seven.

He could find little solace in the first choices for his new household; to Saint-Simon they were an "uninspiring group." The marquis de Denonville, appointed Gentleman of the Handle (his unenviable duty was to hold the wide sleeves of the boy's coat and prevent him from tripping) was a "decent enough fellow, and courageous, but of an innocence not far removed from idiocy, and notoriously incapable." Two others, Dupuy and L'Eschelles, both renowned at Versailles for their godliness, were "honorable, well-read, and highly esteemed, but the most boring men in all France, relieved only by a few clerical jokes." Left to this high-minded, humorless group, what would keep the prince from becoming just another studious churchmouse?

The answer to this lay in the appointment of the two highest officers in the young prince's household. As governor, the king appointed Paul, duc de Beauvilliers; for chief tutor, he selected the same Abbé Fénelon whose theories on education had so inspired Mme de Maintenon. With their profound influence, these two men would transform young Bourgogne from "the holy terror" into the hope of France.

The duc de Beauvilliers was one of the most respected nobles at Versailles. So high was the king's esteem that he had already been granted two other important offices at court: in addition to his new post as governor, Beauvilliers was First Gentleman of the Bedchamber and sinecure president of the Council of Finance. (Mme de Sévigné quipped: "The King made three men out of one duke, and Saint Louis himself could not have chosen better.") Forty years of age when he took control of Bourgogne, Beauvilliers was a tall, thin man, with a long and ruddy face, an aquiline nose, and a sunken mouth with a pleasant smile; his eyes were "intelligent and piercing . . . usually serious and concentrated in expression."

As a young man he had been passionate and hotheaded, flourishing in Louis XIV's Court of Love and marrying, in 1671, the second daughter of finance minister Colbert. That same year saw the transformation of the dashing young hedonist: in Saint-Simon's words, "God touched him . . . and I believe I can say that since that day, he never lost His presence." He renounced the fleshly pleasures of his youth, and though he made no attempt to conceal his piety and devotion to God, neither did he censure or attempt to proselytize: "He was sincerely humble, although grateful to what he owed his rank, and so detached from worldly things that I do not think the saintliest monks could have done better." Even-tempered, polite and honest, his simplicity and sagacity, equally blended, were legendary. He was an extremely close friend of Maintenon's: at the height of their friendship, she "dined with [the Beauvillierses] once or twice every week, with a handbell on the table, so that they might have no servants about them, and might converse without restraint" — a signal token of her favor. Consequently, his appointment led Maintenon's critics to declare she intended to surround the prince with her own crowd, and introduce him into her camp osmotically. The criticism is unfair to both the royal educator and the new governor: from the moment of his appointment to the end of Bourgogne's life, Beauvilliers made it plain that his sole objective was the spiritual and intellectual education of his future king as the most perfect Christian prince in Europe.

François de Salignac, the abbé Fénelon, was born in August 1651 to an ancient, noble, but impoverished family of Périgord. He had been ordained in 1675 and given the parochial duties of the parish of Saint-Sulpice in Paris, but his career truly began in 1678 when he was appointed director of the Nouvelles Catholiques, an academy founded by the archbishop of Paris in 1634 to "provide girls converted from Protestantism with a safe retreat from the persecutions of their relatives and the artifices of heretics." His tremendous success within this institution, plus his own ambition, won him entry into the great homes of France and a number of influential friends — among them the duc de Beauvilliers. In fact, it was the duchesse de Beauvilliers who had enjoined Fénelon to pen his revolutionary *Traité de l'education des filles,* originally private guidelines for the instruction of the Beauvillierses' daughters, only published afterward at the direction of their grateful mother. Four years later, at Beauvilliers's urging, Louis XIV appointed Fénelon to the Bourgogne household.

Saint-Simon drew a vivid portrait of the ambitious churchman:

He was a tall, thin man, with a large nose, eyes from which fire and intellect streamed like a torrent, and a physiognomy the like of which I have never seen in any other man, and which, once seen, could never be forgotten. It combined all things, and its contradictions produced no want of harmony. It united gravity, gaiety and courtesy; it equally expressed the man of learning, the bishop, and the *grand seigneur*. But its prevailing characteristic, as in everything about him, was elegance, refinement, grace, modesty, and above all nobility. It was difficult to take one's eyes off him. His manner was in complete accord with his appearance; his perfect ease was infectious to others, and his conversation was distinguished by that grace and good taste which are only acquired by constant intercourse with the best society and the great world.

High-minded yet never unrealistic, urbane as well as pious, Fénelon accepted his new position with the conscientious zeal of a knight on quest. He regarded it his mission not only to educate the prince but, through and with him, to reform the state — a mission for which the abbé never doubted his qualifications.

Fénelon saw the potential young man hidden deep in the indulged hellion, and observed that, like most passionate children, Bourgogne was capable of sincere affection. He recognized that the prince's quickness and penetration were remarkably keen, and that he was frank and truthful to a fault. Unlike his predecessors, for whom the pupil was secondary to the position, Fénelon strove diligently to gain the trust, affection, and confidence of the prince.

He met with overwhelming success. His methods for bringing home to his charge the gravity (because of his destiny) of Bourgogne's faults and for instilling in him the desire for amelioration were many and varied. Once, having patiently and silently endured a particularly violent temper tantrum, Fénelon arranged for the members of the suite to remark on how ill the prince looked, until the alarmed young boy summoned the royal physician. Fagon (in on the ruse) methodically examined him, then asked in perfect innocence if he had lately found something irritating. The prince replied affirmatively. Fagon nodded gravely: of course, that was the answer, and after listing the maladies resulting from excessive anger, he added archly that he had known of several cases where such offensive conduct had produced immediate death. With alacrity, Bourgogne apologized to Fénelon.

Another time, the inquisitive boy came upon a carpenter making repairs in one of the palace galleries, and found his tools of the trade particularly intriguing. He pestered the workman until the carpenter, pretending outrage, cried out, "Off with you, Prince! When I am in a temper I break every bone in the bodies of those who come near me!" The frightened boy ran to his tutor, crying that the carpenter must surely be a wicked man. Fénelon gave a knowing smile and replied, "Then what would you call a prince who beat his *valet de chambre* when the poor fellow is doing his best to serve him?"

Pride remained an even greater obstacle than temper, and Fénelon ruthlessly applied his cure. One significant episode appears in the memoirs of the marquis de Louville: giving in to a fit of pique, the prince cried out arrogantly, "No sir, no! I will not be ordered about. I know your place, and who I am!" Without a word, Fénelon left the room. He returned the next day, looking very sad, and quietly spoke: "Do you remember saying yesterday that you knew my place, and yours? It is my duty to inform you that you know neither. You imagine yourself above me; perhaps the servants have told you so; I have no hesitation in saying that I stand far above you in learning and experience. You think me happy to be your tutor. You deceive yourself. I accepted the post in obedience to the king; not at all for the doubtful pleasure of instructing you. So that you may be undeceived, I am taking you to His Majesty to beg him to find you another tutor, who I pray may be more successful." The devoted pupil, in floods of tears, implored and received forgiveness. Small wonder that Fénelon's favorite fable, often recounted to Bourgogne, was that of Bacchus and the faun: "How dare you make fun of the son of Jupiter?" — "How dare the son of Jupiter have quite so many faults!"

One similar tantrum — quickly repented of — resulted in a royal pledge: "I promise M. l'Abbé de Fénelon, on the word of a prince, to do at once what he tells me, and to obey him the moment he gives me an order; and if I fail in this, I will submit to any kind of punishment and disgrace. Written at Versailles, the 27th of November 1689. L O U I S." With the very next outburst, this note was promptly produced — punishment, of course, was waived and the lesson well learned.

Gradually, Fénelon established complete ascendancy over the heart and mind of the prince, and the transformation he brought about in the tempestuous boy was deemed by his contemporaries no less than a miracle. Mme de Maintenon wrote: "Since the First Communion of the Duc de Bourgogne, we have observed the gradual disappearance of all the faults which, in his childhood, inspired us with great anxiety for the future. His progress in virtue is remarked from year to year."

Saint-Simon was even more fulsome: "God, who is the master of hearts, worked a miracle in this prince. From the abyss he emerged affable, gentle, kindly, tolerant, modest, humble . . . compatible with the duties of his position."

(Despite the many wondrous changes he wrought, not even Fénelon could break the prince of his two favorite pastimes: watching flies drown in oil and blowing up frogs with gunpowder. These edifying hobbies were discontinued only after Adelaide made her revulsion perfectly clear. But lest Bourgogne be unfairly thought too puerile, it must be noted that *he* did not share enthusiasm for *her* favorite — being dragged by the heels across the manicured lawns of Marly and Versailles.)

Like Mme de Maintenon at Saint-Cyr, Fénelon was now afforded the opportunity of putting into practice his theories of education, the change of gender requiring only modest areas of revision. As noted, his ideas contained a heavy, and surprisingly modern, emphasis on exercise and hygiene, both largely ignored by the age. The harsh discipline so prevalent in the seventeenth century was discarded, except as a final resort. His maxim "A mind governed by fear will always be the weaker for it" was followed scrupulously. Learning could not be crammed into a resisting mind, so Fénelon appealed to Bourgogne's imagination and natural curiosity. "Give [him] well-bound books, even books with gilt edges. Children love to hear absurd stories . . . Be sure to use this to good advantage, and when you see that they are in the mood to listen, tell them some short, pretty tale. Choose animal fables that are innocent and well contrived. Narrate them quite simply and explain the moral." With a pupil like Bourgogne, this practice was turned to useful advantage by the study of fables (later historical essays) where pride and obstinacy brought about self-destruction.

Fénelon was especially fortunate that his pupil possessed an extraordinary intelligence and matching thirst for knowledge. Though taught no living language other than French, Bourgogne was steeped in Latin, and by the age of eleven had read Virgil, Homer, Horace, Livy, and portions of Tacitus. His knowledge of his own country was prodigious, not only in history but geography as well — one instructor declared that the prince knew the terrain of France as well as he did the park of Versailles. Yet all this was accomplished with only four hours of the day spent in the schoolroom, in strict accordance with the Fénelon principle "The fewer formal lessons there are, the better." "An infinite amount of instruction," Fénelon maintained, "more useful even than lessons, can be imparted in the course of pleasant conversations." Mme de Maintenon heartily endorsed this idea first at Saint-Cyr and later with Marie Adelaide, although her efforts, primarily with the latter, would be crowned with far less success than Fénelon's.

Bourgogne thrived under the spartan simplicity of Fénelon's regime. He rose daily at quarter to eight, and dressed at once without ceremony, though his rank demanded his presence at the *levers* performed by his father and grandfather. Having satisfied etiquette, the boy was free until his first lesson at ten. Luncheon was at one, and brief: boiled beef or stewed chicken, bread and two glasses of beer, cider, or light burgundy, after which his lessons took a lighter turn — music and dancing, sometimes drawing. With his care for exercise and physical well-being, Fénelon sent off his pupil each afternoon at two for a round of tennis (his favorite) or some other game with the gentlemen of the household.

In the summer months, Bourgogne returned to study with Fénelon from three to five, then went riding or walking until seven; in winter, this schedule was reversed. After forty-five minutes allotted for his "private amusement" — he could read any material he chose — the prince dined with his younger brothers on roast mutton or veal, usually with a little chicken, followed by cakes and fruit. Games were permitted between supper and bedtime: an engraving of the period shows the three brothers practicing the royal game of fortresses. A model fortress was erected on a small billiard table, and the players had to push their balls through the gates of the fort with special cuesticks — the princes' first lesson in the kingly science of warfare. Bedtime, set at nine o'clock, was generally flexible: a productive day might see it extended fifteen or twenty minutes, just as one filled with arguments or tantrums might find curfew advanced to after supper — after, for Fénelon did not believe in sending a child to bed hungry.

While the abbé nurtured the prince's mental health, the duc de Beauvilliers developed his physical stamina. Bourgogne had inherited his father's love for outdoor sport and the traditional Bourbon passion for hunting. This was a blessing in his governor's eyes: Beauvilliers firmly believed that "a delicate prince [was] good for nothing," and worked the boy like an athlete in training. The prince walked or rode daily, regardless of the weather, and the intensity with which he attacked a round of tennis was praised and loudly encouraged — as Beauvilliers felt it beneficial for young men to run and sweat. Coughs and colds were ignored; the delicacy of his early years was shed as

Bourgogne approached adolescence — a fact attributed both to his tutor's theories and his governor's ban on bleedings and purgatives.

Beauvilliers initially recommended that the prince follow the chase on foot, but his love of hunting quickly brought an end to such strenuous exercise. Since his first stag hunt at the age of thirteen, his grandfather (himself one of France's finest shots) had taken a keen personal interest in his apprenticeship to the gun and the hounds. The king reserved a small warren for the exclusive use of the royal grandsons at Noisy, where they hunted rabbit, and he often visited the School of Pages to observe the boys' special classes in swordsmanship and the use of pistols. Under the king's watchful eye, Bourgogne developed as a fine horseman, adept at both blade and gun.

Of course, life had its little rewards, too. The king indulged his grandsons with troupes of jugglers and acrobats, while Fénelon devised holiday excursions to Paris, for dinners at the Tuileries or afternoon visits to Notre Dame and the Hôtel des Invalides. The court pampered the royal children as well: in 1694, Cardinal von Fürstenberg gave a fête for the three young princes, complete with shooting galleries and carousels.

But unquestionably, the greatest treat of them all came but once a year: on the journey back to Versailles after the court's annual fall visit to Fontainebleau, the princes (accompanied only by their valet, Morau) were permitted to stop for the night in the village of Plessis, at the house of the king's old barber, Prudhomme. For a few precious hours, they were free of governors and tutors, free of etiquette and the ever present court, free to run and jump and play — to be the little boys they were. What Adelaide took for granted in the fields, the gardens, and the gently sloping vineyards of the Vigna, was but a rare and fleeting respite for her future husband and his brothers.

The duc de Bourgogne entered his teens a vastly altered character from the *enfant terrible* of five short years before, exciting the hopes of a court long since disillusioned by his father. Though somewhat on the short side, the young prince was handsome enough, with a long dark face; Saint-Simon declared that "the top half was perfect, the most beautiful eyes in the world, and an expression that was lively and always piercing." His chin was perhaps a bit too pointed, but his lips and mouth were attractive "when he kept them closed . . . Although his teeth were not ugly, his upper jaw was so prominent that it covered the lower one, which was unfortunate when he spoke or laughed." His thick chestnut hair fell in rich curls around his shoulders; his general

manner was always affable, while refined and dignified, and his countenance affirmed that "he possessed enough intelligence for two." His
legs, "well-turned and graceful, with small and shapely feet," unfortunately did not show themselves to advantage in the saddle; his riding
master, Denonville, cried in despair that astride a horse, the prince
resembled nothing so much as a pair of tongs.

The difficulties of his birth had left him with a crooked spine; though
barely discernible through his childhood, this deformity worsened
with age, raising one shoulder higher than the other. The royal surgeon
devised an iron collar and cross which the prince wore for years, even
during public ceremonies.

Apart from causing him considerable discomfort, this "harness"
had no effect, and as the years passed his handicap grew more pronounced. Madame, who never much liked the boy, cruelly called him
"a hunchback," yet Saint-Simon noted: "It is surprising that the Prince
never saw (or never wanted to see) himself as crippled" — a self-
delusion that forced the court to take added precaution against loose
talk and indiscreet name-calling. Lest this rather glaring physical im-
pairment seem incompatible with the judgment of Bourgogne as
"handsome," it must be remembered that the seventeenth-century
practice of inbreeding, and the general disregard for physical well-
being, had produced courts largely composed of malformed dwarfs
and amorphous freaks. Wigs and powders, laces and brocades attempted to disguise artificially the neglects of nature, but they could
not entirely hide the debilitation that pervaded Versailles. The
maréchale de Luxembourg had humps both in front and back; the duc
du Maine had a clubfoot. When the duc de Vendôme submitted to the
mercury cure for syphilis — probably the single greatest killer at the
French court — he returned without his nose; the prince de Vaudé-
mont's bones were decalcifying so quickly that the young man could
barely walk. Women fared no better — to be considered beautiful it
was enough not to be misshapen. In this world of infirmity, congenital
and acquired, the twisted spine of the young Bourgogne was accepted
as a course of nature.

The prince's moral education was founded on *Les Aventures de
Télémaque,* a trenchant political treatise composed especially for him
by the abbé Fénelon, "to do no more than instruct M. le Duc de
Bourgogne while amusing him with tales of adventure." A baroque
Pilgrim's Progress, based on Greek mythology, it chronicled the jour-
neys of Telemachus, the son of Ulysses who, guided and advised by

Minerva, searched the world for his father. It also contained several allusions to the present reign, and a good deal on the art of government and the uses and abuses of power — observations scarcely calculated to win the approbation of the Sun King. Louis XIV could hardly be expected to have endorsed the ideas of Mentor, who persuades the kings of the world to peace: "War is sometimes necessary, but it is the shame of the race . . . Do not tell me, O kings, that I should desire war to acquire glory. Whoever prefers his own glory to sentiments of humanity is a monster of pride and not a man; he will gain only false glory, for true glory is found only in moderation and goodness . . . Men should not think well of him, since he has thought so little of them, and has shed their blood prodigally for a brutal vanity."

Even more offensive to royal sensibilities is an imaginary conversation between Louis XII and François I, in the "Dialogues with the Dead." Louis, having questioned the uses of special taxes, comments to his successor: "I will wager that your mistresses had a bigger share of them than the officers of your army, and that is why the people are ruined, the war still rages, justice is corrupted, the Court given over to the follies of sex-mad women, and the whole country plunged into misery." The book, published two years after Fénelon's disgrace and banishment, would surely have hastened the tutor's downfall had the king been aware of it: as it was eventually, the printer of *Télémaque* was arrested, and all copies were immediately confiscated.

But political philosophy was subordinate to Fénelon's larger purpose — he intended with his allegory to instruct the prince on the course and nature of true love, and to warn him against the perilous mortal sin of adultery. Three women appear in *Télémaque,* representing the three forms of love: sensual Calypso is carnal love, sinful love to be avoided with horror; Eucharis typifies the gentle courtly love that one embraced with noble purity; and last there is Antiope, the love that is eternal, the pure virgin to be sought and won in marriage, a reward to be earned and prized forever. Composed as it was even while negotiations for Adelaide's hand were nearing conclusion, it seems plain that *Télémaque* was preparing its reader to fall in love with his chosen bride — nor is there any indication that the lesson was not avidly ingested.

The accident of his birth made the duc de Bourgogne the most highly prized matrimonial catch of his generation. Even Madame (swallowing her dislike) cast an eye on the boy, her grandnephew, and deemed him the perfect husband for her daughter; to what higher glory could she aspire than mother-in-law to the king of France? As early as April 1692, she confided in her aunt Sophia: "It is to be hoped that after all our waiting we shall finally be able to catch the Duc de Bourgogne; he would not be a bad morsel." But the waiting came to naught, and the disappointed Madame settled instead on being mother-in-law to the prince of Lorraine.

The exiled English royal family experienced similar dreams and similar disappointment. Madame reported to Sophia, July 27, 1696: "They were saying the other day at Saint-Germain before the little English Princess that the Duc de Bourgogne is to wed the Princesse of Savoy. The good child began crying bitterly, exclaiming that she had always believed that the Duc de Bourgogne would wed none but herself, and that if he was really going to wed a Princesse of Savoy she would never marry, but retire into a convent. Since she has been told the news she has remained mournful and cannot be consoled." (The princess never did enter the religious life, but remained unmarried to the end of her days.)

The marriage of an heir presumptive was a matter of major state policy; when policy decreed the import of an alliance with Savoy, the matter was inexorably resolved. The fourteen-year-old prince was no less curious than the rest of the court on the subject of his future wife: when her portrait, dispatched from Turin by Tessé, was unveiled at Versailles, the prince was observed to spend long hours at a time gazing on the painted canvas. And falling under Adelaide's spell as well, to hear the courtier Barbezieux: Bourgogne was joined in the gallery one afternoon by his brothers Anjou and Berri. Young Berri asked his oldest brother if he looked forward to being married and whether his wife would make him happy, and received strong affirmatives to both questions. Then he asked Bourgogne what he would do should his wife forbid him to hunt, and the reply was no less emphatic: "Then I should not hunt." "This brought a furious protest from [Berri] that if he himself ever married, his wife might do as she pleased at home; but if she got in the way of his pleasures, he would soon show her who was master . . . No one knows what the Duc de Bourgogne replied." Bourgogne was a true grandson of Louis XIV, who grew blindly furious with anything that disrupted *his* hunting — yet his capitulation to love was well under way and, had Adelaide but spoken a single word, the prince would surely have quit the chase for the rest of his days.

It did not occur to anyone that the prince might wish to journey south to welcome his prospective bride. While the king, Monsieur, and the dauphin left Fontainebleau to meet the princesse at Montargis, Bourgogne stayed behind in the schoolroom. But the boy's curiosity was naturally intense, and on the day scheduled for the royal party's return — November 5, 1696 — Beauvilliers consented that he might drive south as far as Nemours to greet his future wife. He left Fontainebleau at noon, his governor at his side; the ride to Nemours was short, and the royal cortège had already arrived when Bourgogne and Beauvilliers entered the village. His impatience at bursting point, Bourgogne did not wait for his coach to cross the bustling town square, but jumped from the cabin while still some distance off and ran across the plaza to his grandfather's carriage. At last confronted with his bride-to-be, the poor boy flushed with embarrassment.

While Adelaide's arrival revitalized the Sun King's slumbering pleasure palace, her first year in France produced no change in the life of the duc de Bourgogne. While the delightful little fiancée scampered through the gardens and hearts of Saint-Cyr, her studious bridegroom poured over gilt-edged tomes of Greek philosophy, just as before; his hunting and riding, his ferocious tennis matches, went uninterrupted, for the future consort played only with the king.

On alternate Saturdays, the prince was admitted to Adelaide's apartments for thirty minutes of carefully chaperoned conversation ("to inspire him with a desire to return to her," the Savoyard ambassador explained to her father), and apart from their attendance at daily mass, these fortnightly visits were the young couple's only encounters. As the clock chimed the hour, the princesse would flit off to Maintenon's apartment, to delight her new grandfather and doting aunt; the prince returned to the suite he shared with his brothers and the sensible supper that Fénelon had ordered.

The king's attitude toward his grandson during this last year before his marriage was clearly ambivalent. His pride in the boy's attainments — which caused him to boast at Bourgogne's thirteenth birthday that France no longer need fear the rule of a minor — battled with his urge to suppress the growing adolescent and keep his new plaything, the princesse of Savoy, all for himself. It was the less possessive Maintenon who forced her husband to see that the boy was proving a fine young man, and that to ignore him did irreparable damage — to the succession no less than the successor. With great pomp and pageantry, the king created Bourgogne (together with the duc d'Anjou) knight of the

Order of the Holy Ghost. Following the solemn inaugural ceremony, it was favorably remarked that the two princes had conducted themselves with grace and dignity, and appeared "not to be unduly conscious of the heavy brocaded mantles which weighed on their youthful shoulders." But these mandatory introductions into royal service were still woefully sporadic, and Madame was highly critical of the king's indifference to his grandsons' social education: "They are very badly brought up. They eat alone, go out alone together, and never appear in public. When there is an *Appartement,* they arrive just as the band is striking up and leave as soon as it stops." The boys would never learn to comport themselves with the blend of dignity and affability required by their station, Madame argued. Indeed, their painful lack of polite intercourse was already leaving its mark: "The eldest has a sharp way of speaking; the second hardly utters, and when he does say something, he stammers." The little duc de Berri was Madame's favorite and could do no wrong: "The youngest is always cheerful and seems pleased when anyone speaks to him. He is quite merry and at ease, and does not stand stiff as a ramrod when addressed, as do his elder brothers." But the king, absorbed entirely in his love for the little princesse, felt no compulsion to alter the comfortable pattern of their days.

When change did at last occur, its effects were anything but comfortable for the duc de Bourgogne. His secure and idyllic world was shattered about him, and he was forced to enter the adult world without the support and guidance of his adored teacher.

Ostensibly, Fénelon's fall from grace and favor was due to his championship of Mme Guyon during the Quietist controversy; in truth, it was due to jealousy. Louis XIV certainly had no cause for envy, but in his advancing years, he suddenly found himself jealous of his wife's friendship with his grandson's tutor — an innocent relationship, to be sure, but one that took some of the attention the megalomanical king deemed undividedly his. Archbishop Bossuet had far more valid motives: thirty years before, the king had entrusted to him the education of the dauphin, and if the resulting product was less than successful, it did not in any way diminish the king's respect or friendship for the archbishop. Since Fénelon's appointment as tutor to Bourgogne, Bossuet had watched his success with suspicion and mounting alarm. On the eve of the Quietist controversy, he — like most of the court — realized that "at any moment the post [Fénelon] held might place him foremost among rulers" — for if Louis XIV died, the eyes of the nation would focus not on Bossuet's pupil, who would never be more than a crowned nonentity, but on Fénelon's. After more than a quarter century of preeminence, this was more than the proud archbishop could endure. Bossuet further detected the royal prejudice against Fénelon, and was prepared to use it to his own advantage. Only some catalyst was required.

The Sun King's revocation of the Edict of Nantes in 1685 put an end to religious tolerance in France. However, religious controversy was far from ended; while revocation appeared to check the rise of Protestantism within the realm, it brought into sharper focus the growing dissension in the French Catholic church. The importance of religious belief in this period cannot be overstressed. More than one historian has observed that religion was, to the seventeenth-century mind, what politics has become for its twentieth-century counterpart. No other topic was argued so fiercely; careers could be made or broken on the basis of one's adherence to dogma — as Fénelon's so aptly demonstrated.

The early years of the Sun King's reign saw the rise of a theological system labeled Jansenism (after its founder, a Dutch monk). The Jansenists advocated predestination and denied the Roman Catholic concept of man's free will — such freedom, they argued, was lost forever with the sin of Adam, and redemption lay, not in the good works or the exemplary lives condoned by the Church, but through the grace of God *alone*. Although this earned the sect the lasting (and dangerous) enmity of the Jesuits, Jansenism achieved striking popularity in France — until it was condemned as heresy in 1653 by Pope Innocent X. Louis XIV's aversion to religious deviation in general, and Jansenism in particular, was legendary: during the War of the Spanish Succession, the king refused to assign a certain officer to Bourgogne's staff because the man was suspected of Jansenist proclivities; when the prince assured his grandfather that this was not true, that the officer was, in fact, an atheist, Louis XIV at once approved the appointment.

Despite the papal ban and the royal displeasure, Jansenism continued covertly throughout the century; during its last decade an offshoot appeared called Quietism. Its theories were propounded by a fascinating woman, Mme Guyon. Born of wealthy parents and married at an early age to an elderly barrister who left her a widow at twenty-two, Mme Guyon was intelligent but eccentric, prone to religious hysteria. Her husband's death produced in her a severe melancholy, and at this critical juncture she discovered mysticism; it cured her melancholy but left her in a mental state not far from insanity (at one point she believed herself pregnant by Jesus Christ). She spent five years doing missionary work under the Catholic bishop of Geneva, and during this time, formulated her doctrine of Quietism, which she set down in her *Short Method of Prayer* in 1687.

She began with the statement that religion depended entirely on prayer, then defined her concept of it — "not the formal offering up of specific petitions, but the state of the heart in which it is united to God in faith and love." Prayer became a mental state, "the silence of the soul," and from this silence arose a disinterested, pure love and an unquestioning resignation — the essence of Quietism. "When we have given ourselves to God in abandonment, then God becomes central to the soul, and all which is the opposite of God gradually dissolves itself."

The Jesuits perceived at once two dangers in the Quietist theory. First, an indifference to morality, resulting from Mme Guyon's claim that indifference to salvation is the highest of pure love; the budding mystic had written that "to commit the sin that one most abominates is to offer God the greatest sacrifice." Second, the self-confidence she advocated, the direct and sole reliance on God, denied the laws of tradition and convention with which the Church had ruled people for centuries. The mystic and her dangerous ideas had to be suppressed.

For a time she was imprisoned and wrote a number of brief treatises that soon came into vogue; her literary success led to her release in 1688. More importantly, it attracted the attention of Mme de Maintenon and Abbé Fénelon.

Mme Guyon was introduced to the "holy set" of Versailles — Mme de Maintenon and her friends — and quickly charmed the king's secret wife. At first Fénelon was not so taken in: "[She] has a bad reputation; she makes use of an appearance of piety, and is not to be trusted," he wrote shortly after their first meeting. But before the year was out, he too had fallen beneath her spell, and would ultimately prove a more loyal friend than Maintenon.

It was, ironically, Mme de Maintenon's friendship that began Guyon's downfall. She allowed her new friend access to Saint-Cyr, and Quietism ran through the school like an epidemic. The bishop of Chartres (who was a director of Saint-Cyr, as well as Maintenon's personal confessor) sniffed danger at once and warned Maintenon that he was under obligation to bring the matter to the king's attention. The royal educator panicked, knowing full well her husband's inexplicable bigotry; she ousted Mme Guyon from her precious school and severed all communication with her, then went herself to the king and requested that he send the *Short Method of Prayer* to Rome for a ruling. In 1689 the pope condemned the book and Maintenon hoped that the incident was closed forever.

It might have been, but for Fénelon. Appalled by the callous treatment the king's wife had shown her erstwhile friend, he rallied to Mme Guyon's defense. At his instigation, the *Short Method* was sent to Archbishop Bossuet, asking him to examine and judge it for himself. This was Fénelon's fatal error.

Bossuet proceeded to ensnare his unsuspecting rival under the aegis of Church legality. His proposal was to set up a conference at Issy to examine and rule on Guyon's ideas — provided, he stipulated, that the mystic and Fénelon both submit to whatever decision was reached. His condition was accepted, and the Conference of Issy convened in July 1694. When its labors were concluded in March 1695, it resulted (not surprisingly) in an unqualified condemnation of Quietism, a decision Fénelon was bound by honor to accept.

But while the Conference of Issy had met, Fénelon had achieved a triumph of his own: in February 1695, Mme de Maintenon persuaded Louis XIV to appoint him archbishop of Cambrai (in Flanders), raising him to the same ecclesiastic level as Bossuet.

On March 10, 1695, the Articles of Issy were presented to Fénelon for signature. Bossuet later claimed that the new archbishop signed them as they stood, though admittedly with great reluctance. Fénelon maintained that he had refused to sign until four additional articles, all in his favor, were inserted into the document. Regardless of the truth, the result was that both Bossuet and Fénelon were dissatisfied and both were determined to publish their own defense of the issue.

Bossuet worked speedily, anxious to have the first word. In July 1696, he completed his treatise *On the States of Prayer,* a purported commentary on the Conference of Issy, and a stinging renunciation of Mme Guyon. Cleverly, he devised a trap: he forwarded his manuscript to Fénelon for reaction and sanction, knowing that with consent Fénelon "must admit error in his own expressed opinions, and thus weaken his position in the Church forever," while "the consequences of refusal were incalculable, and might possibly be fatal to his career."

Fénelon entered the trap with his eyes wide open. His code of honor bound him to continue his support of Guyon, despite the loss of friends or reputation that such support might cost. "If I supported this explanation of her system," he wrote Bossuet, "I should help to convince the world in general that the imputation of her is true, and that she is, in consequence, the most accursed being on earth. I have often seen her; it is well known that I have, and I respect her. I could not esteem her without going to the very foundation of her theories."

With Fénelon's refusal to sanction *On the States of Prayer,* Bossuet's course was set; as one historian wrote: "The most powerful brain in the kingdom was at work to compass [Fénelon's] downfall." But Fénelon himself unwittingly assisted: one month *before* Bossuet's publication, Fénelon's own book *Maxims of the Saints* appeared. Fénelon claimed his work drew the distinction between true and false mysticism; in truth, it was a blatant defense of Guyon.

Bossuet was furious, as much at the timing of publication as at the contents of the treatise. As he prepared for battle, he discovered happily that alliances had shifted. The king understood little of the theological arguments at stake, but did understand that his wife had spent far too much time in support of a man whose ideas smacked of heresy. He had taken Mme de Maintenon to task, and the woman was terrified of the possible consequences to herself should she continue defending the archbishop of Cambrai. As swiftly as she had turned on Mme Guyon, she now cut loose Fénelon, and henceforth numbered herself among his bitterest critics. Bourgogne's tutor no longer had a chance.

With the king, his secret wife, and the sycophantic court now firmly in his camp, Bossuet closed his trap around Fénelon. The archbishop of Cambrai had no alternative but to plead permission from the king to refer the matter to the Vatican. The pope's response was predictable: *Maxims of the Saints* was prohibited and twenty-three of Fénelon's propositions were condemned. Bossuet had destroyed his rival.

Reprisals were swift. On August 1, 1697, Fénelon was ordered to retire to his bishopric in Cambrai — in effect, perpetual banishment. The defeated prelate obeyed, and immediately left Versailles forever, carefully avoiding a painful farewell to his devoted pupil.

Bourgogne was devastated by the loss — and all the more by the king's injunction forbidding him to correspond with Fénelon. With great weeping, he begged his grandfather to soften his decree, but offended Majesty was immovable. The separation was equally hard on Fénelon, as he wrote Beauvilliers, although "as for everything else, I am glad to be well away from it all; I sing the song of deliverance." He assured Beauvilliers that young Bourgogne would never be out of his thoughts and urged the prince's governor to continue the work they had begun. "I must love the Duc de Bourgogne in spite of his worst faults. I beseech you to let nothing lessen your friendship for him; let it be disinterested friendship rooted in faith; it is your part to nourish him . . . Encourage without flattering him, instruct without wearying him . . . Tell him such truths as you must needs tell him, but shortly, gently, with respect and tenderness."

And so under the guise of protecting him from dangerous heresy, Bourgogne was separated from the most important influence in his young life. He accepted the king's ruling as law, as he had been trained ever to do. However he outwardly acquiesced, inside he never forsook his revered teacher and friend. Four years were to pass before he was permitted any communication, but his first letter to Fénelon made it plain that the affection and inspiration he derived from the archbishop had in no way diminished: "Versailles, 22 December 1701. At length, my dear Archbishop, I have a chance of breaking our silence. I have suffered much in that time, but nothing that hurt me more than the impossibility of telling you all that I felt for you. Your misfortunes have made my love the warmer instead of chilling it. I think with delight of a time when I shall see you again, but I fear that time is still a long way off . . . I cannot tell you here how I loathe the treatment you have received, but one must accept the will of God and believe it is all for our good." Such acceptance was indeed the great lesson Fénelon had taught, the one that would hold the prince in good stead for the rest of his life.

9

Bourbon Munificence

LIKE HER FIANCÉ, Adelaide approached the wedding sustaining the loss of a cherished figure from the past: her personal maid since birth, Mme Marquet. It will be remembered that Louis XIV ordered the entire Savoyard retinue to turn back at the frontier. Marquet alone was permitted to follow the princesse to Fontainebleau, and remained in her service at Versailles. Certainly his darling's reliance on her safe, familiar maid contributed largely to the initial relaxation of Louis's decree, but Marquet's obvious devotion to her tiny mistress, and her strict policy of nonintervention, had earned her the respect and trust of the king and his wife. When Mme Marquet requested leave to return to her family in Turin, the king consented at once. "The Princesse is so easy with me now," he explained to Tessé, "and so comfortable with her ladies, that she has absolutely no further need for her Piedmontese maid." Marquet's farewell audience with the royal couple was filled with fine praise and finer gifts — the king presented a purse of one thousand louis d'or and Maintenon a dinner service of solid silver. Overwhelmed by this (typical) display of Bourbon munificence, the simple Marquet stammered her gratitude and took her leave.

Farewell to the little princesse was far more difficult; Adelaide cried bitterly when saying goodbye to her beloved confidante. Symbolically, she presented Marquet with her original trousseau brought from Savoy (and already outgrown). By French standards, it was not much of a collection, but remembering the costly gold lace and silk embroidery, the quantities of cloth of gold and silver for which the stingy father of the bride had given his reluctant consent, the gift was of no mean value. Even more prized — for sentiment as well as cost — was a miniature of the princesse in a diamond-studded frame.

Adelaide cried for several days after her nursemaid's departure for Savoy. Though she was never to see her native land again, her interest in her family and their people remained steadfast. Her steady correspondence with her mother and grandmother, however shallow or sparse, gives ample evidence of a fidelity that never failed her; indeed, when her extreme youth through the first quarter of the correspondence is taken into account, Adelaide's modest output assumes voluminous proportions.

Throughout her first years in France, Adelaide's letters to Turin cry out for assurances of affection ("I wish I could express what I desire for your happiness . . . and how much I hope that you will love me always" is one variation on the recurrent theme). As she grew more comfortable and secure in her new life, the princesse felt a need to convey her own assurances: after lauding the king and Mme de Maintenon, she hastens to add: "But I shall love you everywhere, my dear grandmama," and shortly before her death, having been ill for "the last seven days," Adelaide still managed to pen a note to the duchess Anne Marie, "in order not to miss a week in assuring you myself of my tenderness."

With Marquet's removal, Adelaide's last link with Savoy, the Vigna, and her carefree childhood was lost; even for a child in wonderland, sadness was inescapable. But this shrewd little girl had already mastered two lessons: one public — that her position within the Versailles hierarchy did not allow for the indulgence of personal grief; and one private — that Louis XIV was averse to contact with any sort of human unhappiness and especially from the little girl whose happiness had become his primary concern. Hidden away in her closet, Adelaide wept comfortably in the arms of her new "Nanny," Mme Nogaret, till a visit from Louis brought a quick recovery, as Sourches observed: "She showed great courage and quickly dried her eyes, for fear of troubling the King."

While time alone would have sufficed to blur Adelaide's nostalgia, her nature was never one to dwell on sadness or regret. "I know that henceforth I am to be the happiest person in the world," she had boasted a year before on the Franco-Savoyard border; this, the princesse was learning, was easier to say than do, but the continued indulgence of the king and her own household became ample compensation for the loss of an old friend — not to mention the surefire excitement of wedding preparations.

At Adelaide's birthday celebration at Marly the year before, the king had set her wedding date for December 10, four days after her twelfth birthday (the marriage contract had stipulated that Marie Adelaide could not wed the duc de Bourgogne until she had attained her majority). As the time approached, the old king's impatience grew: early in the fall of 1697, he advanced the wedding again — to the day after her birthday.

The king's plans and dreams for his grandson's union were suddenly threatened when illness struck his treasured princesse in November. The early winter was long and bitter, and the canal at Versailles froze over three times before the new year. Adelaide, never particularly robust, took to her bed with a heavy cold. However trifling her indisposition, Louis XIV was frantic with concern; he visited her sickroom daily, and for one entire evening, the state affairs of the mighty Sun King went untended while Grandpapa sat on the edge of the bed and played proverbs. By the end of the week, the princesse was well again; her first request was to go sledding with the king.

Monseigneur, her prospective father-in-law, had also paid daily visits during Adelaide's brief illness (his attentions doubtless motivated by duty, since he had little use for children), but fear of contagion had barred all communication with Bourgogne. As the princesse recovered and the wedding date drew near, Louis XIV stepped up the process of familiarization. The fortnightly "interviews" were increased to once a week — still, of course, under the careful supervision of the duchesse du Lude. Despite the discomforting presence of their chaperone, it was noticed that the attitudes of the young couple — her complete, childlike indifference and his awkward adoration and embarrassment in her company — had markedly improved. The Savoyard ambassador, invited to witness one of their meetings, wrote to Victor Amadeus: "From the outset, the young couple began to converse familiarly, and concluded more sadly, when they perceived that the moment when they must separate was at hand."

These encounters grew longer and more intimate. As the weather once more turned bad, forcing the court indoors, the prince and princesse were allowed to dance together for the first time. On November 26, they rehearsed the steps of their stately wedding dance in the presence of the king, Mme de Maintenon, and honored guests. Adelaide shone: she loved dancing and she loved being praised — and if an objective witness like Saint-Simon felt that "she moved with an unconscious grace, like a goddess walking upon clouds," imagine the compliments that fell from the lips of her proud Grandpapa! One week later, on December 2, the marriage ceremony itself was rehearsed before the same august audience and rows of empty chairs.

Shortly before the wedding, Adelaide wrote Madame Royale that she looked forward to her status as a married woman, imagining all sorts of new freedoms; but "I assure you, in my change of state I shall be always the same through life." By return post came word of a tragedy that once more threatened Adelaide's high spirits and anticipation: the birth and immediate death of a brother, Savoy's longed-for heir. Mme de Maintenon was visiting the dauphin at Meudon when she heard the news, and she quickly returned to Versailles to find the princesse deeply upset, crying bitterly. This painful reminder of home required more compassion and understanding than had Mme Marquet's departure. Maintenon's gentle voice spoke long and low, with soothing words of comfort and reassurance.

The duc de Bourgogne's wedding was even more historic than his birth: the last (and only other) grandson of a reigning king to be married was Charles the Wise in 1350. Free to set precedents to befit the illustrious occasion, Louis XIV was determined to present a display of unrivaled Bourbon munificence. Since his marriage to Mme de Maintenon, he had dressed with the utmost simplicity — always in a plain brown suit with an open vest of blue or red embroidered satin, without rings or jewels save for his shoe buckles and the brooch in his white-plumed hat. Now he ordered an "elegant new suit," and hinted broadly that the court had best follow his example.

"That was enough," Saint-Simon recalled, "for everyone, excepting priests and lawyers, to disregard their purses, or even their rank. There was hot competition in splendor and originality, with scarcely enough gold and silver lace to go round; the merchants' booths emptied in a very few days ... Unbridled extravagance reigned throughout the Court." Saint-Simon was hardly a dispassionate observer: he and Mme de Saint-Simon spent twenty thousand livres on their costumes for the wedding. The silk merchants and Parisian jewelers estimated later that over five million livres' worth of goods had been sold for the occasion. The activity rose to such a pitch that the king professed regret at having made his suggestion, "that he failed to understand how husbands could be so foolish as to ruin themselves for their wives' clothes" — he might just have rightly said for their own. But secretly Louis XIV was heartened by the lavish turnout; all his life he loved rich materials and fine workmanship, reveled in elegant attire, and was ever ready to praise another's magnificence and taste. As Saint-Simon suspected, "he made his little protest on principle, but was enchanted to find that no one heeded him."

As if to further belie his token plea for moderation, Louis XIV lavished the bride with wedding presents: a brilliant set of diamonds worth half a million livres, and a necklace of twenty-one large and flawless pearls.[1] Louis also provided the wedding bed, dressed in exquisite linen and covered in a counterpane of lace, valued at fifty thousand livres. The king personally chose the embroidery pattern for Adelaide's wedding gown, providing one more example of his elegant manners and legendary politeness: having made his selection, Louis XIV was assured by the fatuous embroiderer that all other work would be put aside until the wedding gown had been completed. The Sun King would not hear of such a thing. "He told him most explicitly to finish all that he had on hand, and only then work on his order, and he added that if it were not finished in time the Princesse would do without it."

Mme de Maintenon's gifts were two, appropriately one temporal and one spiritual: a handsomely crafted casket, filled with an assortment of costly jewels and inset with a miniature portrait of the duc de Bourgogne, and an album of serious reflections and recommendations for the new bride, written in Maintenon's own fine hand. The king's wife, deploring "false delicacy" on the subject of marriage, felt duty bound to dispel her little darling's illusions and misconceptions. The album was divided into three sections: "Regarding God" and "Regarding the World" are echoes of Maintenon's lectures at Saint-Cyr, lessons Adelaide had been studying for almost a year, but "Regarding Your Honored Husband" is full of sound advice as well as practical piety: "Let M. le Duc de Bourgogne be your closest friend and confidant; take his advice; give him your own. Make of yourselves one person, according to God's ordinance." "Do not expect as much affection as you bear for him. Men, as a general rule, are less affectionate than women." "You will be unhappy if you are overcritical of his friendships. Pray God that you be not jealous." "Never seek to recover his love by complaints, miseries, or reproaches. The only way is by gentleness and patience; but I hope that M. le Duc de Bourgogne will never subject you to such ordeals."

The treatise is studded with the royal educator's personal observations, from practical — "Speak, write and act as though before a thousand witnesses; for sooner or later all becomes known" — to altruistic — "Have compassion on the unfortunate; God has placed you in your high position to do good. The power to serve others and make them happy is the true compensation for the fatigues, discomforts and constraints of your position."

After Adelaide's death, the missive was found in her favorite jewelry box, the one Maintenon had given her. Louis XIV ordered that it be kept as a cherished remembrance for her descendants, although it is unknown whether any of those descendants ever opened the little album again. Providentially, Marie Adelaide herself prized the counsels of the royal educator; although convenient lapses of conscience would invariably bring her trouble, the shrewd little princesse already demonstrated an astonishing receptiveness to advice. In almost every difficulty for the rest of her life, Adelaide relied on the wisdom, guidance, and support of *"ma tante"* and was never disappointed. "Do not hope that your union will bring you perfect happiness. The best marriages are those in which each suits to the other with gentleness and patience."

Louis XIV felt that the household of the princess of Savoy was unsuitable for the duchesse de Bourgogne. He added to her entourage a maître d'hôtel, superintendent, secretary, physician, and personal surgeon — and such a number of menials and stable staff that her household swelled to five hundred. The most prestigious of these new positions Louis blatantly offered to the highest bidder: the marquis de Villacerf, for example, paid two hundred thousand livres for the privilege of supervising Adelaide's kitchen. M. Ricourt, son of the King's Apothecary, purchased the office of Physician for twenty-two thousand livres, and fifteen thousand bought the post of surgeon for M. Dionys (the son of the royal *accoucheur*, Dionys obviously envisioned a lucrative family monopoly).

The king hoped to raise at least two million livres from the sale of these offices, to help defray the wedding costs — costs that continued to soar. Bolts of sheer linen arrived daily for the new bride, along with gold plate and baroque silver "of the most costly description" to grace her table. A new livery, resplendent in gold and silver lace, was designed for her gentlemen, and for her carriage, itself "as fine as the King's," Master of the Horse Tessé was authorized to purchase "twenty dapple-grays with white tails, and eight beautiful blacks . . . from the north of Holland; another dozen from Naples, and seven more from North Italy."[2] The postnuptial celebrations with which Louis XIV intended to honor the future queen of France were to last until Christmas, and included two balls, an opera, and a display of fireworks.

December 6, 1697, was Marie Adelaide's twelfth birthday. On the morning of the seventh, she rose at dawn to dress for her wedding. Her bridal gown was dazzling: the underskirt, trimmed with silver ribbons, was decorated in rubies and diamonds from the Crown collection; her overdress was cloth of silver, embroidered in silver thread and set with rubies. Around her small neck hung the king's matchless pearl necklace, while her train, twenty-five feet long, was stitched thick with rubies, pearls, and spun silver.

After her hair had been dressed and jeweled, the princesse received first the felicitations of the royal family, then the good wishes of her ladies and servants, who hurried off to find themselves seats in the extra stands added to the royal chapel.

The court had risen early as well and assembled in the bridegroom's apartments. For his wedding day, Bourgogne cut a dashing figure: his suit was simple black velvet, and his mantle was cut of the same cloth but covered in golden embroidery and lined with cloth of silver, and diamonds flashed from his fine lace jabot and his white-plumed hat. He marched across the marble halls, the court in tow, and arrived at Adelaide's door to escort his bride to the king's study.

There the entire royal family waited to witness the private betrothal ceremony. Louis XIV's wish for opulence was rewarded; *Le Mercure* reported to its readers: "Never had splendor of apparel been carried so far," and the raiments of the royal family alone (which Madame afterward described in detail for her aunt) support the newspaper's contention. The king's new suit was in cloth of gold, the seams delineated with heavy golden embroidery and the coat studded with precious stones worth over ten million livres. The father of the groom was also dressed in cloth of gold, covered in intricate golden embroidery. The flaming Monsieur, delighted with his brother's request for magnificence, "wore all his big diamonds" — as buttons on his embroidered black velvet suit. Madame is modest in her description of her own costume: "My dress was of gold, covered with raised flowers of black chenille, and my ornaments were pearls and diamonds." But she beamed with maternal pride when Mademoiselle's attire aroused universal admiration: "My daughter wore a gown of green velvet, embroidered with gold; the gown and underskirt were studded all over with rubies and diamonds, and so was the corsage; the embroidery was so exquisitely made that each flower stood out as if it were embossed; her headdress consisted of several *enseignes* [circlets] made of brilliants, and ruby *poinçons* [stickpins] with a golden ribbon completely covered with diamonds."

The betrothal was brief, and shortly before noon the royal procession formed. First came the bridal couple, escorted by Monseigneur and Monsieur, their nearest (French) relatives. The king marched beside the ambassador of Savoy, who represented Victor Amadeus; they were followed by the royal princes and princesses, headed by Madame; then the nobles and ladies of the royal households, in strict accordance to their rank. The procession passed slowly through the Hall of Mirrors and the sumptuous state apartments, before descending the Grand Staircase to the royal chapel; these state rooms were crammed with excited spectators, and *Le Mercure*'s qualification that "in the chapel, they kept excellent order" suggests a spontaneous outburst of affection and loyalty from the crowd that the refined nobility would have deemed unseemly.

Inside the chapel, the bride and groom knelt on satin cushions at the foot of the altar while the cardinal de Coislin, bishop-elect of Metz, performed the public betrothal ceremony. Madame explained: "The King, Monseigneur, Monsieur and I stood around the betrothed couple. When the moment came to say 'I will,' the bride bowed four times, but the bridegroom only twice, because he had only to ask the consent of his father and grandfather, while the bride asked Monsieur's and mine as well, since we are her grandparents." This distinction was also observed in the wedding ceremony that immediately followed.

The duc de Bourgogne placed a ring on Adelaide's finger and presented her with thirteen pieces of gold, the symbol of all his worldly goods. The marriage vows were exchanged, and Marie Adelaide of Savoy became the duchesse de Bourgogne. Cardinal de Coislin continued with the nuptial mass. At the offertory, the duc and new duchesse rose to present the prescribed gifts: after paying their obeisance to the altar, the king, and Monseigneur, they were each handed a wax taper and ten gold coins, and with admirable solemnity approached the prelate and offered their tokens.

The nuptial mass concluded, the parish registry was signed: first by the king, then Monseigneur, and then the newlyweds. Witnesses for the bridegroom were his two brothers, Anjou and Berri; for the bride, her grandparents. The king had strictly curtailed the number of royal signatories, out of consideration for his illegitimate children who,

Saint-Simon explained, would "have felt humiliated at not signing, whereas the Princes might have objected to their doing so." The wedding procession formed again and the royal family returned to Adelaide's apartment. Madame sniffed: "The bride took her rank as Duchesse de Bourgogne directly behind the King," escorted by her husband and his father.

In the antechamber of the new duchess, a large horseshoe table was set for twenty-one, and the entire royal family (including the bastards) sat down to a public dinner. Madame enjoyed this *grand couvert* more than most: "I was not dull at the table because I was next to my dear duc de Berri, who kept me laughing. 'I see my brother,' he said, 'winking at his little wife, but if I liked I could make eyes at her too, because I have known how to ogle for a long time now. You have only to look at them hard, out of the corner of your eye.' As he said this, he imitated his brother so funnily that I could not help laughing."

Following the *grand couvert,* the royal family adjourned to Adelaide's bedchamber. Louis XIV left almost at once, for "the affairs of state claimed him above his own pleasure," and the other members of the family headed for their apartments and a few hours of rest. The bride was allowed to remove her heavy robes and nap peacefully, but briefly. At six o'clock, dressed again in full state, she received the Savoyard ambassador and the many Italian nobles who had journeyed to Versailles for her wedding; the princesse "smiled graciously and offered them her hand."

At seven, the new duchess returned to the king's apartments — apparently with greater ease than her grandmother, for Madame complained: "There was such a crush that I had to wait a quarter of an hour at each door before I could enter." The king, who had been quietly visiting with Mme de Maintenon in her salon, fared no better; neither did the exiled King James II and Queen Mary of England, who kept the French royal family waiting forty-five minutes while they tried to push their way into the king's drawing room. Queen Mary, dressed in cloth of gold trimmed with black flowers and diamonds, was charming and beautiful, if not particularly clever, and had grown intimate with Mme de Maintenon in the nine years since her flight to France. James II, clothed in golden velvet with gold buttons, was Louis XIV's peer, an anointed king, whose presence was always a comfort to the aging French monarch — although the rest of Versailles found him stubborn and opinionated, a tremendous bore whose troubles were entirely of his own making.

Once the royal party convened, they joined the courtiers that filled the Hall of Mirrors to watch the fireworks display; Nicolò Erizzo, the Venetian ambassador, declared them "the most magnificent display that the world has ever seen," but their splendor was marred by heavy winds and rain, and the show ended abruptly. Undeterred, the royal revelers sat down to an enormous supper. The dethroned English queen presided between the two kings, but Erizzo noted: "Amid so much rejoicing, one could see tears in the eyes of the king and queen of England, unhappy spectators of this magnificence . . . While they thus celebrate the marriage of the duc de Bourgogne, in London King William makes his triumphal entry."

After supper, the female wedding guests went to prepare the bride for bed, "men being rigidly excluded by order of the King." The nuptial bed was now unveiled and acclaimed: a veritable masterpiece in the art of upholstery, its green velvet coverlet embroidered in silver and gold. Surrounded by her ladies and half the court, Adelaide undressed and accepted her nightgown from Queen Mary. In the adjoining anteroom, the young bridegroom undressed, seated on a folding stool. He was attended by his grandfather and all the royal princes: his nightshirt was handed by the king of England and his orange silk dressing gown by the king of France.

When the little bride had been put into bed, the duc de Bourgogne entered the room and took his place beside her. This marked the consummation of the day's events — if not of the marriage, which was prohibited for at least another year. Louis XIV proudly displayed his royal grandchildren before the foreign ambassadors and his court; "a gentleman was immediately dispatched to hasten to the duke of Savoy with the news."

The king and queen of England were the first to leave; when Louis XIV retired to perform his ritual *coucher,* the fawning court obediently followed. The bride and groom were left alone — alone, that is, with Monseigneur and a crowd of their household officers, the duc de Beauvilliers stationed to the right of the bed and the duchesse du Lude to the left. Monseigneur, sitting at their feet, chatted quietly with his son and daughter-in-law for fifteen minutes. Then he ordered his son to return to his own room, and over the protests of Lude, told the boy to kiss his bride good night. Saint-Simon reported that Adelaide "ran forward, threw herself into his arms and gave immense proofs of her satisfaction," but her lady-of-honor did not share her enthusiasm: in the morning, Lude complained to Louis XIV of this innocent but unauthorized kiss, and the king took it very much to heart, swearing

A view of Versailles

Louis XIV

Above left:
Philippe, duc d'Orléans,
younger brother of Louis
XIV and grandfather
of Marie Adelaide.
At court he was known
simply as Monsieur.

Above right:
Queen Marie Thérèse,
wife of Louis XIV, and
her only surviving child,
the young Dauphin, on
their way to a court ball

Left:
Madame de Maintenon,
Louis XIV's secret
second wife

Monsieur the Dauphin,
Louis XIV's son and heir

Below:
The Dauphin and his family, c. 1687.
The Dauphine, Marie Anne of
Bavaria, cradles the infant duc de
Berri; the duc d'Anjou, later Philip V
of Spain, sits on a cushion; the five-
year-old duc de Bourgogne is at the
right.

Marie Adelaide of Savoy, shortly after her arrival at Versailles

The Menagerie at Versailles, Louis XIV's gift to Marie Adelaide

Françoise Marie and Louise Françoise de Bourbon, Louis XIV's daughters by the marquise de Montespan. With their half-sister, the princesse de Conti, they formed the core of the Meudon Cabal.

Marie Anne de Bourbon, princesse de Conti, Louis XIV's daughter by Louise de La Vallière

Marie Adelaide, duchesse de Bourgogne

Louis, duc de Bourgogne

The duc de Villars

Philippe, duc de Chartres. The son of
Monsieur and his second wife, he
ruled as regent for the child king
Louis XV.

The duc de Vendôme, a
hero in the War of the
Spanish Succession and
a mortal enemy of the
duc and duchesse de
Bourgogne

he would not have his grandson so much as kiss the tip of the bride's little finger until it was time for them to live together as husband and wife. The impish duc de Berri declared his brother too meek, and said that *he* would never have left his bride's bed.

As Versailles retired for the night, the new duchesse de Bourgogne drifted into well-earned sleep, alone on her wedding night. The extreme youth of the royal newlyweds had eliminated the necessity of a honeymoon; just as well, since the elaborate festivities planned by Louis XIV would leave the new couple scarcely a moment to themselves in the coming fortnight. Not until after Christmas would life return to normal and these children to their schoolrooms.

Louis XIV meant to demonstrate his granddaughter's supreme position at the earliest moment possible. Sunday, the day after her wedding, the duchesse de Bourgogne held her first *cercle,* or reception, in her Grand Cabinet. Adelaide, in red velvet (her favorite color), sat on the royal dais, surrounded by the princesses of the blood and the royal duchesses, all in magnificent court dress. The little girl received her guests with poise and charm, if a bit too much affability and obvious happiness for those sticklers for etiquette who demanded perpetual blandness from their royalty. The king honored her first party with an appearance, although on his arrival an awkward silence fell on the intimidated guests.

Following Adelaide's reception, the king gave a glittering *appartement.* The plenteous buffet in the Salon of Abundance, the gaming tables in the Apollo room, and the oboes and violins that filled the music room with the strains of Lully recalled for more than one veteran courtier nights of similiar parties, nights of indescribable gaiety from their, and their master's, exuberant youth. The duc de Bourgogne, now a married man, no longer waited behind with his brothers till the musical interlude signaled their appearance; with his wife on his arm, he proudly entered the state apartments directly behind the king, modestly receiving the court's obeisance with noticeable twinges of embarrassment. (Guests of honor or not, bedtime was observed: at nine, the duke and duchess kissed their grandfather goodnight and scampered off to their separate bedrooms.)

On Monday morning, Adelaide drove with Mme de Maintenon on an official visit to Saint-Cyr. There was much to report to her wide-eyed schoolmates, and she had been allowed to bring her wedding gown to model for the girls; one nun felt the elaborate gown was "so heavily embroidered with silver she was scarcely able to support it," but Adelaide, basking in so much friendly praise, replied that it was no heavier than it had been on Saturday. She attended a Te Deum in the convent church, and then the school choir recited verses in her honor; it was dark before the princesse and the royal educator finally returned home.

Tuesday the newlyweds received an official call from the children of James II and Queen Mary. That night, they enjoyed a special treat: dining alone with Mme de Maintenon in her apartment. In a gown of rose-colored satin edged with silver, Adelaide merrily flitted about the room, and at table insisted that *she* would serve her husband and *tante;* Bourgogne watched her every move with adoring eyes, Maintenon was delighted to notice.

For Wednesday, the eleventh, Louis XIV had arranged Adelaide's first grand ball. The king ordered special lighting for the Hall of Mirrors, already a suitably opulent setting for so special an occasion; the Venetian ambassador was dazzled with the results: three enormous chandeliers hung from the richly painted ceiling, thirty-two multi-branched candelabra sat on gilded pedestals, and eight great pyramids of silver, draped in crimson velvet, held 150 candles each — over five thousand tapers illuminated the great gallery. "Between the reflections from the mirrors and the diamonds," Erizzo wrote the doge, "this place was rendered brighter than if it had been lighted by the rays of the sun."

As with the royal wedding, sartorial magnificence was de rigueur, and the princes and nobles continued their attempts to outdo each other in lavishness. Erizzo computed the cost of the least sumptuous of costumes at twelve thousand livres, the most expensive at thirty thousand, "not including the precious stones, which were numberless and priceless." Guests began to arrive at six as the orchestra tuned in its corner of the hall. At seven, the great mirrored doors flew open, and His Majesty appeared with his young guests of honor.

Adelaide had chosen a gown in cloth of gold, her hair and neck sparkling with diamonds, though her husband, frugal if not just practical, gave another wearing to his black velvet wedding suit. The newlyweds opened the ball with the ritual *branle,* or round dance. Dipping and gliding in well-rehearsed measures across the parquet floor, the princesse tried in vain to maintain an air of gravity, fast becoming aware of the criticism of her "unseemly enjoyment" of pageantry. She was more successful with decorum in her second, slower dance, the *courante,* a rhythmic walk interrupted by curtsies and *pas doubles.* Under the steady scrutiny of the court, Adelaide performed these complicated maneuvers gracefully and excited a favorable reaction; much complimented too was her bearing in the *minuet,* and the vivacity with which she executed the athletic *passe-pied* — a dance extremely difficult to perform in a seventeenth-century boned corset. But Adelaide adored every type of dance, and in this, her first grown-up ball, she all but refused to quit the floor when called to supper.

For those lacking the stamina of the young duchess, a staggering buffet appeared at eight, carried in by one hundred lackeys. With their skillful artistry, they transformed one corner of the ballroom into a garden of flowers, fruits, and sweetmeats. Twelve tables (covered with moss and verdure instead of tablecloths and flanked with fragrant orange trees) were laden with baskets of fresh fruit, silver trays of marzipan, and crystal goblets of sweet liqueurs and ices.

"At that hour," rhapsodized the Venetian ambassador, "the grandeur and *brio* of France was made manifest, and one understood how poor and miserable are the attempts of other countries to imitate it. The presence of the King gave luster, and at the same time, imposed a restraining influence on the fête, in which the silence and constraint were so great that one would have imagined oneself in the midst of a Senate of grave men rather than in a ballroom."

But the overwhelmed ambassador had conveniently closed his eyes to the squalor beneath the surface, to ugliness that on this particular night emerged in harmful, as well as scandalous, incidents. The duc d'Aumont, whom the king had charged to organize the celebration, was unfortunately a man lacking in judgment, calm, and coolness. D'Aumont quite simply invited too many guests, and as the rush for seats mounted and the buffet lines grew threatening, he lost his head. Several disorderly scenes resulted. Monsieur was knocked down and trampled by courtiers, and the king himself narrowly missed the same abuse; many escaped with insults and bruises while others were crushed and beaten in the confusion. Despite the French court's reputation for refined superiority, such unedifying scrapes were all too common at Versailles. No doubt with a sense of relief Louis XIV closed the ball at half past ten, retiring to his private apartments for an intimate supper with the young couple.

The second wedding ball, three nights later, was no less magnificent and much more fun: fewer guests had been invited, minimizing the inconvenience so recently endured. Adelaide, perhaps to complement her sober young mate, wore a dress of black velvet, covered with diamonds; "her hair was braided with pearls, and the rest of her coiffure was so full of diamonds that one might say without exaggeration that the eye could scarcely endure such dazzling splendor." Again she danced for hours; again she consented to withdraw only after an express royal command.

Although unofficial rejoicing continued for the rest of the year, the royal celebration of the duc and duchesse de Bourgogne's wedding concluded on the seventeenth with a performance of the opera *Apollon et Issé* at the Trianon theater. With music by André-Cardinal Destouches and libretto by Houdart de La Motte, it was an inescapably boring work, relieved only by the sumptuous decor provided by the artist Berain. But for Adelaide, her first opera was an evening of enchantment. The little girl sat enraptured throughout, now laughing loudly, now sobbing uncontrollably; she showed so keen an interest and afterward asked so many questions that the king and Mme de Maintenon decided she had been overexcited by such intensive Bourbon munificence and that a respite, at least until the Christmas festivities, was of top priority.

Like all his associates, the Venetian ambassador was pressed from home for his observations on the characters of the young royal couple, and asked to speculate on the future of their union. With candor and insight, Erizzo reported: "The Duchesse is highly gifted, but *scarse di bellezza* [lacking in beauty]. Her husband is a serious youth, sufficiently well-informed to be called a scholar, and yet of a passionate disposition. It is fondly hoped that these two human beings will come to understand each other. At present, and on account of their youth, their souls are no less apart than their persons." And their persons were no less apart than before their wedding day. A dazzling fortnight, center stage in wonderland, then the lavish rituals of a Christmas court — and in the new year of 1698, Bourgogne returned to his tutors and his priests, and Adelaide to Saint-Cyr, Lude and her ladies, and cozy evenings by the fireside with Grandpapa and his wife.

But Grandpapa was not yet finished with this particular round of royal spectacle. While the rest of his court indulged in Twelfth Night tomfoolery, the Sun King was closeted with his top military advisors, preparing a summer sequel to the royal wedding.

The notion of a military camp, conceived by Louis XIV in the first days of 1698, gratified more than one royal wish. On a strictly personal level, it would afford the Sun King the pleasure of a splendid display of arms, a demonstration of French military superiority of which he never tired. Branching out from this, the camp would provide fresh diversion and enjoyment for the king's new granddaughter and, chief among its aims, teach his grandson the principles of warfare — so far as could be done in peacetime. Widening still further, the military camp would be a clear and compelling example of national policy.

All Europe recognized that the peace which had brought to a halt the long, debilitating War of the Palatinate less than a year before was, in reality, little more than a truce, an uneasy respite until the impending death of the heirless king of Spain would force them all back onto the battlefield to determine his successor. The most calloused of continental statesmen, with no personal malice toward the imbecilic Carlos II, prayed for his immediate demise — a fortuitous stroke of timing that would give the former allies the advantage over an exhausted and sorely weakened France. Carlos would perversely survive for another two years, but Louis XIV wished to immediately dispel any impression that his ability to wage successful warfare had been diminished. Recognition of this political motivation was tacit, of course: under the sole pretext of his grandson's martial education, the king called for a camp at Compiègne in the first weeks of September, to be commanded by the maréchal de Boufflers under the duc de Bourgogne. An inordinate number of troops was allotted for the review, and several illustrious generals chosen to participate; to ensure a dazzling success at Compiègne, Louis XIV made it understood that he desired the attendance of the entire court.

The Sun King had previously established three such camps, but they had been small, practical reviews of the national force. The scale of Compiègne was staggering: 35,000 infantrymen, 3,000 cavalry troops and several batteries of artillery — more than 60,000 soldiers — were assembled under canvas for a display of every conceivable wartime military operation.[3]

Nor was size its only distinction, Saint-Simon noted: "In smartness, it was the marriage of the duc de Bourgogne all over again," for Louis XIV hinted broadly that he expected not only a splendid outfitting of his troops, but a healthy rivalry in surpassing each other as well. Such rivalry and ostentation was sheer wantonness, warned Saint-Simon: "Not only were all the troops superbly equipped — indeed, it would have been hard to single out any particular unit for a prize — but their commanders added horses, harnesses, and all the magnificence of the

Court to the warlike splendor of the men themselves, and junior officers ruined themselves buying uniforms grand enough for any State occasion."

In other aspects as well, the camp at Compiègne resembled more a *grand divertissement* than a military review. The officers' tents were open to all visitors, and mere captains offered their guests delicious and abundant refreshment. Saint-Simon marked out six lieutenant generals and fourteen brigadiers as "especially generous," but he reserved his highest compliments for the presiding maréchal de Boufflers, who "by his liberality, the perfectly organized and most delicious refreshments offered in the greatest abundance, his admirable taste and supreme courtesy during the entire time of the camp, by night and day and at all hours . . . showed the King himself an example of how to give royal entertainment." Certainly the Sun King had scant need for any such lessons — indeed, he had given Boufflers one hundred thousand livres to defray the costs of Compiègne, although judging from the descriptions of the maréchal's munificence, this was but a drop in the ocean. Every type of hot and cold beverage was served from Boufflers's constantly replenished buffets, including wines, both French and foreign, and the choicest of liqueurs. Immense quantities of venison and game arrived daily at the camp; fish from Normandy, Brittany, Holland, and England — and from the distant Mediterranean as well — appeared by post chaise at precisely timed intervals. Even the water supply had been considered: Boufflers knew the wells of Compiègne could not survive the exhausting demands of the court *and* the army, so water from every available spring for miles around the city was appropriated and delivered to the camp in regulation water carts.[4]

Boufflers supervised the construction of wooden guest houses, furnished in the comfortable style of Parisian *hôtels,* and enough spare tents were erected to form an entirely separate camp. Kitchens, butteries, pantries, and servants materialized from the air — "Impossible to think of anything that was not provided, for the poorest wayfarer as well as the most honored and invited guest."

Despite the maréchel's careful preparation, the turnout of curious spectators was overwhelming and, as the haughty Saint-Simon sniffed, "for the first time dukes were billeted in pairs." Yet so magnetic was the Sun King's pull, so tantalizing his promise of spectacle that men and women flocked to the camp and endured gratefully all manner of deprivation: to Saint-Simon's amazement, the ladies of the court — who had never before been allowed to attend such an exercise —

"treated as outmoded decorum discomforts which one would not otherwise have dared suggest to them."

The royals themselves descended on Compiègne September 1, 1698. Louis XIV, in his gilded state coach, traveled with the duchesse du Lude and his two illegitimate daughters; Mme de Maintenon, as always, followed in another carriage — not from any great desire for propriety, but because she could not abide the king's passion for driving with the windows wide open. Adelaide, who for weeks had been agog with excitement, had the pleasure of choosing her own companions for the journey from Versailles. Her great friends, Mlles d'Aubigné, d'Ayen, and de Chevreuse were selected at once, and the vivacious Mme de Dangeau, no less a favorite than her husband, rounded out their party in the guise of chaperone. One courtier, observing the passing carriage of giggling schoolgirls, noted that their ages combined just barely exceeded that of His Majesty — who in five days would be sixty.

Bourgogne traveled in a separate carriage with his brothers, no less enthusiastic than his wife but certainly better prepared in his expectations. Recently, he had completed an extensive study of the theories and strategies of warfare — a logical step in his royal education and not merely in anticipation of Compiègne. He had prepared for the camp with youthful thoroughness: in June, on one of the hottest days of the summer, he walked his horse from Versailles to Maisons and back, in order to become accustomed to the marching pace of the troops he would lead before the king.

Monsieur and his wife elected to remain behind at Saint-Cloud. Though in his youth he had exhibited real flair for battle, Monsieur in middle age found the handsome young officers too temptingly inaccessible and opted instead for his boudoir, with his pots of rouge and scent and his chevalier de Lorraine. For Madame, the sight of the Sun King's massive army promised to revive the awful memory of their destruction of her homeland a decade before. Her absence left open the position of "royal grumbler" — surprisingly filled on this occasion by Mme de Maintenon. The old lady felt no great urge to endure the rigors of army life at her advanced age, and could see no reason why such hardships should be forced upon her. To the archbishop of Paris she complained, "It seems to me that a charitable assembly would be more fitting for me than a military camp, but They must have everything Their way" — leaving no doubt as to the identity of "They."

Louis XIV had devised a complete program of exercises for his troops to perform, including a skirmish, a cannonade, a partition of the army into two forces, and a full-scale battle. The river was to be forded, then later crossed by boat; following the siege, assault, and capitulation of the fortress, there was to be a retreat by columns "without confusion or disorder." To broaden the scope of his grandson's education, Louis further assigned the duc de Bourgogne to such subsidiary services as the supply of victuals and forage, and the organization of a hospital service.

The sixteen-year-old prince gloried in his role of honorary commander and in the soldier's life he lived at Compiègne. The first one awake each morning and the last to bed each night, his days were literally spent in the saddle. He presented his troops to the king, and directed all their operations. He rode with his cavalry and fought with them bravely to repulse their attackers; facing reversals, he rallied his shaken men and returned them to the field of combat (to the enormous satisfaction of his grandfather and the pride of his wife). His youthful daring and his thirst for experience often led him into danger and one narrow brush with death: while his army crossed the river one night by pontoons during a heavy rainstorm, Bourgogne's horse took fright and bucked, tossing its rider into the dark floods below; yet, through it all, the prince "showed himself fearless."

Moreover, he was "enthusiastic, ardent, and solicitous for the comfort of his troops," and spent every available moment visiting their campsites and chatting with the foot soldiers. This keen interest in all aspects of army life was clearly inherited, for Louis XIV was scarcely less involved at Compiègne than his grandson. The king rather smugly displayed his military knowledge for the admiration of the ladies in his entourage, but his investigation into each operation of the camp was exhaustive: while overseeing all troop maneuvers, he also found time to inspect the cantonments and victual arrangements, the distribution of forage, and the feeding and watering of the horses.

Adelaide was intrigued and delighted with the novelty of camp life. She dined frequently at Boufflers's sumptuous table; just as often, she stood for hours in the mess tents, graciously distributing rations to awestruck old soldiers. She aptly demonstrated her total commitment to the duties of the first lady of France — which, given her age, must surely have taken the armed forces by surprise. Boldly she walked or rode through the lines, talked with the soldiers, called at their tents, and sampled their camp bread. On one visit, she won the lifelong devotion of the army grenadiers by pleading with her husband to issue them an extra ration of beer. The princesse was also taken to inspect the many abbeys and convents in the area — doubtless at the insistence of Mme de Maintenon, but certainly with the complete concurrence of the restless, actively curious little girl.

The morning of September 13, Marie Adelaide scribbled a short note to Madame Royale: "I never thought, my dear grandmama, that I should find myself in a besieged town, and be waked by the sound of cannon as I was this morning." It was an experience both alarming and exhilarating. "I hope we shall soon get out of this state," she wrote, while confessing in the next sentence: "It is true that I have great pleasure here." For that Saturday morning, the king had arranged the penultimate event in his military spectacular, the siege of the fortress of Compiègne. An old line of ramparts, overlooking the entire plain, sprawled across the castle on the side that faced the open country; it had been raised level with the king's lodgings, and from there, the royal party would view the day's proceedings. Huge crowds of spectators — among them several distinguished foreign guests — had already gathered when the king, the princesse, and the irritated Mme de Maintenon took their places; Saint-Simon was "in the semicircle around the King, very close to him, not more than three paces distant, with no one in front of me."

The day was perfect, the loveliest weather possible, and Saint-Simon declared: "It was the most beautiful sight that can be imagined to see all that army, and the prodigious number of spectators on horse and foot, and that game of attack and defense so cleverly carried out." Attack and defense were not merely well executed, but highly visible: "display being the only purpose, neither side concealed themselves." Again young Bourgogne inspired favorable comment. He gave the order for the first trench to be dug before the resisting citadel, and then demanded full explanations for every detail of the siege. He stormed the walls at the head of his battalions with as much pride and determination as if a real enemy threatened from above.

But for Saint-Simon, the most memorable display occurred, not in the foray below, but three paces before him: the unprecedented effrontery and disgusting familiarity exhibited by the former royal governess toward the mighty, imperious Sun King.[5] This "spectacle which the King presented to his entire army and the huge masses of onlookers" was so vivid and revolting to Saint-Simon "that forty years hence I shall be able to describe it as though it were yesterday:

Mme de Maintenon sat there in her sedan-chair, facing the plain and the troops, with the three glass windows closed. On the left-hand shaft sat [Adelaide]; behind her, forming a semicircle, stood [the king's daughters]. By the right-hand window was the King, standing . . . His hat was off most of the time, and every now and then he bent to speak to Mme de Maintenon through the glass, explaining what was going on and the reasons for each maneuver. Whenever he did so she was sufficiently polite to lower the window four or five inches, never so far as halfway, for I noticed particularly, and I must admit to having been more taken up with this scene than by the movements of the troops. Occasionally she opened the window first to ask the King some question, but most often it was he who first leaned down to give her information, not waiting for her to address him; but sometimes when she paid no attention he rapped the glass to make her open. He did not speak to anyone else, save to give orders . . . and sometimes answered [Adelaide], who tried hard to persuade him to speak to her. Mme de Maintenon pointed things out to her and communicated in sign language from time to time through the front window, but did not open that, and the young princesse screamed back a few words in reply . . . [The king] bent to talk and the continual stooping must have made his back ache considerably.

Saint-Simon's hatred for Mme de Maintenon, rooted in his contempt for her base origin, and his resentment for the honors so unsuitably bestowed upon her reached monumental proportions following this imagined slight to his monarch's dignity. But his credibility is strained as he describes the witnessing courtiers: "All had the same expression of ill-concealed apprehension and shamed astonishment . . . All were acutely embarrassed"; and still more farfetched is the purported reaction of the army in the field far below: "It was the same with those in the plains; even the soldiers asked about the sedan-chair, so it became necessary to silence the officers and discreetly prevent the troops from asking questions." Saint-Simon's final pronouncement — "You may imagine the effect upon the foreigners . . . All Europe heard of it, and the incident was as much talked of as the Camp itself" — is hyperbolic; the courts of Europe had buzzed with speculations on the French king's inexplicable attachment to this quondam governess for well over a decade by the time of the camp at Compiègne and such behavior was hardly newsworthy any longer.

Petty outrage apart, the day was enormously successful, and by late afternoon, the fortress of Compiègne fell (as prearranged) to the victorious duc de Bourgogne. The young heir to the throne derived "great pleasure and much profit" from the whole adventure, though in the final presentation still to be made, the prince's military education was very nearly thwarted by a surprising, almost comical incident of pride and human willfulness.

The closing event of the camp was "a pitched battle of all arms." Bourgogne, assisted by Boufflers, took to the field in opposition to the marquis de Rosen (later maréchal). The arrangement, of course, was that the prince's side should carry the day, but in midbattle, owing to some misunderstanding, the opposing army found itself in an unexpectedly favorable position. Rosen, who was understandably less than thrilled with orders to lose, rallied his troops so successfully that the tables were turned, and the king was at last obliged to send him a direct order to retire from the field. Louis XIV was much amused by the incident, and wryly remarked, "The Marquis de Rosen apparently does not care to be beaten!" For Bourgogne, it was the finest exercise in the entire program, a delicious taste of the martial glories he felt certain one day awaited.

The camp at Compiègne was slowly dismantled, and as the summer ebbed, the king returned to Versailles, as delighted with his grandchildren's performances and their growing aptitude as he was with the general success of his military demonstration. These protracted maneuvers at Compiègne stood out far above the other *grands divertissements* of the reign — for lavishness, if not downright prodigality. Historians fond of neatly packaging the risings and fallings of power have marked the Peace of 1697 as the beginning of Louis XIV's "sunset": but as accurate as this assessment might seem three centuries later, it was by no means apparent to the Sun King's contemporaries. Unquestionably, the tacit objective of the Compiègne camp was achieved: all Europe was impressed and intimidated by the undiminished strength of the Grand Army. The political buzzards hovering over the wasted Carlos of Spain could no longer view his early demise so desirable, nor could they contemplate the inevitable scramble for his throne with the same confidence they had felt only a month before. Compromise and coalition, however ill fated, now became crucial to the balance of power. Ironically, it was Louis XIV himself — at Compiègne — who cemented the Grand Alliance bent on destroying his continental hegemony.[6]

10

Youthful Desires

THE CLOSING YEARS of the seventeenth century were the happiest of Marie Adelaide's life. Her future was settled, her destiny assured — although she was not the kind to reflect gravely on an intangible tomorrow. In the delicious today, her smallest wish was granted, her slightest desire satisfied.

While her primary occupation remained making Louis XIV happy, marriage and age increased her ceremonial obligations. The added exposure brought an end to the novelty of the little princesse of Savoy. The court was growing used to its future mistress, and the faultfinders slowly emerged, to no one's great surprise. Transformed into the duchesse de Bourgogne, defacto queen of Versailles, Adelaide had become a public personage, the newest slave to the all-demanding etiquette. This relentless master had small regard for age: be she twelve or twenty, the heir's wife was expected to maintain her own court and, at all times, uphold the solemnity and dignity personified in the first lady of France. Though the success of her first *cercle* had been less than overwhelming, the new duchess obligingly began her weekly receptions. She presided with good-natured resignation, her demeanor improving markedly with repetition, but her inexperience, her ignorance of the convolutions and endless regulations of protocol, gave rise on more than one occasion to social blunder — petty from our perspective, but of vital import at the court of the Sun King.

One afternoon, the princesse held a reception for the wife of the new Dutch ambassador, Mme de Heemskerke, who arrived at the Salon of

Nobles accompanied by her sixteen-year-old daughter. As etiquette decreed, Adelaide bestowed a kiss upon the envoy's wife, but when the daughter suddenly offered her cheek for the same royal salute, the startled princesse looked to the duchesse du Lude to discover the required response. Lude shook her head no, but M. de Sainctot, the king's *introducteur des ambassadeurs* (motivated, it appears, by the desire either to advance the social prestige of the Heemskerke family or to embarrass the king's new granddaughter), pushed the Dutch girl forward and barked at the princesse, "Kiss her, madame. It is required." Adelaide went crimson and, terrified of causing a scene, quickly complied.

The triumphant Sainctot next escorted his guests to Madame's apartments. The ceremony of reception was repeated and once again the young girl stepped forward to be kissed. But Madame, who was far better versed in the minutiae of etiquette than young Adelaide, and who was obsessed with her own rank and prerogative, drew back haughtily. Sainctot persisted, playing his trump card: "Mme la duchesse de Bourgogne has just honored Mlle de Heemskerke with a kiss." "So much the worse," sniffed Madame. "Because you have made her commit a blunder, you will not make me follow her in it." The story raced through the circles of Versailles, Madame's smug satisfaction quite equal to Adelaide's embarrassment.

Not long afterward, the princesse received the English ambassador, Lord Jersey. As preordained, she sat in a solitary armchair at the center of a large semicircle of backless seats, called taborets. The stools on her right — the seats of honor — had been usurped by high-ranking duchesses before the ceremony had commenced, and the royal princesses, arriving fashionably late, had been forced to take their place at Adelaide's left. Last to enter the room was the princesse d'Harcourt, a proud and arrogant old woman, once a celebrated coquette, now "a great fat creature, with a mottled complexion, ugly thick lips, and hair like tow." Finding no seat available on either side, the old princesse furiously stalked up to the duchesse de Rohan, sitting modestly among the other duchesses, and demanded her seat. Rohan respectfully declined to move — whereupon the cantankerous d'Harcourt, with a strength that belied her age, plucked the startled duchess from her seat, wheeled her around, and plopped down in her place.

Marie Adelaide watched this disgraceful spectacle from her royal chair with alarm, but so intimidating was the old princesse that she dared not speak a word; her silence was taken by the spectators to condone d'Harcourt's inexcusable behavior. The offended duchesse de Rohan complained to Louis XIV, and the king demanded a public apology.[1] But the damage, already done, was irremediable: the outraged gossips of Versailles laid full responsibility on the shoulders of the duchesse de Bourgogne, "who had not found word or gesture to rebuke the erring woman."

But Adelaide's embarrassment was more than compensated for by the Sun King. Like Ariste, in Molière's *School for Husbands,* he lavishly indulged her every whim: "I've continually complied with her youthful desires, and thank Heaven, I don't repent it. [Plays and balls, clothes, linen and new fashion] — these are pleasures we should allow young women when our circumstances can afford it." Louis XIV's circumstances certainly afforded it.

On her arrival, Adelaide had been given the king's fabled menagerie; now, Louis ordered Mansard to renovate the pavilion (just outside the aviary) for the princesse's exclusive use. Marie Adelaide forwarded to Madame Royale the plans for *her* menagerie: "The King has ordered Mansard to spare nothing. Imagine, my dear grandmama, what it will be."

The suite of small rooms around the octagonal salon was entirely done over at a cost of fifty thousand livres. The princesse was allowed to choose all the furnishings herself; the king instructed his architect to brook no other interference, then immediately interfered himself: "Let there be children everywhere." There were no bedrooms in the pavilion, as it was designed purely for entertainment, and the king could not bear his darling to sleep anywhere but under his roof. The menagerie became Adelaide's favorite retreat. In the newly created kitchens and pantries, she relived her childhood at the Vigna, baking pies, making cheeses and butter for the king's table. She fed and tended the baby animals, and played endless rounds of blind man's buff; best of all, she held private tea parties just for herself and Grandpapa. "It is true that the King's kindnesses to me are wonderful; but I love him well also."

Her letters to Savoy during this period make plain Adelaide's enchantment with her new life. Comically, much of each letter is devoted to reasons why she doesn't write much in the first place, but her brief notes were treasured none the less in Turin: "Versailles, 13 February 1698: I hope, my dear grandmama, that the Marquis de Ciré [a Savoyard noble sent by Victor Amadeus to congratulate Louis XIV on the wedding celebrations] will tell you agreeable things of this country, and partly of myself, who have a great desire to please you. I envy the pleasure that he will have in giving you an account of everything; you will have no difficulty in understanding how happy I am. My only desire is that it will long continue . . ."

"28 February 1698: I hope to remedy, when I have learned how to write properly, the faults which I now commit, and to make you understand then, my dear grandmother, that I write to you seldom, because I write very badly, but that I do not love you less tenderly. I am going to the ball . . ."

December brought Adelaide's thirteenth birthday, her first wedding anniversary (which she neglected to mention to Madame Royale), and feverish preparations for Christmas court, but no cessation of pleasure for the teenaged princesse: "9 December 1698: I could not write you by the last courier, my dear grandmama, because I am out continually, and every evening I go to see the King. I am sure that this excuse will not displease you, and that you will think that my time is well employed, when I spend it with the King. His kindness to me cannot be expressed, and since I know the interest you take in my happiness, I am very pleased to assure you it is perfect . . ."

Duchess Anne Marie received similar reassurances: "16 December: I do not dare to tell you, my dear mama, that I could not have the pleasure of writing to you sooner, because I have very little time to myself. I am shown every day something new and beautiful. The King continues his kindness to me, and I am very happy. Love me always I beg you, and be assured of my respect for you."

"The King" dominates Adelaide's correspondence, just as he dominated her life. It is interesting to note that over this two-year period, her husband's name appears only once: "10 January 1699: . . . I am not yet free enough with the duc de Bourgogne to do the honors of him. I am only pleased that you are satisfied with his letter." Yet this comes as no surprise, for the marriage had virtually no effect on their respective routines. Six weeks after the wedding, Louis XIV had proudly boasted to the Savoyard ambassador: "The marriage goes better and better. The young couple are now in love, and their love will increase when they are put together"; but as Adelaide's own words reveal, the old king saw just what he wished to see.

The young duke and duchess continued to live apart, the only change being that Bourgogne was now permitted to visit his wife daily and talk to her "without restraint," provided that one of her ladies remained in the room. Three times a week they dined together informally with Mme de Maintenon. However comforting the bride may have found these perpetual chaperones, the groom, whose Bourbon blood was no less passionate than his forefathers', soon chafed with impatience.

At an age when both his father and grandfather had begun their sexual educations, Bourgogne was still chaste. Even more, as his confessor, Père Martineau, wrote: "He has not yet been known to succumb to the ordinary vice of youth." The prince was extremely bashful, Martineau observed: "Always modest in his looks, always reserved in his speech, his conduct is based on the maxim of Tertullian: 'To be chaste is not enough. One must look chaste.' One of the lords who has seen him most often and most intimately assures me that the modesty of the most virtuous of ladies excels not that of the Prince."

But patience is not a quality often found in adolescents, even in the most virtuous of princes, and all too soon this true grandson of Louis XIV found himself an opportunity. Enlisting the aid of a sympathetic waiting woman, Mme Quentin, Bourgogne hid himself one evening behind the thickly brocaded curtains in his wife's bedchamber. Allowing time for the watchful Lude to fall asleep, the ardent young husband emerged from hiding and approached the object of his desires. But the vigilant governess woke instantly, and after a severe tongue-lashing, the prince was ordered back to his own bedroom. The next morning brought a summons to the king's study, and Bourgogne had no delusions as to the purpose of the interview. Louis XIV appraised the fidgeting boy for a long silent moment, then spoke gently, but firmly: "I have ascertained, monsieur, that something has happened which might be injurious to your health; I must beg you not to let it occur again." The red-faced prince protested that his health had never been better, but nonetheless promised to observe the king's wishes; inwardly he could not resist the bitter reflection that at sixteen his grandfather had not been similarly inhibited, for reasons of health or otherwise.

Clearly some outlet had to be found. The standard royal remedy — an older, instructive mistress — was unthinkable to the pious young prince. He began to hunt daily with his father, and capped the long hours of the chase with furious sets of tennis. He developed bold skills at cross-country riding for, despite his unprepossessing appearance in the saddle, he was an expert horseman. One day, while trying out a new mount in the company of his undergovernor, M. de L'Echelle, and several members of his suite, Bourgogne took to the high road from

Versailles to Paris and raced without a stop as far as Sèvres. There he cried passionately, "Let him who loves me follow!" At an even more rapid pace, he galloped on, soon outdistancing all his companions. Arriving at the gates of Paris, he slowed to allow his horse to breathe and discovered himself alone. Nonplussed, he turned and rode back to Versailles — having covered more than ten leagues in less than ninety minutes.

Study, both religious and secular, served too in distracting the passions of young manhood. He came to regard the strict rules of prayer, fasting, and above all, conduct — established by the Church of Rome — as his only hope for salvation, his defense against his two great failings: exaggerated pride (imagined, thanks to Fénelon) and lust (real, thanks to Adelaide). He was not so bad as he imagined himself to be, and certainly no worse than any other boy in the awkward teen years. But Fénelon had so developed his conscience that slowly, inexorably, he became its abject slave; as Père Martineau commented, "Those who hitherto had regarded his pious exercises as mere childish devotions found in [them] their own refutation, and those who had feared that his entry into the married state might cause him to change his conduct found reason for relief."

Even without the inspiring presence of Fénelon, Bourgogne studied diligently. His new favorite was political philosophy; in preparation for his destiny, he read and analyzed Plato's *Republic*. His thirst for knowledge was unquenchable, and the duc de Beauvilliers hit upon a novel idea that won the king's wholehearted endorsement: orders were dispatched to the intendants throughout the kingdom to send the prince detailed reports on transportation, manufacture, and agricultural production in the districts under their jurisdiction. They speedily complied. Endowed with tireless (and understandable) energy, a passion for detail, and an astonishing memory, Bourgogne absorbed this stupendous mass of statistical information and displayed, before the king and court, so astounding a mastery of this knowledge that one retired nobleman, the comte de Boulainvilliers, wrote: "Word has reached me already, buried deep in the country, of the rare gifts of the Duc de Bourgogne . . . When I learned that all the intendants in the kingdom were ordered to send him an exact report . . . and that he himself framed the questions, I must confess that my heart leapt with hope for the future."

While Bourgogne worked, Adelaide played. There was less and less time for Saint-Cyr; court functions increasingly demanded her attendance, but so too did the many amusements available to a young married woman.

Versailles had come to life again. For fifteen years Mme de Maintenon's austerity had cast a gloom over the royal pleasure palace; the disillusioned old king, grown virtuous with advancing age, had adopted an air of piety in deference to his secret wife; the nobility, ever ready to emulate their master, had quickly turned Versailles into "a Court of repentant old men and pious dowagers." Then young Adelaide, gay and reckless, irrepressible and always in motion, changed everything. The darkness shrouding the palace was thrown off; laughing voices rang once more through the great mirrored galleries, the gardens and groves. Men and women, especially the latter, who had so recently complained that Versailles was a monastery in court dress now flocked eagerly to sample its delights and pleasures.

Louis XIV welcomed this "renaissance" of Versailles, and the next five years saw tremendous redecoration of his monument to absolutism. Considering himself too old to begin a major construction project — the creation of a new and larger chapel, begun in 1699, was scarcely on the level of a Marly, let alone Versailles — Louis contented himself with extensive interior redesign. New marble fireplaces materialized, and with them new tapestries, mirrors, and painted ceilings. The king's apartments were reapportioned and enlarged, and the Grand Salon (at the apex of the palace, overlooking the Marble Courtyard) was made into the royal bedchamber: for the ceiling of his new bedroom, Louis XIV ordered the creation of "a richly ornamented mosaic ground, in the middle of which a beautiful figure representing France would be seated on trophies beneath a rich canopy attached at the top and held at the corners by genii, and the corners of the ceiling adorned with figures of Fame."

At his private retreat, the Trianon in the Versailles park, the king created an entirely new apartment for himself (his third there), adjacent to those of Mme de Maintenon and Marie Adelaide; significantly, Bourgogne, his brothers, and his father continued to live in the opposite wing.

In the palace gardens, men worked day and night, clearing new paths, planting new trees and shrubs, and recreating whole sections of the park; Madame wrote that it seemed each morning as if the fairies themselves had been at work. One new grove was christened in Adelaide's honor, and other alterations were made solely for her pleasure. Two courses were laid for *mail* (the precursor of golf) because the princesse was fond of the sport. The game had long since passed out of fashion at Versailles, but predictably, once Adelaide was observed playing it with the king and Monseigneur, it became the latest rage.

The restrictions on entertainments previously held unsuitable were slowly relaxed. On October 30, 1698, Adelaide and Bourgogne, with the ducs d'Anjou and Berri, drove to Paris for their first visit to the Comédie Française, where they were treated to a performance of *Le Bourgeois Gentilhomme*. Doubtless much of Molière's biting social satire was lost on these innocents; nevertheless, Madame informed her aunt, the childlike rapture in the royal box was a delight for the entire theater: "The Duc de Bourgogne quite lost his eyes; the Duc d'Anjou was so delighted that he sat in ecstasies, with his mouth wide open; the Duc de Berri laughed so much that he nearly fell off his chair." As for Adelaide, who Madame observed "understands better how to disguise her feelings," she "controlled herself very well at the beginning, laughed but little, and contented herself with smiling; but now and then, she forgot herself, and rose from her chair in order to see better. She was also very amusing in her way."

To further his daughter-in-law's artistic tastes, Monseigneur (an ardent patron) escorted the princesse in early January on her first visit to the Paris Opéra, where she heard *Le Carnival de Venise;* while she professed having enjoyed the spectacle, opera never captured Adelaide's imagination in the same way as drama. A few weeks later, she attended her first serious play — Racine's *Bajazet* — and was so enthusiastic that Grandpapa declared henceforth she could go to the theater as often as she liked.

This permission was further (though hardly needed) proof of the king's inability to deny the princesse anything, because Louis XIV's mistrust of actors had trebled following a disgraceful incident two years earlier. A troupe of Italian players had settled in Paris several years before and, against the urgings of the more reactionary element at court, the king had tolerated the ensemble, "as long as they keep the butt of their overflow of filth and profanity to their own kind." But in 1697, the troupe gambled with a play entitled *The False Prude* — a great gamble indeed, since the title role was a thinly veiled caricature of Mme de Maintenon.

Predictably, all Paris rushed to see it, but the king — and certainly his wife — had been pushed too far. At the end of the fourth performance of *The False Prude* a royal warrant arrived declaring the immediate closure of the theater and ordering the entire troupe to leave the kingdom within one month. Saint-Simon, with his obsessive hatred for Maintenon, laid all responsibility for this censorship at her door: "There was quite a fuss, and although the players lost their establishment through boldness and folly, she who had them banished won nothing, because of the talk that surrounded such a ridiculous event." But the husband's indignation was no less than his wife's, nor had any measure been taken without his absolute consent. The vibrant young king who had encouraged Racine and defended Molière from the outraged clergy had long since quit the stage of France; the religious, narrow-minded old monarch in his place made it perfectly clear he would brook no criticism or parody.

Yet Adelaide adored the theater — therefore drama flourished anew. The king wanted to spare his darling the inconvenience of a long carriage ride to Paris, so troupes were frequently summoned to Versailles for command performances. During the annual autumn stay at Fontainebleau in 1699, plays were performed every evening, to the delight of the princesse. Not that she attended each performance: Dangeau noted the absence of the duc and duchesse de Bourgogne at one Sunday presentation. "They never go to the play on Sundays," he explained tersely, with no doubt just whose idea that was. The pious boy on the verge of manhood, slowly assuming responsibility for himself and his wife, plainly intended to be master in his own house (though, technically speaking, he didn't have one).

A logical outgrowth from this passion for theater was Adelaide's brief career as an actress. It began at Sceaux, the country home of the duc and duchesse du Maine. Anne Louise Benedicte de Bourbon, wife of the king's bastard son and of royal blood herself (her father was Louis XIV's cousin, the mad prince de Condé), was a tiny woman with an enormous ego. She eschewed the court at Versailles, feeling her position there less than she deserved; at Sceaux she could and did reign as queen. The fairyland she created was a world of magic and romance, where guests marveled at the ingenious and endless rounds of amusement provided by their indefatigable hostess — all springing from Anne Louise's absolute terror of being alone, even for a few minutes. The fairy duchess fancied herself an actress (though contemporary report makes plain the fact that this was just one more of her delusions), and with no effort at all, she persuaded her young niece to join her in the insipid romances she found so inspiring.

In the fine tradition of the theater, Adelaide began with walk-ons and minor roles, but the roar of applause and the fulsome flattery of courtier spectators quickly turned the young girl's head, and in no time at all she was demanding larger parts. Louis XIV and Mme de Maintenon watched this budding career with trepidation: how could they allow the wife of the heir to the throne to continue prancing about the stage at Sceaux, where *the public* was permitted? Their remedy was logical, if characteristically extravagant: a private theater was erected in Mme de Maintenon's apartments at Versailles.

It was inaugurated on December 5, 1699, with a performance of *Johathas,* a "devotional play" in three acts written by a protégé of Maintenon's, Duché de Vancy. The cast, if not professional, was certainly illustrious: supporting Marie Adelaide was her old friend Françoise d'Aubigné, together with the comte d'Ayen and other members of the distinguished de Noailles family. The audience, no less august, consisted of the king, Mme de Maintenon, Monseigneur, and the duchesse du Lude. The applause of so small an assembly was not enough to satisfy the starstruck princesse, and a second performance was scheduled for the officers of the Bourgogne households and the remaining members of the royal family — except Bourgogne, who could not be induced to attend. From what Dangeau wrote after this second performance we get a fair idea of Adelaide's talents — or more accurately, from what he did *not* write; he dissected the play in great detail and described the reactions of the audience, including the king ("very touched"); he had high praise for the acting abilities of d'Aubigné and d'Ayen; and he said *not one word* about Marie Adelaide. Modern critics would not have been so kind, but then modern actresses do not call kings Grandpapa.

The princesse must have gleaned that her talents were less than exceptional, for she decided not to perform again for two years. When at last she did appear onstage, it was in the tragedy *Absalom,* also by Duché de Vancy. This production was approached with far more seriousness than the first: the cast rehearsed for over a month, coached by the celebrated actor Michel Baron. *Absalom* was presented on January 19, 1702, for an audience of forty — the king and Mme de Maintenon, the royal family, and honored members of their households. The comte d'Ayen played the title role; Françoise d'Aubigné was his wife, Thares; Monsieur's son, the duc de Chartres, took the small part of David, and Adelaide, wearing a magnificent dress covered with crown jewels, appeared as Absalom's daughter. The evening was a great success. Mme de Maintenon wrote that she cried like a fool, and that the king had great difficulty in holding back his own tears. "Although the subject was the death of Absalom, they changed one or two things to make it more pathetic. For instance, they pretended that he returned to die before the King in the presence of his wife and child." Once again, d'Aubigné was praised for her thespian talents; once again, Adelaide's performance was virtually ignored, save for Maintenon's trenchant observation "[She] is better in serious plays than in comedies."

Apparently the princesse concurred: for her next project, she chose to revive Racine's *Athalie*, written a decade earlier for the girls at Saint-Cyr. Mme de Chailly, who had played the title role at the school, was invited to repeat her performance; d'Ayen once again was given the male lead, Joad. Françoise d'Aubigné was originally slated to play Josabeth and Marie Adelaide the much smaller role of Salomith, when suddenly the princesse developed an aversion to rehearsals, and declared that she found the play "too cold." Mme de Maintenon divined the real cause of her discontent: she held a conference with her niece Françoise, and the two girls switched roles. Thereafter, Adelaide maintained that *Athalie* was "a very fine play."

The first performance was at Versailles on February 14, 1702. Backstage jitters were abnormally high: the large audience included not only the king, Mme de Maintenon, and the royal family, but a correspondent from the newspaper *Le Mercure de France*. In his subsequent review, the "impartial" reporter showed himself a true courtier, for surely stage fright has never been so generously excused: "The Duchesse de Bourgogne played Josabel [*sic*] with all the grace and the intelligence imaginable . . . her performance was joined to a certain timidity, which ought perhaps to be accounted modesty, rather than nervousness."

Two additional performances of *Athalie* were offered, but the closing of the play brought an end to Adelaide's stage career. Perhaps she had grown tired of watching her efforts eclipsed by the more talented d'Aubigné. Perhaps she could no longer ignore the indifference of her family: Louis XIV attended all her performances, but no longer pretended any great enthusiasm; pious Bourgogne would *not* attend, even out of loyalty to his wife; and Mme de Maintenon, picking up her martyr's pen, complained to the princesse des Ursines: "You take too much trouble to please them; it is not worthwhile. You also try to do these things too well, too richly, with too much regard for the great ones . . . What a bore everything becomes!" When Maintenon insisted the theater be dismantled — she objected to the havoc it created in her precise and ordered household — Adelaide did not demur. Watching plays was just as much fun as being in them, and at Versailles there were alternatives aplenty for satisfying youthful desires.

As the princesse was now allowed to attend the theater, the ban was lifted on balls and masquerades. Louis XIV celebrated her thirteenth birthday with a *bal masqué* in the Hall of Mirrors. Adelaide and her ladies appeared dressed as the nine Muses; the Sun King deemed himself either too old or too regal to come in costume, so it was left to Bourgogne to adopt his grandfather's favorite guise, the god Apollo. Watching his heirs as they dipped and swayed in precise choreographic patterns, the old king recalled the days of his radiant youth, when *he* was Apollo, performing the same steps for the admiration of La Vallière and the scintillating Montespan, days when the promise of a glorious future still lay before him. Now he sat complacently with his secret wife, content, for one evening, to surrender center stage to his grandchildren.

Because of Adelaide's passion for dancing, balls — masked or otherwise — again became the rage at Versailles, and the court rushed to curry her favor with innumerable galas. The elaborate entertainments they devised were carefully tailored to the interests of the child-woman they honored. One typical party, given by the king's son-in-law, M. le duc, on his estate at Saint-Maurice, began with a merry-go-round with gilded horses, where grabbing the golden ring brought exquisite and expensive prizes — in this Dangeau noted that Adelaide "enjoyed herself exceedingly." The party next moved indoors for a round of games, followed by a concert of operatic selections. M. le duc provided an impressive supper for his guests and arranged a lottery in which everyone held a winning ticket.[2] Dancing went on till five in the morning, when at last the little princesse was persuaded to start for home.

On the road, she was suddenly struck with the desire to visit the marketplace of Les Halles in Paris, to see the fresh produce arriving from the country. Then she stopped at the Church of Saint-Eustache to hear mass — a move more practical than pious, since it excused her from noon mass at Versailles and allowed her to sleep in. At last the royal carriage clattered into the cobblestone courtyard of the palace, and Adelaide ran upstairs to the king's apartments, waking him with a good-morning kiss and sitting on his bed as she described the pleasures of the night before. Grandpapa was patently enchanted, but neither time nor etiquette stood still: Lude was summoned to collect her charge, and as Louis XIV began his day with the ritual *lever*, Marie Adelaide ended hers — at least until four or five in the afternoon.

Her professed weakness was for masked balls, and she spent hours planning costumes for herself and her friends or practicing the complicated court dances with Dangeau and her ladies. Exotic costumery fired her imagination, and on one occasion gave vent to her budding royal megalomania. The morning before a costume ball given in her honor, Marie Adelaide sent her coach to fetch her confessor, Père Lecomte. The priest arrived, assuming the princesse required absolution. "No, Father, you must design me a Chinese lady's dress. I know you lived there, and I want to wear it tonight." Taken aback, Lecomte insisted that he was ill-equipped to comply with her request, that he had dealt more with the men of China than the women, that his expertise was in salvation not fashion. But Adelaide, unaccustomed to being crossed, persisted: that evening, she appeared in an "authentic" costume, designed by the clergyman turned couturier.

The most spectacular entertainments, naturally, were those presented by the king. An unusually large number of balls were given during the winter carnival season of 1699. In late January, Louis XIV provided two celebrations within one week at Versailles; these were but preludes to the extravaganza he offered at Marly, beginning on February 4. To indulge the princesse, he had vast numbers of costumes brought from Paris, and placed at the disposal of his guests. *Le Mercure,* which noted later that "nothing was wanting to please the eye, delight the ear, or gratify the taste," reported that the revelers changed their disguises four and five times in the course of the evening.

The masked ball began at ten o'clock, and Madame described its unique opening: "A lady broad as a tower entered the ballroom. It was the Duc de Valentinois, Monsieur de Monaco's son, who is immensely tall, wearing a cloak right down to his feet. In the middle of the room, it flew open, and out sprang Harlequin, Scaramouche, Punchinello, and all the other characters from the Italian comedies. M. de Brionne was Harlequin, my son [the duc de Chartres] Punchinello, the Duc de Bourgogne was the Doctor." The dauphin arrived with another party of stock commedia dell'arte types, while Adelaide appeared in "a beautiful fancy dress, in the gay Spanish fashion, with a tiny little cap."

The dancing went on till two in the morning, but the party, far from ending, began afresh at sundown the next evening, and the zany antics continued:

At half past seven, maskers with guitars appeared, dancing the opening scene of an opera. It was my son, the Comte d'Ayen, Prince Camille, and M. de La Vallière in ridiculous male attire . . . The Dauphin, M. d'Antin, and M. de Brionne came dressed as ladies, in dressing gowns and shawls, and with towering edifices of blonde hair, much higher than usually worn. These three gentlemen are almost the same height; they wore quite small black and red masks with patches, and danced with high kicking steps. D'Antin kicked so hard that he upset M. de Brionne, who fell on his bottom at the feet of the Queen of England. You may imagine what a shout of laughter that caused.

The silliness was infectious: the waggish duc de Berri disappeared from the ballroom, returned disguised as Baron de La Crasse (Baron of Filth), and regaled the crowd with a comic solo dance.

The approach of Lent signaled the traditional end of carnival madness. Then as spring gave way to warm summer weather, the court moved outdoors for its amusements.

Since Adelaide enjoyed fishing, it quite expectedly came into fashion again. She also delighted in summer water parties, and in his journal, Dangeau described one such evening, June 10, 1699, at Trianon: "At six o'clock in the evening, the King entered the gardens, and after promenading for some time, took a seat on the terrace which overlooked the canal . . . Monseigneur was in a gondola, with the Duc de Bourgogne and the princesse de Conti. The Duchesse de Bourgogne was in another, with the ladies whom she had chosen; the Duchesse de Chartres and Mme la Duchesse in others. All the King's musicians were on a yacht. The King remained until eight o'clock, listening to the music." Old Louis XIV was no longer the center of every party, and his retiring no longer brought an end to the festivities. "When the King re-entered the château, the gondolas went to the end of the canal, and the party did not return till suppertime." The king had originally planned to join Adelaide in her golden barge, but rheumatism and his doctor changed his mind, "although the weather was very fine . . . Monseigneur and the Duchesse de Bourgogne walked in the gardens and on the terrace above the château till after midnight, when Monseigneur went to bed, and the Duchesse entered a gondola with some of her ladies, and remained on the canal till sunrise." Reluctant still to bring an end to the party, Adelaide insisted on staying up until Mme de Maintenon left for Saint-Cyr at seven — only then did she consent to go to bed, "without appearing the least fatigued by so long a vigil."

These nocturnal escapades continued through the summer. Adelaide would rise well past five in the afternoon, then run to Mme de Maintenon's apartments where Grandpapa awaited. When the king was compelled to return to the business of government, the young princesse blithely trotted down to the canal, where a row of pretty colored tents had been pitched for her use, and passed the night with swimming, dancing, and card games, returning to the palace as the first rays of sunlight warmed the sky.

Certainly the governess in Mme de Maintenon objected to such behavior, but if she worried over its effects, she kept her own counsel: a happy Adelaide meant a happy Louis XIV, and the king's secret wife had no intention of upsetting the balance.

Best of all possible treats for the pampered princesse, her avowed "favorite happiness," was hunting with the king. At Marly, during the last summer of the seventeenth century, Louis XIV presented Adelaide with a hunting costume of red velvet with gold facings. The princesse was so thrilled by her appearance in this riding habit that she commissioned a portrait of herself wearing it. The king (and even more, Mme de Maintenon) considered her still too young to ride with the hounds on her own horse; beside the old Sun King in his two-seat chariot, Marie Adelaide would race for hours through the forests outside Marly and Fontainebleau, free from the restraints of etiquette and expected only to make the king smile. These privileged excursions were such fun that, on one occasion, Adelaide successfully concealed a painful toothache for fear of missing the day's hunt — and returned to the palace with a raging fever.

"She was the planner and center of every diversion; all were given for her, and the King enjoyed them only in so far as they gave her pleasure." The words were written by Mme de La Fayette in 1670, describing Minette, but they could have just as easily been written for Minette's granddaughter, for by the close of the century, Adelaide's ascendancy over Louis XIV was at its apex. Their closeness was apparent to all Versailles, as Sourches recorded: "The King entertains for her all the affection and all the kindness which it is possible to conceive." Now Louis XIV never passed a day without seeing his precious darling: if he were confined to his bed, Adelaide was immediately sent for, and when her frequent toothaches kept her in her rooms, he returned the courtesy. They walked or drove together every day, and when the time approached for their afternoon excursion, it mattered not in the least to the princesse if the king was closeted with his ministers or involved in important affairs of state. Ignoring the feeble protests of the royal usher, she would boldly knock on the council chamber door, and Louis would abruptly dismiss his advisers, lest his young companion be kept waiting.

The court, whose respect for the person and the presence of the king bordered on veneration, was amazed — and sometimes scandalized — by Adelaide's flippant attitude toward the master of France. One afternoon she chattered by the fire with Maintenon as the king worked quietly across the room. Anne Stuart had recently ascended the throne of England, and speculation on her character was high. Adelaide ventured her opinion: "*Ma tante,* it cannot be denied that England is better governed under a queen than under a king, and do you know why? Because under a king, a country is really ruled by women, and under a queen, by men." No one else would have had such audacity, but Adelaide had taught Louis XIV to laugh again — and privately, at least, to laugh at himself.

The results of unfettered indulgence are inevitable, though surprisingly neither Louis XIV nor Mme de Maintenon appear to have given much thought to the effect on the princesse's character. Adelaide, vivacious and impressionable, was all too human — the king's attention and the endless flatteries of the court quite naturally went to her head. Her manners — the modesty and courtesy that had inspired such admiration at the time of her arrival in France — deteriorated with alarming speed; the enchanting little girl was fast becoming an insufferably spoiled adolescent.

It was the critical Madame (who else?) who first observed the detrimental effects of such leniency. As early as September 18, 1698, she complained to her aunt, the electress of Hanover, that the king and Mme de Maintenon were "absolutely spoiling the Princesse. When she goes for a drive, she does not remain in her place for a moment, but seats herself upon the knees of all who happen to be in the same coach, and jumps about like a little monkey. All this is considered charming."

Nor were Madame's criticisms confined to Adelaide's public deportment: "In her own apartments, she is absolute mistress, and people do everything she wishes. Sometimes she takes it into her head to go and ramble about the gardens at five o'clock in the morning.[3] Everything is permitted and admired. Any other person would give his child a whipping if she behaved in this way. A time will come, I am sure, when they will regret having allowed this child to act just as she pleases."

Madame's disgust did not wane and Adelaide showed no signs of improvement. On October 22 she wrote: "*Mon Dieu!* How badly in my opinion is the Princesse being brought up! This child makes me pity her. In the middle of dinner, she begins to sing, she dances on her chair, pretends to bow to the servants, makes the most hideous grimaces, tears the chickens and partridges on the dishes with her hands, thrusts her fingers into the sauces. In short, it is impossible to be worse brought up, and those who stand behind her exclaim, 'What grace she has! How pretty she is!' "

Others, too, complained of Adelaide's behavior, and those who earlier had criticized her indifference to and ignorance of proper etiquette now discovered more serious failings. The princesse de Conti and Mme la duchesse found their nephew's wife unbearably irritating and rude: what right had this presumptuous girl to address the dauphin in the familiar instead of the polite? Mme la duchesse complained — with some justification — that while Adelaide could steal a horse, *she* got into trouble for even looking over a hedge. Mme de Sévigné's correspondent Mme de Coulanges deplored the spiraling extravagances inspired at court by the new duchess: "The King wishes the Duchesse de Bourgogne to do from morning till night just as the fancy takes her. It is enough for him if she enjoys herself. Her life is all excursions to Marly or Meudon or drives to Paris and back for balls, operas, and masques, with the courtiers at daggers to win her favor. Those ladies who take part in these diversions need to have their purses well-lined, for the expense is quadrupled."

Even more serious was the duchesse de Bourgogne's increasing inability to conceal her dislikes. In the case of the old princesse d'Harcourt, few courtiers would have disagreed with Adelaide's feelings — no one, least of all the princesse, had forgotten d'Harcourt's disgraceful scene at Lord Jersey's reception when she had forced the duchesse de Rohan from her seat. But Adelaide's revulsion for the fat, ugly princesse grew so obsessive that she persecuted the old woman in a barrage of practical jokes, many of them on the far side of safety. One evening at Meudon, Adelaide and her ladies invaded d'Harcourt's bedchamber and pelted the sleeping woman with snowballs; later during that visit, she made twenty Swiss Guards report to d'Harcourt's room just before dawn — each beating a kettledrum. At Marly, she had the garden outside d'Harcourt's guest suite lined with petards — the victim approached in her sedan chair and, as the bombs began exploding around her, the forewarned footmen dropped the chair and left the old princesse screaming in terror.

The court laughed conspiratorially at these obnoxious pranks, but it was baffled by Adelaide's growing aversion to the duchesse du Lude. The beautiful governess, with her charm and her perfect manners, had guided the little princesse through the labyrinth of court life loyally and ably, and heretofore had received total courtesy and cooperation. Now the adolescent wife found her duenna a nuisance and made no effort to conceal her distaste; her predawn escapades into the Versailles gardens more often than not were merely to vex the conscientious Lude, whose anxious calls in the still night air went maliciously unanswered. Mme Dunnoyer, one of Adelaide's attendants, felt the princesse was irritated by Lude's fussing, her constant complaints of poor health, and her relentless vigilance; more probably, the teenage girl resented this last figure of authority remaining in her path.

Scorn, bred with arrogance, surfaced in Adelaide's distastes, so completely at odds with her natural inclination to content and excuse. Jérôme Pontchartrain, the chancellor's son, was one more victim of her violent dislike — to the king, she shamelessly referred to him as "your one-eyed monster." One night at the royal table, she made loud, demeaning jokes on the appearance of one particularly homely officer — the poor man, of course, could do nothing but sit in embarrassed silence. At last the king stopped her, barking loudly, "To me he is one of the best-looking men in my kingdom since he is one of the bravest."

Madame did not hesitate to blame Adelaide's teenage rebelliousness on her old adversary, Mme de Maintenon. Conveniently forgetting her earlier criticism of how "politic" the little girl was who ignored all but the king and his secret wife, she now declared that Adelaide's "virtuous mother had brought her up with sound principles, and when she arrived in France she had very good manners, but 'the old slut,' in order to obtain her affections and sole control over her, has allowed the Princesse to have her own way in everything, nor has she exercised any restraint over her caprices."

Adelaide's "virtuous mother" was, after all, Madame's stepdaughter: it is not surprising that at this same time, the princesse's confessor records a letter from Duchess Anne Marie, complaining of the haphazard education her daughter was receiving and expressing her deep concern for Adelaide's future. The king's devotion was all well and good, but what would happen to the princesse after his death? Her headstrong daughter seemed bent on making enemies: "She shows no respect for the people of the Court, but is forever poking fun at them and mocking them." Bourgogne, who in time would be Adelaide's sole support, she still treated with polite indifference. Instead of nurturing his love, she took it for granted; "all her endeavors are turned to pleasing Mme de Maintenon." Here Anne Marie plainly echoes Madame, for her stepmother had remained her major source of information from Versailles. The closeness revealed in their correspondence helps to shed light on the curious fact that, during this period, far more letters exist from Adelaide to her grandmother than to her mother. It has been suggested that much of the latter correspondence was destroyed during the siege of Turin in 1706, though there is no explanation of why Madame Royale's letters did not suffer a similar fate. Rather, there developed a period of estrangement, certainly not uncommon between mothers and adolescent daughters; perhaps, in Adelaide's case, her difficulties with Lude at Versailles and her mother in absentia were really the same rebellion. The princesse found it far easier, and more gratifying, to write to a complacent grandmother than to a reprimanding mother. One particular incident speaks volumes: on April 26, 1699, Anne Marie at last gave birth to a son. Adelaide wrote on May 18: "You have attained the summit of happiness, my dear grandmama, since you find it in having a grandson. Your joy increases mine." No letter to her mother exists. (It must be happily noted here that with the birth of the prince, the happy home life so long denied the suffering Anne Marie was at last realized. Victor Amadeus forsook all extramarital dalliance — the contessa di Verrua left Turin and resettled in France — and remained a faithful and loving husband until his wife's death in 1728.)

Both Madame and her stepdaughter were unfair in exonerating Louis XIV, for much of Mme de Maintenon's well-intentioned discipline was undermined by Grandpapa's indulgence. But Madame vented her criticisms for a reason far larger than merely describing for her family the court life of Versailles: she knew without question that her letters were opened and read before they were posted. Her Hanoverian aunt had once ventured to blame the mail's irregularity on the inclement winter; the fault, Madame retorted, lay not in bad weather, but in bad people. "So as to show me that [my letters] were opened, they mix them all up so much together that it often takes me a quarter of an hour to sort them."[4]

For once, Madame decided to make use of the royal spies and communicate to the king opinions she would never dare say to his face. Apparently her plan succeeded. The king's rebuke at the royal table was not an isolated incident; shortly afterward, Mme de Maintenon recorded another case of royal discipline: "[Adelaide] undertook a piece of work, to execute which she sent for a woman who embroiders, and this woman spent the whole of yesterday with her without [Adelaide's] ever thinking of giving her anything to eat. I asked the woman in the evening if she had eaten; she said no, and I made her dine and sup both. The King . . . reproved the Princesse severely; she tried to laugh at such a matter . . . [but Louis insisted that] the poor woman would not be much pleased to find that while she worked hard, those she worked for let her go hungry."

Eventually, even Madame noticed signs of improvement. When her daughter, Elisabeth Charlotte, left Versailles following her marriage to the duc de Lorraine, Madame was enormously pleased by the sincere grief Adelaide showed at parting: "[She] has at last proved that she is kindhearted, for she was too sad to eat, and did nothing but weep bitterly after she had bidden adieu to her aunt." More important, after dining with the princesse in public that December, she happily informed her aunt that Adelaide "now eats quietly and soberly." Characteristically, she took credit for the change: "My letter did some good, and I am pleased to see that they thought me right."

In the fall of 1699, the young duchesse de Bourgogne was nearing her fourteenth birthday. One afternoon, the duchesse du Lude requested permission to appear before the king while he was meeting in council. She informed His Majesty and his ministers that evidence observed during Adelaide's toilette indicated that she was "now able to conceive." The news spread like wildfire through the halls of Fontainebleau, where the court was in residence. Such an important affair of state could hardly be kept secret.

Louis XIV ordered a new apartment in Versailles prepared for the duc de Bourgogne. Until now, he had resided with his brothers in the south wing of the château; a suite of rooms, next to his wife's, was now deemed suitable — rooms still occupied by the prince's former governess, the maréchale de La Mothe. The maréchale was induced to vacate, having received the royal promise she would continue in her position as governess when the new generation of royal babies appeared. Bourgogne's new apartment, on the first floor of the palace, overlooked the royal courtyard, communicating both with the king's antechamber and Adelaide's Grand Salon. Here he lived until his father's death in 1711, when he took up residence in the dauphin's apartment.

The redecoration was scheduled for completion in mid-October, when the court would return to Versailles. In the meanwhile, the young couple required some instruction in preparation for their new life together. The king, sparing his heir the embarrassing father-son talk, took it upon himself to answer his grandson's questions, while Mme de Maintenon gently explained the reproductive process to Marie Adelaide. The princesse, despite her outward shows of assurance, was by nature timid and bashful, and she heard the lecture with alarm and apprehension. In his *Memoirs,* the baron de Breteuil noted: "At his *Petit Coucher,* the King said to us, in speaking of the Duchesse de Bourgogne, that for four or five days now she had been shedding tears of bashfulness and fright." As for Bourgogne, the Venetian ambassador was convinced that he was "still too green, and incapable of ardor in conjugal affection by reason of the lukewarmness of his desires." But Erizzo saw only the prince's public side: privately, his love for his young wife had increased enormously in the two years since their marriage and he anticipated consummation with all the fervor and gusto to be expected from a love-struck seventeen-year-old — feelings that Adelaide, despite her initial trepidation, came to share. Her longtime friend, Mlle d'Ayen — certainly a better placed observer than the Venetian ambassador — stated that during this waiting period at Fontainebleau, "the husband and wife sought each other continually, and often withdrew together to a place apart. Those who watched them carefully saw that they were in love, that they passionately desired to be together."

On October 21, 1699, Louis XIV left Fontainebleau without ceremony, driving to Versailles with his grandchildren. That evening, Adelaide dined privately with Mme de Maintenon in the latter's apartment; Bourgogne took his supper alone with the king, where he received final instructions. The princesse retired to her bedchamber at ten, so unexpectedly early that, with the exception of one *femme de chambre,* none of her ladies were there. Bourgogne left the king and went to undress in his new apartment before joining his wife. This was done with all the impatience of youth — so quickly that Louis XIV, who had informed his grandchildren that he would come alone to see them in bed, arrived too late; tactfully, he did not enter the nuptial chamber.

There was time enough, however, for the bridegroom's valet to dress his hair in honor of the occasion; the baron de Breteuil, having the honor to hold Bourgogne's candlestick, noticed that "[his] hair was frizzled, and the magnificence of his *déshabillé* and his toilette savored of marriage . . . He quitted his apartment with a courageous and rather sprightly air." Closing the door behind him, he was alone with his wife for the first time in their lives — and so the duc and duchesse de Bourgogne began their married life.

The next morning, courtiers commented favorably on the prince's "air of fatigue" at the king's *lever*. Adelaide rose at nine o'clock, performed a hasty toilette and escaped all curiosity by leaving at once for Saint-Cyr, where she spent the entire day. The consummation of her marriage was announced in *Le Mercure*, and foreign newspapers carried the story as well; in Paris, there were celebrations, and all too quickly ribald songs appeared, so many that the lieutenant of police gave orders for his men to confiscate them (without success). The most popular — and the dirtiest — of these were attributed, correctly, to Mme la duchesse.

Dangeau, having noted the consummation in his journal entry of October 22, added that "at first, he will only pass alternate nights with her." This arrangement lasted a scant three weeks. Bourgogne's long-suppressed ardor increased perceptibly, for on November 11, Dangeau confided in his diary: "The Duc has formed the habit of sleeping every night with the Duchesse. He no longer desires to sleep apart." It was a happy ending for more than just the royal couple, as Mme Dunnoyer observed: "Our young couple are very happy to have gained their liberty, and the duchesse du Lude is released from the duty of observing their conduct, which was no small affair."

Married in deed as well as in spirit, the couple was still strikingly dissimilar. The groom was serious and studious, pious to the point of severity, ruled in every action by an inflexible sense of duty and the stern precepts of his religion. The bride was kind, affectionate, and intelligent, but impulsive, thoughtless, and insatiable in her pleasures. Yet they were happy together, for she returned his adoration with honest esteem. Too young and carefree to empathize with his gravity or his conscience, she nevertheless made a sincere attempt to understand her husband. As she informed Mme de Maintenon, "I am not content with doing the will of the Duc de Bourgogne, but I even enter into his views, which is no small matter for me. For you must understand, *ma tante*, that he sometimes offers them to me in three degrees — the good, the better, and the perfect, just as the Abbé Fénelon would do, and leaves me free to choose. Sometimes I have a good mind to declare for neutrality; but, by what enchantment I know not, I always conform to his wishes, even in spite of myself."

A good beginning indeed — but even bad marriages have good beginnings. For the duc and duchesse de Bourgogne, the road ahead was paved with difficulties — some common to all marriages, some peculiar to their own. With their new life as husband and wife, a new century lay before them, the age which Maintenon had prophesied that Adelaide should glorify. Yet the new age opened ominously.

11

A New Century:
Beginnings and Endings

As THE EIGHTEENTH CENTURY dawned over Europe, the
supremacy of France remained unchallenged. Its phenomenal expansion during the last four decades, though not undisputed, had been
unchecked. From Sun King to cobbler, Frenchmen everywhere considered themselves invincible, and with no one yet prepared to shatter
their illusions, they imagined the glories of the past but a prelude to a
triumphant future — and the eventual reign of Bourgogne and Adelaide.

No less than his people, the fading Sun King looked hopefully to the
rising young stars of Versailles. Long resigned to disappointment in his
immediate heir, Louis XIV studied the next generation with great
expectation. Following the well-publicized consummation of his marriage, the duc de Bourgogne was released from the care of the duc de
Beauvilliers and awarded total responsibility of his own household.
The prince was next nominated to the Council of Dispatches (regu-
lating internal affairs), an appointment that raised several eyebrows
since no one so young had ever before been admitted there — but the
king wished to initiate his successor into the business of government
as quickly as possible and a seat on the councils of State and Finance
could not be obtained without prior service in Dispatches. Louis XIV
also added three more nobles to Bourgogne's staff of gentlemen-in-
waiting and proposed a substantial raise in the allowance settled at the
time of his marriage. Bourgogne declined the increase, remarking to
his grandfather that he had enough money for the present. The king

persisted, and the prince promised that if, at some future time, his allowance proved insufficient he would at once take the liberty of informing His Majesty.

As for his beloved Adelaide, Louis XIV expected her to preside at the center of his newly resplendent Versailles. Imbert de Saint-Armand described the princesse at the turn of the century: "[She] is now one of the most attractive of women. Without her, all would wither at this Court, which would resemble a magnificent convent. The flowers would be less fair, the fields less gay, the streams less clear. Thanks to her seductive charm everything revives, all lights up under the rays of a vernal sun." For this reason as much as to welcome the new century, the king inaugurated the most brilliant carnival season France had yet witnessed; from Candlemas to Ash Wednesday came an uninterrupted procession of festivities, and Marie Adelaide reigned supreme as Queen of the Carnival.

Mme de Coulanges wrote to her country correspondent, Mme de Grignan: "You cannot conceive, Madame, the extent of the frenzy for all kinds of pleasure which now exists" — and the daily round of pageants, balls, and operas defied her description. Monseigneur, the prince de Condé, and all the leaders of court society rushed to organize parties in honor of the princesse who so delighted in them. The duchesse du Maine was pregnant and bedridden, but her condition did not prevent her from sponsoring no fewer than twenty balls for her young niece: guests danced in the expectant mother's bedroom as she smiled benignly from her pillows.

The most wonderful entertainment of the carnival season was given by Mme de Pontchartrain, wife of the chancellor (and mother of Adelaide's "one-eyed monster"), at the Hôtel de la Chancellerie on February 8, 1700. *Le Mercure,* rapturous as ever, explained that Mme de Pontchartrain "contrived to combine in one evening all the diversions usually indulged in during the carnival period, namely, those of comedy, fair and ball." Adelaide entered the courtyard, "which was brilliantly illuminated by torches," and was received by the chancellor and his wife (and their son — though the princesse was successful in masking her dislike before the watchful gaze of the *Mercure* reporter).

Inside, the ballroom was lit with "ten chandeliers and magnificent gilded candelabra. At one end, on raised seats, were the musicians, hautboys and violins, in fancy dress with plumed hats. Above the fireplace was a full-length portrait of the Duchesse de Bourgogne . . . Beyond the ballroom was another room, brilliantly lighted, in which were [more] hautboys and violins; this was reserved for the maskers, whose numbers were such that the ballroom could not have contained them all." After dancing for an hour, Adelaide was escorted to an adjoining room, a temporary theater, for the presentation of a comedy written by Dancourt expressly for the occasion. "All the actors belonged to the Comédie Française; their acting was perfection, and they were much applauded."

Following the performance, the guest of honor was taken to yet another room, where five booths had been arranged in a semicircle, attended by vendors dressed in costumes from different countries: a French pastrycook, an Italian *limonadiere,* a Provençal seller of oranges and lemons, a sweetmeat peddler, and an Armenian merchant with tea, coffee, and chocolate; "they were from the King's musicians, and chanted the merits of their wares to the guests." Adelaide sampled from each booth, then returned to the ballroom, "and amused herself until five in the morning . . . When [her hosts] escorted her to the foot of the staircase, she informed them, in the most gracious manner, that the entertainment which they had just given her had afforded her great enjoyment, and that she was extremely pleased with it."

Adelaide's taste for such entertainments was insatiable; moreover, she disliked her friends' leaving them before she did. Saint-Simon wrote that once he attempted to slip away unnoticed, but was informed by a sentry that the duchesse de Bourgogne had given orders that no one was to be allowed through the doors until after her own departure. He added that he and his wife passed the last three weeks of the carnival season "without seeing the day."

No less popular that carnival season were Adelaide's extravagant masques. In one pageant, she appeared as the goddess Flora, "in the midst of a posy of young girls as smiling and spring-like as herself." In a playing card ballet, she was the Queen of Hearts to Bourgogne's King. Her penchant was for the exotic — a sultana in gorgeous Oriental robes or an enchantress shimmering with diamonds — but at one masque, she arrived as the peasant milkmaid/bride (to Bourgogne's baker/bridegroom) to play a scene from *A Village Wedding;* "as ready to dance with a vulgar comedian as with a Prince of the Blood," was Mme de Maintenon's sour comment.

Her boundless zest infected her grave but adoring husband. Freed from his governor and finding liberty not without its attractions — and desperately anxious to please his wife in everything — Bourgogne steadily relaxed and soon had taken to dance, to drink, and to gambling with the same passion he had shown as a child for military training. For a time he found "great amusement" in theater, but Dangeau noted that music was his true love: he attended all the concerts held regularly at Versailles, and often went to the Opéra in Paris with his father (music and hunting were their only shared interests). After much rehearsal, he was able to assume a role in Lully's opera *Alceste* when it was performed before the king and court. Naturally, his increased participation in court life brought an increase in his popularity, and those who had previously dismissed the prince as a pious bookworm now curried his favor as much as they did his wife's; his aunt, the princesse de Conti, attempting to win his affection, spent a small fortune transforming her gallery into a private theater for his use, filling it with beautiful paintings and elaborate, moveable scenery.

Carnival season came to a climax, the Tuesday before Lent, with three separate balls: the first in the salons of the king, the second in the duchesse du Maine's apartments, and the last in those of the Grand Equerry, the comte d'Armagnac. The Bourgognes attended all three, and while the bleary-eyed prince's appearance at the final fête was brief and perfunctory, his wife remained until dawn, leaving only to attend early mass at the parish church of Versailles, and making her way to bed, "not in the least tired," sometime after seven.

Lent offered all too brief a respite, one more welcomed by her exhausted entourage than by the young princesse. The forty days of abstention passed quickly, and the rounds of fun began afresh.

Such incessant pursuit of pleasure — days of the chase, of fairs and water excursions, nights of opera galas and balls — would have strained the health of any normal young girl. Adelaide's constitution was, at best, delicate. For one thing, her teeth had become a chronic problem, causing attacks of indigestion and severe migraines ("I have been unwell with inflammations and headaches" is a recurrent phrase in her correspondence to Savoy). As she continued to run herself well past her endurance, she suffered increasing bouts of fever, finding relief in generous doses of self-prescribed quinine. Some sort of restraint was imperative, her doctor pleaded, but those who best loved and worried for the princesse — the king, his wife, and his grandson — had long since lost control of her.

The inevitable occurred in August 1701, when Adelaide fell seriously ill at Marly. (Saint-Simon's less than medical opinion held that her sickness was brought on by swimming in the Seine for three days in a row and then consuming an inordinate amount of fresh fruit.) She suffered great pain, and burned with so high a fever that she was quickly returned to Versailles and placed in the hands of the king's own physician. Fagon, no medical pioneer, dutifully subscribed to the precepts of seventeenth-century medicine: the ailing duchess was given a purgative and "a broth seasoned with cordial powders." She complained of pains in her head, so he bled her from the arm and, the next morning, from the foot. Yet the fever persisted, and Fagon administered two ounces of emetic wine from Spain; Adelaide immediately vomited and seemed to find some relief. She was then given three potions which, Fagon assured the frantic king, "purged her violently and successfully" — so successfully, in the doctor's opinion, that the entire process was swiftly repeated.

By the thirteenth, she had lost consciousness, doubtless the result of such ruthless medication, and would awaken with fits of delirium. Fagon was now seriously alarmed and called for a consultation with Bourdelot, Adelaide's private physician, and Boudin and du Chaine, the attendant doctors for Bourgogne and Berri. The patient regained consciousness, saw the four medicine men huddled around her bed, and gave herself up as lost; calling for her confessor, she begged the doctors to let her die in peace. Outside the sickroom, the entire court waited in suspense; inside, the king and Mme de Maintenon sat in mute despair, and Bourgogne made no attempt to hide the steady flow of his tears.

The morning of the fifteenth, Adelaide's temperature began to drop and the pains in her head diminished. The doctors were overjoyed and rushed to administer a laxative with a strong dose of quinine. By nightfall, the fever had vanished, and on August 16 the duchesse de Bourgogne was pronounced convalescent.

Le Mercure, publishing every intimate detail of the royal illness, ended: "The Duchesse de Bourgogne has shown during the course of her sickness all the high spirit, courage, resignation, patience and piety that could be, qualities rare enough at her age." A relieved Louis XIV ordered Te Deums sung in all the churches of Paris. That evening, Dangeau recorded: "[She] is very gay, and not so weak as might be expected after so severe an illness and so many remedies," but such optimism was unfounded, for it was several weeks before the princesse could leave her room, and for a long time after that she was forced to spend most of each afternoon in bed. Mme de Maintenon nursed her with selfless devotion and during Adelaide's recuperation organized quiet card parties with the ladies of the household to divert her restless patient. Louis XIV visited the young invalid daily, sitting unceremoniously on a small folding chair at the foot of her bed; Saint-Simon had no doubt that the princesse enjoyed her convalescence: "She was easily amused, and though she preferred gambling, was as happy and as cheerful spending an afternoon reading and sewing with her 'serious ladies,' as she called the older members of her Household."

The gravity of her illness made no impression on the princesse, for her return to court life was marked with a full resumption of all the pleasures she had forgone for so many months. But her husband, who never once left her bedside for five consecutive days, was profoundly affected. Once Adelaide had safely passed out of danger, Bourgogne penned a moving letter to his former governor:

> God has shown me many mercies, my dear duke, as you yourself have witnessed. Yesterday He accorded me yet another for which I will never cease to thank Him. I was within an hour of losing the Duchesse de Bourgogne; only imagine the blow that would have been to me . . . I was in the depths of despair. I prayed to God. Before Him, I confessed my sins, with loathing, for I was firmly convinced that He had chosen that way to punish me. I beseeched Him to cast on me the burden of them all, to spare that poor innocent, and if she had sinned, to let mine be the guilt. He took pity on me, and thank God, the Duchesse de Bourgogne is now entirely out of danger . . . I cease not to thank God for his mercy, for He clearly intended to punish me; but He has withheld His anger and taken pity on me.

Bourgogne's irrevocable conviction was that his wife's brush with death had been a divine warning against the pleasures he had lately come to enjoy. Gradually he drew back into his puritanical shell. Dancing was the first casualty: "It was my misfortune," he declared, "to lack adroitness at that exercise." Theater followed next, and even his love of music suffered in his atonement. So Adelaide's illness of 1701 did mark a real turning point — not for the patient but for her spouse.

The life of the princesse had been spared; others found themselves victims not of illness but the passage of time. Louis XIV, once so dazzlingly handsome, was a venerable sixty-two at the turn of the century; Madame felt that "he [was] still a fine and imposing-looking figure," though she conceded his "countenance has strangely altered." His secret wife was three years his senior and holding up admirably;

an Englishman who watched her set off one day for Marly with the king wrote: "There is about her whole person an indefinable charm which old age cannot destroy."

But the other principals from the Court of Love (now just a distant memory) had suffered the vicissitudes of age, if they had not disappeared altogether. Madame reviewed the king's former mistresses: "Those I once knew as beauties have lost more than myself; none would recognize Mme de La Vallière; Mme de Montespan's skin resembles a piece of paper that children have twisted about, her face is covered with innumerable little wrinkles, her beautiful hair has become as white as snow, and her face is red." (Madame was being neither hard nor unfair: of herself she wrote that she had become "an ugly little creature.") Even the mincing Monsieur could no longer successfully conceal the ravages of dissipation with his long black wigs and his pots of powder and rouge; his wife wrote: "Monsieur says openly . . . that as he is beginning to grow old, he has no time to lose, and will do everything and spare nothing to amuse himself up to the last, that those who survive him will know how to spend their time after their own fashion but . . . that he intends, so long as he lives, to attend to no one but himself — and he acts as he talks."

A new court appeared, a second generation, and predictably, those they replaced condemned them mercilessly. La Bruyère wrote that Versailles was a place where old people were gallant, polite, and polished, while the young were hard-hearted and ferocious, without any manners at all. Mme de Maintenon complained: "I find the females of today insupportable with their ridiculous and immodest clothes, their tobacco, their drink, their greed, their vile manners and their idle hands." But the new court thrived while the old court perished: the Fates, as if to prove the Sun King had outlived his time, systematically removed those major contributors to the glory of his reign. Gone were wise and capable ministers like Colbert and Louvois, brilliant and fearless generals like the maréchal de Luxembourg. Even those artists who had so brilliantly translated the king's conception of absolutism into the phenomenon of Versailles were leaving the stage they had so lovingly created: Le Vau and Le Brun were dead, the landscape genius Le Nôtre died in Paris in 1700, and "young" Mansard, fifty-four as the century began, had less than a decade left him.

As one by one the figures of his youth and his prime deserted him, Louis XIV turned to Marie Adelaide for solace and assurance — needs that increased with alarming rapidity. The great tragedian Racine fell late in 1699; the poet had long since lost favor at court because of his flirtation with Jansenism, but out of fondness (and respect) the king had allowed him to remain at Versailles, made him court historian, and genuinely deplored the death of this master of the French theater.

The death in 1701 of the king's valet, Alexandre Bontemps, at the age of eighty, was another painful blow. Bontemps had served Louis XIV since his birth, held the position of governor of Versailles for forty years, and had been a witness at the king's secret marriage to Maintenon in 1683. One of the most powerful men at court, he was completely without pretense and wielded his influence sparingly. He spoke to his master like a gruff, old nanny, and with his death, the Sun King lost yet another vital link to his childhood.

Bontemps was quickly followed to the grave by the marquise de Montespan. This death, Louis XIV felt, was of small consequence; to Adelaide he privately confessed that, so far as he was concerned, Athénaïs had been dead ever since she had left Versailles twenty years earlier. Still, the death of a woman who had borne him five children was one more painful reminder of universal mortality.

It was the loss of his brother Monsieur, in June 1701, that gave Louis XIV his greatest grief in this season of death. For the rest of his life, his conscience was tormented by the thought of responsibility — for Monsieur died within days of a violent argument with the king over Philippe, the duc de Chartres, Monsieur's only surviving son.[1]

Born in 1674, Chartres was a young man of medium height, with black hair, a wide, pleasant face, and a noble, relaxed manner. He was highly gifted, far more than his cousins, the dauphin and the royal bastards, Maine and Toulouse; Saint-Simon praised his "great poise when under stress," his kindness, affability and charm, his "singular memory," and his natural eloquence with "abstract sciences (which he could explain clearly), affairs of state, finance, justice, war, Court politics . . . [and] all sorts of arts and technical subjects."

But he was doomed by his position in the royal family: Louis XIV, jealous of his nephew's obvious superiority over his own sons, continually thwarted Chartres's ambitions, while advancing those of his illegitimate children, despite their overwhelming lack of merit. Young Chartres had been compelled, by false promises of advancement, into marrying Françoise Marie, the king's second daughter by Mme de Montespan.[2] The marriage, though fruitful, was a total failure. Frustrated at every turn by his all-powerful uncle, Chartres gave himself up to a life of debauchery and boisterousness. "He could not do without it," said Saint-Simon. "He thrived on noise, turbulence and excesses. He threw himself into the weirdest and most scandalous debauchery, as though he wanted to be unequaled as a rake. He spiced his orgies with blasphemous speeches and found a delicious refinement in holding them openly on the holiest days, such as Good Friday."

Madame adored and supported her son, all the while deploring his libertine ways and stubborn nature. She once declared that, at his christening, the fairies had given him every gift, but the one fairy she had forgotten to invite had taken her revenge by decreeing that her sisters' gifts should all be useless to him. "My son," she complained to her aunt in May 1701, "has often pained me by his disobedience. When I begged him not to do a thing, he did it immediately, many times before my eyes. When I tell him that I cannot bear to see him mix with certain people, he speaks to them more than before; he once told the King that I was the cause of his bad conduct, because I hate those that he bears in affection." Madame had little fear of Louis's believing this justification, but even as she wrote, the king's anger toward his son-in-law/nephew was mounting to new heights.

Chartres's wife was pregnant — so was his mistress, a fact he announced to all with great relish. His mortified wife complained of ill usage to her father, and early in June Monsieur was summoned for an audience with his brother. Louis expressed displeasure at his nephew's escapades, but Monsieur appeared indifferent, flippantly noting that a king who traveled to the battlefront with his wife and *two* mistresses all in the same coach (as Louis XIV had done in Flanders in 1667) was hardly one to blame people who flaunted their affairs and upset their wives. The king grew furious as his brother recalled those happy but sinful days and chided him for having no authority over his son.

It was now Monsieur's turn for outrage: he demanded to be informed how he was to deal with an adult son who had nothing to do but cool his heels in the galleries of Versailles and watch while his royal brothers-in-law were loaded with appointments, households, governorships, and other honors. His indignation mounted by the moment, Saint-Simon reported: "His son, he added, was in a worse plight than any gentleman of France of comparable age who could serve with the armies and earn promotion and rank; that idleness was the mother of evil; that it was hard for him to see his only son falling into dissolute habits with bad companions and indulging in harebrained schemes, and that it was beyond endurance to be asked now to reproach the high-spirited boy, unjustly thwarted, without blaming the one who had brought him to pass."

The king was flabbergasted: never before had Monsieur spoken so passionately, with such anger or intensity, and not only was this an effrontery to his royal person, but deep inside he knew his brother's accusations were valid. Still, the Sun King had no intention of giving in, even less of admitting a mistake: seething beneath his imperturbable façade, Louis XIV coldly answered that there was soon going to be a war, and ample opportunity for his nephew to distinguish himself; further, he would soon be forced into wartime economies and would not fail to begin by cutting off Monsieur's allowance.

A servant interrupted, announcing dinner, and with great effort, the royal brothers went in to table. Monsieur had gone crimson, and the king remarked it was quite obvious he ought to be bled, and that he had a good mind to pack his brother off to his room and have it done at once, by force if necessary. Table conversation was stilted at best, but as true Bourbons, neither found his appetite diminished. After consuming their usual enormous meal, Monsieur took leave of the king and returned to his château at Saint-Cloud, "the former still furious, and the latter much vexed."

Later that night, a message arrived from the duc de Chartres that his father was ill. Louis XIV, who otherwise would have rushed at once to his brother's bedside, was still too angry and suspected a ruse in this timely indisposition. He sent no reply and retired to bed.

At three in the morning, a second courier arrived with a more detailed report. The king was informed that Monsieur "had been seized with exhaustion before supper, but felt better after being bled and had been given an emetic . . . Supping as usual with the ladies, he was in the act of pouring a glass of wine, when he had suddenly stammered and pointed with his finger . . . It was all over in a moment, and he fell into the arms of M. de Chartres in a fit of apoplexy. They carried him to his bedroom, shook him, walked him up and down, bled him copiously, and administered a powerful emetic."

Louis XIV, accompanied by Mme de Maintenon, hurried off to Saint-Cloud, to find that Monsieur had lapsed into a coma. Throughout the night he kept vigil in the adjoining room, battling with his emotions while Maintenon soothed him in her low, gentle voice. Saint-Simon thought that "these sad moments must have reminded him of their old affection. He may have blamed himself for precipitating Monsieur's death by their quarrel; he may also have felt some disquiet, since

Monsieur was the younger by two years and had appeared quite as healthy as himself, if not more so."

At eight the next morning, the royal couple heard mass in the chapel at Saint-Cloud. Adelaide had driven over from Versailles and was with the king when the doctors informed him that his brother was past all human aid. Together with Mme de Maintenon, she persuaded him to tarry no longer and ordered the coachman to drive them to Marly. As they left, the king encountered Chartres, and both men burst into tears. Louis XIV mumbled a few kind words, and Chartres fell to the ground, clasping his uncle around the knees and crying, "Alas! Sire, what will become of me? I am losing my father, and you do not love me!" The Sun King was deeply moved and embraced his nephew warmly, "speaking very lovingly."

With the king's departure the crowds gradually dispersed, and Monsieur was left to die on the daybed in his study surrounded only by lackeys and servants, "most of whom from love or self-interest appeared deeply distressed." Madame was not present; she was herself in bed with a terrible cold. She told her aunt, "A quarter hour after I heard a great noise, Mme de Ventadour entered my apartment, as pale as death. 'Monsieur feels ill,' she said. I immediately ran into his room; he recognized me, but could not speak plainly enough to be understood. I could only make out these words, 'You are ill; go away.' He was bled three times, given eleven ounces of emetics, Schaffhouse water, and two bottles of English drops . . . Towards six A.M. they saw that the end was approaching, and forced me to leave the room. I was in a fainting condition. They put me to bed, but I could not stay still." Shortly before noon, June 9, 1701, Monsieur the duc d'Orléans died of a stroke, aged sixty-one.

At Marly, the king received word of his brother's death from his doctor, Fagon. He retained his composure, but the next morning when Chartres paid a visit at the king's *lever*, Louis was more emotional. "[The king] spoke to him very kindly, bidding him henceforth consider him as his father, and promising to protect his honor and interests and to forget all the past small vexations. He said further that he hoped Chartres would forget them also, and that these promises of affection would persuade him to return the King's proffered love." Saint-Simon added smugly: "You may well imagine that M. de Chartres answered in a proper spirit."

Like her son, the new widow sorely needed some reassurances. Tradition held that following her husband's death she should retire from the court — ideally, to a convent to pray till the end of her days for both their immortal souls, but more realistically, to the seclusion of her estate at Saint-Cloud. The vigorous forty-eight-year-old Madame felt no inclination to relinquish the heady prerogatives joined to her position in the royal hierarchy or to sever her connection with the mighty and the powerful at Versailles. After wisely destroying Monsieur's voluminous correspondence — mostly scented love letters from his young men — she hastened to Versailles and arranged an interview with her archenemy, Maintenon: "I remembered how many times I had been advised to make friends with the lady . . . so I asked the duc de Noailles to tell her from me that I was so touched by the manner in which she had expressed sympathy for me that I begged her to come and see me. This she did at six o'clock." For the first time, Madame invited the king's unacknowledged wife to sit in her presence. She came to the point with no elaboration — asking Maintenon to intervene with the king and allow her to remain at court. "I asked her to be my friend. I owned that I had been angry with her because I had thought that she injured me in the king's estimation, but I would willingly forget everything if she would be my friend in the future."

Mme de Maintenon did not reply at once, but drew a letter from her bodice and handed it over. Madame at once recognized it as one of hers. She had known for years that her letters were being read — letters in which she freely referred to Maintenon as the old horror, old ape, manure heap, witch, or slut. The letter she now perused said that no one really knew for certain if "the old brute" was the king's wife or his concubine; even more dangerously, it described in graphic detail the miseries and privations of the French poor — one of Louis XIV's better-known sore spots. Small wonder Madame dissolved into hysterics. Smiling with triumph and magnanimity, Mme de Maintenon spoke at last, promising that she would arrange for her sister-in-law to remain at Versailles. "She made me many charming and eloquent speeches, and swore to be my friend, and we embraced one another."

Madame knew well there were other fences to be mended. " 'But it is not enough,' I continued, 'to tell me that the King is displeased with me — you must also tell me the way in which I can re-enter into his favor.' She advised me to speak plainly to him. I followed this counsel . . . The King embraced me, begged me to forget the past, and promised me his affection in the future. He also laughed when I said to him in the most natural fashion, 'If I did not love you I should not have hated Mme de Maintenon when I thought that she had injured me with you.' So all ended happily."

All ended well, if not truly happily: Madame remained at court (and enjoyed a position of even greater prestige when her son became regent in 1715), but her "friendship" with the king's wife was short-lived. Chastened at first into modifying her epithets, her animosity eventually resurfaced, and by December 1707, she was writing her aunt: "I have to pay a visit to the all-powerful lady when at Marly. My nature is not at all to her taste. I am not flattering enough. Flattery is a difficult art . . . To be adept at it, one must have been born in France or Italy." Another two years and she was as venomous as ever: "She persecutes me always, but she does not dare insult me openly, for she believes me as vindictive as herself." Madame then offered a surprising new conjecture: "As she is aware that the King, whom I love and greatly respect, has no dislike for me, and that we get on well together, she is afraid lest he should attach himself to me rather than to the Duchesse de Bourgogne. This is the reason why she keeps us as much apart as possible." It is extremely doubtful that the king's wife ever seriously worried that the cantankerous old Madame would control the king's affections.

Monsieur's loss was keenly felt at Versailles. He was flamboyant, to be sure, and often outrageous; but he was also the leading expert on court etiquette (after his brother), a charming raconteur, and a surprisingly devoted and generous father. For seventeen years he had maintained a steady correspondence with his daughter Anne Marie; the duchess of Savoy suffered deeply at his death — all the more since the news arrived at the very time she faced the loss of her younger daughter, Marie Louise, leaving in September to wed the new king of Spain.

Her older daughter likewise grieved: this was Adelaide's first encounter with death and it shook her greatly. "I loved Monsieur very much," she wrote her mother sadly after his funeral, noting that she and her grandfather had shared an irreverent sense of humor and took much enjoyment in each other's company. Mme de Maintenon saw in Adelaide's prolonged, heartfelt sadness evidence of further maturity: on the afternoon following Monsieur's death, the princesse was discovered sitting quietly in a corner of her bedroom, "looking very wretched." The sight of his corpse, laid out in the flickering candlelight of the Saint-Cloud chapel, affected her so painfully that she fainted, and two days after the funeral, Louis XIV found her weeping in her apartments. "He ordered the duchesse du Lude and the other ladies-in-waiting to distract her. She allowed herself to be comforted, but she was observed to mourn the death of . . . Monsieur for a long while in private."

Such mourning had to be done in private: one of Louis XIV's more striking characteristics was his lifelong aversion to sadness and grief. Tears were intolerable, unhappy faces unwelcome in the enchanted world of Versailles. Following the funeral of one prominent court lady, Mme de Maintenon wrote: "The death of Mme d'Espinois was a surprise and nothing more. The King rids himself of unhappy ideas as soon as possible." The death of his own brother was no exception, as Saint-Simon recorded with disapproval: "Shortly after two o'clock, that is to say just twenty-six hours since Monsieur's death, the Duc de Bourgogne invited the Duc de Montfort to play a hand of *brelan*. '*Brelan!*' cried Montfort, amazed. 'You must have forgotten; Monsieur is not yet cold!' 'Indeed, I know it,' said the Prince, 'but the King will not suffer anyone to be dull at Marly. He has ordered me to set everyone playing and to show the example myself.' . . . Before long, the entire drawing room was full of gaming tables."

But the Sun King's insistence on ignoring death never appeared so politic as in the spring of 1701, for six months earlier there had occurred another death — one of international significance. In November 1700, the feeble Carlos II of Spain had finally expired, and the time bomb that had threatened Europe for more than thirty years at last was detonated.

As the new century opened, Europe was united in an ardent desire for peace. The desultory War of the Palatinate (concluded to no one's satisfaction by the treaty of Ryswick in 1697) had left the continent exhausted, depleted of manpower and matériel. A pacifist Parliament ruled in England; to the east, the infidel Turk again battered at the gate of the Hapsburg empire, and Emperor Leopold I, struggling for the survival of Vienna, had not time, money, men, or inclination to wage war in the west.

The Sun King's camp at Compiègne had succeeded in intimidating his European rivals with the recuperative power of the French war machine; but despite the ostentatious display, France was also tired. It had encountered more strenuous opposition in the recent eight-year war than ever before, and the effects told; true, it had rebounded remarkably, but the braggart stance of Compiègne was largely to im-

press, for the aging Sun King shrank at the thought of another protracted conflict.

Spain wanted war least of all. In terms of territory, it was still the
greatest empire in Christendom, encompassing most of Italy and Morocco, the Catholic Netherlands (roughly, modern Luxembourg and
Belgium), Mexico, most of Central and all of South America save for
Brazil, the Philippines, the Canaries, and the bulk of the West Indies.
But the military and naval power needed to control so vast and scattered an empire had diminished steadily in the seventeenth century:
supremacy on the seas was conceded to the Dutch and English, and on
land to the Sun King's Grand Army.

Internally, the situation was even worse, for Spain had become the
victim of its own wealth and greed. The proud Spaniards scorned trade
and industry, relying totally on the flow of silver and gold from the
New World (an influx all too frequently interrupted by the fleet ships
of England and Holland). Europe prospered greatly in the seventeenth
century — Spain did not. Commerce declined rather than expanded:
in 1700, shipping between Spain and America was seventy-five percent
less than it had been a century before. All manufactured items were
imported — offset only in part by the export of Spanish wine, oil, and
wool — and since the balance of payments were made in bullion, the
Spanish ports had degenerated into mere clearinghouses, where incoming gold from America was duly recorded, then shipped out immediately for London or Paris or The Hague.

The Spanish countryside reflected the shriveling economy; once-
renowned cities like Valencia and Cordova suffered from highly visible
decay, and farms everywhere lay abandoned, their owners victimized
by exorbitant taxes — including a general sales tax of fourteen percent. Transport was so primitive and the road system so badly maintained that even the coastal towns and the cities on navigable rivers
found it cheaper to import necessities than to buy them within the
country. Infant mortality was high, and so was emigration: Seville and
Toledo suffered severe losses as the poor, the starving, and the bankrupt fled to the New World, and the population of Madrid — four
hundred thousand in 1600 — dwindled to half that number within
one hundred years.

The monarchs of the seventeenth century were surprisingly symbolic of their lands: the brash young Sun King aptly personified the
expanding power of France in the latter half of the *grand siècle,* and
nowhere was the decline of Spain better represented than in its pathetic
king, Carlos II.

Carlos had ascended the throne in 1665, at the age of four. The formal regent during his minority was his mother, Queen Mariana of Austria; the real rulers of Spain were the queen's Jesuit confessor, Nithard, and her lover, Fernando Valenzuela. At the age of sixteen, Carlos assumed the reins of government — or at least attempted, with his feeble faculties, to preside over the disintegration of his patrimony.

Interbreeding of the Spanish and Austrian branches of the House of Hapsburg had been the persistent tradition of two centuries: the king's parents had been uncle and niece; his grandparents, first cousins. Carlos was the last of his line, and in him, the genetic defects of such concentrated inbreeding created a wizened, misshapen parody of a human being. His body was so deformed and debilitated that he was carried in the arms of a nurse until he was ten. His jutting Hapsburg chin was so prominent that he could not chew food and his tongue was so large that his speech was virtually unintelligible. His malformed brain rejected the scant education it was offered (he could barely read or write), but clung to the legends and superstitions of Roman Catholicism: one leading Spanish historian observed that he firmly "believed himself to be possessed by the Devil."

Inevitably, this pathetic creature became the pawn of ambitious clergy and court factions. For obvious reasons of state, he was married — twice: first to the lovely, loveless Marie Louise d'Orléans, older sister of the duchess of Savoy, and following her death in 1689, to a German princess, Maria Anna von Neuburg, a puppet in the hands of the Austrian emperor. Both marriages were fruitless, and the king's impotence was common knowledge. Lame and epileptic, senile at thirty-five, and forever on the verge of death, Carlos II continued to survive year after year, baffling the doctors in Madrid and the courts of Europe, while politicians everywhere pondered the troublesome question of who was to inherit the king of Spain's vast possessions.

This was a question of enormous political complication in the continental balance of power, for the major claimants were each representatives of the major powers. In addition to the sorry Carlos, Philip IV of Spain had produced two daughters: the older, Marie Thérèse, had married Louis XIV, and the younger, Margaret Thérèse, had been the first wife of Emperor Leopold I. Through their wives, both monarchs now put forth their claims: Louis on behalf of his son, the dauphin; Leopold on behalf of his grandson, the little prince of Bavaria — and later, with blatant greed, for himself by virtue of his mother, Maria, a sister of Philip IV.

Leopold argued that neither his mother nor his wife had been required to renounce their rights of succession at the time of their marriage, as Marie Thérèse had been forced to do; Louis retorted that Spain had never paid his wife's dowry as agreed in the marriage contract, and that her relinquishment of any share of the Spanish inheritance had been contingent on *full* compliance with the treaty terms. No dowry, no renunciation of rights. The notion of Spain united with France sent shivers down the European spine, but no less welcome was the idea of a combined Holy Roman and Spanish empire under one omnipotent Hapsburg. Some arrangement satisfactory to all the European powers was demanded; without it, war between France and the empire was inevitable.

It devolved on the two leading statesmen of the age, Louis XIV of France and William III of England, to work out some sort of settlement, for it was generally understood that if these two archrivals could reach a compromise, their combined clout could impose the solution on all the other parties concerned. Early in March 1698, William dispatched his trusted adviser, Lord Portland, to open negotiations in Paris. Portland's embassy had a secret purpose as well: to obtain from Versailles full recognition of William as king of England.[3]

Portland emphasized his master's success as England's first constitutional monarch by arranging a lavish and impressive entrance into France. Madame wrote her aunt, on March 18: "Last Sunday, my Lord Portland made his entry into Paris. His equipages and liveries were very magnificent. He had six coaches, twelve outriders, twelve pages, fifty courtiers, and a great following of English lords." He was received at court with full ambassadorial honors, although Madame wryly noted, "It amuses me that they sing the praises of the ambassador sent by the same king whom they burnt and dragged through the streets in effigy some years before."

Portland created a most favorable impression at Versailles and was highly successful with Madame. In a letter to her aunt, she wrote: "I had the pleasure last evening of holding a long conversation with my Lord Portland. He told me that he had often had the honor of seeing you, and that he admired exceedingly the perfection with which you speak English."[4] Less taken with the English emissary were the staunch, but dwindling, supporters of the exiled Stuarts, and notably Monsieur, former brother-in-law of James II (Minette was his youngest sister).

[My husband] does not approve of my Lord Portland's coming to see me so often, and as he cannot forbid him to, he tries to set me against him. "This lord," says he, "only comes to see you that he may get information out of you." "That would be more to be feared from you," I reply, "who know all the state secrets, but I, who know nothing, cannot be made to say anything, and I much enjoy his company, for he talks to me of those I love and honor." . . . [Monsieur persisted:] "This will much displease the King and Queen of England at Saint-Germain." "I cannot help that," I answer. "I pity them and would willingly do anything for them, but I cannot help esteeming King William for he deserves it, and I do not hide this from them. I cannot refuse to see the ambassador of a king recognized as such, and one that the King and yourself received with every courtesy, and who comes with many kind messages from the King his master to me, asking for my friendship. All this makes me treat him well, and reply to his courtesies, and the King and Queen at Saint-Germain are wrong if they find fault with it."

James II and Queen Mary *did* rage (ineffectually) at Saint-Germain that their French brother should receive and bargain with an agent of their usurper. But Louis XIV was nothing if not a political realist: together with Portland and his foreign minister, Torcy, he tackled the problem of the Spanish succession.

Each candidate's claim was formalized and evaluated. There were three: representing the French was now the young duc d'Anjou, the dauphin's second son (Monseigneur's right of inheritance had been settled on Anjou because the dauphin and his oldest son, Bourgogne, stood in direct succession to the French throne). The emperor's personal claim through his mother was settled on another second son, from Leopold's second marriage, the archduke Karl — for the same reason that produced the Anjou candidacy. The third, and clearly compromise, candidate was the four-year-old Bavarian prince, great-grandson of the late King Philip IV of Spain.

The result of the Portland embassy was the Treaty of Loo, or the First Partition Treaty. It stipulated that Spain, the New World, Sardinia, and the Spanish Netherlands — the bulk of the empire — would go to little Prince Joseph Ferdinand of Bavaria. As compensation for the loss of a scepter, the French claimant would receive Sicily and the Spanish ports in Tuscany, while the prosperous duchy of Milan would go to the Austrian archduke. Louis XIV found these terms acceptable and signed the treaty with William on October 11, 1698. Emperor Leopold held out with reservations, until one month later — November 14, 1698 — when Carlos II drew up his will and named the prince of Bavaria his official heir. The problem of the Spanish succession had been neatly — and peacefully — solved.

This convenient solution lasted just over two months. Europe was shocked and appalled when the little prince suddenly died on February 6, 1699. The extraordinary and timely coincidence of his death could not fail but excite suspicion, and rumors abounded that the child had been poisoned — by secret order of his jealous grandfather, the emperor; to this day, the true cause of death remains a mystery. But from causes natural or other, the corpse was still a corpse, and the European powers found themselves once again back at the starting point.

In secrecy, Louis XIV and William III arrived at a Second Partition Treaty in June 1699. It was indicative of the Sun King's strong desire for peace that he was willing to surrender his grandson's claim to Spain: now that there would be only one loser, however, he expected more ample compensation to be made. Under the new terms agreed upon with England and Holland, the Spanish Empire would be disbanded; Archduke Karl would receive Spain itself, the Spanish Netherlands, and the American colonies, while Anjou would acquire Naples, Sicily, and the duchy of Milan. A provisional clause allowed the emperor two months in which to accept or reject the proposed arrangement: Leopold, with a covetous eye on the vast tracts of Italian territory soon to fall into French hands, rejected the plan outright. On March 13, 1700, the Second Treaty was formally ratified — but only by France, England, and the Dutch United Provinces.

Time was running out, both for the hope of a peaceful settlement to the Spanish succession and for the Spanish successor. Carlos the Sufferer, approaching his thirty-ninth birthday but looking more like seventy-nine, sat vacantly for hours on end staring at the mummified remains of his ancestors, resting in enviable repose on eternal beds of porphyry and black marble in the royal mausoleum at the Escorial. But somewhere in the jumble of his rotting brain, one thought remained resolute: unity. Rumors of this secret Second Treaty had trickled into the court of Madrid — Carlos, like Spaniards everywhere, was aghast at the thought of his great heritage being chopped up and parceled out to the major contenders. As death at last mercifully promised to end his suffering, Carlos II swore to pass his vast dominions *intact* to one candidate or the other. But which?

A palace revolution occurred during Carlos the Sufferer's last dying months. It began, not in Madrid or the Escorial but in Rome, where the newly elected Pope Clement XI, reversing twenty-five years of anti-French policy, openly supported the accession of the duc d'Anjou. Through his influence (and the influence of French gold arriving, secretly and daily, in enormous quantities in Madrid), the archbishop of Toledo, primate of Spain, was induced to take up the French banner. The archbishop, together with several loyal priests, established himself in the royal sickroom and barred entry to the queen and the queen mother — both well-known Austrian sympathizers. As Carlos hovered on the brink of release, the archbishop remained in constant vigil at his side, reminding his master over and over that only Louis XIV had enough power to prevent the dissection of the Spanish Empire and to use it as a true bastion of Catholicism. Carlos II acquiesced on October 7, 1700, signing his last will and testament and bequeathing everything to the duc d'Anjou. Three weeks later — on November 1 — Carlos the Sufferer expired.

News of the Spanish king's death, and the terms of his will, reached the French court at Fontainebleau on November 9. The courier arrived early in the morning, interrupting the king in council. With no visible signs of emotion, Louis XIV read the will silently. Afterward, he said nothing except that the king of Spain had died; that there would be a formal court mourning; and that there would be a meeting of ministers at three o'clock that afternoon in Mme de Maintenon's apartments. The undisclosed topic (as everyone knew) would be the Spanish will.

The meeting was attended by Monseigneur, the duc de Beauvilliers, Chancellor Pontchartrain, and Foreign Minister Torcy, as well as Mme de Maintenon. The king finally divulged the contents of the will. Carlos had left the entire Spanish Empire to Anjou, with one stipulation: the crowns of Spain and France were never to be united. Should Louis XIV not accept this condition, or should he have any intention of taking even the smallest province from the Spanish domain, the inheritance would pass — intact — to Archduke Karl, with a similar restriction on union with Austria. Given the close and covert dealing between the archbishop of Toledo and the French ambassador in Madrid, it is probable that Louis XIV had advance knowledge of the terms in the will.

Carlos II had placed the choice, and the responsibility, solely on the Sun King, and Louis XIV weighed his options and their implications: to accept would court the possibility of war, besides violating the Second Partition Treaty signed only nine months before (he could, and did, argue that when the emperor rejected the partition plan, he nullified the entire treaty, releasing the other involved parties from commitment). If he rejected the will, this peerless prize would fall into the hands of his greatest adversary, the Austrian emperor. The royal advisers were asked for their opinions.

Monseigneur and Torcy were unequivocal in favoring acceptance, reminding Louis XIV of England's prevailing mood of pacifism as well as the disorganization and dissension within the United Provinces. Chancellor Pontchartrain would not commit himself to either side, but the duc de Beauvilliers was strongly opposed to accepting the crown, and warned the king that another costly war would be the ruin of France. (Mme de Maintenon said nothing — at least not at the meeting.) After four hours of intensive debate, the king brought the session to a close, still refusing to commit himself and saying only that so grave an issue deserved a night's sleep before resolution.

The next morning, the court waited in suspense. Louis XIV's first act after his *lever* was to summon the Spanish ambassador, and word spread rapidly that acceptance was in the offing. But their interview was brief and still the expected announcement was withheld.

While the court and the world held its breath, Louis XIV continued to deliberate, calling even for the opinions of his family. His daughters, Mme la duchesse and the princesse de Conti, felt the crown should be accepted, and for once were in agreement with their "irritating" niece, who remarked to the duchesse du Lude, "The King would be a fool to refuse the crown of Spain for his grandson." When on the thirteenth Adelaide pressured the king for his decision, he stopped her wheedling with the observation "Whatever course I take, I am quite sure that many people will condemn it."

The court, long practiced in the reading of the royal mind, detected in the noncommittal king a bend toward acceptance. "Everyone is whispering, 'Don't repeat it, but the King has accepted the crown for Anjou,' " Madame informed her aunt; she too felt certain of the outcome. "I keep silence; but when hunting, I heard the Duc d'Anjou behind me. I stopped and said, 'Pass, great King! Let Your Majesty pass!' I should have liked you to have seen how astonished the good child looked at my knowing the news."

Six days had gone by since the news first reached Fontainebleau; Louis XIV could vacillate no longer. He left for Versailles the morning of the fifteenth with Adelaide, the princesse de Conti, and the duchesse du Lude, arriving at four in the afternoon. He spent the evening alone with Adelaide and Mme de Maintenon, and finally came to a decision.

The next morning the king summoned the Spanish ambassador to meet with him and the duc d'Anjou in the council chamber, and the court scurried expectantly into the Hall of Mirrors. The suspense was soon to end.

Suddenly, the great doors to the council chamber were flung open for the entire court (something never before done and much remarked upon). Out stepped the seventeen-year-old duc d'Anjou, between his grandfather and the Spanish ambassador. In a loud voice, Louis XIV proclaimed, "Messieurs, behold the King of Spain! His birth has called him to that throne, also the will of the late King. The whole Spanish nation deserves to have him and asks me to let him go. It is the will of Heaven, and I gladly obey."

Turning to the new king, he said, "Be a good Spaniard; that is your first duty now; but never forget that you were born a Frenchman, and foster the unity between our two nations. That is the way to make them happy, and to preserve the peace of Europe."

The Spanish ambassador kissed the hand of his new master, then threw himself at Anjou's feet. As he rose, the other members of the Spanish embassy followed suit; after them, the French court fell to its knees in homage to His Most Catholic Majesty, Philip V, king of Spain. Overcome with emotion, the Spanish ambassador turned to Louis XIV and cried out, "Il n'y a plus des Pyrénées; elles sont abîmées!' — "The Pyrenees have ceased to exist!"

It was a sentiment an uneasy Europe could not share.

12

Eliminating the Pyrenees

THE CROWNED HEADS of Europe would have taken issue with the Spanish ambassador's boast on the disintegration of the natural boundary between France and Spain, yet none would have argued with Saint-Simon's proud assertion that, for France, the eighteenth century opened "in an incomparable blaze of glory and prosperity."

Louis XIV gambled on the current European mood and won — however unsettling the idea of a Bourbon king in Spain, it was, at the moment, a development few seriously wished to dispute on the battlefield. True, William III of England openly broke down when informed of Anjou's succession, crying that the work of his lifetime was being destroyed, but Parliament had already demobilized the army, adopted the slogan "No Foreign Entanglements," and shown no inclination whatever to challenge the legal execution of the late king's last will and testament. Without the English commitment, William (who was also *Stadholder,* or chief executive, of the Dutch United Provinces) was powerless to rally Holland against this French takeover of half the known world. By the end of December, both London and The Hague had recognized Philip V.

Nor did the entire diplomatic corps at Versailles respond to Anjou's elevation with the enthusiasm of their Spanish confederate. Most discomfited of all was the new Austrian ambassador, who arrived at this untimely moment to announce the birth of a son to the queen of the Romans, wife of the emperor's older son, and found himself instead witness to the defeat of his master's younger one.

No less embarrassed, if far less evident, was the conte di Vernone, the Savoyard ambassador. For some time past, in great secrecy, the enterprising Victor Amadeus had been negotiating a share of the Spanish settlement for himself — negotiations now patently fruitless. In far-off Turin, the duke was furious at Anjou's accession to an undivided empire: "We had always suspected that the offers made by France were not intended sincerely." His ambassador at Versailles was concerned with saving face (a rather needless task since the French court was largely unaware of their covert dealings) and maintaining the proper attitude: "I did no more than bow very low to the new King, who stood facing His Majesty, and I then immediately, but not too pointedly, continued my conversation with King Louis, who said how much he hoped that Your Royal Highness would rejoice in this happy event that gives promise of abiding peace."

Victor Amadeus felt little reason for rejoicing, though his November correspondence with Vernone showed that his hopes for an arrangement which would bring him the duchy of Milan were not altogether dashed. Only after he was advised by his ambassador of the general opinion in Holland — "There will be little opposition, and [the French] will feel themselves perfectly safe; thus they will alter none of the intentions of the will" — did Victor Amadeus resign himself to the will of Carlos the Sufferer, instructing Vernone to join with the other foreign ambassadors in presenting his congratulations.

The duke of Savoy's acquiescence was a great relief to Adelaide, who had been alarmed by her father's sulking attitude. Her happiness trebled when she interviewed Vernone at her toilette and was apprised of the personal letter Victor Amadeus had sent to the Sun King: "In this latest extension of Your Majesty's glory, by the acquisition of the entire Spanish empire on behalf of the Duc d' Anjou, my gratification cannot be too highly estimated, considering, as I do, that blood so august as Your Majesty's is rightly destined to fill the greatest thrones in Europe."

Louis XIV easily overlooked the duke's sarcasm and his sour reference to the "entire" Spanish Empire, for his happiness and pride were near bursting, and he confessed to the Spanish ambassador: "I still think this is all a dream."

Equally pleased with the turn of events was the proud father: Monsiegneur went about court boasting, "Few people can speak of the King, my father, and the King, my son." He seemed blissfully unaware of the prophecy made at his birth that he would be the son of a king, and the father of kings, but never a king himself — a prediction that time proved true.

Meanwhile, the seventeen-year-old boy who had been magically

transformed into sovereign ruler of half the world accepted the obeisance owed his new station with a shy and diffident air. Philippe
d'Anjou was a fair, handsome young man; his aunt felt that he looked
"very Austrian," and he did bear a striking resemblance to his Hapsburg ancestor, Philip II of Spain. Madame judged him not so quick or
intelligent as his younger brother, the duc de Berri (her personal favorite), "but he has other excellent qualities: he has a warm heart, is
generous (a rare quality in this family), and truthful; nothing can
persuade him to tell a lie. He will also be a man of his word; he is
merciful and courageous."

His family meant everything to him. He was devoted to his father
and brothers, in particular Bourgogne, for whom he had all the fervent
hero worship of a younger brother. Outside the royal circle, Philip had
almost no ties or friendships: in his correspondence following his move
to Spain, the only figure at Versailles he ever inquired after — and only
once — was Mme de Maintenon's old friend, the duchesse de Beauvilliers. His feelings toward accepting the Spanish throne (not that
anyone thought to ask for them) were at best ambivalent: the glorious
fate that beckoned was too attractive to resist, yet it required him to
forsake the family and home he loved above all else.

For a time, the court of Versailles was treated to an honor never
before imagined: two reigning monarchs in residence under one roof.
The situation demanded new procedures of etiquette, devised on the
spot. Louis XIV naturally set the tone himself. That first evening, he
personally escorted the new king to bed, and said with a deep and
graceful bow, "I wish Your Majesty a pleasant sleep tonight," smiling
with great relish as he emphasized "Your Majesty." It was unseemly
for the king of Spain to sleep in a room with his brother and their tutor,
as the duc d'Anjou had done the night before. A magnificent canopied
bed was installed in one of the state apartments, the Mercury Salon,
and for the last three weeks of his life at Versailles, Philip V of Spain
slumbered beneath the protecting gaze of the gods' own messenger.

A question of etiquette rose the next morning when the royal family
entered the chapel for daily mass. Traditionally, the members of the
family knelt on a step before the balustrade in the King's Gallery, with
only one hassock for Louis XIV's use. The king immediately offered
this cushion to Philip, who very tactfully declined; to demonstrate his
grandson's equality, Louis ordered the hassock put to one side and the
two kings knelt together on the carpet. The next day, two cushions
were placed side by side in the gallery.

At his first public supper following his elevation, Philip V sat to his grandfather's right, in an identical armchair, and appeared somewhat chagrined at seeing his older brother and his wife relegated to folding chairs at the end of the table. Since the first few days of the new reign were devoted to paying formal visits to the members of the French royal family, Louis XIV carefully decreed that there be no stools or chairs in the room — to spare the boy's kin the mortification of having to stand in the presence of His Spanish Majesty. However uncomfortable this arrangement, the royals all deferred except for Adelaide: seeking out her longtime playmate in his study, she stood respectfully for a few minutes, then plopped herself down in a comfortable side chair and declared that she preferred to sit when she saw no useful purpose in standing.

Adelaide also demonstrated her attitude toward the cold and rigid formality of protocol in a harmless prank that upset the sticklers and delighted the new king. Philip V received a deputation from the Académie Française in the Mercury Salon. Adelaide hid herself in the drapes of the royal bed, and as the long-winded speechmakers droned their congratulations, she treated her brother-in-law to a sideshow of funny faces and deft mimicry, making it all but impossible for Philip to keep a regal demeanor.

The date of the new king's departure for Spain was set for December 4, 1700. He was to be accompanied as far as the border by his two brothers, the duc de Beauvilliers, and a suitably impressive French escort. (After taking their leave at Saint-Jean-de-Luz, the French party was to return by way of Languedoc and Provence, in order that Bourgogne might see as much of his future realm as possible.)

This journey to the Pyrenees posed even greater challenges to protocol than Philip's brief sojourn at Versailles, for the younger brother, a present sovereign, clearly took precedence over the older, heir to the land through which they now traveled. Louis XIV neatly devised a solution, though one hardly welcomed by the three affectionate brothers: because of the question of armchairs, the new king would eat his meals alone; because of the matter of the hassock, he would hear mass alone; and at public receptions, where the gradations of armchairs, armless chairs, and low stools could present endless difficulties, everybody would stand. One concession to privacy and fraternal intimacy was made: while on the road, the three brothers could picnic together in one coach.

The morning of December 4 the court waited in the Hall of Mirrors to pay its last compliments to the departing king. In the privacy of the king's study, the royal family said farewell with great emotion. Adelaide wept openly, and when Philip V presented her with a magnificent pair of diamond earrings that had once belonged to his mother, she broke completely and fled the room. The family exchanged other tokens, and Louis XIV (also unable to hide his tears) handed his grandson a list of Royal Instructions, meticulously compiled in the king's own hand.

Beside providing useful advice for the fledgling monarch, the instructions afford an illuminating look at the Sun King's concepts of absolutism. That his grandson's (and his own) birthright was divinely ordained Louis XIV had no doubt: his first dictum was "Never omit any of your duties towards God"; later, in Rule Three, he elaborated: "Cause God to be honored in all places where you have power; procure His glory; give the example. It is one of the greatest forms of good that kings can do."

There was much advice from the veteran to the novice on the abstract responsibilities of monarchy: "Love the Spaniards and all your subjects attached to your Crown and to your person; do not give preference to those who flatter you the most; esteem those who, for a good cause, venture to displease you, for these are your real friends . . . Make your subjects happy; and with a view to this, only engage in war when you are obliged, and after you have well considered and weighed the reasons with your Council . . . Endeavor to keep your finances in good order."

There was also much reflection on the specific position of Philip V:

See that your Viceroys and Governors shall always be Spaniards . . . Give evidence of your gratitude to the late King and to all who sided with choosing you as his successor . . . Have great confidence in Cardinal Portocarrero [the pro-French archbishop of Toledo] and show him your pleasure in the course he has pursued . . . I think you should do something considerable for the Ambassador who had the task to ask for you and to be the first to greet you in the quality of a subject . . . Have no dealings with the Queen Dowager beyond what you cannot help; arrange for her to leave Madrid and not to go out of Spain; wherever she is, keep an eye on her conduct, and prevent her from mixing up herself in any affairs; regard with suspicion those who have too much to do with her.

Louis XIV realized that a new and alien king might not at once win public approval, therefore Philip was to "throw some money to the

people when you are in Spain, and especially when entering Madrid."
Very important: "Do not appear astonished at the extraordinary figures you will meet; never make fun of them; each country has its
peculiar manners, and you will soon become accustomed to what at
first will seem most surprising to you."

On the whole, Louis's instructions were well intentioned, and for an
apprentice ruler like Philip, highly valuable. However, one theme re-
curred throughout, a tragic, if human, flaw in the royal philosophy
that, once followed, would lead inexorably to continental war: "Never
forget that you are French . . . Keep all Frenchmen in good order . . .
Have entire trust in the duc d'Harcourt [the French ambassador to
Spain]; he is a clever and honest man, and will only give you advice in
accordance with your interests . . . Live in close union with France,
since there is nothing so advantageous to our two Powers as this union,
which nothing can withstand." This idea of a union that nothing could
withstand, this elimination of the Pyrenees, was the very thing of
which all Europe lived in dread.

When the great mirrored doors to the gallery were flung wide, the
French court beheld a weeping royal family. For the last time, Louis
XIV presented the king of Spain to his nobility. His voice shaking with
emotion, he cried, "Behold the Princes of my blood and yours! Our
two nations must now regard themselves as one. Our interests must be
the same." And amid great cheers, Philip V, the first Spanish Bourbon,
entered his coach and left Versailles forever.

Begrudgingly, Europe accepted the accession of Philip V, hoping fervently that the stipulation made by Carlos — the perpetual separation
of France and Spain — would be honored by the voracious Sun King.
No one wanted war, least of all Louis XIV — so he maintained. Yet his
subsequent actions plainly contradicted his avowed desire for peace,
and first confused then alarmed the major powers. The truth of the
matter was that Louis XIV had become convinced that a continental
conflict over a French king in Madrid was ultimately unavoidable, and
he was determined to prepare as fully as possible for it. It was this very
conviction that largely determined his acceptance of the throne of
Spain in the first place — if a struggle for the Spanish inheritance was
impossible to avert, then he preferred his candidate to be on the throne
before it all began.

And so rather than allay European fears of French domination, the
Sun King blatantly encouraged them. In February 1701 — just as the

new king made his triumphant entry into Madrid — Louis XIV issued letters patent, duly registered by his parlement, upholding Philip V's succession rights to the crown of France. William III was deeply disturbed by this flagrant defiance of poor Carlos's will, but still could not rouse his passive Parliament. But his luck and the tide were turning. A few days later news arrived in London that the exclusive rights for the importation of Negro slaves to South America had been signed over by the Spanish government to a French company — a serious blow to British commercial interests.

British and continental fears grew even greater with Louis XIV's next move: though still officially at peace, he marched his armies into the Spanish Netherlands, appointing himself a sort of "real estate agent" come to claim his grandson's property from the old management on behalf of the new. Those forts under Spanish control welcomed the French invaders, and the few Dutch holdings, recognizing the futility of their resistance, surrendered to the superior force. By springtime Namur, Charleroi, Ath, Mons, Nieuport, Oudenarde, and Ostend — virtually the entire Spanish Netherlands — had been absorbed into the kingdom of France. With the exception of Maastricht (still firmly in Dutch hands), Louis XIV had bloodlessly regained in one month all the territories he had lost during eight years of war.

With the French army on their very border, the Dutch grew frantic, and at last the English Parliament was sufficiently alarmed to take action. On June 8, 1701, the House of Commons authorized William III to "seek allies"; the brilliant John Churchill, duke of Marlborough and captain-general of the English army, was appointed ambassador extraordinaire and dispatched to The Hague, his mission to negotiate a treaty of alliance between the English, the Dutch, and the Hapsburg Empire.

It might be supposed that Marlborough's task was a relatively simple one: the emperor, furious at the loss of the Spanish crown and declaring the will of Carlos II invalid (he maintained that it was signed under duress), had already begun marching his troops into Italy with the intention of taking the entire peninsula for himself; the Dutch, with the Grand Army on their doorstep, lived in daily dread of invasion. But the negotiations were in fact quite difficult to conclude, and consumed the months of July through September, often threatening to break down completely.

For one thing, the French diplomatic corps had secret orders to divide the prospective allies with enticing offers of territory and money, and at all costs to prevent the formation of another Grand Alliance. Secondly, Marlborough was forced to contend with the widespread English mood of wariness at another foreign entanglement; Parliament's reluctance to make a major contribution to the continental defense force all but checked his bargaining powers. These difficulties might well have succeeded in preventing a coalition, but for a surprising turn of events: Louis XIV's inexplicable behavior at the deathbed of the ex-king James II of England.

Following the Glorious Revolution of 1688, which had toppled the Catholic James and replaced him with staunchly Protestant William and Mary, the fugitive monarch, his wife, and their infant son (destined to enter history as the Old Pretender) appealed for succor from kinsman Louis XIV.[1] Never did the Sun King demonstrate the generosity of his nature more nobly than in his relations with his fallen cousin during the last, sad years of James II's life. True, much of the honor accorded to the dethroned James was Louis's affirmation of his belief in the eternal sanctity of coronation, but his courtesy and consideration for James and Mary remained steadfast, long after they had ceased to play any part in European politics. The royal exiles were given the king's own palace at Saint-Germain, and the French treasury paid to feed and clothe them and the large entourage that had followed them from England. When James made his unsuccessful attempt to regain his throne in 1690, it was a French ship that took him to Ireland, French troops that fought and lost. At Versailles, the Stuarts were given precedence over everyone else and addressed as "Your Majesties" (even after the treaty of Ryswick compelled Louis to recognize William).

These signal tokens of affection and respect were hardly inspired by the character or the person of the defeated king. James II was cold and charmless, a bigoted reactionary, utterly incapable of sustaining the affections of those who served him. Charles II had said of him, "You see my brother? When he becomes King, he will surely lose his kingdom through religious zeal and his soul through ugly queans [mistresses], for he has too bad taste to choose fine ones." Madame, whose admiration for William III was considerable,[2] regarded his predecessor as little more than an idiot. In a letter to her aunt on July 30, 1690, she observed: "The King of England is not quick in repartee; sometimes he would be wiser if he kept silence," and related a conversation between James and a gentleman-in-waiting on the unsuccessful Irish invasion earlier that year:

"Sire," said M. de la Rougere, "what became of the French who were with Your Majesty?" "I know nothing of them," replied the King. "How so? Your Majesty knows nothing of them? Were they not with you?" "Pardon me," said the King, "but I am going to tell you all. The Prince of Orange [William III] arrived with forty thousand men, and I had only half that number; he had forty cannon, I only sixteen; I saw that he was placing his left wing towards Dublin, and that he was going to cut off my road, and hem me in; so I went away, and returned here." "But I have heard tell of a certain bridge that Your Majesty abandoned to the enemy. I suppose you had no need of it." "Oh! as for that bridge — I defended it very well, but the enemy sent troops and a cannon, and this same cannon forced my troops to retire, so the Prince of Orange passed over it."

A military strategist he clearly was not; his success in private life was no greater than in public, as Madame discovered when the royal couple paid a visit to Saint-Cloud in August 1690: "Monsieur, as usual, was talking of his jewels and furniture, and ended by saying to the King, 'And Your Majesty, who has so much money, have you built some fine palace?' 'Money!' observed the Queen, 'He never had any. I never saw him with a halfpenny!' The King answered: 'I once had some, but I did not purchase gems and furniture, neither did I build palaces; all mine went in making fine ships, cannons and muskets.' 'Yes,' said the Queen, 'and much good it did you. Everything has gone ill with us.' "

Everything had indeed gone ill: in 1701, James was an embittered old man of sixty-seven, a king in exile for thirteen years, his health rapidly failing. Early that summer he attended a church service and, as the choir sang "Our inheritance is turned to strangers; the crown is fallen from our head," he suddenly collapsed to the floor, the victim of a stroke. His condition remained grave for several days; when he began to show some improvement, he was taken to the spa at Bourbon for recuperation.

He returned to Saint-Germain at the end of August, but suffered another stroke at once. The French royal family hurried to his bedside. Madame found him "in a pitiful state; he can still speak and knows everybody, but he looks very ill and has a long beard." Louis XIV was deeply distressed to see his fellow king in extremis, and even more moved when the dying man gasped out his last request: that his thirteen-year-old son, the titular prince of Wales, be acknowledged as the true and only king of England.

Louis XIV hastily called a cabinet meeting to discuss the proposal. His ministers were unanimously against recognition of the pretender. The minister of war pointed out that this would be in direct violation of the treaty of Ryswick; acknowledgment of the Catholic claimant would both infuriate and unite Protestant England, strengthening Marlborough's hitherto weak position at the negotiating table in The Hague. Furthermore, it would be obvious to all the world that "King James III" was a mere French puppet and his chances would be ruined from the outset. Louis XIV quietly listened to the arguments presented (apparently the wisest and most logical course — inaction — occurred to no one); he dismissed his advisers and returned to Saint-Germain. Taking a seat beside the dying James, the Sun King announced, "I come to tell Your Majesty that, whenever it shall please God to take you from us, I will be to your son what I have been to you, and will acknowledge him as King of England, Scotland and Ireland."

Recognition of the Old Pretender, whatever Louis XIV's true motives, would prove the strangest, and certainly most expensive, error in his life. Reprisals were swift: the English ambassador, Lord Manchester, did not return with Louis from Saint-Germain, but quit France immediately, not even taking leave of the king. William III heard the news in Holland, at his house in Het Loo; he turned scarlet, and pulled his hat down low, unable to hide his distress. Then he sent orders to London for the immediate dismissal of the French ambassador.

James II died on September 6, 1701. On September 7 in The Hague, the Grand Offensive and Defensive Alliance was concluded between England, Holland, and the empire. With his recognition of "James III," Louis had provided William and Marlborough the sorely needed prod for a sluggish Parliament. In English eyes, the incipient War of the Spanish Succession would now be a war for the British succession as well.

While Louis XIV occupied the spring and summer months of 1701 antagonizing his northern adversaries, Emperor Leopold I had not waited to take action. Leopold refused to believe that Carlos had willingly signed over his patrimony to Spain's ancient enemy; to support his contention, he pointed out that the postmortem on the Spanish king had shown Carlos's brain and heart "grievously infected with disease." The rich Italian peninsula lay within his grasp, provided that Hapsburg armies got there before their Bourbon counterparts. Immediate mobilization was ordered, and by the end of May 1701, 25,000 troops under Austria's greatest general — Prince Eugene of Savoy[3] — had invaded northern Italy and menaced the plains of Verona.

More than ever before Louis XIV had need of an unconditional alliance with Victor Amadeus. Control of the safe pass was vital: unless French troops could be moved across the Alps as quickly as possible to bolster the small Spanish force awaiting them, the Milanese territories would fall to the imperial army. Furthermore, the Sun King's troops required winter quarters on the Italian peninsula, since a retreat back to French territory would entail great expense and a loss of valuable time. The king pressured his ambassador in Turin for a new treaty ensuring unqualified cooperation with the duke of Savoy.

But twenty years of bullying and bargaining had taught Louis XIV nothing about his chameleon nephew by marriage: the Savoyard gnat had risen from the defeat of his previous resistance to buzz once more about the proud French lion.

Two generations of marital alliance between Savoy and France had not achieved the subjugation the Sun King envisioned. It was, of course, extremely gratifying to Victor Amadeus that the king was so enchanted with his daughter; but to the duke's mounting irritation, Louis XIV's overbearing attitude toward the small Italian duchy remained set. Their difficulties were further, and seriously, compounded by Louis's duplicity on the question of the Spanish succession — long before the death of Carlos II brought matters to a head.

As early as December 1696, Tessé had reported to Versailles that Victor Amadeus had spoken with him of the problems that would arise on the death of the king of Spain — referring in particular to the duchy of Milan. Acquisition of Milan was the lifelong dream of Victor Amadeus; he had insisted on the inclusion of a secret clause in Adelaide's marriage contract that France would attempt to procure the duchy for Savoy should Carlos II die "during the present war." Carlos was still alive as the Peace of Ryswick was framed, and while in the duke's opinion Louis XIV was still honor-bound to uphold his obligation, he knew better than to blindly trust the crafty old Sun King. Could France, he now demanded of Tessé, be expected to fulfill in peacetime a promise made in war?

The Frenchman adroitly evaded commitment, and requested immediate instructions. Louis XIV replied:

> I was aware that the smallest sign of reopening of the succession would inspire the Duke of Savoy to wish for some profit for himself . . . He requires my help, believing that my own advantage will lead

me to prevent the Emperor from adding [Milan] to his other possessions. The Prince should be persuaded that I, more than anyone, have
his real interests at heart . . . The time, however, has not yet come for
measures to be taken. The health of the King of Spain has always been
so poor that the slightest mishap makes [the Spanish] fear for his life.
His age gives cause to hope that the dreaded tragedy is still far distant,
for a tragedy it would be, bringing the danger of war closer than ever
before, with each claimant nation armed and ready to uphold its
rights by force. You know all that I have done to bring peace to Italy.
All my endeavors would prove useless, foreign armies would at once
reenter it, were it thought that I was taking preparatory measures
with the Duke of Savoy for the conquest of Milan. I therefore much
approve your reply on that subject, and counsel you to avoid going
into details. Simply assure him that if the King of Spain dies, he will
find me ready to do all that may contribute to his personal advantage.

But the ambitious duke of Savoy was not to be mollified by vague
and hollow promises, nor did he mean to sit quietly by while Europe
partitioned off the Spanish Empire. He had claims of his own, and not
without justice: he was a descendant of the infanta Caterina, daughter
of Philip II of Spain (in 1585, Caterina had married Charles Emmanuel
I of Savoy). Moreover, he hurried to point out, the will of Philip IV,
which excluded the Sun King's wife and her descendants, had enu-
merated the order of succession: his son Carlos and his heirs; his third
daughter, Margaret Thérèse (wife of Emperor Leopold) and her heirs;
his sister, Empress Maria (mother of Leopold) and her heirs; and *then*
the House of Savoy. If France had no wish for an Austria south of the
Pyrenees, the only legal alternative was Victor Amadeus.

The French responded to this argument with two points: Philip IV's
right to dispose of his son's inheritance in advance was itself ques-
tionable; and should that right be allowed, there still remained two
princes with superior claims, the Bavarian prince and Archduke Karl.
Still, the duke's rights merited some consideration and, as Victor Amadeus reiterated, he wasn't asking for the entire empire — only Milan.

Victor Amadeus had been incensed by the First Partition Treaty,
which altogether ignored his claims, and he made no secret of his
displeasure to the new French ambassador (the comte de Briord had
replaced Tessé in December 1697). In January, Briord informed Versailles that he was all but barred from the duke's presence, that courtiers had secret instructions to avoid him, and that the speaking of
French within the ducal palace was now frowned on. By return post,

Louis observed: "It now appears to me that a revision of the existing treaty might be the means of preventing the Emperor from conquering the whole of Italy, and at the same time bind the Duke to oppose him for the sake of my advantage. It is in my interests to pursue this policy . . ."

Revision became unnecessary when the death of the Bavarian heir rendered the First Partition Treaty useless. In a secret dispatch to Victor Amadeus, Louis XIV proposed an astonishing new plan: by virtue of his Spanish descent, the duke should inherit the throne of Spain and its colonies in the New World, while the rest of the empire would be absorbed by France. Savoyard reaction was predictable: the court of Turin was agog with excitement, and Briord wrote to his master: "Everyone here, poets, people, and the gentry alike, all speak with the same voice, and regard the Prince as the next King of Spain."

Just as Louis XIV had expected, appealing to the duke's greed was the surest way to cloud his otherwise astute political judgment. Had Victor Amadeus been able to assess the French proposal rationally, he would have seen its impossibility at once: given his treachery in deserting the League of Augsburg in 1696, it was inconceivable that William III should ever accept him on the throne of Spain.[4]

Sure enough, William rejected the plan outright. Undaunted (and probably relieved), Louis XIV proceeded to play a double game: while secretly arranging with William the terms of the second treaty, he continued his assurances to Victor Amadeus that he was doing everything within his power to obtain for him the duchy of Milan (or some equitable settlement). It should be said in the Sun King's defense that, at least in the initial stages of negotiation, some attempt *was* made to include Victor Amadeus in the partition plans, evidenced by two secret dispatches to the French ambassador in London. The first suggested that the duke be given the kingdom of the Two Sicilies (the southern half of the Italian peninsula and the islands of Sicily and Sardinia) in exchange for Savoy and Nice, which would then revert to France; the second proposed that Victor Amadeus should surrender Savoy to France in return for the crown of Spain exclusively. Both ideas were rejected by the English, and it is doubtful the French king ever had any real hope of success for either plan, knowing as he did the British animosity to the turncoat duke of Savoy.

When the terms of the Second Partition Treaty were published, Victor Amadeus was livid at again being excluded, with all his fury directed toward the Sun King. When the French ambassador requested an audience and the duke's endorsement of the treaty, Victor Amadeus refused both, saying he was "too small a prince to enter into so important an affair, in which it had not been thought necessary to give him either part or portion." Briord wrote Louis XIV that later in his private apartments, the duke was heard to rant and bellow over this "latest French humiliation."

The Sun King was now genuinely alarmed. It was imperative that Savoy be kept from any dealings with the emperor, so throughout the summer months of 1700, a number of conferences took place between Louis XIV, his foreign minister, Torcy, and the Savoyard ambassador, Vernone, on possible amendments to the treaty.

The plan that emerged from these discussions was simple enough: the prince of Lorraine, to whom the second treaty awarded the duchy of Milan in return for his neutrality, would be given instead the kingdom of the Two Sicilies; Victor Amadeus would then receive Milan, surrendering to France Nice and Savoy; lastly, the Sun King and the duke would sign an offensive and defensive alliance. But this arrangement, mutually advantageous to Louis XIV and Victor Amadeus, was not adopted — for the gnat gambled with time, and lost. Motivated by greed and his lifelong resentment of the French lion, the duke declared this settlement insufficient, demanding also the city of Monteferrato (part of the duchy of Mantua), the Genoese port of Finale Ligure, and the retention of the valley of Barcelonnette, which would allow him continued access to France.

Louis XIV was unprepared to meet these fresh demands; negotiations continued as summer turned to fall. When word reached Turin of the impending death of Carlos II, Victor Amadeus realized the error of his delay: he hurriedly advised Vernone to accept whatever conditions France offered and get the Sun King firmly committed on paper. Fate intervened, and the Franco-Savoyard treaty was still unsigned when Fontainebleau discovered that Carlos the Sufferer was no more and the duc d'Anjou was king.

Victor Amadeus watched helplessly as all his dreams evaporated, his spirits hardly improving after a smug letter from Louis XIV informing him of Anjou's accession: "My brother and nephew, I am so well persuaded of your devotion to my interests that I cannot doubt your pleasure at learning of my decision to accept, on behalf of my grandson, the Duc d'Anjou, the succession of the entire empire of Spain, to which his birth, the testament of the late Catholic King, and the voice of the Spanish peoples unanimously entitles him . . ." Nor would the

duke have appreciated the dispatch received at the same time by Phelypeaux, the latest French ambassador to Savoy: "Tell His Royal Highness that I am persuaded he will rejoice to see a monarchy to which the
testament of the late King of Spain may conceivably summon his
descendants and make them safe from any form of partition . . ."

Victor Amadeus did *not* rejoice; rather, he contended that the Sun
King could not now withdraw from his earlier (though unsigned)
arrangement, except with dishonor: "What! Is this all that comes of
my hopes of benefiting by his expressed affection, and the honor of
becoming his near relation — an honor which I flattered myself I was
doing him. Oh! I might have expected this!" Phelypeaux, commenting
on the duke's outburst, added, "The Duke is brimful of honor, pride,
arrogance and ambition. All these sentiments would have been satisfied by the acquisition of Milan, of which he had believed himself as
firmly possessed as of Turin. Nothing can compare with his pain at
seeing his hopes dashed, and of all the Spanish succession, nothing
remaining to him, beyond the honor of offering his congratulations."

With Carlos II's testament affirming the legality of his every move,
Louis XIV was under no compulsion to offer the duke one acre of the
coveted Milan. But he needed the duke's alliance, should war break
out, so he stepped up the vague assurances to Victor Amadeus that he
would "lose no opportunity of furthering his interests." When it was
reported to Versailles that the wily duke was tiring of empty French
promises and, worse still, was seeing more and more of the Austrian
ambassador, the Sun King ordered Phelypeaux to force a commitment
for or against the Franco-Spanish cause.

The gnat was not about to succumb to more leonine pressure: he
refused to promise or sign anything, and Phelypeaux was left with his
sarcastic comment that "he was glad to think that his country could
be of some service, and hoped that his army might be also." Louis XIV
was desperate to wrest from the duke a safe conduct for his troops,
who idled along the border while their presence was required in the
troubled Tyrolean valleys. He wrote to Tessé, conferring in Milan with
the Spanish governor, and ordered him to leave at once for Turin.
Tessé was more familiar with the duke's subtle and elusive character
than any other Frenchman, but he had no better luck than Phelypeaux;
all too soon he was complaining that Victor Amadeus's "strange,
suspicious, irresolute, ill-natured, self-seeking conduct . . . [was]
enough to try the patience of a saint."

Without the promise of some reward for his cooperation, Victor

Amadeus chose to remain noncommittal. No written guarantee of safe conduct was forthcoming: "The King of France is powerful enough to send troops through my country whenever it pleases him; he does not need my consent" — a clever evasion since both parties were fully aware that an unwarranted French entry into Savoy could be construed as an invasion, and would justify the duke in calling for Austrian aid. When Phelypeaux raised the question of provisions and accommodations, Victor Amadeus snapped angrily that he was not an army contractor and would not concern himself with such matters.

Though infuriated by the duke's resistance, Louis XIV realized that concessions were unavoidable. He dispatched to Turin a new treaty of alliance: in return for Savoy's pledge of eight thousand infantry and thirty-five hundred cavalry (plus, of course, safe conduct permits across the Alps), Victor Amadeus would be named generalissimo of the French and Spanish troops in Italy; he would be given a monthly subsidy of fifty thousand écus for the duration; and — what Louis XIV clearly considered the "bait" — a marriage between the new king of Spain and the duke's second daughter, thirteen-year-old Marie Louise, would be arranged at once. (Philip V's feelings on this match were of no greater importance than his brother's had been four years earlier, but deeply devoted to Marie Adelaide, he happily welcomed the idea of marriage to her sister.)

Victor Amadeus was not particularly thrilled with the prospects of yet another Bourbon marriage. However appealing the idea of his daughter on the throne of Spain, he perceived it was the Sun King's intention to further bind him to French interests. It was himself, not his daughters, he wished ultimately to elevate, so he demanded the inclusion of one more secret clause in the treaty: if Milan was in French (or Spanish) hands at the end of the approaching war, or if it had been awarded to the prince of Lorraine as stipulated under the Second Partition Treaty, Louis XIV would guarantee its reversion to Victor Amadeus in exchange for Savoy, Nice, and Barcelonnette.

The Sun King's response, strictly honorable, was a grave mistake. He had been advised repeatedly by Phelypeaux that the duke's heart "[was] still set on Milan . . . If he should be disappointed, a desire for vengeance will lead him to side with the Emperor." But despite these warnings, he responded that it was impossible for him to make any such promise or dispose of lands in direct violation of the late king's will. The best he could do was pledge to preserve the prewar status quo in Italy — which in effect would quash all Victor Amadeus's dreams of aggrandizement.

Phelypeaux, anticipating the duke's objection, protested to Versailles, but to his great surprise, Victor Amadeus accepted the king's conditions and signed the treaty on April 6, 1701. In truth, there was little else he could do: with France on his left, the army of Spanish Italy on his right, and the emperor too far away to help, annihilation was a very real threat. He had no choice but to bend again to the Sun King's will, albeit with a bitter heart.

From that moment, his determination to desert the French cause was reborn: immediately following the conclusion of the Franco-Savoyard alliance, Victor Amadeus sent a secret dispatch to Vienna, assuring the emperor that he had been compelled to sign the treaty or risk the extermination of his country; as for the marriage plan (for the emperor had been negotiating concurrently to win Marie Louise for his son Archduke Karl), he wrote that he had been overwhelmed by its suddenness and forced to agree, but politically it meant nothing to him. To his ambassador, the marquis du Prié, the duke sent instructions to reiterate to the emperor that his signature was given under duress — and to pave the way for his eventual defection.

According to Sourches, Marie Adelaide was performing her toilette when the news arrived that the treaty had been signed at last. She "jumped for joy" at her father's commitment to the French side and her sister's engagement to her beloved brother-in-law. The Sun King's pleasure was no less than his granddaughter's. The new bride would amply fulfill all their hopes; Marie Louise deservedly earned the affection and esteem of Philip V and captured the hearts of the Spanish nation. But the duke of Savoy would show his true colors all too soon.

In the spring of 1701, there was still no official declaration of war; however there was, in Spanish Italy, an invading force of twenty-five thousand Austrian troops. Leopold I employed this formidable tool to prevent Pope Clement XI from formally investing the new king of Spain with the crowns of Naples and Sicily. To a small degree, he succeeded: formal investiture was postponed "for various reasons," but His Holiness let it be known that he accepted Philip V's nomination to those benefices and regarded him as "the sole and rightful King of Spain, Naples, and Sicily." As Saint-Simon observed: "Thus it had become necessary [for the French] to prepare for active war in Italy."

Immediate complications arose — all difficulties stemming (predictably) from the reluctant generalissimo of the French and Spanish troops in Italy. Several anxious weeks passed and still Victor Amadeus delayed in taking to the field. The French commanders who awaited him — the prince de Vaudemont and the maréchal Catinat — grew steadily more suspicious of the duke's loyalty to the cause of the two crowns.

For Catinat, suspicion gave way to certainty when he observed that the imperial troops were able to cross the Adige River, unopposed, and score a major victory at Carpi on July 9. The duke's force had appeared at the eleventh hour, but his movements had been so dilatory that Catinat informed Versailles, "It was not natural that the armies of the Two Crowns, seventy thousand strong, should have to retire before thirty thousand Imperial troops." Louis XIV refused to comment, afraid to antagonize his vital ally, but the gruff Catinat held no such qualms: in war council the morning after the defeat at Carpi, he spoke out, his eyes directed on Victor Amadeus: "Not only is Prince Eugene kept informed on all the movements of our army, on the strength of the battalions and their destinations, but he is always acquainted with every project discussed in Council." Victor Amadeus wisely ignored the maréchal.

Catinat continued his complaints of suspected treachery to the king. But Savoy was strategically too important at this juncture and, callously, Louis XIV sacrificed his loyal maréchal rather than offend his dubious ally. Using terms of bitter reproach, the Sun King announced that the maréchal de Villeroi would succeed to the Italian command; Catinat, still faithful despite this shabby treatment, made a submissive reply to the king and craved permission to remain with his men, serving under Villeroi.

The appointment of François de Neufville, second duc de Villeroi, raised several eyebrows, for the courtier-maréchal lacked any real knowledge of warfare, and was unanimously condemned by his fellow soldiers. One general called his tactics "mean and unmasterly"; another described him as "presumptuous and ignorant"; a third wrote: "He knows how to avoid serious engagements and executes minor ones badly."

Villeroi was the son of Louis XIV's former governor. Three years younger than the king, he had been raised with Louis, and they remained intimate friends for life. Since childhood, Villeroi had openly worshiped Louis XIV as his hero, and the king, protective and patronizing, looked on him as a younger brother; the only time the word "favorite" ever slipped from his mouth was in reference to Villeroi.

Unfortunately, Villeroi's arrival at camp only exacerbated the situation. His arrogance and his superior attitude toward the far more capable Catinat led the entire army to despise him, while his insulting familiarity toward Victor Amadeus — whom he pointedly addressed as "Monsieur" rather than "Your Royal Highness" — infuriated the duke and his Savoyard troops. One instance of Villeroi's blatant rudeness found its way back to the galleries of Versailles, repeated by incredulous courtiers: while addressing the staff of officers, Victor Amadeus opened his jeweled snuff box and took a pinch. Villeroi, standing close by, reached over without a word and helped himself to the snuff. The duke flushed scarlet at this presumption, threw the box to the ground, and barely able to conceal his fury, gave orders that the box should be refilled.

A second catastrophic French defeat that summer — the battle of Chiari in September 1701 — was solely the responsibility of the vain, inept Villeroi, who engaged in battle despite the unanimous protest of his general staff. But the crowning act of his ludicrous career in Italy came on February 21, 1702. Villeroi's troops had occupied the town of Cremona for the winter, but so little attention had been given to fortifications that Prince Eugene was able to steal into the city by night and take possession of it without the French troops even being aware of their presence till the following morning. A skirmish followed, and the imperial troops were forced to retreat — but several hundred prisoners were taken, including Villeroi himself. The loss of their idiot commander put the army in excellent spirits, and a lampoon made its way through the ranks: "Français, rendons grâces à Bellone / Notre bonheur est sans égal. / Nous avons conservé Crémone / Et perdu notre Général." ("France, give thanks to Bellona [the Roman goddess of war] / Our luck is unequaled. / We have saved Cremona / And lost our General.") To the army's great joy and relief, Villeroi was quickly replaced with the duc de Vendôme.

Villeroi's insufferable insolence toward Victor Amadeus had strengthened the duke's resolve to join with the emperor of Austria and the newly formed Grand Alliance. At this critical juncture, only a sense of loyalty to his daughters and their husbands might have prevented him from taking this drastic step. But if Villeroi had pushed him to the brink, Philip V — a true and typical Bourbon — now nudged him over the edge.

Philip deemed it politic to present himself to his beleaguered Italian subjects. In April 1702, he set sail for Naples, to take formal possession of the kingdom of the Two Sicilies. He intended to journey as far north as Milan, and so a meeting with his parents-in-law was hastily arranged. Victor Amadeus, together with Anne Marie and Madame Royale, left Turin for Alessandria; the ladies waited there while the duke traveled on to meet his son-in-law in the nearby village of Acqui.

During the preparations for this visit, Victor Amadeus insisted that Philip owed him all the honors due a sovereign, citing as his precedent Philip II's reception of the duke's great-grandfather, Charles Emmanuel, when he had journeyed to Spain to marry the infanta Caterina. The Spanish protocol officers had led the duke to believe these honors would be strictly observed; but, alas, the inordinate pride of the Bourbon dynasty had not been taken into account, and unwittingly, the arrogance of the grandson was to undo the alliance of the grandfather.

At their first interview, nothing occurred to shatter the duke's illusions. Philip alighted from his coach and warmly embraced his father-in-law. He apologized that his carriage was too small to offer the duke a seat (true or not, Victor Amadeus accepted this without question), then invited him to dinner that night. Victor Amadeus left this first meeting happily enough, but when he entered the king's dining room that evening, he noted with suspicion two identical armchairs. Again Philip V greeted the duke with great courtesy, then as they approached the table, took for himself the right-hand chair and offered his father-in-law the left. The duke was outraged; an identical left chair, as all the world knew, was always occupied by the person of *inferior* status. Mortified and insulted, Victor Amadeus left without another word.

The party was to reconvene the following day at Alessandria, and Philip V aggravated the already precarious situation with a further slight to the House of Savoy: rather than advancing to receive the duchess and Madame Royale, the king remained stationary at the door of his apartment, making the ladies come instead to him. The duke was now livid. Strained, brief, and meaningless polite conversation followed; Philip retired and the duke at once called for a carriage to take his offended family back to Turin, without making their farewells to the proud — and tactless — young king of Spain.

To our eyes, the observation of such nuances of etiquette appear inconsequential, but to Victor Amadeus, the visit gave indisputable evidence of the contempt with which these overbearing Bourbons viewed his own noble house. Removed forever was any sense of loyalty, any scruples over defection. It mattered not at all that his eldest daughter considered herself "a proper Frenchwoman," even less that his youngest daughter was queen of Spain. He would, at the earliest possible moment, turn his back on all prior commitments and join arms with Europe against the army of the Two Crowns.

Nor did he doubt for a moment that he would be welcomed — albeit as a prodigal — since, despite the animosity of William III of England and the warranted mistrust of Leopold of Austria, Savoy's defection was vital. Only by banding together in one great force could the European powers hope to shatter the French hegemony and prevent the elimination of the Pyrenees.

13

Lessons in Love and War

THE OFFICIAL DECLARATION of war came on May 15, 1702, more than a year after the imperial invasion of Italy. The Grand Alliance — the life dream of William III — included Great Britain, Holland, Austria, Denmark, and all of Germany save Bavaria (and was joined by Savoy in 1703); their opposition was the army of the Two Crowns, France and Spain.[1] The opponents were better matched than might be expected: true, under the treaty terms agreed on at The Hague the previous September, the Dutch pledged a force of one hundred thousand, the Hapsburgs eighty-two thousand, Britain an army of forty thousand and a navy of equal size, and eight thousand soldiers from Duke Frederick of Brandenburg[2] — a quarter million men, a most impressive force; but the Grand Army of France *alone* numbered four hundred thousand.

It was, like so many European conflicts, a war of relatives in opposition to each other: Louis XIV and Emperor Leopold I were first cousins as well as brothers-in-law; Louis was also first cousin (once removed) to Queen Anne of England; Anne's field opponents included two half brothers, the pretender "King James III" and the duke of Berwick (James II's illegitimate son by Arabella Churchill); Berwick was pitted against his uncle, the duke of Marlborough; the Austrian commander, Prince Eugene of Savoy, against his cousin the duke of Savoy; and Victor Amadeus, following his defection, against both of his daughters' husbands.

The structure of war in the seventeenth and eighteenth centuries

bears little relation to our twentieth-century achievements of ruthless-
ness and brutality. War was based on strict rules of conduct and
founded on the structure of civilized behavior. Armies met to settle
precisely stated grievances and, military antagonism aside, there was
no hatred between forces: following a battle, both sides (and especially
the victor) returned to the field to rescue the wounded, and meticulous
records were kept for the subsequent exchange of prisoners. War was
waged only during the spring and summer months; with the onset of
cold weather, both sides retired to their winter quarters and passports
were issued to high-ranking officers enabling them to cross enemy
territories and make their way home for Christmas. Following precise
strictures of etiquette, opponent generals treated each other to every
courtesy and compliment, sending presents of fruit and fowl, allowing
private letters to pass unopened, and showing great concern for each
other's health — when Victor Amadeus sustained his severe illness in
1692, the French general he had so recently encountered on the battlefield sent him large quantities of mineral water and offered to
procure for him the best available French doctor.

Even the age-old problem of displaced nationals was treated logically and with true charity. Queen Anne's proclamation of war ended
with the following passage: "We henceforth strictly forbid the holding
of any correspondence or communication with France or Spain or
their subjects. But because there are remaining in our Kingdoms many
of the subjects of France and Spain, We do declare our Royal intention
to be, that all the subjects of France and Spain who shall demean
themselves dutifully towards us, shall be safe in their persons and their
estates."

Such polite warfare offered the young nobility tremendous opportunities to distinguish itself and, despite the misgivings of the duc de
Beauvilliers, the outbreak of war was greeted at Versailles with great
enthusiasm. Young men, restless and bored with the endless monotony
of pleasure, were infected with war fever and hurried off to join their
regiments and make their names. After all, anything but victory was
unthinkable.

In spite of the war — or perhaps because of it — the season at Versailles was an exceptionally brilliant one. The queen of the court was
a young lady of sixteen now, growing taller and maturing rapidly.
Adelaide was not a classic beauty — her cheeks were too full, her lips
too thick, and her forehead too prominent — but many of her features
were, in themselves, quite beautiful: her dark chestnut hair was thick

and luxuriant, her eyebrows finely shaped; her smooth Italian complexion was clear, and her eyes, Saint-Simon declared, were "the most eloquent and the most beautiful eyes in the world." Her slender figure was changing too, lengthening and rounding, and proportioned well: "not much bosom, but what there was was admirable." The years of courtly breeding had produced in her an exquisite grace, which Saint-Simon likened to that of a goddess walking on the clouds: "Grace accompanied her every step, her manners, and her most ordinary conversation. An air always simple and natural, often rather naïve, but seasoned with wit, aided by the ease peculiar to her, charmed all who approached her and communicated itself to them."

She was the unquestioned center of the court, and universally adored, and everyone from cabinet ministers to chambermaids strove to please her. Her waiting staff worshiped their mistress to the point of idolatry: Domingo, her Spanish butler, refused to marry, saying he could not share his affections with anyone but Marie Adelaide. When the princesse died, the heartbroken butler took to his bed, receiving no one but his confessor, and followed his goddess to the grave within the year. She became as indispensable to the court as to the king: "Everybody missed her when she was away; when she reappeared, the void was filled. In a word, she had attached every heart to her."

The object of this adoration was hardly ignorant of it, or of the physical changes she was now experiencing. Writing her grandmother in January 1702, she declared: "It seems to me that I am no longer young; my childhood has lasted but a short time!" Still, she behaved with a recklessness characteristically adolescent: her serious illness in the summer of 1701 had no effect on her spirit, for with her recovery, she threw herself into pleasure and amusement more strenuously than even before. Of course, those nearest and dearest to her — the king, Mme de Maintenon, and Bourgogne — who had been driven to the brink of despair during her sickness, watched with poorly concealed alarm as she returned to her former ways, but no one could deny her anything, nor were they willing to risk her irritation with feeble pleas for moderation.

During Adelaide's recuperation, Mme de Maintenon had organized small card parties to amuse her patient. Unwittingly, she paved the way for the princesse's new passion: gambling.

Up to this point, Adelaide's tender age had kept her from the card tables, but gaming had been a principal distraction at the French court for several decades. The young Sun King's taste had been nurtured by Cardinal Mazarin, who imported from Italy a game called hoca, a forerunner of roulette. When hoca declined in popularity, the vogue shifted to various games — hombre, piquet, lansquenet — and a game called la bassette, played between a banker and four bettors. Mme de Sévigné wrote of la bassette: "One can easily lose one hundred thousand pistoles at it in a single evening" — assuming one was not royal, or a royal mistress: the marquise de Montespan, on Christmas Day, 1678, lost two million pistoles at la bassette and four million one evening the next March. Even the virtuous Queen Marie Thérèse could not resist the gambling bug and on her death left a debt of three hundred thousand francs. Monseigneur was greatly addicted; so too was Monsieur, whose losses were so heavy on one occasion that he was forced to pawn his precious jewels. In his heyday, Louis XIV had played moderately, but with the approach of middle age, his fondness intensified; Saint-Simon wrote of the fifty-year-old monarch: "Now nothing interests him anymore but play — play at high stakes, that follows him everywhere in all his travels. At Marly . . . he has installed a great many tables." Under Mme de Maintenon's restraining influence, the king came to control his addiction: in the late 1680s, he banished la bassette and hoca from the court, "judging it prudent to prohibit them in the interests of his subjects' welfare," and set limits on the extent of an evening's loss; but these rules were more often than not ignored.

Several court critics deplored this insatiable passion that dominated the galleries and salons of Versailles. The Jesuit preacher Louis Bourdaloue warned: "Play without limit and without regulation is no longer an amusement, but a business, a profession, a trade, a fascination; it brings inevitably in its train the neglect of duty, the ruin of families, the dissipation of fortunes, the mean trickery and knavery which result from greed of gain, insanity, misery and despair" — but no one paid him any attention either. Madame wrote her aunt one winter that four officers, faced with insurmountable gambling debts, had committed suicide: "They would have done better to amuse themselves with innocent German games, and confined themselves to drinking milk." The diarist Charles Auguste de La Fare was outspoken on what he termed "the deterioration" of the French court: "Nothing is now to be seen but gaming, confusion and bad manners . . . When the Duchesse de Bourgogne entered Society, she found it hard not to succumb to the fashionable vices, of which drunkenness and lansquenet are the most ruinous."

Indeed Adelaide found it hard not to succumb. She had inherited from her father his Italian love of gambling, and she joined in the excitement with her standard gusto — all the more because, with Grandpapa standing by ready to pay her debts, she stood no chance of courting ruin or disgrace. She played with good humor and remained in high spirits even when luck ran against her, except for one occasion: entering the gaming room at Marly one evening, she discovered that the young duchesse de Berri had taken *her* favorite seat at the table. Barely able to hide her annoyance, the princesse took another chair and began to play. Her losses were matched only by her sister-in-law's winnings, and outraged by the usurper's luck, Adelaide suddenly rose and shouted angrily, "Get up, madame, you are in my seat!" The red-faced duchess threw her cards on the table and fled the room in tears; Louis XIV, watching from another table, said nothing.

But another incident is more typical of the gentle duchesse de Bourgogne and her lighthearted attitude toward gambling: again at a Marly card party, she was playing with the comtesse de Rupelmonde, wife of a colonel in the Walloon regiment of the Spanish army. The colonel had retired for the night, and sent his footman to whisper to his wife to join him. But the footman gave his mission instead to a soldier of the Swiss Guard, who marched into the crowded salon and barked out, in a heavy German accent, "Madame Rupelmonde, go to bed! The Colonel is already there, and has sent me to fetch you!" The mortified woman (enjoying a streak of good cards) tried to ignore both the summons and the laughter that filled the room, until Adelaide, laughing loudest of all, told the countess to be content with her winnings and obey her husband.

Lansquenet quickly became Adelaide's favorite game. Unlike dancing or acting, cards could be enjoyed every night, and her visits to her father-in-law's estate at Meudon multiplied when she discovered that Monseigneur played daily with Mlle de Choin and the princesse de Conti. This fervent novice was no match for such seasoned professionals: once at Meudon Adelaide lost twelve thousand pistoles in a single sitting. She hurried back to Versailles and begged Mme de Maintenon to cover her debt — and *not* to tell Bourgogne or the king.

The indulgent Maintenon complied, begrudgingly and not without a stern lecture; a few hours later, she received this letter from the princesse:

Friday, Midnight. I am in despair, *ma tante*, at always committing follies, and giving you reason to find fault with me. I am firmly resolved to correct myself, and not to play again at this wretched game [lansquenet], which serves only to damage my reputation and to diminish your affection, which is more precious to me than anything. I beg you, *ma tante,* not to speak to me about it, if I keep my resolution. If I fail only once, I shall be delighted for the King to forbid me the game, and to endure everything which may result from the bad impression which he will form of me. I shall never console myself for being the cause of your sufferings, and I shall not forgive this accursed lansquenet.

Pardon then, *ma tante,* my past faults. I hope that my conduct hereafter will generally make amends for my follies, and that I shall be worthy of your affection. All that I shall desire in this world is to be a princesse whose conduct renders her estimable, and this I shall strive to deserve in the future. I flatter myself that I am not yet too old nor my reputation too tarnished, for me to succeed in time. I am overwhelmed by all your kindness, and by what you have sent me to enable me to pay my debts . . . I am in despair at having displeased you. I have abandoned God, and He has abandoned me; but I trust that, with His help, which I ask of Him with all my heart, I shall get the better of my faults, and restore to you your health, which is so dear to me, and which I am the cause of your having lost. To my sorrow, I should not dare to flatter myself that you will forgive my faults, nor to ask you to give me back again, *ma tante,* an affection of which I have rendered myself unworthy. I trust, however, that in time I shall merit it once more and I shall have no other occupation.

Maintenon's lecture had hit the mark — for the moment. It must be remembered that this abject repentant, "not yet too old," was a girl of sixteen, and one used to the gratification of every whim. Adelaide *did* give up lansquenet for a season — but instead she played at brelan, hombre, and reversi, and lost just as often as before. Eighteen months after the princesse's resolution, Mme de Maintenon observed with disapproval: "High play is still her passion."

Louis XIV continued to wink at her losses and pay her debts without question, but when, in the summer of 1707, the lure of lansquenet called too strongly and Adelaide tried to pass off as a harmless hunting party a gambling orgy with Mme la duchesse at La Bretesche, the king exploded and finally ordered her never to play the game again. Mme de Maintenon felt it was the princesse's blatant deception that had pushed Louis XIV to the limit; she detailed their conversation in a letter to Adelaide's companion, Mme de Dangeau, July 16, 1707:

The King told me yesterday that he had been surprised to find the card-players at La Bretesche, so I knew she had been deceiving us . . . The King said to me: "Was not a dinner, a ride, a hunt, and a collation enough for one day?" Then he added: "I shall do well to tell these gentlemen that they are not paying their court to me in an acceptable way by playing cards with the Duchesse de Bourgogne." I told him that lansquenet had always been a source of trouble to me, from my fear lest it should lead her to do something which might injure her and place her in an equivocal position. We then talked of other matters . . . but the King returned to the subject and said to me: "Ought I not to speak to these gentlemen?" I answered that I thought that such a step would hurt the Duchesse de Bourgogne, and that it would be better for him to speak to her and keep the affair a secret. He told me he would do so today, and it is in order to warn her that I have written . . .

Here we are then, and sooner than I expected, on the verge of that estrangement I have always dreaded. The King will think that he has offended her by forbidding her to play lansquenet, and will be more distant to her; and it is certain that she will be angry and more cold towards him. I shall think the same, but I am not yet sufficiently indifferent to the world's good opinion as to suffer it to be believed that I approve such conduct . . .

Mme de Maintenon had no desire to be present at the dressing-down of the royal pet, and made it clear where *she* intended to spend the dreaded day: "If after speaking to the Princesse you could come out to Saint-Cyr, I should be glad; but I doubt whether, after so painful a conversation, you will be in a state to appear. If you find it possible to approach the Duchesse de Bourgogne, you might give her this letter to prepare her for answering the King, and then you can speak to her in the evening at more length. You can imagine, Madame, what a night I have passed. Let us pray God for our Princesse, who is drowning herself in a glass of water."

The interview must have been extremely painful for both parties, but the "dreaded estrangement" of the hurt young woman and the disappointed grandfather was blessedly temporary: within the week, all was forgiven and forgotten.

Despite the promises of reform she was often required to give, Adelaide never fully mastered her gambling addiction. As she grew older, she also grew more adept at concealing her weakness: at the height of her betting frenzy, she organized a weekly card party at the shop of her Parisian dressmaker, Mme Lebrion, in the rue de La Vieille Monnaie, where she would play for bolts of material instead of money. But unlike a great many at court, she never failed to honor her debts (if not always with her own money), nor did she ever cheat, though such practice was common and accepted among the jaded court gamblers.

After some initial hesitation, Bourgogne too gave in to the temptations of gaming. Soon he became as ardent a gambler as his wife, playing three times a day, either at Versailles or with his father at Meudon. But his innate arrogance made him a highly irritable card player — one who could not bear to lose. Dangeau noted: "People dreaded playing with him because he could be dangerous when losing, which, from pride and a hatred of meeting defeat, even when caused by bad cards, he could not endure."

At first the prince confined himself exclusively to brelan and small stakes, but once smitten, he joined Adelaide at the lansquenet tables and was seen to lose as much as fifty thousand pistoles in one night. An appeal to the king for money always resulted in a prompt and generous settlement, usually far in excess of the losses he had incurred. Louis XIV told his grandson that he was glad the prince came directly to him and should continue to do so in order to play without anxiety: for royalty to lose at cards was no matter, since they should demonstrate a perfect indifference to money (a maxim followed more consistently by Adelaide than her husband).

In the years since their wedding, Bourgogne's passion for his wife had trebled; Adelaide did not return her husband's devotion in full measure, although her affection for him was genuine. When the prince journeyed to the Spanish frontier with the new king Philip V, the young couple experienced their first separation, one which apparently gave Adelaide time to reflect on her husband's finer qualities. On Bourgogne's return to court after a two-month absence, Dangeau noted: "It would have been impossible to testify more joy than they have both shown at seeing one another again."

To the rest of the watchful court, the royal couple certainly appeared to be in love, although the willful, headstrong Adelaide showed no inclination to continue in the tradition of blind obedience and empty-headed loyalty established by Bourgogne's mother and grandmother. One courtier noted: "She continually opposes her husband. They agree on nothing; yet their hearts are as one"; a view supported by another noble observer: "I do not suppose there has ever been a married couple with such different characters who loved one another so dearly."

Bourgogne nicknamed his vibrant young spouse "Draco," after the Athenian tyrant said to have written his laws in blood — a rather curious pet name, but probably best explained in one of the many

verses composed by the infatuated husband: "Draco, what sweet ser-
vitude / To be the slave of duty and of you." Corneille and Racine had
little to fear from this would-be royal bard. One typical ode, written
from the front where the prince languished in love, began: "Draco,
you would command the universe / To serve your pleasure and your
sense of fun. / What won't men do for you, and to what height not
climb, / Since I, your husband, write to you in rhyme?" At least Bourgogne had the good sense to end with an honest admission: "Loved I
you less, my verses might be better."

On one occasion, while Adelaide teased him to reveal the decisions
made during a secret session of the Council of Dispatches, Bourgogne
extemporized: "Draco! My heart is thine alone / For it is mine to
give. / Thine too the secrets of my soul — / When they are not the
King's."

Of course it was enormously flattering to receive such attention
from so important a figure at court (even if it was one's husband), and
Adelaide, whose simple nature was motivated by a need to give pleasure to others and feel their love in return, responded graciously to
Bourgogne's devotion. But a subtle, stealthy change had begun in the
prince, an unforeseen change that soon would place their relationship
in serious jeopardy.

The fears so patently evident in the king and Mme de Maintenon
during Adelaide's illness in the summer of 1701 were trivial compared
to the severe emotional trauma suffered by the duc de Bourgogne.
Watching his beloved writhe in agony seared his very soul, and the
sudden possibility of life without his darling Draco awakened terror in
his heart. Adelaide's brush with death was all too clearly a divine
warning, a personal admonition to the already pious prince. "I never
cease from thanking God for His mercy," Bourgogne wrote during her
recuperation, "for He clearly intended to punish me; but He has withheld His anger and taken pity on me."

Adelaide's recovery convinced her husband to put an end forever to
his "evil ways." His days of wild oats — the relatively harmless pleasures he found at the gambling table or in escorting his wife to balls
and theaters — were numbered. Progressively he withdrew from the
enjoyments of the court; Dangeau noted in early 1702 that the prince
had given up dancing (judging from accounts of his limited terpsi-
chorean talents, this was no great sacrifice) and that there were other,
more desirable qualities which "the Prince hopes to acquire, in order
to make up for what he lacks." Dangeau, one of the more "serious-

minded" courtiers, applauded his new gravity, expressing the view of that court element which anticipated a new, enlightened age under Bourgogne's rule: "One sees every day that his mind is set on nobler and more admirable acquirements."

But the diarist's feelings were far from universally shared, and even the king found his grandson's well-expressed distaste for parties and theatricals irritating. One day he remarked that the prince seemed to derive very little pleasure from the plays so artfully and painstakingly presented for the court's enjoyment. Bourgogne replied smugly, "I have the pleasure of accompanying Your Majesty." "As to that," the king snapped, "you are free to do as you please." Instead of taking the royal rebuke as a warning, Bourgogne increased his self-restriction, and his appearances in the royal box grew less and less frequent. "[He] never now attends," Dangeau noticed, "which makes people think that he has quite given up the theater."

Personal rejection of amusement was bad enough, but the prince was given to discouraging others from such "sinfulness." "I see that the duc de Bourgogne is going back to his old life," his step-uncle, the comte de Toulouse, wrote to the duc de Gramont. "What you tell me about the comedies is really too bad. It would be far better if he tried to enjoy them, instead of keeping other people away. But that he will never do."

He also resolved to control his Bourbon propensity to overeat and drink. Though he had never reached the stage of permanent inebriation later achieved by his indolent brother and sister-in-law, the duc and duchesse de Berri, Bourgogne had developed a hearty taste for the grape and had left the table under its influence on more than one occasion. His guilt now focused on an exquisite pair of silver wine coolers, which he had admired greatly in Paris and ordered specially for his table. He preferred to drink his wine cold and took great pleasure in the finely crafted silver beakers, but his conscience nagged him for the sin of extravagance, until he ordered the coolers melted down to become "food for the poor." Such selflessness was not a quality the court found desirable in a successor to Louis le Grand.

Gambling was a vice more difficult to abjure than cool wine. His rationalization, we learn from his confessor, Père Martineau, was "the reflection that love of gambling is, at bottom, merely a low and sordid desire for gain, and consequently unworthy of a prince, who should have no feelings that are not noble and elevated." The prince began by refusing to wager during Lent, and though Easter Monday invariably saw him back at the gaming tables, he now avoided lansquenet. It was great proof of his iron will that, although he continued to play for the rest of his life, Bourgogne restricted himself only to ready money, shunning the all-too-available credit and confining his losses to whatever amount he had brought to the table — a rule he strictly imposed on his fellow players. When Adelaide required a fourth, he dutifully joined her table, even if the game in progress was the dreaded lansquenet. But he insisted on keeping the stakes at a very low level; not surprisingly, his wife soon sought a different partner.

It should not be assumed that he divorced himself entirely from all court activities, for his stringent conscience was equally matched by his sense of duty, to both his position and his wife. To the former he was not negligent, lest he should incur the wrath of his grandfather for failing to uphold his God-given obligations, and he graciously consented to escort his wife to the many balls and pleasure outings given in her honor — provided they did not fall on a Sunday or a holy day of obligation. (When a court ball was arranged for the Feast of the Epiphany, the prince refused to attend, even after the king personally advised him to appear.) But his obvious discomfort at these entertainments soon made his absence preferable to his attendance; even Saint-Simon, one of Bourgogne's most loyal supporters, was forced to concede that "he made everyone feel ill at ease by his air of disapproval, and his insistence on literal accuracy (a relic of his schoolroom days) stopped all conversation. Moreover, he appeared always distracted, always impatient to be gone, like a man who feels that his time is being wasted."

"Wasted time" decreased at a dizzying rate and, as he gave himself up to God, Bourgogne became a virtual recluse. The greater part of his day was spent in prayer and scriptural studies; he remained closeted with his confessor for hours on end, and composed, for his own edification, a tract entitled *Reflections for Every Day of the Week*. He no longer accepted a quickly said mass at Fontainebleau or Marly as a sufficient observance of the Lord's Day, but attended three services every Sunday. While even the most religious of courtiers took Holy Communion once or twice a year, the prince received the sacrament weekly, and fasted with such assiduity during Lent that he grew "as thin as a withered vine branch." "You cannot imagine the piety of the Duc de Bourgogne," Madame informed her Hanoverian aunt. "It is not hypocrisy, but really heart-felt devotion; he is melancholy, and goes about dreaming."

The only indoor amusement which he still allowed was music. He studied harmony and composition, but in order to justify so profane an interest, he took great pains "to adapt religious hymns to the finest airs of opera, in order to sing them without impiety."

The court was alternately amused and disgusted by such holy austerity, and the prince became the butt of many harmless, but pointed, pranks. One court lady launched into effusive praise of his eyes; Bourgogne immediately squinted, in an effort to prove her wrong. The comtesse d'Estrées one day playfully tried to kiss him, and he violently averted his head. When she doubled her efforts, he grabbed a brooch from his frock coat and viciously scratched her. Madame was derisive: "Never was such prudery seen; even Joseph escaped his seductress with the loss of his coat, but neither struck nor scratched her."

In his terror of temptation, his aversion to feminine company (apart from those of age or religious piety) reached manic proportions. As one observer, Proyart, remarked: "He considered himself at the Court as in the midst of a voluptuous isle . . . He was continually on his guard against the insidious artifices of those perfidious nymphs who contended for the glory of triumphing over virtue." Such precious virtue was all too tiresome and even Adelaide partook of the new sport of Bourgogne baiting. One night, she announced her intention to retire, knowing her ardent husband would follow fast on her heels. In the royal bed, she put in her place Mme de La Vrillière, eighteen years old and one of the loveliest ladies at court, then hid herself behind the window curtains. The unsuspecting husband entered the room, blew out the candle, and jumped into bed. Suddenly the curtains were flung wide, and there stood his wife, feigning outrage. "Well, Monsieur, so much for your virtue! I find you in bed with one of the prettiest ladies at Court!" Then she betrayed the prank by bursting into laughter. Bourgogne went purple: he dragged poor La Vrillière out of bed and threw her to the floor, screaming "Shameless hussy!" and striking at her until the frightened young woman ran from the room — and Adelaide continued to laugh. It was not without a trace of contempt that she later remarked, "I should like to die before the Duc de Bourgogne, just to see what would happen here. I am certain that he would marry a 'gray sister' of the Filles de Sainte-Marie [a particularly strict order of nuns]!"

Such virtue and propriety were rare in a young man, rarer still in a Bourbon. His exaggerated concept of the seriousness of his station hardly appealed to his sixteen-year-old wife, who was too vivacious, too lighthearted and frivolous, and quite simply too young to share such sentiments. It hurt the princesse that he preferred religion to her and her amusements; as she grew more aware of the court's mounting scorn for the "royal monk," her own attitude underwent a change. She became indifferent, at times plainly irritated. She had always been adept at mimicry, taking almost cruel delight in poking fun at the physical handicaps of others. With Bourgogne, the potential for such mockery had unfortunately increased with the years, for the physical deformity of his back and shoulder had steadily worsened: by the spring of 1701, Madame was writing: "The Duc de Bourgogne is more deformed than the Duc de Luxembourg. The latter is merely a hunchback, but the Prince is quite awry. One of his legs is much shorter than the other, and so much so that, when he wishes to stand up, the heel of one of his feet is in the air, and he only touches the ground with his toes."

Spurred on by laughter and applause, Adelaide developed a perfect imitation of her husband's lopsided gait and mannerisms. Someone was cruel enough to inform Bourgogne of his wife's skillful impersonation; that evening, for the first time in years, the prince slept in his own room and sent word to Marie Adelaide that "he was greatly displeased at her conduct, and that, though she would place him under an obligation by informing him at once of his defects of mind or character, so that he might hasten to correct them, there was nothing witty in holding his physical infirmities up to ridicule."

Adelaide took his censure very badly, no doubt experiencing pangs of guilt at her own heartlessness, and so Bourgogne kept to himself for more than a week. Finally, Louis XIV intervened and peace was restored. This spat was the only disagreement of any consequence to disrupt the harmony of their first years together, but it remained a sad and ironic fact that, in Bourgogne's strenuous quest to perfect his nature, he succeeded in alienating the one person he loved above all others.

Madame wrote: "The Duc de Bourgogne is much in love with his wife, but she not at all with him, and I believe that once she has borne a young prince or two, she would see the good man depart for the celestial regions without great grief." Madame could be — and usually was — extremely catty but, for once, there might have been an element of truth in her trenchant observation.

There existed in Louis XIV's relationship with the duc de Bourgogne, from before his grandson's marriage until his death, a subliminal element of competition for Marie Adelaide. The doting grandfather and the faithful husband unconsciously vied for the attention and affection of their mutual paragon; given their respective positions, it was a foregone conclusion that a king should triumph over a prince. Doubtless this emotional war played a part (however small) in the Sun King's decision to send his heir to experience the real war outside the borders of France.

Louis XIV was never so monstrous as to contemplate his grandson's elimination on the battlefield: every precaution was taken to ensure the prince's safety and he was under strict injunction *never* to come in contact with the enemy. But sending the duc de Bourgogne to review the army in Flanders neatly solved several potential difficulties. On a public level, it allowed the future commander in chief an enviable view of the daily workings of his armed force; it also afforded a promising young man his first taste of glorious combat. Privately, it was hoped a separation might relieve some of the growing tension between the prince and his wife, all too noticeable within the family circle. Last, and certainly not least, it allowed old Grandpapa the pleasure of his darling's undivided attention.

And so the duc de Bourgogne was authorized to join the French army of Flanders, to view its position and "consult" with its co-commanders, the maréchals Boufflers and Tallard. The prince left Versailles in April 1702 — without a personal staff and accompanied only by his valet, Suaméry. His journey north would take him through Cambrai, refuge of the exiled Fénelon; quite naturally, he requested leave to call on his former tutor. The king's anger with Fénelon had not softened in the five years since the archbishop's disgrace, but he reluctantly granted permission for a short visit — provided they were not left alone at any point during the meeting.

There had been no communication between student and teacher since Fénelon's exile except for Bourgogne's anguished letters during Adelaide's illness. The reunion was emotional for them both. They embraced tenderly at the door of the post house of Cambrai, then moved inside. The valet dutifully discharged his royal orders and remained by his young master's side, but (Saint-Simon wrote) "the Prince's piercing and expressive eyes said much more effectively than his words what was passing in his mind, and the Archbishop, whose eyes were no less eloquent, responded with all his being, while maintaining the most scrupulous reserve." Under the circumstances imposed, their interview was brief; just before he entered his carriage, Bourgogne again embraced Fénelon and was able to whisper something private to his beloved tutor. Wiping back his tears, he then entered the coach and proceeded to the front lines. .

The French campaign of 1702 was hardly successful — before its conclusion, six Flemish fortresses were lost, and the allies gained control of the rivers Rhine and Meuse. But for the duc de Bourgogne the summer was something of a personal victory. Freed from anxieties over his wife and away from the intimidating presence of his grandfather, he slowly bent his dignity and relaxed. The general staff was impressed with the intelligent questions he put to them and the keen potential he demonstrated; when he returned to Versailles in the autumn, he was preceded by Boufflers's glowing praise of his courage and bravery, and his "cheerfulness under fire" — though, given the king's concern for his heir's safety, "in the general vicinity of fire" would have been more accurate.

The prince received a hero's welcome. It was after midnight as he entered the Marble Courtyard, and the court was performing a graceful exit from the *grand coucher* when he appeared in the doorway of the royal bedchamber. Louis XIV interrupted his grandson's deep and ceremonious bow, throwing wide his arms and crying out, "Well! Aren't you going to kiss me?" They embraced heartily, their great emotion evident to all; then the king broke off and said with a laugh, "Go quickly to the Duchesse de Bourgogne; she will be waiting impatiently to see you!"

Adelaide was *not* waiting impatiently. She was preparing for bed when news of her husband's arrival reached her. She "ran to the King's Cabinet by way of the Great Gallery, although she was *en déshabillé*," Dangeau noted. "Their embraces were warm and tender. She carried him off to her apartments and into [her private room] . . . sent for food for him, and he was served by the waiting women. The meal lasted but a short time, such was his impatience to find himself alone with her."

But joyful as their reunion was, Adelaide discovered soon enough that time and separation had done little to stem their changing characters or ease the rising friction of their differences. Bourgogne returned to the front in the spring of 1703, happier and more comfortable than ever before, full of love and full of confidence; as for Adelaide, it was Mme de Maintenon who noticed it first: "I do not think I have ever seen a passion so unpleasant to her who is the cause of it."

The Sun King's confidence in Boufflers was shaken by the striking losses suffered in the Flanders campaign of 1702. Though the maréchal was not relieved of his post, Louis XIV felt it unwise to return Bourgogne to the Low Countries to witness another possible season of defeat and demoralization. (Actually, the campaign of 1703 ended far more successfully for Boufflers than that of the year before: greatly outnumbered by the allies, the French army in Flanders nonetheless maintained an effective resistance and gave up only three — relatively minor — fortresses from the more than thirty still under their control.)

Louis XIV and his advisers had decided on a major offensive against the empire. Though the largest bloc, it was the weakest of the allied powers — and all the more at this time since, early in 1703, Prince Eugene had been forced to quit the Italian peninsula and speed to Hungary to suppress an internal uprising. With Italy now unencumbered and the pathway cleared, the French high command turned its eyes to vulnerable Vienna and regrouped its forces: the army in Italy, under the successful duc de Vendôme, was to enter the Tyrolean valley from the south at Lago di Garda. The eastern army was divided into two corps: the first, under Maréchal Villars, was to cross the Rhine and the Black Forest, effect a juncture with the elector Maximilian of Bavaria (the Two Crowns' only German ally), and enter the Tyrol from the north; joining up with Vendôme's troops, this impressive force was to advance on the Austrian capital. The other corps of the eastern army was assigned to Maréchal Tallard: it was to maneuver along the Rhine and keep in check the allied force stationed there under Prince Louis of Baden. To this division Louis XIV appointed the duc de Bourgogne.

The prince was anxious to take a more active and less advisory role in the forthcoming campaign. With this in mind, it would have been far better had he followed Villars, who united successfully with the Bavarian elector and captured the cities of Augsburg and Ratisbon.[3] Tallard was an indifferent general at best and, unlike Boufflers, he resented his nominal subordination to the young heir to the throne. He tended to blame Bourgogne for his own many errors in judgment: for one, through Tallard's negligence, the prince of Baden was able to elude their force, cross the Danube, and retake Augsburg. Tallard and Bourgogne's only real accomplishment in this campaign was the capture of Breisach, a city on the eastern bank of the Upper Rhine, vital to the allies for the transport of war matériel.

Their siege began in late August and strictly followed the two distinct stages prescribed by seventeenth-century war etiquette: first, the town itself was besieged until the defensive force conceded that it could no longer withstand an assault. The town then surrendered, while its battalions took their positions inside the city's fortress. Under the rules, the assailants were now expected to take the fort as well, although the articles of capitulation usually included a clause stating that if the fortress were not relieved within a set time period, it would also be surrendered.

Breisach fell on September 6, 1703. When Bourgogne returned to court later that month, he found himself accorded all the praise and glory for the siege and lauded as a great military hero. Court poets vied to extol his graces; one wrote: "Prendre Breisach en treize jours, / C'est une plus belle besogne / Ces exploits vigoureuz et courts / Sont du goût du Duc de Bourgogne." ("Taking Breisach in thirteen days / This is the finest piece of work / Such quick and vigorous exploits / Suit the taste of the Duc de Bourgogne.")

But the lavish praise, gratifying as it must have been, was not entirely accurate, for the keen and inspired soldier of 1702 was a very different man in 1703, as Bourgogne's letters to Versailles revealed. In the sixteen letters written during the siege of Breisach, not one single reference was made to the army or its actions. For in that summer in 1703 the duc de Bourgogne endured a personal emotional crisis — predictably, brought on by his adored, but negligent, young wife.

While her husband was stationed in Flanders during the campaign of 1702, Marie Adelaide had written him daily. When Bourgogne arrived at the Rhine the following spring, he waited impatiently for word from his darling Draco, but weeks passed without any communication. At last a note arrived, very short and inconsequential; it was followed within days by another (of equal brevity) and then by total silence.

The lovesick prince dared not complain of such remissness directly to his wife, but he vented his frustrations in a letter to Mme de Montgon, one of Adelaide's older and more cherished attendants. Dated June 12, 1703, Bourgogne admitted his astonishment "at not having yet received anything from you, and still more at the irregularity of your illustrious mistress, who allows an interminable time to pass without writing to me more than two letters . . . I have decided not to begin by reproaching her; nevertheless, I am unable to bear this with patience, and I was really angry yesterday evening at not receiving any letters by the courier who arrived from Franche-Comte. I would that you had seen me at supper, looking as gloomy as a chimney, speaking to no one, with my hat pulled down to my eyes." The letter ended: "As for the naughty one of whom I have spoken, tell her that, if in the future I do not receive letters from her more often, I shall quarrel with her, and shall not write to her during the whole campaign" — followed by the pathetic confession "I greatly fear that these threats will be useless, since I should certainly be the more severely punished."

Bourgogne's cry went unheard; he wrote Montgon on June 17 that he still had received nothing from his wife: "I am delighted to learn from you that she is well, but speaking often of the Duc de Bourgogne, inquiring after his health, and not finding his memory altogether repugnant, does not tally with leaving him twelve days without a word, and I always come back to that, because it vexes me so."

The poor boy's exasperation mounted as June gave way to July and still no word arrived from Marie Adelaide. "This letter, Mme de Montgon, must serve as my reply to two from you, which I received at almost the same time. Both drove me crazy with their descriptions of the charms of your royal mistress . . . Tell her that I am charging you to learn from her own lips whether she loves me, and to give me her answer in her own words."

Clearly the princesse had to do something to alleviate her husband's emotional torment. One afternoon, while her physician was drawing blood in an effort to relieve her nagging toothache, she hit upon an idea. Handing over the vial of her blood to Mme de Montgon, Adelaide directed the woman to write her compliments to the prince ("weakness from the operation" prevented her doing it herself), making sure the source of the "ink" was noted. Montgon found this rather excessive, if not downright disgusting, but the princesse insisted.

Far from repelled, Bourgogne was transported into ecstasy: "I cannot wait another moment before sending my reply. I am not sickened by that adorable blood, for I have already kissed it a thousand times, and shall do so a thousand times more before the day is over." The prince was not one to be outdone: "This letter, as well as the little sketch, is scrawled entirely with the blood which love caused me to shed on the instant, and if she says she would shed all for me, I would assuredly keep none back of my own. But we must preserve it for each other, and unite our hearts, like those which I have sketched here with my own blood." By now his passion for Adelaide had banished from his mind all thoughts of war and glory.

You must promise me faithfully, to carry this letter to her so soon as you receive it. Endeavor to see her in private, go on your knees before her and, after kissing both her hands for me, offer her the blood which has been shed for her alone. I know not whether you will entertain doubts about my sanity; but can I do enough to prove to this queen how much I love her, although she is already well aware of it? Let me know how she has received [my letter], and her very words, and ask her, at the same time, if she does not love me . . . I thank you a thousand times for this ingenuous letter, and I shall keep it all my life, for the sake of the precious ink which has been used."

But Bourgogne's euphoria was short-lived. By the end of July, he was back to moaning: "I have written her six letters in the past week, and five successive couriers have arrived with nothing, a proof that she has not written for at least nine days." He conceded once again the futility of his continued threats to stop writing himself: "If, on her side, she did the same, I should be a hundred times more punished than she would be." The anguish he endured from her indifference mounted: "She, apparently, no longer cares for me at all, who would not hesitate to shed my blood in order to give her fresh proof of my love . . . ; who would expose myself to frightful perils for her sake; who would sacrifice everything for her." He tried to shame his wife into writing: "I say nothing of the promise which she made me on my departure, to write to me at least twice a week; but, even if she were not bound by her word, ought she not to do so of her own free will?"

He feared that she might for some reason be angry, "in which case tell her I shall endeavor to make amends as soon as possible," or that his long and frequent letters might bore her — "Is she tired of being so passionately beloved?"

Still no word arrived at camp, and the frantic prince resorted to other tactics: "Remind this coquette that, at the very minute she reads my letter, I might be risking my life in the trenches, into which the cannon and musket shot fall constantly, and where the dead and wounded are all about me . . . Picture to her also the arrival of a courier with the news that I am dangerously wounded, in which condition my only thought would be that I might perhaps never see her again . . . I think that it will be well for you to read this passage to her, in order to tell me exactly what you may be able to divine of the sentiments of her heart, from the effect which it produces upon her."

It seems to have produced no effect, for her chilling silence remained unbroken. The siege of Breisach and the war itself had long ceased to matter to the anguished husband. In his distraction, he decided that Adelaide was again seriously ill, and that news of her condition was being withheld from him deliberately. "If anything were to happen in conformity with my gloomy presentiments, I should take a walk along the palisades . . . to find there the end of my sorrows; and I should think myself fortunate, if she were ill, to get some bullet-wound which would reduce me to the same condition." In his torment, he implored his grandfather to recall him to court.

When at last Adelaide broke her silence, her letter was cold and cruel, advising him to remain with the army and not yet return to Versailles. Confused, almost brokenhearted, Bourgogne turned to the duc de Beauvilliers for comfort:

> 12 September. I received this morning a long letter from the Duchesse de Bourgogne, in which she begins by telling me that she has not written sooner because she was too angry, and then, after having exhorted me not to hasten my return like last year, she continues as follows: "The King has been greatly surprised that you are so soon demanding permission to return, as the campaign is not yet very far advanced, and you are still engaged in the Siege, and this inclines him to think that you do not care for war any more than the others, and has annoyed him very much, which you will apparently understand from the letter that he has written you." I confess that this has caused me some surprise, since I have found nothing to correspond to it in the King's letter.

The prince's observation was accurate. There *was* nothing in Louis XIV's letter to indicate royal displeasure. Adelaide had reasons of her own for desiring her husband's continued absence, and his continuing unawareness of those reasons — at the time and after — was a blessing for the poor tortured soul. For while the duc de Bourgogne received his lessons in warfare, the duchesse de Bourgogne was taking lessons in love.

For any young woman possessed of a healthy inclination toward romance, there could be no more perfect spot on earth to dally and dabble than in the park of Versailles. Its shaded walkways and well-hidden groves provided idyllic settings for lovers to tryst; what could be more romantic than being courted by a dashing young nobleman, while the moonlight filtered through concealing fir trees and the jets of a nearby fountain splashed softly in a gilded basin?

For Adelaide — gay and vivacious, alluringly trembling on the threshold of womanhood — the incessant attentions and flatteries of court gallants were growing daily more difficult to resist. She was an obviously intelligent young lady, but giddy and flirtatious too, "as every young person would be who had been allowed such great liberty," Madame (for once) said in her defense. "If she had been with people who would have exercised over her the control she needed, one might have been able to make something good of her, but I fear, from the way she is allowed to behave, that she will furnish her husband with matter for mortification."

Certainly the changes maturity worked in her husband triggered many of the subsequent changes in Adelaide. Saint-Simon's initial assessment — "I do not think she felt much attraction for the person of her husband, nor that she responded eagerly to the attraction he felt for her" — was not strictly accurate: all her life she responded well and kindly to demonstrations of affection, and all the more from her wedded spouse; her frank, undisguised pleasure at Bourgogne's return in 1701 from the Spanish border, and in 1702 from Flanders, left no doubt in the mind of the court what her true feelings were for her husband. But his growing piety, his relentless, tormenting conscience, could find no empathy in the fun-loving princesse. "You must agree," she once remarked to him, "that in you I have married the hardest-working man in France." Nor did she leave much question as to her opinion of such excessive diligence: "In truth, there is no need for a descendant of Henri IV to submit himself to so wretched a slavery." She resented her husband's lack of interest in her various amusements, and was mortified by the mockeries he provoked in the sophisticated courtiers who surrounded her. To be honored and adored by one's spouse was very pleasant; but when that devotee was dull and severe, forever censorious, pleasure soon evaporated. It was with mixed feelings that she bade her husband farewell in the spring of 1703, for she was relieved to be free of his company — but unsure about seeking out that of others.

It was in this uneasy atmosphere that temptation entered her life, in the person of twenty-one-year-old Armand de Brichanteau, marquis de Nangis. Wonderfully handsome and equally gallant, Nangis was, according to Saint-Simon, "a model of perfection . . . He was trained for love and intrigue by his grandmother and mother, past mistresses in those arts . . . His only talent was for pleasing the ladies, and winning the trust of those most desirable by a discretion beyond his years." When the war broke out, Nangis had been given a regiment, and in the opening campaign had displayed "keenness, industry and brilliant courage." At the same time Bourgogne left to join the army along the Rhine, Nangis was taken ill at the front and returned to Versailles for an extended recuperation. He was a tremendous success with the ladies of the court, whose husbands and lovers had forsaken them for military glory. They vied for the honor (and great pleasure) of nursing the handsome marquis; all too quickly, this competition — and its prize — came to Adelaide's attention.

In the beginning, the princesse confined her budding interest to long, silent stares, "speechless messages" that no gentleman could fail to interpret: in the sophisticated French court, where silence implied consent, verbal communication had long been rendered unnecessary. At first, only the ladies of Adelaide's most intimate circle were aware of the feelings Nangis sparked in their mistress, but her excitement whenever her eyes fell upon the dashing young horseman became impossible to conceal. "I have heard my late mother declare," remembered Mme de Louvigny, "that [Adelaide's] household first suspected her partiality for the Marquis de Nangis because she reddened whenever he appeared." But if Adelaide was unbothered by propriety — and her position — her staff was not: "They so well understood the danger of that show of impropriety that they made it their business to see that she did not have cause to blush too often; they kept watch over her."

The marquis himself was not unresponsive to Adelaide's overtures: what finer honor could there be than the favor of a future queen? Soon the court reeled with gossip that Nangis had arranged an afternoon tryst with the princesse in her pavilion at the menagerie and, on the pretext of helping her make cakes, had spent several hours locked alone with her. (The rumor was certainly baseless since, under orders of the king, the princesse was *always* accompanied by one or more of her women; still, it proved that Adelaide's flirtation was far from unnoticed.)

However innocent their baking session, there was trouble brewing in the wings, for Nangis was not, in Saint-Simon's phrase, "heart free." Mme de La Vrillière, "as pretty as Cupid and possessed of all his charm," had been his mistress for some time past. She was the daughter of Mme de Mailly, lady-in-waiting to Marie Adelaide, and consequently a member of that circle that enveloped and protected the princesse. (Adelaide herself had a special fondness for the woman dating from their practical joke on Bourgogne, when La Vrillière took her place in bed and received a royal thrashing.)

All too quickly, La Vrillière spotted her royal rival. "Far from yielding gracefully to the Princesse, she made it a point of honor to keep her conquest, outdo her rival, and carry him off as her prey." She comforted herself with violent rages of jealousy, and Adelaide retaliated by treating her former friend with cool disdain — "a most remarkable and fascinating spectacle."

For Nangis, these cat fights were more than embarrassing, for they underlined the awkwardness of his position: he truly loved La Vrillière, and lived in terror of her temper, for a public outburst could mean the ruin of them all. On the other hand, resistance to so powerful a woman as the future queen of France (a woman unlikely to endure, much less yield to, a rival) could just as likely bring disgrace, possibly exile. Saint-Simon was maliciously gleeful — "His perplexity, for those in the know, provided endless entertainment" — but for the poor marquis, it was a period of considerable dilemma.

Adelaide soon tired of her would-be lover's vacillation and became as jealous as her competition. Relying on rather adolescent logic, she attempted to force the issue by making Nangis jealous for a change, and looking about Versailles, her eye fell upon the marquis de Maulevrier.

His connections at court were impeccable: his late uncle was Louis XIV's brilliant minister, Colbert, and his father-in-law none other than Adelaide's great champion, Tessé. Maulevrier was not "the right stuff for gallantry"; far from handsome, he was coarse and vulgar-looking, but he was clever and high-spirited, highly imaginative in the ways of love, with "unbounded ambition so little restrained by good principles that it came very close to madness." His wife was attractive, if somewhat silly; but despite her appearance of sweetness and light, she was "spiteful to the last degree." As Tessé's daughter, she was on close terms with the princesse, enjoying the privilege of riding in the royal carriage and sharing in the rounds of games held in Adelaide's apartments; through her, Maulevrier gained his entry into the charmed circle.

With Nangis, Adelaide was the huntress; with Maulevrier, she was clearly the prey. He "appeared continually before her, and finally, fired by Nangis's example, dared to sigh." Whether or not the princesse really felt something for this ardent suitor, she recognized his potential to prod the sluggish attentions of Nangis, and her smiles grew noticeably more frequent.

Maulevrier was inspired with heady notions of royal favor and foolishly compromised the princesse by sending her a love letter, using as intermediary her head housemaid, Mme Quentin. The romantic young girl was suitably touched by his declarations, and with no thought to the danger involved, sent a reply, again through Mme Quentin. "So much was known to her household," recalled Saint-Simon. "I shall not add how much else was believed."

Unquestionably, the cynical court believed the worst: Saint-Simon, while doubting that Adelaide's relationship with Nangis ever became physical, was not so sure of her relationship with Maulevrier. Only those who knew her best had no doubt that her flirtations were strictly platonic. Her childhood friend, Marguerite de Caylus, Maintenon's niece, wrote: "Let us believe in flightiness and indiscretion, rather than in wrong-doing, of which there is no proof . . . I doubt whether the affair ever went so far as people thought; I am convinced that the whole intrigue took place in looks, and at most, in a few letters."

Examination of Adelaide's character, and the circumstances of her life at court, fully support Marguerite's assessment. It is true that the princesse was wild and headstrong, but her sense of royal honor had been nurtured since birth; nor could she totally ignore her husband's slavish devotion, as boring and irksome as it was at times. She could never bring herself to deliberately hurt him; neither could she delude herself that any serious entanglement would pass unnoticed at Versailles. Flirting was a harmless new amusement, but she had no wish to court the wrath of Louis XIV — and she was in no doubt as to the magnitude of that wrath should even a hint of indiscretion reach the royal ears. Besides, her feelings for Maulevrier, less intense than those she entertained for Nangis, had never approached a serious level: she was amused by his audacity and charmed by his persistence, but he was never more than a tool she wielded to spark the jealousy of her other cavalier.

Even had Adelaide been so reckless as to contemplate the taking of a lover, her rank and its importance within the Versailles structure would have prevented her from doing so. For royalty, the double standard of the sexes was nowhere more strictly observed than at the French court. Kings and princes were expected, even encouraged, to keep a string of mistresses, but queens and princesses were to be pure and chaste — and above reproach. The ladies of Adelaide's entourage were ever mindful of this fact and had no intention of letting their mistress succumb to the ways of the flesh. If Adelaide was intimidated by the thought of the Sun King's fury, her staff was terrified of it. Night and day, they kept unflagging vigil, for their positions, their futures, even their freedom, depended on it.

Still — however innocent her liaisons — the princesse was playing with fire. Her gambit had paid off: Nangis, alarmed at this new rival, hesitated no longer and, braving the abuse (verbal and physical) of La Vrillière, he stepped up his courtship. Meanwhile, Maulevrier was ordered to the army (probably the work of Mme de Maintenon, who saw everything and said nothing) but, loath to leave clear the field for Nangis, he "feigned a chest malady, took to a diet of milk, pretended to lose his voice, and so far controlled himself that no intelligible words passed his lips for more than a year." The ruse worked and Maulevrier was allowed to remain at court. (Ironically, he *did* develop consumption two years later.) He worked his "illness" to great advantage, as Saint-Simon remarked: "His idea was that by thus putting himself under the necessity of whispering to everyone, he might be able to whisper to the Duchesse de Bourgogne before the entire Court, without impropriety or suspicion that he said anything secret. He contrived in that way to say whatever he pleased to her every day . . . People became so used to this maneuver that they ceased to notice, except to pity him for his distressing impediment." Nangis, for one, felt no such pity!

And through it all, the anguished cries for a little attention still poured in from the soldier away at the front. Juggling two suitors and an injured husband, while tremendously ego-bolstering, required talents far greater than those possessed by the naïve teenage princesse. Adelaide's feelings of guilt, as she welcomed Bourgogne back to Versailles in September 1703, were doubtless mixed with a sense of relief that her complicated flirtations had concluded without incident.

Sad to say, her relief was ill founded, for the fires she had kindled would smolder for a time, then blaze anew. Her lessons in love had not yet ended, any more than had Bourgogne's lessons in war. Indeed, for them both, troubles were only just beginning.

14

Father and Son

AT THE END OF OCTOBER, one month after the Duc de
Bourgogne returned to Versailles, Dangeau noted in his diary: "There
is no longer any doubt of the condition of the Duchesse de Bourgogne."

While of course it would be absurd to suggest calculation on Adelaide's part, it *was* a very timely pregnancy. The news that trickled in
from the front lines remained grim — the first two years of the Spanish
War had been devastating, with France forced to sustain losses of men
and territory enough to eliminate several of its lesser opponents — and
still the struggle continued. The threat of Savoyard defection, feared
from the very moment of Philip V's accession, grew daily more probable, putting the turncoat's daughter in a most awkward situation. The
princesse, the king, and the entire nation felt sorely in need of some
glad tidings, some boost in morale: a new heir was the perfect answer.

Up to this time, Adelaide's inability to reproduce had been the result
of neither indifference nor a lack of effort. The young couple had been
living together as man and wife for four years and were fully cognizant
of their obligation to perpetuate the Bourbon dynasty. If the French
court was too polite to remind the princesse of her primary function —
the breeding of a king — her relatives and friends across the Alps were
not so delicate: Victor Amadeus availed himself of the spiritual services of Père Valpré, a Barnabite monk (and Adelaide's former confessor), who wrote the princesse: "In my daily prayers for the preservation of Your Highness, I petition God no less for your fruitfulness,

which seems to me somewhat tardy. Either my own prayers or the will of Your Highness must be lacking in efficacy." Duchess Anne Marie, herself pregnant for the eighth time, added her entreaties to those of the brusque Valpré, and Tessé sent an antique basin for holy water, surmounted by a figure of the infant Jesus: "May this child of white coral awake in you, night and day, the thought that you owe us a similar child, and let nothing hinder you in this, neither fears for your fine figure, nor any other thing."

If Adelaide did have such fears, they had been quickly dispelled, for within a fortnight of the consummation of her marriage, rumors flew through the court that she had conceived. Louis XIV ordered the taking of all precautions, but by the end of October, it was obvious their hopes were ungrounded. In early November, they rose again, Dangeau noting in his journal that the doctors were "convinced" Marie Adelaide was pregnant; by November 22, this too proved to be a false alarm.

Twice in the early months of 1702 Adelaide exhibited the appropriate symptoms, and on both occasions, time and further examination ended speculation. (Small wonder the doctors grew steadily more reluctant to diagnose her condition!) In the summer of 1702, she *did* conceive, but refused to take (even commonsense) precautions, and by autumn she had miscarried.

A satirical verse entitled "The Frequent Miscarriages and False Alarms of the Duchesse de Bourgogne" made its rounds through the court during the opening years of the eighteenth century: "Unaware of what the gossips say / She shyly tells the doctor all; / In his ear, whispering low, / The oft-repeated question, / Am I? Or am I not?"

Very often she was — but not for very long. She had inherited Anne Marie's difficulties in carrying a child to full term; like her mother, she would conceive far more often than deliver. Moreover, Adelaide was still a young girl in her teens: it takes little imagination to understand her preference for riding, rowing, and late nights of dancing or gambling over the disfigurement, the enforced inactivity, and the general nuisance of childbearing. There was time enough in the future, she felt, for such "obligations." For the present, pleasure was sufficient.

By the spring of 1703 — when Adelaide started her dangerous lessons in love with Nangis and Maulevrier — her enemies at court began to whisper that the king was considering packing off to Turin the apparently barren young princesse.[1] When Adelaide learned of the rumor, she became hysterical and ran at once to Mme de Maintenon's apartments, throwing herself at the old lady's feet and sobbing bitterly. Maintenon did her best to allay the poor girl's fears; she complained to the king of this vicious rumor, and after he had assured the weeping princesse of his continued love and devotion, Louis XIV ordered a full investigation to discover who had initiated the lie. (The court generally believed the culprit to be the king's daughter, Mme la duchesse, which might explain why the perpetrator was never officially discovered.) The incident deeply affected the young princesse; for the first time, she understood the personal value of a son and heir.

By the end of October, the fact of her pregnancy was well established. Louis XIV was transparently delighted: he was determined, at all costs, to avoid another miscarriage and immediately forbade Adelaide to ride, hunt, or dance until after the birth of the child. (To spare her temptation, the king decreed there were to be *no* balls given during the carnival season of 1704, an order that pleased no one, least of all the expectant mother.) When driving, her coachman had instructions to avoid all bad roads, in fact to walk the horses most of the ride. In Adelaide's sixth month, the *accoucheur* Clément — with full royal approval — ordered her to remain in bed until her delivery. Of course, the mother-to-be protested, but for once, Louis XIV refused to let her have her way. He wanted an heir, and he was determined not to be disappointed again.

The king's concern for her condition, however restrictive, was welcome proof to the princesse of his favor and affection — a sorely needed proof indeed. For by the end of 1703, as Adelaide completed her first trimester, the probability of "the Savoyard question" became a reality; for the second time in his life, Victor Amadeus deserted his French ally and joined France's enemies.

The insensitivity and arrogance of his son-in-law Philip V of Spain, the supercilious attitude of the French generals technically under his command, and above all the Sun King's refusal to guarantee *any* of his territorial claims had forever soured Victor Amadeus to the French cause and sealed his determination to defect. Though this resolution came as early as May 1702, the pragmatic duke, with his acute sense of timing, had delayed publishing his transfer of loyalty. With good cause: the replacement of the inept Villeroi with the capable Vendôme in February 1702 had brought about a stunning reversal of French/ Spanish fortunes on the Italian front. Vendôme relieved the besieged Mantua, checked the obstinate advance of Prince Eugene in the battle of Suzzara, and forced the imperial army to fall back behind the Mincio River, where he held them at bay for the remainder of 1702 and most of 1703.

Clearly it would be an imprudent move for Victor Amadeus to announce his defection in the wake of such victories. However, since under the treaty terms with Louis XIV he was bound only to offer his assistance for a period of two years, he consoled himself with the idea that he could not be accused of treachery if, at the end of that time, he refused to re-ally himself with France and Spain. Recalling the animosity and the distrust — on both sides — after his defection a decade earlier, his consideration of this factor was well founded. So he remained in Turin throughout the campaign of 1703, playing (predictably) with both antagonists — wrangling for more equitable terms from the emperor and pestering Louis XIV with the old idea of Milan in exchange for Nice and Savoy.

The arrival of Vendôme in Italy and the phenomenal success that carried his threat to the very gates of the empire convinced Vienna that Savoy's support of the Grand Alliance was imperative. The emperor stood ready to pledge *anything* in order to gain control of the safe pass and block the Sun King's land route into Italy, as he proved with the question of Montferrato.

During the bargaining summer of 1703, Victor Amadeus let it drop to both Versailles and Vienna that he "keenly desired" the Montferrato territory, a possession of the duke of Mantua. The reactions to this hint told all. Louis XIV spent months negotiating with Mantua, his old ally, only to be told that "although he was but a little prince, [Mantua] was a very proud one, and no sum of money from Their Majesties of France and Spain could induce him to part with any portion of his dominions"; the French response to Savoy's duke was that his wish was sadly beyond the powers of the Sun King. The emperor, on the other hand, promised not only Montferrato, but also the rich province of Alessandria if Victor Amadeus would join the allied cause.

But the emperor was all too familiar with the delaying tactics employed by the duke of Savoy and when the negotiations dragged on and on, he devised a clever ruse to bring the endless bargaining to a conclusion. Copies were made of several letters to Victor Amadeus, letters that explained in great detail the compensations to be made after the duke's defection. These copies were entrusted to a Neapolitan officer who was then given orders to get himself captured by the

French. The soldier obliged, however unwillingly, and as planned the French discovered the "secret" documents and assumed that the new alliance had already been forged. When the first rumors of this new development hit the French court, the imperial spies at Versailles made certain they were suitably embellished, and by the second week of September 1703, a livid Sun King was convinced that he had been once again betrayed.

Orders to Vendôme in Lombardy were dispatched posthaste: immediately surround and disarm the Savoyard unit (a force of over six thousand men encamped at San Benedetto, near Pavia), arrange for them to be conducted into France as prisoners of war, and proceed directly to Turin. To Victor Amadeus, Louis XIV wrote harshly: "Monsieur, I perceive that neither religion, honor, nor your own signature are any guarantee; therefore I send my cousin, the Duc de Vendôme, to inform you of my wishes; he will give you twenty-four hours to decide."[2]

The wishes of the old French lion were clear enough: the fortresses of Vercelli and Coni were to be handed over as surety of the duke's continued loyalty to the Two Crowns; a refusal to do so would spark the immediate invasion of Savoy.

The gnat refused to kowtow: "Sire, I am not intimidated by menaces. Concerning the unworthy proceedings used towards me, I shall take such steps best suited to me. I can give no further explanation and refuse to listen to any proposals." He ordered the arrest of every Frenchman within his states, including the ambassador, Phelypeaux, and prayed that Vendôme's threatened advance was mere bluff.

It was: with the Imperial troops so close on his heels, Vendôme could not detach sufficient divisions to effect an invasion without leaving vulnerable the rest of his force. He was compelled instead to wait for reinforcements from France. Victor Amadeus took full advantage of this delay; on November 8, 1703, he signed a pact with Emperor Leopold, pledging unqualified support for the allied cause — in return for Alessandria, Montferrato, and the duchy of Milan.

The duke's second defection put his pregnant daughter in a most difficult position. She considered herself a "true and loyal French woman" and deplored her father's treachery and ingratitude. She was also a daughter of the House of Savoy, devoted to her parents and her grandmother (now her official enemies) and haunted by fears that now she had lost them forever.

From the beginning of her life in France, her letters to Turin had been filled with such phrases as "love me always, and be assured of the tender feelings I have for you," and she had required constant pledges of her family's continued interest. After her father's defection, she assumed a pleading, almost desperate tone, "begging you for that you have always shown me" and crying plaintively: "No one in the world feels more interest in you than I." Throughout this difficult time, her husband proved himself no support at all. Thoughtless or heartless, he remarked one day that should he be sent to the Italian front (one of Adelaide's recurring nightmares), his wife would be hard-pressed to decide for whom to pray first, her husband or her father, and that she would do better to keep them both remembered — hardly an observation calculated to lighten the pregnant girl's burden.

Moreover, the switch in Savoyard loyalty could not help but focus attention on Adelaide's birth and heritage. The Meudon cabal, a group of dissatisfied courtiers led by the king's daughters who seized every opportunity to besmirch the princesse's reputation, whispered through the halls and corridors that the duchesse de Bourgogne was a traitor, a spy for her father. Of course Louis XIV did not believe this for a moment and took steps to stop the gossipmongers; serious questions as to Adelaide's involvement in espionage would not surface until the siege of Turin in 1706. Nonetheless, it was one more cross to bear.

The princesse derived some consolation in the establishment of a correspondence with her sister, Queen Maria Luisa of Spain. Given Adelaide's intimate and long acquaintance with the Spanish king (now her brother-in-law on two counts), it is not surprising that her curiosity about the royal household in Madrid was, from the start, insatiable. "I agree with you, my dear mother, that news from Spain comes slowly," she wrote early in 1702. "I would like to know all that she [the queen of Spain] does from morning till night, to satisfy the interest that I feel. I am, however, more easy now that I feel a true affection exists between the King of Spain and her."

This "true affection" had been achieved with some difficulty: the first meeting of the seventeen-year-old king and his thirteen-year-old queen had been something of a disaster. The king had ridden out from his capital to meet the bride at Figueras, not far from Barcelona: he encountered a hysterical girl, weeping bitterly for her home and her mother. That evening, a banquet was arranged to honor the royal couple, with Spanish and French dishes to be served alternately. This complimentary arrangement was ruined by the haughty Spanish court ladies, who deliberately spilled the French dishes to the floor and only served the Spanish ones. Royalty was expected to remain unruffled and aloof in the face of such boorishness, but the strain on the exhausted and emotionally overworked Maria Luisa had been so great that, after the meal, she exploded, refusing to join the king in his private apartments and demanding to be sent back to Savoy.

After so inauspicious a wedding night, the king rose alone in the morning and went hunting; in her private rooms, the queen was given a firm and pointed reprimand by the princesse des Ursins, who said that Philip was full of compassion for his wife's homesickness and anxious to make her feel comfortable in her new land, but was, for now, "greatly disappointed."[3] The king's coldness to her that entire day, and his decision to spend the evening alone in his study, was Maria Luisa's "punishment" for her tantrum; happily the punishment was brief. After three days of marriage, Maria Luisa had discovered just how charming her husband could be when he wanted; by the end of the week, the young couple was firmly on the road to love, and the princesse des Ursins assured the Sun King: "I believe, Sire, that I may say with confidence that the Queen's only thought at present is to please the King and his subjects." While Adelaide (so much older and wiser!) was pronouncing her own judgment to the duchess of Savoy: "What she did [on her wedding night] was only a piece of childishness, and had no consequence. I hope that she will give nothing but joy," the bride rhapsodized to her mother: "The King, our King! He becomes every day more charming. At first I did not like him, when he was so serious."

Tessé, now stationed at the court of Madrid, understood the strain that Savoy's defection put on the royal sisters. It was he who urged Marie Adelaide to write and commiserate; when she did, he wrote of his enormous gratification: "One of the things that most pleases the Queen is the regularity with which you write to her by every post. It goes to confirm my belief that when you make up your mind to do something, you do it better and more charmingly than anyone else." Tessé liked and admired the young Spanish queen, though he remained firmly under the spell of her older sister: when Adelaide asked him for a full description (she had not seen her sister in more than five years), Tessé replied that, while there was a small resemblance between them, Adelaide was definitely the better looking of the two. Like her sister's, the queen of Spain's teeth were very bad, but "her complexion is good, though her lips are not so red as yours, nor does she possess Your

Highness' 'roving eye.' " (Tessé was fond of saying that when Adelaide entered a room, she was able to take in every detail within seconds — even those things she was not supposed to see.)

Though Tessé's heart belonged to the older sister, he did not hesitate in serving the younger. The circumstances facing the new king and queen — battling all of Europe for the right to wear their crowns — reduced them to a penury unimaginable at the opulent French court, and Tessé frankly made use of Adelaide's renowned generosity. "I have committed myself to a promise," he wrote the princesse in 1703,

> on behalf of your sister, the Queen. It will set you to some small expense, and a command to Mme de Mailly [Adelaide's mistress of the robes], but nothing costly . . . This, Madame, is the need. The Queen returned from hunting wearing a jacket, hat and wig. The hat she wears nearly as elegantly as you do yours; she does not absolutely need a new one. But truly, Madame, you would not wish to see your sister, a Queen, in a wig, jacket and skirt of the kind she is wearing . . . The King said to me, "Confess it frankly, is not the Queen abominably dressed?" I shrugged my shoulders, and then made so bold as to say, "Madame, will Your Majesty not ask my mistress to send you a well-cut riding habit?" "I should indeed be glad of one," she replied, "but I dare not, for I would not be a burden to my sister." "Let me undertake it all," said I (being certain of excellent results). "Very well," said the Queen, "but nothing grand, just a well-cut jacket, with gold sleeves, in the simple style my sister wears when she hunts from a carriage; since I do not nor will I ever ride on horseback . . ."[4] To be brief, what we require from you is a jacket and skirt of red, blue or grey cloth, with a bank or two of gold braid, or a few rosettes, but no finery. We also need a wig, for hers is dreadful. All these to be exactly what you would choose for yourself, and if possible, done with such speed that our courier may bring them back with him.

As he anticipated, it was indeed possible: Adelaide was delighted to play the part of older sister and mentor — to have (for a change) something pleasant to occupy her mind. The riding habit and wig were quickly followed by parcels of clothing and food, then countless letters describing the experience of pregnancy for the young bride. When a Spanish heir, the prince of Asturias, was born in 1707, his delighted aunt rushed to send an exquisitely embroidered layette — as well as sheets of experienced advice for the new mother.

"What a cruel war this is," Mme de Maintenon complained to the princesse des Ursins, "which arms sister against her brother, a father against his children, and subjects against their legitimate princes! Our Duchesse de Bourgogne suffers greatly from this state of things; I am very much alarmed for the safety of her infant." It was the expectation of her infant that provided the one spot of joy and hope in an otherwise dismal winter.

A son would more than atone for his treacherous Italian grandfather, and Adelaide prayed fervently for a boy. The king's hopes were emphasized on New Year's Day, when he distributed more than four thousand pistoles in gifts to his court, but his expectations were tempered with concern for his darling's safety. He arranged for a papal dispensation so the expectant mother could eat meat on Fridays and forgo fasting during Lent. Dangeau noted on January 25: "[She] has felt the first stirrings of her child," and Adelaide was immediately forbidden to travel anywhere but in a sedan chair.

In her fifth month alarming complications developed, reported to Turin by the duchesse du Lude: "For three days past, we are in strange apprehensions concerning the Duchesse . . . She has felt pain and was put to bed. Then it was found that her child has turned and is very low; but they say this is not a bad thing. She has terrible fears of delivery, and is thereby in a sad enough state. The child moves and is big, and from its frequent moving, seems in good health."

By May, the princesse was totally confined to bed; from the twenty-second on, she heard mass twice daily and received communion every morning. Louis XIV visited three times a day to check her progress, and Mme de Maintenon seldom left her side. No less solicitous was Bourgogne, and during the last months of Adelaide's pregnancy, a new closeness blossomed between husband and wife: Mme de Maintenon wrote the princesse des Ursins that Adelaide "is not at all well . . . and her condition requires many remedies and much care," but that her husband was always nearby and extremely supportive and encouraging — despite the fact, Maintenon chuckled, that he was "furious [that] they were prevented from living together."

The first labor pains came the afternoon of June 23. The *accoucheur* Clément was sent for at once and arrived to find Louis XIV, Bourgogne, and Mme de Maintenon already present. As the night wore on, it became apparent the delivery would be long and difficult. Louis XIV, overcome with emotion, refused to leave the chamber, sitting by the bedside and holding Adelaide's hand, just as he had done at the birth of her husband two decades before. Bourgogne was not so stoic: he found Draco's cries and moans too painful to hear and fled the room, locking himself in his private cabinet and praying fervently until his brother Berri came with good tidings.

At half past five, the afternoon of Wednesday, June 24, 1704, the duchesse de Bourgogne was delivered of a son. The infant was so large and robust "they were required to cap him with a three-year-old's bonnet and with difficulty bound his arms to his sides." He was wrapped in swaddling clothes sent by His Holiness the pope, and immediately baptized the duc de Bretagne. He was shown to Bourgogne, who kissed him, then cried tears of relief; the new father handed his son to the governess of the Children of France to be taken to the royal nursery. (This was Bourgogne's own former governess, the maréchale de La Mothe, who had surrendered her choice apartment at Versailles to the prince four years earlier with anticipation of the moment now at hand.) The king and the duc de Bourgogne then excused themselves from the crowd of well-wishers and retired to the chapel, where they knelt together for forty-five minutes giving thanks.

The news of little Bretagne's birth was announced by a salvo of rockets fired from the balconies of the palace, and the waiting throng went wild. For the first time in French history, there were *three* direct heirs to the throne, and Frenchmen everywhere rose to the occasion with magnificent demonstrations of loyalty.[5]

Immediately the mansions of the great nobles throughout the Versailles village were brilliantly illuminated. Processions formed in the street, to the blast of bugles and beat of drums, and crowds surged into the Great Courtyard of the palace shouting "Vive le Roi!," "Vive le Duc de Bourgogne!," and (loudest of all) "Vive la Duchesse de Bourgogne!" The marquis de Villacerf, Adelaide's maître d'hôtel, ordered silver coins thrown from the windows, and the officers of her household distributed bottles of wine among the cheering masses. Forty-six cannons, parked along the Grand Avenue of Versailles, fired eight salvos each; the guild of masons and stonecutters, with muskets on their shoulders and bearing an illuminated triumphal arch, marched in military order to the gates of the palace and discharged a volley of their own. In Paris, the celebrations were even more frenzied; bonfires were lit along the quays, bread and wine were distributed to the poor, and in the Place de l'Hôtel de Ville, the citizens danced all night as the bells of every church, abbey, and convent in the city pealed their jubilation.

The next evening, the king ordered a dazzling display of fireworks at Versailles. The climax of this spectacle was a gigantic allegorical figure of France, with all her heraldic adornments, holding the newborn prince in her arms and presenting him to the heavens. Court poets proclaimed "the incomparable Adelaide," and throughout the château motets and madrigals, all composed in her honor, were performed.

Louis XIV assessed the mood of his people: thoroughly weary of war, their illusions of invincibility shattered by the stunning victories of Marlborough and Prince Eugene, they were in vital need of something to hope for, something to believe in. To this end, the celebrations for the birth of little Bretagne were celebrations of the system, a reaffirmation of monarchy as the living symbol of France — and the people responded eagerly.

From the largest cities to the smallest villages, enthusiasm generated festivities unmatched in recent memory — even by those for the baby's father two decades earlier. In Paris, churches, schools, and government buildings remained illuminated for one entire week. City guilds responded with no fewer than seventy banquets to honor the royal parents.[6] Even the bad and the mad were invited to share the general jubilation: the inmates of the prison at Petit Châtelet were permitted to set off bonfires on the roof of their jail tower, and at the asylum of Petites-Maisons, the warden not only distributed wine to passersby but ordered all the cell doors open and lavished food and drink upon his patients, "with such generosity that some of the poor lunatics regained their sanity, for nothing repairs a deficiency so much as a plenitude of victuals, and those who recovered their senses drank the health of all the Royal Family."

Court notables contributed to the national euphoria with their own brand of lavish celebration. Two days after Bretagne's birth, Dangeau gave a magnificent supper party in Adelaide's honor at his town house in the Place Royal. Cascades of light flooded the square (appropriately illuminating the equestrian statue of the king in its center) and an orchestra of twenty-four violins filled the still summer air with Lully and Couperin. When this sumptuous fête acquired a large and curious throng of spectators, Dangeau gallantly ordered refreshments served to the ladies in the crowd. The marquis de Courcelles, a gentleman in the princesse's household, organized a fireworks extravaganza that exploded for hours over the Seine; the architect Mansard provided a stunning entertainment at his own city mansion, where performers from the Paris Opéra sang in a garden lit by ten thousand carefully concealed candles.

The heart of this massive outpouring of emotion was the eighteen-year-old duchesse de Bourgogne. Adelaide's popularity reached its zenith with the birth of her son in a well-deserved tribute not only to her youth and her grace, but to her other fine qualities as well: her simplicity, her good nature, and her generosity of heart (and purse).

The great and powerful of Versailles were far better known to the populace than they ever imagined: maids and valets spoke freely of the comings and goings of their lords and ladies, of their quirks and their idiosyncrasies — and always to enraptured audiences. Of course, the greatest curiosity was focused on the royal family. All Paris had known of Monsieur, with his high heels, his pots of paint and his pretty boys, just as they knew of the extraordinary piety and great promise of the duc de Bourgogne. And their princesse, they knew well, was "always considerate for the humbler of the servants of the King, even the last and least of them." She was not haughty or arrogant, like the king's illegitimate daughters, and her liberality at alms giving was widely appreciated. She smiled at the cheering crowds, gaily and unaffectedly. It is a signal token of her tremendous hold on the affections of the French that in this period replete with malicious and ribald rhymes, scurrilous ballads, and satiric couplets — from which not even Louis XIV was exempt — not one single verse existed attacking the duchesse de Bourgogne, "our Princesse."

Adelaide's recovery from childbirth was slow. She remained bedridden for three weeks, rising for the first time (to visit the nursery) on July 17. On the twenty-ninth, she gave an audience to several prominent courtiers, but remained in bed throughout their visit. She was allowed to go outdoors for the first time on August 3, and the next day Louis XIV whisked her off to Marly. She had missed the lavish rejoicings of late June, and Grandpapa was determined to make amends with the most spectacular entertainment his royal mind could devise.

At Marly, the young mother was to walk the gardens with the king, to be hailed and honored from each of the twelve guest pavilions that lined the Reflecting Pool. In the first house was the goddess Flora, bringing flowers and fine verses; Pomona, in the second, offered heaping baskets of fruit and sweetmeats, while next door Cupid presented liqueurs and ices of every conceivable flavor and color. In the fourth and fifth pavilions, lesser goddesses showered the princesse with ribbons and parasols, and beautiful fans thickly encrusted with emeralds, rubies, and diamonds. In the sixth house, Adelaide — who loved to spin — found a gilded spinning wheel beside a Chinese lacquered table that held two hundred pounds of unspun silk. The seventh and eighth pavilions were filled with curiosities from India and the Far East, and a wondrous new telescope awaited in the ninth. An exquisite dinner service, finely wrought in silver, was her present in the tenth house; in the eleventh was the same dinner service, done this time in gold. In the last guest house, a goddess presented the princesse with a portrait of herself, her baby on her lap, in a frame so thickly jeweled that it took two pages to hold it. The entire pageant was devised by the poet Bellocq — and unfortunately it was spoiled by rain.

Not one to let inclemency ruin his fun, Louis XIV followed this Marly extravaganza with a public festival at Versailles. As the royal family sat down to dinner in the warm night air, fifty cases of fireworks exploded above their heads, opening the ceremonies. Throughout the evening, a torchlit procession of allegorical chariots made its way up the Grand Avenue of Versailles into the Great Courtyard. The splendor of the first of these chariots gives ample indication of the night's opulence: appropriately, it carried Mars, the god of war, come to pay homage to the earthly Sun King. Mars sat on a throne six feet high, starred with golden lilies and encrusted in jewels, each bearing the name of one of the twelve great military victories of Louis XIV.[7] He wore a helmet sparkling with diamonds and topped with a white ostrich plume (a deliberate compliment to the white plume Louis XIV sported every day); in his hand he carried a jeweled javelin, and at his feet there burned an immense globe of fire between the standing figures of Minerva and Bellona. The chariot was drawn by four cream-colored horses and driven by two of Jove's messengers, classically dressed and sounding their trumpets. Twenty-four soldiers, dressed as Roman centurians and carrying lanterns, provided an escort for the war god.

As this stunning spectacle entered the Marble Courtyard, Louis XIV and Marie Adelaide appeared on the balcony above: Mars rose majestically from his jeweled throne, declaiming in rhymed couplets the glorious birth of a great-grandson destined to complete the Sun King's work. As Mars concluded his paean to the House of Bourbon, another volley of fireworks burst in the air above the awestruck crowd — and the stage was cleared for the second chariot. Throughout the night, the procession unfolded, each tableau more magnificent than the last; the final cases of fireworks concluded the entertainment and welcomed the rising sun.

On August 12, 1704, Louis XIV held a *fête de nuit* in Adelaide's honor at Marly. The royal circle — including "King James III of England" and his mother, ex-Queen Mary — was entertained during supper in the great banquet hall by an orchestra of violins and hautboys, while outside the clear call of hunting bugles sounded in the glades. The fountains and pools of the Marly gardens glittered in the light of one thousand torches. The king, in a rare gesture, ordered the iron gates to the park thrown open for the public, and "half of Paris" turned out to savor the woods and walkways, the enchanted arbors, and the perfect summer night.[8] After supper, the guests moved onto the terrace. Darkness fell shortly before nine, and the first illumination rose in the night sky — an enormous triumphal arch, with letters of fire across it proclaiming "FOR ADELAIDE." A specially designed assortment of tableaux and representations followed, all paying homage to the glowing young woman who sat in a gilded chair beside the king.

But the Fates were determined to temper joy with sorrow: even as the court reveled in these spectacular royal diversions, word was trickling through of a disastrous military defeat in Bavaria. By the end of August, all France knew of Marlborough's triumph at Blenheim — though few outside the Sun King's intimate circle understood the implications of this allied victory.

The battle of Blenheim all but destroyed the fabled war machine of Louis XIV. Three of his armies went into the conflict — those of Villars, Tallard, and the elector of Bavaria — a force of more than 150,000 men. After the battle, sixteen thousand survivors straggled back into France. The French military domination of Europe had been shattered, and with it, Louis XIV's dreams of an invasion of Austria. After Blenheim, the king understood that unqualified victory was no longer possible; though careful to maintain his brave and haughty front, his sole objective thereafter was to find a dignified way out of the war.

In the face of this adversity, the Sun King's pride, in his people and his granddaughter, never wavered. Stoically, he refused to cancel the elaborate fête designed by the city of Paris to honor the new parents on August 27.

It was, on the whole, an unsatisfactory evening. Adelaide appeared on the balcony of the royal apartments at the Louvre, overlooking the Seine. With her to receive the wild acclamations of the Parisian crowds were Bourgogne, Berri, and Monseigneur. The spectacle opened with a joust performed by the watermen *on* the river — a lighthearted spoof of the chivalric tournaments of the Middle Ages, performed with oars and boathooks. The customary fireworks display was next. Unfortunately, it had been planned well in advance of Blenheim and one (rather ironic) allegory presented the Seine and the Tagus (France and Portugal) in triumph over their symbolic enemies, the Rhine and the Thames. The general response to this bravado — now so patently false — was disgust, and several felt it was a blessing when a sudden downpour put an end to the fireworks show.

At least one feature of the evening was successful: a magnificent supper was served to the royal party by the municipality. Two tables, of twenty courses each, were spread for the guests. Adelaide and Bourgogne presided over one, with Berri and Monseigneur at the other, and as Saint-Simon noted succinctly: "There was lavish spending on eating and drinking." At half past one, the royal party entered their carriages and drove through the streets of Paris, down the rue Saint-Honoré, passing Pont Neuf (with its statue of Henri IV, founder of the House of Bourbon) and on to Meudon where the king awaited them. (That same evening saw more successful celebrating in London — for the victory of Blenheim, with bonfires, fireworks, and the incessant tolling of bells: "Never were such demonstrations of joy since the laying of London stone.")

The next night at Meudon, Monseigneur gave yet another *fête de nuit* to honor his daughter-in-law, with fireworks by her favorite artist, Claude Audran; this brought to a close the royal festivities for the birth of the duc de Bretagne.

Not that they ended without criticism. Many felt such wanton and extravagant spending was inexcusable during wartime — and all the more deplorable since the war was going so badly. Saint-Simon was condemning: "The time was at hand, when they would repent their premature rejoicing, their reckless expenditure of money, their foolish demonstrations, so improper in the circumstances."

It was customary in the French royal family to leave children totally to the care of a large staff of nurses and governesses. The new baby's father, grandfather, and great-grandfather had seen precious little of *their* parents during the nursery years, and there seemed no reason now to depart from tradition. Adelaide did not hold her son until she left her bed on July 17 for her first visit to the royal nursery. The official obligations of her station — she was, after all, the untitled queen of France — placed heavy demands on her time; even had she been so inclined, there was little room in her crowded schedule for the tending of a newborn child.

Still, like many new mothers, she was fascinated by this tiny creature she had made, and once she had returned to public life, the frequency of her "surprise visits" to the nursery would have astonished most of her predecessors. "I cannot help telling you about my son, who is very well," she crowed to her grandmother on September 1.[9] "He would be rather pretty if he were not covered with the itch, but I hope that when we get to Fontainebleau, he will have no more of it."

The rash did vanish, though perhaps it was an indication of deeper, more serious trouble. The baby continued to thrive in the early months of 1705, then sudden and senseless tragedy struck. On the morning of April 13, the ten-month-old infant was seized with inexplicable and violent convulsions. The doctors were summoned at once — much to the unheeded disgust of Madame. "Doctors have no idea of the care that children require," she had written in 1676. "They will never listen to anything, and have already dispatched a heap of children into the next world."

A diagnosis was reached and a remedy devised, with no consideration of the patient's age: the poor infant was given a powerful emetic and bled several times from the arm, with predictable and horrifying results. "Nature was so exhausted," Dangeau wrote, "that none of the remedies could save him, and he died at seven in the evening."

The court was stunned at the loss of the little prince and deeply moved by the obvious grief of his parents. Adelaide suffered severely. Four years earlier, her first experience with death (that of Monsieur) had left her profoundly shaken: "I have felt [it] much more than I expected," she had confessed to Madame Royale. Now the loss of her firstborn child, the child in whom so many hopes had rested, was a shattering blow. She showed much "piety and resignation," though unable to share in the philosophical outlook of the king, who explained to the royal confessor, Père de La Chaise: "If he had lived, royal princes are exposed to so many dangers to health that there is always ground for apprehension; since he has died, he will become an angel in heaven."

But as so often is the case, misfortune brought with it growth, and in her first letter to Turin after Bretagne's death, we glimpse a new and maturing Marie Adelaide: "25 April 1705. I cannot, my dear grandmother, be longer without comforting myself with you in the sorrow that has befallen me. I am convinced that you have felt it, for I know the affection you have for me . . . If we did not take all the sorrows of this life from God, I do not know what would become of us. I think

He wants to draw me to Him, by overwhelming me with every sort of grief. My health suffers greatly, but that is the least of my troubles . . . The assurances of affection which you give me bring me consolation. I have great need of it in my present state."

Adelaide's "present state" did not pass quickly: two months later, Mme de Maintenon wrote the princesse des Ursins: "The Duchesse de Bourgogne wept yesterday for her son as on the day of his death, because it was that of his birth."

The duc de Bourgogne also felt bitterly the loss of his son, but his letter to his brother the king of Spain (written at the same time as Adelaide's to her grandmother) proved the success of his upbringing — to the extent that he could no longer distinguish between public misfortune and private sorrow:

> I have not written you, my dear brother, since the loss of my son, and I believe that the affection which you entertain for me will have caused you to feel it keenly. It would have been desirable, not only for my sake, but for that of affairs in general, that this misfortune should not have befallen us, but men ought always to submit blindly to that which comes from above. God knows better than ourselves what is right for us; He has life and death in His hands, and has taken my son to a place where I ardently desire to rejoin him one day. However to desire that is not sufficient, I must work for it . . . The position in which you are, my dear brother, and for which I am destined in the course of Nature (though I desire that the time may be very far distant), this position, I say, is as full of dangers as there are duties to discharge, and these dangers are so much more pressing as the duties are great; but, at the same time, what degree of glory is reserved in Heaven for those who discharge them worthily!

(While the grief-stricken parents resigned themselves to the mysterious workings of the Lord, the more earthbound Madame reported to her niece: "The poor little Duc de Bretagne died last Monday. I am firmly convinced that the doctors dispatched the little prince to the other world with their bleedings and emetics. But no one ever listens to me.")

Because of the infant's age, Louis XIV decreed there should be no funeral ceremony. The tiny corpse was taken at night to Saint-Denis (the eternal resting place for the French royal family) in a coach without pall or trappings, escorted by a company of torch-bearing pages. Inside the carriage sat the bereaved father, the now ex-governess Mme de La Mothe, and the cardinal de Coislin, who had blessed the little boy at his birth. In compliance with another — and gruesome — royal tradition, the cardinal carried on his knees a little silver urn, bearing the heart of the dead baby. The cortège moved slowly through the streets of Paris (where, Saint-Simon said, "the public was deeply moved by the loss") and on to Saint-Denis; in the dead of night, without any ritual, the duc de Bretagne was laid to rest.

Louis XIV, with his characteristic aversion to displays of grief, forbade the wearing of mourning, even by the baby's parents. The day after the interment, the royal family left for Marly. The king was loath to alter in any way his daily routine and insisted that Adelaide join him in the hunt. Dutifully, the princesse obeyed; but this time, not even the Sun King could ease her sorrow or banish her sadness. Her health — never robust and weakened by years of exhaustive pleasuring — steadily deteriorated after her son's death. At the end of April, Bourgogne wrote Philip V of a new medicine the doctors were giving Adelaide: "I think they will soon repeat the dose, and then give her a bath, after which she will be drinking the waters of Forges, so as to dispose her to repair as speedily as possible the loss which we have suffered."

The doctors strove, with some success, to repair her body. The mending of her spirit was not forthcoming.

15

"Every Sort of Grief"

THE BIRTH OF LITTLE BRETAGNE won Adelaide the
greatest popularity she had yet enjoyed; with his tragic death, an
element of pathos entered into the national adulation. Her trials were
far from over: the next twelve months would prove a landmark year
in her short life, truly a year filled with "every sort of grief."

While the death of the child could have brought new closeness to the
stricken parents, their sorrow instead became a wedge between them.
It was a one-sided estrangement, however, and a surprising shift in
their relationship: Adelaide turned to her pious husband for solace and
support, confident that his unwavering love and devotion would
steady them both in accepting their loss. She found nothing of the kind.

The princesse, and the entire court, failed to realize how deeply
shaken Bourgogne was by his son's death. It was always his nature to
blame himself (and still worse, to punish himself) for the misfortunes
of others. In 1701 he had read his wife's illness as divine censure of his
"wild and dissipated" life. Now the death of this innocent baby, in the
middle of a war France seemed destined to lose, was further proof to
him of Almighty displeasure — with him, with France, with the war,
with the eighteenth-century world itself. He became gloomy and mo-
rose, suffering renewed outbursts of the violent temper, "often displayed at the wrong moment," that he had so diligently tried to master.
Even Mme de Maintenon, who had long encouraged Bourgogne's
religious proclivities, described as "uncouth" this new piety that held
him in its grip. Still passionately fond of music, he labeled *all* concerts

"sacrilegious" and refused to attend them, even though he knew this infuriated the king. His fulfillment of courtly obligations fell off sharply, increasing the burden for his emotionally drained wife. Adelaide found that he expected her to bear far more than just his ceremonial duties: engulfed in guilt and imagined neglect of little Bretagne, Bourgogne displayed an "angry passion" to his wife, as if she herself had caused the child's death.

This painful change in the king's heir alarmed the entire court, including his staunch defender, the duc de Beauvilliers; it was the ex-governor who apprised Fénelon (still in far-off Cambrai) of the distressing royal metamorphosis. Fénelon responded with a long, advice-filled letter, admonishing his former pupil to moderate his puritanical ways and soften his harsh, unwarranted treatment of his wife. The prince should not oppose Adelaide in every matter, great and small; the manner in which she observed Lent, for example, should be the decision of her doctor, not her husband. "If you wish to inspire her with a love for religion, make it appear sweet and gentle, and avoid all that is irksome; allow her to realize for herself the value and pleasantness of virtue, simple and unadorned. In all things that do not entail serious moral laxity . . . appear cheerful and easy. In short, comply with her wishes and be patient."

Fénelon's excellent advice, had it been followed, might have alleviated much of the pain the royal couple endured separately in the latter half of 1705. But the archbishop's sage counsel had no effect. Bourgogne continued to immure himself in his private chapel, praying fervently for the soul of one son and the delivery of another. In his rare public appearances, he looked "as black as thunder and most disdainfully superior," provoking one courtier to declare him "a nuisance to everyone, and perhaps to [Marie Adelaide] also."

If her husband was difficult, her suitors were now equally disagreeable. Both Nangis and Maulevrier had been at court when Adelaide's condition was first announced and remained throughout her pregnancy, but the bearing of an heir had acted only as a partial deterrent: Maulevrier, still shamming illness, continued to whisper words of passion in the young lady's ear and Nangis, with jealousy of his rival outweighing fear of his mistress, continued his assiduous courting. Balancing two illicit admirers, encouraging their honey-coated flatteries and cavalier attentions without surrendering to their passion, required an expertise that Adelaide did not possess. While the princesse vacillated, Nangis and Maulevrier chafed. The enforced hiatus of royal pregnancy had done nothing to dampen their ardor — in fact, for Maulevrier, whose mental health had never been accepted as completely satisfactory, the waiting only aggravated his obsessive envy. In the summer of 1705, it was noted at court that Nangis's mistress, Mme de La Vrillière, had been "for some time in exceeding ill-humor." Maulevrier concluded that his rival had at last gained the true favor of the princesse[1] — or, as Saint-Simon put it, "he thought it revealed that Nangis was happy and he wished him not to be . . . At last rage and jealousy drove him to the point of sheer folly."

One morning, as Adelaide left daily mass, Maulevrier presented himself at the royal box. Dangeau, who generally escorted her back to her apartments, was absent and the princesse very properly took her suitor's proffered hand. The equerries and ladies of the household drew back respectfully and the couple proceeded through the crowded state apartments. Maulevrier, still using his "throat trouble," whispered furiously in Adelaide's ear all the while they walked. From Saint-Simon's description, it was an encounter she would not soon forget. "He roundly abused Nangis to the Princesse, called him every name under the sun, threatened to tell all to the King, Mme de Maintenon and her husband, almost crushed her fingers in a frenzy of passion, and so escorted her to her door."

The princesse was stunned: shaking uncontrollably and on the verge of fainting, she ran to her private room at the back of the apartment and cried for her "Nanny" — her favorite waiting woman, Mme de Nogaret. Adelaide tearfully revealed to Nogaret all that had occurred, "saying that she had felt ready to drop, and did not know how she had survived or ever reached her apartments." Old Nogaret, who had never before seen her charge so upset, advised her to be as careful with Maulevrier, "a man quite incapable of self-control," as with a dangerous lunatic and, above all else, "to avoid being compromised" — rather conveniently forgetting the letters she herself had delivered the summer before.

Maulevrier's mischief for the day was not yet over. Leaving the princesse, he searched for Nangis and found his rival in the Hall of Mirrors. With no provocation, he threatened the startled officer, "making all manner of attacks, as though he had been insulted and wished for satisfaction." Wisely, Nangis refrained from picking up the quarrel — not because "the very idea of quarreling made his blood run cold" (Saint-Simon's unfair slur), but because he realized that to do so was to risk exposing them all to royal wrath. "He saw his whole future at the mercy of a raving lunatic, and accordingly, resolved to avoid Maulevrier as much as possible, to appear very rarely at the Court, and to remain silent."

Being "at the mercy of a raving lunatic" was only one sort of grief for the princesse. A few days after the chapel door incident, Adelaide was visiting with Mme de Maintenon in the latter's private room. She had long been in the habit of riffling through whatever papers might be lying about. In her first years in France, the king and his wife had found this endearing; now such behavior was so ingrained that, had they chosen, they could no longer put an end to it. Adelaide's eye spied her own name in a letter written by Mme d'Espinay, a member of Monseigneur's court at Meudon and a longstanding critic of the princesse. She blushed as she read the first lines, hurriedly dropping the page on the desk.

"What are you reading, pet?" asked Mme de Maintenon innocently. "What is the matter?" The embarrassed princesse showed her the letter. "Well, so I have a letter from Mme d'Espinay. When people are inquisitive, they sometimes learn more than they bargained for. Read the whole letter, madame, and if you are wise, profit by it."

Adelaide read with horror Mme d'Espinay's complete account of her year-long flirtation with Nangis and Maulevrier. A stern lecture from Mme de Maintenon followed, warning her that people at court were becoming aware of her dalliances and reminding her of the consequences she faced if the king or her husband ever discovered the news. Drained of all color, struggling to keep her composure, Adelaide returned to her rooms — again, "Nanny" was called to her private room for another outburst of tears and rage. Her wise counsel was to be especially nice now to Mme d'Espinay, to let no one know that she had read the letter — and again, *to be careful*. Difficult as it was to mask her true feelings, Adelaide accorded Mme d'Espinay every respect and honor, and the old lady died several years later never knowing that her letter had earned for her the lasting enmity of the duchesse de Bourgogne.

For six long weeks, Adelaide lived in agony, knowing that her affairs were the talk of the court and facing the dread terror of exposure. It was her beloved Tessé who finally came to the rescue: Saint-Simon declared he never knew "who it was that informed Tessé" of the gravity of Adelaide's situation — if not his daughter, it is reasonably safe to assume it was Mme de Maintenon. The discreet old diplomat persuaded Maulevrier, his son-in-law, to accompany him to Spain, "with the promise of astronomical rewards." To guarantee the young lover's acquiescence, Tessé enlisted the aid of Fagon, the king's personal physician, "a man of great sagacity, kind-hearted and well able to take a hint." Fagon announced it his professional opinion that, since every known remedy for a weak chest and a lost voice had failed, Maulevrier had no choice but to seek a warmer climate; he added darkly that if he remained in France, the coming winter would assuredly kill him.

This diagnosis was given out to the court, and although Maulevrier's departure was suspiciously well timed, no one had any reason to doubt the verdict of the king's trusted doctor. More important, the story was fully accepted by those for whom it had been protectively devised — Louis XIV and the duc de Bourgogne. In a perfect demonstration of his unawareness of the gossip that rocked the court, Bourgogne recommended his wife's rejected suitor to his brother, the king of Spain: "Since he is particularly attached to me, as his wife is to the Duchesse de Bourgogne, the interest I take in the Marquis de Maulevrier will serve him as sufficient recommendation to you."

To Adelaide's enormous relief, Tessé and Maulevrier departed for Spain in October 1705. But Maulevrier's conduct at the court of Madrid was no more honorable than it had been at Versailles: his madness was worsening, and manifested itself in increasing cunning and audacity. Having gained entry into the royal circle through the goodwill of the very man he had tried to cuckold, he transferred his affections to the young queen of Spain, courting her as assiduously as he had her older sister. Saint-Simon hinted that his advances were "not entirely rebuffed," although there is little historical evidence to support his opinion. Nevertheless, rumors and speculation reached such a level that Gramont, the French ambassador to Spain, was obliged to report them to Louis XIV.

The king's reaction was swift: Maulevrier was prohibited from receiving any further honors from the king (or queen) of Spain and ordered to join his father-in-law at the siege of Gibraltar. There his quirkish behavior and disintegrating sanity could no longer be ignored: Tessé sent him back to Madrid for a brief sojourn, and in a private letter to Louis XIV, requested that the king recall him to France. Within the month, Maulevrier was back again at Versailles — to discover many changes.

The first change, that of his own stature at court, was a pleasant surprise: Mme de Maintenon, who took an avid interest in Spain and the Spanish court, obligingly forgot the true reason for his absence and graciously welcomed him back. She granted him several private interviews, often upward of three hours, asking "a thousand questions" about the king and queen, the current situation in Madrid, and seeing to it that Louis XIV himself was present at many of these audiences. Saint-Simon judged this new prominence the beginning of the end: "This sudden rise to a pinnacle of favor after facing imminent ruin completely turned Maulevrier's head; he began to despise the ministers and ignore the warnings sent him by Tessé."

His protracted acquaintance with the queen of Spain provided him with an ideal excuse for gaining a private audience with Adelaide. But the changes he discovered in the princesse's circle were far less pleasant than his new importance to the king and Mme de Maintenon.

For in Maulevrier's absence, Nangis had not triumphed, nor had Adelaide learned her lesson from the painful events of the previous summer. In his first public interview with the princesse, Maulevrier came face to face with a new and formidable rival, the abbé de Polignac.

Melchior de Polignac was forty-five when he met the twenty-year-old duchesse de Bourgogne. Fifteen years earlier, Mme de Sévigné had declared him "one of the men of this world whose disposition appears the most agreeable." Even Saint-Simon, who disliked him heartily, complimented his good looks, his conversation, his highly cultured tastes, and the wonderful fascination of his manners: "[He] was a man to gain all hearts. He desired to please the valet and the maid, as well as the master and the mistress. To succeed in this, he stopped at no flattery." Not even with the king: one day, as he followed Louis XIV through the gardens of Marly, it began to rain. When the king remarked that Polignac's fine outfit would be ruined soon, he replied, "It is no matter, sire, the rain of Marly does not wet."

He had served as French ambassador to Poland, but his inability to secure the Polish crown in 1698 for the French candidate, the prince de Conti, resulted in his disgrace and banishment.[2] During his three-year exile, he published his *Anti-Lucretius,* a philosophical poem in Latin that attracted the attention of the duc de Bourgogne and, ultimately, Louis XIV. The king arranged for his election to the Académie Française and Polignac again returned to royal favor.

His taste for the sciences, no less than his sympathetic religious views, endeared him to Bourgogne, who soon introduced the abbé into his wife's circle. Then, Saint-Simon explained, "the agreeable situation

in which he saw Nangis permanently and in which he had seen Maulevrier temporarily, excited his envy . . . He sought to share in the same
happiness. He took the same road. He strove to get a hearing; he was
heard." It began with Adelaide unburdening her heart to this kindly,
older — and very handsome — listener, and in no time, she was once
more braving the watchful Swiss Guards to rendezvous with him in the
Marly gardens.

The rise of Polignac's star eclipsed even that of Nangis; Maulevrier,
finding himself now out of the running and all but forgotten, was
pushed to the brink. Furiously he demanded a private audience with
the princesse and was emphatically refused it. Mme de Maulevrier,
exhausted by her husband's insulting, manic behavior, now salved her
wounded vanity by making overtures (with delightful irony) to
Nangis. The marquis responded, doubtless relishing this unexpected
twist.

For Maulevrier, the realization that he was being cuckolded by his
most bitter enemy was more than his mind could bear and he went to
pieces. He bolted himself up in his room and screamed "vile abuse" for
hours on end to those outside. Then he left court and moved to Paris.
He kept inside his house all day and, in the dead of night, would hire
a cab to take him to a distant Carthusian monastery where he would
walk in the garden and whistle to himself till dawn. He wrote incessantly, long recriminating letters to Mme de Maintenon and Marie
Adelaide; the ladies, one alarmed, the other terrified, did not respond.
He paid one last visit to Versailles and made a terrible scene when the
princesse refused again to see him privately.

Back in Paris, his behavior grew so erratic that the doctors were
summoned. He suffered from hallucinations, babbling wildly to an
imaginary Adelaide and arranging the assassination of Nangis. In rare
moments, he was gentle and withdrawn; most of the time, he spoke of
being mortally ill and on the verge of death.

The end came on Good Friday, 1706. Eluding the servants that kept
vigil over him, Maulevrier ran into a hallway behind his apartment,
broke open a window and threw himself into the courtyard below. His
head shattered on the cobblestones and he died instantly. "Such was
the end of that ambitious man," Saint-Simon moralized, "whose wild
and dangerous passions drove him out of his mind and deprived him
of his life, the tragic victim of his own hand."

When news of Maulevrier's death reached Versailles, Adelaide was
with the king in the chapel, observing the stations of the cross. In-

formed in the presence of the watchful court, she remained unmoved; but privately (Saint-Simon heard), "her tears flowed unchecked," and for several days after, her eyes were noticeably red and puffy. "They might well have been tears of compassion, but they were not so charitably interpreted."

Maulevrier's death brought matters to a head, and within days. "At Marly, after Easter," Saint-Simon recalled, "we found Mme de Maintenon looking depressed, uncertain, cross and quite unlike her usual self with the Duchesse de Bourgogne." She had every reason for being "unlike her usual self": Bourgogne and the king were dangerously close to discovery of Adelaide's lessons in love, and the possible consequences — for the princesse and her "aunt" — were too dreadful to contemplate. Maintenon was resolved: however innocent, however harmless, the fun had to end immediately. "They were closeted together alone and for long periods, from which the Princesse emerged in tears."

Mme de Maintenon was never one to move slowly once she had set a course. Maulevrier at least was already out of the picture. Nangis had had three years to recover from his illness: he was recommissioned and returned to the army. He continued to distinguish himself in successive campaigns, and while he remained a popular and respected member of the court, he was never again involved with the duchesse de Bourgogne save for reasons of official ceremony.

Polignac was not so easy to eliminate. Maintenon enlisted the aid of Foreign Minister Torcy and then the pope: the abbé was appointed auditor of the Rota — in essence, honorable exile to Rome. But Polignac, enjoying the supremacy afforded by the death of one rival and the departure of the other, was most reluctant to quit Versailles and its pleasures. He delayed his move to Rome throughout the summer months. At last he was compelled into action and left in early October, 1706. His farewell to Adelaide was emotional and not particularly well disguised: "The Duchesse de Bourgogne wished him a prosperous journey in a manner very different from her usual . . . Few believed in the headache that kept her all day long extended upon a couch in Mme de Maintenon's room."

So the matter of three too many suitors was resolved, but not without repercussions. For the first time in her life, Adelaide was subjected to the public ridicule of the broadsheets: a few days after Polignac's departure, Madame was walking in the Versailles gardens and discovered two verses, "as rude as they were apposite," scribbled across a balustrade and several pedestals. Typically, "she was neither discreet nor benevolent enough to hold her tongue." Yet Adelaide was too popular a figure, too well beloved by all Versailles, to suffer for long the malice of anonymous enemies. Court response was extremely atypical — "the verses had little influence because everyone united in suppressing them" — a fine tribute to the princesse's extraordinary hold over her people.

Of course the question was once again asked — how far did she go with Polignac? And once again, the answer seems to be nowhere at all. The princesse certainly responded positively to her suitor's advances, but it is improbable their relations ever entered into the physical. The palace was too well stocked with spying Swiss Guards and conscientious attendants to allow a major indiscretion, even had Marie Adelaide been so inclined. And she was far from inclined: the death of her son had been a shattering experience from which she had not yet fully recovered. Moreover, in the summer of 1706, when Polignac resisted his exile and stepped up his courtship, the princesse discovered herself pregnant once more and was too preoccupied by fears for the safe delivery of this child to flirt with danger.

Polignac's departure brought an end to Adelaide's lessons in love, lessons more beneficial for their pain than for their pleasure. She had learned the vital importance of maintaining the propriety of her station by coming perilously close to abandoning it. Maulevrier had taught her a hard truth — that princesses, no less than princes, are seldom loved for themselves. Above all, she realized that the carefree, irresponsible days of her youth were truly over.

Happily, maturity brought her closer to Bourgogne. With her pregnancy, his moodiness disappeared, and she began at last to appreciate his many finer qualities, buried beneath his insecurities. She recognized the true worth of his selfless devotion. Ever so slowly, but steadily, she was falling in love with her husband.

Adelaide was pregnant in the summer of 1706 and filled with apprehension, for twelve months earlier she had miscarried. The circumstances of this miscarriage reveal a good deal of the ambivalence innate in Louis XIV.

One of the king's most sterling qualities, acknowledged by friends and foes alike, was his extraordinary courtesy and sense of fairness. The daily chambermaid was treated to the same chivalry as a princesse of the blood; once, when a mistake occurred in the ceremony of the *lever* and the anxious audience tried to pay court by abusing the erring valet, Louis XIV silenced the throng by saying, "Let us remember that he is much more upset about it than I am." On another occasion, he went out of his way to obtain justice for the duc de Rohan, a man he openly detested. The king underwent an operation on an anal fistula in 1686; when his chief surgeon, Charles Tassy Félix, understandably intimidated by his patient, panicked in midprocedure, Louis calmed him by saying, "Do not treat me like a king. I wish to recover as though I were a peasant."

But there was another side to all this, a selfishness and inconsiderateness that were simply baffling. To think of the comfort of others, when it crossed his own plans, was inconceivable to Louis XIV. For example, the king enjoyed passing his carriage ride between Fontainebleau and Versailles in the company of one or two young ladies of the court. He would thoughtfully provide refreshment during the journey, and the royal invitation was an honor highly cherished. But the honor did not always outweigh the rigors of the experience: the Sun King, notoriously passionate about fresh air, insisted on making the trip with all the carriage windows wide open, regardless of the weather.

Worse still, the carriage stopped for the king's convenience *only*. For a passenger to request permission to answer a call of nature meant immediate and total disgrace.

Once, the duchesse de Chevreuse was invited to join in the six-hour ride to Fontainebleau. The coach had just pulled out of the Great Courtyard when the duchess felt, too late, a need to relieve herself. Every mile aggravated her discomfort, but she knew that nothing could be done until they reached their destination. Halfway there, the king ordered the carriage stopped and their meal served. Since Louis XIV showed no sign of leaving the coach to relieve himself, the duchesse was forced to remain in her seat. The poor woman could not refuse the royal hospitality, though the little she ate and drank only worsened her predicament. Back on the road, the jostlings of the royal coach were agonizing, and several times she felt near to fainting. At last, at nightfall, they arrived at Fontainebleau. The duchess's brother-in-law, the duc de Beauvilliers, awaited them in the courtyard, and as she alit from the carriage, the tortured young woman hissed her problem in his ear. Curtsying graciously (and with great pain), she hurried off with Beauvilliers. She cried that she would never make it to her rooms, and the duke hurried her into the palace chapel nearby, mounting guard while the miserable creature finally emptied her bladder — in a holy-water font.

The results of the Sun King's insensibility to others, as Adelaide sadly proved, were not always so amusing. In the critical first months of her pregnancy in 1705, she was under careful scrutiny by the royal doctors. One evening following supper with the king at Marly, she was suddenly taken ill and carried to her bed. Fagon prescribed complete immobility, but the king was scheduled to leave the next morning for Fontainebleau and insisted that she accompany him.

The long ride over poor country roads proved too much: on arrival, the princesse was put to bed immediately, and two hours later she miscarried. Louis XIV was walking in the gardens when the news was brought to him. (The precise formula prescribed by etiquette to announce a miscarriage was employed: "Sire, Madame the Duchesse de Bourgogne has been injured.") Several of the gentlemen attending the king offered their condolences, bemoaning "the greatest misfortune in the world," adding their hopes that, after so many such accidents, the princesse might still be able to conceive and deliver. Then Louis XIV stopped everything with a startling outburst: "What does it matter to me who succeeds me? Even if the Duchesse were never to have another son, is not the Duc de Berri of an age to marry and have children? Since she was to miscarry, thank God it is over and I shall no longer be nagged by a pack of doctors and old women. I shall go and come at my pleasure and shall be left in peace!"

Saint-Simon reported the reaction: "A silence so deep that an ant might have been heard walking . . . All eyes were lowered; scarcely anyone dared to breathe. Everyone seemed stupefied. Even the servants and the gardeners stood motionless. This silence lasted more than a quarter of an hour. The king broke it by leaning over the balustrade to speak about a carp."

But at the French court it had long become impossible to distinguish the king Louis XIV from the man Louis de Bourbon: had Saint-Simon possessed a superhuman objectivity, he might have seen a tired old man, severely shaken — horrified to be so confronted with his own thoughtlessness and terrified by the consequences of his lack of consideration

From then on, it became the law at court that every precaution imaginable was to be taken when the duchesse de Bourgogne was expecting.

"God . . . overwhelms me with every sort of grief," Adelaide had written in the spring of 1705. Since then she had suffered one more debilitating miscarriage and, through the madness of Maulevrier and her own folly, come dangerously near to public disgrace. New and greater grief awaited in the field of war, where her family was now the enemy.

When the news of her father's defection reached Versailles, the princesse was horror-stricken. She sobbed uncontrollably, as much for herself as for her family. Her fear for her future was grounded in historical precedent, the case of her own mother-in-law: when the late dauphine's brother, the elector of Bavaria, had likewise defected from the French cause in the mid-1680s, poor Marie Anne Christine suffered severely from the effects of royal disfavor. That the duke of Savoy's *second* defection had no damaging effect on the status of his daughter is further evidence of the triumph she had achieved at the court of Louis XIV. In fact, to signal his continued favor, the king multiplied the number of balls and fêtes presented at Versailles, and wisely, Adelaide "took care not to miss one of these diversions. It was for her that they were invented, and she employed the occasion to her advantage."

But public smiles gave way with increasing frequency to private tears. The war news, from all fronts, was distressing, and by the opening months of 1706, the situation facing the Two Crowns in Flanders, Germany, and Spain was critical.

The battle of Blenheim completely reversed the fortunes of both sides, and one of its effects was to put the Sun King on the defensive, for the first time in his reign. In the winter following this disastrous setback, herculean efforts were made within France to repair her enormous losses in manpower and equipment. Universal conscription was adopted, taxation was severely increased, and all exemption abolished. (The clergy alone was compelled to contribute six million livres to the war effort.) These measures were successful: to the allies' amazement, the French army that took to the field six months after Blenheim was greater than ever before. Apart from the force held in reserve for Philip V of Spain, the Sun King was able to send one hundred squadrons and one hundred battalions into Italy under the duc de Vendôme, and two hundred sixty squadrons and two hundred battalions along the northern frontiers, divided into three armies on the Upper Rhine, the Moselle, and in Flanders.

Despite this extraordinary show of strength — a force of 200,000 — the army of the Two Crowns found itself outnumbered by an allied army of 250,000 soldiers, and the campaign of 1705 proved as disastrous as that of the year before.[3]

Marlborough succeeded in piercing the Lines of Brabant, a string of fortresses from Antwerp to Namur some sixty miles long, which stretched across Flanders and protected France from northern invasion. In mid-July, the allies broke through the French defenses at three points — Elixem, Wange, and Orsmael — and gained control of some fifty miles of the lines. The stalemate in the northern theater was broken.

Louis XIV was shaken by the fall of the lines and distressed that his defensive strategy had proved such a failure. Writing to Villeroi, the commander in Flanders, on July 21, he carefully avoided the temptation to censure: "Although I am convinced of your vigilance and the pains which you have taken to be carefully informed of the movements of the enemy, it is nonetheless most disagreeable to see them in the middle of the Low Countries, masters of the Lines and several important posts, and my army compelled to retire before them to avoid its entire defeat." He knew his childhood playfellow well enough to understand that the insecure Villeroi was racked with remorse: "I blame you in no way for what has happened." However, it was time to rethink their strategy, to return to the offensive: "Our affairs having definitely changed their character, we must forget a kind of warfare which is suited neither to the genius of the nation nor to the army you command . . . You should not in the future avoid them with too much care; you should make war as we have in the past; hold the field, take full advantage of your position. Do not expose yourself to a general engagement without need, B U T D O N O T A V O I D I T W I T H T O O M U C H P R E C A U T I O N : because if the enemy perceives this they will take advantage of it."

Marlborough's stunning victories all but destroyed the last shreds of Villeroi's waning confidence; to the minister of war, Chamillart, he confessed piteously: "Would God that the King's interest could be served by my renouncement of command. I would reduce myself with pleasure." Instead, he was left to preside over the continuing debacle: the forts at Aerschot and Diest were abandoned, and Leau and Monluc were surrendered without a fight. Villeroi had once labeled his adversary a "mortified adventurer," but as the foiled French army crept back to its winter lodgings, it was not Marlborough but Villeroi who struggled with mortification.

Maréchal Villars, commanding the army along the Moselle River, studied the reversals of his confederate with mounting alarm. He feared greatly that his own force would soon come face to face with the seemingly invincible Englishman's, but (to his poorly concealed relief) Marlborough confined his attentions to the Lines of Brabant throughout the summer.

In Paris, there was much speculation as to why Marlborough, whose force far outnumbered Villars's, avoided such a confrontation. Madame, always eager to recount a good story, informed her aunt (July 9, 1705) of the current Parisian explanation: "They say that [Marlborough] believes in and consults wise men and fortune tellers. Well, there is one at Frankfurt who has a great reputation; he sent for her and tried to force her into telling him whether he would have a successful campaign. She is said to have told him that Fortune would favor him, provided that he avoided giving battle to a general who wore on his sword a knot of ribbons given him by a beautiful princesse." Marlborough immediately dispatched a spy to Villars's camp, to observe the maréchal's sword; being advised that Villars wore an unadorned sword, he prepared to attack. "But next day, my lord Marlborough sent another spy to the French camp, who returned saying that this time Villars *had* ribbons on his sword. Immediately others were sent to find out from where they came, and his valet declared that they had been given him by the Princesse de Conti; so my lord Marlborough went away without giving battle." Madame found this tremendously funny, and added wryly: "If Villars' people had been quicker they would have declared that he held those ribbons from me, and so, thanks to the deceit, my lord would have been beaten according to prophecy."

Whatever the true reason, Villars was spared an encounter with Marlborough. Nor was he destined to have another opportunity, for in planning his campaign for 1706, Louis XIV made several changes in command. Vendôme was removed from Italy and his position on the peninsula was taken by Villars, in joint command with the king's nephew, the duc de Chartres.[4] Madame wrote (June 24, 1706): "My quiet life will soon be filled with anxieties and fears, for my son starts in a week's time for Italy."

The opening months of the 1706 campaign continued the downward spiral of fortune for the Two Crowns. Villeroi's army suffered another tremendous defeat at Ramilles on May 23. Even the capable Vendôme was powerless to check the allied advance in the Low Countries, and by midsummer, virtually the whole of Flanders was under allied control. In Spain, the meteoric English commander Peterborough marched toward the capital, scoring victory after victory; Philip V and Maria Luisa were forced to flee Madrid for Burgos, while the allied army entered the city and proclaimed their candidate, the Austrian archduke Karl, King Carlos III.

But in northern Italy, the situation was quite the opposite. Despite the irregularity of news and the abundance of wild rumor, Madame was able to write — with accuracy — "My son is before Turin, and I greatly fear that [the allied army] is even now advancing towards him, and will give him much trouble. I am in great anguish." Her anguish was fully shared by the young duchesse de Bourgogne.

The luck that had marked the martial fortunes of Victor Amadeus never failed him quite so drastically as it did after his second defection from France. He had been forced by circumstance (and imperial trickery) to show his true colors earlier than originally planned, and the Grand Alliance had insufficient time to send him desperately needed reinforcements. All too quickly he found himself in the center of the storm, with the Spanish troops in Milan at his eastern door and the French in Provence to the west.

French reprisals had been swift and vengeful: the county of Nice was overrun, and three separate forces invaded Savoy, each by a different route. Susa and Vercelli fell easily, and the French continued to advance on Turin. The fortress of Verrua heroically withheld siege for over two months, capitulating only after the governor had blown up his own fortifications and bastions. The imperial troops, off in the Tyrol, were themselves too preoccupied to be of any assistance; while they were being driven back across the Adige River by Vendôme, every Savoyard city of import fell systematically to the French horde. It appeared that nothing could prevent a siege of Turin and the annihilation of Savoy — indeed, sentiment ran so highly against the treacherous Victor Amadeus that all of Versailles seemed obsessed with the destruction of his capital. Preparations for the siege occupied the court and the Grand Army in the early months of 1706.

Quite naturally, Adelaide viewed this turn of events with apprehension. She had lived in France now for almost a decade, and with every word of her correspondence, every thought, movement, and gesture, proclaimed herself a Frenchwoman; but her father and mother, her grandmother, and her two little brothers (whom she had never met) were in mortal danger, and the country she nostalgically recalled now faced extinction. Vehemently she urged the duke to come to terms with the Sun King, using her correspondence with the duchess to state her case:

3 May 1706. I have had no letters from you by this courier, my dearest mother. I hope however they will arrive in a few days.
 We have had very good news from Barcelona, and from all sides agreeable tidings are reaching us.[5] All that is passing in Italy affords

me cause for reflection . . . I confess the truth, my dearest mother, that it would be the greatest pleasure that I could have in this life if I could see my father brought back to reason. I cannot understand why he does not make terms, especially in the unfortunate situation in which he now finds himself, and without any hope of being succored [by the Austrians]. Does he still wish to allow Turin to be taken? The rumor afloat here is that it will not be long before the siege is begun. Conceive then, my dear mother, the state in which I must be in, sensitive as I am to all that concerns you! I am in despair at the situation to which my father is reduced by his own fault. It is possible that he believes that we should not grant him favorable terms? I assure you that all that the King desires is to see his kingdom tranquil, and that of his grandson, the King of Spain, also. It appears to me that my father ought to desire the same thing for himself, and when I reflect that the power of making it so is in his hands, I am astonished that he does not do it.

I fear, my dearest mother, that you will think me very bold in writing all that I have; but I cannot restrain myself, feeling as I do my father's position. I feel that he is my father, and a father whom I deeply love. Therefore, forgive me if I write you too freely. It is my intense desire that we should escape these difficult moments that causes me to write as I do . . . I send you a letter from my sister, who is as vexed as I am at all that is happening.

Victor Amadeus cared little that his daughters were "vexed," and he ignored their pleas for peaceful capitulation. In a final effort to avert what was daily becoming inevitable, Adelaide took up her pen and tried to reach her father personally: ". . . I own that affection may feel somewhat wounded at seeing you arrayed against both your daughters. But as for me, I will never be against you, and I can only regard you as the father whom I love as my own life. But that is not saying enough; I would willingly sacrifice my life for you; your interests are the sole object of my present desires . . . I venture to tell you that it depends on you alone to make me the happiest person in the world." But the price of making his daughter the happiest person in the world was French subjugation — a cost too dear for the parsimonious duke of Savoy.

At the end of May 1706, Turin was invested by a force under the command of the duc de La Feuillade, son-in-law of War Minister Chamillart; the actual siege began June 3.

That same morning, Victor Amadeus received a delegation from La

Feuillade. He was offered papers of safe conduct for the duchess, Madame Royale, and the two little princes, and shown an order from the Sun King prohibiting the shelling of the royal quarters — would the duke kindly advise them of their location within the city? Victor Amadeus loftily replied that as long as his capital was besieged, his quarters would be wherever his presence was of greatest service; as for the passports, His Majesty of France need not have bothered, for the duke was still master of one of the city gates and his women and sons were free to leave the city of their own accord, should such desperate measures be required. To further demonstrate their confidence and their faith, the entire Savoyard ducal family took part in a procession of the Sacred Host through the city streets, even as the shells began to fall; their courage and dedication inspired the people to new heights of loyalty.

Such bravery was laudable, but the need to evacuate the ducal family was fast made plain; despite the Sun King's assurances, the ducal palace was a major target and rendered uninhabitable within days. At first, Victor Amadeus favored escape down the river to nearby Chivasso, but then decided this retreat was not safe enough; when the republic of Genoa extended sanctuary, the offer was immediately accepted.

The journey was a long and tedious one, for continued warfare had left most of the roads impassable, and sedan chair was the only possible mode of transport. It took six weeks for the refugees to reach their destination at Multedo, on the outskirts of Genoa. There a handsome residence was made available for their use, and they remained until September.

It was unquestionably a painful summer. "I pity my mother," Adelaide wrote to Madame Royale on July 25, "who, for additional sorrow, is anxious about the illness of her children and yet is obliged to travel with them in such excessive heat and over such dreadful roads." The health of her little boys was but one of Anne Marie's concerns: her husband was fighting to save his capital and his country, while outside Turin's walls, her stepbrother Chartres helped direct the siege. Frantic letters arrived daily from her daughter in Spain, where Archduke Karl lurked outside the very gates of her palace. Even Adelaide, longing to be "the happiest person in the world," gave cause for concern: when in June the princesse had discovered she was again pregnant, Anne Marie agonized at the thought of another miscarriage.

Adelaide, no less than Anne Marie, was tormented by the trials that beset her family. In June she wrote her grandmother to announce her condition and added: "My health is not so much injured as it might be; I am pretty well, but in a state of sadness which no amusement can lessen . . ." She closed her letter with a pathetic plea: "Do not deprive me of your letters. They give me much pleasure; I need them in the state I am in. Send me news of all that is dearest to me in the world." Those "dearest in the world" were en route to safety in Genoa and could not write; Adelaide understood this, but her terrors multiplied. "I cannot be reconciled to your trials," she wrote at the end of July. "I see them increasing with extreme sorrow; there is not a day when I do not feel them keenly, and weep in thinking of what my dear family — whom I would give my life to comfort — is suffering." The siege of Turin continued, as did the unbearable silence from Genoa; not surprisingly, hysteria crept into Adelaide's correspondence. "God is trying me by ways in which I feel it most; I must resign myself to His will, and pray that He will soon withdraw us from the state in which we are. As for me, I feel I cannot bear it longer if He does not give me strength."

Once his family had been safely evacuated, Victor Amadeus stayed, not in the city but with his few remaining troops at Chivasso. There he awaited the promised arrival of Prince Eugene and his Tyrolean reinforcements. It was entirely due to Marlborough's efforts that this liberating army was making its way west: the sluggish emperor Joseph I already considered Savoy lost, and it took all of Marlborough's great powers of persuasion to convince him that a serious effort must be made to retain the safe pass.[6]

The siege of Turin lasted four months. *All* the city inhabitants — from the priests to the women and children — worked courageously, diligently in the defense of their homes, and examples of personal bravery and dedication grew so numerous as to become commonplace. The story of Pietro Micca is one such instance of exalted loyalty, however apocryphal: Micca, a soldier from the village of Andorno, discovered the enemy on the point of entering the capital through a breach in the town wall. He also discovered a mine nearby. There was no time to light the fuse and run for safety, but Micca did not hesitate. Shouting to a comrade to recommend his wife and children to the duke's mercy, he set fire to the powder, and in the explosion was hurled several feet into the air, then buried with a detachment of enemy troops beneath the ruins and debris.

While such acts of valor and heroism took place inside the city walls, Victor Amadeus worked bravely from without. Every morning, the duke would sally forth with a small band of infantry to scour the countryside. His plan was to distract La Feuillade from the siege, and the French commander, realizing the master stroke if he could but capture the turncoat duke, played neatly into the trap. Day after day, Victor Amadeus gave no rest to his pursuers: from Moncalieri he was tracked to Carignano, from Carignano to Carmagnola, then he was reported to have been seen in the mountains near Saluzzo, then in the village of Coni . . . The chase was always close, but the prey was never caught.

Meanwhile Prince Eugene was drawing near. He had crossed the Adige River and marched along the southern banks of the Po. Time was running out for the beleaguered Turin, and his arrival promised its only chance for survival. What happened next was true irony, for the French themselves effected the failure of the siege of Turin.

At this critical juncture, Louis XIV ordered the duc de Vendôme to Flanders, there to replace the incompetent Villeroi. The duc de Chartres and Maréchal Marsin were ordered to leave the siege of Turin with a suitable detachment and march northeast to relieve Vendôme. Versailles was not as yet aware of Eugene's advance, but Chartres had followed his progress no less keenly than the Turinese. He wrote Vendôme, begging him to remain a few weeks longer to "help repair mistakes already made" (Vendôme had done nothing to hinder Eugene's crossing of the Adige, although his troops were only a short distance away) and urging him to pursue the imperial saviors. According to Saint-Simon (who, it must be noted, was a lifelong supporter of Chartres), Vendôme knew too well of his own responsibility for mistakes already made and, hoping to shift all blame onto Chartres, he refused to stay and departed at once for Flanders.

Eugene inched closer and closer still. Confrontation was inevitable; Chartres ordered Marsin to prevent the imperial troops from crossing the Tanaro, their last obstacle outside Turin. Chartres was hardly a military genius — an encounter was not just the wisest plan of action, it was the only plan of action possible to stop the liberation of Turin. But perhaps by virtue of his birth and his proximity to Louis XIV, the duc de Chartres was immune to the general malaise that infected the French high command — intimidation, to the point of petrification, by the Sun King. Louis XIV's pull, even from distant Versailles, was so great that no move could be made without royal knowledge and approval. Marsin refused to engage the formidable imperial force without a written order from His Majesty. When Chartres persisted, Marsin produced letters patent from the king, granting him absolute power over their unit. (This was a perfect instance of the king's ambivalence toward his nephew, appointing him commander, then placing final authority in another's hands.) Mortified, resigned to the enemy's unchecked advance, Chartres led his detachment back to Turin, to reinforce La Feuillade and await Eugene.

The French camp outside Turin, in contrast to the inspired unity of purpose within, was a model of chaos, rampant with petty jealousies. Commander de La Feuillade was a young Villeroi: insolent and presumptuous, inept at the strategies of warfare (his unmerited appointment was solely the work of his wife's father, Chamillart). In the field, La Feuillade refused to follow the advice of the older, more experienced officers in his staff; against all counsel, he played straight into Victor Amadeus's hands, wasting precious time and men, chasing across the countryside in futile pursuit. That he conducted the entire operation with no regard for the principles of siege was demonstrated in the fact that, after a summer of coercion and bombardment, Turin still had not fallen.

With the return of Chartres and Marsin outside the city, there followed a long, heated discussion on the imminent arrival of Prince Eugene. Again Chartres urged an immediate march against the imperial troops, to prevent their juncture with the duke of Savoy. La Feuillade insisted they maintain their position and wait for Eugene to offer battle — ignoring or ignorant of the fact that by spreading his lines over fifteen miles, he had effectively neutralized the superiority of their number. Marsin, "who wished to keep in the good graces of the son-in-law of the all-powerful minister," sided with La Feuillade. The decision was made to sit and do nothing; Saint-Simon wrote graphically: "The throat of France was cut."

At last, on August 28, Eugene's forces met with those of Victor Amadeus at the Chapel of the Madonna della Grazie on the hill of Superga, outside Turin. As he welcomed his cousin and scanned the massive French army in the field below, the duke of Savoy made an impromptu vow: if the French invaders were repelled, he would return to this very spot and erect a basilica/mausoleum for his family in thanksgiving.[7]

On the morning of September 7, 1706, the Savoyard-imperial troops swept down from the hills. The French, with their superior force, waited confidently behind their entrenchments, watching the allies across the open plains. But the long French line held several weak points and was pierced easily. Moreover, the French soldiers had been demoralized by the obvious dissension among their leaders, confused by the contradictory orders they had so often received.

In the intense battle that ensued, discipline, purpose, and the united efforts of Victor Amadeus and Eugene of Savoy carried the day. The French force was routed completely. Marsin was killed; Chartres, after a great display of courage, was wounded; La Feuillade led a retreat, "in utter confusion," back to the fortress of Pinerolo, abandoning his artillery, his supplies, even his money wagons. Turin was liberated and the Savoyard cousins entered the city in triumph.

The failed siege of Turin was, for the French, as disastrous as the battle of Blenheim, for in losing Turin Louis XIV lost Italy. The Grand Army was evacuated from Savoy, save for the few garrisons that maintained the forts still under French control; one by one, these fortresses were compelled to open their gates and surrender to the advancing imperial force. Victor Amadeus and Eugene then took Mantua, and the duchy was ceded to the emperor. As promised, Montferrato was conferred upon the exultant duke of Savoy. The victorious cousins next made further gains in the Milanese valleys: Novarro opened its gates to them without a struggle, and with the fall of the Castle of Milan in March 1707, all of northern Italy was securely in their hands. The kingdom of Naples was their next target, and the Bourbon reinforcements were driven out in less than one month. With land routes now blocked and the British fleet in complete control of the Mediterranean, the pragmatic Neapolitans made a hasty peace with the empire, recognizing "Carlos III" as their liege lord and king. Less than twelve months after Turin had been relieved, the army of the Two Crowns was without an acre of land on the Italian peninsula.

Naturally, news of Turin's liberation was badly received at Versailles, although Louis XIV refrained from any mention of it before Adelaide. For the princesse, who had suffered a summer of agonizing suspense on top of a pregnancy, this unexpected turn posed something of a new dilemma, for to rejoice in her father's victory meant to celebrate her grandfather's defeat. She knew her reactions to every war dispatch were closely scrutinized and she held her public emotions firmly in check, waiting for the outrage to subside.

The Sun King had taught his court that failure was unacceptable. France was the greatest power in Christendom, glorious and invincible; since honorable defeat was inconceivable, it followed logically that only through dishonor, deceit, and/or treachery could an enemy triumph. The debacle of the siege of Turin could not be attributed to dissension at the French camp or to superiority of purpose in the Savoyard-imperial force since, in the mind of the French court, neither of these factors even existed. Any explanation, however implausible, was preferred to an admission of failure. And the perfect scapegoat existed, under the king's own roof.

The courtier Duclos was the first to point an accusatory finger: "This fascinating child, so dear to the King, nonetheless betrayed France, by informing her father, the Duke of Savoy and our enemy, of all the military plans which she found means of perusing. The King discovered the proof of this in the Princesse's desk after her death. 'The little rogue was deceiving us,' he said to Mme de Maintenon."

Several historians have accepted Duclos without question; others subscribe instead to the romantic notion that La Feuillade, madly in love with the duchesse de Bourgogne, secretly promised her *not* to take Turin — and that Adelaide, in turn, persuaded Mme de Maintenon to arrange covertly for the city to be warned of attack.

Even the briefest examination proves the absurdity of both theories. Duclos's contention — that Marie Adelaide secretly supplied her father with military plans — is easily dismissed. First, a total lack of corroboration removes much of Duclos's credibility: apart from this (often unreliable) source, not one other contemporary so much as hints at filial espionage; even Madame, whose feelings for Adelaide were at best ambivalent, and whose position in the royal family would surely have made her privy to any discovery of deceit, mentions nothing of the kind.

Second, it is hardly consistent with the Sun King's character that important military plans should be left about casually for general inspection. Louis XIV, Virgo by birth and by temperament, was quite orderly in his habits, naturally discreet and secretive in all his affairs. Military documents, following his perusal, were filed and carefully guarded at Les Invalides in Paris; no information of a classified nature remained for long at Versailles. If, by some remote chance, papers *had* been left about and if, by an equally remote chance, Adelaide *had* been able to appropriate them without detection, in what possible way could the information then be transmitted to Savoy? The princesse was allowed to correspond with her relatives in Turin (at this point, in Genoa), but like Madame's, all her letters were opened — and even censored — before they left the palace. The use of a secret messenger is unlikely: Adelaide was surrounded by an ever present entourage, who reported her every word and gesture to the king and his wife. She would have been hard-pressed to deliver such documents to a spy who, in turn, would have been hard-pressed to escape Versailles without rigorous examination by the Swiss Guards. Crossing the border into enemy territory was impossible without a royal warrant, and even then, subject to exhaustive inspection. Carrier pigeon — from Versailles to Turin — appears the only possible method of conveyance, a solution befitting a ridiculous charge.

The romantic theory of La Feuillade's passion for the princesse fares even worse. The twofold contention — that Adelaide seduced the young commander and that Mme de Maintenon willingly betrayed her husband and country by warning Victor Amadeus of the intended siege — assumes behavior unthinkable for either woman. Would Adelaide, still smarting from the lessons she had learned from Nangis, Maulevrier, and Polignac, recklessly court disgrace with yet another flirtation? She had recently suffered a miscarriage, her relations with her husband were improving daily, and she would soon be pregnant again — was this a time to seduce a vain and notoriously loose-tongued courtier? Is it even worth the space to suggest that Mme de Maintenon would blithely deceive her royal spouse and aid a petty prince she had never met, a prince whom her correspondence reveals she held in very low esteem, if not open contempt?

If simple logic does not suffice, then chronology is enough to destroy this theory. A projected siege of Turin could hardly come as a surprise to Victor Amadeus. The duke knew well how much the French desired his capital; twice in the previous war the city had been threatened by Catinat. Long before his rupture with the Two Crowns at the end of 1703, Victor Amadeus had begun strengthening the fortifications of Turin. In addition, as Saint-Simon tells us, the siege of Turin was originally planned for the summer of 1705 and would have been executed, had not "incessant bickering" caused its postponement for a year. No secret of the army's intentions had been made at that time — and Victor Amadeus had over one year to prepare for a French attack.

Mlle d'Aumale, one of the major proponents of the "passion" theory, offered as testimony the final audience between the duchesse de Bourgogne and La Feuillade before the latter joined the army in Savoy: in a low voice, Adelaide whispered: "Do not drive my father to extremities." Her great charm and pathos "made him resolve not to grieve her by ruining the duke of Savoy" and, in his last meeting with Chamillart, he remarked to his father-in-law that the taking of Turin would be "exceedingly painful" to the duchesse de Bourgogne. During the siege, d'Aumale averred, La Feuillade confessed: "If I succeed, I shall have the greater glory, and it will not be for want of having done everything to ensure failure."

Charming and very romantic — and not one word of truth. La Feuillade had been in command of the army in Savoy since February 1705 and did not appear at court between that time and the siege; nor would Adelaide have spoken in this vein prior to February 1705, for the siege was as yet unplanned. La Feuillade's conduct during his four months outside Turin showed no great desire to spare the princesse pain; often he quit the siege and weakened his lines to give chase to the marauding Victor Amadeus, with hopes of taking him prisoner. As no less a historian than Voltaire noted: "It is difficult to believe that the same general should have desired to fail before Turin and take the Duke of Savoy prisoner."

Much later it was suggested that Marsin and not La Feuillade was Adelaide's pawn to avert the destruction of her homeland. The French historian Michelet advanced the idea that Marsin was admonished by Marie Adelaide before leaving for Turin "to make him promise that he would offer the advice which would be the least dangerous for her father" — for this reason, Michelet felt, he opposed Chartres's wish to attack the imperial force. Again, facts belie conjecture. Marsin was in Alsace and *not* at Versailles when he received orders to proceed to Italy. He traveled to Savoy via Switzerland; he did not even enter France, let alone stop at the court. And one last question should be posed: would any of these soldiers, either for love of the princesse or secret reasons of their own, willingly and consciously have brought disgrace on their native land?

Saint-Simon, whose proximity to the royal family increased the strength of his conviction, held no doubts of Adelaide's complete innocence. True, he admitted, she had access to secret information: "By her graces, her wheedling and cajoling manners, [she] had become so familiar with the King and Mme de Maintenon as to take the greatest of liberties." But those liberties were affectionate, not treasonous: "With the King she was particularly playful, her arms ever round his neck, sitting ever on his knee, teasing him with her chatter, turning over his papers, opening and reading his letters, whether he would or no."

The tone of Marie Adelaide's correspondence also refutes all slander. Time and again, she proudly calls herself "a true Frenchwoman."

It is not the liberation of Turin that would make her "the happiest person in the world," it is the reconciliation of France and Savoy. Savoy was the land of her past, the home of her parents — and she would never cease to love it. France was the land of the present, and more important, the land of the future. Queen Maria Luisa of Spain was incensed that her sister's honor and loyalty should be thus impugned — and outraged when her own fidelity came into question. "How is it possible," she wrote Tessé, "that I should be suspected of communicating with my father to send him information? I know that this is being said; but should I likely wish to dethrone my husband and myself, for my father's advantage?"

The argument was just as applicable to the future queen of France.

16

"Where Glory Awaits"

W H E N   T H E   P R I N C E S S E discovered herself pregnant that
spring of 1706, precautions more stringent than ever before were
taken. The first of these new rules was a ban on her long walks through
the Versailles gardens. "Frequent walks injured the Duchesse almost
before it was known that she was pregnant," Bourgogne had explained
to Philip V following her last miscarriage, tactfully forgetting the fate-
ful ride to Fontainebleau with the king. "We can console ourselves
with the reflection that it will not be long before she is [pregnant]
again" — insensitive, but accurate.

"Our Princesse is taking great care to carry her child to the end,"
wrote Mme de Maintenon in early autumn. "She is fairly well, but
extremely sad." Her parents struggled for survival in Italy, her sister in
Spain; in the Low Countries, Marlborough continued to wax triumphant; at home, her husband pressed daily for another command,
another chance to risk his life — and when this was refused, vented his
frustration on her. Maintenon sympathized fully with Adelaide's lot:
"This is a terrible state for a person of her age." The wise old woman
perceived too a deep and unexpressed fear: "For one who has, I think,
without speaking of it, much uneasiness about her approaching confinement, and many fears lest she should have a girl."

"I should like to comfort her," Mme de Maintenon admitted, "but,
on the contrary, I distress her." There was precious little at this time
that did not distress the princesse. The king wished his pet to be as
vivacious and entertaining as ever — but the king did not have to

experience morning sickness or forgo the simple pleasures of fresh air and exercise. The court expected its first lady to discharge her duties and preside over its amusements, failing to comprehend the anxieties of a young woman watching her body swell to ungainly proportions and fearful that the smallest jolt should bring about another miscarriage. The daily wonders of bearing a child in one's womb no longer held any fascination for Marie Adelaide. She retired to her rooms and the protective company of her ladies, to wait impatiently for delivery.

The safe (though premature) birth of a son on January 8, 1707, went far to relieve Adelaide's depression. Mercifully, the long and difficult labor she endured in 1704 was not repeated. Labor pains began late the night of the seventh, and the child was delivered at eight o'clock in the morning — so quickly that there had not been time to move the princesse to a labor bed, and the *accoucheur* arrived only moments before the child was born. The only members of the court present were Mme de Maintenon and the duchesse du Lude — not even the king arrived in time. (Alone of Adelaide's three delivered children, this second one entered the world without the comforting presence of his royal great-grandfather.)

The little boy was immediately sprinkled with holy water. "Thank God, he is now a Christian," Louis XIV remarked to the officiating cardinal de Jeanson. Other rites attached to the birth of a Child of France were faithfully performed: the baby was wrapped in swaddling clothes blessed by the pope and given the blue ribbon of the Order of the Holy Ghost. He was styled duc de Bretagne — Louis XIV, only mildly superstitious, did not hesitate to reemploy the title. Once more the aged maréchale de La Mothe was pressed into service, for the sixth and final time.[1] Pressing the infant tightly to her withered breast, she was carried through the crowd by sedan chair to the royal nursery.

A Te Deum was sung at the Versailles chapel that morning, and France braced itself to rejoice. But Louis XIV did not intend a repeat performance of the extravagant celebrations of three years earlier. The critical conditions at the front lines rendered such rejoicing inappropriate, and the old king *was* superstitious enough to avoid courting a similar fate for his second great-grandson. "More and more sensitive to the sufferings of his people, the King had orders conveyed to Monsieur d'Argenson, lieutenant general of police in Paris, to prohibit any out-of-the-way expenditure on the celebrations of the birth." To the nobles of Versailles similar commands were issued, and Dangeau heartily endorsed the king's proclamation that "it was his desire that the joy of his subjects should be manifested only by their anxiety to pray." The only celebration at the court was a modest display of fireworks at Marly, designed by Cotte and Gabriel — a huge step down from the earlier "birthday party," but one indicative of the sharp need for economy.

But economizing or not, the new baby was third in direct line to the throne of France, a position (in the eyes of Louis XIV) that demanded a certain level of magnificence. Before reaching the advanced age of one week, the duc de Bretagne was allotted a household of no fewer than twenty-two people, all devoted to his care and service. In addition to his governess, the duchesse de Ventadour, and her grandmother La Mothe (the undergoverness), there was a governess of the nurses, Mlle la Lande. La Lande supervised a staff of five: Mme Desperier, who rocked the royal cradle and changed the royal diapers; Catherine Gaubert, whose job it was simply to carry the royal infant; a wet nurse, Mme Catherine Maison (paid two thousand livres for her milk), and two reserve nursers. The tiny prince further required the services of a private physician (at a salary of six thousand livres a year), two waiting women, two laundrymaids, and two valets.

In the middle of this elaborate entourage was the infant prince, a healthy and vigorous baby with a thick head of black hair and a robust temper, gifts from both his parents. Adelaide was entranced: "I am delighted, my dear grandmother, that you exhort me to give you frequent news of my son; I assure you I do not need to be urged to do so." She was candid in her opinion — "He is not handsome as yet, but strong and lively" — but quick to excuse: "He is only two months old, and I should not be surprised if, in a few months, he became quite pretty." She proclaimed the often stated and seldom followed vow of universal motherhood: "I believe that I shall never be blind about my children, and that the love I have for them will make me see their defects and so try in good season to correct them."

In keeping with tradition, Adelaide's visits to the royal nursery were sporadic and brief. "I go very seldom to see my son," she confessed to her mother, adding sadly, "in order not to grow too attached to him." Attachment was, of course, inevitable. "I take the greatest pleasure in his gentleness and quietness." Her frustrated maternal instinct came into frequent conflict with the objective professionalism of the nursery staff. "Yesterday I went to see my son," she wrote the duchess of Savoy, "and I wanted to whip him, for he is becoming extremely naughty and very stubborn" — which was, of course, *not* the baby's fault: "Mme de Ventadour spoils him terribly." But in the end, the royal mother had good sense enough to trust the experienced women who tended her son. "As long as I know he is in good health, I am satisfied; that is all I need wish for as yet."

The safe and easy delivery of Bretagne did not alleviate Adelaide's fears of childbirth. Now that she had provided an heir for France, she clearly felt herself free of immediate obligation. In June, five months after Bretagne's birth, she wrote to Madame Royale: "I believe, my dear grandmother, that you will share my joy that I am not pregnant. I have been in fear of this for a long time; but thank God my uneasiness on the subject is now at an end."

Whether or not Madame Royale shared her granddaughter's sentiments is unknown, but Mme de Maintenon unequivocally did not. "It is certain, Madame," she wrote to the princesse des Ursins in Madrid, "that our Princesse is too much afraid of becoming pregnant. Yours [the queen of Spain] is so reasonable that I trust that she will not get these ideas, which I believe to be very wrong in the sight of God. They ought still, for many other reasons, to wish for children." There can be little doubt that Maintenon's views were frequently aired during their quiet evenings *à trois*, while the king worked swiftly through state papers, his wife and his pet knitting and chatting by the fire. Mme de Maintenon was finding it progressively harder to get through to the headstrong young woman she had helped create. "The Princesse is not yet sufficiently alive to her true interests," she complained a few months later to the princesse des Ursins; but with one child dead and several miscarriages, with full understanding of the male attitude in the royal family ("We can soon have another"), it is not surprising that twenty-two-year-old Marie Adelaide chose for a time to indulge in the pleasures of the court rather than the rigors of childbirth.

As always, Mme de Maintenon stood in the wings, ready with quiet disapproval of the young woman's "reckless" fun. "Our Princesse makes great efforts to amuse herself, and only succeeds in making herself giddy with fatigue," she complained to Madrid on April 10, 1707. "She went yesterday to dine at Meudon followed by twenty-four ladies; after that, they were to go to the fair and see some famous rope dancers, return to supper at Meudon, and play cards, no doubt, till daybreak. She must have come home this morning — ill perhaps, certainly serious, for that is the usual result of all her pleasures."

But the king understood, as Mme de Maintenon did not, that Adelaide's taste for enjoyment (which afforded him as much pleasure as it did her) had been painfully stifled for too long a time by death and war. He welcomed the return of her old spirit. He was grateful for her support of his determination to keep the image of Versailles untarnished by the misfortunes of war — although, according to Mlle d'Aumale, Adelaide's common sense made her "conscious, as the King was not, that the time for feasting was past." He generously encouraged her revels, though he was adamant that standards be maintained, and to Adelaide's disappointment, he quarreled long with his son over one projected entertainment. Mme de Maintenon recalled: "Monseigneur wanted to give a public ball to which society in general should be admitted; he was absolutely determined about it and with him, the Duchesse de Bourgogne. The King, with charming gentleness, opposed it, and told Monseigneur that it was not proper, if he wished the Duchesse de Bourgogne to be present, that all sorts of men and women could be present also. The Princesse, on her side, could see no harm in it." In such disagreements, one opinion always prevailed: "with charming gentleness," the ball was canceled.

There were other consolations to be sure. "We are much occupied with a grand ball here," Adelaide informed her grandmother soon afterward. "I am prepared to amuse myself much. Every day I practice getting my breath to dance well, which I think will be very difficult, for I have absolutely forgotten how to dance and I have grown very heavy, which is not good for dancing." (The weight was not due to excess in diet, for she was once again pregnant; she miscarried four months later.)

Marie Adelaide, duchesse de Bourgogne, was in her early twenties. She had lived at the French court for over a decade and had passed through praise (as a novelty) and censure (as a spoiled, rebellious adolescent). She had made enemies, for Saint Louis himself could not have lived in that hotbed of intrigue and factions without incurring the enmity of at least one element. But by and large, she was regarded not only as the court's queen, but its idol as well.

Saint-Simon assessed the secret of her success: "Complaisance was natural to her. It flowed from her, and was bestowed on every member of the Court." Stories of her thoughtfulness, her kindness and generosity, were eagerly recounted and augmented her popularity. One day she was driving rapidly from Paris to Versailles when her carriage knocked down and seriously injured a man in the streets of Sèvres. Instantly, Adelaide ordered the driver to halt and stepped out of the coach. She directed her footmen to carry the injured man into the nearest house, where she herself dressed the wounds. When she realized that the man was dying, she sent for a priest and remained by his side until he expired. Reaching Versailles two hours later, she was too grief-stricken to attend the king at supper, spending the evening praying alone in her room. The next morning, she sent for the dead man's family and offered them her abject apologies and a large bag of silver coins.

On another occasion, her sense of fairness won for her the undying devotion of the Swiss Guards. A new captain, Courtenvaux, had not yet been informed that his men were under secret instructions from the king to patrol the grounds of Marly at night and report their findings each morning to Louis XIV's valet. Finding several guards out on this mission without his knowledge, Courtenvaux was outraged and threatened heavy punishments, while the soldiers (confident in their covert orders) remained obstinately silent and appeared unmoved. The incident was reported to the king, who sent at once for the innocent Courtenvaux and flew at him with so unusual a fury "that not only the soldier trembled, but the entire Court present." The poor captain was dismissed amid a storm of threatened penalties, and slunk away in confusion. Only Marie Adelaide had the courage to plead his cause. That evening she spoke, first to Mme de Maintenon, then directly to Louis XIV. Her defense of the unfairly punished captain was so eloquent, so heartfelt, that Grandpapa's anger melted and Courtenvaux was reinstated as captain of the Swiss Guards.

Her relations with those familiar to her — her household and favored members of the court — were no less gracious or affable than her dealings with strangers. She lived on terms of equality and freedom with her ladies. Mme d'Ayen she called "sister," while Mme de Nogaret had graduated from "Nanny" to "the Well" — because, Adelaide was fond of saying, the truth poured forever from her lips. Walking with her companions in the gardens of Marly or Versailles, she eschewed the notion that they must keep a respectful distance behind royalty. She grabbed their arms and walked beside them, chatting away with a breeziness that shocked the proper duchesse du Lude and outraged the imperious Madame: "She walks on foot and uncorseted, in the avenues of Marly, and sits anywhere in church, even among the waiting women!"

For ten years, she had studied the ways of the court, mastering its endless ceremonies and rituals, the daily minutiae of etiquette. She understood fully the import placed on such rites by the king and the reactionaries of Versailles; in public, her observance of protocol was flawless. "She showed herself serious and reserved, respectful with the King and timidly proper with Mme de Maintenon" — such was the general verdict. But her shrewd instincts warned her that the day of magnificent, hollow pageantry and mundane obsequiousness, the day of the Grand Monarch, was fading with the dawn of a more enlightened age; in private, she became careless of etiquette, indifferent to infractions of courtly conduct. The younger denizens of Versailles flocked to her salon for the same reason that the older members shunned it: one did not stand on ceremony, forced to repeat empty formula phrases that passed for conversation. One simply had fun.

With her Italian temperament she was prey to sudden caprice. Her affections fluctuated with her tastes, and her whims reflected her mood of the moment. Yet even this weakness, Saint-Simon noted, was redeemable, for she was perfectly conscious of it, and "admitted it with a charming ingenuousness which went far to make amends."

Men have left more favorable descriptions of the princesse in this period than women, but the fairer sex was not immune to her charms. Mlle d'Aumale declared her manner "unsurpassed," and the princesse des Ursins had high praise for "a look that penetrated to the heart, particularly when she was a trifle animated." Adelaide was entirely without physical vanity: "No woman appeared less concerned with her looks, or took less precaution to conserve them." She knew she was no classic beauty and was always the first to poke fun at her own thick lips and rotting teeth. Writing to her grandmother, she mentioned suffering another of her interminable toothaches, adding wryly: "My health is coming back to its usual state."

Still, she understood the value of appearances, and for court balls or masques, for formal state occasions, she took great pains to seem glamorous and dressed with a magnificence that befitted her station. In everyday costume, she was satisfied with much less. More than once, Louis XIV reproached her for such indifference to clothes. Her toilette was now performed as quickly as possible, and what little remained of ritual was allowed only as concession to the king. The daily dressing of her hair she found a torturous ordeal: the princesse fidgeted for long hours while her ladies constructed elaborate pyramids of hair, lace, and jewelry, experimenting and gossiping endlessly until Adelaide would stamp her foot in disgust, "regardless of company." She made no effort to hide her delight when the knell tolled for these complex, well-engineered hairstyles: the king condemned these structures of curl and wire, ribbon, brooches, pins and buckles, and they were quickly abandoned. One morning, she had appeared at the king's door with her hair worn low, curled very simply and without any accessories, and Grandpapa had been enchanted. The style was christened *la petite Bourgogne* and immediately became the rage at court.

Whatever Adelaide's initial motivation for gaining the favors of Louis XIV and his secret wife, ten years of their company had produced in her a sincere and tender love for the aging royal couple. They had truly become her family: she looked to them for support, encouragement, and guidance, and when she erred, for forgiveness. They in turn (and particularly the king) found sustenance in her vivacity. Louis XIV could not be without her company for more than a few hours at a stretch. To the astonishment of all Versailles, Adelaide was accorded the right of entry into the council chamber, regardless of the hour or the importance of the business being discussed — so great was the King's dependence on her.

Of course, reconciling one's enemies is more difficult than appeasing one's friends, but even in this the charming duchesse de Bourgogne was making progress. From the time of her arrival in France, two of her sharpest critics had been her step-grandmother, Madame, and the Venetian ambassador, Nicolò Erizzo. The ambassador had taken an instant dislike to the little girl: "She fawns most abjectly on Mme de Maintenon, calls her Aunt in public, but in private mocks her as Grandmama." (The irony of this unlikely charge is that Grandmama was indeed more accurate than Aunt.) After a decade of close scrutiny and reams of censure, Erizzo was softening: "Those who judged her with the most severity are all agreed that she [has] corrected herself with age, and that her will, her rare spirit, her sense of the rank she is about to hold, triumphed in the end over her first impetuosity and petulance."

Madame was not so easy to win over, for criticizing the young princesse appears to have been one of her chief pleasures in life. "[She] attends Mass wrapped up in a nun's hood in the hope of appearing devout, and pretends to weep . . . She drinks two bottles of strong wine without any ill effects . . . [She] is such a flirt that she makes eyes even at her equerry" — and so on and on. By 1708 a confrontation was in the offing; Madame exploded her rage in a letter to Chartres, stationed in Spain: "She is rude to me every day at the King's table, and when I am about to help myself, sweeps the dishes away from under my very nose. She looks past me when I visit her, and says nothing or giggles about me with her ladies. It is all the old rag bag's doing [Mme de Maintenon]. She wants me to complain so that she may say there is no living with me and get me sent to a convent, but I am saying nothing and never complain[!]. I laugh at all they do, and tell myself that she is not immortal, that nothing lasts, and that they cannot get rid of me unless I die."

Madame *did* complain — and Chartres listened. Eventually something vaguely akin to a reconciliation occurred.

Our Queen of Spain is so angry at the insolent manner with which her sister behaves to me, that she sent a message to her by my son, recommending her to make peace with me, she also wrote such an angry letter about this that the King asked my son what it was all about. He added that he approved of the advice given to the Princesse and hoped she would never more do anything to anger me. Whereupon, the Duchesse de Bourgogne charged my son to tell me that her only desire was to be friends with me. I immediately went to her and said, "Madame, my son has just caused me great pleasure by telling me that you will behave more kindly to me in the future. I also will try not to cause you any displeasure. I never intended to do so, so have been more unfortunate than guilty." She became as red as fire, and seemed quite put out of countenance. "You took my timidity for aversion," said she. "And why," I replied, "should you be timid with one who only wishes to appease and honor you?" "Let us forget the past," said she, "and I hope that you will like me better in the future." "I certainly shall," I answered, "if you behave better towards me." Whereupon we began talking of other things.

Like Madame's reconciliation with Maintenon following Monsieur's death, this truce — at least on Madame's side — was short-lived. Liberal criticism of the princesse soon reappeared on the sheets of her voluminous correspondence. It was not in Madame's nature to "bury the hatchet," so her praise of Adelaide, conceded only after the princesse's death, rings all the more true: "In the three years before her death, [she] changed entirely for the better. She gave up playing pranks and drinking too much. Instead of behaving like an unruly child, she became polite and sensible, conducting herself in a manner befitting her rank, and no longer allowing her young ladies to be familiar or stick their fingers into her dish."

Voltaire, in his *Century of Louis XIV,* had fine words of praise for the young woman emerging from the dangerously protective cocoon in which she had been wrapped by the doting old Sun King: "[She] grew in grace and merit. Inspired to emulate the much-lauded example of her sister, the Queen of Spain, she multiplied her own gifts for pleasing. Hers was not a perfect beauty, but she had the same look as her son, a grand manner, a noble figure. These advantages were embellished by her wit, and even more so, by her passionate desire to gain the goodwill of everybody."

The last few years had been a watershed time for Marie Adelaide. In 1704, she had been a giddy and frivolous teenage girl, hell-bent on pleasure, flirting with delicious danger and handsome young noblemen, indifferent to the present, thoughtless of the future. The young woman who welcomed the new year of 1708 was an altogether different creature. She had buried one son and endured the suicide of a frustrated, insane suitor. The anxiety she had suffered over the fate of Savoy had been a personal education in the cruelty of war. She now knew another side of life, one far removed from balls and fêtes, from jewels and gowns and the pampering to which she had grown accustomed. A mature duchesse de Bourgogne reflected to Mme de Maintenon: "*Ma tante,* I am under infinite obligation to you; you have had the patience to wait for my reason."

Saint-Simon recorded that the duc de Bourgogne quit the campaign of 1703 and returned to Versailles in September by direct order of the king; Bourgogne's own correspondence proves that, while mercifully ignorant of Adelaide's dalliance with Nangis, the prince was intensely eager to be reunited with his wife. As preparations for the campaign of 1704 began, he confidently awaited another commission; to his surprise and patent disappointment, he was ordered to remain at court. In 1705 his hopes rose again and once again were dashed. In 1706 he dared not hope; just as well, for still he stayed at Versailles.

Different reasons have been put forth to explain Louis XIV's refusal to give his grandson another command post at the front. One explanation has it that Louis XIV had been informed of Bourgogne's "reckless bravery" during the Siege of Breisach and was loath to court further danger. Another possibility was the issue of royal heirs: Adelaide's pregnancy was an established fact in the advent of the 1704 campaign, and thoughtfully the Sun King wished the expectant father present at the birth of his first child; then, when the baby died (in the opening month of the 1705 campaign), even greater pressure was put to bear on the duc and duchesse de Bourgogne to produce another son.

The incompatibility of Bourgogne's character with army life has also been suggested. The prince's all-absorbing piety and his efforts to run the army like a monastery had a demoralizing effect on the soldiers — understandably, since under Bourgogne the punishment for breaking a fast was more severe than that for desertion in the face of the enemy.

Louis XIV was aware that while his grandson greatly enjoyed the soldier's life, he had little, if any, interest in strategy. The good reputation he had thus far enjoyed in the field was due more to luck than to skill; like many a loving grandfather, the Sun King wished to protect the young man's reputation. Further, he hoped that age would cure Bourgogne's indecisiveness, a trait already observed in the French high command. And finally, with the war going so badly, Louis XIV simply may have wished to spare a future king of France the disgrace of defeat.

Whatever the motivations, the duc de Bourgogne remained at court, humiliated and bored by enforced inactivity. He immersed himself in his religion more than ever before. Those who had found him "too holy" at the turn of the century now found him positively unbearable. His proselytizing tripled. Even Fénelon, in far-off Cambrai, grew sufficiently alarmed to risk the royal fury by writing directly to his ex-pupil, pleading for moderation: "Do not spend long hours in prayer; but pray a little every morning, at some quiet moment . . . God does not require of all Christians austerities like those practiced by the ancient hermits"; once again his wise counsel fell on deaf ears. The frustrated prince nagged at his wife and argued incessantly with his father; the king, struggling to maintain a brave front for the world, was outraged at having to contend with a scowling, disapproving young ascetic in the intimacy of his family circle. At this point, in Saint-Simon's trenchant phrase, the duc de Bourgogne was "no ornament to the Court."

In 1707, it appeared that Louis XIV at last would end his grandson's forced idleness and return him to the front. The eradication of French and Spanish forces on the Italian peninsula (following the liberation of Turin) had left vulnerable the southeastern frontier of France, and Victor Amadeus and Prince Eugene suddenly found an incursion into Provence propitious. For the first time since the outbreak of the war, France faced invasion. Louis XIV ordered south a sizable force under his most competent general, the duc de Vendôme. Certain of ultimate victory in Provence, envisioning even the recapture of Savoy, the Sun

King felt that this was the moment for Bourgogne to return to the army. On August 13, it was announced that Vendôme would be joined by the ducs de Bourgogne and Berri — the latter (twenty years old) without a command, the former to share equal authority with the old maréchal.

The court found it strange that the king proposed sending Bourgogne into direct conflict with his father-in-law; either Louis XIV felt no qualms or he imagined the presence of his daughter's husband might act as a deterrent on the duke of Savoy. Adelaide was naturally distressed and reportedly "wept a great deal," but she said nothing of it to her husband. Bourgogne, thrilled at finally being permitted to march again, felt no embarrassment whatever for his assignment. He had written Vendôme as the latter marched south: "You are presented with a brutal task; I hope and believe that my father-in-law will listen to reason, and that you will not need to be harsh." Harsh no, but certainly successful: "You will contrive, Monsieur, to show him that his best course is to trust the King who wishes only to be sure of him, and not at all to injure him." It is unlikely that, having endured four months of brutal siege less than one year earlier, Victor Amadeus was ready to believe the Sun King had no wish to "injure him," nor (contrary to the imaginings of Louis XIV) would the presence of Bourgogne have compelled him to reconsider his course.

But none of this was ever tested. Early that summer, the allied forces invaded Provence and laid siege to Toulon. The city proved more difficult to capture than they had anticipated, and with the intelligence that Vendôme and his sizable force were drawing nearer each day, Prince Eugene and the duke abandoned their plans. The siege of Toulon was aborted and the army beat a hasty retreat back across the border into Savoy. Adelaide's relief that her husband and her father should thus be spared a confrontation was matched only by Bourgogne's chagrin at losing his command. He consoled himself by reasoning that, after offering him a position in 1707, the king was morally bound to employ him in 1708.

Louis XIV and the French high command entered into the campaign of 1708 with more optimism than they had felt since the outbreak of the war. The year 1707 had proved a remarkably good one for the army of the Two Crowns. The failed siege of Toulon raised French military morale, which was reinforced by successes elsewhere in the theater of war. Along the Upper Rhine, at Stollhofen, Maréchal Villars scored a stunning victory over the margrave of Bayreuth and wrested central Germany from allied control. The duc de Vendôme, leaving Provence and marching north, made substantial gains in Flanders without having to engage the enemy once. In Spain, the army of the Two Crowns (under the duke of Berwick and Madame's son, Chartres) enjoyed extraordinary success, recapturing the entire Mediterranean coast. On May 19, Madame received a letter from her son: "The town and country of Valencia are at last conquered. It is a beautiful country, full of orange trees, jasmines, pomegranates, and all kinds of fruit, far more pleasant than the horrible country by which we have passed before reaching it. Our enemies have retired seven leagues from here and are going towards Catalonia. I do not apprehend any difficulty in taking Aragon." There was none.

And so with high hopes and higher expectations, Louis XIV sat down to the planning table in the opening months of 1708. It was decided that the chief war effort should be made in Flanders against Marlborough. Conditions there offered the greatest encouragement: two years of Dutch occupation had aroused in the Belgians such hatred for the allies that the major cities now openly favored the return of the Spaniards, and it was generally believed that one considerable victory for the army of the Two Crowns would suffice to unlock several city gates for the oncoming French. In addition, it was common knowledge the Dutch were growing tired of this endless conflict; Louis XIV hoped that the winning of Flanders might knock Holland out of the war altogether.

Wanting a lion's share of success for his grandson, the king was inclined to assign him to this northern army. Sourches noted in his journal: "On 30 April, after dinner, when the King returned from hunting the stag, he proceeded to the Duchesse de Bourgogne's apartments, and informed her that the Duc her husband would set out on 14 May, with the Duc de Berri, his brother, to take command in Flanders, where he would have under him the Duc de Vendôme." To his other brother, the king of Spain, Bourgogne wrote of his great joy: "You will readily understand how glad I feel. My brother Berri is as pleased as I am; but the King has forbidden him to show anything, and he controls himself astonishingly well. It is a great pleasure, after a lapse of four whole years, to be returned to the service, to not have to live uselessly at Versailles or Marly or Fontainebleau."

But the prince's great pleasure must surely have been tempered with reservations at the appointment of Vendôme — for it was impossible to find a greater contrast in characters than those of the ducs de Bourgogne and Vendôme.

Louis Joseph, third duc de Vendôme, was of royal blood, albeit left-handedly: his grandfather, César, was the illegitimate son of Henri IV by his mistress Gabrielle d'Estrées. His father had married the beautiful Laura Mancini, the oldest sister of Marie Mancini, Louis XIV's first love. When Laura died, the widowed duke entered the priesthood and rose to the rank of cardinal.

The son had little in common with his holy father. Vendôme was fond of saying he "derived his talents from a more distant source" — Henri IV — and he shamelessly exploited his kinship with the Sun King. Louis XIV's admiration for his grandfather bordered on reverence: perhaps he felt the elevation of his grandfather's bastards would justify that of his own, but whatever the reasons, he "tolerated in Vendôme what he never would have pardoned in a Son of France." Saint-Simon had scant regard for Vendôme and labeled him a man who "combined the most nauseous of all vices [homosexuality] with a ravenous pride, an intolerable insolence, and a filthiness of person which revolted all." Saint-Simon tended always toward exaggeration, but in this particular case, only just — for all contemporary accounts agree that Vendôme *was* shamelessly immoral, overbearing, slovenly, and dirty. His lust for young men was well known and the handsomest soldiers were commandeered for his tent and, in peacetime, his castle at Anet. Twice he underwent the cure for syphilis, losing most of his nose in the process. His sloth was legendary — on more than one occasion he barely escaped capture because he refused to leave a comfortable lodging. The squalor with which he surrounded himself defied description. His bed was always filled with dogs, bitches who littered even while he slept; Vendôme shrugged this off with the remark that everyone was as filthy as he was, but none had the honesty to admit it. In the field, he could usually be found on his portable toilet: he rose late, immediately mounted his chair, and spent the morning there, writing dispatches, giving orders, and eating a huge breakfast in the company of two or three friends. Once, the duke of Parma had cause to deal with Vendôme. He sent him the bishop of Parma, who was visibly taken aback at being received by the general on his chamber pot, and then even more startled when, in the middle of their conference, Vendôme stood up and wiped himself! The indignant bishop left without another word and informed his master the duke that under no circumstances would he ever return to Vendôme's camp.

The question is obvious: how could such a man ever have risen to the rank of maréchal of France? And the answer is, very simply, that Vendôme was the greatest French general since the duc de Luxembourg. As Voltaire observed: "In the day of battle, he made amends for all, by his presence of mind and by a genius which danger rendered all the more dazzling." Vendôme was a brilliant strategist. He had an unfailing instinct for the enemy's position during a battle, a hawk's eye for weak spots along their lines, and a sure talent for recognizing the exact moment when a charge might produce the greatest success. Despite his sexual proclivities, the soldiers adored him, for he would drink and joke among them like any enlisted man, and their implicit faith led them to forgive much of his unsavory character. Voltaire was emphatic: "He was the only general under whom the duty of serving [king and country] did not drive the soldiers to the combat. They fought for the duc de Vendôme; they would have given their lives to extricate him from one of those false positions in which the impetuosity of his genius sometimes involved him."

His military record was flawless. Commissioned as a subaltern in the Garde du Corps in 1673, he rose purely by his own merit to the rank of lieutenant general. He showed ability and courage in campaigns through Holland and Germany, and with the outbreak of the War of the Palatinate, was created maréchal. His brilliance then reached its zenith: at Steinkirk, his inspired cavalry charge against the English ensured victory; transferred from the Low Countries to Savoy, he all but destroyed the army of Victor Amadeus at the battle of Marsaglia. In the opening years of the War of the Spanish Succession, he enjoyed continued success on the Italian peninsula while elsewhere his contemporaries endured defeat.

When Vendôme returned to Versailles after the campaign of 1706, he was hailed as the greatest general France had ever produced. Saint-Simon described his triumphant reception: "Scarcely had he ascended to his chamber when everyone rushed there . . . He was sent for by the King and Monseigneur . . . [He] went to the salon, carried rather than accompanied by the crowd which surrounded him. Monseigneur stopped the music in order to embrace him. The King left his cabinet, where he was at work, came out to meet him, and embraced him several times. Chamillart the next day gave a fête in his honor, which lasted two days . . . Never was triumph equal to his; each step he took procured a new one for him."

The enthusiasm of the Parisians was even greater: to honor him, a special performance of Lully's *Roland* was staged, and despite the doubling of ticket prices, the performance was completely and immediately sold out. Streets of cheering crowds shouted "Vive Vendôme!"

as he drove to the Opéra. Inside, the acclamations continued till the opera began, and at its conclusion, no one would leave before him. Such tributes would have turned the head of a far more humble man, and Vendôme, who directed his staff to address him (incorrectly) as "Your Highness," reveled in his glory. So greatly did his pride swell that when Louis XIV offered him the unprecedented title "Maréchal General of the Camps and Armies of the King," Vendôme refused the honor because the letters patent made no mention of his royal birth. This was the man Louis XIV had chosen to command the army in Flanders with the duc de Bourgogne.

It seems astonishing that the king imagined the two could work together harmoniously, but Louis XIV — a past master in self-deception — deluded himself that he had made an inspired choice. He felt certain that Bourgogne's presence would rally the soldiers with a new vigor; the zeal with which the prince discharged his duties would shame Vendôme into improvement just as his caution would offset Vendôme's recklessness; best of all, Bourgogne's moral severity would temper Vendôme's notorious laxity. (One imagines that, had Louis XIV chosen, he could have persuaded himself that the sun rose in the west and set in the east.)

Few shared the Sun King's confidence: Vendôme's aunt, the duchesse de Bouillon, told her nephew plainly: "You will be sorry. You will find that whatever you decide with [Bourgogne] in the morning will be reversed by him at his *petit coucher*." Saint-Simon foresaw a clash and held no doubts as to the victor: "While Vendôme emerged from it covered with glory, the Duc de Bourgogne would be ruined at the Court, in France, and in all Europe." When the duc de Beauvilliers argued with him, applauding the wisdom of the king's decision, the little duke cut him short: "The stronger character will overcome the weaker, and the stronger will be Vendôme." Even the duke of Marlborough condemned the Sun King's move; writing to the lord treasurer, Godolphin, he declared: "The Duc de Bourgogne will prove to be more of a burden and embarrassment to Monsieur de Vendôme, and no benefit to him whatsoever."

Vendôme himself was far from thrilled by Bourgogne's appointment. The prince would nominally command him and would share in the glory he wanted alone. He despised Bourgogne as a "sanctimonious bookworm" and fully expected that the officers in Bourgogne's staff would encourage him to question Vendôme's decisions and thwart his every plan. It was hardly an auspicious beginning.

The duc de Bourgogne left Versailles on May 14, 1708, the sixty-fifth anniversary of his grandfather's accession to the throne (no coincidence; Louis XIV planned it that way). *Le Mercure* reported to its readers that his farewell to his wife was very tender and "the extent to which the Princesse was affected after the departure of her husband revealed to the whole Court the grief by which she was overwhelmed and the affection which she entertained for the Prince." Bourgogne felt anything but grief: "It is hard to describe the joy which departure imprinted on him. For a long time past, he has been longing to make the journey. One might almost say that he left on wings for the place where glory awaits."

As in 1702, Bourgogne stopped en route to visit Fénelon in Cambrai. This time, Louis XIV had not forbidden private conversation between them, and while teacher and student had not met in over six years, it was obvious (to Saint-Simon) that their feelings were unchanged. "The young prince embraced his preceptor tenderly several times, and said aloud that he would never forget the great obligations under which he had placed him, and though he said nothing which could not be heard by others, he spoke only to him, and the intensity of the gaze which he fixed on the archbishop, coupled with the first words he addressed to him, atoned for all that the King had forbidden, and thrilled the spectators." Unbeknownst to Fénelon or the prince, it was their final meeting. Like so many others, the archbishop felt a grim foreboding which he expressed to Beauvilliers: "I should not wish to put . . . the Duc de Bourgogne with Monsieur de Vendôme." Apart from his being "of a hard, stubborn and headstrong temperament," the maréchal was simply "too dangerous."

Vendôme had established headquarters at Mons, in Flanders, and rode south to meet the approaching Bourgogne and Berri at Valenciennes. Their first interview went smoothly. Arriving at camp, Bourgogne immediately paid a visit to Vendôme's tent. Glass in hand, he said, "Monsieur de Vendôme, let us drink to success in the campaign." Vendôme stood up, and mindful of protocol, raised the rim of his glass to touch the base of the prince's, but Bourgogne stopped him, saying, "Let us have no ceremony for we all regard you as the father and leader of our armies." Vendôme quickly succumbed to such flattery and a few days later wrote: "I perceive in the Duc de Bourgogne an intelligence and amiability that will, I believe, stand every test." That very same day, Bourgogne revealed to Chamillart surprising insight into Vendôme's character: "You know how gently M. de Vendôme needs to be handled. If one approaches him tactfully, one may persuade him to change even those opinions on which he is most headstrong."

On May 26, the co-commanders reviewed the army of Flanders, and Bourgogne professed himself "very satisfied." He had good reason for satisfaction: not only did their force of 110,000 men outnumber Marlborough's army of 90,000, encamped to the south of Brussels, but it was composed of many of the best regiments in France and commanded by a majority of highly experienced officers. It was exceptionally strong in artillery, and was motivated equally by the father of the army and the heir to the throne.

Everything necessary for victory was present — except for strong, efficient leadership. For the joint command was doomed to failure. Louis XIV's commissions were so vague that neither his grandson nor his cousin really understood the extent of their authority; each thought all final decisions his own, while neither was willing to assume final responsibility. These misconceptions would soon be painfully obvious.

There was general agreement in the French high command to engage Marlborough's numerically inferior army in battle before Prince Eugene (marching along the Moselle River) could arrive with reinforcements. But at Mons, disagreement rose as to where and when. Vendôme favored a march east, laying siege to the town of Huy to provoke the encounter. Bourgogne pushed for a more dramatic plan: a march north toward Brussels and Marlborough's camp. He argued that if indeed the Belgians were as anxious as rumored to oust the allies, where better than at the very lines of their defense?

Surprisingly, Vendôme concurred, and at the end of May, the French army moved north by night to Soignies. Marlborough was compelled to move his troops south to Halx. Confrontation appeared in the offing; to London, Marlborough wrote: "There will soon be the opportunity of action, not only because the French will take advantage of their superiority in numbers, but because of the impetuous nature of the young prince [Bourgogne], who is full of ambition and eager to acquire a reputation." But, to Marlborough's great surprise, the French did not attack: instead they dropped back to the east, at Braine-l'Alleud near Waterloo. Though their new position still threatened Brussels, no action was taken.

Responsibility for this about-face lay squarely on the shoulders of Bourgogne and Vendôme. Squabbling had now begun in earnest, and with each disagreement, the obstinacy of the co-commanders necessitated the intervention of the Sun King. Vendôme still pushed for the siege of Huy, despite Bourgogne's argument that the town was too unimportant to be descended upon by so powerful an army. The king was asked to break the deadlock: his decision was to back Bourgogne. Vendôme shifted his strategy and revived the idea of a surprise attack on Brussels. But Bourgogne, whose indecision in the field had been noted before, vacillated once again, arguing now that such a plan was too hazardous. Again Louis XIV was called upon to mediate: again he backed his grandson.

These disagreements occupied the entire month of June. With the allied army a scant four leagues away, the French force idled at Braine-l'Alleud. Vendôme, in bad temper, sulked in his tent, while Bourgogne congratulated himself in a letter to Philip V: "We have been here very peacefully since the beginning of the month . . . We are free to move right or left as best pleases us, always in advance of the enemy, who wait to learn what we propose to do . . . Let us hope that the campaign will continue in the same way, and that with God's help we may come to a good and favorable peace." (For all that had been accomplished on this campaign, which Bourgogne felt "had commenced so well," the army might just as well have remained in its winter quarters.)

Blame for this waste of a month should rest more properly on Vendôme, for it was the responsibility of this experienced soldier to insist on a bold (but not foolhardy) plan of action; Bourgogne, eager to prove himself — as Marlborough correctly assessed — would certainly have agreed to any such proposal. But the vicious streak in Vendôme's character was slowly emerging, an attitude that if he gave this royal nuisance enough rope, he would hang himself and thus leave Vendôme to carry on the job of winning the war. The fact that this attitude was in direct contradiction to the best interests of France apparently did not occur to the proud maréchal, and therein lies much of the tragedy of the campaign of 1708.

For his part, Bourgogne did not look upon June as wasted time. He had started methodically to discipline the army and to crack down on the horrible extravagance practiced by the higher-ranking officers. His obvious concern for the comfort of the common soldier won him admiration in the ranks — but this was sadly offset by their wariness of his excessive religious displays, and more than one infantryman questioned the wisdom of a prince-general who spent the entire morning in prayer while the duke of Marlborough worked tirelessly only twelve miles away.

The inactivity of the French army mercifully ended in July with the arrival of the comte de Bergeyck. Bergeyck had been the minister of finance for the Spanish Netherlands until the allied occupation had forced him into exile. He had intrigued for months with the Flemish burghers to open their towns and cities to the French, and having obtained an audience with Bourgogne and Vendôme, he urged a quick descent on Bruges and Ghent, promising no resistance from either city.

Again there was disagreement. Vendôme (for once) thought the plan too hazardous, and proposed instead a long detour to the south, but Bourgogne, fired with excitement, insisted on a sudden march straight across the Dender River to Ghent. He devised a brilliant ruse: his advance force, under General Grimaldi, made a feint in the opposite direction and Marlborough was completely taken in. The main army broke camp at seven, the evening of July 4, 1708, marching all night and the next day toward Bruges. At three o'clock, the morning of the sixth, they entered Bruges and the city surrendered without opposition. By dawn, they were on the move again; by nightfall, Ghent had also capitulated. The exhausted French army had marched continuously more than thirty miles, often in pouring rain, but their achievement was spectacular: in one stroke they had regained all of western Flanders, effectively cutting Marlborough off from his North Sea base at Ostend. This, Bourgogne felt certain, was the glory that awaited him.

Marlborough was devastated by this sudden, unexpected French triumph, the kind of strategic coup he had effected so often in campaigns past. As the Prussian envoy to the allied camp informed his king: "The blow which the enemy dealt us did not merely destroy all our plans, but was sufficient to do irreparable harm to the reputation and previous good fortune of Milord [Marlborough], and he felt his misfortune so keenly that I believed he would succumb to this grief early the day before yesterday, as he was so seized by it that he was afraid of being suffocated."

Word of Bourgogne's success reached Louis XIV at Fontainebleau at eight in the morning, July 8, and the king went immediately to awaken Adelaide with the news. The prince was the hero of the hour, and his wife and grandfather beamed proudly, while "the whole Court went wild with delight." To celebrate, an elaborate picnic expedition was staged in the woods outside Fontainebleau three days later. The French court gamboled and feasted, congratulating itself on its good fortune and proudly toasting the victorious heir to the throne.

They were blissfully unaware that at that very moment the fatal battle of Oudenarde was taking place.

Winston Churchill labeled the battle of Oudenarde "the first twentieth-century battle": "The chance encounter by forces of unknown strength, the gradual piecemeal broadening of the fighting front, the increasing stake engaged willy-nilly by both sides, the looseness and flexibility of all the formations, the improvised and wide-ranging maneuvers and, above all, the encircling movements of the Allies . . . present us with a specimen of modern warfare which has no fellow in the rest of the eighteenth century." Alone, this would suffice to make Oudenarde noteworthy. But the battle stands apart for still another reason: in one day, an entire year of French victory was reversed.

Prince Eugene, learning of the fall of Bruges and Ghent, left his advancing army and raced north to meet Marlborough. He found the duke shattered by the sudden loss of western Flanders — "pretty consternated," as Eugene wrote to the Austrian emperor — but Marlborough's spirits rose at the sight of his respected confederate, and the two men retired at once to plan a strategy. They resolved to rest Marlborough's troops for another few days at Assche, while Eugene's reinforcements finished their race for Brussels. Then, with this force a comfortable distance away, Marlborough's army would advance across the Scheldt and prevent the French from seizing Oudenarde, forcing a battle if necessary.

Again the allies were (unconsciously) aided by the French high command. The stunning triumph of Bruges and Ghent had done nothing to ease the tensions between the co-commanders. Doubtless Vendôme's jealousy for the high praise accorded Bourgogne further aggravated their discord, and the long arguments over their next move forced another appeal to Versailles, affording the allies precious extra time. At last the order from Versailles arrived: attack Oudenarde from the western bank of the Scheldt and ensure the siege by maintaining a strong position nearby at Lessines. The French army duly set forth, marching south. But Marlborough had divined this strategy and set his own force in motion. The race for Lessines was on.

As the overly confident French crawled, the allies sped. The morning of July 10, the allies crossed the Dender River and took possession of Lessines — an extraordinary march of thirty miles in thirty-three hours. The French, astonished to discover their destination already occupied by the enemy, halted briefly at Voorde, then turned westward for Gavere, a few miles north of Oudenarde.

Bourgogne and Vendôme hastily convened a war council. The position they found themselves in was unique: the surprise march to Lessines had put Marlborough's force between the French army and the French border, isolating the co-commanders deep in the heart of Flanders. One French option was to march and attack (and the battle of Oudenarde would have been fought one day earlier), but agreeing for once, neither Vendôme nor Bourgogne wished to take the offensive and launch a battle. It was decided to cross the river at Gavere the following morning, thus maintaining control of the Scheldt, and await a junction with the French reinforcements under the duke of Berwick, now marching west from the Moselle River. In this, the co-commanders made two fatal errors: they calculated (incorrectly) that Berwick's forces would join theirs before Eugene's met with Marlborough, and they underestimated the speed with which Marlborough could move when the occasion demanded. This second error was pointed out to them the very evening of their war council, when word arrived that the allies were already on the march from Lessines toward Oudenarde. Alarmed, Bourgogne urged that they cross the river that night, to outstrip the enemy and reestablish communication with France; Vendôme, according to Saint-Simon, reacted "with contempt, as was his custom," and refused to budge till daylight.

The French troops slept peacefully that night on the eastern bank of the Scheldt at Gavere; at the same time, some twelve miles down river, the allies worked feverishly to erect pontoons. Before daybreak, nine bridges stood ready for use by Marlborough's force.

As July 11, 1708 dawned, the French army began their leisurely preparations to cross the river. Passage for the advance guard of twenty squadrons and seven Swiss battalions, under Lieutenant General Biron, was delayed for several hours, as the French bridges were not yet completed; when his force finally crossed the Scheldt shortly before noon, Biron was stunned to find the *entire* allied cavalry and twelve battalions under General Cadogan waiting for him on the summit of rising ground outside the city.

Biron sent word immediately to Vendôme, who typically had not risen till ten and was, at that very moment, still eating breakfast. (In a subsequent dispatch to Louis XIV, Vendôme justified his behavior with the lie that he had concluded thirty hours in the saddle the day before.) The maréchal found it too incredible that the allies, spotted just outside Lessines the night before, should be able to march seventeen miles, erect their temporary bridges, and move their entire force across the river in less than twenty-four hours — and he simply refused to believe Biron's messenger. "If they are there," he cried, "the devil must have carried them. Such marching is impossible!" Two more frantic dispatches from Biron at last convinced him that the impossible had indeed occurred.

At half past one, Vendôme sent Biron an order for immediate attack, assuring the lieutenant general he would come himself with an ample force to support Biron's charge. Ordering Bourgogne to follow slowly with the main body of their army (still crossing the river), Vendôme rode off leisurely at the head of the cavalry right wing.

But the time wasted in convincing Vendôme of the enemy's presence across the river had strengthened the allies' advantage. When Biron finally received the charge order, he found himself in no position to do so: wildly outnumbered by an ever increasing enemy force, unfamiliar with the terrain, Biron could do nothing but sit and wait for Vendôme's arrival. Not till after two o'clock was Vendôme spotted on the Ghent road. He angrily demanded the reason why Biron had not yet attacked; on being informed that a marsh lay between his troops and those of the enemy, Vendôme turned his force westward — leaving Biron completely unsupported.

While these mistakes were being made, Bourgogne was marching the main body of the army down the slopes of the Norken Stream, above the plains of Oudenarde. Seeing that battle had not yet begun, he decided *not* to cross the Norken, but to wait on the high ground behind for further developments. And so, as the opening positions for battle were taken, the French army was hopelessly, helplessly divided: Vendôme's force was moving west, leaving Biron's battalions isolated and perilously exposed to assault, while the bulk of the army sat watching from a low hill across the stream.

At three o'clock, a roar of musket fire opened the battle of Oudenarde. Cadogan's force charged the badly outnumbered Biron. At once the allies gained the upper hand. The Swiss regiments under Biron were broken and scattered, and fled toward the main French army. At the same time, the allies charged Vendôme and the right wing and again met with instantaneous success: within one hour, the allies had captured ten French standards, three battalions, and countless officers.

At four o'clock, Bourgogne — out of communication with Vendôme since the battle began — ordered a portion of his force to cross the Norken. He sent sixteen squadrons, under General Grimaldi, to counter Cadogan's attack. Had this movement been a prelude to a general attack by the left wing, a French victory might well have ensued. But Bourgogne, lacking any word from Vendôme and confused by the contradictory advice of his staff, still refused to move. Grimaldi's pitiful force, obliged to charge through woodlands and marshes, was quickly repulsed by Cadogan and retreated back to their initial position, observing with Bourgogne and the left wing.

The prince desperately needed to confer with Vendôme, but the maréchal was nowhere to be found. As commander of the army, his true place was on the hill of Roycgem with Bourgogne, but instead he remained on the battlefield. The common soldiers doubtless found his presence inspiring — indeed, they fought with "devoted courage" — but his position allowed no opportunity to assess the course of the battle and destroyed the effectiveness of any French strategy. This became painfully evident when, at five, Vendôme sent the order that the prince should launch an eastern attack with the (still observing) left wing. The order reached the hill: Bourgogne's advisers, unaware of the maréchal's predicament, maintained that this advance over the marshy terrain was out of the question, whereupon the prince refused to issue the command. He sent back Vendôme's aide-de-camp, Captain Jenet, to explain to the maréchal why his left wing remained immobile, but Jenet was killed before he could deliver his message.

Tragedy was now inevitable: the uninformed Vendôme prepared for another assault on Cadogan, confident of support from the left wing. His troops charged, while the left wing — some thirty thousand men — watched impassively from their nearby hilltop. Such reckless bravery does not excuse Vendôme from his share of the blame for the ultimate defeat at Oudenarde. Consciously or not, he was reinforcing the contrasting images of the co-commanders — the pious prince who watched dispassionately from above and the hearty general who risked his life along with those of his men — a contrast that would plague the dual command for the remainder of the year, and Bourgogne for some time after that.

The battle continued through the last few hours of daylight. Shortly after six, Vendôme launched his third attack. But his forces were dwindling fast, while one third of his army still idled at Royegem. At seven, Marlborough brilliantly played his final, and decisive, card: sixteen battalions of infantry under the prince of Orange, poised and ready just south of Oudenarde, now came into play. Swinging wide around the fortress-city, they charged onto the battlefield from the west. The entire French right wing was now surrounded, their defeat assured.

From his perch at Royegem, the heir to the throne watched the destruction of his grandfather's army. Panic swept through the ranks. Mercifully, darkness fell, and a soft summer rain; at nine o'clock, Marlborough ordered a general cease-fire.

It was the dark that saved the French from total annihilation. Even so, two thirds of the army had disappeared, ninety-five standards had been captured, and seven thousand French prisoners were taken.[2] Shortly after ten, the defeated French command met in the village of Juysse, behind the Norken. Bourgogne and Vendôme had not seen each other since early that morning; the maréchal arrived disheveled, dusty, and furious — with the enemy, with himself (for excellent reasons), and with Bourgogne.

What was to be done next? Bourgogne opened his mouth to speak, but Vendôme turned on him savagely and ordered him to hold his tongue: "Your Royal Highness must remember that you only came to this army upon condition that you obeyed me!" This was, of course, patently false — although, had this been the king's intention, then total responsibility (which Vendôme soon tried to shift onto Bourgogne) would have been the maréchal's alone. Moreover, his outburst was highly treasonous, but wisely Bourgogne kept silent.

Vendôme then harangued his disillusioned staff, averring that the battle was far from over and proposing to fight again in the morning. Only one young officer concurred with the father of the army, while from one after another came disheartening reports on the extent of the disaster.

Finally, Vendôme was forced to agree to a general retreat. "Oh, very well, messieurs! I can see clearly what you wish. We must retire then." Turning to Bourgogne, he snarled, "I know that you have long wished to do so, Monseigneur." Once again, the prince remained silent, while the general staff stood frozen in astonished horror. Vendôme gave the order to retreat to Ghent, and the meeting broke.

The remnants of the French army straggled north throughout the night and early next morning. Vendôme reached Ghent at eight o'clock the morning of the twelfth and watched his men move through the city toward Lowendegem, where Bourgogne had set up headquarters. To vent his disgust, Vendôme squatted in the middle of the street and emptied his bowels. Then he ran to his tent and, refusing to receive any more reports, slept for the next thirty hours.

In assigning blame for the debacle at Oudenarde, "should haves" bounce freely from one commander to the other. Vendôme should have crossed the river with greater speed that fatal morning; Bourgogne should have seen how desperately in need of reinforcement Biron was; Vendôme should have maintained a perspective and not remained in the middle of the fray; Bourgogne should have followed without question Vendôme's order to charge. To Bourgogne's credit, he avoided the temptation to point his finger at Vendôme; the reverse was not true. Regardless of blame, the French army never fully recovered from the shock.

From Versailles, Madame wrote her aunt, Sophia: "I am aware that a battle has been lost, but I know nothing in detail, for we are forbidden to speak of it, and those with the army are forbidden to write anything home in their letters."

News of the disaster came piecemeal to Versailles, first on July 14. As the king emerged from a meeting of the Council of Finances shortly after noon, Dangeau recorded, a messenger arrived from the duc de Bourgogne, "bearing with him the sad tidings of a great battle in Flanders, wherein we did not have the advantage."

The messenger did not report the particulars of Oudenarde, informing the king that dispatches from both Bourgogne and Vendôme were on their way by separate courier. Later that evening, a second messenger appeared, "but he brought none of the details that might have enabled us to know what had happened. All that we have learned is that there has been a disaster."

Knowledge of the discord between Bourgogne and Vendôme led the court to immediate speculation on where responsibility would rest, and the arrival of the co-commanders' dispatches fired divided factions. Bourgogne's note, written in his own hand, carefully avoided observation on his confederate's failings; Vendôme was not so taciturn: "I shall give Your Majesty no details, merely have the honor to inform you that the enemy would not have been successful, had we not freely given them the victory by our retreat. We had gained some ground; lost neither guns, baggage, nor flags, and we had captured one flag, a standard, and a pair of kettledrums. That, Sire, is the truth; and I am heart-broken, because for a whole hour, I believed the battle won, and *had I been supported,* as it was my right to be, our victory would have been complete." Vendôme's version, contrary to his assertion, was *not* the truth. But it was accepted without hesitation at Versailles and it signaled the beginning of a very difficult period for the duc de Bourgogne — and his duchess.

Louis XIV faced the defeat at Oudenarde with his customary resignation. Mme de Maintenon wrote the princesse des Ursins that "the King supports this latest mischance with full submission to the will of God, and displays his usual courage and equanimity." He tried in vain to pacify his defeated co-commanders. To Bourgogne he wrote: "I am extremely sorry that the first occasion on which you have figured has not had a more successful issue. Do not be discouraged. You should rather try to hearten the officers and troops with words of good cheer. It is at times like these that men of high rank need to encourage their inferiors . . . Do nothing without careful consideration."

That same day he attempted to placate Vendôme. Though acknowledging that differences between the two commanders made it impossible to "avoid a situation whose consequences could not be otherwise than disastrous," he added tactfully: "I am sending word to the Duc de Bourgogne that, to prevent any such embarrassment in the future, he should consult with you as to the next move. I recommend him to show you all the respect that is your due because of the manner in which you constantly expose yourself to danger. Most of all, I desire him to have in you all the confidence deserved by your zeal for the glory of my armies, for his own glory, and for that of our nation. Finally, I commend you to him for your long service at the head of my armies which, under your command, were never defeated."

The king's letter to Vendôme was more an epistle of policy than honesty. Reading it, the maréchal had every reason to assume that Louis XIV absolved him of all blame, but the reactions of those two women closest to the king give strong evidence of his true feelings. Mme de Maintenon's version of the battle of Oudenarde, confided to the princesse des Ursins, was doubtless supplied her by her royal spouse: "M. de Vendôme, who believes according to his wishes, insisted on fighting a battle; he lost it, and we are in a far worse plight than before, as much by our losses as by our fear of the consequences and the enemy's apparent superiority." Adelaide, having received a private communication from Bourgogne and a note from her brother-in-law Berri, was heard to exclaim that her husband was surrounded by "monstrously stupid people."

But Vendôme was not to be pacified by the Sun King. His anger over defeat had robbed him of much good reason and he penned a letter of lies and wild incriminations: "The Princes [Bourgogne and Berri] are a fearful burden on an army. When night fell, they were within a hair's breadth of capture. I still tremble when I think of it. I do not know what Your Majesty plans; but it appears to me that the movements required during the remainder of the campaign do not in any way require their presence."

The king's refusal to recall his grandsons infuriated Vendôme and he continued to attack Bourgogne's conduct on the battlefield: "I could never have believed that fifty battalions and nearly one hundred twenty squadrons of our finest troops would have been content to spend six hours watching us do battle, for all the world as though they were seated in a box at an opera. [Bourgogne] admits that he was wrong not to have followed his first instincts . . . I shall ask Your Majesty not to lay the blame on me, since you must concede that my decisions are not always accepted."

In contrast to Vendôme, whose incessant protestations smack of secret heartfelt guilt, Bourgogne maintained a posture of silence. He believed there to be three people at court whose support was unconditional — his wife, his former governor, Beauvilliers, and Mme de Maintenon (his direct link to the king) — and to these three alone he expressed his true feelings. His letter to Adelaide no longer exists, but his note to Beauvilliers makes plain how deeply he felt the responsibility for this military disaster:

> Our spirits are very low; our situation critical; we are in great difficulties and much mortified. I trust that when God has sufficiently punished us, he will not quite abandon us, but will bring us to a happy issue from this time of affliction . . . Pray to God more than ever before, that He may grant me wisdom and courage, whatever may befall, and that He may teach me increasingly to recognize my own weakness and unworthiness, which I think prosperity had somewhat concealed from me; for I did not have then perfect faith in God. Should He still find a use for me, it would be an act of pure mercy, for I have not been as faithful as, after His recent goodness, I had promised to be.

Sure of Mme de Maintenon's affection for himself and his wife, the prince was able to write more passionately to her. He did not hesitate to praise Vendôme's heroics, or to enumerate his mistakes, but his resentment of the maréchal's overbearing obstinacy mounted with each sentence:

> In fact, Madame, neither in the direction of a campaign nor in battle does he act as a general should, and the King is gravely mistaken in having so high an opinion of him. I am not the only one to say this;

the entire army says the same. He had never gained the confidence of the officers, and has lost that of the rank and file. He does nothing, as it were, but sleep and eat, for truly his health no longer supports fatigue, and he is thus unable to fulfill his necessary duties. Consider also his extraordinary conviction that the enemy will act as he desires and that, since he has never been defeated, he cannot be vanquished in the future (something which now he can no longer claim). Pray reflect, Madame, whether the interests of the State are well served in such hands.

Vendôme's rude remarks on Bourgogne's limited authority over the troops obviously rankled still, for next the prince begged that the king grant him not just the right to advise, but "the casting vote, in concert with the Maréchals of France, and other able and experienced officers" — if Vendôme was intent on placing all blame upon his shoulders, then let him assume the responsibilities involved as well. He closed his letter, as always, with an invocation: "The worst of all would be to lose courage, and it is at the worst moments that one most needs it. Let us hope that God does not abandon us entirely, and that the future may not be as bad as we fear."

The immediate future would be even worse than feared: glory did not await the French army in the remainder of the 1708 campaign, or for some time still to come. Most certainly it did not await the troubled young duc de Bourgogne or his worried wife.

17

The Cabal

HAD VENDÔME CONTENTED HIMSELF with angry letters to the king and War Minister Chamillart, his continual attacks on Bourgogne would have done little damage to the prince's reputation. But shrieking his own innocence to the skies, the maréchal allied himself to a court faction dubbed the Meudon cabal (by Saint-Simon), thus ensuring maximum exposure for the controversy. Ironically, it also paved the way for Vendôme's downfall.

No court, by the definition of its nature, can be without factions, and the Meudon cabal had existed on the fringe of Versailles society for several years before Oudenarde. It developed as a logical course of fallible human nature. Louis XIV — the focal point of all France — had directed the state for more than half a century, but not even sun kings are immortal and Louis was fast approaching seventy. He and the progressive element of his court looked forward with keen anticipation to the eventual reign of Bourgogne, an enlightened Louis XVI. But there still remained a future Louis XV in the sorry person of Monseigneur the dauphin.

The Sun King had long abandoned all hope of making something out of his lethargic and hedonistic son, pinning his hopes instead on the next generation. As he had barred his brother, the feckless Monsieur, from all affairs of state, so he excluded Monseigneur from the business of government. The dauphin watched with envy while his oldest son rose to prominence, gaining entry into council rooms where he himself had no access and fulfilling obligations that rightfully belonged to the heir alone. Good feelings turned ill as he saw his daughter-in-law reigning as uncrowned queen of Versailles while his own wife, Emilie Joly, went unacknowledged. He retired to his country seat at Meudon, to hunt and sulk; there, with all conditions ripe, the cabal was born.

Chief supporters of the slighted dauphin were the duc d'Antin (Mme de Montespan's only legitimate son) and the duc de Luxembourg (son of the illustrious maréchal). The duc du Maine eventually joined the intrigue, with feelings of neglect similar to those of his half brother, but the acknowledged leaders of the group were Monseigneur's illegitimate sisters, the princesse de Conti and Mme la duchesse.

Marie Anne, the king's only surviving child by the ingenuous Louise de La Vallière, had been married at fourteen to her distant cousin, the prince de Conti, who fell promptly and deeply in love with his wife — and died not long afterward. Not so fortunate was Louise Françoise, Louis XIV's oldest daughter by Montespan, who married Conti's younger brother Louis, duc de Bourbon, in 1685: M. le duc was an alcoholic woman-beater and was quickly banished from his wife's bed and company. The beauty of both princesses was legendary: the duchesse de Durras wrote of the princesse de Conti: "She is love itself, and they are frightened to let her keep any pages more than ten or twelve years old." [1] Saint-Simon, who generally despised the royal family, admitted that the countenance of Mme la duchesse proved her unquestionably "the offspring of tenderest love," although Madame's description of her niece was probably closer to the mark: "Her wit shines in her eyes, but there is some malignity in them also. I always say that she reminds me of a pretty cat which, while you play with it, lets you feel its claws."

The princesses enjoyed fine positions at court, for the king had acknowledged paternity and legitimized them both before the advent of Mme de Maintenon. Mme la duchesse, in particular, was on more familiar terms with Louis XIV than any of his children, though this did not save her from frequent paternal lectures on her drinking (she could drink any woman, and most men, under the table), on her smoking (she enjoyed a pipe with a Swiss Guard or two in her private apartments), or on her biting and often slanderous wit.

The princesses had always heartily disliked each other — until the arrival of Adelaide bound them together in common resentment for this "upstart" Savoyard who usurped pleasures and prerogatives previously theirs alone. They fumed with thinly veiled hostility, year after year, while Adelaide's hold over the old Sun King grew stronger and more impregnable. Feeling they could not change the present, they looked to the future, and the first objective of the Meudon cabal became the permanent estrangement of Monseigneur and his oldest son so that, once the dauphin ascended the throne, the influence now enjoyed by Bourgogne (and Adelaide) would be destroyed and supplanted by their own. Alienating father and son was no difficult task. Monseigneur was not particularly fond of his oldest son to begin with, and the king's blatant preference had already joined jealousy to his dislike. Although Bourgogne had long tried to disarm the dauphin's hostility with a show of deference and courtesy to his father's morganatic wife, Monseigneur stood unmoved, and Meudon rapidly became a haven for all who opposed the young Bourgognes.

But the Meudon cabal harbored a second dream as well, one rooted impatiently in the present and much harder to achieve: the effective destruction of "the Bourgogne influence" *before* the Sun King's death. They realized that to accomplish this end through Adelaide was all but impossible; their only hope was to damage the young princesse through her husband. They had waited years for an opportunity to arise, and in the summer of 1708, their moment arrived.

Even before the battle of Oudenarde, Vendôme's sympathies rested heavily with the Meudon faction. His younger brother, the grand prior of France, was a great favorite of Monseigneur's and an ardent member of the cabal. To him, Vendôme released all his bitterness, and the grand prior, conniving with Mme la duchesse, devised a scheme to use the warrior-hero to their own advantage. Published letters suddenly appeared throughout France — as the nation was learning of the July slaughter in Flanders — letters that praised Vendôme for his military brilliance and faulted Bourgogne for the humiliating defeat. They were written by Vendôme's secretary (and cousin), the comte d'Evreux, who had been with the army throughout the early summer months. They dealt a serious blow to the duc de Bourgogne's image with his future subjects; equally damaging were the scurrilous ballads that soon appeared (most of them attributed to Mme la duchesse): "Our timid, pious Louisot / With his confessor, Martineau, / Is no more than an idiot . . ."

Just as Adelaide had come under suspicion of espionage after the failed siege of Turin, so her husband now was proffered as scapegoat for the failures of the French high command. Both accusations were patently false, but they indicate the desperation felt by a nation, invincible for half a century, struggling for survival in a losing war. Adelaide had ridden out her storm; the siege of Turin had been but one isolated incident and controversy died as quickly as it was born. For Bourgogne (and for France) the disaster of Oudenarde proved the prologue to a tragic campaign.

Losses in dead and wounded had decimated the French army of Flanders. Marlborough's assertion in late July was no hollow boast: "If it had pleased God that we had had one hour's daylight more at Oudenarde, we had in all likelihood made an end to this war." But the Sun King's military machine was still capable of astonishing recovery. It should be remembered that Berwick and his army had been marching westward from the Moselle River for several weeks past. On July 12, he learned from the governor of Mons that "there had been an engagement . . . that the enemy had had the advantage, and that our army was retreating towards Ghent in great disorder."

Happily, Berwick had inherited much of his uncle Marlborough's genius, for he instantly perceived the danger now facing the Sun King's greatest Flemish fortress, Lille.[2] He ordered his army to encamp south of Lille at Douai, then alone traveled north to the city to prepare the fort for possible siege.

Prince Eugene's army, which had been slowly marching north from Germany without its leader, had finally reached Brussels. Consequently, the small Flemish province now housed four armies — Marlborough's at Wervik, west of Lille; Eugene's at Brussels, east of Lille; Berwick's at Douai, south of Lille; and the remains of the Bourgogne/ Vendôme force at Ghent, north of Lille. Whoever could first effect a junction would gain a tremendous advantage.

With half of the French force in Ghent, blocked from its own frontier by *both* Marlborough and Eugene, France lay perilously open for invasion. Indeed, this was Marlborough's idea, which, "if it succeeded," he wrote, "would put a happy end to the war." Fortunately for France, he could sway neither the ever cautious Dutch nor (more important) Prince Eugene to his bold and brilliant plan, so the idea of invasion was dropped.

Vendôme, for one, never believed the allies would risk an invasion with a hostile force so close to their rear. Consequently, he entrenched himself in a strong position behind the canal running from Ghent to Bruges, expecting Marlborough to attempt a recapture of the two cities. But Marlborough had another idea, one Berwick had divined.

He made preparations for an extremely vital project: the siege of Lille.

Lille was the capital of French Flanders, and outside Paris, the most important city in France. Its fortifications had long been regarded as an unqualified masterpiece: its outer ramparts, studded with huge bastions, enclosed a wide, river-fed moat. Within the great moat were triangular island defenses, called half-moons, from which the city force could open fire, should attackers breach the outer defenses. On the far side of the moat was the city wall, protected at regular intervals by more bastions. The citadel, at the northwest corner of the city, was still more formidable: the main wall, again covered with bastions, was defended by *two* lines of ramparts and *two* moats. Within the city garrisons, fifteen thousand French troops were billeted. Louis XIV had wrested Lille from Spain half a century before and had sworn never to lose it.

To breach so magnificent a defense was a formidable task, requiring an immense amount of siege equipment. The allied undertaking was further complicated since, after the fall of Bruges and Ghent, their waterway communication lines were under French control. To Marlborough, the solution lay in transporting siege matériel by land from Brussels, which meant passing dangerously close to Vendôme's force — hardly an ideal option, but the only one available.

At the beginning of August, the siege train left Brussels: an immense convoy of sixteen thousand horses transporting eighty heavy cannon, twenty mortars, and three thousand ammunition wagons. On August 12, it arrived outside Lille: not one attempt to stop it had been made.

Blame for this must rest totally with Vendôme. Berwick was fully aware of the incoming siege equipment and had repeatedly informed Vendôme of its progress, but the maréchal still refused to believe the allies would attempt anything but the recapture of Bruges and Ghent, and refused to budge from his entrenched position. The very day the convoy set forth, Vendôme had written Louis XIV, ridiculing the "siege fear" at Versailles: the roads were "absolutely impracticable on account of rain," and the successful transport of any heavy equipment over land was out of the question.

Bourgogne can hardly share credit for this myopic vision: not only had he recently been censured for not following the counsel of his "distinguished" co-commander, but since the devastation of Oudenarde, he appeared to lose all confidence in his own judgment and experienced an increasing horror for war and bloodshed. Timidly, he had suggested that Vendôme heed Berwick's warnings; being shouted down peremptorily, he had returned to his tent for long hours of prayer and meditation.

On August 13, Marlborough reported to the lord treasurer, Godolphin: "This day Lille is invested; I pray to God to bless the undertaking. What I most fear is the want of powder and ball for so great an undertaking." The siege itself was Eugene's responsibility; Marlborough's charge was to wait nearby with a field army, should the French attempt to relieve the city. But the first days passed into a week and still there was no sign of the French army. Louis XIV sent urgent dispatches demanding the preservation of Lille, Bourgogne pleaded for a march south to the beleaguered fortress — and still Vendôme did nothing. "So wise a commander as Prince Eugene," the maréchal maintained, "would not venture upon such an enterprise." At last Berwick (who personally despised Vendôme) was able to convince him of the crisis they faced, and on August 27, two full weeks after the siege of Lille began, the French army of Flanders marched south. Leaving the comte de La Mothe and a corps of twenty thousand men to cover Bruges and Ghent, Vendôme and Bourgogne covered twenty-five miles in three days. On August 30, they made their junction with Berwick, on the plains outside Lessines, a combined force of one hundred ten thousand men.

Marlborough, still covering Lille, was informed of the French junction that day, but was unmoved. "If God continues on our side," he wrote Godolphin, "we have nothing to fear, our troops being good, though not so numerous as theirs. I dare say that, before half the troops have fought, success will declare, I trust in God, on our side."

Still obsessed with self-vindication, Vendôme urged an immediate attack on Marlborough, but Berwick disagreed. He stressed that the allies' position was too strong to risk another Oudenarde defeat. The two generals looked to Bourgogne to settle their dispute; the prince, sadly but justifiably terrified of the responsibility, deferred the matter to Louis XIV. The delay would prove disastrous.

At Versailles, suspense enervated the court; nothing was known, save that Bourgogne and Vendôme had left Ghent on August 27. "Every day increased the uneasiness," Saint-Simon wrote. "The princes and the chief nobles of the Court were with the Army. Everyone at Versailles feared for the safety of a relation or friend. Prayers were offered everywhere. Gaming, conversation, ceased. Fear was depicted upon every countenance. If a horse passed a little quickly, everybody ran without knowing where. Chamillart's apartments were crowded with lackeys, since everyone wished to be informed the moment that a courier arrived. The King wrote to the bishops to request that they should offer up prayers suitable to the danger of the time."

No less than the court, Adelaide was infected with this general terror and found her role as the king's contented pet increasingly difficult to sustain. By the time of the armies' junction, her nerves were close to breaking point. Saint-Simon reports an exchange between Grandpapa and his darling extraordinary in its atypicality: "The King observed one evening that the Duchesse de Bourgogne appeared deeply depressed. He seemed surprised and asked the reason, and then tried to cheer her with his relief and satisfaction at learning the armies were at last united. 'And the princes, your grandsons?' she retorted sharply. 'I am anxious about them,' he said, 'but I expect that all will be well.' 'I am also anxious,' she replied, 'and that is why I am low and out of spirits.' "

At last, on September 7, a courier arrived at the palace from the French command in Flanders — requesting orders! The king was infuriated by his generals' indecision. He sent his war minister north to reconcile Berwick, Bourgogne, and Vendôme — and with him, orders for an immediate attack.

Wily Marlborough had taken full advantage of the delay. He placed his army in so strong and impregnable a position that even Vendôme now refused to launch an attack. And so the plan adopted by the three commanders (and sanctioned by Chamillart) was to stop the allied siege by waylaying the fresh convoys of ammunition and supplies en route from Brussels, Antwerp, and Oudenarde. On September 15, the French army fell back to Tournai; three days later, Chamillart returned to Versailles.

News of the retreat to Tournai brought fresh disgrace for the duc de Bourgogne. The Meudon cabal, waiting impatiently since Oudenarde for more fuel, seized the opportunity to hold him personally responsible for an action taken in joint decision. Perniciously they declared that, had the father of the army been given sole command, he would straightaway have attacked and defeated the allies, forcing them to abandon the siege of Lille. "They revived the worst that was said of [Bourgogne] after Oudenarde," Saint-Simon recalled, "and denied the earlier favorable reports which until then no one had contradicted." Their persecution took an insidious turn:

They did not question his courage or say anything obviously disparaging, but they spoke of his religion, saying that the thought of so much blood spilt, so many men dying, unconfessed, filled him with horror, and that he could not bring himself to give battle and bear the responsibility before God . ∴. [They] exaggerated his lengthy sessions at table, his parties of battledore and shuttlecock . . . turned to ridicule his fruit in oil, his absent-minded way of crushing grape-pips, his theories on anatomy, engineering and other abstract sciences, but more especially his too long, too frequent sessions with Père Martineau, his confessor.

Their poison was effective; within days, "it was thought disgraceful to speak with moderation of the son in his father's house." In far-off Cambrai, Fénelon sighed: "As for our little prince, his reputation has been damaged incalculably; not a soul has a word in his favor."

Not a soul — except his wife. The princesse was now an intelligent young woman of twenty-two. The Meudon cabal, aiming to destroy the young prince and princesse, brought them closer together than before. The strength of the cabal would ensure the victory of the couple.

In the wake of her newfound feelings for Bourgogne, Adelaide somewhat belatedly discovered education. She reasoned she could best serve her husband by cultivating an interest in those areas where he excelled, and while the court frolicked through its annual pilgrimage to Fontainebleau, she remained indoors, reading philosophy and studying languages. A bemused Mme de Maintenon commented: "That will not last long," but the princesse was absorbed enough to compose a lengthy philosophic discourse in Latin — which, of course, enchanted her husband. Maintenon still played the skeptic: "Do not be alarmed," she wrote the princesse des Ursins. "Our Princesse will never be a scholar or a wit. It amuses her to listen to learned talk," though the royal educator had the grace to concede: "I think that a slight acquaintance with the arts and sciences is as good a distraction as card-playing all day." Adelaide's fling at academia was short-lived: not because of "student apathy," but because the growing threat of the cabal forced her, figuratively, out of the schoolroom and into the fray.

Rising to her husband's intellectual level would have to wait; she rose instead to defend his honor. No one at the court ever expected such loyalty from the pleasure-loving princesse, the indifferent wife. Even Mme de Maintenon was taken aback: "I confess that I did not believe that she loved the Duc de Bourgogne as much as we now see. Her affection makes her very sensitive."

Discarded for a time was her innate timidity. She attacked with a bold vigor that astonished friends and foes alike. Insults to her husband were taken as to her, and she returned them in kind. Offenders were unwelcome in her salons or in her company anywhere. Her popularity, which she now firmly affixed to her husband's, proved steadfast and formidable: almost overnight a "Bourgogne faction" rose at court in their support. Madame chronicled developments: "The entire Court is in a ferment. Some are trying to gain the favor of the all-powerful dame [Maintenon], others that of Monseigneur, others again that of [the Bourgognes] . . . The Duchesse de Bourgogne wishes to rule both the Dauphin and the King; she is jealous of Mme la Duchesse and had made a pact with the Duchesse d'Orléans [Madame's daughter-in-law] to thwart her."

Other pacts were made. Marie Adelaide relied on the support and counsel of Mme de Maintenon throughout the crisis, but realized it was not enough. One of her first "victories" was the reconciliation of *ma tante* and the duc de Beauvilliers. Since Fénelon's disgrace, Maintenon had turned her back on her former friend, the archbishop's defender, and they had not been on speaking terms for several years. Adelaide convinced her that, in the struggle to save Bourgogne, old differences must be forgotten; Beauvilliers was the most illustrious member of the court who still supported the prince and his cooperation was imperative. He was duly summoned to a private audience in Maintenon's rooms.

It was not a moment too soon. The support of these two well-placed figures — the king's secret wife and his closest adviser — grew ever more important as summer faded and the campaign of 1708 plunged deeper into the mire. The plan to curtail reinforcement of the siege of Lille from Tournai was at the start successful, insofar as effectively barring all interior transportation. But fear and hesitation born at Oudenarde had nurtured delay and in delay was defeat. With the Flemish waterway systems closed before him, Marlborough drew on supplies from England via the port of Ostend. In the last days of September, word reached the French command that a convoy of seven hundred wagons, with an army escort of five thousand, was due shortly to leave the port. Vendôme sent orders to La Mothe, who still covered Ghent, to intercept the train. With his ever mounting caution, Bourgogne sent reinforcements north, but La Mothe did not wait for their arrival. On September 28, he attacked the covering force in the valley of Wynandael — and was repulsed, with a loss of three thousand to four thousand men. Two days later, the wagon train arrived intact at the allied camp outside Lille. The city was doomed.

With the defeat at Wynandael, Bourgogne abandoned all hope of succor for Lille and wrote his grandfather for royal consent to certain measures he proposed "in anticipation of this loss." Vendôme, the experienced courtier, presented a more optimistic, and illusionary, picture to the throne-chair general at Versailles. Then he raced north to assume command of La Mothe's force and in a daring act reminiscent of the Dutch a generation before, he opened the canal sluices of Nieuport and flooded the area surrounding Ostend, hoping thereby to put an end to further enemy communication. Once again he was outwitted by Marlborough: the English general had wisely commissioned the construction of a fleet of flat-bottomed boats on the chance of just such an action; unharassed, allied supplies now floated down the countryside.

From Versailles there came repeated, urgent orders to attack and save Lille but, as Saint-Simon admitted, "the army near Tournai was in a state of complete torpor that overcame even the Duc de Bourgogne." Vendôme was no less lethargic in Ghent, though in the final days of October he was at last sufficiently aroused to march south. It was far too late: on October 23, Lille fell.

The city had endured more than two months of siege. All powder and ammunition had been consumed. All meat as well; rations had been reduced to the barest of minimums. The city could no longer accommodate its sick and wounded. On October 20, the enemy had finally breached the outer defenses in three different places and drained the moat — further resistance was futile. The casualties of the siege, once the figures were published, horrified Europe: within the city, two thousand were dead and twice that number lay sick or wounded; the allies admitted to three thousand dead and more than eight thousand wounded, of whom more than half eventually died. To War Minister Chamillart, Vendôme wrote: "It is a pity that the town of Lille should have capitulated, and I am mortally sorry for it . . . But if we can manage to stay where we are for some time longer, I will answer for it that the enemy will be more impeded than ourselves." Fine words, and hopeful — but perfectly hollow.

In the last week of November, the French command in Flanders, its members now barely civil, held one last war council. The army was demoralized and decimated, yet Vendôme urged a final confrontation with Marlborough along the Scheldt River. Predictably, Berwick disagreed and, having gained ascendancy over the prince, saw to it that Bourgogne concurred with him. But Vendôme, driven to find some victory in a campaign of defeat, overrode both objections and attacked Marlborough the morning of November 27.

The ravages of a summer of failure were evident, and again the French were roundly trounced, leaving eight hundred wounded and dead as they beat an ignominious retreat. It seemed the ultimate humiliation of a devastating season, but the fates were not so kind. There remained one more bitter pill to swallow. As the army of Flanders crept brokenly into their winter quarters, the indomitable Marlborough continued his offensive and marched north. On December 11, he invaded Ghent: before the year was out, both Ghent and Bruges were again under allied control. Marlborough returned to his winter quarters on December 30 and the campaign of 1708 — possibly the most inglorious in the entire history of the French army — was ended.

Chief among the culprits for the debacle must be the Sun King himself. His waging of council-chamber warfare from the safe luxury of Versailles had hampered his armies before and would again, though seldom to such an alarming extent. More inexcusable was his division of responsibility between two such incompatible personalities as Vendôme and Bourgogne. Rather than solving this problem, so painfully obvious by midsummer, with the transfer of one commander or the other, Louis XIV aggravated the situation with the addition of Berwick. As Chamillart later wrote: "M. de Vendôme and M. de Berwick are two great men, but they will never be seen sleeping with their heads in the same nightcap. When one said a thing was white, the other said it was black, and this did not fail to cause frequent and considerable perplexity for the Duc de Bourgogne."

Bourgogne's letters following Oudenarde indicate that he did feel a measure of responsibility himself, but in his defense, it should be noted the prince was twenty-five years old and without experience. Eager for counsel, he was surrounded by advisers who themselves could not agree on a single plan of action, and whose primary motivation too often was sending him home alive and safe, not fighting the enemy.

Forcing the prince to mediate between the headstrong Berwick and the stubborn Vendôme had brought into sharper focus the greatest weakness in his character — an inability to take command; self-awareness of this defect only increased Bourgogne's torment. Lastly, his obsessive piety, controversial in the halls of Versailles, was damning in the field camps. By late autumn of 1708, the common soldiers no longer bothered to hide their sneers, and as the Prince returned from mass one morning, he was accosted by a crusty old veteran: "You will certainly win the Kingdom of Heaven, but as for the kingdom of this world, Eugene and Marlborough know how to seek it better than you." His staunch defender Saint-Simon reluctantly admitted that "his conduct lent too much color to the accusations leveled against him, and was severely judged, even by his most devoted friends." None was more devoted than Fénelon, and the archbishop himself rebuked Bourgogne: "Your piety tries to govern an army like a nunnery, and wears itself out in little trifling details, while it neglects everything that is essential to your honor and to the glory of the arms of France."

Mme de Maintenon had a kinder word. To the princesse des Ursins, she wrote: "What was our prince, who has not yet had much experience, and finds himself in the most difficult position conceivable, to do, except trust a man [Berwick] who enjoys the confidence of the King? How could he decide or discover by himself that the counsels which were being given him were too timid, or that he ought to abandon himself to the guidance of M. de Vendôme, against whom three quarters of the army are bursting with indignation?" But hers was decidedly the minority opinion. Even the king was unsure just what to think; his reply to Bourgogne's formal request to return to court was curt: "It was to be desired that you should have had more satisfaction in this campaign."

As the prince journeyed south to Versailles, he doubtless pondered the tenor of his reception there. One thing only was certain: it would in no way resemble his sendoff eight months before.

The close of 1708 was a period as difficult for Adelaide at home as for her husband in Flanders. In her private war against the Meudon cabal, she suffered vicissitudes that drew heavily from his continued misfortune. The cabal was growing in power, meeting with less and less resistance — not because the Bourgogne faction was dwindling, but because the sporadic news from the front was rigidly censored, and bewildered courtiers no longer knew what was truth and what was fabrication.

Daily, the Meudon party grew bolder. Their minions infiltrated the theaters and gaming rooms of Paris, spreading their vicious rumors; they secretly printed broadsheets lambasting the duc de Bourgogne, and devised offensive songs (usually the work of Mme la duchesse), which they set to familiar tunes to ensure their popularity. One invoked Fénelon: "Acknowledge your pupil, my lord of Cambrai, / When Lille is blockaded, he's far from the fray. / In action takes never a part; / His face is so doleful, his mien so sad / That — answer me — is not the sanctified lad / A Quietist after your heart?"

In another blast, Bourgogne was depicted as refusing to go into battle for fear of sending souls to hell; the cruelest ballad of all accused him of hiding in a mill and refusing to budge while his soldiers fought and died. Vendôme, of course, was presented as a true hero thwarted at every turn by "this devotee, this shuttlecock-player, this poltroon, trembling at the mere sound of a cannon."

Monseigneur turned completely against his oldest son. While never close in the past, the dauphin now made no attempt to conceal his distaste and Saint-Simon recorded his expression of disgust when Chamillart read to the king in council the dispatch announcing the siege of Lille: "Halfway through this reading, Monseigneur made as if to go, but the King called him back to hear the rest; after which, he departed without saying a word." That evening, at his *coucher*, Monseigneur "praised the Duc de Berri to the skies and did so repeatedly, yet never once did he mention the Duc de Bourgogne."

Of far more importance was the king's attitude, and here the Bourgogne faction had matter for grave concern; Saint-Simon feared that, despite his darling Adelaide, even despite his secret wife, Louis XIV was "already half convinced . . . In public he more than once protested bitterly that he failed to understand why there was no attack, even on the entrenchments . . . In an incredibly short space of time, it became dangerous to praise the Duc de Bourgogne in the slightest degree, whilst those who extolled M. de Vendôme at his expense might be sure of pleasing the King and Monseigneur." It seemed as if all France had joined the cabal.

Beauvilliers and Saint-Simon spent many anxious hours in conference, exploring ways to rehabilitate their young prince in his grandfather's eyes. They felt it of vital importance the princesse be advised of their plans, through a medium such as Mme Nogaret. But Adelaide was not one to wait inactively: on her own account, she sent Nogaret to the duc de Beauvilliers and asked to be informed of where exactly she stood with the king and what she might do or not do with safety in the matter of her husband. For the first time in her life, she had reason to question her influence over the Sun King: Louis XIV loved peace at home and hearth even more than he did his young darling, and the new, defensive Adelaide was not at all to his liking. When she called upon him to support his grandson, he delivered what amounted to a public snub.

As the siege of Lille dragged on remorselessly, the princesse battled with forces bent on her destruction. During the day, she wrote long and regularly to Bourgogne in Tournai, her letters apprising him of the latest developments at court. Her correspondence was Bourgogne's only respite: "Nothing shows me better the affection which you have always said she felt for me," he exulted to Mme de Maintenon. "I realize more and more her affection for me, and you may be sure that it does not diminish my love for her . . . I only wish she had a more fortunate husband; but she could not have one who loves her more dearly."

Now the reverse was equally true. The princesse agonized over the safety of her husband's life and honor. "She passed whole nights in the chapel, when the people believed her in bed," said Saint-Simon, "and drove her women to despair." Mme de Maintenon wrote: "She watches the King's face continually. If she thinks she reads in it sorrow, she is in despair. She can talk of nothing save that which occupies all her thoughts. She strives to amuse herself, but without success; her heart palpitates at the arrival of every courier; she fears for her husband's life; she fears for his reputation; she would like to see him expose himself like a grenadier, and yet to return without a scratch; she would like a battle to take place, so that he might win it, and yet she dreads it. In short, nothing escapes her." In her correspondence with the princesse des Ursins, the king's wife observed: "I think as you do, regarding M. le Duc de Bourgogne, and I agree that it would be wisest to tell him only half of what his wife is suffering. She is now fasting for his sake, and you will readily admit, Madame, that this is the last thing one might have expected of her affection for him. Amid all her different worries, she no longer has any life of her own."

The strength, loyalty, and determination demonstrated by the duchesse de Bourgogne predictably softened more than one heart, and public opinion slowly wavered. Adelaide was far too wise to demand that the king remove Vendôme at so crucial a time in the campaign, but together with Mme de Maintenon (and with much difficulty) she persuaded Louis XIV to put an end to the slanderous reports circulating Versailles and Paris. Publicly the king ordered Vendôme's secretary, the comte d'Evreau, to be silent on the subject of Oudenarde and the army co-commanders; d'Evreau, terrified for his position at court and encouraged by his mother, the duchesse de Bouillon, immediately issued a second letter that contradicted his first and declared it a forgery. No one was fooled — but d'Evreau's recantation was seen by all as a major victory for Marie Adelaide.

Then Bourgogne's innate charity very nearly destroyed all his wife's hard-won success. Wisely, d'Evreau absented himself from court, but he shamelessly appeared before Bourgogne at army headquarters, and the prince forgave and welcomed back the prodigal. In the weeks that followed, Bourgogne appeared almost excessive in his favoring of Vendôme's cousin-accomplice, which more than one disgusted officer read as an admission of guilt. For the pious young prince, turning his cheek was the duty of a true Christian, but the court found his behavior naïve and ludicrous, and the army despised his affront to honor. As greater numbers quit the Bourgogne camp and drifted toward Meudon, Adelaide was forced to redouble her public criticism of Vendôme.

Despite a brave exterior, the maréchal had been shaken by the ferocity with which "the Big Two" — Marie Adelaide and Mme de Maintenon — launched their counterattack. He brazenly approached Bourgogne — neither to apologize nor excuse himself, but to request the prince to intervene on his behalf with the princesse. "His impudence," Saint-Simon felt, "clearly showed how timidity and piety may draw contempt upon even the most godlike beings."

More surprising than Vendôme's temerity was Bourgogne's compliance: "It is not very difficult to justify the Duchesse de Bourgogne to me . . . and I am only too much inclined to be favorable to her in everything. But the affection of which she has now given me such signal marks makes me apprehend that she might have gone a little too far in certain speeches." His appeal received an appropriate reply, Saint-Simon noted proudly. Adelaide wrote her husband that "she would never like nor respect M. de Vendôme again. She asked him to inform the latter that she had nothing to say to him and could very well understand the reasons for his concern. She added finally that nothing would ever persuade her to forget M. de Vendôme's conduct, and that for her part she would always regard him with loathing and contempt."

Vendôme had attempted to retain his dignity by offering the princesse a chance to reconcile through the injured third party. But her reply made plain that she would accept no terms but unconditional surrender. The prince donned a face of embarrassed regret before the maréchal; inwardly he exulted. "I have told her already several times," he wrote Mme de Maintenon, "that I am satisfied with what she had replied to me as to this, and my present fear is that I may have pained her a little by what I wrote to her. I beg you to tell her so once more, and to make her see how charmed I am with her affection and confidence. I flatter myself that I deserve them, and I shall endeavor more and more to merit her esteem."

Nightly the princesse prayed for some victory to resuscitate her husband's honor; daily the dispatches from the front returned bad news. The fall of Lille incriminated Vendôme *with* Bourgogne for the first time since the campaign began, and despite the cabal's efforts to block them, songs against both commanders appeared in the streets: "They hazard neither limb nor life, / Nor yet their honor in the strife. / One plays with shuttlecocks all day, / The other roosts on his *chaise-percée.*"

But this implication of the old maréchal made little difference to Adelaide. This latest shame, the loss of Lille, was a tremendous setback. Mme de Maintenon sadly dubbed her "the unhappiest [person] in the world . . . [She] weeps plenty of tears, but they are tears of courage and true affection, without admission of any weakness. She sees an incomprehensible outburst against Monsieur her husband. He is held to blame for all our misfortunes, when the decision has not once been his."

Nervous strain took its toll on the princesse's health: she suffered from "a swelling on one of her sides," which greatly alarmed Mme de Maintenon, and the old inflammation of her gums reappeared, painfully robbing the few hours of sleep still left her. In public she continued to fight — in private she battled with despair. One evening she appeared on the threshold of Mme de Maintenon's apartment, drawn and pale: "*Ma tante,* my heart is bursting. I am afraid of being a trouble, but I do so much want to weep with you." Her husband extolled her: "Her spirit is far indeed from being what is called a woman's spirit," and *ma tante* concurred: "Three-quarters of the people here share my opinion that [her] conduct is truly admirable, and would be highly commendable in an old dowager-queen. She spends her days either in the chapel or else writing letters to the army . . ."

In September, Adelaide had bravely convinced herself that once the army officers returned to court the coming winter, the truth would prevail and vindicate her husband. But in the intervening months, Lille fell and Ghent and Bruges were recaptured; by December, the princesse was deeply agitated "as to the Prince's probable reception," and she sought the advice of his friends on how best to see and instruct him before he met with the king.

Saint-Simon's suggestion was typically devious: he advised that the prince "time his journey so as to arrive an hour or so after midnight and thus be free to go straight to her and avoid meeting anyone else" — advice that failed to consider the notorious Bourbon pride. Fénelon's counsel was more beneficial: prior to his departure south, the prince received a lengthy epistle from the archbishop: "Nothing becomes you better than your disposition to forgive everything" — but the much maligned Bourgogne ought not to hesitate to justify his actions by condemning those "truly at fault.'" He should honestly admit to all his faults and errors; after that, he should enumerate Vendôme's: "laziness, negligence, rashness, obstinacy. Seeing nothing for himself, listening to no advice, deciding everything without regard to risks . . ." Most important of all was how to approach the king: "If you speak out strongly and nobly, you will gain the King's respect. If, on the other hand, you appear nervous and ineffectual, the whole world, which has been waiting for this moment, will conclude that there is nothing to be hoped from you, and that you are not concerned to reestablish your good name, not even at the Court."

The duc de Bourgogne rode into the Great Courtyard of Versailles at seven o'clock, the evening of December 8, 1708. Saint-Simon, who watched him from an upstairs window, thought he looked "prosperous, gay and smiling." Etiquette demanded that he see no one before making his report to the king; with a gaggle of curious courtiers trailing behind, he marched confidently into his grandfather's presence.

Wife and grandfather awaited him in Maintenon's rooms: the king, Saint-Simon heard, "changed countenance several times," and Adelaide openly trembled and "flitted about the room trying to conceal her agitation by wondering which door the Prince would use for his entry." The doors were flung open, and there stood the duc de Bourgogne. "The king . . . moved two paces to meet him, and embraced him with a sufficient show of tenderness." Adelaide and Maintenon sighed in relief, though here their worry had been groundless: Louis XIV, with his rigid concepts of royalty, would never have humiliated his grandson in the presence of the court. Greetings and pleasantries were exchanged, then the old man turned and pointed to the princesse, saying with a smile, "Have you no greeting for her?"

For a quarter of an hour, they chatted of roads and journeys and lodgings, then the king dismissed his grandson, "saying that it would not be right to keep him longer from the joy of the Duchesse de Bourgogne's company," and added significantly that there was time enough for later meetings. Plainly relieved, the prince bowed graciously and retired with his wife to their private rooms.

They were closeted together for over two hours. Adelaide advised him of the shape of court opinion and analyzed the tenor of the king's welcome. Louis XIV appeared to have already pardoned the prince but, she warned, Monseigneur would require far more diplomacy. The dauphin had been to the theater that evening and when he entered the Grand Cabinet shortly after eleven to await supper, he found his daughter-in-law, but not his son. Saint-Simon felt the reunion of father and son went worse than expected, though not from want of effort on Adelaide's part:

> The Duchesse de Bourgogne, troubled that her husband did not hasten to salute Monseigneur, went herself to find him, and returned saying that he was powdering; but observing that Monseigneur was not pleased with his lack of eagerness, she sent to hurry him. The maréchale d'Estrées, a silly giddy creature . . . attacked Monseigneur for waiting so tranquilly to see his son, instead of going himself to embrace him. Monseigneur answered curtly that it was not for him to seek the Duc de Bourgogne, but for the Duc de Bourgogne to come to his father . . . At last he came. The reception was fairly good, but by no means like that of the King.

The supper bell mercifully interrupted their awkwardness, and the royal family went in to dinner.

The subsequent arrival of the duc de Berri during this supper warned Adelaide that victory was not yet theirs: "At the sight of [Berri] all hearts seemed joyful. The King embraced him tenderly. Monseigneur looked at him in the same manner, but dared not embrace him in the King's presence. Everyone present seemed to court him. He remained standing beside the King during the rest of the supper; the talk was only of post-horses, roads, and trifles of that kind. The King also spoke with the Duc de Bourgogne at table; but with quite a different air and manner than that he used for the Duc de Berri."

Bourgogne's high spirits despite the disastrous campaign — due as much to reunion with his wife as to advice from Fénelon — was viewed by the court as "unsuitable," but two days of silence from the king, who was "fully occupied working with his ministers," were effectively sobering. On Thursday, Louis XIV's weekly holiday, Bourgogne was at last sent for and locked away in conference with the king for more than three hours. "I had feared lest his piety should restrain him on the subject of M. de Vendôme," Saint-Simon confessed afterward, "but I learned later that fortified by his wife he had spoken out and not spared him." Calmly and logically, Bourgogne presented his case before his grandfather. Saint-Simon still had reservations: he could have been more forceful, "but at least he did say all, and better than could have been expected, considering who was speaking and who listening." In the end, he begged for a command and another chance in the next campaign — with a smile, Louis XIV promised him both.

Following his interview, Bourgogne sent a quick note to Beauvilliers: "I thought I should tell you this, so as to give you a good night's rest!" He declared himself well pleased and confident of the king's continued favor: "He did not seem to be against making further use of me. I dare to think that I am sure of re-employment, should I desire it; and that I most heartily do."

Bourgogne had appeased his indulgent grandfather; pacifying his overtly hostile father was another matter, one that required his wife's considerable charm and tact. The morning after the prince's audience with the king, Adelaide and Mme de Maintenon drove to Meudon to pay a call on Monseigneur's morganatic wife, Emilie Joly. The conciliatory nature of their trip was evident at once: contrary to the rules of etiquette, the princesse insisted that Emilie Joly sit in an armchair throughout their visit and treated the former maid with a deference never before accorded her. She quickly succumbed to her (unofficial) daughter-in-law's persuasions and promised to speak with the dauphin about his treatment of Bourgogne. That very evening, Monseigneur held a dinner party in honor of his son and daughter-in-law; whatever private hostilities lay unresolved, his wife saw to it that appearances were maintained.

The cabal had waited on tenterhooks since Bourgogne's return to Versailles, their hopes rising and falling with each new development. Mme la duchesse had not expected so warm a welcome from the Sun King, but her spirits revived as Berri's entry met with markedly more enthusiasm. When it became evident that Louis XIV's affection for his first grandchild was undiminished, the cabal looked to the dauphin to "maintain hostilities," and Monseigneur's supper party was another setback. The conspirators breathlessly awaited Vendôme's arrival at court, sure that the returning war hero would quickly set the scales again in their favor.

The duc de Vendôme reached Versailles on December 16, just as the king was leaving his study for lunch. Louis XIV "embraced him with such a glad look that the Cabal found cause for rejoicing," Saint-Simon wrote. But their happiness did not last long, for the pressure continually exerted by the duchesse de Bourgogne had had its effect, and Vendôme found his royal master courteous but distant. "[Vendôme] monopolized the conversation while the King was at table, but it was nothing but small talk," and when the maréchal pressed Louis XIV for an immediate private interview, he was told the king would receive him in Mme de Maintenon's rooms the next day. Vendôme withdrew from the royal presence and called at once upon Monseigneur, who "received him warmly and kept him a long time" — but it was also quickly apparent that the dauphin felt intimidated by his father (and indirectly by Marie Adelaide). Monseigneur gossiped of court matters and carefully avoided any mention of the dismal campaign.

The maréchal then made the error of trying to compromise the dauphin with an invitation to Vendôme's estate at Anet. "To his huge surprise," Saint-Simon noted gleefully, "he received a vague response, which nonetheless made it perfectly clear that Monseigneur had no intention of visiting him ever. Vendôme was visibly embarrassed and hurriedly left." Small wonder that when Saint-Simon encountered the proud old general on a private staircase minutes later, Vendôme appeared "vexed."

His royal interview the next day was not encouraging: he was with the king for less than an hour and Mme de Maintenon never left the room. Chastened by her presence, Vendôme held his tongue on the subject of the prince. The maréchal then paid a duty call on the duc de Bourgogne. The reunion could hardly have been pleasant on either side, although Bourgogne displayed his customary Christian charity and entertained his adversary with great kindness as if the disasters of their co-command had never occurred. In a major breach of protocol (which surprised no one), Vendôme did not call on the duchesse de Bourgogne once during his week at Versailles. Doubtless he feared a public upbraiding from the uncrowned queen, but this insult to royalty further strengthened Adelaide's position.

Court opinion took the royal cue and swung perceptibly toward the Bourgognes. The cabal grew desperate. To curry popular support for Vendôme, they publicized the maréchal's "persecution" at the palace; for the first time, their vicious lampoons directly attacked Marie Adelaide: "Princesse, you are welcome to dance, / And share all the pleasures of France, / For you cause us no harm by your joy. / But when Vendôme you attack, / Your husband to back, / You work in your father's employ."

Such base charges, whatever their effects on the Parisian mobs, made no dent in feeling at Versailles, where even the dimmest of courtiers could perceive victory for the princesse, defeat for the cabal — and the sacrifice of Vendôme on their private battlefield. Adelaide's strenuous effort had been rewarded: the king soon let it be known that, while Vendôme was not in disgrace, he was certainly not in royal favor. The maréchal de Boufflers, who had commanded the fortress of Lille and bravely resisted the allies for two months, returned to Versailles the day after Vendôme, and the contrast in their respective receptions was striking. The king received Boufflers warmly, embracing him several times and overwhelming him with praise. Louis XIV declared that, having served so well his king and country, Boufflers might name his own reward. The maréchal humbly replied that such a mark of favor was in itself sufficient, to which the king said: "Very well! M. le Maréchal, let me make you a suggestion . . . Here and now, I create you a peer of France, and present you with the reversion of the governorship of Flanders for the benefit of your son, and for your own, the entrée of a first gentleman of the bedchamber." [3] Boufflers dropped to his knees, stunned by such unparalleled rewards. The court — and Vendôme — easily read the writing on the wall.

Once proud and sure, now shaken to his very soul, Vendôme tried in vain to salvage his position. He "stooped" (Saint-Simon's word) to asking *everyone* at court to visit him at Anet — "whereas in times past he had made it a favor, inviting only the great and the rich, and not deigning to notice ordinary mortals." But with the royal disposition so patently clear, there were precious few willing to court social suicide with an acceptance. "Many people sent excuses, others failed to honor their engagements, and all began to consider the distance a drawback — a journey of fifteen leagues, which in earlier years had seemed no more tiring than going to Marly." The chagrined old maréchal retired — alone — and dreamed of revenge.

Effectively banished from Versailles by the princesse, he planned a return to favor by way of Meudon and Marly, and was bold enough in late January 1709 to request permission to visit the king at his private estate. "The king received the request most graciously," the marquise d'Huxelles noted, "but [Vendôme] has been forbidden even to mention the campaign, a favor granted to the Duchesse de Bourgogne, who bears a grudge against him." "Bears a grudge" was an understatement: she had no intention of resting until Vendôme was permanently removed from royal favor.

Vendôme went to Marly first on February 6 and again on the fifteenth. Watching him in the salon, Saint-Simon concluded that the effects of his "exile" at Anet had been, at best, negligible: "[At Marly] he resumed all the arrogance of his days of glory, his haughty bearing, his loud voice, and his habit of monopolizing every conversation. To see him there, although sparsely surrounded, one might have thought him master of the salon, and with Monseigneur, and even with the King, when he dared to be so bold, he had all the air of a favorite."

The doors of Marly would not remain open to him for long. He requested and received permission to accompany the royal family on its post-Easter excursion. On the first evening of their stay, Adelaide and her father-in-law sat down to the brelan table, and discovered themselves one player short. The dauphin thoughtlessly sent for Vendôme to join their card party.

Softly, but very distinctly, Adelaide informed Monseigneur that the presence of Vendôme at Marly was sufficiently painful to her without being obliged to play cards with him. The dauphin realized his blunder and quickly sent for another card player, so that when Vendôme approached the table, he endured the mortification of being dismissed and watching another take his place. Saint-Simon was delighted by the old maréchal's embarrassment: "He turned upon his heels, left the salon as quickly as he could, and soon after retired to his own room, there to storm at his leisure."

While he fumed in private, the princesse worked on her own. She ran to Mme de Maintenon, repeated the incident, and persuaded *ma tante* to join her protests to the king at allowing Vendôme within their private circle.

Their combined efforts were successful. The next morning, the king's valet de chambre, Blouin, appeared at Vendôme's door and informed the maréchal that he must no longer expect invitations to Marly, as his presence was "distasteful" to the duchesse de Bourgogne. Vendôme was livid and left Marly at once for the house of a friend in nearby Clichy. Still he refused to concede defeat and doubled his visits to Meudon where he felt certain of welcome. Yet the situation at the dauphin's country seat had changed as well: with the partial reconciliation of father and son, engineered by Marie Adelaide and Emilie Joly, the Bourgognes were now frequent guests at Meudon. Two months after the card party incident at Marly, Adelaide's opportunity to expel her enemy once and for all arrived.

One afternoon the princesse, with the king and Mme de Maintenon, drove to Meudon for dinner. Vendôme was there as usual and brazenly presented himself at the door of the royal carriage, forcing Adelaide to acknowledge him. With an undisguised sneer, she gave the merest pretense of a bow, turned her head, and entered the château. The reckless Vendôme did not stop there: after dinner, he approached her card table and offered himself as her partner. So marked was the snubbing he received, said Saint-Simon, that he was forced to leave the room "to hide his confusion." He spent the rest of the evening alone in his bedroom; Adelaide spent the rest of the evening upbraiding her father-in-law for his lack of consideration. And she did not stop there: when the royal party returned to Versailles, Adelaide took her complaints to the king and Mme de Maintenon. How hard it was, she declared, to be treated so poorly by Monseigneur, "for while [the king] had banished Vendôme from Marly, [Monseigneur] continued to receive him at Meudon." She demanded retribution.

Vendôme was at a card table when the duc d'Antin arrived from Versailles. D'Antin marched up to the maréchal, gravely inquiring when the hand would be finished. Vendôme asked him why, and d'Antin replied that he had delivered the message entrusted to him. Vendôme was perplexed: "But I gave you no message." "Excuse me," d'Antin answered pointedly, "have you forgotten that I must give you an answer?" Vendôme accompanied him to a small private room, where d'Antin informed him that the king had just given orders to Monseigneur to never again invite Vendôme to Meudon. The maréchal reacted predictably: "He was seized with a perfect transport of rage, spitting out every insult he could call to mind" — but with total futility. The next day Monseigneur returned to court and Vendôme fled to Anet. Adelaide had won her war.

The maréchal deluded himself that the king would still be obliged to give the father of the army a command in the forthcoming campaign. He underestimated the damage he had done by blaming everyone else for the failure of 1708. Chief among those whom he had criticized following Oudenarde was Bourgogne's adviser, General Puységur, who had remained with the army during the months of the "winter war" at court. Puységur visited Versailles in April and the king granted him a long audience. Informed of Vendôme's accusations, he defended himself and his actions, and turned the tables by laying all blame on

Vendôme. General Puységur was a man of the highest integrity; he submitted several statements that corroborated his version of events, and Louis XIV could no longer doubt that Vendôme had deceived him. A courier was dispatched to Anet, and the maréchal was informed that he would no longer enjoy the benefits of a lieutenant general on the active list.

The destruction of Vendôme was now complete — in France at any rate. One year later, Philip V requested that his grandfather permit the maréchal to command an army in Spain — and actually asked his brother Bourgogne to support Vendôme's candidacy! The prince complied, the king consented, and Vendôme left for Spain. His campaign of 1710 was tremendously successful. Obsessed with exoneration, he pushed himself to his limits and scored major victories at Brihuega and Villa-Viciosa. Philip V loaded him with honors, but the years of debauchery — and syphilis — took their toll, and Vendôme died suddenly in Valencia in June 1712. Philip V ordered public mourning and buried the maréchal in the royal vaults at the Escorial; scorned in France, he died in Spain a hero.

Adelaide's victory did not go unheralded. Saint-Simon wrote: "We saw the great colossus, swollen with pride, collapse at the mere breath of a young princesse, as shrewd as she was courageous, and saw her rewarded with well merited applause." The court realized that she could no longer be regarded as a spoiled child, a pet to be flattered and amused. "All those who were attached to her were charmed to see of what she was capable, and all who were opposed to her or to her husband trembled."

In destroying Vendôme, she effectively destroyed the cabal: Mme la duchesse and her jealous cohorts continued to meddle and plot, but their power had been broken forever and, unwillingly, they conceded defeat. Saint-Simon called it "a pleasure" — "to see them artfully and basely making their overtures to those of the opposite party whom their arrogance had caused them to hate and despise; and particularly to see with what embarrassment, what fear, what terror they began to crawl before the young Princesse."

Almost single-handedly, Adelaide had vindicated her husband and proved her mettle. She had always held his love and now she had truly earned and deserved his respect. The Church had joined them together more than a decade before, but in 1709, the duc and duchesse de Bourgogne had become, in every sense, partners in marriage.

18

"Misfortune Is the Rule"

THE YEAR 1709 saw Marie Adelaide riding a new wave of popularity, and Mme de Maintenon, for one, could not have been prouder. "After having endured so much criticism for the mistakes I have made over her education," she wrote the princesse des Ursins,

> after being blamed for the freedom with which she gadded about from morning to night; . . . after seeing her accused of the most shocking deceit in her attachment to the King and the affection with which she honors me, I now find everyone singing her praises, believing her to have a kind heart and a noble spirit; admitting that she is capable of holding a large court in awe of her. I see her now, adored by her husband and dearly loved by the king . . . I am acquainting you of my view on this account, Madame, being persuaded that you also will be pleased, for you perceived sooner than others the fine qualities of our dear princesse.

Even that indefatigable critic Madame was changing her tune; only a few months before she had labeled Adelaide "a badly trained plant," and complained to her aunt: "I cannot count upon her friendship . . . The only things I insist upon from her are that she should not mock me before my face, that she should answer when I speak to her, not contradict me flatly, and behave with politeness during my visits." With the new year, she informed the electress of Hanover: "[She] has greatly improved and is now living on excellent terms with her husband."

It was this new relationship with Bourgogne that brought about much of the "improvement" Madame noticed. The fortitude, the zeal with which she had fought and beaten the cabal had convinced the love-hungry prince beyond all doubt of her true affection, and happily ushered in a period of domestic harmony. The private war she had waged for honor increased his already excessive devotion; proudly he wrote: "She has assuredly a solid mind, much good sense, an excellent and very noble heart" — then with insight he added: "Perhaps the pleasure that I have in speaking of her prevents me from perceiving that I do it too often and at too great a length."

For her part, Adelaide had come to respect her young husband, with his striking intelligence and his conscientious devotion to God and the state, and also to share in his interests to a much greater extent than ever before. She never lost her sense of humor, nor her easy enjoyment of pleasure, but, having at last discovered purpose in her life, she grew more serious-minded and (following Bourgogne's example) more conscious of the propriety demanded by her station. Her religion was never as tormenting or relentless as her husband's, but her recent years of adversity had strengthened her faith and deepened her devotion to God. In the old days, she had visited Saint-Cyr nearly every day, to romp in the gardens and play games with the younger schoolgirls; now she accompanied Mme de Maintenon to services in the chapel, and was no longer flattered when her presence occasioned an inevitable distraction for the novices. *Le Mercure de France* reported one such incident: as Adelaide knelt at her prie-dieu fingering her rosary beads, a group of curious nuns and students gathered behind the grille to watch her, hooking back the curtains with their fans. "The Princesse was not amused; she went over herself and with a very set face pulled the curtains closed, not only over the smaller gratings, but over the large ones as well; whereupon there was confusion and the sound of a speedy retreat." On another visit, it came to the princesse's attention that one of her pages had developed a crush on a Saint-Cyr schoolgirl and had even ventured to write her a letter. Adelaide was furious at the young man's indiscretion in the house of the Lord and ordered him never again to attempt such communication. She was not so hardhearted as to dismiss the page (as Mme de Maintenon might well have done), but he never again accompanied her to Saint-Cyr.

With Adelaide's popularity once more on the ascendant, it was natural that public opinion toward her husband should improve as well. At the same time the king disclosed that Vendôme would not receive a command in the forthcoming campaign, he appointed the duc de Bourgogne co-commander with maréchal d'Harcourt of the army of the Rhine. It was a clear indication of where the Sun King placed responsibility for Oudenarde, and it altered significantly the court's attitude toward his grandson.

This rehabilitation of Bourgogne was further advanced in an inspired plan suggested by d'Harcourt. In the time left before the opening of the war season, he proposed to give the duc de Bourgogne daily lessons in the art of warfare — instructions obviously neglected in Fénelon's schoolroom and, in view of the 1708 campaign, crucially needed. Bourgogne responded enthusiastically to the idea — even more when d'Harcourt suggested that the princesse might also attend their sessions. This was not a courtier's flattery: d'Harcourt recognized Adelaide's intelligence, her innate common sense, and had observed her husband's increasing reliance upon her judgment. He hoped the prince would find his wife's presence inspiring and abetting. Nor was he disappointed — by either pupil. Impressed with Adelaide's sound and concisely expressed opinions as the lessons progressed, he found himself reserving the important topics of discussion till after her arrival. The princesse was as delighted as her husband with her inclusion at these meetings. She had long wished that Bourgogne would discuss with her matters of importance, and she perceived now how much closer it drew them together.

In the end, unfortunately, their long hours in the classroom came to nothing, for Bourgogne's appointment as co-commander was revoked. The reasons were purely financial. After seven years of inconclusive warfare, the French treasury stood on the brink of bankruptcy, and Foreign Minister Torcy felt compelled to inform the Sun King that it was impossible to provide the duc de Bourgogne (or any other royal prince) with the expensive entourage deemed necessary for a Child of France. The critical nature of his finances was no surprise to the Sun King: he had already been forced to melt down the fabled solid silver furniture in the Versailles state apartments and to eliminate the king's bounty, gifts of money he distributed each New Year's Day. The fervor of Torcy's arguments convinced him that further sacrifice was imperative. Accordingly, he canceled his grandson's appointment and relieved his nephew, the duc de Chartres, of his command in Spain.

Bourgogne was crushed. He pleaded with his grandfather to let him go to the Rhine as a simple soldier, arguing that this would make an excellent impression on the troops, dispelling the unfavorable attitudes still lingering from the year before. But for Louis XIV, the maintenance of royal dignity and the display of royal ostentation were inviolable concepts, and he refused even to consider the idea. Sadly the prince accepted that he would play no part in the campaign of 1709. Though he did not know it, his military career was over.

Bourgogne moped and sulked for several days, hoping this might perhaps move his grandfather to relent. But Louis XIV had matters on his mind far more pressing than a downcast prince with frustrated dreams of martial glory. His nation had fallen under the grip of a new and horrible misfortune, an ordeal that by comparison made the War of the Spanish Succession seem trifling. It would be known simply as the winter of 1709.

An unusually cold frost settled on France in the first week of December 1708. It remained until Christmas. Despite the cold — and more important, because of the devastating campaign just ended — Louis XIV provided Versailles with the most brilliant Christmas the court had witnessed in several years. Nightly, there were masquerades and supper parties, and comedies by the royal theatrical troupe. The English royal family in exile threw a great ball at Saint-Germain, and at Sceaux, the duchesse du Maine provided a fête of balls, concerts, and theatricals that lasted three days. At Marly and Meudon, the festivities seemed endless. With his habitual ostentation, the Sun King gave a brilliant dinner party at Versailles to commemorate the Epiphany: guests sat at four tables — presided over by the King, Monseigneur, and the duc and duchesse de Bourgogne — and were served a feast of sixteen courses, then treated to a masked ball in the Hall of Mirrors. As the courtiers danced, their diamonds sparkling in the light of a thousand candles, the drama outside unfolded.

On that January sixth 1709, the temperature began to fall; in three days, it had dropped to twenty-one degrees below zero (Centigrade). On the eighth, the Seine and the other rivers of France were frozen; even the Rhône, one of the fastest rivers on the continent, was covered with ice. Still the temperature plunged: by the end of the week, the canals of Venice were frozen over and, at the mouth of the Tagus River in Lisbon, the ice was so thick that horses and wagons could pass from one bank to the other. By midmonth, all communication between Britain and the continent was suspended; massive blocks of ice rendered the English Channel unnavigable. Along the Atlantic coastline, inlets and bays froze hard enough to bear transport. In the forests of

Sweden and Norway, live elk became dead ice-statues. Everywhere in Europe cattle and sheep, squirrels and birds — even the rabbits in their burrows — perished in the unrelenting cold.

Snow fell on January 25 and mercifully raised the temperature. Then followed a week of clement weather. The rivers thawed, and in the south, the trees began to bud. Europe dared to hope the worst of the winter had passed, but on February 6, the second frost descended. It was longer and harsher than the first; this bout of extraordinarily cold weather lasted until March 6.

"It was the second frost that destroyed everything," Saint-Simon wrote. "The fruit trees were killed; no walnuts, olives, apples or vines survived." "It is impossible to keep Lent, because all the vegetables are frozen," Adelaide informed Madame Royale in February. "The archbishop will be obliged to allow three meat days a week." Vegetables were not just frozen, they were ruined — and for the common man, meat three days a week *outside* Lent was an unattainable luxury.

At Versailles, the court suffered. The palace, with its vast marbled halls and elongated windows, was difficult to heat even in moderate winter weather; in that February frost it became impossible. Wood fires burned incessantly, but had no discernible effect on the temperature. Madame described a supper party of the king's: a roaring fire burned one's face, while one's feet and hands seemed encased in ice. Bottles of water and wine burst in the cupboards of those rooms containing fireplaces, and when Saint-Simon dined with the duc de Villeroi, "splinters of ice fell into our glasses from the bottles on the chimneypiece, after being brought there straight from his tiny kitchen where there was a blazing fire." The ink froze in marquise d'Huxelle's pen even as she wrote. Many older courtiers died from the cold and related illnesses, including the maréchale de La Mothe (the venerable governess of Bourgogne, his brothers, and his sons) and Maintenon's old friend Mme d'Heudicourt.

While the rich suffered and, in some cases, perished in icy splendor, the poor suffered and, in most cases, perished in miserable squalor. Louis XIV ordered firewood distributed to the poor of Paris, but this had even less effect there than in the gilded galleries of Versailles. Madame's assessment that "people are dying from the cold like flies" was appallingly accurate: in Paris alone, 24,000 died between January 5 and February 2.

Louis XIV went to Marly in early February to escape the illness rampant at Versailles. There he learned that the nation's seed corn had died in the ground — there would be *no* harvest that summer. Worse news followed: the English fleet, mooring for the winter in the Mediterranean, had intercepted the vital grain supplies en route from North Africa. In the sixty-seventh year of the Sun King's glorious reign, the people of France faced imminent starvation.

News of the crop failure spread quickly, and in the ensuing panic, merchants scrambled to hoard the remnants of last year's harvest. The price of bread soared. "The dearth is frightful," Madame reported. "One cannot go out without being followed by people who are black with hunger. Everywhere one sees people dropping, literally dead of starvation."

She recounted to her aunt the heartbreaking story of a woman caught stealing a loaf of bread in a Paris bakery. "If my misery were known to you," the poor thief told the policeman, "you would not wish to deprive me of this loaf. I have three little naked children at home who asked for bread; not being able to bear it, I stole this." The policeman made her take him to her home, where there were, indeed, three children covered in rags and shivering. He asked the oldest, "Where is your father?" and was told, "Behind the door." The officer looked — and found that the man had hanged himself. "Similar things happen every day," Madame concluded. She *did* exaggerate when she reported the rumor that "children have eaten one another," but the situation was critical: in a scene darkly portending the events of 1789, the market women of Paris marched on Versailles to bewail their misery to the Sun King.

Louis XIV was deeply concerned and made serious efforts to relieve his starving people. "Various decrees were published concerning wheat," wrote Saint-Simon. "Searches were instituted for hoarded grain, and commissaries were sent into the provinces." These government agents were ordered to purchase the remaining grain in the areas where it was cheapest and make it available in the provinces where the prices had reached exorbitant levels.

But with human fallibility, there was much speculation: "The gentlemen of the Finance Department have seized . . . all the corn in France, and are selling it at their own price, to the King's advantage, not forgetting their own." Greed and avarice destroyed the Sun King's well-meant efforts, and aggravated the crisis. "All that this policy achieved," Saint-Simon felt, "was to increase the poverty and the prices to a disastrous level at a time when calculation showed there to have been enough wheat in the country to feed the entire nation for

two years, without reckoning on a harvest." Madame, with her eternal
grudge against the king's wife, accused Maintenon of being one of the
speculators: "When she saw that the harvest had failed, she bought up
all the corn remaining in the markets. She has made a vast amount of
money, but people are dying of hunger." (The accusation was false: on
the contrary, Mme de Maintenon took to eating only black bread to
set an example for the privileged denizens of Versailles.)

The duc de Bourgogne was also moved by the abounding misery. In
the king's council, he demanded detailed information on the true condition of the people although (Abbé Proyart pointed out) "there was
nothing he could do beyond suffer the misery of being unable to assist
them." And suffer this misery he did: "At one meeting, it was observed
that the Prince had burst into tears."

Under Bourgogne's guidance, the first government food program
was organized, and "the contributive tax on the property owners and
inhabitants of the village of Versailles" was levied to aid the poor and
starving of the town. No "householder" was exempt, not even royalty:
the king was assessed 4,220 livres, Monseigneur 2,110, Bourgogne
397, and so on down the scale of the palace hierarchy. Seven officers
were appointed to manage these funds and to supervise the distribution of bread. Food cards were issued to the poor; these were presented
at the designated centers, bread was provided, and the card then
snipped with a pair of scissors. The program, revolutionary in concept,
ran smoothly and efficiently. For the remainder of 1709, the poor of
Versailles were kept supplied with bread and firewood.

The prince did not stop there. He opened his purse with Christian
charity, but with such humility that none but his closest friends and the
priests who distributed his alms were aware of the depth of his generosity. The king provided him with a monthly allowance of twelve
thousand livres for private expenses: Bourgogne kept one thousand for
himself, and gave away the rest. He told his confessor that he would
have stripped his apartments as well, but he felt that the furniture truly
belonged to his grandfather. However, he did not hesitate to sacrifice
his fine collection of precious stones, many of them jewels bequeathed
from his mother. "M. l'abbé," he said, "since we have no money, and
the poor are dying of hunger, take these stones and change them into
bread."

One afternoon the princesse called her husband to view a pair of fine
silver inkstands she contemplated buying him. Bourgogne examined
them carefully, praised the style and craftsmanship, and inquired after

the price. Then he made no further comment and appeared to have lost all interest in the stands. Adelaide asked if he did not like them. "On the contrary, they please me enormously — but the poor!" Mme de Maintenon stepped in: "Truly, Monsieur, your poor would be excessively mean to grudge you an inkstand after all you have done for them!" — and she persuaded him to accept the gift. The prince acquiesced with good grace; but a few days later, Adelaide noticed that the inkstands were gone and understood his latest sacrifice for the hungry.

Such noble charity made an impression on the princesse. At first she resented his giving all "their" money away and sourly remarked one day that she too could use a little charity. Quietly he handed her a list of people he intended to assist, with the amount of each donation noted, and told her to strike off the names of those whose need she felt in all good conscience to be less urgent than hers — those moneys she could have. Adelaide had every intention of crossing off several names and collecting a tidy sum for herself; but reading the list of so many peasants ruined by the failure of the crops and facing starvation, she softened. Returning the paper, she told her husband, "I must allow that these people all deserve more pity than myself."

It was a lesson she did not quickly forget: soon afterward, Bourgogne was secretly informed by one of Adelaide's maids that, without a word to anyone, his wife had not only donated a sizable sum to charity but had arranged for forty people of Versailles to be fed daily at her personal expense. "I am absolutely delighted," Bourgogne commented, "and what pleases me most is that she did it out of kindness, and wants no one to know."

Louis XIV alone appeared reluctant to curb his lifelong instinct for extravagance. True, he announced that he could no longer feed the ladies on Marly excursions or pay for any entertainments except his own, but he feared that a major change in his customary munificence would be interpreted by his enemies as another admission of defeat. He refused at first to cancel the winter's program of feasts, and ordered the court to celebrate carnival season as richly as it had in years past. To the surprise of most courtiers, it was the "pleasure-driven" duchesse de Bourgogne who opposed the king's plans and urged him to abandon his designs. The magnificent supper parties and elaborate balls were canceled — at the insistence of their very inspiration. "I shall not have much trouble in giving you an account of the amusements of this Carnival," she wryly informed her grandmother. "It has been very dull up to this time, and I think it will end in the same way."

There was little the Sun King could offer the privileged grumblers of Versailles besides theater: this he provided in abundance. It was a time for comedy, a time to laugh and forget the privations and troubles of reality; in the first few months of 1709, the royal theater troupe played twenty-two nights at the palace — with *Tartuffe* and *Le Malade Imaginaire* their most frequent offerings. Otherwise, by way of amusement, a few of the heartier members of the court braved the elements to ice skate on the Grand Canal or slide down the snow-covered terraces. Adelaide was tempted to join in the fun: "I have a strong desire to drive out on a sledge, for I never have done so." But the princesse, like so many court denizens, had heavy reservations: "I own I have not enough courage on account of the bitter cold" — and with the vast majority she remained indoors.

As the winter died slowly and spring brought no relief from famine, the general unrest grew. For the first time in his long reign, Louis XIV was personally attacked in speeches throughout the land. A sacrilegious version of the Lord's Prayer appeared in the streets of Paris: "Our Father that art at Versailles, / Thy name's no longer hallowed. / Thy Kingdom is no longer great / Nor is thy will done on the earth or the sea. / Give us this day our daily bread / For we cannot buy it. / Forgive the enemies who have defeated us, / But not the generals who let them win. / Fall not to the temptations of La Maintenon, / And deliver us from Chamillart. Amen."

An even more defamatory lampoon made the rounds. It evoked the English Revolution of seventy years past, and forecast the French Revolution of seventy years hence: "The Grandpapa's a braggart, / The son's an idiot, / The grandson has a cowardly heart, / Oh! What a gallant lot. / I pity you, poor Frenchmen, / Beneath their rule, oh God! / Do now as did the Englishmen, / A wink to you is like a nod."

Food riots broke out in cities everywhere, and Paris seethed with discontent. One afternoon in early spring, Monseigneur proposed to Adelaide a visit to the Paris Opéra — recently reopened after the winter had forced the cancellation of all public entertainment. As the royal coach entered the city, it was surrounded by an angry crowd of women, screaming for bread and "displaying the wretched fare to which they were reduced." The dauphin was able to quiet the mob only by emptying his purse and throwing all his silver through the window. When at last a path was cleared, the royal party changed course and returned in silent apprehension to Versailles.

This instance of mob intimidation was positively harmless in comparison to an August riot that very nearly developed into full-scale insurrection. Madame described it: "Entering Paris by the Porte Saint-Martin, I saw everyone running this way and that, some crying 'Oh! My God!', all having perturbed countenances. The windows were full of people, there were even some on the rooftops. Down in the streets, the shopmen were putting up their shutters, and everyone was closing his doors." Madame entered the Palais Royal — which was also shut — confused and afraid; there she met an old acquaintance who lived in Paris. " 'Are you not aware, Madame, that there is an insurrection here which has lasted since four o'clock this morning?' I thought her crazy and began to laugh, but — 'I am not crazy, Madame,' she said. 'What I tell you is true, so true indeed that forty people have already been killed.' " Madame demanded details.

> Work is going on at the Porte Saint-Martin; each workman is given three and a half pence and a loaf of bread; there were two thousand working there. But this morning there suddenly arrived four thousand crying for bread and work. As this demand could not be met, and a woman behaved very insolently, they took her and shut her up. Then began the tumult; six thousand others joined the four thousand first, and they delivered the woman. Many servants out of work joined the crowd, and cried out to the others to come and pillage; so saying they emptied several bakers' shops. The guards were called, and told to fire on the mob, but the latter quickly perceived that this order had only been given to frighten them, for the soldiers' muskets were not really loaded. "Let *us* attack them!" cried they, "their muskets are not loaded." Hearing this, the guards saw themselves obliged to shoot several.

By noon, conditions in the city were critical. Full-scale revolt was averted only by the courage and tact of Maréchal Boufflers, who "happened to pass by the place where the tumult was greatest," and who skillfully invoked his enormous popularity to quiet the rioters. "He got down from his coach, harangued the mob, threw them several handfuls of money, and declared he would inform the king that although money and bread had been promised, the people had received nothing. The insurrection was immediately calmed; the people threw their hats into the air exclaiming, 'Long live the King and Bread!' "

Madame noted that "the Parisians are a good sort of people to be so easily calmed." Her predilection for them was due no doubt to their commonly shared sentiments: "Although the King is popular, they hate Mme de Maintenon." With undisguised glee, she related to her aunt: "On seeing me at the window, a crowd assembled calling out blessings on my head, but they began saying such horrible things about a certain lady that I had to withdraw and shut the windows. None of my people can show themselves, for as soon as one of them is seen at a window, they recommence their observations, saying freely that had they their will she should be cut to pieces and burnt as a witch."

Louis XIV was shaken by the Parisian riots but compassion for the hungry mob prevented any reprisals. Mme de Maintenon — who was unmoved, but not unaware, of the Parisian enmity — was alarmed to see the unmistakable marks of stress and tension in her husband's face. Characteristically, "he contains himself, and keeps his thoughts to himself," she wrote the princesse des Ursins. "Your love for him would be vastly increased, Madame, if you could see with what courage and fortitude he endures the misfortunes that strike him from more than one direction."

More than one direction indeed — for it must be remembered that throughout this trying time a war was still in progress. The nadir of French fortunes came in 1709: her armies abroad and her people at home were struggling simply to survive. In this climate, the Sun King found he had no options: he was ready at last to sue for peace.

Since the disastrous defeat of his forces at Blenheim in 1704, Louis XIV had ardently desired peace — albeit on French terms. In four successive campaigns, his armies had been ejected from the Italian peninsula, lost their footing along the Rhine, and (in the fiasco of 1708) surrendered nearly all of their Flemish conquests. Saint-Simon observed — and Louis XIV could not help but see — that the entire structure of the French war machine was "visibly deteriorating... The troops [were] unpaid, disheartened by bad leadership, and therefore never successful; the finances were bankrupt, the generals and ministers incapable, promotions came only by favor or intrigue, no faults were punished, no inquiries held, no councils of war. It was equally impossible to fight or make peace. Silence and misery were everywhere."

And now, nature unleashed catastrophe on the exhausted, disillusioned nation. The king, immured in magnificent Marly, pondered his dwindling alternatives and kept his own counsel, leaving the court — and the world — to speculate wildly. An alarmed princesse des Ursins wrote Mme de Maintenon in March of the rumors circulating through

Madrid that the Sun King was prepared to accept the allied candidate as king of Spain, if the allies would compensate his grandson with the tiny kingdom of Naples and Sicily. She was doubtless disheartened by a reply that in no way contradicted the speculations or allayed her fears: "We have suffered a series of disasters, from which France can recover only after a long period of peace, and now famine, the latest and worst of our misfortunes, has us in its grip. I must allow that in all my fears for the future, I never foresaw our being reduced to desiring the abdication of the king and queen of Spain. No words, Madame, can express my sorrow at the thought." Ursins was horrified: "It would be a shameful peace," she harped. "An atrocious peace," Maintenon sadly conceded — but a compulsory one.

Late in April 1709, the king assembled his full council. With tears in his eyes, he announced that Foreign Minister Torcy was to leave at once for The Hague — to sue for peace at any price. After more than half a century of triumph, the Sun King was forced to admit defeat.

On May 4, Prince Eugene informed the Austrian emperor that an unknown man bearing the passport of a courier had entered Brussels en route to Holland; beyond all doubt, Eugene declared, the man was Torcy. He was certain of Torcy's mission and thrilled by the prospects. "All the facts go to show that France is quite unable to prolong the war, and we can, therefore, if we wish obtain everything we ask for. We have only to hold together and preserve a good understanding among ourselves."

At The Hague, the allied negotiators were soon as jubilant as Eugene. The terms agreed to in the peace discussions exceeded their wildest dreams and made plain the plight of France: to the demand of total French evacuation from Flanders, Torcy acceded; to the insistence that the *entire* Spanish empire must go to the Austrian "Carlos III," Torcy acceded. When the question arose as to what measures Louis XIV was prepared to take to ensure the compliance of Philip V, Torcy replied that the soon to be ex-king would be given three months to accept the allied terms, at which time the entire French force on the Iberian peninsula would withdraw.

The extraordinary concessions Louis XIV was ready to make are ample evidence of his desperation. He assumed too that the allies' need for peace, if not as critical as his own, was nonetheless heartfelt. What he failed to perceive was the rabid resentment of a Europe that had endured fifty years of French expansionism. As the leader of the Dutch peace party, van der Dussen, wrote: "The policy of this province . . .

depends upon more than five hundred persons, most of whom regard France as brought to bay, and who are so embittered by memories of the past that they are resolved without compunction to make an end once and for all of their puissant foe." Put more simply: a bow from the haughty Sun King was not enough; they wanted him on his knees.

The allied demands increased — demands the harassed French foreign minister continued to accept. By the end of May, Torcy informed the negotiators that his king no longer insisted on Naples and Sicily for his grandson. Still the allies wanted more. What *real* guarantees could France give, they demanded, for the capitulation of Spain? After all, Philip V had held the crown for almost a decade; his one-year-old son had been created prince of Asturias (the Spanish equivalent of dauphin or prince of Wales) and was accepted by the Spanish parliament as heir to the throne. Philip showed no inclination to step down merely to gratify an old man's wish for peace; with true Bourbon spirit, he professed that "God, and not his grandfather, had placed him on the throne and was not now deserting him. His people were showing themselves loyal, and he could not abandon them." To the Sun King, he proudly declared, "I will only give up my crown with my life." Faced then with this reality, the allied negotiators deemed the evacuation of the French army from Spain inadequate: why, they argued, should *they* face a chance of continued war in Iberia while France settled back to enjoy peace?

With this dilemma foremost in mind, the allied negotiators presented their final, and fatal, demand. The morning of May 27, 1709, Torcy was handed a preliminary treaty. The wily diplomat skimmed quickly, then returned to two separate clauses he read again with mounting alarm. Article 4 stipulated in part: "If it should happen that the said Duke of Anjou [Philip V] does not consent and agree to the execution of the present convention . . . the Most Christian King [Louis XIV] and the Princes and States concerned in the present treaty, shall in concert take convenient measures to secure the full execution thereof." This was further clarified in Article 37: "Unless the King of France executes all that is above mentioned, and the whole monarchy of Spain is delivered up and yielded to King Carlos III as is stipulated by these articles, within the limited time, it is agreed that . . . war shall continue." These articles, read in conjunction, compelled Louis XIV himself, under pain of continued war, to obtain the surrender of his grandson — if not through diplomacy, then on the battlefield.

These demands were not a complete surprise to the French envoys;

one of the English party, Lord Townshend, described their reaction when the proposal was first raised earlier that week: "The French Ministers absolutely refused an amendment which might, they said, possibly engage their master to a condition so unnatural as to make war with his grandson." Marlborough himself opposed the demand, Townshend noted: "[He] even suggested schemes to turn the article so as *not* to commit His Majesty to war against Spain." But Marlborough was overridden by the vengeful Dutch, and this appalling condition was incorporated into the treaty.

Torcy skillfully evaded commitment: of course, he said, the document must now be forwarded to Versailles for approval by the king. When pressed by the Dutch to affix his signature before dispatching the document, the foreign minister refused politely. Another member of the French party, Abbé de Polignac (Adelaide's former suitor) was not so politic. Turning to one vindictive burgher, he sneered, "It is easy to see that you are unaccustomed to victories."

Secretly Torcy certainly rejoiced that the Dutch with their outrageous demands had themselves doomed the possibilities of peace and provided the Sun King with a valid justification to reject the entire treaty. Forwarding the document to Versailles on May 28, Torcy advised: "Your Majesty is thus entirely free to reject absolutely these conditions, as I trust the state of your affairs will permit." Nor was Torcy's faith in French pride — royal or otherwise — misplaced: on his journey home, he stopped at the headquarters of Maréchal Villars at Douai and showed him the terms of capitulation. Villars was outraged at the Dutch presumption, and with great indignation requested that Torcy inform the king he could rely on total support from the army in rejecting the loathsome document.

Torcy arrived at Versailles on June 1. Court reaction to the treaty was neatly expressed in a letter from Madame: "Peace is impossible, the terms are too iniquitous. It is a wicked and pagan thing to wish to force a grandfather to fight against a grandson who has always treated him properly and obediently. I am sure that God will find some means of punishing him who suggested this evil idea."

The king received his foreign minister in Mme de Maintenon's apartments where, according to an English spy, he "seemed sad and gloomy." The council met the next morning to debate acceptance or rejection. The terms of surrender were read aloud and, despite their severity, a number of ministers favored acceptance. Chamillart implored the king to consider the gravity of the food shortage within the realm, and confessed that not a single regiment had received their wages for over a year. Maréchal d'Harcourt refused to take up his post as commander of the army on the Rhine without proper assurance of enough food and money to maintain his troops; Villars, despite his patriotic boast to Torcy, had written home: "I have corn enough for one month."

In this atmosphere of pessimism and defeat, the dauphin rose to speak. Monseigneur, usually so apathetic, was incensed by the thought of abandoning his son, a crowned monarch. He berated the council for the "despicable action they were ready to take," and, to the astonishment of all present, censured even his father. Shaking with fury, he reminded those ministers in favor of peace at this price that he would be their master someday, and that "if the King by their advice abandoned his son they should render a long account to him." With that threat, he turned abruptly and quit the chamber.

The council deliberated for another hour; when Torcy emerged, he was immediately accosted by the dauphin, who demanded to know what decision had been reached. Before the entire court, Torcy announced that France would not forsake the king of Spain. It was learned afterward that Louis XIV had dryly remarked in council that if he must continue fighting, he would sooner fight the Dutch than his own flesh and blood.

The king's address to the French people announcing his rejection of the treaty was a masterpiece of patriotism. "I have sustained this war with the high hand and pride which becomes this realm," he began loftily; then turned immediately to the universal wish for peace: "I have also put in motion the measures I thought necessary in fulfilling my duties and making known the love and tenderness I have for my people, by procuring by my labors a peace which will bring them rest for the remainder of my reign so that I need have no other care than for their welfare . . . I have given ear to the proposals of peace which have been made to me, and I have exceeded perhaps on this occasion the limits of prudence in order to accomplish so great a work." He stressed heavily his willingness to compromise with the allies in order to achieve his end: "I may say that I stepped out of my own character and did extreme violence to myself in order promptly to secure repose for my subjects at the expense of my reputation, or at least of my own particular satisfaction, and perhaps of my renown."

However, the Sun King, the mighty State of France, would *not* submit to the humiliations demanded by the Dutch. "Seeing at this hour that my most vehement enemies have only wished to play with me and that they have employed all the artifices they could to deceive me as well as their allies by forcing them to contribute to the immense expenditure which their disordered ambition demanded, I do not see any other course to take than that of considering how to protect ourselves securely, making them understand that a France thoroughly united is stronger than all the powers they have got together at so great pains, by force and by artifice, to overwhelm her." France had endured adversity in the past and triumphed over it. She would do so again. "Our enemies will learn from the efforts we shall put forth that we are not in the condition they would have people believe, and by means of the help which I am asking of you and which I believe to be indispensable, we shall be able to force them to make a peace which shall be honorable to ourselves, lasting for our tranquility, and agreeable to the Princes of Europe." With their Sun King's stirring words ringing in their ears, Frenchmen everywhere resolved to fight anew.

On June 3, 1709, the allied negotiators were informed that Louis XIV had refused their terms for peace and offered no counterproposals. The war resumed.

Disheartened as he was by the failure of the peace talks, Marlborough was convinced nevertheless that a total French collapse was imminent. "All the wheat is dead everywhere that we have seen," he wrote from Flanders on July 4. "It grieves my heart to see the sad condition of all the poor country people for want of bread; they have not the same countenance they had in other years." One week later, he wrote: "The poverty of all the poor people we see is such that one must be a brute not to pity them."

But France and her master refused to kowtow. "The King is so determined to continue the war," Madame wrote her aunt, "that he has sent all his gold plate to the mint to be melted down into money." He also pawned or sold many of the crown jewels and, inspired by his example, courtiers and rich city merchants followed suit. The Dutch effort to bring France to her knees resulted instead in raising her patriotic zeal to fever pitch. The very character of the war changed. No longer did the army fight to preserve a king south of the Pyrenees; it fought to preserve French honor.

Nor was this rejuvenated spirit dampened by the reversals that opened the campaign of 1709. The French fortress at Tournai, in Flanders, fell to the allies on September 5, and Mons shortly afterward.

Villars, who in June had been ordered to avoid a battle at all costs, now received an injunction to force a confrontation: though greatly out-numbered, he clashed with Marlborough in the fields outside Malpla-quet on September 11.

What Marlborough labeled succinctly "a very murdering battle" proved to be the biggest and bloodiest encounter of the entire war. Fifteen thousand French soldiers died that day, and the allies — victors nevertheless — sustained a loss of twenty thousand. (Going into bat-tle, the allies had twenty thousand men more than the French.) "Noth-ing but tears and despairing countenances are to be seen here," Ma-dame wrote from Versailles as news of this fresh defeat arrived. "Misfortune is the rule; one weeps for a son, another for a son-in-law; a third for a father or a nephew." Even in the face of such losses, France enjoyed a victory of sorts: the staggering loss of manpower at Mal-plaquet put an end to the allied hope for an invasion of France. "Never was a lost battle so advantageous and glorious," Adelaide crowed to her grandmother in Turin. "That is to me a great consolation."

Far more doleful a consequence of the battle of Malplaquet was the recall of French troops from Iberia. The move was purely an act of national security. With one sixth of his army wiped out, Louis XIV found that the defense of his own realm no longer allowed for the protection of his grandson's. "In the midst of all the calamities which it has pleased God to inflict upon my kingdom," he wrote sadly, "the war in Spain has become impossible to sustain; it is no longer a ques-tion of personal preference. I stand as a father to my subjects, and I must think of their welfare . . . I am well aware that my reasoning will appear hard to my grandson, the King; but it is more painful to me than to him to be obliged to refuse him assistance when I can see it is so sorely needed. I feel for his needs with all the affection of a parent who has always loved him with a particular love. He will feel for me, also, if he can grasp the state of my kingdom." Philip V felt conflicting emotions, compassion and dismay: eventually he persuaded his grand-father to leave twenty-five battalions in Madrid, not as a fighting force but to guard the royal family and to provide an escort should they be forced to flee Spain.

Christmas 1709 saw the conclusion of eight years of bloody and indecisive warfare. "I never knew such wretched times as these!" Ma-dame bemoaned. "Would to God that a satisfactory peace could be arranged to put an end to this state of things!" Writing Madame Royale on December 9, Adelaide echoed her step-grandmother:

"When will come the long desired day when we can speak frankly on so many things about which we are forced to keep silence now? This war has lasted so long! I believe that all of those who are making it desire its end; and yet, in spite of that, it continues."

"All of those who are making it desire its end" — Adelaide's assessment was more accurate than she knew.

The Dutch leaders had good reason to regret their selfish abortion of the first peace talks: so desperate had the need for peace grown that the province of Utrecht and the city of Amsterdam threatened to cut off all war supplies unless the possibilities of a new conference were immediately investigated. England, sated with Marlborough's phenomenal success, was thoroughly weary of futile continental entanglement. The carnage of Malplaquet had done irreparable damage to the Whig ministry that had allowed it; the government's tenuous hold on power was further jeopardized by Queen Anne's growing estrangement from her former friend and confidante (and ardent Whig), the duchess of Marlborough. "Lord, when will all this bloodshed cease!" had been the queen's reaction to the victory of Oudenarde; quickly it became the cry of all England.

Winston Churchill observed: "The end of 1709 marked the zenith of Britain in Europe, of the Whigs under Queen Anne, and of Marlborough's career. Thereafter, all fell with odd rapidity." Sarah, duchess of Marlborough, was the first to go, dismissed from her post as Mistress of the Robes and banished forever from the queen's presence. The Whig government, under Lord Treasurer Godolphin, quickly fell from power, replaced by a Tory administration that demanded peace; Marlborough himself, after a decade of glorious service, was relieved of command and charged (unjustly) of embezzlement.

The climate seemed propitious for negotiation. On March 10, 1710, the Sun King sued again for peace. Once more his willingness to recognize the Austrian "Carlos III" and even to contribute money to the allied cause in Spain demonstrated his sincerity; once more his magnanimity was insulted. The allies proposed not peace, but a two-month truce — during which the French army *alone* would expel Philip V from Spain. The Sun King published this term and, with universal French support, rejected it outright. Reluctantly, Europe entered another season of stalemated warfare.

There next occurred an event of such appalling irony that in one stroke, an entire decade of war was rendered meaningless. On April 17, 1711, the thirty-two-year-old emperor of Austria, Joseph I, suddenly died of smallpox. He left no direct male heir, and the crown devolved to his younger brother — none other than "Carlos III" of Spain.

The allied leaders were stunned: ten years before, they had gone to war rather than allow one major power to gobble up the entire Spanish Empire. Now their de jure king of Spain was de facto emperor of Austria, and victory would bring about the very thing they had battled to prevent.

News of this bizarre turn of events reached Versailles on April 24. "Last night," Madame wrote, "we received news that the Emperor had died of smallpox . . . What a miracle it would be if this event should bring peace to us!" Torcy himself conveyed the news to the king and Bourgogne. "They hailed it as though it had been a great victory, although the Duc de Bourgogne's conscience prevented him from appearing to rejoice."

Next day, Louis XIV sent word of the emperor's death to the Spanish court at Saragossa (where Queen Maria Luisa was battling unsuccessfully with tuberculosis). "This death is a sign from heaven," exclaimed Philip V. He composed at once a lengthy letter to the new emperor (in Barcelona, where he had recently proclaimed himself king of Spain) offering condolences and proposing a "fair settlement," whereby Karl would assume the throne of Austria and Philip would maintain his crown in Spain. The letter was returned unopened and the emperor persisted in styling himself "king of Spain." But his confederates plainly preferred a Bourbon grandson to a merger of two vast empires under one Hapsburg, and to all Europe it was obvious that peace was finally at hand.

In England, Emperor Joseph's death removed the final Whig argument for continuing the war. "We are all great fools to get ourselves killed for two such boobies [Philip and Karl]," snorted Lord Peterborough. His feelings were shared by Parliament: before the end of the month, it had voted to withdraw from the Grand Alliance. Britain's departure assured an end to the war. At Marly, the Sun King exulted: "This will do for us everything that we could desire."

A preliminary peace agreement was signed between England and France on October 8, 1711. Nine weeks later, Adelaide informed her mother: "The conference will be held at Utrecht, and will begin on the twelfth of next month." She was hopeful, but realistic: "They would not make such advances if they were not veritably resolved to conclude a peace . . . It is only the new emperor who still will not listen to it;

but when he finds himself alone he will surely come to it. They say it is his usual way to make difficulties."

The new emperor, Karl VI, then behaved most usually: persisting with his claim to Spain, he charged his general, Prince Eugene, to continue the war, and coerced the beleaguered Dutch into half hearted assistance. Eugene steadily pushed south through Flanders in the direction of Paris, but his defeat by Villars at Denain on July 24, 1712, so weakened his force that he was compelled to retreat. This French victory rattled the Dutch into opposing the Hapsburg might, and the English government seized its opportunity and at last persuaded the Dutch States-General to come to terms with the Sun King.

On April 11, 1713, after fifteen months of argument and compromise, the powers of Europe — with the notable exception of the emperor of Austria — signed the peace treaty of Utrecht. All prewar territories of France were returned, the Dutch surrendering Lille, Aire, and Bethune to Louis XIV. (The Dutch were allowed to keep control of the rest of the Low Countries until peace with the Austrian Empire could be reached.) Nice was returned to Savoy, and Victor Amadeus was awarded the kingdom of Sicily. France surrendered to England its valuable slave trade monopoly, and Spain ceded Gibraltar and Minorca. After more than a decade on his throne, Philip V was proclaimed throughout Europe the true and only king of Spain.

The difficult Emperor Karl struggled to resist, but his treasury had long been drained and Eugene protested that his paltry force of forty thousand men could not possibly meet with Villars's army, 120,000 strong. On March 6, 1714, the treaty of Rastatt was formalized: in exchange for recognition of Philip V, France restored the occupied territories along the Rhine (except for Strasbourg and Alsace) and agreed to the Austrian occupation of northern Italy and Belgium.

Thirteen years of war had achieved little more than might reasonably have been expected from skillful diplomacy in 1701. Certainly Philip V emerged a winner, the throne at last undisputedly his. Crafty Victor Amadeus had played both sides and won glory beyond his wildest dreams — a throne of his own. Both Austria and England had good reason to rejoice: the emperor, now in control of Milan, Naples, and Belgium, would be the greatest force on the continent for the next quarter century, and Britain, now unquestioned mistress of the seas, had begun her age of phenomenal expansion with the acquisition of Newfoundland and Nova Scotia.

The greatest loser in the War of the Spanish Succession was Louis

XIV. He had accomplished his purpose — his grandson sat firmly on the Spanish throne — but it had cost him his sea power, his economy, and more than one million subjects. He had brought France to dizzying heights; now he watched helplessly as it fell to the wheel of fate. France would not recover from the Sun King's dream of eliminating the Pyrenees until a Corsican general rose from the debris of the Revolution.

19

Mother and Matchmaker

IN APRIL 1709 AT VERSAILLES, as the Grand Canal thawed and trees cautiously sprouted their leaves again, Adelaide discovered that winter and war had brought a change. "There can be no balls," she informed her grandmother, "because there is no one to dance." For one thing, the male population of Versailles was drastically reduced; in addition, "several ladies are pregnant, and those who are lately married come from convents and do not know how to dance." For a princesse who delighted in dancing, it was indeed a privation. "There are but nine ladies who can do so, and half of those are little girls. I should be the old woman at a ball, which takes away all my desire for one." The old woman of twenty-three observed, "I do not know what folly possesses the women now, but at thirty years of age they think they are past dancing; if the fashion lasts, I ought to make the most of the time that is left me."

If dancing partners were now at a dearth, the warmer weather did allow the revival of another passion: riding. Adelaide gathered together a group of noted beauties — the maréchale d'Estrées, Mmes de La Vrillière, Polignac, and Tonerre, and Mlles de Charolais and Listenois (all, like the princesse, superb horsewomen) — and dubbed her band "the King's Amazons." Daily they rode for long hours through the green glades of Versailles and Marly, their cavalcade quickly gaining renown for its beauty, its youth, and its exuberance. Naturally, exclusion from the circle provoked jealousy, and when the Amazons were joined by the bold Mme de Rupelmonde, whom Saint-Simon judged "an intriguing young woman and little concerned to preserve her virtue," gossip spread like brushfire of scandalous afternoons behind locked doors at the menagerie.

The fame — or notoriety — of "the King's Amazons" spread as far as the front: one evening following a long march Maréchal Villars commented that he was tired of riding "like the harlots in the train of the Duchesse de Bourgogne." His flippancy was met with loud guffaws, but somehow the remark filtered back to Versailles, where it met a far different reaction. Adelaide was outraged, and a nasty scandal threatened. Louis XIV demanded an explanation from Villars. The old maréchal was greatly embarrassed and (to his discredit) thrust all blame on one of his subordinates. He accused his aide, d'Heudicourt, of being indiscreet in repeating "words used in mess, among soldiers, and not intended for polite ears." Apparently the king was satisfied with this explanation — or else deemed his general too valuable for sacrifice; with royal sanction, Villars imprisoned the unfortunate scapegoat d'Heudicourt at the fort of Calais, a hard lesson in the compliance demanded of soldiers in the service of the Sun King.

Still, Villars's barb hit a nerve: the incident (plus another pregnancy) put an end to Adelaide's brief career as an Amazon and her group was disbanded with an alacrity equal to that of its formation.

It was not through any lack of effort on Adelaide's part that the little duc de Bretagne was the king's only great-grandson: despite her often expressed fears, she was pregnant at least once a year. When, in March 1708, she found herself again expecting, she immediately gave up horseback riding. In April, she wrote her mother she was "growing visibly stouter," and cautiously took to her bed. Two months later, complications developed and the *accoucheur* Clément was hastily summoned. Although the princesse had no pain, Clément concluded that she had somehow been injured, and two days later she miscarried. How much the deterioration of her condition was due to anxiety — Bourgogne and Vendôme had begun to battle each other as well as the allies — can never be ascertained.

In June 1709, she again suspected herself pregnant; by July she was certain, and an official announcement was made. The king and Mme de Maintenon were naturally delighted. The expectant mother was rather less enthusiastic: "You reproach me," she wrote Madame Royale, "that it is some time since I had a child, and I could not obey you better than by becoming pregnant. Nevertheless, I confess I would have wished not to be so punctual in fulfilling such commands."

The standard precautions were taken. Dangeau noted in his journal on August 15 that the princesse heard Vespers in the royal chapel, but was too "indisposed" to walk in the procession. One month later he wrote that she was "in much better health than during her earlier pregnancies," and save for familiar bouts of morning sickness, Adelaide concurred. "I have been for three days very ill," she informed her grandmother on September 23, "having vomited at intervals, which fatigues me greatly . . . Otherwise, my health is good." She was already sure of the unborn child's gender: "I hope very much to give you another grandson, and I do not doubt it, for I am as I was with the two others."

In October, the deputies of the Estates of Languedoc, under the bishop of Béziers, called at the palace to present their felicitations to the expectant mother, and Adelaide received them from bed. Though the bishop was famed throughout France for his eloquence, the princesse complained afterward that his long speech had "bored her to tears" — a remark that greatly amused the king. Later that same month, the elector of Bavaria arrived for an official visit to Versailles. Louis XIV, wishing to show his precious ally every hospitality, entrusted to Adelaide the task of entertaining her kinsman.[1]

This was a favorite role — one in which she excelled — and she employed all her charms to dazzle the impressionable elector. At their first meeting, she remarked that she was delighted to renew her old acquaintance; surprised, the elector maintained that she could not possibly remember him. Ah no, Adelaide replied with a smile, she had a very clear memory of him sitting in her mother's boudoir and regaling the ladies with his droll imitation of the old emperor. The elector blushed, then laughed, enchanted by the princesse.

"The Duchesse de Bourgogne surpassed herself, and it has already come to our ears that the Elector was charmed," wrote Mme de Maintenon after his return to Bavaria. She insisted however on her share of the credit: "Our princesse owes her success to me; she wished to appear in a scarf, on the pretext that she was pregnant, and in a state of undress which suits her worse than anybody. With much trouble I persuaded her to dress, and even to put on her jewels." Maintenon's efforts were well worth her pains: dressed from head to foot in rose-pink and white, Adelaide was an entrancing sight, though, "in truth, I was surprised: she did not look to be five months gone with child." She didn't look it because she wasn't: Adelaide had miscalculated her dates, and was not as far along as she believed, though of course this would not be known for several months. "Now that I have passed my eighth month," she wrote Madame Royale on December 9 (actually she was in her seventh month), "I am very languishing. The changes of month always affect me in my pregnancies, so that I hope in a few days I shall be over it."

The new year of 1710 opened; believing herself in the final weeks, Adelaide retired to her bed to await delivery. Bourgogne spent his available free time in her rooms, and she flattered her husband's taste for music (a taste she had revived in him, then rapidly came to share) by arranging private concerts in the antechamber, performed by Mssrs Buterne, Descoteaux, Vixe, and Fourcray (her respective teachers of the spinet, flute, lute, and bass viol). The solicitous father-to-be returned the compliment by ordering a small theater to be built in another anteroom. The royal company played there for the princesse's amusement and, with Louis XIV and Mme de Maintenon invariably making an appearance, Adelaide carefully selected the fare herself — *Le Misanthrope* for the king, the tragic *Polyeucte* for Maintenon, and for herself, always a farce.

On January 22, Adelaide felt pain in her kidneys, but this turned out to be a false alarm. Two days later, she supervised a marionette performance for the three-year-old Bretagne, a postbirthday present. The carnival season had begun, but in view of her condition, Louis XIV thoughtfully banned court balls until after his granddaughter's delivery. To compensate the disappointed courtiers, the princesse borrowed an idea from her step-aunt, the duchesse du Maine: small informal dances were held in her apartments which she watched from her bed "without visible fatigue."

By February 5, the miscalculation of dates had become obvious; to distract his impatient wife, Bourgogne arranged the performance of three comedies that week in her little theater. At last, late in the night of the fourteenth, labor pains began. The king had taken to keeping a suit of clothes beside his bed in order to dress quickly; when he arrived in Adelaide's bedroom, Bourgogne and Mme de Maintenon were already present, along with Clément. The labor was painful, and more than one gentleman was compelled to leave the room, unable to watch the princesse suffer. At three minutes past eight in the morning, February 15, 1710, the future King Louis XV was born.

Le Mercure observed that this early morning birth was "enchanting the astrologers, for it has been recognized, from time immemorial, that children born in daylight are more fortunate than those born at night."

With strict attention to etiquette, the new baby — styled the duc d'Anjou on the spot by a beaming great-grandfather — was sprinkled with holy water by the cardinal, wrapped in swaddling clothes, and carried to the nursery in a sedan chair. His birth was heralded at Versailles by the ringing of the great palace bell, and the king ordered Te Deums sung in all the churches of the realm.

He recalled the public disappointment when war reversals had prohibited any major celebration for the baby's older brother in 1707; now, despite his grave economic plight, Louis XIV gave permission for official rejoicing, and the people, in desperate need of good cheer, responded eagerly. They hailed the birth of this prince as an omen of returning peace and prosperity, the perfect issue from "the princesse of peace" they had welcomed in 1696. In Paris, the provost of merchants gave a grand banquet at the Hôtel de Ville, followed by a brilliant fireworks display in the Place de Greve which extolled the three cardinal virtues desired in a prince — wisdom, knowledge, and greatness of soul. There were bonfires in all the principal squares of the city and gun salutes fired hourly along the Seine. However, at Versailles and Marly there were no special court festivities: the public celebrations throughout the land had shown Europe that France was *not* on its knees and the king, prudent for once, saw no need to reinforce the notion at his own expense.

Adelaide was enchanted with her new son. "He is the prettiest child in the world," she bragged to her grandmother, "and I believe he will become a great beauty. Though it is of no consequence after they grow up, one likes better to have a pretty child than an ugly one." For his part, the little duc de Bretagne was put out at being upstaged by a new brother and made no attempt to hide his annoyance.

The baby prince thrived under the skilled care of his governess, the duchesse de Ventadour, but nevertheless Adelaide fretted over his health and progress. "I know that children often withstand illness better than grown-up people," she conceded to Madame Royale, "but that does not stop me, however sensible I try to be, from worrying dreadfully whenever my sons are in the least unwell." She made her first public appearance following her confinement on April 3, driving in state to Meudon for dinner with Monseigneur, but she returned home early to pay a visit to the nursery.

Her maternal instincts were developing steadily, though she was not entirely blinded by mother love. Nine months after Anjou's birth, she penned a charmingly candid progress report to her mother. "I am

always afraid to bore you by talking of my children," she began in-
genuously, then proceeded to do just that. "The elder is getting sense
enough to know he has a grandmother, and that he loves you. He
grows immensely and, consequently, is very thin; he is well-made, but
rather ugly. The little one is not the same; he is a fat dumpling and very
handsome; he will soon have four teeth, and is in fine health. As soon
as he is one year old I will send you his portrait; I dare not have it
painted any earlier, for they say it brings ill-luck. I do not believe that;
but the case of my eldest makes me prefer to risk nothing."

The princesse gradually returned to official obligations; by the end
of May, she had resumed her weekly receptions in the salon at the
menagerie. But the old days of Versailles splendor were past, destroyed
as much by their own cost as by the war. The aging Sun King no longer
maintained much state, more and more seeking refuge from military
and economic woes in the privacy of Marly. By 1710, he was spending
more than a third of the year at his hermitage, justifying such hiber-
nation with the claim that the air at Marly was purer than at Versailles.
He still followed the hunt in his barouche with all his old fervor — in
July 1710, Dangeau recorded a stag chase through a violent rainstorm:
"The ladies came back wet to the bone, and several of them badly
grazed, so ardent was the chase" — but the king was seventy-three and
the years told terribly on him. Harassed by defeat, by famine and
insolvency, he craved the security and comfort of his family circle. In
the past, he had always dined alone at Marly; now he welcomed the
soothing company of Adelaide and Bourgogne, and took unabashed
delight in the endless prattle of a young mother and the occasional
boast of a proud papa.

With the happiness of his oldest grandson's family so apparent, the
king's thoughts soon focused on his youngest grandson's lack of a
mate; thus began Adelaide's brief career as a matchmaker.

The duc de Berri was twenty-four years old, blond like his father,
and — also like the dauphin — tending to overweight, "with a hearty
and rather beautiful face that emanated glowing health." The most
approachable of Monseigneur's three sons, he was thus the most popular and ultimately the most spoiled. Madame always had a soft spot
for this grandnephew and called him "my Berri." His enjoyment of
court life — in which he was so different from the pious, self-critical
Bourgogne — won him the approval of several court factions. Even
Saint-Simon, who pronounced him "rather dull-witted [with] no ideas
or imagination," admitted he was "the best of men, the kindest, the

most compassionate and accessible, lacking in pride and vanity but not in dignity or in awareness of his own rank."

He was devoted to his oldest brother, even more so to his brother's wife. "For the last few years, the Duc de Berri has been entirely taken up with the Duchesse de Bourgogne and her ladies," Madame observed in 1708. Not that she approved: "Since in that circle they have no more notion of good breeding than cows in a cowshed, they treat him like a servant, and he forgets his rank." Adelaide and her ladies petted and fussed over the sweet young man, teasing him good-naturedly; accustomed from birth to the groveling of court sycophants, Berri delighted in their casual disregard for rank and station. Two years after Madame's first observation, she again picked up a critical pen: "Day and night he is to be found in [Adelaide's] rooms, waiting on her ladies as though he were a lackey. One of them makes him bring her a table; another her sewing; a third sends him on an errand. He stands about or perches on a taboret, while the young women loll in armchairs wrapped in shawls or lie full-length on chaises-longues." She feared that such subservience would come to harm him once the young man took a wife or mistress — *if* he were to take such a step. For in the art of love, Berri was surprisingly un-Bourbon: Saint-Simon wrote that the prince had had several opportunities for love affairs, but "had not known how to embark on them, conduct them, or bring them to a successful conclusion."

Berri's position as a Grandson of France entitled him to a foreign bride of royal birth, but for the last eight years, the chief Catholic states of Europe had been at war with France and the two exceptions — Spain and Bavaria — could not produce a princesse of marriageable age. With no end to the war in sight, Louis XIV was forced to lower his standards, and he looked about his own court for a suitable bride.

The choice was soon narrowed down to two princesses (incidentally, both granddaughters of the king and therefore cousins to the bridegroom): seventeen-year-old Louise Elisabeth, Mlle de Bourbon, daughter of Mme la duchesse, and fifteen-year-old Marie Louise Elisabeth d'Orléans (called Mademoiselle by the court), whose parents were the king's nephew, the duc de Chartres, and his other natural daughter by Montespan, Mlle de Blois. (The fact that the mothers of both candidates were illegitimate was much remarked upon, but accepted as an indication of the dearth of appropriate young ladies.)

Instantly, the court split into factions. Mme la duchesse naturally favored her own daughter and was joined in this by her stepbrother the dauphin and the remnants of the Meudon cabal. Adelaide had other ideas: she dearly loved her young brother-in-law and feared that an alliance with Mlle de Bourbon would take him from her side and force him into the Meudon camp. She also had a personal reason for supporting Mademoiselle's candidacy: more than anyone, Adelaide understood the power that novelty held over the Sun King — her own case being a prime example — and she dreaded a possible rivalry with the high-spirited Mlle de Bourbon. Mademoiselle was not ugly, but she possessed few qualities that might endear her to the old king, making her an infinitely safer choice. Finally, the young girl and her parents had always been friendly to Adelaide and Bourgogne, and the princesse wished in particular to compensate Chartres for his unfailing support at the time of the cabal controversy.

Ordinarily, Mademoiselle would have had immediate preference over Mlle de Bourbon, being a daughter of the head of the younger branch of the royal family. But this did not take into account family feelings. Louis XIV's relationship with his nephew — never an easy one — had been of late more strained than ever: ugly rumors had surfaced that, during his two Spanish campaigns, Chartres had conspired with the imperial forces to grab the throne for himself and, despite his nephew's fierce denial of the charge, the king was not yet fully convinced of his innocence. Mme de Maintenon detested Chartres (who was, after all, the son of her archenemy, Madame) and her feelings would play no small role in the decision. Then there was the age factor and, because Mlle de Bourbon was two years older and closer in age to the duc de Berri, it was assumed by most at the court that ultimately she would be chosen.

Saint-Simon wildly opposed an alliance with Mlle de Bourbon and claimed afterward that he aroused in Adelaide a sense of "her great duty to herself, which was in danger of being stifled" should the Meudon faction gain so strong a foothold in the royal circle. Certainly the diarist did work tirelessly in the ensuing contest, yet no one but Adelaide, through her sheer persistence, could have successfully overcome the objections of so formidable a trio as the king, his wife, and his son.

She opened her campaign with a clever ploy. One spring evening, she brought along the young Mademoiselle when paying her nightly visit to Mme de Maintenon, knowing the king and Monseigneur would be present as well. As they sat together, Adelaide loudly praised the girl to her face; Mademoiselle blushed becomingly and, once she had taken her leave, the duchesse de Bourgogne remarked casually that she would make a perfect wife for Berri. Monseigneur swallowed the bait: flushed and angry, he snapped that "indeed that would be a fine way to punish his cousin for his misconduct in Spain," and stormed out of the room. Adelaide feigned astonishment. Turning to Mme de Maintenon, she artfully asked, "*Ma tante*, have I said something stupid?" The king was irritated by his son's unwarranted outburst and had no doubt who was fueling this cousinly enmity. He remarked sharply that if Mme la duchesse continued to spread her vile gossip and influence her stepbrother, she would find herself in serious trouble.

After so victorious an opening, Adelaide worked tirelessly to promote her candidate. Despite the heavy demands of her station, she took Mademoiselle under her wing, preparing the girl for the great position she felt, with growing confidence, would one day be hers.

Predictably, Mme de Maintenon was the first to surrender to Adelaide's persuasions, and the old lady's acquiescence ensured that of the king. Under Saint-Simon's careful direction, Adelaide made her final move: with Maintenon in tow, she drove to Meudon and called upon Emilie Joly to enlist her support and to personally explain why Mademoiselle should be selected. The dauphin's secret wife was transparently delighted that the princesse should ask for her assistance, and the subsequent pressure she exerted at last compelled her husband to consent.

The engagement was announced on June 2, 1710, to the delight of all but Mme la duchesse. The duc and duchesse de Chartres at once called upon Monseigneur with their congratulations and found him still at table with Adelaide and Bourgogne. There were kisses and embraces, and many toasts for the future fathers-in-law and the affianced couple. "The Duchesse de Bourgogne, perfectly radiant, enlivened the whole party," Saint-Simon wrote, "and the Duc de Bourgogne, so glad of the marriage and to see it so happily arranged, lifted the elbow with such joyful utterances that the next day he could hardly believe he had made them."

The bride's grandmother, Madame, was next to hear the news:

This evening, about seven o'clock . . . the Duchesse de Bourgogne, with her ladies and her husband, came running in exclaiming, "We bring you the Duc de Berri, because the King has just announced that he is to marry Mademoiselle. The King is coming to tell you, and Monseigneur also. We have come on ahead." I replied at once, "As soon as I too may speak, let me assure you, Madame, that I shall always be grateful for all the trouble you took to bring this affair to a happy conclusion. I also know," I said, turning to the Duc de Bourgogne, "that you too have wished for it; and for that I thank you a thousand times." To the Duc de Berri I said, "Come and kiss me. Now you are more than ever 'Madame's boy,' as the Dauphine used to say. I shall keep you close in my heart and love you dearly; but I am too old to see you often, for I can no longer assist you. Be merry and contented, and I shall rejoice in your happiness."

The engagement was a triumph for Adelaide, further proof of the unassailable strength of her position at court. She busied herself with wedding preparations, and found the king placing more responsibility in her capable hands. "The Duchesse de Bourgogne becomes more sensible every day," Mme de Maintenon proudly wrote the duc de Noailles, June 13. "She is to be trusted with the feeding and education of the Duchesse de Berri, who for some time is not to have an establishment of her own."

Like the birth of Anjou five months earlier, the approaching royal wedding did much to boost the sagging morale of the nation and the court. "There is no talk of anything here but the marriage of the Duc de Berri," Adelaide informed her grandmother on June 23. "Though it will take place without any ceremony (for the times do not allow amusements or great expenses), all the ladies are none the less busy with their finery." Such preoccupation had never much appealed to the princesse, who complained: "This does not render conversation very lively . . . for really nothing is talked of but headdresses, costumes, petticoats, and milliners, and though I am a woman, I never take much pleasure in such discussions."

By the end of the month her patience with this "frivolous chatter" had been exhausted: "I have a great desire for the wedding to take place and end all discussions about it. They are only waiting for the dispensation from Rome [for the first cousins to marry]." Just as tiresome were the long-winded compliments presented by all the diplomatic corps: after an entire afternoon of pedantic speeches, Adelaide was heard to whisper to her husband, "How fortunate one doesn't get married every day!"

The wedding was set for July 6. The evening of the fifth, the bridal couple signed their marriage contract in Adelaide's bedroom before the entire family. The groom declared his bride to be "the prettiest person in the world . . . Helen of Troy was not half so beautiful!"

Madame, of course, disagreed: "In point of fact, she is not pretty at all, either in face or figure. She is thick-set, with long arms and short hips; her discontented face is marked by smallpox; she has red eyes, a ruddy complexion, and looks much older than she is." Lest she be thought too harsh, she hastened to add: "What is perfectly beautiful about her is her throat, her hands and her arms, which are very white and well-formed."

The Berri wedding, in contrast to that of Adelaide and Bourgogne thirteen years earlier, was a quiet, simple affair. "The Duc de Berri was married yesterday," Adelaide wrote on July 7, 1710. "It was all as magnificent as the season and the times would allow. There was no fête." The bride and groom dined alone with the princesse in her private rooms, then spent the afternoon playing cards in the Salon of Peace.

Marriage to a royal grandson gave the new duchess precedence over her formidable grandmother; artfully, the girl cooed, "Push me forward, Madame, so as to propel me in front of you. I need time to grow accustomed to that honor." But in truth, she needed little pushing. Now that she had attained the position she desired, the shy and simple demeanor was cast aside, and the true nature of her character emerged. Adelaide and Saint-Simon quickly came to regret their handiwork. "If I had known," sighed the little duke, "the half-quarter — what do I say? — the thousandth part of what we have unhappily been the witnesses to . . ."

As quickly as he had fallen in love, poor Berri fell out, and small wonder. "His great love for her, plus his natural kindness and accommodation, did not take long in spoiling her completely . . . He had to deal with a proud, haughty and pig-headed woman, who despised him and let him know it . . . She made herself unbearable by bragging about her vices, mocking religion and jeering at Berri because he was pious."

Among her many failings (and Saint-Simon averred that "except for avarice, she was the incarnation of all the vices") were intemperance and gluttony: at the very first reception Adelaide held in her honor, the girl drank till she passed out. Madame recounted:

The Duchesse de Berri fainted dead away. We thought it was a stroke, but when the Duchesse de Bourgogne poured some vinegar over her face, she returned to her senses and began to vomit most abominably. Who could wonder? — after hours of continuous stuffing with glazed

peaches, chestnuts, a confection of red currants and cranberries, dried
cherries, with quantities of lemonade, and then fish for supper and
wine on top of that. She had felt sick, had tried to restrain herself, and
had fainted. She has recovered today; but though I tell her that she
will really be ill one day if she overeats so gluttonously, she will not
heed me.

The dutiful granddaughter had disappeared along with the dutiful
bride, and by September Madame noted: "The Duchesse de Berri
comes often to see me because it is the King's and my son's wish, but
she does not really care for me."

The new duchess degenerated from bad to worse, and Saint-Simon
painfully chronicled the misdeeds of this "Messalina of Versailles":

> At each of the many informal meals she took, she became dead drunk,
> and threw up whatever she had eaten; she even berated Berri for not
> keeping up with her . . . She lost no time in having affairs, which
> were conducted so indiscreetly that her husband found out about
> them . . . She often treated her father with an arrogance that had
> many frightening implications [it was widely believed that they were
> involved in an incestuous affair]. Her daily and interminable sessions
> with her father, where it was clear that her husband was not wanted,
> put him in a rage, and there were many stormy scenes between
> them . . . She did all she could to make M. de Berri, who was gen-
> uinely pious and completely honest, give up religion. She persecuted
> him for his diligent and self-sacrificing observance of lean and fast
> days. She mocked him so that sometimes he broke the fast, and
> embarrassed him by her acid jests. Since she could not convince him
> without arguments that brought out how painfully scrupulous he
> was, she scoffed all the more and added to his grief.

Gluttony and drunkenness were deplorable, but ever present at Versailles. So too was extramarital dalliance. However, Louis XIV drew
the line at irreverence, and very quickly the duchesse de Berri found
herself at odds with the king and his wife. "Last Tuesday, I went to see
the all-powerful lady," Madame wrote in October. "She told me to
send away my ladies. This was serious; my heart began beating, for I
thought she was about to scold me." Maintenon came directly to the
point. "The King had told my son and his wife to watch over the
conduct of their daughter, and he had said nothing to me thinking that
I should do so naturally, but hearing lately that I had said nothing to

her, he had ordered Mme de Maintenon to tell me, from him, that I was to speak severely to the young woman."

For once, the two adversaries were in agreement:

"Although it will be a painful thing," I replied, "yet I will do my best to please His Majesty in this matter; this will show him that I am always ready to obey him in all things, but I hope that His Majesty will inform the Duchesse de Berri that I speak to her by his desire; this will impress what I say more powerfully on her." He did so . . . That same evening the father, mother, and daughter came to see me. I began on the matter immediately, thus: "My dear child, you are aware that I have only scolded you once since your marriage; I had never meant to do so again, but the King has ordered me to speak to you, and explain to you why he did not take you to the hunt the other day; the reason of it is that you have seriously displeased him by your conduct . . . I will not speak to you of the Lord God; I leave that to your confessor. I will only remark that it is very bad taste in a person of your age to boast of your disbelief in the Divinity. You do not only arouse God's anger, but cause men to despise you. I do not tell you all this from ill-humor or from anger, but only in obedience to the King, and because your father's kindness and your mother's laziness prevent their reproving you when you behave foolishly by drinking overmuch, contradicting the King, ill-treating your husband, and quarreling with the Duchesse de Bourgogne."

The girl responded to this tongue-lashing with meek contrition, and Madame was able to report success to Maintenon. But the repentence was painfully short-lived, and in no time at all the duchesse de Berri had again incurred the royal wrath. "How annoying and tiresome are obstinate children!" Madame cried in January 1711. "After having spent the whole of Tuesday morning scolding the Duchesse de Berri, and explaining to her how to ask pardon of the King, she ended by answering, 'I should have indeed a bad memory, Madame, if I forget all that you have told me.' "

Her conduct became so outrageous that the king banned her from his presence, and the girl's distraught mother begged for her readmission. The plea was met with a qualified refusal, and once again Madame was called into the fray:

I followed the King into his cabinet; "I hope that Your Majesty will forgive my following you without being invited," I said. "I will go away the moment I have finished what I came to say . . . My son and his wife inform me that you will not receive the Duchesse de Berri, nor allow her to beg your forgiveness for having displeased you, till I have joined my entreaties to theirs. This is what I have come to do." "What, Madame, do you advise me to already receive Mme de Berri?" "It is not my place to advise you," said I, laughing, "but I beg of Your Majesty to afford that consolation to Mme de Berri, for she has been truly punished."

Madame had always enjoyed a special place in her brother-in-law's heart, and Louis XIV eventually relented: " 'Your advice is good, and is worthy of your good sense. I will receive Mme de Berri tomorrow evening, you can tell her this.' "

As before, their reconciliation was brief. Fear of the Sun King kept a rein on Mme de Berri's excesses, not fully unleashed until after Louis XIV's death and her father's assumption of the regency. Adelaide watched the disintegration of the Berri marriage with great sorrow and resolved never to play matchmaker again.

Ironically, the scandalous conduct of the duchesse de Berri had one positive result: its diametric contrast to the propriety and fine character of the duchesse de Bourgogne served to augment the national love affair with Adelaide and greatly enhanced her prestige at Versailles. More than one courtier breathed a sigh of relief that the future belonged not to the Berris, but to the Bourgognes. The fact that Monseigneur still barred the way to King Louis and Queen Adelaide was one that many, in secret, deplored. No one could foresee, as the year 1710 faded, that this obstacle would soon be eliminated.

20

"I Shall Be Their Queen"

FEW FRENCHMEN ALIVE in 1711 could recall a time when Louis XIV had not been king. In May of that year he would celebrate the sixty-eighth anniversary of his accession, and though he had reached the venerable (and considering the medical practices of the era, astonishing) age of seventy-two, his health remained good and his faculties still intact. His immediate heir was no longer young — the dauphin would turn fifty that year — and except for one serious illness in 1701 (brought on "by eating too much fish" in Lent), had never known a day's sickness in his life. Monseigneur's heir was a vigorous young man of twenty-seven with two sons of his own. The Sun King took great pride in pointing out that the succession to the French throne had not been "so well assured for centuries."

Within the space of fifteen months, the royal family of France would all but disappear, the "well assured" succession left to its sole survivor, a child of two.

The new year opened, like so many others, with martial preparations for a spring campaign as the war dragged on inconclusively. The denizens of Versailles, having borne two years of privation, struggled to revive some vestige of their former glory. Carnival season opened, demanding banquets and balls, hunting and card parties; till Lent at least the palace sparkled as before. Adelaide's time was divided between presiding as first lady of the court and giving solace to the old king and his wife in the privacy of their family circle. The circle still held irritants, to be sure — the duchesse de Berri for one, and the vicious-tongued Mme la duchesse. But as the Sun King sank into twilight, he simply banished unpleasantries from sight. Factions and rivalries had become tiresome, so too the call for regal splendor; how much more pleasant to sit by the fire, while Bourgogne played or sang, and Adelaide and Maintenon discussed the children over needlework.

The dauphin's prolonged absences from the court had increased in recent years. He had displayed scant interest in the affairs of state — nor had he ever been encouraged otherwise — and in government circles his presence was scarcely missed; the king, absorbed with the Bourgognes and their growing brood, hardly minded the absence of his timid son. Shut off from the power and responsibility of Versailles, though never from its pleasures — he continued to hunt there several times each week — and cursed (it appeared) with an everlasting father on earth as well as in heaven, Monseigneur retired to his estate at Meudon, the only kingdom fate would allow him, and into a private circle more impenetrable even than his father's. He carved a realm all his own: his "consort" Emilie Joly at his side (her ample bosom still supplying him percussion), his widowed stepsisters, the princesse de Conti and Mme la duchesse (M. le duc had died in 1710) as constant companions, frequent visits from his favorite son, young Berri, and a retinue of devoted servants to provide for every need. He rode or hunted daily, made constant excursions to the Paris Opéra, and still derived great pride from his reputation for giving the finest entertainments outside of Versailles. By and large, he approached his middle years craving quiet domesticity and the joys of simple country living. The defeat of the Meudon cabal three years before had soured him forever to political intrigue, and as his father lived on — and on and on — he came to accept that he would be, at best, a stopgap king, a brief interlude between Louis *le Grand* and Bourgogne. Mme la duchesse might continue to scheme and dream, her resentment of Adelaide growing each year, but her brother had at last settled into the life of a country squire.

He drove to Versailles on April 5, 1711, Palm Sunday, to attend services with the royal family and remained at court for three days. On Wednesday the eighth he returned to Meudon, accompanied by the duchesse de Bourgogne.

Along the way, they spied a priest bearing the Holy Sacrament. The pious dauphin immediately halted the carriage, stepped down, and knelt to pray before the Host. He inquired where the priest was heading and was told the Sacrament was intended for a sick man in the nearby village, a victim of the smallpox epidemic that had raged through Europe for several months past. Monseigneur had suffered a mild case of smallpox as a child — so mild that his doctors felt he was, in all probability, still susceptible to the disease. This country priest's mission seemed to upset the dauphin terribly; that evening, he remarked to his physician, Boudin, that it would not surprise him if he contracted smallpox himself. The epidemic had claimed many victims in France, he noted; why not the heir to the throne?

The next morning, he rose early to hunt, but suddenly fainted while he was dressing. Boudin put him to bed at once and sent a messenger to inform the king. Already Monseigneur was running a high temperature, but Boudin stressed firmly that there was no cause for alarm. The king received his message returning from mass; he flippantly remarked that no doubt Monseigneur was suffering from indigestion, and left the palace for the afternoon at Marly.

Adelaide was still at Meudon, where she was quickly joined by Bourgogne. Neither had ever been particularly well treated by the ailing dauphin; Adelaide, even more than her husband, felt no great love for the Meudon clique, but Saint-Simon made plain their determination to forget past slights and offer solace and assistance. Adelaide, he wrote, "cannot have been deeply grieved by what her mind must have told her was a possibility, but she fulfilled all the duties of a daughter-in-law, and fed [the dauphin] with her own hands," while Bourgogne, "always careful to do his duty, did it now in full measure, and despite grave suspicions of smallpox, which he had not had, refused to leave Monseigneur's beside." That afternoon the prince wrote to King Philip, apprising him of their father's condition: "You will be extremely anxious, my dearest brother, when you read this letter; but I trust that by that time we shall be free from worry."

By Friday morning, the dauphin had worsened and the doctors admitted at last that it was indeed smallpox. Word was sent at once to Louis XIV at Versailles. Immediately following mass, the king (whose fearlessness in the face of infection was well known) and Mme de Maintenon departed for Meudon. Adelaide and her husband greeted the king, who ordered them to leave Meudon at once to avoid contagion. Back at Versailles, they found themselves mobbed by anxious courtiers; Bourgogne announced they could supply no information except that the king had banned from Meudon anyone who had not suffered the disease.

Louis XIV installed himself in an apartment above Monseigneur's. Daily, he spent long hours in the sickroom, watching silently as Emilie

Joly nursed his son, relieved for brief intervals by Mme la duchesse or the princesse de Conti. The court at Versailles waited breathlessly for each successive courier, wondering in whispers what fate held in store for the heir.

The Sun King, who allowed neither illness nor death to interrupt the workings of state, deputized his oldest grandchildren to preside over and maintain the court. They complied, albeit less than wholeheartedly. "The Duc and Duchesse de Bourgogne held open Court," Saint-Simon remembered, "and all the courtiers were there assembled, all Paris flowed in; and as discretion and caution were never French qualities, all Meudon came too, and people were believed on their word that they had not entered Monseigneur's apartments. *Lever* and *coucher,* dinner and supper with the ladies, public conversations after each meal, walks in the gardens — these were the times to pay court, and the apartments could not hold the crowd." [1] Although couriers arrived every fifteen minutes, bringing "hope and confidence" that "the course of the malady [was] all that could be wished," the eyes of Versailles focused not on Meudon, but on the king's young deputies, admiring "the majesty and cheerful gravity of the Prince and Princesse, their cordial greeting to all, their continual attention to speak to everyone amiably among the crowd . . . In this way, five days went by; each individual thinking ceaselessly of future contingencies, and trying in advance to adjust himself to any event."

While efficiently discharging their new obligations, the prince and princesse fretted dreadfully at the king's prolonged stay at Meudon. "I have taken the liberty to write to the King regarding something of even greater importance to the State than the health of Monseigneur," Bourgogne wrote Mme de Maintenon over the weekend.

> You will readily understand that I mean his own well-being. There is no one who does not tremble when he considers that the King is all the time in danger from bad airs, not only of smallpox, but of other diseases that are equally malignant and even more to be feared. I realize, Madame, that the King has a duty to his family; indeed, I am only too well aware of it by the order he gave me not to approach him. But I also know that he owes still more to his subjects, and that if their vote were taken, he would not unnecessarily expose himself to a risk, from which God, I trust, will protect him, but which nonetheless is very real.

Adelaide's note to Maintenon, written at the same time, indicated that her relationship with the old Sun King was, if anything, stronger than ever: "I am beside myself but much more on the King's account and your own than on account of Monseigneur, for I have an idea he will get over it easily. We will see how it can be managed that I see the King, for in truth I have no great desire to enter the house. I make the same reflection for myself as for you, that if ill should befall me I should gain no thanks from anyone. I must, however, see the King, otherwise Versailles will become unbearable. For me the spot where the King is not is lifeless." A visit with his precious darling was no less imperative for old Grandpapa, though Bourgogne was compelled to remonstrate to Mme de Maintenon: "Pray, Madame, reflect on all that I must think and fear, loving her as I do, if I see her going to Meudon, and believe that only the King's gratification could prevail over my disquiet." Good sense prevailed in the end: the princesse was ordered to remain at Versailles.

Monseigneur's condition had improved by the thirteenth, and he received a deputation of the fishwives of Paris, with whom he was extremely popular and who had walked all the way to Meudon to see him. "They threw themselves at the foot of the bed, which they kissed several times, and, in their joy, declared that they would have a Te Deum sung when they returned to Paris." Enormously touched by their devotion, the dauphin smiled weakly but remarked that it was still too early for celebration.

The next day he took a turn for the worse and by the afternoon of the fifteenth had lapsed into unconsciousness.

The doctors kept the king and Mme de Maintenon ignorant of Monseigneur's relapse. Louis XIV was at table and "nearly fell backward" when his own physician rushed in crying that all was lost. The king bolted from the table and ran to his son's room, but was stopped at the door by the princesse de Conti. She confessed to her father that the dauphin could no longer recognize anyone. With numb compliance, he remained outside in the anteroom, joined soon by Mme de Maintenon.

"What a sight met my eyes!" she related afterward to the princesse des Ursins. "The king was sitting on a daybed, dry-eyed, but shaking from head to foot, surrounded by the weeping members of his family and their people. It seems that before my arrival he had tried to enter his dying son's bedroom three or four times, terrified lest he should expire before Père Tellier was able to give him Extreme Unction." Mme de Maintenon urged their return to Versailles, since the doctors had conceded the dauphin was past help, but Louis XIV refused to leave.

Last rites were administered to the insensible patient; at seven that evening, Monseigneur appeared to be sinking. Shortly after eleven, April 15, 1711, the dauphin, "the son of a king and father of kings, but himself never a king," expired.

Only then did Louis XIV leave his station outside the deathroom. He tried to weep but tears would not come; in a dry, broken voice, he ordered a carriage and sent word to Versailles that he was driving on to Marly, but wished to meet for a moment with Adelaide as he passed through the village outside the château. A grief-struck servant thoughtlessly brought round Monseigneur's personal coach. Louis XIV glanced at the familiar carriage, shuddered, then quietly asked the driver to bring him a different one. As he drove from the Meudon courtyard for the last time, a crowd of servants and household officers lunged at his coach. "Have compassion!" they cried, "we have lost our master, and will starve to death!" But the Sun King saw and heard nothing, and the carriage clattered through the gates and down the road.[2]

News of Monseigneur's death reached Versailles within the hour; stunned courtiers instinctively flocked to the Bourgognes' apartments. "I quickly dressed and rushed over," Madame recounted.

> I found the most harrowing scene imaginable. The Duc and Duchesse de Bourgogne looked stunned and deathly pale, neither of them saying a word. The Duc and Duchesse de Berri lay on the floor, leaning their elbows on one of the daybeds and sobbing so loud that the noise could be heard three rooms away. My son and his wife wept silently, and did what they could to quiet the Berris. Ladies were sitting on the floor all around the Duchesse de Bourgogne, and they too were weeping. I accompanied the Berris to their apartments, and they went to bed, but didn't cease to weep.

Madame intended to race to Marly and offer solace to her brother-in-law, but "the Duchesse de Bourgogne told me that the King had forbidden any of his family to go to Marly that night; we were to wait until next morning." She left the scene of desolation at half past two, but Saint-Simon wrote that the lamentations continued till seven in the morning, when the duc de Beauvilliers arrived and ordered all assembled to bed.

Throughout the night, Adelaide's bearing was "so adroitly composed of pity, compassion and concern" that it was universally read as deep sorrow. She did not suffer altogether a want of real emotion, but it was less for the death of her father-in-law than for its effect on her husband. Bourgogne suffered the devastation common to children at odds with their parents during life, suddenly racked with guilt at their death. His conscience dictated that he immediately inform his brother in Spain, but the task proved too difficult: "The subject of this letter is so dreadful, my dear brother, that I have not the strength to tell you of it. I share your grief, which will only be too much like my own." He sat at one side of the room, reliving the sorrows of the past, deathly pale and weeping silently. His wife tightly gripped his arm, pressing a lace handkerchief discreetly into his hand, and now and then dabbing at her own eyes.

When she retired to a private room in order to dress for her rendezvous with the king, Adelaide was served by one of her ladies, Mme de Levis, who cynically remarked to her mistress that "since she had no reason for affliction, playacting would be horribly out of place." Adelaide replied with quiet dignity that "there was no question of playacting; she was touched by the pity and the pathos of the scene; she responded out of seemliness, and that was all." Her conduct throughout the coming days was perfectly correct, and no more; one admires her honesty in sparing the court an embarrassing display of grief that would have fooled no one. False sentiment was not in her character. "I have truly been touched by the death of Monseigneur," she wrote her old friend, Françoise d'Aubigné, "but I am reconciled to it like the others; like everyone else, I shall soon recover."

Louis XIV had asked to meet with Adelaide in the avenue near the stables. Just before one in the morning, a message arrived that the king was approaching. Saint-Simon watched the princesse gather up her scarf and shawl, and with her ladies, descend the Grand Staircase. "She bore herself with her usual grace, erect and resolute, her eyes scarcely moist, but betraying her inner turmoil by the stealthy glances which she cast around her."

The reunion, after six days apart, proved brief: while Louis XIV's need for consolation from his darling overshadowed his standard caution for her well-being, his wife was not so impractical. As Adelaide approached their carriage, Mme de Maintenon's voice broke the still night air: "What are you doing, Madame? Do not come near us, we are infectious!" The chastened king mumbled that he would speak with her at Marly in the morning, and Adelaide returned to the palace.

After a few hours of troubled sleep, the Bourgognes left Versailles and joined the king at Marly. They were as shaken by his appearance as was Madame, who had arrived some hours before them: "He is a prey to such affliction that he would soften a rock. He does not fret, however, he speaks to everyone with a resigned sadness, and gives his orders with a great firmness, but the tears come to his eyes every moment, and he stifles his sobs." There were no tears (to the great surprise of his suite) at the first meeting with his heir, but when the chief ministers appeared soon afterward, the king broke down, and Beauvilliers noted that his voice was so choked he could barely be heard.

The body was interred that same day at Saint-Denis. As always with the death of kings and princes, there were rumors of foul play, and the haste of the funeral (due in fact to the body's putrefaction and the misplaced fear of contagion) further fueled the gossipers. A lampoon appeared in Paris, accusing Mme de Maintenon of poisoning the dauphin: "Ce-git le Sire de Meudon, / Qui vécut sans ambition, / Et mourut sans confession, / Dépêché par la Maintenon." ("Here lies the master of Meudon, / Who lived without ambition, / And died without confession, / Polished off by Maintenon.")

Louis XIV and Mme de Maintenon remained in seclusion at Marly for four days, seeing no one but Adelaide and Bourgogne. When the king reemerged on April 19, it was only to announce his intention to stay at Marly for yet another three months (though a list of invited guests was posted soon after).

There were, however, official calls of condolence to be received, and on April 20, the king returned to Versailles to face the court. Standing beside his desk, dressed in mourning costume, Louis XIV remained impassive as the black-robed courtiers filed past with their curtsies and bows. Crowds of Parisians flooded the château, on this day guaranteed admission to the royal presence, and the procession seemed interminable. At sundown the exhausted monarch returned to Marly to regarner strength for subsequent delegations. Wisely these were crammed into a single (though overwhelming) day: a week later Louis received the entire diplomatic corps, the papal nuncio, special envoys from the greater and lesser powers of Europe, the provost of Paris, and delegates from the parlement, the Chamber of Accounts, the Grand Council of State, the Académie Française, and the guilds and corporations of Paris.

Each lengthy address read in the throne room was immediately repeated in the Salon of Nobles for the king's new heirs. The beleaguered prince and princesse had every reason to deplore the revival of this ancient custom, suspended since the days of Henri II; Dangeau noted that they returned to Marly that evening "much fatigued by listening to the great number of speeches, although they said that many had been extremely eloquent." (Characteristically, Bourgogne refused to see the delegation of actors, maintaining they were "persons useless to the state.")

That evening, after his wife had retired for a night of well-earned sleep, the new heir wrote his feelings candidly to his brother:

> I wrote only a brief word to you, my dearest brother, on the fifteenth of this month, regarding the tragedy that has come upon us. I do not doubt that, with your kind heart, you have been deeply afflicted, and I am sure that you have felt for me also. I have been deeply shocked and profoundly stirred, and was unwell for several days, that is to say I was listless, and without appetite. God be thanked I am better now.
>
> This is a blow from the hand of Him whom we must submissively adore . . . I know, my dear brother, that you were well-assured of Monseigneur's affection; it was not by my intention that I did not enjoy the same love . . .

Louis XIV ordered official mourning for one year, but as Saint-Simon remarked: "Never was mourning briefer than that which followed the death of this prince, and as to the King no man so reluctant to give way to his feelings found himself so promptly restored to his normal state." It was not, as some have unfairly judged, that the king was unmoved by his son's death. By making himself the incarnation of the state, Louis XIV surrendered the personal grief that is the right of every private individual; furthermore, he insisted that those who shared his charmed existence share also his stoicism. Courtly activities resumed almost at once, and six weeks after Monseigneur's death, the ban was raised on all gambling except lansquenet. Only the doors of the royal theater remained shut, a tribute to the late heir's generous patronage. Within three months, Monseigneur was forgotten.

The Sun King's obsession with correctness of form had caused him instant concern on the proper title for his new heir. The very day Monseigneur was laid to rest, Louis XIV raised this subject to his council. Strictly speaking, the dauphin was the oldest son of the reigning monarch, thus the heir to the throne; could Bourgogne, as grandson of the reigning monarch, properly assume the same title? Precedents in the case were inconclusive: historically, French kings had granted the title *only* to oldest sons. On those occasions when the heir had been someone else — a cousin or a brother — he kept his original title until the moment of accession (for example, the founder of the Bourbon dynasty, Henri IV, cousin of the last Valois king, had remained Henri of Navarre till he took the throne).

It was Torcy in the end who confirmed the king's own inclination, pointing out that since no one now stood between the duc de Bourgogne and the king, the title dauphin did apply.

The king's next question was not so easily resolved, but was pondered and debated on in council for an entire week. At issue was the proper form of address in conversation. The late dauphin had always been addressed as Monseigneur, but the title had no base in history. Louis XIV had first employed it as an endearment and since his son's correct title, "Monsieur," applied also to the king's brother, the duc d'Orléans, "Monseigneur" had conveniently served to avoid confusion.

Half a century of usage had given the title a certain cachet, and Louis XIV proposed to bestow it formally on his grandson. The council disagreed and, in the end, the king settled on "Monsieur le dauphin."

The real motivation behind the council's stand was doubtless hidden from the king: for years, Louis XIV's bastards had pushed to elevate their status at Versailles, to the disgust of all but their royal parent. They had appropriated "Monseigneur" for their own use, subtly insinuating their connection to the legitimate Son of France and, because the title had no official place in the rules of etiquette, their presumption had gone unopposed. The council removed all prestige from the term by refusing to confer it on Bourgogne, and their neat turn of the tables, done in strict adherence to the Sun King's own rules, delighted the court.

The new heir's own feelings appeared ambivalent. "You will have heard that the King thinks it best that I should assume the title of Dauphin," he wrote Philip, "which reminds me at all moments of the loss I have sustained." For her part, the new "Madame la dauphine" was enormously gratified by the elevation and deeply moved when the king, to demonstrate his affection and his confidence, granted to her all the dignities enjoyed by the late Queen Marie Thérèse — dignities never before conferred on a dauphine. With baroque imagination, these honors were manifested by three symbols — the ship, the padlock, and the wand — and were presented to Marie Adelaide with great ceremony. The ship, representing dominion over the seas, was an exquisite miniature done entirely in silver, which housed the royal saltcellar, table linen, and serving plates. The padlock, French dominion on land, was a thickly jeweled casket containing the late queen's cutlery, and the wand, a scepter symbolizing Adelaide's station, was presented to be carried by the royal maître d'hôtel.

To befit their new station, Bourgogne was offered his father's monthly pension of fifty thousand livres. His response, which met with enormous approval both at Versailles and in Paris, was characteristic: he declined the increase, declaring himself content with his present allowance of twelve thousand a month and asked that the vacant pension be applied instead to the needs of the state. As dauphin, he was obliged to increase his household suite, and he engaged many of his late father's servants.[3] Yet apart from this augmentation of outer trappings, there was little change in the life-style of the new heir to the throne.

There was, however, a tremendous personal change in the duc de Bourgogne. In 1710, less than a year before Monseigneur's death, the duc de Beauvilliers asked Saint-Simon to write a detailed evaluation of the prince's character. (Whether or not Beauvilliers was aware of the little duke's considerable ability as a diarist is open to question; nevertheless, his choice was an inspired one.) Saint-Simon was conscientious in his objectivity; while he did not hesitate to praise Bourgogne for his "keen spirit — active, piercing, stiffening itself against difficulties, and literally superior in all directions," he noted that the prince "felt his faults, acknowledged them and sometimes with such vexation that he recalled their fury."

Greatest of these faults, Saint-Simon believed, was the prince's obsessive piety, his remorseless struggle to lead the perfect Christian life: "This desire for perfection, the ignorance, the fear, the little discernment which always accompanies a dawning devotion, made him excessive . . . inspired him with an austerity which exaggerated everything, and gave him a constrained and, without his knowing it, censorious air." He recalled a Christmas court at Marly, when Bourgogne adamantly refused to attend a ball on the Epiphany since "he believed that he ought not profane it by turning from the duties he owed to so holy a day to a spectacle which, at the best, was only endurable on ordinary occasions." Not even the king (who was greatly annoyed) had been able to sway his grandson, and as Saint-Simon dryly observed: "It was useless to put out to him that, having given the morning and the afternoon to the services of the Church, and several other hours to prayer in his cabinet, he could, and ought, to give up his evening with the respect and compliance of a son and subject." It was this reconciliation between his private inclinations and his public duty as prince and heir that Saint-Simon felt demanded the most urgent attention.

And that was precisely what happened after Monseigneur's death. While the dauphin lived and the cabal flourished, while the prospects of Monseigneur's rule threatened to blight his own career, Bourgogne had been forced into constraint and fear. Now, enemies dissolving into flatterers, the prince lost his shyness, his disapproving frown, and grew both approachable and affable. Instead of locking himself away in long hours of prayer, he began to mingle with the court. Gradually he developed a confident ease with his future subjects. Saint-Simon was ecstatic: "One beheld this prince, diffident, unsociable, self-centered, a stranger in his own house, embarrassed everywhere, become little by little easy, dignified, gay, agreeable, presiding over the groups that gathered about him, like the divinity of a temple who receives with kindness the homage to which he is accustomed, and recompenses the mortals who offer it with his kindly regard."

His years of study now proved their value: the court listened to him at last, and marveled at his vast knowledge of history, politics, science, and even finance. People found themselves coming, not merely to pay court, but to enjoy the conversation of so cultured and informed a gentleman. "From the Court to Paris, and from Paris to the depths of the provinces, his reputation flew so rapidly that the few people formerly attached to him asked one another if they could believe what was reported from all sides."

In the depths of the provinces, Fénelon was delighted by the reports of this transition. His deep love for his pupil had never blinded him to Bourgogne's failings; only the summer before, Fénelon had severely reproached him: "Sending out dispatches from your study, in which you perpetually confine yourself, is wasting precious time which you owe to the State. Do you not avoid acquaintanceship with other men out of laziness? Is it not arrogance that leads you to shun Society, trumping up excuses that are mere quibbles in comparison with your duty to study men? Is it not self-indulgence to amuse yourself alone in your study on the pretext of being engaged in secret work?" The archbishop composed a tract, "An Examination of Conscience on the Duties of Royalty," which he forwarded to Beauvilliers. It seems certain that Bourgogne not only read it but, coming as it did at this critical time, took all its lessons to heart. One month after Bourgogne's elevation, Fénelon was able to tell Beauvilliers: "I hear that our little prince is doing better, that his reputation is rising, and that he is to have more power." But, the archbishop warned, these wondrous changes were but a beginning: "He needs your support to gain practice in State affairs, thus learning to see things for himself and make his own decisions. He needs to work with other men, in order to discover their good qualities and learn how to use them, despite their faults. You must encourage him to give reports to the King, so as to lighten his burden, and assist him in coming to decisions by tactfully offering advice. If he can do this with deference and a show of zeal, he will give no offense and soon come to be trusted."

Trust did come, and quickly. The king "saw the change that had come over him, and treated him with ever growing affection and esteem." The slight, but perceptible, coolness that had lingered after the campaign of 1708 vanished altogether. Louis XIV proudly presented the new dauphin to the Assembly of the Clergy, and Dangeau recorded his speech: "Here is the prince who will soon succeed me, and who, by his virtue and his piety, will render the Church still more flourishing, and the kingdom still more happy."

The piety which had provoked such steady criticism now received universal acclamation. Mme de Maintenon observed: "At first jeered at by all the Court, he has become the admiration of the most pronounced Libertines . . . His piety has so transformed him that, passionate though he is, he has become even-tempered, sweet, complaisant. One would say that this is his real character, and that virtue has become natural to him."

Even Madame experienced a change of heart. In her first letter following her nephew's death, she confessed that "the Dauphin and myself are not great friends," and added (incorrectly), "It is indeed true that the King has every reason for regretting the Dauphin's death." Three months later, her thoughts were quite different: "I assure you that the Dauphin deserves the praise awarded to him." While still "somewhat bigoted, he does not preach" (except to his closest friends), though his religious principles remained as strong as ever. When he refused to attend a state performance at the Comédie Française, arguing "the best theater for a dauphin's energy is the improvement of the provinces," Madame confronted him. "What will you do when you become the master? Will you prohibit operas, comedies, and other plays? Many people are of the opinion that, if they were stopped, their place would be supplied by even more reprehensible amusements." "I should weigh carefully the arguments for and against," Bourgogne told his great-aunt. "I should examine the inconveniences, which might arise in either eventuality, and then I should choose the course which would entail the least."

Inspired by an heir at last worthy of the succession, Louis XIV broke his own tradition of half a century and opened all business of government to the new dauphin. He invited his grandson to share the authority he had so jealously guarded in the past, and "ordered the Ministers of State to work with the Duc de Bourgogne whenever sent for, and whether sent for or not, to make him acquainted with all public affairs." Councils took to meeting in Bourgogne's apartments, and councillors came to admire "his unstudied eloquence and the good sense in all that he said." Best of all (Saint-Simon crowed), the councils, the court, and all of France "derived from him the much-needed and yearned-for comfort of seeing before them a future master eminently capable of sovereignty because of his great benevolence and the good use to which he showed that he would put it."

Bourgogne's governmental obligations rose, compounded by mounting social responsibilities as deputy for his aging grandfather, and it soon occurred to Beauvilliers that the prince was in sore need of a "private secretary."

The meaning of the term has changed greatly in two centuries. The post did entail "secretarial" duties, but more important, what the prince required was an honest and indisputedly trustworthy agent to serve as his eyes and ears in absentia, to keep him informed of the real sentiments concealed beneath the obsequious masks of professional courtiers. Both the king and Mme de Maintenon approved the plan, in principle — provided the right man for the job could be found and provided the entire operation could be done without stirring up jealousies at court. Beauvilliers agreed wholeheartedly to their stipulations and replied that he knew of the perfect candidate. And so the duc de Saint-Simon joined the charmed circle that surrounded the Sun King's heirs.

The little duke and his wife had lived at court for several years, but only recently had come to the attention of Adelaide and her husband. A friendship had blossomed between the princesse and the lovely Mme de Saint-Simon (it was through Adelaide's efforts that she was appointed lady-in-waiting to the duchesse de Berri), and since 1708, Bourgogne had been quietly grateful to Saint-Simon for his public support in the Vendôme controversy. Beauvilliers, recalling the duke's candid evaluation of the prince, approached him with the idea — warning, however, that the very nature of the position would require them to proceed with the utmost caution.

Saint-Simon was naturally thrilled by the prospect, though he felt it imperative to first determine the extent of Bourgogne's regard for him. "One evening, in the Marly gardens, I joined the Dauphin, when he had only a small following. Emboldened by his gracious smile, I whispered into his ear that events, of which he had known, had hitherto kept me from him, but that I now hoped to show my devotion more openly, trusting that this would not displease him."[4] He replied, also in a whisper, that he 'looked forward with pleasure to seeing me more often' — I quote his exact words, because his ending was particularly gracious."

While careful to avoid Bourgogne in court society (in order to divert suspicion), Saint-Simon took every opportunity to arrange for private, nocturnal meetings in the glades and arbors of the palace gardens.

It was just such an exchange at Marly that finally resolved Bourgogne to accept Saint-Simon for the post. The little duke encountered the prince and princesse ending an animated conversation which (he quickly surmised) involved a question of etiquette. Boldly, but very politely, he inquired what the matter was. Bourgogne replied that a forthcoming state visit to the English court at Saint-Germain was being needlessly complicated by a dispute over seating arrangements. Princesse Louisa, having come of age and apparently still bitter that Bourgogne had married Adelaide and not her, refused to give precedence to the dauphine by surrendering her armchair for the more correct (and less comfortable) taboret stool.[5] Bourgogne proposed a solution often used in the past by his grandfather — everyone would remain standing — but nonetheless he defended vigorously the importance of gradation in rank and the need to maintain an established order. It was music to Saint-Simon's ears: "What a joy to hear you speak in this way!" he cried. "How right to be meticulous in ceremony, for when that is neglected, nothing remains to inspire respect!" Bourgogne concurred and Saint-Simon deftly turned the conversation to his pet subject — safeguarding the hereditary rights of the French peers.

Their long, lively discussion dispelled the last of Bourgogne's reservations. Three days later, Saint-Simon was summoned to attend the dauphin in his private apartment.

Before this interview, Beauvilliers set down the rules: Saint-Simon must arrive and depart through a secret back door; publicly, he must visit the prince only in the company of other courtiers, and then rarely and for brief periods of time — "often enough for the visits not to appear unusual yet not so often as to suggest any suspicion of favor." During these visits, Bourgogne was to take no special notice of the little duke. (If this strikes us today as rather conspiratorial, it must be remembered that only through such subterfuge could Saint-Simon retain the anonymity necessary to keep his master well informed of public opinion at court. It was typical for Beauvilliers to arrange this type of espionage; such discretion had won him the king's trust and favor for over a quarter century.)

The meeting was a great success. The duc de Bourgogne, fully assured of Saint-Simon's trustworthiness, launched into an attack of the royal ministers for the way in which they had slyly wrested extensive powers from the king. He spoke of his grandfather only in terms of gratitude and deep affection. When Saint-Simon tentatively suggested that Louis XIV remained in ignorance of many things that should be brought to his attention because he himself made it impossible for people to speak freely with him, Bourgogne was impressed with the insight. Generously, he conceded the truth of Saint-Simon's remark, citing the king's deplorable upbringing and the many pernicious influences inherent in so large a court; the king's mind, his heir maintained, was essentially virtuous and noble, but the world had led him astray, and the proof of Almighty displeasure was the present unhappiness of France.

Saint-Simon next broached the subject of the king's bastards, and their encroachment into royal privilege: again their views were parallel. Bourgogne used the question of the title "Monseigneur" as his example and admitted that, resenting deeply the rise of these illegitimate offspring, he himself had been secretly instrumental in the decision to style himself "Monsieur." The two men envisioned a new, enlightened order, a France governed along the lines of eighteenth-century England, a France where greedy professional administrators would be replaced by the peers and great landowners of the realm.

Following this encounter, Saint-Simon rapturously depicted the new dauphin as "pious, tolerant, just and enlightened, ever striving to improve his mind . . . I savored the pleasure of enjoying his full and most precious trust at our very first interview." Their second meeting was, for the duke, even more gratifying: "I clearly foresaw the destruction of those hammers of the State [the administrators] and other enemies of the high nobility . . . who, revived by this prince, would be restored to their rightful status."

In the months that remained of Bourgogne's brief tenure as dauphin, there were many such sessions at Versailles or Marly or Fontainebleau, all enshrouded in secrecy. Duchesne, the dauphin's confidential valet, would wait at the back door till no one was nearby, and then admit the duke to his master's study. Saint-Simon would bustle in, his pockets filled with notes, ready to apprise the prince of the latest in mood and temper at the court, and to plan together a glorious future.[6]

Bourgogne opened his soul to Saint-Simon, affording the diarist an illuminating study of the prince. Their papers reveal a multitude of projects for the reform of church and state: the decentralization of the administration and the establishment of local councils; the abolishment of the intendants and their tax inequities; the recall of the States-General; the restoration of the great noble families to the political importance deprived them by the Sun King (Saint-Simon's personal dream); the redistribution of clerical benefices, putting an end to the scandalous contrast between the wealthy bishops and the starving country priests; the rigorous suppression of court luxuries to set the country an example of economy; and the establishment of a non-aggressive foreign policy.

A France under Bourgogne's rule is one of the greatest "what ifs" of history. Could his extensive reform have prevented the monarchy's downhill slide into revolution, or had the cancer already eaten too deeply into the social system? Certainly he would have been the most virtuous king of France since Saint Louis and would have strengthened the moral authority of the Crown as greatly as his son's subsequent licentiousness destroyed it — as to that, Louis XV would doubtless have proved a very different monarch had he been raised by his parents instead of the depraved duc de Chartres. Bourgogne's favorite maxim was that kings exist for the sake of their people, and not people for the sake of their kings. If he had been unable to avert the Revolution, he still might have stemmed its excesses; as one critic remarked, Bourgogne might not have saved the monarchy, but at least its sun would not have gone down in blood.

One afternoon, the secret sessions were threatened with exposure. The duke had advised the dauphin to bolt the door of his apartment. Bourgogne protested — "The Dauphine never comes in at this time" — but Saint-Simon replied that it was not the duchesse de Bourgogne he feared, but the courtiers who dogged her every step. Unconvinced, the dauphin set to work.

His hands were filled with secret papers when suddenly the door opened and there stood Adelaide.

Our eyes glazed, our bodies remained as still as statues, our silence, our utter consternation lasted fully the time of a slow Pater Noster. The Princesse spoke first. She was perhaps a little disconcerted to find that her husband, whose every secret she thought she knew, had been concealing something from her. Turning to the Prince, she said in a quivering voice that she had not expected to find him in such good company, and then she smiled, first at him, then at me. I had just sufficient time to return her smile and lower my eyes before the Prince replied, smiling also, but rather less warmly, "Well, Madame! Since you do find me so well occupied, perhaps you will have the goodness to leave me."

Adelaide promptly took her cue, and with another gracious smile to them both, left the room. "Now, Monsieur, had you only consented to bolt the door!" But Bourgogne was unperturbed. "You were right and I was wrong, but there is no harm. Fortunately she was alone, and I can vouch for her silence."

Saint-Simon was not as confident of the dauphine's discretion. Nor was the duc de Beauvilliers; when informed by Saint-Simon of her accidental discovery, he "went quite pale with fright." But they both misjudged the princesse, whose implicit trust and support of her husband was unequaled: to the day of her death, not a single word of this discovery ever passed her lips.

Adelaide was far too busy adjusting to her change of status to create any difficulties for her husband, even had she been so inclined. The grace, the dignity, and the extreme tact with which she approached her new role delighted all Versailles. "The new Dauphine," Mme de Maintenon proudly reported to the princesse des Ursins, "in taking a more exalted place, becomes more courteous and attentive than she has ever been . . . She makes herself adored by everybody." Even the harping Madame sang her praises: "The Dauphine is making herself popular owing to her courtesy," she wrote her aunt. "Last Monday [Adelaide and Bourgogne] invited me to dinner; no one could have behaved more suitably than they did on that occasion; they even waited on me personally."

Maturity had brought with it wisdom, and her elevation a previously unseen discretion — not only with her husband and his private secretary, but with the old king as well. One afternoon, she visited Grandpapa in Mme de Maintenon's rooms, when Foreign Minister Torcy entered with the king's personal correspondence. Adelaide rose politely, and excused herself, offering to retire to another room so the king might read in private. Louis XIV was touched by the gesture; he insisted she remain and even showed her some of the dispatches. "Her great flow of spirits does not deaden her sensibility to misfortune," Mme de Maintenon noticed, "and there is no Frenchwoman more devoted to the welfare of this country than she."

With her lively, intelligent interest in public affairs, and in particular the progress of the war, her patriotism was exemplary. Dangeau recorded (August 6, 1711) that as the court at Fontainebleau waited anxiously for news of Villars's encounter with Marlborough, she was invited to join a card party. "With whom do you expect me to play?" Adelaide snapped. "With ladies who have their husbands — or with fathers who have their sons — engaged in a battle which must be, according to all appearances, a bloody one? And can I be tranquil myself when it is a question of a state affair of the greatest importance?" She called for a carriage and abruptly left the salon, drove along the high road to Paris, and awaited the arriving courier.

Elevation to dauphine freed Adelaide forever from future persecution by Mme la duchesse, and more than one court faction joined the princesse in rejoicing. Still, no rise within the Versailles hierarchy could be accomplished without figuratively stepping on several different toes: in this case, the most prominent feet belonged to her troublesome sister-in-law.

Prior to Monseigneur's death, the Bourgognes and the Berris enjoyed more or less equal rank at the court; in April 1711, Louis XIV decided the difference in their status should be officially observed. Before, Adelaide had knelt in the royal chapel on the same square of red velvet as the duchesse de Berri; now she was provided with a cushion of her own and instructed to kneel in front of all the other ladies. The imperious young Mme de Berri deemed this an intolerable insult. It was only the beginning.

The king next doubled Adelaide's household escort, increasing her royal guards from twelve to twenty-four, then posted two Swiss Guards outside her apartment door to lead distinguished guests to her audience chamber. This was a signal honor, for the Swiss Guards had been formed for the exclusive use of the king. Mme de Berri's jealousy intensified. Then Louis XIV decreed that at the dauphin's *lever,* the duc de Berri would hand his brother the royal shirt and at the dauphine's toilette, his wife should proffer the chemise. Berri had no problem with this new responsibility, but his duchess exploded at the affront to her dignity. She sobbed and screamed, vowing never to submit to such humiliation. She expected her husband's support for her resistance — her upbraiding was so violent that Berri, fearful of her wrath, was obliged to send excuses and not attend his brother's next *lever*. He begged his father-in-law to reason with the obstinate duchess. Chartres alone had a modicum of control over the girl; still, it took some time to persuade her to obey the king's express command.

Even after she had conceded, Mme de Berri delayed her performance for three days. When at last she appeared, she made no effort to hide her irritation. "In the end, she attended the Dauphine's toilette; handed her her petticoat, and finally, offered her *la sale*." [7] Saint-Simon thought her behavior churlish, and had nothing but praise for Adelaide's reaction: "The Dauphine pretended to have heard nothing and not to have noticed the inexcusable delay. She received the Duchesse's servings with all the kindness imaginable, and with the most unaffected signs of fondness. Her great desire for a happy relationship with her sister-in-law persuaded her to overlook this latest prank as though it were she, and not the Duchesse de Berri, who had everything to gain, and nothing to lose by forgetfulness."

Another clash soon followed — this one, surprisingly, with Louis XIV. The princesse had long been slapdash in dress. Like Madame, she preferred the easy comfort of riding clothes or loose morning dresses (which she wore constantly at the menagerie) to the restricting corsets and heavy, cumbersome skirts of ceremonial attire. For years Mme de Maintenon had disapproved of such indifference — "If she would only go to bed earlier and take a little more care of her dress she would be quite perfect. The casual style which she favors is not becoming to her, nor does it suit her rank" — but doting Grandpapa had never felt royal intervention in the matter necessary.

His son's death changed his feelings: as dauphine (and queen already in all but name), it was Adelaide's duty to create a more regal impression. "Dress with greater care," Mme de Maintenon advised within days of Monseigneur's death, "since your untidiness displeases His Majesty. It is important for you to wear jewels, so as to draw attention to the clearness of your complexion and the neatness of your figure." With the court deep in mourning, Adelaide countered, the time was hardly appropriate for ostentatious display; even were she disposed to it, the impropriety of suddenly covering herself in jewels and costly materials would certainly invite courtly censure. To placate Grandpapa, she took special pains with her appearance the following day, but when Louis XIV professed himself still dissatisfied, she resorted to a charming and harmless subterfuge. She had her jewels transported secretly to Mme de Maintenon's apartments. Before visiting the king each day, she would array herself as he wished. After he left, she would remove them all and then return to her own rooms. "Thus," Saint-Simon confirmed, "she contrived not to offend the King's taste, and not to shock the susceptibilities of the Court at such a time."

The conflict over her appearance was based on more than just the simple tastes of a young woman bred in the easy, relaxed atmosphere of the Alpine countryside transplanted to the most stilted court in Europe. Adelaide's wardrobe was perpetually in "a state of disorder," and for this Saint-Simon unequivocally blamed her Mistress of the Robes, Mme de Mailly: "Although the expenditure on her wardrobe was more than double that spent on the late Queen, the Dauphine was so notoriously deficient in everything that day after day ladies were obliged to lend her furs, sleeves, and other such fancies of which she stood in need. The indolence of Mme de Mailly left everything in the hands of chambermaids."

Saint-Simon exaggerates, for Adelaide's wardrobe could hardly be called deficient, but his hint of massive misappropriation is correct. Materials and accessories were constantly being purchased — "Desmaretz, the Controller-General of Finances, was continually in dispute with the Mistress of the Robes on the subject of her extravagance" — yet the bulk of these trappings somehow never made their way into the dauphine's cupboards. Adelaide had always endured this in silence, but as Louis XIV demanded more and more finery with less and less available, her patience neared the breaking point.

A new and extraordinary honor from the king cleared the way for a solution. To the court's great wonder, it was announced that henceforth the dauphine would have complete control over her household, including the disposal of all positions within that might in future become vacant. It was a privilege withheld from both the queen and the late dauphine, and Versailles found it difficult to believe the king truly intended her to enjoy unchecked authority. One gentlemen ventured to remark to His Majesty that he presumed the princesse would render an account of all her actions to the king; Louis XIV at once set him straight. "I have sufficient trust in her not to wish her to render me any account whatever, and I leave her absolute mistress of her Household. She would be capable of more difficult and important matters than that."

One of the princesse's first acts was to take control of her wardrobe from Mme de Mailly, who was dismissed for having done too well for herself at Adelaide's expense, and entrust it to her cherished Mme Quentin. Saint-Simon led the applause at this change: "Henceforth, Mme Quentin, an honest and understanding person, concerned herself with the Princesse's robes and regulated well the expenditure on them."

There was great conjecture on the motivating forces behind the honor, but the decision to give the dauphine control of her household was the king's alone. Adelaide herself never would have dared request such a privilege. Saint-Simon explained: "She would have lost his esteem forever if she had made the slightest effort to obtain it." But once the power was hers, "it may be imagined that she was clever enough not to abuse her privilege." She knew the king too well to do anything without being certain of his approval.

Her Italian subtlety in dealing with Louis XIV proved Adelaide her father's daughter. She never openly sought a favor, preferring to convey the hint of her wishes in a glance from her eloquent eyes. She had no taste for intrigue — probably since, in her position, she had no need of it. Without appearing to exert influence, she had her way in everything. There was no need to court partisan popularity; she concerned herself instead with the advancement of the worthy. When the death of the marquis de Bellefond left vacant the post of captain and governor of Vincennes, Louis XIV was confronted with several candidates, and Adelaide with an equal number of bribes in return for her support. Spurning all offers, she demurely pressed the claims of her own choice, the marquis du Châtelet, a brave and impoverished noble whose wife was one of her favorite ladies-in-waiting. Châtelet was appointed to the post, and the triumph of merit over intrigue made a vivid impression on the court: "It was generally remarked," wrote Saint-Simon, "that the most modest and retiring of the Dauphine's ladies had been rewarded by a royal favor" — and no one doubted whose handiwork the favor was.

Once spring gave way to summer, Versailles slowly returned to life. The palace salons reopened, and though the ban on lansquenet remained in effect for the rest of the year, brelan and other forms of gambling reappeared. It was a far cry from the pleasure-filled summer courts of the past, for mourning prohibited dancing and the theater, but Adelaide took consolation in the joys of the chase. All summer long, the court galloped through the forests of Marly and Fontainebleau in pursuit of deer and wild boar.

One afternoon, a large crowd of Parisians gathered in the Bois de

Boulogne to observe the royal hunters. Dangeau wrote that Adelaide left the group to chat with the spectators, "and said so much that was civil and kindly that they went home charmed by her appearance and simplehearted friendliness." The day was one long treat for all: after the hunt, the duchesse de Bourgogne rode to Passy, where the duchesse de Lauzun had arranged a magnificent meal in her honor — so large was Adelaide's new entourage that Lauzun was forced to seat the party in shifts. "They played brelan and papillon, and did not return to Versailles until after midnight."

Louis XIV had long been aware of the treasure he possessed in Marie Adelaide; in that golden summer, the princesse's popularity eclipsed not only that of the entire royal family, but his own as well. Happily he exploited his charming and gifted granddaughter. Adelaide had always attended military reviews and other functions solely as a private spectator. At the first royal review of the king's musketeers after Monseigneur's death, Adelaide made her appearance on horseback and rode through the ranks between the king and Bourgogne, amid cheers and acclamations. Encouraged by the tremendous response of his soldiers, Louis XIV stepped up the number of her official engagements.

On August 8, 1711, the dauphine dined in state for the first time since her elevation. She was served by M. de Villacerf, the principal maître d'hôtel of Versailles — only thirteen ladies of suitable rank were permitted the honor of sitting while the princesse dined, but a large number of court beauties gathered to stand and watch as their future queen ate, and afterward to attend a gala reception in the Salon of Nobles.

Several days later the new dauphin and dauphine dined publicly together. The crowd was even greater. It was a precise ritual, prescribed by tradition and etiquette: before dinner, their maître d'hôtel, M. de La Croix, presented himself at the Buttery and solemnly washed his hands. His actions were then repeated by the comptroller of the household and the first gentleman-in-waiting. The groom-in-ordinance of the Buttery presented the maître d'hôtel with a silver salver, holding bits of bread that had been dipped in each of the sauces prepared. La Croix returned to him one such sop, which he ate with sufficient gravity — to prove there was no poison — then selected the dishes to be served the royal couple.

This accomplished, the maître d'hôtel took up his wand of office from a nearby usher and the procession to the dining room was formed in strict, inflexible order: first an officer of the King's Bodyguard, shouldering his musket, followed by an Usher of the Drawing Room and an Usher of the Pantry. Next came M. de La Croix, then the gentleman-in-waiting and the comptroller, each bearing a dish, and after them, the other officers of the Buttery bringing the rest of the first course.

La Croix entered the salon to inform the royal couple that dinner was served. Once Adelaide and Bourgogne were seated, La Croix handed his wand and his hat to the Chief of the Goblet: his hands were now free to present, first to the dauphin, then his wife, a golden tray holding a towel dipped in scented water for the washing of their fingers.

Once the prince and princesse had begun the first course, La Croix retrieved his hat and wand and, preceded by two guards and two ushers, returned to the Buttery to scrutinize, test, and taste the second course — a procedure he followed for each of the several ensuing courses. (Adelaide did not share the Bourbon propensity to overeat, nor did she ever show much interest in food.)

But if such duties were onerous, there was ample compensation in delightful private soirées held in Adelaide's salon. Her only requirement for entry was "a light heart and a sense of fun." One new member of court found himself quickly established as a permanent fixture at these carefree evenings.

The sixteen-year-old duc de Fronsac made his first appearance at the Sun King's court on December 15, 1710, when Louis XIV opened the carnival season with a costume ball at Marly. The son of the duc de Richelieu (by the second of his three wives), Fronsac was handsome and precocious, and enjoyed immediate success within the inner circle of Versailles. Mme de Maintenon for one was instantly charmed: "He is sixteen, but looks twelve," she wrote. "For one of his slender build, he has the most charming figure imaginable; he is also one of the best dancers; looks well on a horse; plays cards; loves music and is capable of conversation. He is very respectful, very polite, and most agreeable . . . When it is required, he can be very serious. Everyone finds him such as I have described." A few weeks later she returned again to the subject of Fronsac: "One longs to pet him, like a pretty little boy, and I was just about to chuck him under the chin, when he asked me to sign his marriage contract!" For despite his age, and because of his precocity, Fronsac was already an accomplished gallant and his father swore to stem his womanizing by marrying him to the eighteen-year-old Mlle de Noailles.

Young Fronsac had other ideas. His dancing skills had caught the

eye of the new dauphine, who soon declared him her favorite partner — even the king, complimenting their grace and form, declared
them the handsomest couple on the floor. Adelaide discovered they
shared a common love of music, and she enjoyed his conversation and
presence with increasing frequency. Intensive royal favor completely
turned the boy's head: Fronsac decided that he was in love with the
princesse.

Worse still, he concluded that the feeling was mutual. On the very
eve of his wedding, he threw himself at the dauphine's feet, declaring
his passionate love. Adelaide, who had long regarded him as a delightful but naughty child in need of pampering, petting, and correc-
tion, tolerated his outburst with amusement. With a charming smile,
she gently rebuffed the would-be lover. The flattering attention, the
ardent and handsome suitor, doubtless recalled to her the distant days
of Nangis and Maulevrier. With her customary generosity, she concluded that, having handled the incident firmly but kindly, there was
no reason to hamper the boy's career at court by informing her husband (or the king) of his adolescent infatuation. Her very kindness
exacerbated the situation: Fronsac read her sweet rebuff as modest
encouragement. Under this delusion, he was ready to press his suit.

One morning, as Adelaide finished performing her official toilette
and the ladies of the court withdrew from her chamber, Fronsac was
discovered beneath the bed. She demanded an explanation; Fronsac
replied that he wanted to know what she *truly* thought of him and had
hoped to hear some private comment. Adelaide laughed at the impu-
dent romantic, and sent him on his way with the promise of silence,
sadly unaware that her clemency would provoke a second encounter.

Fronsac did not delay. Two evenings later he quit the salon early,
sneaking into her bedroom and hiding behind a screen. Presently Adelaide entered the room, prepared for bed. When her ladies had departed and she was completely disrobed, Fronsac suddenly emerged.
The dauphine screamed and the women rushed back to the room.
Shaking, but in control, Adelaide covered herself with a sheet and
ordered the boy to leave immediately. Again she swore her ladies to
secrecy. But these gentlewomen, having had time for reflection since
the first incident earlier that week, were no longer inclined toward
silence. They realized that if Louis XIV were to discover Fronsac's
trespass, this silence would be held against them; even more, they
feared for their mistress, lest inaccurate reports reach the king's ears
and perhaps damn her forever in his eyes. They drew lots, the unlucky
winner hastening to the royal study with a full, and accurate, account.

Grandpapa was outraged: within twenty-four hours, and with the full approval of the duc de Richelieu, Fronsac was arrested and conveyed to the Bastille, where he was imprisoned for fifteen months.[8] The Fronsac incident, despite its brevity, is important for two reasons: it demonstrated the passion Adelaide aroused in those who fell under her spell, and it proved — unlike the earlier lessons in love — that the heart of the princesse now belonged solely to her husband.

Adelaide was determined that the Fronsac affair should not spoil the rest of the season; she was also aware that any grief or remorse on her part would be taken by the court as proof of collusion. She redoubled her efforts to amuse both herself and the king, but had significantly less success with the latter.

During their autumn visit to Fontainebleau, Louis XIV appeared unusually gloomy and thoughtful. News from Flanders was still disheartening, and the preliminary peace talks seemed doomed to stalemate. Mme la duchesse was stirring up trouble again, trying (in vain) to breathe scandal into Adelaide's gentle rejection of Fronsac. For once, not even the dauphine's charm could fully rouse the king from depression — a fact that gladdened the black heart of her adversary.

One autumn evening, while Saint-Simon watched the princesse "jabbering all kinds of nonsense and indulging in a thousand childish pranks in order to amuse the King," she spied her old enemies, Mme la duchesse and the princesse de Conti, exchanging glances of disdain. The dauphine waited until the king had entered the adjoining room to feed his dogs; then, taking the hand of Mme de Levis on one side and Mme de Saint-Simon on the other, she said to them excitedly, "Did you see them? Did you see them? I know as well as they do that there is no common sense in what I have said and done, and that it is ridiculous; but he requires rousing, and those kinds of things amuse him."

Then, in high spirits, she began to skip and dance about the room. "Ha! I laugh at them! Ha! I mock them! I shall be their Queen, and I have nothing to do with them, either now or at any time. They will have to reckon with me, and I shall be their Queen!" Her two shocked attendants pressed for some restraint, but Adelaide continued her jubilant refrain: "I mock them! I have nothing to do with them! I shall be their Queen!"

On December 6, 1711, Adelaide celebrated her twenty-sixth birthday. To honor the occasion, Louis XIV suspended court mourning and gave a ball at Versailles. The gala evening was marred only by the dauphine's chronic battle with toothache. "For more than two months it has seized me from time to time," she wrote her mother, answering Anne Marie's birthday greetings. "I have ceased taking care of it, for keeping to my room does me no good, and during the time I am not in it I am thinking and always hoping the pain may not return. I merely avoid the wind in my ears, and eating anything which may hurt me."

Possibilities for peace slowly materialized. "We have today another courier from England," Adelaide wrote on December 13, "which confirms the hope I feel. The conference will be held at Utrecht and will begin on the twelfth of next month." (Peace would not be concluded, however, for another sixteen months.)

The glad tidings shook the old Sun King from his lethargy and his Christmas court sparkled with new vigor. "What glory for our king," Mme de Maintenon declared, "to have sustained a ten years' war against all Europe . . . Now to see it end in a peace which places the monarchy of Spain in his family, and re-establishes a Catholic king in his kingdom — for I will not doubt that that will follow upon peace. The King is blest with a health which makes me hope he will long enjoy the rest he is now to have."

All of France celebrated the Christmas season with a joy unfelt in more than a decade. At Versailles, the king demanded feasting and entertainment, and after a two-year hiatus revived the *appartement* evenings. He relied heavily on Adelaide to lead the merrymaking, and she responded wholeheartedly. "The Dauphine's fertile mind," Maintenon wrote, "avid of pleasure and festivities, is already rapturously planning the program with which she will celebrate the return of peace. She intends to do something on the day that peace is concluded that she has never done before, and will never do again," adding somewhat tongue in cheek, "but she has not yet decided what it shall be."

Meanwhile, Maintenon detailed some "preliminary pleasures": "She is going to the Te Deum at Notre Dame; to dinner with the Duchesse du Lude, in a beautiful brand-new house; then to the Opéra; to sup with the Prince de Rohan, in that magnificent Hôtel de Guise; then to cards and a ball, which will last all night, and, as the hour of her return will be that of my waking, she proposes to breakfast with me on arriving." After a decade of war and tribulation, it was immeasurably delightful to enjoy oneself again: the dauphine personally instructed young ladies fresh from the convent schools in the steps of court dances. She gave a large supper party for the king at the menagerie and followed it with a lavish ball. "Inexhaustible is her capacity for joy," commented Mme de Maintenon — this time, the old lady did not disapprove.

"I wanted to forestall the first day of the year by offering to all my family the wishes I desire for them," Adelaide wrote the duchess of Savoy on December 18. "Not being able to do so, I content myself, my dear mother, by embracing you with all my heart." It was her last letter.

The Feast of the Epiphany closed the Christmas court and Versailles prayed that 1712 might long be remembered as "the year of peace." Instead, they would recall it as "the year of death."

Adelaide entered her twenty-seventh year. Fifteen of those had been spent at the court of the Sun King — years of growing success, power, and influence, years that paled in comparison to the dazzling future that awaited still. The king loved and indulged her above all others, including his own wife. Her husband worshiped her, and her two sons, little Bretagne and baby Anjou, were "the most lovable children that one could desire, sturdy, pretty as a picture, gracious as herself, and displaying much intelligence" (so felt their biased great-grandmother). She was the idol of the court, the heroine of the common people. She stood at her husband's side on the highest step to the throne, and only the life of a tired old man stood between them and the greatest inheritance of Europe. Already she was regarded as queen of France — by its king, its court, and its people. As Maintenon observed: "She has every reason to be happy."

One long winter night soon after Epiphany, the dauphine sat by the fire chatting with two of her ladies. Outside the winds howled, rattling the casements and whistling through the chimneys. Wistfully, Adelaide remarked on how many people had died at Versailles since that ancient time of her arrival. How quickly time passed: already she was twenty-six, a respectable middle-aged woman whose youth was gone! How strange to be old, to find oneself without contemporaries with whom to reminisce!

One of her companions suddenly recalled a long-ago prediction of a Turinese astrologer, a forecast that Marie Adelaide should die in her twenty-seventh year. Reminding her mistress of the prophecy, she scoffed at its absurdity. But Adelaide did not join in the laughter. Gazing intently at the fire, she spoke in a quiet voice. "Well, I must make haste. I cannot enjoy myself for long, for I shall die this year."

Within a month, the prophecy was fulfilled.

21

"Everything Is Dead Here"

HARSH WINTER WEATHER followed a rainy autumn. The smallpox epidemic that claimed Monseigneur faded away, to be replaced by yet another disease. An outbreak of *rougeole pourpré,* a malignant strain of measles, hit Paris shortly after New Year's Day; several hundred died in the first two weeks alone. The epidemic spread and soon reached Versailles: the first of the palace inhabitants to succumb was the marquis de Gondrin, Montespan's only legitimate grandson. Then, several servants in the Bourgogne households fell ill and died. Thus the infection was introduced in close proximity to the royal family; by the end of the month the princesse had been exposed to it.

Marie Adelaide was ripe for infection. The old trouble with her gums had flared up before her birthday and gave her no peace. On January 18, the king ordered a family excursion to Marly, and the dauphine arrived early, planning to welcome the king in person. But her teeth still throbbed and her face was so swollen after the drive from Versailles that the doctors insisted she go to bed instead.

Of course, Louis XIV was not one to be indisposed by the indispositions of others: he required the dauphine's presence in his salon that evening, so Adelaide dutifully made an appearance at seven, "*en déshabillé* and with her head wrapped up." She played cards briefly, the pain in her jaw making concentration difficult. As soon as she could, she retired to Mme de Maintenon's room for her evening visit with the old king and his wife. Louis XIV pressed her to dine with him: she confessed to feeling wretched and asked for her supper in bed. She remained there all next day, rising in the evening, ordered again to appear in the king's salon.

Little notice was being paid to the dauphine's malady but this did not betoken courtly indifference: Adelaide's constitution had never been robust, and courtiers were long accustomed to her frequent indispositions. All were confident these latest pains would soon subside — and the princesse shared in this delusion. Since her serious illness in 1701, Adelaide's health had been in steady, continuous decline. A decade and six miscarriages later, she quite simply lacked the stamina to battle with infection.

On the morning of January 20, she admitted to feeling better. Louis XIV, anxious to have his darling by his side, insisted she resume a normal schedule for the remainder of the Marly holiday. Naturally the dauphine complied. In doing so, she severely taxed her limited strength and further weakened her resistance. At this critical point, exposure occurred.

The court returned to Versailles on February 1. For three days, Adelaide performed all her royal functions, and on the evening of the fourth, gave a private dinner party for the king at the menagerie. She served Italian ragout and a special cheesecake that she made herself; when a fever appeared the next day, the doctor wrote it off to indigestion brought on by the richness of the meal.

His diagnosis seemed confirmed when the princesse was able to rise twenty-four hours later and pass the sixth customarily. But that night the fever returned, and on the morning of the seventh, rose alarmingly. It was Sunday and Adelaide attempted to dress for mass, when she was seized by "a sharp pain under the temple, which did not extend to the dimensions of a ten-sou piece." (So Saint-Simon described it; Mme de Maintenon wrote Madrid of "a fixed pain between her ear and the upper end of her jaw.") The pain was so violent that when she heard the king was coming to visit, Adelaide — for the first time in her life — asked him to stay away.

Throughout the night and all next day, the excruciating pain continued. She seemed immune to every known remedy of the period, all of which were applied: tobacco and opium to smoke, tobacco leaves to chew on, and of course the obligatory bleedings, twice from the same arm in one morning. Nothing brought relief. Mme de Maintenon wrote: "She has convulsions, she screams like a woman in childbirth, and with the same intervals"; indeed, Adelaide, in a moment of respite, admitted the pains surpassed even those of childbirth. The throbbing then eased gradually, and by nightfall her fever had dropped perceptibly — owing, her doctor maintained, to the bloodletting. Just before dawn it rose again, higher than before, and this time bleeding her foot throughout the ninth had no effect on her temperature.

The dauphine's personal physician was Jean Boudin. Formerly attached to Monseigneur, he had entered her service only ten months before and was not yet sufficiently familiar with her constitution. He was, however, sufficiently perplexed to call upon the king's physician, the renowned Fagon, for a second opinion. Fagon, whom Saint-Simon considered "one of the best and cleverest brains in all Europe," had one serious shortcoming: "Although generally well-informed, he could be dangerous for he was easily biased, and, having made up his mind, could hardly ever be shifted."

Fagon diagnosed measles and pronounced that once the rash appeared, her head would clear and the fever abate. The rash did break out that very afternoon, but no clearing of the head followed: to Fagon's puzzlement, Adelaide dropped into a semiconscious state (having been bled continuously for three days). The next turn in her illness was even more baffling, for the spots disappeared entirely on Tuesday and her temperature increased. The bewildered doctors resorted to more bleeding, which did nothing for the fever or the head pains that had returned.

On Wednesday the tenth, Boudin administered a powerful emetic: it brought about a violent reaction, but no positive results. Louis XIV could no longer stay away. Mindless of Fagon's fears of contagion, he entered the sickroom. The risk to the state had kept the king out, but not his wife or grandson. Mme de Maintenon had stationed herself at Adelaide's bedside once the fever began; the dauphin also had remained with his wife and had not slept for more than an hour or two in five days. Maintenon quickly retired so that the king might visit in private, but Bourgogne was reluctant to leave for even five minutes. Eventually persuaded by his grandfather to take some fresh air, he went for a walk in the gardens, but returned immediately to resume his vigil.

The king was left alone with his darling, his composure sorely tried. The princesse tossed fitfully on her bed, consumed by fever, battling with delirium and exhaustion. Lucid for a short period, she listened while the king outlined the latest developments at Utrecht. "I have a feeling there will be a peace," she murmured, adding weakly, "and that I shall not see it." Louis XIV dissolved in tears.

That night her condition declined, with shorter moments of sensibility and longer spells of incoherence. The doctors could no longer hide their uncertainty or their fear, and the Sun King experienced true panic: his decision on the eleventh to evoke the aid of Saint Genevieve, patron of Paris, was an act of desperation. "His Majesty desires that tomorrow at daybreak the coffer should be uncovered and the Sainte exposed to the veneration of the faithful come to pray for the recovery of Madame la Dauphine." Evocation was a very serious measure, taken only at times of national calamity, and required the approval of the parlement. But love and concern for the princesse was by no means confined to Versailles. Without a single dissenting vote, the parlement endorsed the king's request and sent a delegation of its own members to join the mass of supplicants praying to the holy relics for their dauphine's life.

Despite the nationwide plea for divine intercession, Adelaide did not improve. The doctors continued their bleedings and, on the advice of the queen of England's private physician (who had hurriedly arrived from Saint-Germain), applied a second and stronger emetic. Still the treatment was ineffectual — or so the doctors thought. In truth, the harsh purgatives further sapped the patient's dwindling strength.

By the night of February 11, she was judged close enough to death to require last rites. Her private confessor, the Jesuit Père de La Rue, was summoned. There on her deathbed, Adelaide revealed her true feelings on the controversy between Jesuits and Jansenists. La Rue approached her bed, exhorting the princesse to confess: "She looked at him, replied that she quite understood him, and then remained silent. Like a sensible man, he perceived what was in her mind, and like a good man, at once told her that if she had any objection to confessing to him, he begged her not to constrain herself, but only tell him whom she desired, and he would himself go and bring him."

She did have objections, and her choice of last confessor, when it became known, rocked the court: Abbé Bailly, a missionary of Saint-Lazare, "a man much esteemed but not altogether free from suspicion of Jansenism." Unfortunately, Bailly was in Paris and unavailable; the princesse then requested Père Noël, a Franciscan at the parish church of Versailles. Bailly and Noël were great favorites of Bourgogne, whose religious philosophy had been cultivated by the pro-Jansenist Fénelon.

The repudiation of the Jesuits, in addition to creating a minor sensation at court, told that the dauphine understood the full extent of her deterioration. This princesse, whose entire life had been spent in charming but servile obedience to the mighty Sun King, would never have challenged his well-known proclivities had she not accepted fully that her end was fast approaching.

The king and the doctors took advantage of Père Noël's arrival to compel the dauphin to a sickbed himself. For two days, the prince had successfully concealed that he, too, was running a fever; once his condition was discovered, he had battled for the right to remain beside his wife. He returned to his own apartments under protest, and sent hourly for news of Adelaide's condition. The king contrived with Fagon and Boudin to keep his grandson ignorant of the true gravity of the situation, knowing this the only way of forcing on him badly needed rest.

Adelaide's confession to Père Noël was a lengthy one. When the priest had left and Maintenon returned to her side, she had second thoughts on her open rejection of the Jesuits. "*Ma tante,* have I done wrong in taking a different confessor?" "No," came the soothing reply. "It is always permissible. One needs full liberty of conscience." The last rites had transfused serenity to the body wasting on the bed. "*Ma tante,* I feel another person. It seems to me I am quite changed." The old woman struggled to control her voice. "It is because you are nearer to God, Madame, and because He now comforts you." The dauphine faded further into her pillows: "I have no regrets, except that I have offended God." "That sorrow suffices to obtain pardon for your sins, provided you are firmly resolved to commit them no more should God give you back your health." Adelaide smiled weakly and whispered, "Yes, but I fear that if I should recover, I may not do sufficient penance."

Something still preoccupied her for some time. At last she spoke: "One thing troubles me — it is my card debts. M. le Dauphin knows of them. I should much like to see him." Maintenon explained that the prince had been ordered to his rooms, and the king's fears for his health kept them from calling him back. "If M. le Dauphin knows of your debts," she comforted, "you should be tranquil. Be assured that his affection for you will require him to settle them immediately." Adelaide was not appeased: she called for a particular casket, which she said contained a statement of her debts. The box was handed her and she began to search inside; the effort proved too much and she fell back exhausted, mumbling that the casket should be placed at the foot of her bed.

By Friday the twelfth, it was apparent the end was at hand. The princesse was now conscious only at rare moments. In the first of these, she called again for Père Noël. He rushed in and she whispered that the time had come for him to start the prayers for the dead. Maintenon could bear no more and burst into tears. Adelaide gently reproached her: "Oh, *ma tante,* you make me weaken!" The king took her hand, stammering words of consolation, and she smiled up at him with affection and gratitude, but not a word; she admitted afterward to her ladies that she had been afraid to speak lest her courage should break.

Three more glasses of emetic swiftly depleted her strength. In late afternoon, Marie Adelaide asked to see her ladies; to her old friend the duchesse de Guise, she cried out, "Oh! my beautiful duchesse! I am going to die!" Guise stifled a sob. "No! No! God will restore you, in answer to M. le Dauphin's prayers." But Adelaide was past delusion. "I think quite the opposite," she answered. "It is because God loves him that He sends him this affliction." Adelaide peered through heavy lids as her weeping attendants filed past for one last look. A tiny smile appeared across her face. "Today Dauphine, tomorrow nothing," she murmured. "And in two days, forgotten." Then she slipped into unconsciousness.

Night fell and the palace waited in misery and confusion. Mme de Maintenon prayed endlessly in the royal chapel. When her tears made it impossible to read the pages, she fingered her rosary in desperation. Louis XIV sat at Adelaide's bedside, mute with grief, watching the doctors bleed his darling one last time: for their efforts, her temperature rose higher and she sank deeper into the coma.

Suddenly from nowhere, a nobleman appeared beside the bed. Undaunted by the royal presence, he produced a small vial which he claimed held miraculous powders to cure the princesse. The king looked hopefully to the doctors; Boudin knew his patient was past all human aid and offered no protest. The powders brought her back to consciousness, but only briefly. "Oh! How bitter it is!" she exclaimed. A page scurried off to the chapel to inform Maintenon that the dauphine had regained consciousness, and the old woman literally ran to the sickroom. "Here is Mme de Maintenon," the doctor called out. "Do you recognize her?" The response was feeble, otherworldish. "Yes." The frantic old woman grabbed her hand. "Madame, you go to be with God." Adelaide uttered her last words: "Yes, *ma tante,* I go to God." Then she relapsed into her coma.

The end drew visibly nearer. Louis XIV found himself unable to watch his greatest love die; shortly before eight o'clock, he summoned a carriage and left for Marly with Mme de Maintenon. "They were both in the most bitter grief," Saint-Simon wrote, "and had not the courage to go to the Dauphin."

The cardinal de Noailles intoned prayers for the dying and dead. The dauphine's ladies mumbled the responses between their sobs. The clock struck quarter past eight and the princesse exhaled one last time. Marie Adelaide of Savoy, dauphine of France, was dead. She was two months past her twenty-sixth birthday.

The king and his wife were shattered. "The grief I feel at the death of my daughter [sic], the Dauphine," Louis XIV wrote in a personal note to Adelaide's sister, the queen of Spain, "is so keen that I can only say that I share your own on this sad occasion. I know to what degree you will be affected by the loss we have suffered, you bereft of a sister, and I of a daughter whom I loved as tenderly." The Sun King's loss was irreparable. "There will be no moment in my life to come when I shall not mourn her."

Maintenon suffered no less. "This princesse gave life to everything, and charmed us all. We are still stupefied and stunned by our loss . . . Everything is dead here; all life has been removed."

Saturday, February 13, 1712, saw preparations for the dauphine's lying-in-state. Her magnificent dark hair was brushed and curled, her body dressed in a seamless linen shift, her hands folded piously over her heart. Then the doors to the bedchamber were flung wide, and the court filed past for its final glimpse — *Le Mercure* reported that the number of viewers that afternoon was "prodigious."

In the evening, the chamber doors were closed and the autopsy performed. Two witnesses, the duchesse du Lude and Mme de Mailly (both overcome with emotion at this grim experience), watched as Fagon and Boudin opened the body. To the doctors' wonder, no trace of smallpox or measles or any other suspicious symptom was found. The brain and all her vital organs were intact. Ignorance and fear (fear that the dauphine's death might be charged to their handiwork) led the doctors to declare that Marie Adelaide had been poisoned, "on the specious grounds that her blood was all burnt up."[1] Only the surgeon Mareschal, also present, disagreed with this conclusion: he maintained her death was due to natural causes, and he beseeched the king, "for the tranquility and prolongation of his life, to dismiss from his mind ideas terrible in themselves, false, according to all his experience and knowledge, and which bred only cares and suspicions vague and irremedial." Louis XIV had no wish to heap controversy on grief: the autopsy report was immediately suppressed.

The body was placed in a coffin lined in white satin; following royal tradition, the heart had been removed, embalmed, and placed in a separate urn. The casket was mounted on a small platform and surrounded by six large tapers. Two portable altars were erected in the chamber, and masses were said hourly from six in the morning till six in the evening. While four bishops prayed at the altars, six of the dauphine's ladies stood in relays around the coffin. So began the second, more regal, lying-in-state. For two days, Versailles paid court at the catafalque, sprinkling holy water and occasionally kneeling on velvet cushions to pray for the soul of its fallen mistress.

Meanwhile at Marly, the second act of this appalling tragedy unfolded.

When news of his wife's death was broken to the dauphin, he cried out: "Oh God! Save the King!" Abbé Proyart maintained afterward that the prince felt a presentiment that he would never reign. Prostrate with grief and illness, he refused to see anyone except his brother the duc de Berri, and his former governor; Beauvilliers was aghast at his wretched state, though he told Saint-Simon that "never had the Dauphin showed himself so noble as on that fearful day."

Saturday morning Bourgogne left to join the king at Marly. He was carried to the coach in a curtained sedan chair and drove from Versailles with his face hidden from the crowd. On his arrival at Marly, he went at once to the king's bedchamber: Louis XIV, royal slave to custom, was attempting to perform the *lever* as usual, but when his grandson entered the room his composure broke. Falling into each other's arms, the two men wept loudly and without restraint, mindless of the assembly that watched.

The king contemplated hunting that afternoon, but its association with the dead dauphine overwhelmed him and he dismissed his bearer, loader, and pack of dogs. He hoped to bury his grief in government and summoned his ministers, leaving Bourgogne to endure an afternoon of condolence calls. The dauphin's pious resignation impressed everyone: "Whether the doctors have killed her, or whether God has called her back to Him," he told one courtier, "we must adore alike what He permits and what He commands." Presently, Saint-Simon appeared, with word the king wished to see his grandson: "He gave me such a look as nearly broke my heart, and at once left the room." Mournfully, the duke added: "I never saw him again. God grant that I may meet him in that eternal life, to which his virtues will surely have brought him."

Bourgogne presented himself before the king, and again the two men dissolved in tears. But now Louis XIV was alarmed at his grandson's appearance: "His eyes had a strained expression, with something wild about them," and he noticed "numerous marks, livid rather than red, upon his face." He ordered the doctors to take Bourgogne's pulse. Afterward they confessed it had been alarmingly weak; at the time, they remarked that although it was slower than normal, there was no cause for alarm. Still the Sun King begged his heir to go to bed, and Bourgogne meekly consented. The rest of Saturday he saw only his confessor, Père Martineau, and a few close friends; by nightfall, fever appeared.

Sunday morning the prince attempted to follow the king's lead and return to normal life, but his head ached so badly he was unable to rise from his bed. On Monday his temperature dropped slightly, and he seemed to improve. He was filled with grim premonitions: several times that day he told Père Martineau: "Father, I shall not leave this place." When Martineau informed him that everyone at court was praying for his recovery and that he should join his own prayers to theirs "for the sake of France," the prince asked, "Would there be no vanity in my asking God to spare me for the good of France?" The priest assured him otherwise, but Bourgogne shook his head. "Well, God knows what plans He has for me. He is the master. His will is mine. For life or death, let Him decide."

Tuesday the dreaded red blotches appeared and the fever mounted. His terrified physician called for assistance, but Fagon, shaken by Adelaide's death, refused to quit Versailles. Instead he dispatched Desmoulins, the king's second physician. Desmoulins entered the sickroom at Marly and, mindful of his superior's disastrous attempts to cure the dauphine, promptly refused to prescribe any special treatment.

All through Wednesday the fever stayed. That afternoon, the dauphin declared his wish to make a last confession. Martineau challenged him: "Why, Monsieur, are you giving up hope, when the doctors are full of confidence? You must assist their remedies by thinking happier thoughts." Bourgogne was unimpressed. "Thank God, the thought of death does not sadden me. Pray that if God wishes me to live, it may be to serve Him better. If I am to die, pray that I may live with Him eternally." Still Martineau would not concede to alarm, and seeing that he could not budge his confessor, the prince remarked, "Since I may not make my confession today, I had best turn my mind to other things, for there is not much time left."

He called for his household servants, asking each if they were owed any money. He thanked them all for their services to him and his family, then gave assurances that he would recommend them to the king. Next he asked after the families to whom he had dispersed alms regularly and ordered that future provision be made for them. His conscience dwelled on the soldiers killed in battle under his command: he requested that seven hundred livres be sent to the Franciscans, to pray for his forgiveness. When he asked for the names of anyone he had ever harmed or humiliated, a senior officer of his staff broke down. "Ah! Monsieur," he cried, "you have done nothing but good in this world, and all Frenchmen would gladly give their lives for you." Bourgogne tried to smile. "Yes, Frenchmen do indeed deserve the love of their princes. The King will achieve his heart's desire if he can end this exhausting war, and I truly believe that he will succeed in that before long." Then, exhausted himself, he closed his eyes and fell back against his pillows.

Wednesday night passed with difficulty: his temperature increased, though his hands and feet were cold as ice. "This is a dreadful fever," he moaned. "I feel as though I were burning inwardly!" Bourbon pride would not suffer him to be thought a coward: "Perhaps I think this fever so bad," he attempted to rationalize, "only because I have never before been ill, and am not used to suffer pain. After all, what is this pain compared to the flames of Purgatory, where we must expiate our smallest sins?" Père Martineau offered, "One effect of divine mercy might be to let the heat of this fever secure you against the fires of Purgatory, if you would bear it patiently and offer it to God, in penitence." "Most willingly!" Bourgogne responded. "How grateful we should be to God for giving us such an easy means of atonement!"

Still his pains refused to subside, and the dauphin begged to receive viaticum — communion given to a person in danger of death. This required royal approval — approval that Louis XIV (being coddled with hopes of recovery by the doctors) refused to give. "I am not surprised," he said, "that M. le Dauphin, who communicates so often when he is well, wishes to do so in his illness. But he must be reminded that the laws of the Church — which he would not wish to break — forbid communion in viaticum, except in cases of extreme danger. He must trust the doctors rather than his own feelings." Not even an appeal to Mme de Maintenon succeeded; no less than the king, she had convinced herself that Bourgogne *must* recover. "The Dauphin has lived like a saint," she told his officer, "and wishes to die like one. I must commend his sentiments, but I cannot judge his condition."

Bourgogne accepted the royal refusal with good grace, but when his request for extreme unction was likewise denied, he cried out miserably: "Oh! Savior, since no one will believe me, I must leave this world without the consolations which You provide for the dying. You know what my heart desires. Your will be done." The sight of this dying man, consumed with terror for his immortal soul, melted resistance.

Père Martineau presented a solution: after midnight he would be free to perform daily mass, which he offered to say in the prince's room. His plan was quickly adopted. In this way, the wishes of a (possibly) dying man could be followed without breaking the king's express command; at the same time, those present would be freed from the reproach of having denied their prince last rites should the end indeed be nigh. Shortly before midnight, Martineau heard Bourgogne's confession; at the stroke of twelve, mass began. The priest recorded afterward that the prince received communion with ardor — "all his anxieties left him, and his mind was at peace."

However peaceful his mind, his body was racked with pain. He writhed in agony all Thursday morning. Again and again, his thoughts turned to his beloved wife. "Oh, my poor Adelaide! How you must have suffered! Oh Lord, may it have been for her soul's salvation!" He asked if he might see his sons, but the two little princes had been whisked off to Meudon when their mother was first taken ill. Bourgogne understood it was best they remain safely away, mumbling: "I shall see them very soon." His remark was passed to Maintenon as proof that he still hoped for recovery, but the pious old woman knew better. "You do not understand," she told the messenger. "It is in the life to come that he hopes to see them. He says 'very soon' because, in the eye of faith, the longest life is no more than a dream." That afternoon, she paid a final visit to the dying heir. He recalled her noble efforts at educating his wife — memories that brought them both to tears — and he commended to her the training of his sons. Then he spoke of the king: "I know how well he loves me. My death will distress him deeply. Tell him to be of good cheer, for I die full of joy."

At sundown his fever rose again; in his delirium, he called out "Adelaide!" several times. Just before twelve, he was gone. It was February 18, six days after Adelaide's death, six months before his thirtieth birthday.

More than a decade earlier, the young princesse of Savoy had teased her bridegroom: "Your position requires you to have a wife, so should I die before you, what lady would you choose?" The prince had answered gravely: "Should you die, I should not survive you more than a week." He made good his word.

"He passionately loved his wife," Saint-Simon judged. "His grief at losing her broke his heart, and only by a most prodigious effort did his faith survive the blow. It was a sacrifice he offered without reservation, and it killed him." *Le Mercure* concurred: "The Dauphin could not survive his wife. He could not bear her loss. How shall we bear our own? All France is dumb with consternation; her sorrow is little less than despair."

Louis XIV had retired for the night before the duc de Bourgogne died, and no one dared to wake him with the terrible news. But at his *lever* the next morning, he read unmistakable grief in his courtiers' faces, and understood. He was devastated: tears streamed down his withered cheeks, and when he spied his youngest grandson, Berri, in the throng, he walked over and embraced him, murmuring sadly, "My dear child, I have no one now but you."

"The King is overwhelmed by grief," Mme de Maintenon wrote Madrid. Madame, announcing Bourgogne's death to her aunt ("We are again overwhelmed by a terrible misfortune") unconsciously echoed her adversary: "The King is in such grief that I fear for his health. This is a terrible loss for the whole kingdom . . . I have been so frightened by these late events that I hardly know what I am saying. I feel as though we were all going to die, one after the other . . . The sadness that prevails here cannot be described." For once, she had a kind word for Maintenon: "Although the old woman is our worst enemy, I still wish her a long life for the King's sake; everything would be much worse were she to die, and he loves her so dearly that he would certainly not survive her."

The second royal corpse was taken to Versailles for autopsy. Sourches recorded in his journal that "the dead Prince was all gangrene from the feet to the head; his heart was withered; and one of the lungs decayed." Saint-Simon added that when the heart was removed for embalming, "it was without consistency; it dissolved in fluid as they held it in their hands. The blood was decomposed, and an intolerable odor filled the vast apartment."

These findings revived the unwonted controversy of the week before: again (to exonerate themselves) Fagon and Boudin declared there to be "the most violent effects of a very subtle and very violent poison, which had consumed the interior of the body like an ardent fire, the head alone having escaped destruction." Again the surgeon Mareschal declared there to be *no* trace of poison in the body, blaming the prince's death on "a natural venom resulting from the corruption of the blood, inflamed by a burning fever which was less external than internal." And again the king ordered the doctors to keep their findings to themselves.

There were now two bodies to lay on the state bed in the dauphine's salon. For three days, they remained on view, guarded on the right by gentlemen from his household, and on the left by ladies of hers. To foreshorten his misery, the king decreed an abbreviation of these rites; *Le Mercure* noted: "If something was lacking in grandeur it was made up for by the vast crowd of weeping spectators who gathered in such great numbers to file past the coffins that barriers were erected to prevent accidents."

The procession to Saint-Denis, the royal resting place, began the evening of February 23. While royal musicians played a De Profundis, ten of the king's bodyguards lifted the two coffins onto a hearse, then covered them in a single pall embroidered with the arms of France and Savoy. The funeral cortège formed: first, a body of poor pensioners, dressed in long gray cloaks with hoods, each carrying a torch. Next marched two horse platoons, one of sixty gray musketeers, the other of sixty black musketeers — the regiments of which the child Bourgogne so proudly had been a member. After a company of gendarmes came the officers of the Bourgogne households.

Six carriages of mourners followed, each drawn by eight black horses. They carried the royal family's representatives (ironically, the princesse de Conti and Mme la duchesse), the duchesse du Lude, Mme de Mailly, and all the ladies of Adelaide's suite. Then came the king's personal coach, bearing the bishops of Senlis, Autun, and Saint-Omer, as well as the king's almoner, and the parish priest who had heard the dauphine's last confession. The corps of royal pages followed on foot, each bearing a wax taper, then four heralds and the master of ceremonies. Last of all was the royal hearse, drawn by eight horses hooded in black and silver, and surrounded by Swiss Guards.

The cortège made slow progress through the wintery night; it took eight hours just to reach the gates of Paris. Despite the lateness of the hour the streets were jammed and the crowds watched in absolute silence as the procession crossed the streets of the city. It left Paris at three in the morning and arrived at Saint-Denis shortly before six. As the abbey bells tolled mournfully, the bishop of Senlis gave a short oration outside the portals. Then the coffins were carried in. There followed only a brief memorial service, for the funeral proper would come much later: according to royal custom, the catafalque was exposed to public view in the church for forty days.

The year of death had one more victim still to claim. The new dauphin, the duc de Bretagne, was five years old and quite precocious: when a courtier addressed him by his new title, he objected, "Please don't! It's too sad." Despite evacuation to Meudon, Bretagne contracted measles nine days after his father's death. By March 7, his condition was critical. The old king's panic was absolute, and he ordered the immediate baptism of Bretagne and his two-year-old brother Anjou. Burning with fever, his face spotted red, the young dauphin was christened by the bishop of Metz, then immediately turned over to the "care" of the doctors. They administered an adult dosage of emetic and the boy convulsed. They opened his arm and bled him next. One hour after his baptism, the duc de Bretagne was dead.

Little Anjou was spared a similar death, though not from want of trying on the doctors' part. He contracted measles the same day as Bretagne and was spared only through the wisdom and obstinacy of his governess, Mme de Ventadour. Madame explained: "While the doctors busied themselves with the elder child, the nurses locked themselves in with the younger prince. The doctors wished to open a vein because he had a raging fever; but the governess, Mme de Ventadour, strongly opposed this and steadfastly refused to permit it, simply keeping him warm and comfortable. Thus the child was saved."

France was stunned by this final blow. Three members of the royal family dead in one month; three direct heirs to the throne dead in less than a year. Reasons were sought for the inexplicable catastrophe: Mme de Maintenon and the pious read divine retribution for French arrogance, but many more read foul play. Saint-Simon recorded that sinister rumors circulated in Marly as early as January 18 when Boudin, in a crowded drawing room, had blurted out that he had sure news of a plot to poison the dauphin and dauphine. The very next day, Bourgogne had received a letter from Philip V, warning him of danger to himself and with only a vague reference to Adelaide. Saint-Simon admitted that these kinds of rumors, so commonplace in the lives of royalty, were generally discounted. However, he had suspicions about a certain snuff box that had been presented to Adelaide by the duc de Noailles just before her fatal illness. The box contained "excellent Spanish snuff," which the dauphine found beneficial in relieving tooth-ache. When she fell ill within a matter of days, she called for someone to fetch the snuff box from her boudoir — it had vanished and was never seen again. (The duc de Noailles was one of Maintenon's closest friends, the father-in-law of her niece. He stood to gain nothing by the death of the Bourgognes; on the contrary, he stood to *lose* much, since Adelaide's devotion to her cherished schoolmate, Françoise d'Aubigné, had betokened a brilliant future for Françoise's husband and the rest of the Noailles clan.)

The eye of the public, searching for a villian, fell upon the duc de Chartres. He seemed a logical suspect: after all, he was the king's nephew, and only two people — the infant Anjou and the childless duc de Berri — stood between him and the throne. "Some wicked people have spread a rumor that my son poisoned [them]," Madame wrote her aunt. "Being sure of his innocence, I at first thought this a bad joke, not believing for a moment that such a thing could be said seriously; but the King has been informed of it."

Louis XIV was aware of his nephew's profligacy and deplored his dissolute habits, but he also knew that "the Duc's heart was not so black" and that he was incapable of such ruthless and systematic murder. "He [the King] sent for my son, and assured him with great kindness that he attached no belief or importance to the reports. But he advised my son to send, in his own interest, his chemist, the poor and learned Humberg, to the Bastille, to clear him of the accusation."

Apparently, Louis XIV then changed his mind and decided this step unnecessary, for the next day, Madame wrote: "My son sent Humberg to be examined yesterday at the Bastille. The King forbade them to receive him; for, firstly, he does not think my son to be capable of such a wicked thing, and secondly, all the doctors who assisted in the post-mortem aver that they saw no trace of poison in either body, only that the Dauphine died from the measles, and the Dauphin from close air and grief." It was not that Mareschal had finally swayed Boudin and Fagon — despite Madame's assertion, the doctors never did agree on the subject of poison. Rather, Louis XIV decided it best to close the matter forever.[2]

When the funeral services took place on April 18, a third casket had entered the basilica of Saint-Denis. The king himself was absent: too broken to attend the service, he remained on his knees in the chapel at

Marly throughout the day. The maréchal Villars, soon to depart for the front, timidly approached the praying king to take his leave, and afterwards recorded his impressions: never before had he seen the self-control of the monarch yield to the feelings of the man. The king wept without restraint, "and said to me in a voice that went straight to the heart, 'You see in what state I am, Monsieur. Few have known what it is to lose as I have, in the space of a few weeks, a grandson, granddaughter, and their son, all of great promise and tenderly cherished. God punishes me, and I deserve it. I shall suffer less in the next world. But let us now leave sorrowing over my domestic misfortunes and see what can be done to avert those of my kingdom.' "

The funeral decorations at Saint-Denis were executed by the artist Jean Berain, who had created several of the more brilliant fêtes at Versailles. He was inspired by the unprecedented bereavement of the entire nation and he achieved a spectacle as magnificent as anything yet seen in the Sun King's long reign — in Dangeau's opinion, "too brilliant for so sad a ceremony." Each pillar was draped in black velvet, stamped with fleurs-de-lis, gold dolphins, and silver crosses. On a platform in the middle of the choir stood the immense catafalque, in black and gold, with a great gilded crown suspended above it. The pall was covered in gold embroidery, edged in ermine; beside it, on a velvet cushion, glittered the crowns of the dauphin and dauphine.

The duc de Berri represented the king. His wife was chief mourner for Adelaide, the duc de Chartres for Bourgogne. Behind the members of the royal family sat the bishops of France (five to a row), followed by the lords and ladies of Versailles, the deputies of the parlements, and the ambassadors of foreign courts.

The ceremony began at eleven, with a funeral oration by the bishop of Alther, Jacques Mabroul. He extolled first the dauphin, an easy subject — "few princes of his age have been more austere, pious, and conscientious." Then he spoke of Adelaide: he had no intention of establishing an equality of virtue between them, despite all her striking qualities. But he allowed that she had given a noble example of modesty and penitence, "realizing the vanity of pleasures, reproaching herself for having too much indulged in them, growing daily in piety until at last she promised to achieve, in happy emulation, as perfect a virtue as that of the Dauphin, her husband."

Following the bishop's hour-long sermon was a solemn high mass — three and a half hours of incense-filled ritual. Then came the second part of the ceremony: the cloth of gold was removed from the coffins, which twelve ushers lifted onto their shoulders and carried to the gates of the royal crypt. More prayers were said. As the abbey monks chanted the Benedictus and the grand almoner sprinkled a handful of French soil over the caskets, the royal remains were lowered into the vault.

One final ritual, as old as the monarchy itself, remained: the officers of their households surrendered the symbols of their ranks. The knight-at-arms rose, his voice reverberating through the cathedral:

"Monsieur the Marquis de Maillebois, Master of the Wardrobe, bring the royal mantle of Monsieur le Dauphin!"

"Monsieur the Duc de Beauvilliers, First Gentlemen of the Bed-chamber, bring the crown of Monsieur le Dauphin!" This done, the knight-at-arms addressed Adelaide's suite:

"Monsieur the Maréchal de Tessé, acting Knight of Honor to Ma-dame la Dauphine, bring her crown!" Tessé moved slowly, barely able to see through his tears. Sixteen years before, he had negotiated this marriage; he had been friend, guide, and mentor to the young prin-cesse throughout her first years in France. Now he was standing in for Dangeau (himself "too ill" to be present). Years later he would write: "I gazed so long on that dreadful scene that the sight still remains with me."

"Monsieur the Marquis d'O, Principal Equerry to Madame la Dau-phine, bring her royal mantle!"

"Monsieur the Marquis de Villacerf, Principal Maître d'Hôtel to Madame la Dauphine, bring your wand!"

After the wand, covered in black crepe, had been placed on the coffin, Tessé turned to his colleagues, and softly said, "Gentlemen, you are at liberty. Our duties are fulfilled." Then the knight-at-arms pro-claimed in a loud voice: "The Most High, Most Mighty and Most Excellent Prince Louis, the Dauphin, and the Most High, Most Mighty and Most Virtuous Princesse Marie Adelaide, the Dauphine, are dead. Pray to God for their souls!"

The ceremony, lasting six hours, was over.

Bourgogne carried to his grave the secret hopes of those who re-sented the Sun King's autocracy, who dreamed of a new era of peace and prosperity, reform and tolerance. Saint-Simon met Beauvilliers after the funeral and cried out, "We have just buried France."

With Adelaide's death, the last light of the Sun King softly faded. His court continued its time-worn orbit: Versailles to Fontainebleau to Marly and back again, but these outward motions now had no substance. Saint-Simon mourned: "With her departed joy, pleasure, and everything gracious; and darkness brooded over the Court. She had been its life, and if it survived her, it was only to languish. Never was Princesse so regretted; never was one more worthy of regret."

She numbered among the most beloved of princesses, and had promised to become one of France's greatest queens. She personified the charm, the vitality, and the style of her period, as well as the hopes that might have been realized in a new enlightened age — hopes that, like herself, perished too soon. During the reign of their youngest son, the dead couple was eulogized by Voltaire: "From the Duc de Bourgogne all France expected such government as the sages of antiquity imagined, with its austerity softened by the graces of the Princesse, graces even more appealing than the philosophy of her husband. The world knows how all these hopes were dispelled by death."

Two and a half years remained to the aged Sun King — hollow and lonely years. Peace was finally achieved, but like its master, France was too exhausted, too bitter to enjoy it. Slowly, inexorably, the clock wound down . . .

Louis XIV fell ill on Wednesday, August 14, 1715. His death, from gangrene in the leg, was ugly and protracted. He suffered excruciating pain for over two weeks, Mme de Maintenon faithfully at his side. Nearing the end, he confessed to his wife his sorrow, that he had never been able to make her happy. He was concerned for her future, but she cut him off: "I am nothing. Don't waste your time over nothing." Then he smiled, and with a roguish twinkle, told her that, given her age, it was a great comfort to know she would soon be joining him.

The day before he died, Louis XIV summoned his five-year-old great-grandson. "*Mignon,* you are going to be a great king. Do not imitate me in the taste I have had for building, or for war; try, on the contrary, to be at peace with your neighbors. Render to God what you owe Him; recognize the obligations you are under to Him; make Him honored by your subjects. Try to comfort your people, which unhappily I have not done . . . My dear child, I give you my benediction with all my heart."

His last words were: "Oh God! Haste Thou to succor me!" and then he lapsed into a coma. Early in the morning of Sunday, September 1, 1715, four days before his seventy-seventh birthday, the Sun King died.

Adelaide's youngest son, her "fat little dumpling," was proclaimed King Louis XV. The *grand siècle* was over. A new age had begun.

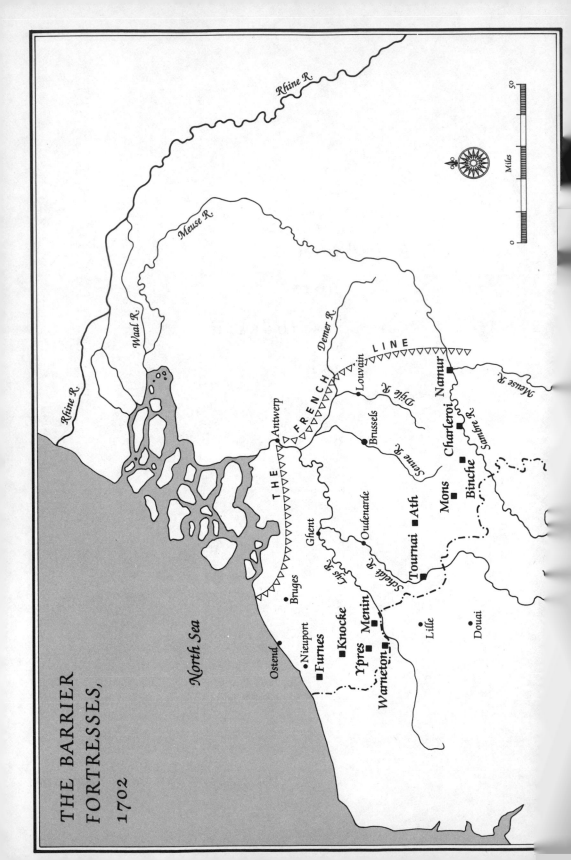

THE BARRIER
FORTRESSES,
1702

North Sea

Rhine R.

Meuse R.

Waal R.

Rhine R.

Demer R.

THE FRENCH LINE

Louvain

Brussels

Antwerp

Dijle R.

Senne R.

Namur

Charleroi

Meuse R.

Binche

Mons

Sambre R.

Ath

Tournai

Oudenarde

Schelda R.

Ghent

Lys R.

Bruges

Menin

Knocke

Ypres

Warneton

Lille

Douai

Nieuport
Furnes

Ostend

Miles

0   50

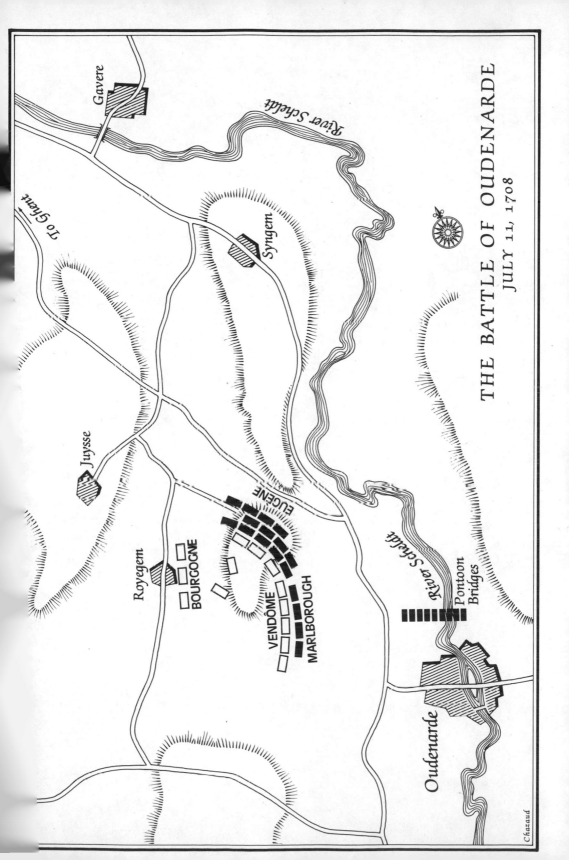

THE BATTLE OF OUDENARDE
JULY 11, 1708

Gavere

River Scheldt

To Ghent

Syngem

Juysse

Royegem

BOURGOGNE

EUGENE

VENDÔME

MARLBOROUGH

River Scheldt

Pontoon
Bridges

Oudenarde

Chazaud

Notes

I. THE STATE OF FRANCE

1. The legend of the Sun King's last exchange with his father is apocryphal: the little boy was brought to the royal bedside, and Louis XIII, dying of tuberculosis, asked, "Who is there?" With no hesitation — so the story goes — the child piped, "Louis XIV."

2. One year later, when Marie Mancini married Prince Colonna, constable of Naples, the bridegroom was surprised and openly delighted to discover his bride a virgin.

3. Louis's brother Philippe, though officially styled the duc d'Orléans, was given the courtesy title "Monsieur" and was always so addressed at court. Consequently, both his wives were addressed as "Madame." Louis's son, the dauphin, was addressed as "Monseigneur," a title of the king's own devising with no precedent in court history.

4. Like all other quotations not otherwise attributed, this observation is the duc de Saint-Simon's.

5. Minette had died in 1670. Despite his penchant for handsome young men, Monsieur dutifully contracted a second marriage to Princess Elisabeth Charlotte of the Palatinate in 1671.

6. Fastidious for his time, Louis XIV changed his linen three times a day, but was also proud of the fact that he had never bathed in his life.

7. We should note at this time that the *lever* performance — dressing before an assembly — extended down through the Versailles hierarchy. Both the king's brother and his son held *lever* ceremonies of their own — though, obviously, earlier than the king's. So did the more prominent nobles of the court: consequently, the average courtier, who sought patronage wherever he could, attended as many of these rites as possible, and generally rose well before sunup, dressing himself in unceremonious candlelight.

8. The autopsy performed after the Sun King's death in 1715 revealed

that his stomach had double the capacity of that of a normal man of his size and that his bowels were twice the usual length.

2. "THIS FORTUNATE MARRIAGE"

1. The fortress of Pinerolo is a case in point: fighting the duke of Mantua in 1635, Richelieu requested that the duke's father lend him the fort for the duration. On the settlement of peace, Savoy asked for the fort's return, a claim the French government conveniently ignored. In 1685 — the year of Adelaide's birth — Pinerolo was still in French hands.
2. Monsieur and Madame produced two children of their own: Philippe, the duc de Chartres, the future regent, and Elisabeth Charlotte, who married the prince of Lorraine and was Marie Antoinette's grandmother.
3. Since the death of Louis XIV's queen, Marie Thérèse, in 1683, his daughter-in-law, the dauphine (Marie Anne Christine of Bavaria) had assumed precedence as first lady of Versailles. She occupied the queen's apartments (later Adelaide's rooms) until her death in 1690.

3. THE GNAT AND THE LION

1. Years later, Marie Adelaide would write Madame Royale from France: "I believe, my dear grandmama, that I did not give you much joy . . . because you would have preferred a boy; but from all the kindness you have always shown me, I cannot doubt you have forgiven me for being a girl."
2. After the War of the Spanish Succession, when Victor Amadeus became king of Sardinia, the property was rechristened La Villa della Regina — the Queen's House. It was greatly enlarged during the eighteenth century, but never lost its popularity with the Italian royal family.
3. William III's dream of an anti-French Grand Alliance had become a reality with the treaty of Augsburg, signed July 9, 1686, four years prior to the duke's defection. To distinguish this coalition from the later (second) Grand Alliance — to be forged at the outset of the War of the Spanish Succession — it is here referred to as the League of Augsburg.
4. The war is so named because the initial cause of conflict had been Louis XIV's claim, on behalf of his sister-in-law, Madame, to a share in the German Palatinate inheritance (much against Madame's loudly expressed opposition). The French Army invaded the Palatinate in

1689, where Louvois's systematic and horrifying devastation of the countryside foreshadowed the scorched-earth policy of World War II. Technically, Savoy's entry onto the battlefield occurred in the second year of the war.

5. The loss of this wished-for heir was an even greater than usual blow to Victor Amadeus, for William III had expressed an interest in the expected child during the meeting in The Hague. William and Mary were childless, and their sole heir, Mary's sister Anne, had given birth to fifteen children, none of whom had survived to the age of ten. If the duke's child was a boy, he would be — through his mother — the first great-grandchild of Charles I of England. William's plan was to bring the boy to London, and raise him as his eventual successor. For Victor Amadeus, the prospect of his son sitting on the throne of England was dizzying, and exacerbated his grief at the infant's death.

6. Indeed Tessé was the first of his countrymen to fall under the spell of Adelaide's charm, and he remained devoted in her service until her death. She in return loved and trusted him, returning his support completely and without hesitation: the only scene she ever made with Louis XIV in the forbidden area of government appointments was to plead for Tessé's appointment as maréchal.

7. Vauban, France's leading expert on siege warfare, wrote to the poet Racine that the restitution of so many fortresses to Savoy was the greatest military disgrace since the days of Henri II — but Louis XIV evidently believed the surety of the duke's alliance and the access to the safe pass well worth these formidable concessions.

8. On September 20, 1697, the treaty of Ryswick, signed by France, England, Holland, and Spain, officially ended the War of the Palatinate. France kept Strasbourg and the Franche-Comte, regained Pondicherry in India and Nova Scotia in America, and conceded only to a lowering of French tariffs for Dutch trade. On October 30, a supplementary peace was signed between the Sun King and Emperor Leopold I.

4. WAITING IN THE WINGS

1. The duchesse du Lude, deputized by Louis XIV to take charge of the princesse on her arrival in France, received strict orders to "turn back at the frontier everyone who has accompanied the Princesse, no matter what the uproar." She was additionally commanded to return to the Savoyard delegation every article of clothing Adelaide was wearing, down to her handkerchief; as Tessé remarked to the duke's secretary, "France wants her naked."

2. The Sun King's insistence on the severing of all ties with Savoy was not as cruel or perverse as might at first appear, for his conviction was rooted in painful past experience. When Marie Christine of Bavaria arrived at Versailles to marry the dauphin in 1680, she was permitted to bring with her a sizable German retinue, including her personal maid, Bessola. The new dauphine, painfully ugly and painfully shy, was miserable in the public spotlight at the French court. Her unhappiness was exacerbated in 1683 when the queen's death made her the official first lady of Versailles. Instead of facing her duties and pleasing her father-in-law, the dauphine shut herself in her private apartments, prattling away for hours in German with Bessola, who reinforced her hermetic life and earned the lasting enmity of Louis XIV. The king was determined such dereliction of duty would not be permitted with a second royal bride.

3. Neither Adelaide nor Tessé ever forgot the mix-up: for years after, the kindly old diplomat could bring a smile to her face by reminding her of the only time she had run from him in terror.

4. Rather predictably, Victor Amadeus delayed the settlement of accounts — for an amazing fifteen years! Shortly after Adelaide's death, the merchants who so long ago had provided a trousseau worthy of a queen at last received payment: calculating on a modest interest of five percent a year, these tradesmen — through the duke's delay — lost just under 26,000 francs.

5. Although he had been appointed her Master of the Horse, Tessé was instructed by the king to remain in Turin after Adelaide's departure. Tessé wished to help ease her transition and so requested permission to accompany the princesse, but Louis XIV replied that he had better use for the diplomat where he was — keeping an eye on Victor Amadeus and seeing that the conditions of their agreement were not violated.

5. A PERFECT PRINCESSE

1. As we have seen, Louis XIV's morganatic marriage to Mme de Maintenon was never acknowledged publicly. The dauphine had died in 1690, and while there is strong evidence that Monseigneur secretly married his mistress, Mlle de Choin, this union was likewise never admitted. With father and son official widowers, the supreme position at court devolved upon the wife of the grandson.

2. As a gambler, Dangeau was unrivaled. Mme de Sévigné observed him in 1676 and wrote: "I watched him play, and realized what innocents we all are in comparison with him. He concentrates on the game to

the exclusion of all else, and neglects nothing which he can turn to his advantage. His judgment far outweighs his luck ... One hundred thousand écus every month go into the credit side of his account book." In his famous journal, annotated by Saint-Simon, Dangeau wrote of Mme de Maintenon: "She was so worthy, doing, when she was in favor, so much good and preventing so much harm, that one cannot speak too highly of her." Saint-Simon, who loathed the king's wife with a passion, noted: "See that! Vulgar, filthy, stinking, lying in his throat!" After reading Dangeau's accounts, he decided to revise and edit his own memoirs.

3. Brionne had long made difficulties over rank and precedence: as a prince of Lorraine, an independent principality between France and Germany, he claimed equal rank with the princesse of Savoy, and insisted that he would sit with her. Louis XIV's decree on Adelaide's status technically removed any equality, but Desgranges, well aware of the hereditary stubbornness of the House of Lorraine, neatly solved the problem by arranging that the comte and the princesse never met in the vicinity of chairs.

4. Louis XIV was so touched by the charming innocence of her reply that he sent special orders to the toymakers of Paris, for dolls and games of "such supreme beauty and charm" that the familiar playthings of her childhood in Savoy should be totally forgotten.

5. Though forks became fashionable during the latter part of his reign, Louis XIV stubbornly refused to use one. Till the day of his death, the regal Sun King picked at his food with his fingers.

6. Eau de cologne was Mme de Maintenon's only personal extravagance, and she spent a fortune on delicate and rare perfumes. But this might well have been owing more to necessity than inclination: not only did Louis XIV never bathe, but his upper teeth were rotted and his breath had grown positively vile.

6. "THE GLORY OF THE AGE"

1. This desire for a retreat was apparently genuine, for no sooner had Versailles completed its evolution from private to public showcase than the king built Marly — at a cost of eleven million francs — for the very same reasons of privacy.

2. Louis's new palace originally included marble floors, but it was discovered that the water used to wash them was trickling through the slabs and rotting the beams below. The marble was ripped out and replaced with parquet — shooting building costs further into orbit.

3. Deeply upset over these charges against du Maine, the king vented his

anger by striking a footman for stealing a biscuit from the royal table — one of the only three times in his life that he was seen to lose his temper. "This prince," Saint-Simon commented, "so even-tempered and so perfectly controlled, gave way on this unique occasion."

4. Only two requisites were demanded by Louis XIV: visitors must be reasonably well dressed, and the gentlemen must carry swords — which could be rented for the day from a palace official.

5. Today Adelaide would recognize only one of these rooms — the guard chamber. Her son, Louis XV, entirely redecorated the bedchamber for his wife, Marie Leszczynska, in the late 1720s; forty years later, Marie Antoinette (Adelaide's second cousin, once removed) ordered a full-scale renovation of the dining room and the Salon of Nobles.

6. This piece of sculpture was the king's favorite in the gardens, and its theme — vengeance for those who dared malign a royal mistress — did not go unheeded by the court of Versailles.

7 . A ROYAL EDUCATION

1. Alone of all the Sun King's buildings, Marly was destroyed in the Revolution; the gardens remain today as a public park.

2. Louis's brother Monsieur fared no better: brought up from the start to defer to his older brother, Philippe was reduced to impotence with an education that indulged and encouraged his potential vices and left his virtues dormant. From a brave, witty, and charming little boy, the queen mother and Mazarin created a mincing, effete nonentity.

3. The music for the song performed by the students during this visit was by Lully and is now lost. The words — "Grand Dieu sauvez le Roi / Grand Dieu vengez le Roi / Vive le Roi / Qu'a jamais glorieux / Louis victorieux / Voie ses ennemis toujour soumis / Vive le Roi" — survive today as the British national anthem, "God Save the Queen."

8 . "THE HOLY TERROR"

1. The duc de Bourgogne was the first French royal baby to be delivered by a male midwife.

9 . BOURBON MUNIFICENCE

1. Louis XIV had purchased the necklace for the marquise de Montespan years earlier — at a cost of 150,000 livres. When the fires of

their passion had sufficiently cooled, the marquise politely and correctly returned the pearls.

2. Tessé sent these horses to be trained in the duc du Maine's stables at Sceaux, reasoning to the king: "Your Majesty will readily understand that to buy horses in haste and put them straight to work would mean . . . eight months later [having] to make good unavoidable losses. They must be allowed time to fatten." While he graciously offered to pay for their upkeep at Sceaux, Tessé did not intend to cover their purchase as well, and he ended his letter with a plea for "something on account, until such time as it pleases Your Majesty to command the repayment of the whole sum."

3. Louis XIV wrote in his own hand a "Memorandum of all the subjects in which His Majesty desires that the Duc de Bourgogne shall be instructed and all the Operations to be made by the troops during their stay at Camp." With his obsession with detail, the king not only outlined the operations he wished undertaken, but established rules for the care and feeding of his men and their horses, as well as the organization of an ambulance unit.

4. With this precaution Boufflers displayed his courtier's sagacity, for it was common knowledge at Versailles that the king drank neither wine nor any other alcoholic beverage, abstaining even from coffee, tea, and chocolate. Instead, Louis XIV drank inordinate amounts of water — water he demanded be fresh, pure, and cold.

5. It is vital to recall here that the king's marriage was not officially acknowledged until after his death; while the court was by no means blind to his relationship with Mme de Maintenon and rumors of their union abounded, it was the prevailing attitude at Versailles that Maintenon was simply the last in a long line of royal mistresses, and as such, owned no claim — moral or legal — over her distinguished lover.

6. The Sun King's year of Bourbon munificence, his bold proclamation of French supremacy, achieved one result sure to have appealed to his more practical side: before the camp, Louis XIV had been borrowing money abroad at twelve percent; within a month of the Compiègne bravado, he was able to arrange a series of loans at six.

10. YOUTHFUL DESIRES

1. The old princesse, however, was a longtime friend of Mme de Maintenon's, who interceded on her behalf, with expected success: the very next day, Louis XIV (reluctantly) granted d'Harcourt permission to weekend at Marly.

2. A typical dinner of the period — offered by Louvois to Queen Marie Thérèse shortly before her death — gives an indication of the momentous scale of these meals. It comprised four "services," or courses: the first service offered forty dishes of entrée (partridge, spiced duck, pigeon, etc.); the second another forty dishes of roasts and salads; the third was hot and cold *entremets;* and the fourth, "an exquisite and rare dessert." Melons and oranges rounded off this modest repast.

3. Madame had little fondness for the duchesse du Lude, whom she considered too imperious, yet even she pitied the poor lady, forced to quit the warmth of her bed and accompany her willful young charge on these predawn excursions.

4. Madame wrote, in a letter of September 18, 1692: "Apropos of letters opened at the post, allow me to tell you the story of a thing which happened several years ago. The Grande Mademoiselle [the king's first cousin] received several letters from her business people, and perceived clearly that they had been opened. When answering, she added, 'As M. de Louvois is very clever, and as he will see this letter before it reaches you, I beg of him, when opening it, to add a little advice on my affairs, which will certainly be the better for it'; since then they have not opened her letters."

II. A NEW CENTURY: BEGINNINGS AND ENDINGS

1. In all, the effeminate Monsieur produced eleven children, by two wives and one mistress, and is justifiably acknowledged "the grandfather of Europe": today, every Roman Catholic royal family numbers him among their ancestors, and every king of France after Louis XIV was his descendant — as well as Marie Antoinette and the king of Rome, the ill-fated son of Napoleon I.

2. Madame lived in horror of her children being used in marriage to ennoble her brother-in-law's bastards. She had agonized for months, in 1692, when her daughter, Elisabeth Charlotte, was proposed as a possible bride for the duc du Maine. Her relief at du Maine's engagement to the daughter of the prince de Condé was enormous, and she informed her aunt:

[His] marriage is a settled thing, so one of my troubles is thus lifted from me. I fancy that they have informed the King's old wretch [Maintenon] what was being said in Paris, and that it frightened her. The people were saying that although it was a disgrace for the King to arrange a marriage between one of his bastards and a Prince of the Blood . . . they would allow it, though much against their feelings; but that if the old woman took it into her head to give my daughter to M. du Maine, they would strangle him before the wedding, and that the old woman . . . should not be sure of her life.

But she was not spared so inglorious an alliance a second time, and after hearing of her son's engagement, she stalked the halls of Versailles, discovered him conversing in a gallery, and publicly boxed his ears for giving in to royal pressure.

3. The treaty of Ryswick in 1697 called for French recognition of William's assumption of the crown. Although the Sun King signed the document, the deposed James Stuart, living on French subsidies at Saint-Germain, was styled still "the king of England," and William, "the prince of Orange."

4. Madame's aunt, the electress Sophia of Hanover, was a great-granddaughter of James I of England, through his daughter Elizabeth. A staunch Protestant, she was viewed as the most likely heir after William and his sister-in-law Anne. In 1700, Parliament's Act of Settlement officially conferred the crown on Sophia and her descendants, should Anne die without a direct heir. Sophia died in April 1714; Queen Anne, having carried and lost seventeen children, followed her to the grave that July, and Sophia's son, George Louis of Hanover, became King George I of England.

12. ELIMINATING THE PYRENEES

1. James Stuart's mother, Queen Henriette Marie, was the Sun King's aunt, the youngest sister of Louis XIII.

2. When William's wife, Queen Mary, died in 1694, Madame briefly entertained the notion of offering him her daughter, Elisabeth Charlotte. (William was a closeted homosexual, with no intention whatever of remarrying.)

3. Eugene and Victor Amadeus were third cousins, great-grandsons of Charles Emmanuel I; their intense dislike of each other probably sprang from mutual jealousy.

4. William was never able to forgive Victor Amadeus for betraying the allied cause. When in April 1701, the duchess of Savoy gave birth to a second son, the duke revived the English king's proposal of ten years earlier to import a Savoyard prince and raise him as his heir; William refused to respond to the suggestion. When Parliament's Act of Succession conferred the throne on the House of Hanover that same year, ignoring Anne Marie's claims as niece of Charles II, the duke directed

Count Maffei, his ambassador to the Court of Saint James's, to formally protest. Maffei did — and no one paid any attention.

13. LESSONS IN LOVE AND WAR

1. William unfortunately never lived to see the Grand Alliance in action, but died in London, March 8, 1702, having broken his collar bone when thrown from his horse.
2. The duke of Brandenburg became the first king of Prussia, a title he was granted by the emperor in 1701 for his contribution to the general defense.
3. The pattern of conflict between professional soldiers and would-be warrior-princes (established by Villeroi and Victor Amadeus) was sadly repeated in 1703. Despite their substantial gains, Villars and the elector of Bavaria quarreled incessantly, and once again Louis XIV put political alliance above military proficiency: Villars was recalled to Versailles and replaced by the less outspoken Maréchal Marsin. Had Bourgogne been assigned to this corps, he might successfully have acted as a buffer between the French general and the elector, who was his maternal uncle.

14. FATHER AND SON

1. Despite her enormous popularity, there *were* enemies: the king's daughters, Mme la duchesse and the princesse de Conti, were bitterly jealous of Adelaide's supremacy at Versailles, and led a faction of dissatisfied courtiers known as the "Meudon cabal" (after Monseigneur's estate). They awaited eagerly the death of the Sun King and the succession of Monseigneur — at which time they fully intended to destroy the hegemony of the "upstart" princesse from Savoy.
2. Louis, third duc de Vendôme (1654–1712) was the great-grandson of King Henri IV and his mistress Gabrielle d'Estrées; the Sun King was Henri's grandson.
3. The princesse des Ursins had been appointed (by Louis XIV) to be camerara-major to the new queen of Spain (playing Maintenon to her Adelaide). "Unequaled in grace, intelligence, and charm; most loyal to her friends; delightfully funny, but never vulgar, with an even temper that allowed her to be mistress of herself at all times," Ursins won the love and trust of both the new king and queen and remained their adviser (virtually running Spain) until the queen's death in 1714. She lived in the palace, controlled the privy purse, performed as major-domo at all audiences, and never left her mistress's side.

4. Spanish etiquette (even more severe than French) strictly forbade noblewomen to ride on horseback — lest their legs be exposed to male view. Maria Luisa, raised on country living and an accomplished horsewoman like her sister, felt the deprivation keenly. But, of course, to violate etiquette was simply unthinkable.

5. It was, in fact, an achievement historic on the entire continent of Europe, and duplicated only once: present at the 1895 christening of the future King Edward VIII (afterward the duke of Windsor) was his great-grandmother, Queen Victoria; his grandfather, Edward VII; and his father, George V. But unlike these British counterparts, not one of the three French heirs was destined to occupy the Sun King's throne.

6. While invitations were naturally declined, the prince and princesse were guests of honor in absentia at feasts provided by the master apothecaries, tennis ball makers, glass makers, bonnet makers, hatters, saddlers, watchmakers, wine merchants, belt makers, coach builders, glovers, perfumers, enamelers, gem polishers, gilders, chessmen makers, ribbon makers, pastrycooks, and hawkers of Paris.

7. These were: Lens, Rocroi, Nördlingen, Fribourg, Fleurus, Neerwinden, Steinkirk, Marsaglia, Staffarda, Friedlingen, Spira, and Suzzara. Ironically, this pageant was held on the eve of the battle of Blenheim — the greatest French defeat since Agincourt in 1415.

8. Versailles belonged to the court and to France, but Marly was Louis XIV's personal retreat, and he was extremely selective in choosing his visitors there.

9. Although a state of war had existed between France and Savoy since the end of 1703, the king had graciously allowed his pet to continue her correspondence with her mother and grandmother in Turin. To play it safe, however, all incoming and outgoing letters were carefully scrutinized before delivery.

15. "EVERY SORT OF GRIEF"

1. This conclusion was probably inaccurate: with Bretagne dead a scant three months, it seems doubtful that Adelaide, still struggling with fits of "weeping for her son," would have succumbed to a persistence she had successfully resisted for over fifteen months.

2. The death of King Jan Sobieski left the Polish throne vacant. The Polish Diet was presented with two candidates: Augustus, the elector of Saxony, and the French prince de Conti. Russia, Austria, and the German states were firmly opposed to an extension of French influence into eastern Europe. The czar, Peter the Great, suddenly sta-

tioned troops along the Polish border and the Diet took his hint: Augustus was duly elected king of Poland.

3. These figures should actually be doubled to include the fortified garrisons and depots as well as the service units at the rear of each front; almost a million men served annually in this first "world war."

4. With his father's death in 1701, the duc de Chartres succeeded to the title duc d'Orléans; to avoid confusion, he will still be referred to by his original title.

5. Barcelona had been taken by allied forces in October 1705, but early in 1706, Philip V and Tessé besieged it by land, while the French armada blocked its harbor. While Adelaide was writing, it appeared the city would shortly succumb. Ultimately it did not: the superior English fleet arrived and frightened away the French ships; Philip and Tessé were forced to end their siege, and Barcelona remained an allied stronghold.

6. Joseph I succeeded his father Leopold as emperor on May 5, 1705. Archduke Karl ("Carlos III of Spain") was his younger brother and, as Joseph had no son, also his heir — a fact of tremendous consequence in the War of the Spanish Succession.

7. Victor Amadeus *did* return and start the mausoleum, but transporting materials up the steep hill proved next to impossible; though his basilica "opened" officially in 1731, it was never completed and never used as a royal mausoleum.

16. "WHERE GLORY AWAITS"

1. The second duc de Bretagne figured in the third generation of royal children under the care of the maréchale de La Mothe. She had raised Monseigneur, the dauphin; his three sons — the ducs de Bourgogne, d'Anjou, and de Berri — and the short-lived first duc de Bretagne. With consideration of her advanced age — she was eighty-three in 1707 — she was made undergoverness to the infant prince and surrendered her position as governess to her granddaughter, the duchesse de Ventadour. Yet her vigilance and devotion to the Children of France remained unimpaired: the night of her death (in 1709) she was sleeping in the same room with two-year-old Bretagne.

2. The number of French prisoners taken would have been much greater but for the skill and courage with which the rear guard covered their retreat; commanding the rear guard was none other than Adelaide's suitor, the marquis de Nangis, the only officer to emerge from the battle of Oudenarde with his reputation intact.

17. THE CABAL

1. Another anecdote attests to the princesse de Conti's beauty: she was one of several ladies-of-honor attached to the homely dauphine. Once observing her sister-in-law sleeping, she was moved to remark, "She is just as ugly asleep as awake" — whereupon the dauphine opened her eyes and responded sweetly, "Madame, if I were a love-child, I would be as handsome as you are."
2. The duke of Berwick was the illegitimate son of James II of England and Marlborough's older sister, Arabella Churchill. He had followed his father into exile in 1688, and was naturalized a French citizen in 1703.
3. Boufflers was already lifetime governor of (French) Flanders, but on his death, this office would revert back to the Crown. By presenting him with the reversion, the king assured that the maréchal's son — a boy of twelve — would automatically inherit both the office and its income of one hundred thousand livres a year.

19. MOTHER AND MATCHMAKER

1. The elector was Adelaide's first cousin once removed, his mother — Adelaide Henriette — the aunt of Victor Amadeus.

20. "I SHALL BE THEIR QUEEN"

1. Saint-Simon added snidely that, amidst all this attention to Adelaide and Bourgogne, "the Duc and Duchesse de Berri were nonentities."
2. Within the hour, another carriage — a hired coach from Paris — left Meudon, bearing Emilie Joly. It had not been her decision to leave, but the corpse had blackened and putrefied so quickly that, even with all the windows open, the stench rendered the house uninhabitable.
   One of the king's first acts the following morning was to send condolences to his son's widow, along with promises of protection and a pension of twelve thousand livres (which Adelaide tried unsuccessfully to have increased). Emilie Joly continued to avoid society and spent her widowhood performing acts of charity; she died in Paris in 1730.
3. Monseigneur's servants, for the most part, remained at Meudon: as oldest son, Bourgogne inherited the estate, though he and Adelaide made little use of it during their brief ownership. Monseigneur's col-

lection of jewelry and objets d'art were divided between his younger sons, the king of Spain and the duc de Berri.

4. Saint-Simon had incurred the royal wrath on several occasions with his vocalized concern for the diminishing prerogatives of the peers of France and the rise of the Sun King's absolutism.

5. Technically speaking, Princess Louisa, as sister of a king (the Old Pretender) *did* take precedence over Adelaide, the wife of a king's grandson. But of course this ignored the reality of their situations: Adelaide was wife to the official heir to the throne, while Louisa and her brother-king lived in royal splendor solely through the grace and generosity of Louis XIV.

6. Saint-Simon later confessed that he could not help laughing to himself as he passed courtiers in the salon on his way to the back entrance of Bourgogne's apartment, knowing these were "the very people whose characters were hidden under his coat."

7. *La sale* was the little red tray from which the queen (in this case, the dauphine) was offered her brooches, fans, and handkerchiefs. It could be handled only by ladies of noble birth.

8. Lest images of torture and privation — the legacy of Dumas and Hugo — prevail, it must be stressed that incarceration at the Bastille was far less horrible than one might imagine. Prisoners there were officially "the King's guests" and treated as such: they dined at the governor's table, had fires in their rooms and furniture supplied from the royal warehouses. They were allowed to keep servants and could receive visitors and mail. A loss of liberty was the only drawback to an otherwise comfortable life-style.

21. "EVERYTHING IS DEAD HERE"

1. Saint-Simon rejected the notion of poisoning, and historians have as well. Adelaide *had* contracted measles, indicated by the appearance of the characteristic rash and the fact that Bourgogne was infected while keeping vigil at her bedside. Death resulted, however, not from the disease but the cure: the powerful emetics sapped her resistance, and the unchecked bleedings — the reason her blood appeared "burnt up" — finished her off.

2. It should be noted that the duc and duchesse de Bourgogne and their oldest son were the most illustrious but not the only victims of this measles epidemic: the *Gazette de Hollande,* published at the end of February 1712, announced that five hundred people succumbed to the illness in Paris and Versailles during the first two months of 1712.

Select Bibliography

Barnard, H. C. *Madame de Maintenon and Saint-Cyr*. London: A. & C. Black, 1934.

Barnett, Corelli. *The First Churchill*. New York: G. P. Putnam's Sons, 1974.

Blennerhasset, Lady Charlotte. *Louis XIV and Madame de Maintenon*. London: W. H. Allen, 1910.

Carre, Henri. *The King's Darling*. Trans. by George Slocombe. London: John Lane, 1936.

Churchill, Winston S. *Marlborough: His Life and Times,* 4 vols. New York: Charles Scribner's Sons, 1968.

Durant, Will, and Ariel Durant. *The Age of Louis XIV*. New York: Simon & Schuster, 1963.

Hatton, Ragnhild Marie. *Louis XIV and His World*. New York: G. P. Putnam's Sons, 1972.

Hibbert, Christopher. *Versailles*. New York: *Newsweek* Publications, 1972.

Lewis, W. H. *The Splendid Century*. New York: William Sloane Associates, 1954.

———. *The Sunset of the Splendid Century: The Life and Times of Louis Auguste de Bourbon, Duc du Maine*. New York: William Sloane Associates, 1955.

Mallard, David. *Culture and Society in Seventeenth-Century France*. New York: Charles Scribner's Sons, 1970.

Massie, Robert K. *Peter the Great*. New York: Alfred A. Knopf, 1980.

Mitford, Nancy. *The Sun King*. New York: Harper & Row, 1966.

Nobili-Vitelleschi, Amy. *The Romance of Savoy*. London: Hutchinson and Co., 1905.

Norton, Lucy. *First Lady of Versailles*. Philadelphia: J. B. Lippincott, 1978.

————. (Ed.). *Historical Memoirs of the Duc de Saint-Simon*, 3 vols. New York: Harmony Books, 1980.

Prescott-Wormley, Katherine (Ed.). *Correspondence of Madame, Princess Palatine, of Marie Adelaide, Duchesse de Bourgogne, and of Madame de Maintenon.* London, 1898.

Van der Kemp, Gerald. *Versailles.* New York: Viking Press, 1978.

Ziegler, Gilette. *At the Court of Versailles.* Trans. by Simon Watson Taylor. New York: E. P. Dutton, 1958.

Index

Absalom (Vancy), 199

Absolutism: and Louis XIV, 1, 239–40

Académie Française, 238, 304

Adelaide. See Marie Adelaide (of Savoy)

Alceste (Lully), 216

Alexander VIII (Pope), 57, 58

Alpine Protestants. See Huguenots

Andromache (Racine), 134

Anjou, Duc d' (Adelaide and Bourgogne's son), 439, 450, 454; birth of, 401–3, 407; bout with measles, 453. See also Louis XV

Anjou, Philippe, Duc d' (Bourgogne's brother, Monseigneur's son), 161, 197; Adelaide meets, 98, 101; birth of, 148; childhood of, 150; at Adelaide's wedding, 176; as possible successor to Spanish throne, 230, 231, 232–34. See also Philip V (King of Spain)

Anne (Queen of England), 205, 256, 257, 394

Anne Louise Benedicte de Bourbon. See Maine, Duchesse du

Anne Marie d'Orléans (Duchess of Savoy), 55, 63, 67, 73, 87, 324; early life and marriage of, 32–41, 69; pregnancies of, 40–41, 57–59, 172, 208, 282; and Adelaide, 42–43, 72, 74, 76, 77, 79, 98, 121, 313, 314, 315, 326, 395, 402–3, 438, 439; marital troubles of, 46–49; esteem for Louis XIV, 50–51, 53, 98–99, 100; and Adelaide's education, 50–51, 126, 141, 207; and shroud of Turin, 52; Louis XIV's desire to see, 78; Louis XIV writes to, about Adelaide, 95–96, 97; Adelaide's closeness to, 170, 193, 282–86; Adelaide's distance from, 207–8; and Monsieur's death, 225; meets Philip V of Spain, 254

Anne of Austria (Louis XIV's mother; regent), 5, 7, 8, 12, 98, 123

Anti-Lucretius (Polignac), 304

Antin, M. d', 203, 354, 375

Apollo: Louis XIV and, 1, 18, 104–5, 106, 112–13, 201

Apollon et Issé (Destouches), 182

Appartement evenings: Louis XIV's, 21–22, 179

Arcy, d' (French ambassador to Savoy), 47, 48, 54

Argenson, Monsieur d', 325

Armagnac, Comte d', 216

Army of the Two Crowns, 256. See also War of the Spanish Succession

Arpajon, Duchesse d', 82

Arts: in 17th-century France, 4. See also Music; Theater

Asturias, Prince of (Marie Louise and Philip V's son), 288, 389

Athalie (Racine), 200

Athénaïs (Marquise de Montespan). See Montespan, Mme de

EUROPE IN 1700

SCOTLAND

Edinburgh

North

Sea

IRELAND

Dublin

ENGLAND

London

Amsterdam

Rhine R.

Cambrai

Brussels

Compiègne

Versailles Paris

Seine R.

Loire R.

FRANCE

Bern

SWITZERL

Lyons

Garonne R.

Rhône R.

Turin

Atlantic Ocean

PORTUGAL

Duero R.

Madrid

Ebro R.

Barcelona

Lisbon

Tajo R.

SPAIN

Valencia

SARDINI

Mediterranean *S*

0   100   200   300   400   500 Miles

Chazaud